ACKNOWLEDGEMENTS

My sincere thanks to all those who contributed to the publication of this book. I would especially like to thank Di Tolland, who updated this edition, and Peter Read, who edited it. I would also like to thank the many people who contributed to previous editions, including Graeme Chesters, Verena Dangerfield, Dan Finlay, Pat and Mike Grey, Martin Hills, Linda Hull, Janet Macdonald, Ken Maxwell-Jones, David and Sigrid O'Hara, Veronica Orchard, Linda and Michael Osborn, Jane and Philip Read, Dougal Robertson, Pat and Ron Scarborough, Kitty Strawbridge, Joanna Styles, Julia Thorpe, Diana Tolland, Peter Turner, Karen and John Verheul and Catherine Wakelin. Thanks also to Joe and Kerry Laredo (layout and dtp), and a special thank-you to Jim Watson for the superb cover design, illustrations, cartoons and map.

TITLES BY SURVIVAL BOOKS

The Best Places To Buy A Home
France; Spain

Buying a Home
Australia & New Zealand;
Bulgaria, Cyprus; France;
Greece; Italy; Portugal;
South Africa; Spain;
Buying, Selling & Letting Property (UK)

Buying and Renting a Home
London; New York

Culture Wise
Australia; Canada; England;
France; New Zealand; Spain

**Foreigners Abroad: Triumphs
& Disasters**
France; Spain

Living and Working
America; Australia; Britain;
Canada; France; Germany;

The Gulf States & Saudi Arabia;
Ireland; Italy;
London; New Zealand;
Spain; Switzerland

Earning Money from Your Home
France; Spain

Making a Living
France; Spain

Retiring Abroad
France; Spain

Other Titles
Investing in Property Abroad;
A New Life Abroad;
Renovating & Maintaining Your
French Home; Running Gîtes and B&Bs
in France; Rural Living in France;
Shooting Caterpillars in Spain;
Wild Thyme in Ibiza

Order forms are on page 575.

WHAT READERS & REVIEWERS

'If you need to find out how France works then this book is indispensable. Native French people probably have a less thorough understanding of how their country functions.'

LIVING FRANCE MAGAZINE

'The ultimate reference book. Every subject imaginable is exhaustively explained in simple terms. An excellent introduction to fully enjoy all that this fine country has to offer and save time and money in the process.'

AMERICAN CLUB OF ZURICH

'Let's say it at once. David Hampshire's Living and Working in France is the best handbook ever produced for visitors and foreign residents in this country. It is Hampshire's meticulous detail which lifts his work way beyond the range of other books with similar titles. This book is absolutely indispensable.'

RIVIERA REPORTER MAGAZINE

'A must for all future expats. I invested in several books but this is the only one you need. Every issue and concern is covered, every daft question you have but are frightened to ask is answered honestly without pulling any punches. Highly recommended.'

READER

'In answer to the desert island question about the one how-to book on France, this book would be it.'

THE RECORDER NEWSPAPER

'It's everything you always wanted to ask but didn't for fear of the contemptuous put down. Its pages are stuffed with practical information on everyday subjects.'

SWISS NEWS MAGAZINE

'A must for all future ex-pats. Deals with every aspect of moving to Spain. I invested in several books but this is the only one you need. Every issue and concern is covered, every daft question you have on Spain but are frightened to ask is answered honestly without pulling any punches. Highly recommended!'

READER

'If I were to move to France, I would like David Hampshire to be with me, holding my hand every step of the way. This being impractical, I would have to settle for second best and take his books with me instead!

LIVING FRANCE MAGAZINE

Living and Working
in
Britain

A Survival Handbook

by

David Hampshire

SURVIVAL BOOKS • LONDON • ENGLAND

First published in 1991
Second Edition 1996
Third Edition 1999
Fourth Edition 2004
Fifth Edition 2005
Sixth Edition 2007

Copyright © Survival Books 1991, 1996, 1999, 2004, 2005, 2007
Map and illustrations © Jim Watson
Cover photograph © David Hughes (⌨ www.shutterstock.com)

Survival Books Limited,
26 York Street, London W1U 6PZ, United Kingdom
☎ +44 (0)20-7788 7644, ▤ +44 (0)870-762 3212
✉ info@survivalbooks.net
▢ www.survivalbooks.net

British Library Cataloguing in Publication Data.
A CIP record for this book is available
from the British Library.
ISBN-10: 1 905303-12-2
ISBN-13: 978-1-905303-12-0

Printed and bound in India by Ajanta Offset.

HAVE SAID ABOUT SURVIVAL BOOKS

'The amount of information covered is not short of incredible. I thought I knew enough about my birth country. This book has proved me wrong. Don't go to France without it. Big mistake if you do. Absolutely priceless!'

READER

'A mine of information. I might have avoided some embarrassments and frights if I had read it prior to my first Swiss encounters. Deserves an honoured place on any newcomer's bookshelf.'

ENGLISH TEACHERS ASSOCIATION, SWITZERLAND

'A thoroughly interesting and useful read, it crams in almost every conceivable bit of information that a newly-arrived immigrant could need. A great book to read and have close at hand when you arrive in Canada to begin your new life. The best all-round handbook on Canada.'

READER

'A concise, thorough account of the DO's and DON'Ts for a foreigner in Switzerland. Crammed with useful information and lightened with humorous quips which make the facts more readable.'

AMERICAN CITIZENS ABROAD

'Covers every conceivable question that might be asked concerning everyday life — I know of no other book that could take the place of this one.'

FRANCE IN PRINT

'I found this a wonderful book crammed with facts and figures, with a straightforward approach to the problems and pitfalls you are likely to encounter. The whole laced with humour and a thorough understanding of what's involved. Gets my vote!'

READER

'We would like to congratulate you on this work: it is really super! We hand it out to our expatriates and they read it with great interest and pleasure.'

ICI SWITZERLAND, AG

'If you are thinking of moving to New Zealand this is the book for you. Of all the books about New Zealand I've bought, this is the only one I still refer to.'

READER

'A vital tool in the war against real estate sharks; don't even think of buying without reading this book first!'

EVERYTHING SPAIN MAGAZINE

THE AUTHOR

David Hampshire was born in the United Kingdom, where after serving in the Royal Air Force he was employed for many years in the computer industry. He has lived and worked in many countries, including Australia, France, Germany, Malaysia, the Netherlands, Singapore, Switzerland and Spain, where he now resides most of the year. It was while working in Switzerland that he wrote his first book, *Living and Working in Switzerland*, in 1987. To date David is the author or co-author of 17 books, including *Buying a Home in Florida*, *Buying a Home in France*, *Buying a Home in Italy*, *Buying a Home in Portugal*, *Buying a Home in Spain*, *Buying, Selling & Letting Property*, *Living and Working in France* and *Living and Working in Spain*.

Contents

12. HEALTH   303

13. INSURANCE   331

14. FINANCE 357

15. LEISURE 401

16. SPORTS 431

17. SHOPPING 459

IMPORTANT NOTE

Britain is a diverse country with many faces, a variety of ethnic groups, religions and customs, and continuously changing rules, regulations (particularly with respect to immigration, social security, the National Health Service, education and taxes), interest rates and prices. Note that a change of government in Britain can have far-reaching effects on many important aspects of life. **I cannot recommend too strongly that you check with an official and reliable source (not always the same) before making any major decisions or taking an irreversible course of action. Don't, however, believe everything you're told or read, even, dare I say it, herein!**

To help you obtain further information and verify data with official sources, useful addresses and references to other sources of information have been included in all chapters and in **Appendices A** to **C**. Important points have been emphasised throughout the book **in bold print**, some of which it would be expensive or foolish to disregard; **ignore them at your peril or cost.** Unless specifically stated, the reference to any company, organisation, product or publication in this book **doesn't** constitute an endorsement or recommendation.

AUTHOR'S NOTES

- The term Britain comprises Great Britain (the island which includes England, Wales and Scotland) and Northern Ireland, the full name of which is the 'United Kingdom of Great Britain and Northern Ireland', usually shortened to UK, as in this book; Britain and the UK are therefore to all intents and purposes synonymous. The British Isles is the geographical term for the group of islands, which includes Great Britain, Ireland and many smaller islands surrounding Britain. I have attempted to be specific regarding information applying to Britain or the UK as a whole and things that apply to Great Britain, England, Wales, Scotland or Northern Ireland only. I apologise in advance to those whom I have offended by including them under the banner of Britain or the UK when I should have been more specific.

- Frequent references are made in this book to the European Union (EU), which comprises Austria, Belgium, Bulgaria, Cyprus, the Czech Republic, Denmark, Estonia, Finland, France, Germany, Greece, Hungary, Ireland, Italy, Latvia, Lithuania, Luxembourg, Malta, the Netherlands, Poland, Portugal, Romania, Slovakia, Slovenia, Spain, Sweden and the UK, and to the European Economic Area (EEA), which includes the EU countries plus Iceland, Liechtenstein and Norway.

- All times are shown using the 12-hour clock, times before noon indicated by the suffix 'am' and times after noon by 'pm'.

- Unless otherwise stated, all prices quoted are in pounds sterling (GB£) and include VAT at 17.5 per cent. They should be taken as estimates only – particularly property prices, which change frequently – although they were correct at the time of publication.

- His/he/him/man/men (etc.) also mean her/she/her/woman/women (no offence ladies!). This is done simply to make life easier for both the reader and (in particular) the author, and **isn't** intended to be sexist.

- British English is (or should be) used throughout.

- Warnings, tips and other important points are printed in **bold** type throughout the book.

- The following symbols are used in this book: ☎ (telephone), 🖹 (fax), ✉ (email) and 🖥 (internet).

- Lists of **Useful Addresses**, **Further Reading** and **Useful Websites** are contained in **Appendices A** to **C** respectively.

- For those unfamiliar with the imperial or metric system of weights and measures, conversion tables are included in **Appendix D**.

- A map of Britain and a list of the counties is included in **Appendix E**.

INTRODUCTION

Whether you're already living or working in Britain or just thinking about it, this is **THE BOOK** for you. Forget about all those glossy guide books, excellent though they are for tourists; this book was written especially with you in mind and is worth its weight in crown jewels. *Living and Working in Britain* is designed to meet the needs of anyone wishing to know the essentials of British life, including immigrants, temporary workers, businessmen, students, retirees, long-stay tourists and holiday homeowners. However long your intended stay in Britain, you'll find the information contained in this book invaluable.

General information isn't difficult to find in Britain, and a multitude of books are published on every conceivable subject. However, reliable and up-to-date information specifically intended for foreigners living and working in Britain isn't so easy to find. My aim in writing this book was to help fill this void and to provide the comprehensive, **practical** information necessary for a relatively trouble-free life.

You may have visited Britain, but living and working there is a different matter altogether. Adjusting to a different environment and culture and making a home in any foreign country can be a traumatic and stressful experience, and for most people Britain is no exception. You need to adapt to new customs and traditions and discover the British way of doing things, e.g. finding a home, paying bills and obtaining insurance. For most foreigners in Britain, finding out how to overcome the everyday obstacles of life has previously been a case of pot luck. **But no more!** With a copy of *Living and Working in Britain* to hand you'll have a wealth of information at your fingertips – information derived from a variety of sources, both official and unofficial, not least the hard-won experiences of the author, his family, friends, colleagues and acquaintances. *Living and Working in Britain* is the most up-to-date source of general information available to foreigners in Britain. It isn't, however, simply a monologue of dry facts and figures but a practical and entertaining look at life in Britain.

Adapting to life in a new country is a continuous process and, although this book will help reduce your beginner's phase and minimise the frustrations, it doesn't contain all the answers. What it **will** do, however, is help you make informed decisions and calculated judgements instead of uneducated guesses. **Most important, it will help you save time, trouble and money.**

Although you may find some of the information a bit daunting, don't be discouraged. Most problems occur only once and fade into insignificance after a short time (as you face the next half a dozen!). The majority of foreigners in Britain would agree that, all things considered, they relish living there. A period spent in Britain is a wonderful way to enrich your life, broaden your horizons and (hopefully) please your bank manager. I trust that this book will help smooth your way to a happy and rewarding future in your new home.

Good luck!

David Hampshire
May 2007

1.

FINDING A JOB

Finding a job in the UK isn't always as straightforward as the unemployment figures suggest, even for qualified and experienced people seeking work in the UK's major cities. Nevertheless, many Europeans currently find that the number and variety of opportunities in the UK far outweigh those in their home countries. If you don't automatically qualify to live or work in the UK, however – for example by birthright or as a national of a European Economic Area (EEA) country (see page 24) – you will usually find it more difficult to obtain a work permit (see page 81) than to find a job.

IMMIGRATION

The UK is a small country with a relatively large population, a recent history of severe unemployment among the young and middle-aged, and an expensive social security (welfare) system, all of which makes immigration something of a sensitive issue. Although governments have taken legal steps to reduce substantially the number of non-EU foreigners allowed to settle in the UK over recent decades, the large numbers claiming political asylum, both with and without justification, during the last ten years have meant that these measures have had little effect. In 2002, there were over 500,000 official immigrants to the UK – twice the number of emigrants.

Foreigners are to be found in the UK in many walks of life. There are large groups of people from a number of Commonwealth countries and significant numbers from EU states, North America and elsewhere, which together total 4,905,208 people according to the 2001 census. The total workforce in the UK is around 28.8 million people, including 6,287,000 part-time workers, of whom 617,000 are men.

EMPLOYMENT PROSPECTS

You shouldn't count on obtaining employment in the UK unless you have a firm job offer, special qualifications and/or experience for which there's a strong demand. If you want a good job, you must usually be well qualified and speak fluent English. If you plan to arrive in the UK without a job, you should have a detailed plan for finding employment on arrival and try to make some contacts before you arrive. The internet is invaluable in this respect. It's difficult to find permanent work in rural areas, and it isn't plain sailing in cities and large towns unless you have skills or experience that are in demand. Many people turn to self-employment or starting a business in order to make a living, although this path is strewn with pitfalls for the newcomer.

Before moving to the UK to work, you should dispassionately examine your motives and credentials and ask yourself the following questions: What kind of work can you realistically expect to do? What are your qualifications and experience? Are they recognised in the UK? How good is your English? Are there any jobs in your profession or trade in the area where you wish to live? Could you become self-employed or start your own business?

The answers to these and many other questions can be quite disheartening, but it's better to ask them **before** moving to the UK than afterwards.

UNEMPLOYMENT

The UK's official unemployment rate was 5.5 in April 2007. However, some analysts claim the real unemployment figure is much higher when the 'economically inactive' – people formerly seeking work have simply given up because they cannot find any – are included in the statistics.

Unemployment varies from region to region. In some, it's far higher than the national average, particularly where the emphasis has been on traditional manufacturing, employing semi-skilled or unskilled workers. Such regions include large parts of northern England, Scotland, Wales and Northern Ireland. The inner cities of a geographically wider area suffer from similar problems, and are characterised by long-term unemployment among the middle-aged.

During the last two decades, employees have been hit by a combination of recession and 'restructuring' as many companies slashed their workforces in order to become 'lean and mean' and compete more effectively. An ominous development more recently, which has been gathering pace, has been the export of service jobs to less developed countries by some companies. This could eventually lead to massive job losses.

During the last recession, companies quickly realised that they could operate with smaller workforces and today, the UK's largest employers are continually thinking about how to cut their payrolls. Manufacturing has been in turmoil over the past decade during which it has been hard hit by the high value of the pound, high interest rates relative to Euro zone countries and Japan, the residual effects of the slump in Asia, and economic downturn in important overseas markets. The UK also suffers from low investment, mediocre skill levels, intense global competition and lack of a strategy for the future. The UK economy is in continual decline, and although this occasionally seems to reach a plateau when circumstances are favourable, its long-term future looks grim. Even once bullet-proof industries are fading away or feeling the pinch. Reports about the loss of manufacturing jobs are a perennial feature of news bulletins.

Unemployment, when it strikes, is no respecter of age or experience and managers in their 40s and 50s, who are made redundant, are still finding it increasingly difficult to find jobs, even though the broader economic picture is far more favourable than it was six or seven years ago. Many secure professions such as banking, insurance and the civil service no longer offer 'jobs for life'. The lesson has been learnt that nobody is immune from unemployment. Accountants, bankers, computer experts and doctors have all felt its chilly blast over the past fifteen years. For today's manager, job security comes from having saleable skills (constantly updated with further education and training) and a portable pension to go with them.

AGE DISCRIMINATION

Many senior employees in their 40s and 50s who lose their jobs are lucky to find new employment. In today's job market, being 'too old to work' begins at around 45 in some professions. You can even be too old for some jobs before you reach your 30s, particularly if you're a mature student (many companies have an age limit of around 25 for graduate trainees).

Before the introduction of the New Deal scheme, the outlook for youth unemployment looked bleak, with joblessness among 16 to 24-year-olds running at around 25 per cent. In many regions, young working-class males were in crisis when it came to finding employment and there were four times more unemployed men than women between the ages of 18 and 24. Many youths had no job prospects whatsoever and an increasing number were turning to crime as a 'career'. Now, however, the government claims that, partly as a result of the New Deal scheme, participation in which is compulsory after a set period of receiving unemployment benefit, 95 per cent of young people are in work. This is greeted with marked scepticism in some quarters. It remains to be seen whether it is more than a temporary measure for removing youngsters from the unemployment statistics or in some cases getting them off the streets.

At the other end of the qualifications spectrum, many companies are swamped with applications for each place on their graduate schemes, and encountering graduates forced to take menial jobs isn't that unusual. Between 1994 and 2002, the rate of graduate unemployment hovered around the five per cent mark, but according to the latest figures from the Higher Education Statistics Agency, this has now risen to six per cent. Around 73 per cent are in employment six months after leaving university, while others may be forced to take jobs without pay to gain experience.

CHANGING WORKFORCE

The jobs lost in the '80s were generally well-paid skilled and semi-skilled manufacturing jobs, which have largely been replaced by poor quality, low-paid jobs with few or no benefits. Employment experts believe that the era of secure full-time employment with comprehensive employee benefits and lifetime guarantees has gone forever. This view is supported by the trend for increasing numbers of full-time jobs to be replaced by part-time ones (mostly for women), and freelance and contract labour at lower wages and definitely no benefits. (Some 500,000 managers and professionals now work part-time or on contract.) Only around a third of employees have the security of a full-time job (down from 55 per cent in 1975), while perhaps a further third survive in the twilight world of contracts and casual work.

EDUCATION & TRAINING

The inability of British schools and training centres to provide the skilled workforce necessary for today's marketplace has long been of concern to employers. The UK was seen, until recently, as having one of the least educated and worst trained workforces in the western world. Official efforts to improve matters inspired only limited confidence. The Programme for International Student Assessment (PISA) study of pupil achievement, (commissioned every three years by the Organisation for Economic Co-operation and Development/OECD), tests 15–year-olds in 32 countries in literacy, mathematics and science, and compares the results. It has indicated that much improved standards now prevail in UK schools, a development probably connected with the present government's down-to-earth education policies.

However, a lack of qualified and trained staff bodes ill for the UK's future in an increasingly high-tech world, and in the face of strong international competition, might be a problem on the way to resolution. Fierce debate about the value of many educational qualifications continues but improvement in some areas is undoubted.

Many experts believe the UK's future, like that of most western countries, lies in becoming a high-skill, high-productivity economy, leaving labour-intensive tasks to the fast-growing population of the developing world. But despite general educational improvements, the UK still produces too few specialists in technical and scientific disciplines, the technicians and engineers necessary for the international trade war now being fought from computer terminals.

WORKING HOURS

Although the British don't have a reputation abroad for hard work, many Britons are workaholics, particularly among the managerial and professional classes, and most Britons see themselves as hard-working. British employees work among the longest average hours in the European Union and 12-hour days and work-filled evenings aren't uncommon. Redundancies and cost-cutting have increased the pressure on employees, particularly white-collar workers, many of whom now do the work of two or more people. Stress, anxiety and depression due to overwork are increasingly common complaints and accounted for the loss of over 13 million working days a year, according to a Health and Safety Commission report. See also **Working Hours** on page 56.

COMMUTING

The British are a nation of commuters and it's nothing for people to travel 80 to 160km (50 or 100mi) or even further, to work and back each day by car, train or bus, although this is becoming increasingly difficult on the UK's clogged roads and overcrowded railways. They endure the longest commuting times in Europe, according to a study by the RAC Foundation, with people across the country spending the equivalent of five weeks a year just getting to work. In extreme cases, people can spend up to a third of their salaries on commuting which occupies almost half of their day.

Commuting was expected to reduce considerably by the start of this millennium, when a huge increase in the number of people tele-working (working from home via telephone, modem, fax and computer) was predicted. However, the increase was modest, mainly because the implications of tele-working, i.e. lack of close supervision by employers, often conflicted with prevailing workplace culture. Studies show tele-working has become partly a privilege of rank among the employed, while the majority of tele-workers, as a whole, are self-employed. Tele-working is, however, gaining momentum, with annual increases averaging 12 per cent over the past six years. Nowhere will this development be more welcomed than in the City of London, with its chronic rush-hour problems and general poor quality of life. Over 2.2 million people now work from home on at least one day a week, according to the latest data from the Office for National Statistics. This is 7.4 per cent of the total labour force. Of these, 44 per cent do their main job at home. Expansion is expected to continue and some experts estimate that up to 23 per cent of workers will be involved in tele-working within ten years.

INDUSTRIAL RELATIONS

The huge reduction in strikes in the '80s and '90s has essentially continued, particularly in the private sector, despite some recent disputes in the public services making headlines, and threats of strikes being heard more frequently. Anti-union legislation brought in by the Conservative government in the '80s, helped strengthen the trade union movement, which is now a model of democracy. Unions must ballot members before undertaking industrial action, and some more militant union leaders have found that rank and file members are less keen on strikes than full-time officials who don't suffer the consequences. High unemployment in many areas still deters employees from striking.

FURTHER READING

There are numerous books written for those seeking a job in the UK, including *The Job Search Manual* by Linda Aspey (Management Books), *How to Find the Perfect Job* by Tom Jackson (Piatkus) and the *London Jobhunter's Guide* (Pearson Books). There are also numerous magazines and newspapers, many of which are dedicated to particular professions, industries or trades.

BRITAIN & THE EUROPEAN UNION

Nationals of all European Economic Area (EEA) countries (Austria, Belgium, Bulgaria, Cyprus, Czech Republic, Denmark, Estonia, Finland, France, Germany, Greece, Hungary, Iceland, Ireland, Italy, Latvia, Liechtenstein, Lithuania, Luxembourg, Malta, the Netherlands, Norway, Poland, Portugal, Romania, Slovakia, Slovenia, Spain, Sweden and the United Kingdom) have the right to enter, live and work in the UK or any other member state without a work permit, provided they have a valid passport or national identity card and comply with the member state's laws and regulations on employment. EEA nationals are entitled to the same treatment as British subjects in matters of pay, working conditions, access to housing, vocational training, social security and trade union rights. Their immediate dependants are also entitled to join them and enjoy the same rights.

European Union (EU) legislation is designed to make it easier for people to meet vocational training requirements in other member states. There are, however, still practical barriers to full freedom of movement and the right to work anywhere within the EU. For example, some jobs in some member countries require job applicants to have specific skills or vocational qualifications unnecessary in others. The EU is continually working to reduce such barriers and its website (🖥 www.europa.eu.int/scadplus/leg/en/s19005.htm) is a good place to keep informed of developments. Other more practical barriers include housing availability and cost, and the transfer of pension rights. There are also restrictions on employment in the civil service, when the right to work may be limited in individual cases on the grounds of public policy, security or public health.

During the final decade of the last millennium, a huge gulf opened up between the UK and many other EU states on a wide range of issues, as the Conservative government moved from lukewarm endorsement of the EU project in general, to open hostility to closer European monetary and political union in particular. The UK has always been a somewhat reluctant member of the EU, and originally pinned its future on the now defunct European Free Trade Association (EFTA), the Commonwealth and its 'special relationship' with the US – anywhere but Europe, where logic has always dictated its future lay. Fears of loss of 'sovereignty' were voiced by members of the then government and others, and served to influence many Britons against the closer integration of Europe (except for the young, who are generally more enthusiastic).

The UK, along with Denmark and Sweden, chose to remain outside the Euro currency group of 12 countries (Austria, Belgium, Finland, France, Germany, Greece, Ireland, Italy, Luxembourg, the Netherlands, Portugal, and Spain) when the Euro was launched in January 1999. (Greece originally didn't qualify but joined later.) The election of a more pro-European Labour government in 1997, initially inaugurated a new era of better relations between the UK and its EU partners, and it seemed as though Euro entry was only a matter of time. However, that mood has now evaporated. The British government's recent announcement that joining the Euro zone – while desirable in theory – wouldn't currently be in the national interest has effectively kicked the subject into touch for some years. In addition, the UK's role in the recent invasion of Iraq has caused a breach with the major continental powers, France and Germany, which has dampened their enthusiasm for closer ties. Although the tone of the present government's dealings with Europe remains superficially cordial, its actions aren't radically different from those of its predecessor.

QUALIFICATIONS

The most important qualification for working in the UK is the ability to speak English fluently (see pages 44 and 229). Once you have overcome this hurdle, you should establish whether your trade or professional qualifications and experience are recognised. If you aren't experienced, British employers expect your studies to be in a relevant discipline and to have included work experience (i.e. on-the-job training). Professional or trade qualifications are required to work in many fields in the UK, although these aren't as stringent as in other EU countries.

Theoretically, any qualifications recognised by professional and trade bodies in one EU country should be recognised in the UK. In practice, recognition varies from country to country, and in some cases foreign qualifications aren't recognised by British employers or professional and trade associations. All academic qualifications should also be recognised, although they may be less acceptable than equivalent British qualifications, depending on the country and the educational establishment concerned. A ruling by the European Court declared that when examinations are of a similar standard and differences are not extensive, then individuals ought to be required to take additional examinations only in those particular subject areas which don't overlap, in order for their qualification to be acceptable.

All EU member states issue information sheets about occupations each of which contains a common job description together with a table of qualifications which permit you to practise that occupation anywhere in the Union. They're intended to help someone with the relevant qualifications look for a job in another EU country and numerous trades and professions are covered. To obtain a comparison of British vocational qualifications and those recognised in other EU countries, particularly with regard to the Certificate of Experience scheme, contact Carol Rowlands, Department for Education and Skills, Room E3b, Moorfoot, Sheffield S1 4PQ (☎ 0114-259 4237, ✉ carol.rowlands@dfes.gsi.gov.uk). For a comparison of academic qualifications contact UK NARIC, Oriel House, Oriel Road, Cheltenham, Glos. GL50 1XP (☎ 0870-990 4088, 💻 www.naric.org.uk).

GOVERNMENT EMPLOYMENT SERVICE

Jobcentre Plus is the new name for the government employment service, which is an executive agency of the Department of Work and Pensions. Its task is to provide help for the unemployed, but particularly those who have been jobless for over six months, or who are disabled or disadvantaged. It's responsible for paying them the Jobseeker's allowance through its network of offices, helping them with other relevant benefits, and otherwise assisting them in two ways: by placing people directly in jobs, or by offering guidance and counselling so that they can find the best way to return to employment, e.g. through education or training. Jobcentre Plus offices – currently co-existing with 'Jobcentres' which have yet to be re-named and which perform a similar function – advertise jobs and training courses, operate a number of programmes and training initiatives, and provide a wide range of publications about help available.

Their activities include Employment on Trial, Jobclubs, Jobfinder's Grant, Jobmatch and the New Deal scheme introduced in 1998. The New Deal programme provides advice, support, training and direct work experience for young people aged between 18 and 24, and those aged 25 or over who have been claiming Jobseeker's Allowance for two years or more. It's also open to EU nationals. Information can be obtained from Jobcentre Plus offices or the website 💻 www.newdeal.gov.uk.

The vast majority of jobs advertised in Jobcentre Plus offices and Jobcentres are manual or low paid and don't usually include managerial or professional positions (or jobs for 16 to 18-year-olds which are advertised in Careers Centres). Jobs are displayed on boards under headings such as building, clerical, domestic, drivers, engineering, factory, hairdressing, hotel and catering, industrial, motor trade, nursing, office, receptionists, shops, temporary and latest vacancies (where new vacancies are initially posted).

Such offices are generally self-service, although staff are on hand to provide advice and help when required. If you find a job which is of interest, write down the reference number and take it to one of the staff who will tell you more about the job and arrange an interview, if required. You can register with a Jobcentre Plus office by completing a card and providing details of the kind of job you're looking for. If the office doesn't deal with your profession or industry, they should at least be able to tell you about other sources of information. When a job comes in that matches your requirements, you will be informed. But don't rely on this method. Check the boards regularly, as new jobs are displayed each morning and good jobs don't remain vacant for long. You can usually check on new vacancies by telephone. Many cities and boroughs have their own employment centres or 'job shops' where jobs with the local council are advertised.

European Employment Service

Jobcentre Plus is also responsible for European Employment Service (EURES) operations in the UK. EURES is the European system for exchanging job applications and vacancies between member states, which participating employment services carry out on a monthly basis. Members are the EEA countries. Details are available in all Employment Service offices in each member country, as is advice on how to apply for such jobs. Local offices have access to overseas vacancies held on the National Vacancy Computer System (NATVACS). Applicants are required to complete two ES13 application forms, either in response to advertised vacancies or to make a general application, which is valid for six months.

RECRUITMENT CONSULTANTS

Private recruitment consultants and employment agencies proliferate in all major cities and towns in the UK (in London they even outnumber pubs), and are big business. Most large companies are happy to engage consultants to recruit staff, but this is particularly true if they're seeking executives, managers and professional employees. Head-hunters, as they're known, account for around two-thirds of all top level executive appointments in the UK. Some rather less grand agencies cover a wide range of occupations, but most specialise in particular fields, e.g. computer or nursing personnel; accounting, sales, secretarial and office staff; engineering and technical specialists; catering, industrial and construction workers. Many more deal exclusively with 'temps': temporary office staff, baby-sitters, home carers, nannies and mothers' helps, housekeepers, cooks, gardeners, chauffeurs, hairdressers, security guards, cleaners, labourers and factory hands. Specialist nursing agencies, which are fairly common, also cover related occupations like physiotherapy, occupational and speech therapy, and dentistry.

Agencies, which must be licensed by local councils, don't usually charge employees, but receive a fee from employers equivalent to one to four months of the successful applicant's salary, plus a fixed amount, in many cases. Some agencies act as employers themselves, hiring workers and contracting them out to companies at a higher hourly rate than they themselves are paying. As a result of recent EU legislation, hourly rates paid should include an additional amount in lieu of holiday pay after a qualifying period, if employees don't take a paid annual holiday. Agencies must deduct PAYE income tax (see page 382) and National Insurance contributions (see page 338) if employees don't operate their own limited company. Many agencies also employ freelance staff on a contract basis, e.g. accountants, computer personnel, nurses, technical authors, draughtspersons and engineers (see **Contract Jobs** below).

Employment agencies make a lot of money from finding people jobs so, provided you have something to offer, they will be keen to help you (if you're a computer expert, you may get trampled in the rush to find you a job). If they cannot help you, they will usually tell you immediately and won't waste your time. A list of agencies specialising in particular trades or professions is available from the Recruitment and Employment Confederation, 15 Welbeck Street, London W1G 7RG (☎ 020-7009-2100, 💻 www.rec.uk.com). To find those in your own area, look in the yellow pages under 'Employment Agencies', and in local newspapers, where their advertising is usually prominent. Agency jobs are also advertised on television (TV) teletext and via the internet. If you're using agencies to look for work you will find an outline of your relevant legal rights at 💻 www.rec.uk.com/rec/details-of-members/your-legal-rights-jobseekers.aspx.

CONTRACT JOBS

Contract, or freelance, jobs for specialists in fields such as accountancy, engineering, computing and electronics are available through many employment agencies. Rates vary considerably, but rise to £70 an hour or more for, say, an exceptional computer specialist.

Contract work may be sub-contracted or obtained directly from a particular company. Contractors may work at home or on a client's or contract company's premises. Sub-contractors in the building industry require a special permit in order to be classed as self-employed. The potential for home-based work in the UK is huge, particularly within the computer industry, which is keen to exploit the number of computer professionals (particularly women) wishing to work part-time from home. There are many websites, such as 💻 www.computercontractor.net, 💻 www.contractoruk.co.uk and 💻 www.freelanceinformer.com, aimed at contractors.

Workers for most British consultancy companies are permanent company employees, although they often work full-time for another organisation on a contractual basis. It can become quite complicated. Contract workers who wish to be classed as self-employed must set up a limited company (the most common choice for long-term contractors); otherwise PAYE income tax (see page 382) and National Insurance contributions (see page 338) must be deducted from payments by their employer, e.g. an employment agency.

Non-EEA employees of foreign companies who are living and working in the UK temporarily require a work permit, which must be obtained by their British employer (unless employment is for a very brief period only). Many British companies avoid the need for work permits (and save money) by contracting computer programming and other information technology jobs to overseas companies (e.g. in Eastern Europe and Asia) where labour is much cheaper.

PART-TIME JOBS

Part-time jobs are widely available in offices, pubs, shops, factories, cafés and restaurants, and many young foreigners combine part-time work with study and improving their English. Most part-time workers are poorly paid. The introduction of the minimum wage a few years ago much improved matters – before that rates were often far lower – but they remain little more than the law dictates. This is currently £5.35 an hour or £4.45 for those under 22. Nobody should ever receive less than this. You can use the national minimum wage hotline (☎ 0845-600 0678) to obtain information or to complain if you're being underpaid. Calls are confidential.

Part-time employees formerly enjoyed little protection from exploitation by employers, but the Part-time Workers (Prevention of Less Favourable Treatment) Regulations 2000 and two subsequent amendments to them, have changed that. Part-time workers must now receive the same hourly pay and overtime rate as comparable full-time workers, equal rights to sickness and maternity pay, paid holiday entitlement in proportion to that of comparable full-time staff, and similar access to pension schemes. There should be no difference in the length of service required to qualify for these benefits. The definition of a part-time worker under this legislation is one who works fewer than the normal hours for the business in question. These regulations apply to all businesses, but not all employers, particularly smaller ones, will be aware of them. The Department of Trade and Industry (DTI) website (🖳 www.dti.gov.uk/er/ptime.htm) is primarily intended to inform employers of their obligations, but is useful to anyone needing more details.

Some companies operate a job-share scheme. Many jobs listed below under **Temporary & Casual Jobs** are also available on a permanent part-time basis. See also **Recruitment Consultants** on page 27.

TEMPORARY & CASUAL JOBS

Temporary and casual jobs differ from part-time jobs in that jobs are usually for a fixed period only, e.g. from a few hours to a few months, or work may be intermittent. People employed in temporary, seasonal and casual jobs comprise around six per cent of the workforce. At least 65 per cent of companies use temporary staff at some time, mostly in the summer when permanent staff are on holiday, and usually in clerical positions. Employers usually require your national insurance number (see page 338) and sometimes a P45 tax form (see page 387). For information regarding your legal obligations, contact your local Inland Revenue or Department of Social Security (DSS) office. Some employers, illegally, pay temporary staff in cash without making any deductions for tax or national insurance (see **Working Illegally** on page 44).

Casual workers are often employed on a daily, first come, first served basis. The work frequently entails heavy labouring and is, therefore, intended mostly for men. Pay for casual work is usually low and is sometimes paid cash in hand. Temporary and casual work includes the following:

- Office work, which is usually well paid if you're qualified and the easiest work to find, due to the large number of secretarial and office staff agencies;

- Work in the building trade, which can be found through industrial employment agencies and by applying directly to builders and building sites;

- Jobs at exhibitions and shows, including setting up stands, catering (waitresses and bar staff), and loading and unloading work;

- Jobs in shops and stores over Christmas and during sales periods;

- Christmas work with the Post Office;

- Gardening jobs, both in private gardens and in public parks for local councils. Jobs may be advertised in local newspapers, on bulletin boards and in magazines. Local landscape gardeners and garden centres are also often on the lookout for extra staff, particularly in spring and summer.

- Market research, which entails asking people personal questions, in the street or house to house;

- Modelling at art colleges; both sexes are usually required and not just the body beautiful;

- Security work offering long hours for low pay;

- Nursing and auxiliary nursing staff in hospitals, clinics and nursing homes (who are usually employed through nursing agencies to replace permanent staff at short notice);

- Newspaper and magazine distribution;

- Courier work (own transport required, e.g. motorcycle, car or van);

- Labouring jobs in markets;

- Driving jobs, including coach and HGV (heavy good vehicle) drivers, and ferrying cars for manufacturers and car hire companies;

- Miscellaneous jobs as cleaners, baby-sitters and labourers are available from a number of agencies specialising in temporary work, e.g. Industrial Overload and Manpower.

Temporary jobs are also advertised in Jobcentre Plus offices and Jobcentres (see page 26). See also **Recruitment Consultants** on page 27.

HOLIDAY & SHORT-TERM JOBS

Holiday and short-term jobs lasting from a few weeks to six months are provided by numerous organisations. Before applying for a working holiday or short-term job, it's essential that you check that you're eligible and will be permitted to enter the UK under the existing immigration and employment regulations (see **Chapter 3**). You may be required to obtain a work permit and/or entry clearance (see page 75). You should check the documentation required with a British Diplomatic Post in your home country well in advance of your visit. If you plan to study full-time in the UK and to work during your holidays, you don't require a work permit and, as a result of recent rule changes, need not obtain permission from your local Jobcentre Plus office beforehand. A booklet on the subject called *International Students in the UK – What You Need to Know* can be downloaded from ▫ www.dfes.gov.uk/international-students/workleaflet.pdf.

The Education and Training Section of the British Council, 10 Spring Gardens, London SW1A 2BN (☎ 020-7930 8466, ▫ www.britishcouncil.org) is the national office responsible for providing information and advice on all forms of educational visits and exchanges. Students from North America can consult the Council on International Educational Exchange (CIEE), 7 Custom House Street, 3rd Floor, Portland, ME 04101 (☎ +1-207-553 7600, ▫ www.ciee.org), which represents the British Council Education Section in North America, about temporary jobs in the UK.

The following organisations can help you to find holiday and short term jobs:

- The International Bar Association runs a legal internship programme which enables US students to come to the UK for a maximum of six months. Applications should be sent to the BUNAC office in the US which is at PO Box 430, Southbury, Connecticut 06488. Students from elsewhere should contact the IBA, 1 Stephen Street, London W1T 1AT (☎ 020-7691 6868).

- The Student Exchange Employment Programme (SEEP) is a reciprocal scheme allowing British students to work in the US for four months during the summer and American students to work in the UK for up to six months at any time of the year. In the US, contact the CIEE (see address above). The programme is administered in the UK by the British Universities North America Club (BUNAC), 16 Bowling Green Lane, London EC1R 0QH (☎ 020-7251 3472, ▫ www.bunac.org/uk).

- Vacation Work (9 Park End Street, Oxford OX1 1HJ, ☎ 01865-241 978) publishes *Summer Jobs in Britain*, which lists job opportunities throughout the country, including the salary, hours, conditions, and qualifications necessary. It's updated annually.

Many other holiday jobs are available in a range of occupations. In demand are couriers and representatives (e.g. in holiday camps), domestic staff in hotels, farmhands, fruit pickers, supervisors and sports instructors, teachers, youth leaders, secretaries, nurses and shop assistants. A wide range of contacts for these and other jobs are available on numerous specialist websites, some of the most useful of which are the following:

- www.summerjobs4students.co.uk;

- www.summerjobs.co.uk;

- www.caretaker-jobs.com.

VOLUNTARY WORK

The minimum age limit for voluntary work is between 16 and 18, depending on the organisation concerned. Most of them expect reasonable fluency in English. Usually, no special qualifications are required and the minimum length of service varies from around one month to one year (often there's no maximum). Disabled volunteers are also frequently welcomed. Voluntary work is unpaid, although meals and accommodation are usually provided and sometimes also pocket money. This may be insufficient for your out-of-pocket living expenses (entertainment, drinks, etc.), so you should ensure that you bring enough money with you.

It's essential that, before coming to the UK for any kind of voluntary work, you check whether you're eligible and whether you will be permitted to enter the UK under the immigration and employment regulations. You may be required to obtain a visa or other entry clearance (see **Chapter 3**), so check what documentation is required with a British Diplomatic Post in your home country well in advance of your planned visit. The usual visa regulations apply to voluntary workers and your passport must be valid for the period concerned. For temporary employment in international workcamps, farm camps and other voluntary jobs, a work permit isn't usually required, but a letter of invitation from the relevant voluntary organisation or your employer must be produced. This letter doesn't provide entitlement to any other kind of paid work in the UK.

International workcamps provide an opportunity for people from the UK and many other countries to live and work together on a range of projects, including building, conservation, gardening and community improvement schemes. Camps are usually run for periods of two to four weeks between April and October. Normally, workers are required to work for six to seven hours a day, five or six days a week. The work is usually quite physically demanding and accommodation, which is shared with fellow workers, is normally fairly basic. Most workcamp complements comprise 10 to 30 volunteers from several countries and English is generally the common language. Volunteers are usually required to pay a registration fee and their travel expenses. They may also be expected to contribute towards the cost of their board and lodging. An application to join a workcamp should be made through the appropriate recruiting agency in your home country.

Information about volunteering, mainly intended for people resident in the UK, can be obtained from Volunteer Development England, New Oxford House, 16

Waterloo Street, Birmingham B2 5UG (☎ 0121-633 4555, 💻 www.vde.org.uk) and the National Centre for Volunteering, Regents Wharf, 8 All Saints Street, London N1 9RL (☎ 020-7520 8900). A helpful website is 💻 www.voluntarywork.org.

There are also a number of books aimed at volunteers in the UK. The National Youth Agency (Eastgate House, 19-23 Humbertsone Road, Leicester LE5 3GJ, ☎ 0116-242 7350, 💻 www.nya.org.uk) publishes *Finding Out About Volunteering*, and *Volunteer Action*. The *International Directory of Voluntary Work* (Vacation Work) is a guide to 400 agencies and sources of information on short- to long-term voluntary work in the UK and worldwide.

WORKING WOMEN

Women make up 13.2 million of the total British workforce of 27.9 million. Of these 5.67 million are part-time employees. A woman doing the same, or broadly similar, work to a man in the UK and employed by the same employer, is legally entitled to the same salary and other terms of employment. As in most western countries, although there's no **official** discrimination, in practice this often isn't the case. On average, women nationwide earn 18 per cent less than men, but in London this rises to 23.6 per cent. However, the pay gap between the sexes is narrowing, particularly in senior positions. In recent years, employers have been trying harder to retain their female staff and many are setting up crèches and even 'granny' crèches (for parents) to discourage employees from leaving.

Although women are breaking into the professions and the boardroom in ever-increasing numbers, they often find it difficult to reach the top, where males continue to dominate. The main discrimination among women executives and professionals isn't in salary or title, but in promotion opportunities, as many companies and organisations are disinclined to elevate women to important positions (partly due to fears that they may leave and start a family). This invisible barrier is known as the 'glass ceiling'. Although 'the best man for the job is often a woman', this isn't always acknowledged by employers, many of whom still prefer the standard male candidate aged between 28 and 38.

Job Clubs (organised by Jobcentres and Jobcentre Plus offices) provide help for unemployed women to secure jobs and training opportunities, become self-employed or gain access to higher education. Self-employment among women in the UK has increased steadily during the last 15 years, particularly, according to anecdotal evidence, among women from ethnic minorities, despite the fact that banks and other financial institutions are reluctant to provide finance. Women now start just over 30 per cent of new companies and constitute 26 per cent of the self-employed. A useful website for following current developments is 💻 www.everywoman.co.uk.

JOB HUNTING

When looking for a job in the UK, it's advisable not to put all your eggs in one basket as the more job applications you make, the better your chances of finding the right job. Contact as many prospective employers as possible, either by writing, telephoning or calling on them in person, depending on the type of vacancy. Whatever job you're looking for, it's important to market yourself appropriately. For example, the recruitment of executives and senior managers is handled almost exclusively by consultants who advertise in the British quality national press (and foreign counterparts) and interview all applicants prior to presenting clients with a shortlist. At the other end of the scale, manual jobs requiring no previous experience may be advertised at Jobcentres, in local newspapers or shop windows, and the first suitable able-bodied applicant may be offered the job on the spot.

When writing for a job, address your letter to the human resources director or manager and include your curriculum vitae (CV), along with copies of all references and qualifications. However, writing for jobs from abroad is often a hit and miss business and it's probably the least successful method of securing employment. If you're doing this, it's advisable to tell prospective employers when you're available for interview and to arrange as many interviews as you can fit into the time available. Your method of job hunting will depend on your circumstances, and may include the following:

- Visiting a local Jobcentre or Jobcentre Plus office in the UK (see page 26). This is mainly for non-professional skilled and unskilled jobs, particularly in industry, retailing and catering.

- Checking the TV teletext job service, the internet, and bulletin boards. The internet offers hundreds of sites for jobseekers, including corporate websites, recruitment companies and newspaper job advertisements. You can find them with ease using a search engine. The number of recruiters using this medium is rapidly increasing all the time, and in areas like information technology it is already the principal way of finding suitable employees.

- Contacting private recruitment consultants (see page 27).

- Obtaining copies of British daily newspapers, most of which have 'positions vacant' sections on certain days. The quality daily and Sunday newspapers (see page 470) all contain 'vacancies' sections for executive and professional employees, and also have job advertisements dedicated to particular industries or professions, e.g. the computer industry, teaching and the media. Most local and national newspapers are available free in the reading rooms of libraries in the UK. They can be obtained abroad from newsagents in most cities, or read in cultural and commercial centres and social clubs for expatriates (although they don't always contain the 'appointments' or 'situations vacant' sections). Trade publications are also prime sources of job advertising, but are usually only to be had on subscription or found in major libraries.

- Applying to major agencies acting for British companies. These chiefly recruit key managerial and technical staff and often have offices worldwide.

- Approaching foreign multinational firms with offices or subsidiaries in the UK and making written applications directly to British companies. A list of those working in a particular field can be obtained from trade directories, such as Kelly's

Directory and Kompass, copies of which are available in British reference libraries. They may also be found at British Chambers of Commerce abroad or online at 🖳 www.kellysearch.com and 🖳 www.kompass.com. If you have a professional qualification recognised in the UK, you can write to a British professional organisation for information and advice (addresses are obtainable from British Chambers of Commerce or British Council offices abroad).

● Placing an advertisement in the 'Situations Wanted' section of a local newspaper in the UK published in an area where you would like to work. If you're a member of a recognised profession or trade, you could do the same thing in a publication dedicated to your occupation.

● Networking, basically getting together with like-minded people to discuss business, which is a popular way of making business and professional contacts in the UK. It can be particularly successful for executives, managers and professionals when job hunting.

● Asking relatives, friends or acquaintances working in the UK if they know of an employer looking for someone with your experience and qualifications.

● Applying in person to British companies (see below).

If you're already in the UK, you can join expatriate social clubs, churches, societies and professional organisations. If in business, approaching your country's chamber of commerce can be invaluable. Many good business contacts can be made among expatriate groups.

Personal Applications

Your best chance of obtaining certain jobs in the UK, where success is simply a matter of being in the right place at the right time, is to apply in person. When job hunting, it isn't necessarily **what** you know, but **who** you know. Many companies rely on attracting workers by word of mouth or through their own vacancy boards. Shops, too, often advertise vacancies in their windows. Notice boards are frequently found at newsagents, although jobs advertised on them are generally for temporary or part-time help. It's advisable to leave your name and address with a prospective employer, and, if possible a telephone number where you can be contacted, particularly if a job may become vacant at a moment's notice. Make known the fact that you're looking for a job, not only to friends, relatives and acquaintances, but also to anyone with whom you come into contact or who may be able to help. You can give Lady Luck a helping hand with your persistence and enterprise by:

● Cold calling on prospective employers;

● Checking 'wanted' boards;

● Looking in local newspapers;

- Checking notice and bulletin boards in large companies, shopping centres, embassies, clubs, sports centres and newsagents;

- Asking other foreign workers.

When leaving a job in the UK ask for a written reference (which isn't provided automatically), particularly if you intend to look for further work in the UK, or you believe your work experience will help you obtain work in another country.

SALARIES

It can be difficult to determine the salary you should command in the UK, and getting the right pay for the job is something of a lottery. Salaries can also vary considerably for the same work in different parts of the UK. Those working in London and the south-east are the highest paid, mainly due to the higher cost of living, particularly accommodation (although the disparity between the north and south of England contracts and expands in response to economic developments). Usually, salaries are negotiable and it's up to each individual to ensure that he receives pay and benefits commensurate with his qualifications and experience (or as much as you can get!). Minimum salaries exist in some trades and professions, but generally it's every man for himself. In some companies, trades and professions, along with the public sector, they're decided by national pay agreements with the unions.

Your working hours (see page 23) in the UK may differ from those elsewhere and depend on your profession and where you work. For most executives, professionals and 'white-collar' or office workers, between 35 and 38 hours a week is the official norm, particularly in London and other major cities. 'Blue-collar' (manual) workers theoretically work from 37.5 to 40 hours a week, although for many it's much longer when overtime is included. (There's now a maximum 48-hour week under EU regulations). In reality, actual working hours are longer than in any other EU country.

The huge disparity between the salaries of the lowest and highest paid employees in the UK, is also far wider than in its European partners. At the bottom end of the scale, some 15 per cent of employees earned less than £3.50 an hour before the statutory minimum wage set at that figure was introduced in April 1999. Although this has now been increased to £5.35 an hour for adults and £4.45 for those under 22, many believe it's still too low. At the other extreme, executive and managerial salaries have been increasing in leaps and bounds (288 per cent since 1992 according to research by Incomes and Data Services) and are now far higher than in any other European country. A survey carried out in July 2001 for the magazine *Management Today* found that top executives in the UK earned £100,000 a year more than those in France, who are Europe's second highest paid, and £210,000 more than their German peers. The average salary of the chief executives (CE) of the UK's top 100 companies is over £530,000 a year, plus performance-related bonuses, share options and 'fringe benefits' (known as perks – short for perquisites) such as chauffeured company cars. Corporate 'fat-cat' abuse of salaries and perks is more prevalent in the UK than in any other industrialised country.

Surprisingly, even failure to produce good company results only impacts on 'performance' bonuses enjoyed by CEs in a minority of cases.

Salaries for some professionals have also soared in recent years, e.g. top commercial lawyers who can earn well over a million pounds a year! In contrast, middle managers in the UK are relatively poorly paid by international standards. In the last decade, private sector salaries have increased much faster than those in the public sector and there's a growing pay gap. This has made it increasingly difficult for local authorities to recruit and retain staff, with the result that there are thousands of nursing and teaching vacancies throughout the country.

Many employees, particularly company directors and senior managers, enjoy perks (benefits) the value of which may even exceed their monthly salary. Many companies offer benefits for executives and managers which may even continue after retirement, and may include a free company car (possibly with a chauffeur); free health insurance and health screening; paid holidays; private school fees; cheap or free home loans; rent-free homes; free rail season tickets; free company restaurants; non-contributory company pensions; share options; interest-free loans; free tickets for sports events and shows; free subscriptions to clubs; and 'business' conferences in exotic places (see also **Managerial & Executive Positions** on page 52). The perks of board members in many companies make up almost 50 per cent of total remuneration (to keep it out of the hands of the taxman). In addition, executives often receive a huge 'golden hello' when they start a job, and a similar payment, which can sometimes run into millions of pounds, should they be sacked or resign.

SELF-EMPLOYMENT

Anyone who's a British citizen, an EEA national or a permanent resident (see page 97), may work as a self-employed person in the UK. This includes participating in partnerships and co-operatives, operating a franchise and doing commission-only jobs as well running a private business (for the regulations regarding non-EEA nationals, see **Chapter 3**). Unlike most other EEA countries, there are few restrictions and little red tape for anyone wanting to start a business or enter self-employment in the UK. One of government's main initiatives for reducing unemployment has been to encourage people to start their own businesses.

The number of self-employed has risen dramatically over the past twenty years and is now ten per cent of the labour force, the highest in the European Union, and still rising. Much of the reduction in unemployment figures during the past decade has come about as a result of expanding self-employment or jobs created by small companies. Redundancy (and the difficulty in finding full-time employment) is often the spur for over 45s to start their own business. Those aged 45 to 55 account for a disproportionate number of new business start-ups (although many are hollow 'consultancies', where professionals eke out a living on commission) and nearly a quarter of all men over 45 are now self-employed. However, self-employment isn't a panacea for unemployment. A useful website for the self-employed is 💻 www. homeworking.com.

Research

For many people, starting a business is one of the quickest routes to bankruptcy known to mankind. In fact, many people who open businesses would be better off investing in lottery tickets – at least they would then have a chance of getting a return on their investment! Most experts reckon that if you're going to work for yourself you must be prepared to fail. The key to starting or buying a successful business is exhaustive research, research and yet more research (plus innovation, value for money and service). It's absolutely essential to check out the level of competition in a given area, as a saturation of trades and services is common in many fields.

Finance & Cash Flow

Most people are far too optimistic about the prospects of a new business and over-estimate income levels (it often takes years to make a profit). Be realistic, or even pessimistic, when estimating your income – overestimate the costs and underestimate the revenue (then reduce it by up to 50 per cent!). While hoping for the best, you should plan for the worst and have sufficient funds to last until you're established. New projects are rarely, if ever, completed within budget. Make sure you have sufficient working capital and that you can survive until your business takes off. British banks are extremely wary of lending to new businesses, especially businesses run by foreigners. If you wish to borrow money to buy property or for a business venture in the UK, you should carefully consider where and in what currency to raise finance. Under-capitalisation is one of the main reasons for small business failures, which isn't helped by the routine late payment of bills.

Payment

Late payment of bills is the scourge of small businesses in the UK. A recent survey carried out by Experian found companies were waiting almost 60 days to settle invoices, one of the longest such periods in the EU. Smaller firms pay their own bills on average 20 days earlier. Not surprisingly, many small businesses are bankrupted by late payers. Under legislation introduced six years ago, the Late Payment of Commercial Debts (Interest) Act 1998, small companies have the right to claim interest on the late payment of bills, although most dare not for fear of losing business. In reality, invoices are paid slightly later now than before parliament's intervention.

Loans & Overdrafts

British banks are reluctant to lend to small businesses without security and were blamed by many businessmen for prolonging the last recession and bankrupting sound businesses by calling in loans and withdrawing overdraft facilities at a moment's notice. British banks probably have the worst record of refusing loans to sound businesses in the developed world. During the recession in the '90s, relations between small businesses and banks reached an all-time low and, although they have since improved, they're still poor.

Information & Professional Advice

A wealth of free advice and information for budding entrepreneurs is available from government agencies, local councils and the private sector. Many books are published on self-employment and starting your own business including *Starting Your Own Business, Which? Guide to Working From Home*, and *Which? Way to Drive Your Small Business* all published by Which? Books. Libraries are also another excellent source of information.

A large number of local authority agencies and government departments provide free professional advice and assistance on starting and running a business, including finance and borrowing; marketing and selling; setting up and naming a company; bookkeeping and tax; premises and employment; advertising and promotion; patents and copyright; equipment and computing. These include the government-run Small Business Service (🖥 www.sbs.gov.uk) and Business Enterprise or Business Advice Centres, financed by county councils. To find your local Business Enterprise or Advice Centre, consult your local telephone directory or yellow pages.

The Small Business Service (or the Scottish or Welsh Development Agencies in Scotland and Wales) offer information, signposting (to put you in touch with the right people), confidential counselling, and business development services. The last two services are provided in consultation with business counsellors. The organisation's website offers comprehensive information and links, as you would expect from a service with the resources of the Department of Trade and Industry behind it.

Business Link (☎ 0845-600 9006), a similar organisation, is the national business advice centre, which you can also use to get straightforward information for your business needs, and to access a wide network of business support. A free copy of its 100-page *No Nonsense Guide* to regulations for setting up your business can be ordered on the website (🖥 www.businesslink.gov.uk).

If you wish to start a business in the London area, an array of organisations exists to help, but the main ones are Greater London Enterprise, 20 St Thomas Street, London SE1 9ES (☎ 020-7403 0300, 🖥 www.gle.co.uk), set up by the London boroughs; the London Development Agency, General Enquiries, Public Liaison Unit, London Development Agency, Palestra, 197, Blackfriars, London SE1 8AA (☎ 020-7593 9000, 🖥 www.lda.gov.uk), instituted by the Mayor of London; and Business Link for London (☎ 0845-600 0787, 🖥 www.businesslink4london.com), which offers similar advice and support as well as a free grant search service to assist you to discover who might help finance your undertaking.

Grants, Low-interest Loans & Training

There are also a number of other schemes designed to assist people (particularly young people) in starting a business including Livewire (🖥 www.shell-livewire.org) for

16 to 30-year-olds, the Small Firms Loan Guarantee Scheme, and the Prince's Youth Business Trust (💻 www.princes-trust.org.uk). The latter specialises in helping people aged from 14 to 30 who would otherwise be unable to raise the necessary finance. In addition, local, county and borough councils offer a variety of low-interest loans and grants. Practically all have an internet presence nowadays. The central government also provides a number of financial incentives and training schemes for those who wish to go it alone. Many county youth and community services run self-employment projects for young people, e.g. those aged 16 to 25. Ask your local Careers Centre for information.

Buying a Business

Businesses and franchises are advertised for sale each week in *Daltons Weekly*, *Exchange & Mart* and weekly and Sunday newspapers (e.g. the *Sunday Times*). The online version of *Exchange & Mart* is at 💻 www.exchangeandmart.co.uk/business/index.php. There are also franchise periodicals such as *The Franchise Magazine*, the annual *UK Franchise Directory* and *Franchise World*. However, you should be wary of franchises, which usually take many years to make a profit (often the only ones who get rich are the franchise companies).

Miscellaneous

If you're self-employed, you must pay your own income tax and National Insurance class 2 and class 4 contributions (see page 338). To work as a self-employed sub-contractor in the building trade, you must have a sub-contractor's tax certificate card, without which an employer must deduct 25 per cent for standard tax and National Insurance contributions. The Inland Revenue publishes many leaflets for the self-employed which come under the general title of *Tax and Your Business*, including *Thinking of Working for Yourself* (P/SE/1). Anyone who's self-employed and whose taxable turnover exceeds £58,000 a year, must register for Value Added Tax (see page 381). You must adhere to local noise, safety, hygiene and other regulations, depending on the nature of your business, and you may need to take out insurance against accidents at work or against damage to a third party's property.

Warning

Whatever people may tell you, starting your own business isn't easy (otherwise most of us would be doing it). It requires a lot of hard work (self-employed people work an average of ten hours more a week than employees), usually takes a large amount of cash (many businesses fail because of lack of capital), good organisation (e.g. bookkeeping and planning) and a measure of luck – although generally the harder you work, the more 'luck' you will have!

TRAINEES & WORK EXPERIENCE

Nationals of most countries are permitted to work in Britain as trainees or to gain practical work experience under the Training and Work Experience Scheme (TWES). The scheme is intended to give greater flexibility to British companies 'to assist their international business and trading links whilst maintaining adequate safeguards for British and EU nationals'. It's also designed 'to assist the emerging democracies of Eastern and Central Europe by helping their citizens gain valuable training or work experience in the UK'.

The training to be gained should be of a type that's not readily available in the candidate's home country but will be of use there, and usually applies to professions or occupations in which it leads to the acquisition of professional qualifications. It may be possible to come to the UK under this scheme if the training leads only to the acquiring of an occupational skill, but it is more difficult.

Trainees must be aged between 18 and 54, and work experience applicants between 18 and 35. In both categories applicants must be at the start of their careers. (Obviously people who start a second career have been taken into account). The training or work experience must be for a minimum of 30 hours a week and for a fixed length of time. Work experience permits normally limit time spent in the UK to a maximum of one year, although in exceptional circumstances this can be extended to two years. Trainees occupy full-time positions with a normal salary and conditions of employment for similar on-the-job training in the same specialist area. Their permits allow them to remain in the UK for up to three years.

Work experience differs from trainee positions in that it doesn't usually result in a formal qualification, the worker doesn't fill a full-time position, and wages are paid in the form of pocket money or a maintenance allowance and are much less than would be paid to an ordinary employee (unless a statutory minimum wage is applicable). Applications are considered even when applicants have no previous employment related to the intended work experience, provided they have relevant qualifications and the work experience is closely related to their future career.

Although the training and work experience scheme is intended to develop applicants' industrial and commercial experience, a secondary objective is to improve their knowledge of the English language (where applicable). Applicants must have an 'adequate knowledge' of English before they're accepted. Applicants may not transfer from training or work experience to full employment in the UK and aren't permitted to work under the main work permit scheme for at least two years after the completion of their training or work experience. Trainees must sign an undertaking to return to their home countries once they have completed their training or work experience.

AGRICULTURAL WORKERS SCHEME

The Seasonal Agricultural Workers Scheme (SAWS) originates from the period immediately after the Second World War, when workers were encouraged to come from all over Europe to help with the harvests. It remains essentially unchanged, although it is now restricted to students. Participants, mostly aged between 16 and

25, may undertake any agricultural work provided it is of a seasonal nature. The intention is that they should simultaneously learn something about the UK and improve their English. While the majority come from eastern Europe, the scheme is open to nationals of any state outside the EU. Many participants make the most of the chance to work very long hours to earn pounds sterling (which can be exchanged at a good rate in their home countries) and many return year after year.

Recruitment is carried out **only** by official 'SAWS operators'. They allocate participants to farms and horticultural businesses and ensure that they receive the appropriate wages and conditions. Farmers and growers are required to provide accommodation, but this is usually pretty basic. The overall quota for 2007 is 16,250 and in 2007 40 per cent of the annual quota was allocated to Romanian and Bulgarian nationals. It is expected that the full SAWS quota for 2008 will be drawn from nationals of Romania and Bulgaria. Work cards valid for six months are issued to participants before their arrival, and must be applied for outside the UK.

Enquiries regarding SAWS can be sent to the SAWS Contract Management Team, Work Permits (UK), P.O. Box 3468, Sheffield S3 8WA. You can also email ✉ managed-migration.workpermits@ind.homeoffice.gsi.gov.uk.

AU PAIRS

Single people aged between 17 and 27 are eligible for a job as an au pair in the UK. Those aged under 18 need their parents' written approval. Male au pairs are also permitted under EU regulations and many families now prefer them (although the British government was slow to accept them). The au pair system provides an excellent opportunity to travel, improve your English, and generally broaden your education by living and working in the UK.

Au pairs are usually contracted to work for a minimum of six months and a maximum of two years. If you're a non-EEA national you may work as an au pair on a number of separate occasions, provided the total period doesn't exceed two years. It's also possible to work for two or three months in the summer. Au pairs in the UK must usually be nationals of a European country (see the list on page 24), and they fall into two groups:

- Those who are nationals of EU countries or Norway, Iceland and Liechtenstein can enter the UK with the minimum of formalities, and have the same rights as any other citizens of those states.

- Nationals of other states are bound by restrictions. They must have a letter from an au pair agency or family confirming their invitation to work in the UK as an au pair, plus a letter confirming that they've had a recent medical examination. Citizens of Bosnia-Herzegovina, Bulgaria, Croatia, Macedonia, Romania, the Slovak Republic and Turkey also need an entry visa. **Some nationals must also register with the police within seven days** (see page 109). **If so, this requirement will be stamped in their passport on entering the country.** They must leave the UK after two years. The Immigration and Nationality Enquiry

Bureau (☎ 0870-606 7766) should be able to help with any enquiries, although there are long waiting times before an official becomes available.

As an au pair, you receive free meals and accommodation and have your own room. You're required to pay your own fare to and from the UK, although some families pay towards the fare home for au pairs staying six months or longer. You're normally entitled to a week's paid holiday for each six months' service. In some families, au pairs holiday with the family or are free to take Christmas or Easter as their own holidays, but you should ask permission before making arrangements to go home at these times. Going on holiday with the family does not count as part of your own holiday entitlement. Most families prefer non-smokers and applicants with a driving license. Working hours are limited to five hours a day with at least two full days off each week. You should be free to attend religious services, if you wish. The Home Office recommends au pairs are paid a minimum of £50 a week pocket money (possibly more in London), which means you stand little chance of getting rich unless you marry a wealthy Briton. EU nationals who take sole charge of a pre-school child for more than 15 hours a week should receive a minimum rate of £60. The Recruitment and Employment Confederation (REC) stipulates that au pairs should never have sole charge of children under the age of three.

Au pair positions must be arranged privately, either directly with a family or through a private agency (there's no official government agency). There are dozens of agencies in the UK specialising in finding people au pair positions (both in the UK and abroad), all of which are licensed and inspected by the British authorities. Some agencies offer a two-week trial period, during which either the au pair or the family can terminate the arrangement without notice. Write to a number of agencies and compare the conditions and pocket money offered. Agencies must provide a letter of invitation clearly stating your duties, hours, free time and pocket money (which must be shown to the immigration officer on arrival in the UK). **Agencies aren't permitted to charge au pairs a fee, which is paid by the family.**

Unfortunately, abuses of the au pair system are common and you may be expected to work unreasonably long hours. If you have any questions or complaints about your duties, you should refer them to the agency through which you found your position (if applicable). You're usually required to give notice if you wish to go home before the end of your agreement, although this won't apply if the family has abused the arrangement.

A useful book for prospective au pairs planning to work in the UK or abroad is the *Au Pair and Nanny's Guide to Working Abroad* by Susan Griffith (Vacation Work). A leaflet entitled *Information about Au Pairs* is available from the Home Office, Immigration and Nationality Directorate (IND), Lunar House, 40 Wellesley Road, Croydon CR9 2BY (☎ 0870-606 7766, 🖳 www.workingintheuk.gov.uk). To view the document on the website, click on 'Schemes and Programmes' at the top and then select 'Au pairs' from the column on the left-hand side.

It's possible for responsible English-speaking young women (without experience or formal training) to obtain employment as a 'nanny'. Duties are basically the same as an au pair, except that a position as a nanny is a real job with a real salary!

WORKING ILLEGALLY

There are hundreds of thousands of people working illegally in the UK (including many children), although only a small percentage are foreigners. The vast majority of illegal workers are British or foreign nationals who have the right to work in the UK, but who fail to declare their income (or total income) to the Inland Revenue. The illegal labour market (usually called the black economy) thrives in the UK and is estimated to be worth up to £20 billion a year. It's also estimated that around ten per cent of unemployment claims are fraudulent. Although some unscrupulous employers use illegal labour in order to pay low wages for long hours and poor working conditions.

It's strictly illegal for non-EU nationals to work in the UK without a work permit or official permission. If you're tempted to work illegally, you should be aware of the consequences, as the black economy is a risky business for both employer and employee. A foreigner found working illegally is usually fined and deported and may be refused future entry into the UK. Non-payment of income tax or National Insurance are criminal offences in the UK and offenders are liable to large fines and imprisonment. **Employees without permits have no entitlement to government or company pensions, unemployment benefits, accident insurance at work or legal job protection.**

LANGUAGE

English is the most important and most widely used language in the world and is spoken by some 1.5 billion people as their first or second language. It's the world's *lingua franca* and is the language of the United Nations, international peacekeeping, world banking and commerce, air traffic control, academic research, computers (particularly the internet), space travel, scientific discovery, news gathering and popular entertainment. It's essential for anyone planning to spend some time in the UK. If you're planning to live or work in the UK you will need to speak, read and write English well enough to find your way around, e.g. dealing with government officials, public transport and shops, and to understand and hold conversations with the people you meet. Your English proficiency is important if you have a job requiring a lot of contact with others or which involves speaking on the telephone or dealing with other foreigners who may speak their own 'dialect' of English.

It's particularly important for students to have a high standard of English, as they must be able to follow lectures and take part in discussions in the course of their studies. This may also require a much wider and more technical or specialised vocabulary. For this reason, most universities and colleges won't accept students who aren't fluent in English and many require a formal qualification, e.g. a pass at GCSE or the Cambridge proficiency examination. Prospective students can assess their English fluency by taking the International English Language Testing Service (IELTS) test at British Council offices in over 100 countries.

Whether you speak British or American English (or some other form) is usually irrelevant, although some foreigners have a problem understanding the British (who often don't understand each other's accents) and even Americans initially have some problems understanding the natives (many British still believe the best way to communicate with foreigners is to **shout**). The main difference between standard British English and standard American English is in the spelling (English spelling is a minefield) and pronunciation, plus a 'few' colloquialisms thrown in to confuse the issue. There are many regional accents in the UK, which is the way people pronounce their words, but few dialects, where a unique vocabulary, grammar and idiom is employed. The English spoken by television and radio newsreaders is usually referred to as 'Standard English'.

Some English (or British) people believe they have an historical claim on the English language, but there are approaching five times as many English speakers in the US as in Britain and more people speak English as a second-language (e.g. in India and many African countries, where English is used to communicate across national language barriers) than the number in mother-tongue countries. If you wish to improve your English before starting work or a course of study in the UK, there are language schools throughout the country where you can enrol in a part-time or full-time course lasting from a few weeks to a year (see **Language Schools** on page 229).

If you're working or living in Wales and have children of school age, they may be obliged to learn Welsh – something that has proved unpopular with non-Welsh parents. In the north-western Highlands and Islands of Scotland some 60,000 people still speak Gaelic and this is taught – but not compulsorily – in schools in the region. Similarly, Irish is an optional subject in schools in Northern Ireland.

2.

EMPLOYMENT CONDITIONS

Working conditions in the UK depend largely on an employee's individual contract of employment and an employer's general employment conditions. Some aspects of your working conditions described in this chapter are prescribed by law and, although many employers' pay and conditions are more generous than the statutory minimum, a significant number still offer pay and conditions that are actually illegal. The UK belatedly signed the European Union (EU) social chapter, giving its workers the same rights as those in other EU countries. Fears that this, and the introduction of the minimum wage, would lose 'millions of jobs', to quote one Conservative politician, have proved utterly unfounded.

In recent years, increasing numbers of employees have taken their employers to tribunals. The government assumed, rightly or wrongly, that sometimes these claims were frivolous, and consequently introduced a £100 fee for plaintiffs.

There's often a huge disparity between the working conditions of hourly-paid workers and salaried employees (i.e. monthly-paid), even between those employed by the same company. As in most countries, managerial and executive staff generally enjoy a much higher level of benefits than lower-paid employees. Employees hired to work in the UK by a foreign (non-British) company may receive a higher salary (including fringe benefits and allowances) than those offered by British employers. Citizens of EU member states working in the UK have the same rights as British nationals, for example with regard to pay, working conditions, vocational training and trade union membership. The employment conditions of non-EU nationals are generally the same as British nationals, although their employment is usually subject to the granting of a work permit and its renewal.

Detailed individual rights of employees are explained in a series of booklets and leaflets published by the Department of Trade and Industry (DTI) and the Advisory, Conciliation and Arbitration Service (ACAS). They're available on the internet from the websites of both (🖳 www.dti.gov.uk and 🖳 www.acas.org.uk), by telephone from ACAS Publications (☎ 0870-242 9090) or DTI Publications (☎ 020-7215 5000), or by calling in at a Jobcentre or Jobcentre Plus office.

TERMS OF EMPLOYMENT

Negotiating an appropriate salary is only one aspect of your remuneration which, for many employees, consists of much more than what they receive in their pay packet. When negotiating the terms of employment for a job in the UK, the checklists on the following pages should prove useful. The points listed under **General Positions** below apply to most jobs, while those listed under **Managerial & Executive Positions** (on page 52) may apply to more senior appointments only.

General Positions

- Salary:

  – Is the total salary adequate, taking into account the cost of living in the UK (see page 397)? Is it index-linked?

- How often is the salary reviewed?

- Does it include an allowance for working (and living) in an expensive area (e.g. London)?

- Does the salary include commission and bonuses (see page 56)?

- Does the employer offer profit-sharing, share options or share-save schemes?

- Is overtime paid or time off given in lieu of extra hours worked?

- Is the total salary (including expenses) paid in pounds sterling, or is it paid in another country (in a different currency) with expenses for living in the UK?

● Relocation Expenses:

- Are relocation expenses or a relocation allowance paid?

- Do relocation expenses include travelling expenses for all family members?

- Is there a maximum limit and, if so, is it adequate?

- Are you required to repay your relocation expenses (or a percentage) if you resign before a certain period has elapsed?

- Are you required to pay for your relocation expenses in advance (which may run into thousands of pounds)?

- If employment is for a fixed period, are your relocation expenses paid when you leave the UK?

- If you aren't shipping household goods and furniture to the UK, is there an allowance for buying furniture locally?

- Do relocation expenses include legal and estate agency fees incurred when moving home?

- Does the employer use the services of a relocation consultant (see page 117)?

● Accommodation:

- Will the employer pay for a hotel (or pay a lodging allowance) until you find permanent accommodation?

- Is subsidised or free, temporary or permanent accommodation provided? If so, is it furnished or unfurnished?

- Must you pay for utilities such as electricity, gas and water?

- If accommodation isn't provided by the employer, is assistance in finding suitable accommodation given? What does it consist of?

- What does accommodation cost?

- While living in temporary accommodation, will the employer pay your travelling expenses? How far is it from the place of employment?

- Are your expenses paid while looking for accommodation?

- **Working Hours:**

  - What are the weekly working hours?

  - Are you required to clock in and out of work?

  - Does the employer operate a flexi-time system (see **Flexi-time Rules** on page 58)? If so, what are the fixed (core time) working hours? How early must you start? Can you carry forward extra hours worked and take time off at a later date (or carry forward a deficit and make it up later)?

  - Can you choose between being paid for overtime and taking time off in lieu?

- **Part-time or Periodic Working:**

  - Is part-time or school term-time working permitted?

  - Are working hours flexible or is part-time working from home permitted?

  - Does the employer have a job-sharing scheme?

  - Are extended career breaks permitted with no loss of seniority, grade or salary?

- **Leave Entitlement:**

  - What is the annual leave entitlement? Does it increase with age or length of service?

  - What are the paid public holidays?

  - Is free air travel to your home country, or elsewhere, provided for you and your family and, if so, how often? Are other travel discounts provided?

  - How much paid maternity/paternity leave is provided?

- **Insurance:**

  - Is health insurance or regular health screening provided for you **and** your family? What does it include (see **Health Insurance** on page 344)?

  - Is free life assurance provided?

  - Is accident or any special insurance provided by your employer?

  - For how long is your salary paid if you're ill or have an accident (see **Accident Insurance** on page 342)?

- **Company Pension:**

- Is there a company pension scheme and what (if anything) is your contribution (see **Pensions** on page 340)?

- Are you required or permitted to pay a lump sum into the pension fund in order to receive a full or higher pension?

- What are the rules regarding early retirement?

- Is the pension transferable (portable) and do you receive the company's contributions in addition to your own? If not, will the employer pay into a personal pension plan?

- Is the pension index-linked?

- Do the pension rules apply equally to full **and** part-time employees?

- Employer:

    - What are the employer's prospects?

    - Are his profitability and growth rate favourable?

    - Does he have a good reputation as an employer?

    - Does he have a high staff turnover?

- Women:

    - What is the employer's policy regarding equal opportunities for women?

    - How many women hold positions in middle and senior management or at board level? (If the percentage is low in relation to the number of women employees, perhaps you should be wary if you're a career woman).

    - Does the employer have a policy of reinstatement after childbirth?

- Training:

    - What initial or career training does the employer provide?

    - Is training provided in-house or externally and will the employer pay for training or education abroad, if necessary?

    - Does the employer have an on-going training programme for employees in your profession (e.g. technical, management or language)? Is the employer's training recognised for its excellence (or otherwise)?

    - Will the employer pay for a part or the total cost of non-essential education, e.g. a computer or language course?

    - Will the employer allow paid day release for you to attend a degree course or other study?

- What are the promotion prospects?

- Does the employer provide a free nursery or subsidised crèche for children below school age or a day care centre for the elderly (granny crèche)?

- Are free or subsidised English language lessons provided for you and your spouse (if necessary)?

- Is a free or subsidised employee restaurant provided? If not, is a lunch allowance paid? Is any provision made for shift workers, i.e. breakfast or evening meals?

- Is a travel allowance paid from your British residence to your place of work?

- Is free or subsidised parking provided?

- Are free work-clothes, overalls or uniforms provided? Does the employer pay for the cleaning of work-clothes (workshop and office)?

- Does the employer offer cheap home loans, interest-free loans or mortgage assistance? A cheap home loan can be worth thousands of pounds a year.

- Do you have a written list of your job responsibilities?

- Does the employer provide any fringe benefits, such as subsidised banking services, car discount scheme, cheap petrol, travel discounts, product discounts, sports and social facilities, or subsidised tickets for social and sports events?

- Have your employment conditions been confirmed in writing?

- Is a company car provided? If so, what sort of car? Can it be used privately and, if so, does the employer pay for petrol?

- If a dispute arises over your salary or working conditions, under the law of which country will your contract be interpreted?

Managerial & Executive Positions

- Is a 'golden hello' (similar to a 'golden handshake' when made redundant) paid, i.e. a payment for signing a contract?

- Is private schooling for your children in the UK paid for or subsidised? Will the employer pay for a boarding school in the UK or another country?

- Is the salary index-linked or protected against devaluation and cost of living increases? This is important if you're paid in a foreign currency, which may fluctuate wildly or could be devalued. Are you paid an overseas allowance for working in the UK?

- Is there an executive (usually non-contributory) pension scheme? British executives lead the world on pensions, most of whom retire on around 90 per cent of their net pre-retirement earnings (in stark contrast to people on average pay, who receive among the worst pensions in Europe).

- Is a housing allowance paid or a rent-free house or company flat provided, e.g. when working late in town?

- Are paid holidays provided (perhaps in a company-owned property) or 'business' conferences in exotic places?

- Are costs incurred by a move to the UK reimbursed? For example, the cost of selling your home, employing an agent to let it for you or for storing household effects.

- Will the employer pay for domestic help or towards the cost of a servant or cook?

- Is a car provided **with** a chauffeur?

- Are you entitled to any miscellaneous benefits, such as club membership, free credit cards, or tickets for sports events and shows?

- Is there an entertainment allowance?

- Is extra compensation paid if you're made redundant or fired? Redundancy payments (see **Redundancy** on page 69) are compulsory for all employees in the UK (subject to length of service), and executives often receive a **very** generous 'golden handshake' if they're made redundant, e.g. after a takeover.

CONTRACT OF EMPLOYMENT

Under British law a contract of employment exists as soon as an employee proves his acceptance of an employer's terms and conditions of employment, e.g. by starting work, after which the employer and employee are bound by the terms offered and agreed. The contract isn't always in writing, although under the Employment Protection (Consolidation) Act 1978 (as amended), and the Part-time Workers Prevention of Unfavourable Treatment Act 2000, an employer must provide employees with a written statement containing certain important terms of employment and additional notes, e.g. regarding discipline and grievance procedures. This must be done within two months of your starting work. A written contract of employment should usually contain all the terms and conditions agreed between the employer and employee. No distinctions exist any longer between full-time and part-time workers with regard to rights in the workplace.

You usually receive two copies of your contract of employment (which may be called a 'statement of terms and conditions' or an 'offer letter'), both of which you should sign and date. One copy must be returned to your employer or prospective employer, assuming you agree with the terms and want the job, and the other (usually the original) is for your personal records. There are generally no hidden surprises or traps for the unwary in a British contract of employment although, as with any contract, you should know exactly what it contains before signing it. If your knowledge of the English language is imperfect, you should ask someone to explain anything you don't understand in simple English (British companies rarely provide foreigners with contracts in a language other than English). Your contract (or statement) of employment must contain the following details:

- Names of the employer and employee;

- The date employment begins and whether employment with a previous employer counts as part of the employee's continuous period of employment;

- Job title;

- Place or places of work and employer's address;

- Salary details, including overtime pay and piece-rates, commission, bonuses and agreed salary increases or review dates;

- When the salary is to be paid, e.g. weekly or monthly;

- Hours of work;

- Details of any collective agreement/s which affect terms and conditions;

- Holiday and public holiday entitlements and pay;

- Sickness and accident benefits;

- Pension scheme details, including whether a contracting-out certificate under the Pensions Scheme Act 1993 is in force or not;

- Probationary and notice periods (or the expiry date, if employment is for a fixed period);

- Disciplinary and grievance procedures (which may be contained in a separate document);

- The person an employee should contact, specified by job description or name, if he's dissatisfied with a disciplinary decision.

If there are no agreed terms under one or more of the above headings, this must be stated in the contract. Any special arrangements or conditions you've agreed with an employer should also be contained in the contract. If all or any of the above particulars are contained in a collective agreement, an employer may refer employees to a copy of this or other documents, such as work rules or handbooks, wage regulation orders, sick pay and pension scheme conditions, and the rules relating to flexible working hours and company holidays. Before signing your contract of employment, you should obtain a copy of any general employment conditions (see below) or documents referred to in the contract and ensure that you understand them.

Your employer has no right to alter the terms of the agreement unilaterally, although not all employers are apparently aware of this.

Employment is usually subject to satisfactory references being received from your previous employer(s) and/or character references. In the case of a school leaver or student, a reference may be required from the principal of your last school, college or university. For certain jobs, a pre-employment medical examination is required and periodical examinations may be a condition of employment, e.g. where good health is vital to the safe performance of your duties. If you require a work permit to work in the UK, your contract may contain a clause stating that 'the contract is subject to a work permit being granted by the authorities'. Employees must be notified in writing of any changes relating to a 'required particular' in terms and conditions of employment, at the very latest one month before their proposed introduction. This must be done explicitly and, as noted previously, only in agreement with the workforce. Employers cannot just change contractually agreed terms to suit themselves. Failure to provide a contract or the unilateral change of contractual terms are grounds for taking the matter to an Employment Tribunal. Details of contracts of employment and conditions are contained in the Department of Trade and Industry booklets *Written Statement of Employment Particulars* (PL700), and *Contracts of Employment* (PL810). You can download these from the DTI's website (💻 www.dti.gov.uk).

GENERAL CONDITIONS

In addition to a contract of employment you should receive a copy of an employer's general employment terms and conditions (including benefits, rules and regulations) which apply to all employees, unless otherwise stated in individual contracts of employment. General employment conditions are usually referred to in employment contracts, and employees usually receive a copy on starting employment (or in some cases beforehand). General conditions normally include the following.

Validity & Applicability

General conditions usually contain a paragraph stating the date from which they take effect and to whom they apply.

Place of Work

Unless there's a clause in your contract stating otherwise, your employer cannot change your place of work without your agreement. The place of work refers to a town or area of a large city, rather than a different office or a new building across the street. Some contracts state that you may occasionally be required to work at other company locations.

Salary & Benefits

Your salary is stated in your contract of employment, where salary reviews, overtime rates, piece and bonus rates, planned increases and cost of living rises may also be included. Only general points, such as the payment of your salary into a bank account and the date of salary payments, are usually included in general conditions.

You should generally receive an itemised pay statement (or wage slip) with your salary, if it's paid weekly in cash (rare nowadays), or separately when your salary is paid monthly into a bank account.

Salaries in the UK are generally reviewed once a year, although the salaries of professional employees or all employees in certain 'highly competitive' businesses (where employees are in high demand and short supply) may be reviewed every six months. The salaries of new employees may also be reviewed after six months. Annual increases may be negotiated by individual employees, by an independent pay review board or by a union (or unions), when the majority of a company's employees are members (called collective bargaining). Generally, if the employer needs you badly, and you're dealing from a position of strength, you're better off if you can negotiate your own salary increases. Otherwise, joining a union and letting them do it for you is more effective. A percentage of your annual salary increase is usually to compensate for a rise in the cost of living (**always** applicable in the UK), although some employees (particularly in the public sector) may receive pay rises below the annual rate of inflation.

Commission & Bonuses

Your salary may include commission or bonus payments, calculated on your individual performance (e.g. based on sales) or the company's performance as a whole, which may be paid regularly (e.g. monthly or annually) or irregularly. Some employers pay all employees an annual bonus (usually in December), although this isn't normal practice. When a bonus is paid, it may be stated in your contract of employment, in which case it's obligatory. In your first and last year of employment, an annual bonus is usually paid pro rata if you don't work a full calendar year.

Some employers operate an annual voluntary bonus scheme, based on each employee's individual performance or the company's profits (a profit-sharing scheme), although this may apply only to senior management and professionals. If you're employed on a contract basis for a fixed period, you may also be paid an end-of-contract bonus. When discussing salary with a prospective employer, take into account the total salary package, including commission, bonuses and benefits such as a company car or a low-interest home loan. In industry, particularly in small firms, production workers are often paid on bonus or 'piece-work' rates based on their productivity.

Working Hours

Working hours in the UK are, in reality, the longest in Europe. They vary in theory depending on your employer, your position and the type of industry in which you're employed. For example, the official working week in most manufacturing industries is around 37.5 to 40 hours, while many office employees work 35 to 38 hours a week (a 35-hour week is usually referred to as 9 to 5 or 9am to 5pm). At the other end of the scale, some employees in hospitals, security, catering and hotels may work up to 100 hours a week, although the average in these fields is usually between 50 and 60.

Under the EU Working Time Directive, which came into force in 1998, the maximum working week is now 48 hours (averaged over 17 weeks). For reasons of safety, employees must have rest breaks during the day and a daily rest period of 11 consecutive hours and a weekly rest period of 24 hours. Night-shift working is limited to eight hours a night, averaged over 17 weeks. However, before these formal restrictions on working hours were introduced, an estimated 2.7 million UK workers spent longer than 48 hours on the job each week. Following them, in 2003, 3.4 million men alone are doing so. This illustrates how little impact they've had.

The British government is coming under severe criticism from the EU for allowing workers to sign opt-outs from these working time limitations. The problem is that pressure is put on low-paid employees by employers to work ridiculously long hours when they're taken on; otherwise they don't get work. Professional staff average 9 hours 36 minutes a week of extra and unpaid work. The Government's Labour Force Survey found that two out of three people who work longer than 48 hours a week want to work less. It also found that only one in three knew there was a theoretical limit to the working week. A proposed solution to this is that even an employee who signs – or is forced to sign – an opt-out may work only a maximum of 60 hours a week.

Only some 30 per cent of workers work fewer than 40 hours a week; the average is 43.6 hours. One in six work more than 48 hours a week, while one in ten exceed 55 hours weekly. Shop floor (blue-collar or manual) workers in many companies are required to clock in and out of work, while white-collar (e.g. office) workers may not be, even when working in the same building. Employees caught cheating the clock are liable to instant dismissal.

If a company closes for the period between Christmas and New Year, or on unofficial holidays, you may be required to compensate for this by working extra hours each week. If applicable, this is stated in your general conditions. Your working hours may not be increased above the hours stated in your general conditions without compensation or overtime being paid. Similarly, if you have a guaranteed working week, your hours cannot be reduced (i.e. short-time working) without your agreement. Your hours also cannot be changed without your agreement unless there's a clause (sometimes referred to as a 'mobility clause') in your contract. In reality, an employer is unlikely to change or reduce your hours without agreement if he wants to retain your goodwill and services. If you refuse short-time working and are subsequently dismissed, you can usually regard yourself as being made redundant (see **Redundancy** on page 69), in which case you should receive compensation.

Paid overtime among blue-collar workers is often considered a perk and not something to be avoided at all costs, as in some other countries. Often, one of the first questions a worker asks about a job is, "how much paid overtime is available?". Overtime is a lucrative bonus in some jobs, while in many others it's a matter of economic necessity, without which many workers would find it difficult to survive. It's the only way for low-paid workers, in expensive areas like London, to earn anything remotely like a living wage. In between these two extremes, many salaried employees are required to work long hours for no extra pay, e.g. National Health Service (NHS) junior hospital doctors and most managers and executives. The hours of work of most goods or passenger-vehicle drivers are strictly controlled by law. In general, working hours are a matter of agreement between employers and employees and their representatives (e.g. unions).

Employers cannot normally require people to work excessive hours or unsuitable shift patterns, which are likely to lead to ill health or accidents caused by fatigue (in theory anyway). Many employers are instituting more flexible working hours and often permit employees to take part in job-sharing (where two people share a job), an annual hours scheme (58where employees work an agreed number of hours a year), voluntary reduced time and working part of the time at home.

Flexi-time Rules

Many British companies operate flexi-time working hours, particularly in offices. A flexi-time system usually requires all employees to be present between certain hours, known as the core or block time. For example, from 9 to 11.30am, and from 1.30 to 4pm. Employees may make up their required working hours by starting earlier than the required core time, reducing their lunch break or by working later. Parents of children under six or disabled children under 18 now have the right to apply to their employer to work more flexibly. The employer has a legal duty to consider this seriously. He can refuse only if there are compelling grounds for doing so. A free booklet called *The Right to Request and the Duty to Consider – A Guide for Employers and Employees* (PL520) is available from Jobcentres, Jobcentre Plus offices or can be downloaded from the ACAS website (🖳 www.acas.org.uk). Another useful guide to be had from the same sources is *Flexible Working – A Basic Summary* (PL516).

Few workers now take an hour's lunch break. This is fuelling absenteeism and increasing lost working days caused by stress. Most business premises are open from around 7am to 6pm. Smaller companies may allow employees to work as late as they wish, provided they don't exceed the legal maximum permitted daily working hours.

Overtime & Compensation

Working hours for employees who work a flexi-time system (see above) are usually calculated on a monthly basis. Companies usually allow employees to carry forward extra hours worked and take time off at a later date, or carry forward a deficit and make it up later. Payment may be made for overtime, depending on company policy or your general conditions. Most companies pay overtime for work that's urgent and officially approved, and many prefer salaried (i.e. monthly-paid) employees to take time off in lieu of overtime worked or expect them to work unpaid overtime. Middle and senior management employees aren't generally paid for overtime. When paid, overtime rates are usually the normal rate plus 25 per cent on weekdays and Saturdays, and plus 50 per cent on Sundays. Employees who work on public holidays may be paid double time (a 100 per cent supplement). In some industries and jobs, overtime terms and rates are agreed with a trade union.

Travel & Relocation Expenses

Your travel and relocation expenses to the UK (or to a new job in another area of the UK) depend on your agreement with your employer and are usually detailed in your contract of employment or general conditions. If you're hired from outside the UK, your air (or other travel) costs to the UK are usually paid for by your employer or his agent. You can also claim any additional travel costs, for example the cost of transport to and from airports. If you travel by car to the UK, you can normally claim a mileage rate plus the cost of the ferry or the equivalent air fare.

Most British employers pay your relocation expenses to the UK up to a specified amount. This may be a percentage of your salary, a block allowance or specific expenses such as removal, legal and estate agency fees only. The allowance should be sufficient to move the contents of an average house and you must normally pay any excess costs yourself. A company may ask you to obtain two or three removal estimates, when they're liable for the total cost of removal. If you don't want to bring your furniture to the UK or have only a few belongings to ship, it may be possible to use your allowance to purchase furniture locally. Check with your employer. Generally, you're required to organise and pay for the removal yourself. Your employer usually reimburses you **after** you've paid the bill, although it may be possible to get him to pay the bill directly or make an advance payment.

If you change jobs within the UK, your new employer may pay your relocation expenses when it's necessary for you to move house. Don't forget to ask, as they may not always offer to pay. (See also **Relocation Consultants** on page 117.)

National Insurance

State social security consists of National Insurance (NI) contributions that entitle you to a pension, unemployment and other benefits. NI contributions are compulsory for most residents of the UK and are usually deducted at source from your gross salary by your employer. For details, see **National Insurance** on page 338.

Medical Examination

Many British companies require all prospective employees to have a pre-employment medical examination performed by a doctor nominated by them. An offer of employment is usually subject to an applicant being given a clean bill of health. This may be required for employees over a certain age only (e.g. 40) or for employees in particular jobs, e.g. where good health is of paramount importance for reasons of safety. Thereafter, a medical examination may be necessary periodically (e.g. every one or two years) or may be requested at any time by your employer. Medical examinations are usually required as a condition of membership of a company health, pension or life insurance scheme. Some companies also insist on employees having regular health screening, particularly senior managers and executives.

Cars & Driving Licence

Many British employers provide senior employees such as directors, senior managers and professionals with a company car, although few jobs paying below around £25,000 a year offer a company car as a benefit unless it's necessary to do your job. If you're provided with a company car, you usually receive full details about its use and your obligations on starting employment. If you lose your licence (e.g. through drunken driving) and are unable to fulfil the requirements of your job, your employment is usually terminated (i.e. you're fired), and you may not be entitled to any compensation. If a company car is provided, check what sort of car it is, whether you're permitted to use it privately and, if so, who pays for the petrol for private mileage. Some companies require employees to make a contribution towards the cost of providing a non-essential company car.

Using a company car for private purposes affects your tax position. Many companies offer employees a car allowance rather than provide a company car, which saves employees having to pay onerous taxes. Company cars are replaced on average every three years or after 112,000km (70,000mi). Most companies allow employees to buy second-hand company cars at advantageous prices.

Company Pension Fund

Most medium to large companies provide a company pension fund for employees. They've been traditionally regarded as a good deal, but have attracted attention in recent years for sometimes not being as soundly based as expected. This is mainly been due to the fluctuation in the values of stocks and shares, although these have done well in the last few years), but occasionally because of mismanagement and, every now and again, corruption. Membership isn't compulsory, although most company pension funds offer much better terms than you can obtain privately, for example, from a private pension plan. The amount you pay varies from nothing (non-contributory), reserved for senior staff, to between four and eight per cent of your gross monthly salary, depending on your age and your employer's pension fund. See **Pensions** on page 340 for more information.

Accident Insurance

All employers, including even the smallest trader, are required to have occupational accident insurance for employees working on their premises, whether in a factory, office, shop, warehouse or residential accommodation. The reporting of injuries, diseases and dangerous occurrences was reinforced under additional regulations, which came into force in 1986. An employer is required to notify the appropriate authority immediately in the case of a death or serious injury as the result of an accident, or when anybody is off work for more than three days as a consequence.

Although the primary responsibility for safety rests with the employer, employees are required by law to ensure that they co-operate with their employers and that they don't endanger themselves or anyone else by their acts or omissions. There are usually specific regulations for activities involving high risks, e.g. when operating electrical equipment and certain classes of machinery and the use of chemicals. The number of people injured at work each year in the UK is some 400,000 and there are also around 250 fatalities.

For more information contact the local Health & Safety Executive office. See **Accident Insurance** on page 342.

Income Protection

Income protection in the event of sickness or an accident depends on your employer, your personal contract of employment, your length of employment and whether you're paid weekly or monthly. Most salaried employees (i.e. monthly-paid) automatically receive sick pay when sick for a short period. Usually, you must have been employed for a minimum period before you're entitled to sick pay, e.g. 13 weeks, which may coincide with your probationary period. Employees paid weekly at an hourly rate, may not be paid at all for any illness lasting less than four days, after which time they receive Statutory Sick Pay (SSP).

Your employer may have an occupational sick pay (OSP) scheme, under which you receive your full salary for a number of weeks in the event of sickness or after an accident. OSP is often provided by employers as part of a company pension scheme, although fewer than 50 per cent of all private sector companies have an OSP scheme. For more information, see **Permanent Health Insurance** on page 342.

Miscellaneous Insurance

Other insurance provided by your employer is usually detailed in your general conditions. This may include free life and health insurance, which also covers travel abroad on company business. Free life insurance is typically four times annual salary for top managers and directors. Some companies provide free membership of a private health insurance scheme, although this may apply only to executives, managers and certain key personnel. Check that health insurance includes your family. Companies may also operate a contributory group health insurance scheme, offering discounted subscriptions for individual private membership.

Notification of Sickness or Accident

You're usually required to notify your employer as soon as possible of sickness or an accident that prevents you from working, i.e. within a few hours of your normal starting time. Failure to do so may result in your not being paid for that day's absence. You're required to keep your boss or manager informed about your illness and when you expect to return to work. For periods of under seven days, you're usually required to provide a self-certificate of why you were absent on your return to work, although some employers may require a doctor's certificate. If you're away from work for longer than seven days, you're required to obtain a doctor's certificate (NHS doctors don't provide free medical certificates for absence from work through sickness for periods of less than seven days).

Annual Holidays

Your annual holiday entitlement usually depends on your profession, position and employer, and your individual contract of employment. Holiday pay and entitlements are decided by individual or collective bargaining (e.g. by unions). Under EU rules, employees are allowed four weeks paid holiday a year. Most British companies grant employees four weeks paid annual holiday and around 25 per cent grant five weeks or more (the average is 23 working days a year). Some employers give employees over a certain age, e.g. 50, an extra week's holiday, and offer additional holidays for length of service and for senior positions (but no time to take them!).

Part-time workers have the same statutory rights as full-time workers, i.e. if they work half the hours of a full-time worker, they receive half the paid holiday entitlement. Equal treatment is now mandatory.

A company's holiday year may not correspond to a calendar year, but may run from 1st April to 31st March to coincide (roughly) with the financial year in the UK. Holiday entitlement is calculated on a pro rata basis (per completed calendar month of service) if you don't work a full 'holiday' year. Usually, all holidays must be taken within the holiday year in which they're earned, although some companies allow employees to carry them over to the next year.

Before starting a new job, check that any planned holidays will be approved by your new employer. This is particularly important if they fall within your probationary period (usually the first three months), when holidays aren't generally permitted. Holidays may normally be taken only with the prior permission of your manager or boss, and in many companies must be booked up to one year in advance. Most companies allow unpaid leave in exceptional circumstances only, such as when all your holiday entitlement has been exhausted. If you fall ill while on holiday, your holiday entitlement may be credited to you, provided you obtain a doctor's certificate. If you resign your position or are given notice, most employers pay you in lieu of any outstanding holidays, although this isn't an entitlement and you may be obliged to take the holiday at your employer's convenience.

Public Holidays

Compared with many other European countries, the UK has few public or national holidays, normally referred to as bank holidays, as they're days on which banks are officially closed. Schools, businesses and many shops are also closed on public holidays. The British celebrate no national, independence or revolution day(s), and the only national religious holidays are Christmas and Easter. The following days are public holidays throughout the UK, except where noted:

Date	Holiday
1st January	New Year's Day
2nd January	New Year's Bank Holiday (Scotland only)
17th March	St Patrick's Day (N. Ireland only)
March/April: Variable date	Good Friday
March/April: Monday after Good Friday	Easter Monday (not in Scotland)
First Monday in May	May Bank Holiday
Last Monday in May	Spring Bank Holiday (not in Scotland)
12th July	Orangeman's Day (N. Ireland only)
First Monday in August	Summer Bank Holiday (Scotland only)
Last Monday in August	Summer Bank Holiday (not in Scotland)
25th December	Christmas Day
26th December	Boxing Day

If a public holiday falls on a weekend, there's usually a substitute holiday on the following Monday. An increasing number of British companies close down during Christmas and New Year, e.g. from around noon or 5pm on 24th December to the 2nd January. To compensate for this shutdown and, perhaps, other extra holidays during the year, employees may be required to work extra hours throughout the year, or may be required to take part of their annual holiday entitlement. Part-time staff now have equal rights in this area.

If you're taken ill immediately before or after a public holiday, you may be required to produce a doctor's certificate in order to be paid for the holiday period. You aren't required to work on public holidays unless otherwise stated in your contract of employment. When it's necessary to work on public holidays, you should receive the same or a higher rate of pay than is paid for working on a Sunday (e.g. double the normal rate) and/or time off in lieu. When employment involves working at weekends and on public holidays (e.g. shift working), you're most likely recompensed in your basic salary or paid a shift allowance.

Compassionate & Special Leave

Whether or not you're paid for time off work, or time lost through unavoidable circumstances (e.g. public transport strikes or car breakdowns), depends on your employer, whether you're paid monthly or weekly (e.g. with an hourly rate of pay) and, not least, whether you're required to punch a clock. The attitude in the UK to paid time off depends on your status and position. Executives and managers (who admittedly often work much longer hours than officially required) have much more leeway regarding time off than a factory worker. All employees are allowed by law to take time off work for the following reasons:

- A pregnant woman is entitled to 'reasonable' paid time off for ante-natal care.

- A trade union official is entitled to paid time off for trade union duties and training for such duties, and employees may also be paid to attend union meetings during working hours. Similarly, a safety representative is allowed paid time off in connection with his safety duties.

- Time off for public duties such as service as a Justice of the Peace, juror or court witness, councillor or school governor, or as a member of a statutory tribunal or authority, although your employer isn't required by law to pay you.

- If you're made redundant, you're entitled to 'reasonable' paid time off to look for a new job or to arrange training in connection with a new job.

Many British companies also provide paid compassionate or special leave on certain occasions, which may include your own or a family marriage, birth of a child, or the death of a close relative. The grounds for compassionate leave may be listed in your general conditions.

Paid Expenses

Expenses paid by your employer are usually listed in your general conditions. These may include travel costs from your home to your place of work, which (if applicable) may consist of a second class rail season ticket or the equivalent in cash (paid monthly with your salary). Companies without a company restaurant or canteen may pay employees a lunch allowance or provide luncheon vouchers. Expenses paid for travel on company business or for training courses may be detailed in your general conditions or listed in a separate document. Most companies pay a mileage allowance to staff authorised to use their private motor vehicles on company business, but **it's important to check that business use is covered by your car insurance**.

Probationary & Notice Periods

For most jobs there's a probationary period, which may be two weeks for hourly-paid employees and three months for salaried (monthly-paid) employees. Your notice period normally depends on your method of salary payment, your employer, your profession and your length of service, and is detailed in your contract of employment and general conditions. Probationary and notice periods apply equally to employers and employees. Most monthly-paid employees have a one month (or four-week) notice period which takes effect after any probationary period. This may remain the same for the first four years of service. From 4 to 12 years of continuous service, there may be an extra week's notice for each whole year of service. After 12 years' service, the notice period may be three months or 12 weeks (unless your individual contract specifies a longer period). The notice period may be longer for executive or key employees, e.g. three or six months, or may be extended after a number of years of service, in which case it is noted in your general conditions.

Unless otherwise stated in your contract of employment, there's a legal minimum notice period for full-time employees, depending on your length of service. For the first four weeks of service, there's no statutory minimum and you aren't entitled to notice unless otherwise agreed. After four weeks' service, you're entitled to one week's notice. After two years' continuous service, it's increased to two weeks and is extended by another week for each subsequent year of continuous service, up to a maximum of 12 weeks notice after 12 years' service.

If an employer doesn't give you the required notice in writing, he's liable to pay you in full for the period of official notice (see **Discipline & Dismissal** on page 68). If you resign your job, you must usually do so in writing. If you resign or are given notice, your company may not require you to work your notice period, particularly if you're joining a competitor or your boss feels that you may be a bad influence on your colleagues. However, if he doesn't want you to work your notice, he must pay you in full for the notice period, plus any outstanding overtime pay or holiday to which you're entitled.

If an employer is bankrupted and cannot pay you, you can terminate your employment without notice, but your employer cannot legally do this. Other valid reasons for an employee **not** to give notice are assault or abuse on him or a colleague by the employer, and failure to pay or persistent delay in paying an employee's salary. As the law stands, you can usually leave a job without giving notice and the chances of your employer having any legal rights worth enforcing are negligible. However, you may lose any bonuses or other monies owed to you, plus any possibility of receiving a good reference.

Education & Training

Education and training provided by your employer may be stated in your general conditions. This may include training abroad, provided that it's essential for your job (although you may need to convince your employer). It's in your own interest to investigate courses of study, seminars and lectures that you feel are of direct benefit to you and your employer. Most employers give reasonable consideration to a request to attend a course during working time, provided you don't make it a full-time occupation. In addition to relevant education and training, employers must also provide the essential tools and equipment for a job (although this is open to interpretation). It's compulsory for companies to provide appropriate and adequate safety and health training for all employees (see **Accident Insurance** on page 342).

If you need to improve your English ability, language classes may be paid for by your employer. If it's necessary to learn a foreign language in order to perform your job, the cost of language study should be paid by your employer. An allowance may be paid for personal education or hobbies (flower arranging, kite flying or breakdancing) which aren't work-related or of direct benefit to your employer (unless he's in the flower, kite or dance business).

Pregnancy & Confinement

Time off work for sickness in connection with a pregnancy is usually given without question, but it may not be paid unless authorised by a doctor. You're guaranteed the right to 'reasonable' time off work for antenatal care without loss of pay, irrespective of how long you've been employed (usually a clinic or hospital appointment card must be produced). A pregnant or nursing woman cannot be required to work overtime, and a woman cannot be dismissed because she's pregnant or for any reason connected with her pregnancy. If she's dismissed, she has an automatic claim for unfair dismissal, irrespective of her length of service. It's also illegal to refuse a woman a job because she's pregnant, provided this doesn't prevent her from doing the job.

A mother cannot (by law) return to work during the first eight weeks after giving birth. Pregnant women are entitled to maternity leave and pay, depending on the length of their employment (at least 26 weeks) and income (at least equal to the lower earnings limit for national insurance contributions). Part-time employees have equal rights. In 2007, Statutory Maternity Pay was 90 per cent of a woman's weekly earnings for the first six weeks and £112.75 for the next 20 weeks. All women, irrespective of their length of service, are entitled to 26 weeks' unpaid maternity leave and employment-related benefits such as private medical insurance, use of a company car and pension contributions must continue during this period. Some employers provide enhanced benefits, including the payment of full salary for some or all of the maternity-leave period.

At the end of the 26-week period, you have the right to return to the same job. If you've worked for the same employer for over twenty six weeks continuously, you're entitled to an additional 26 weeks of maternity leave and can return to the same or similar employment up to 52 weeks after giving birth. Most companies count periods of absence for maternity leave as continuous employment for the purpose of calculating an employee's number of years' service, but not when calculating annual holiday. Various official booklets such as *Maternity Rights* (PL958) and *Working Father – Rights to Leave and Pay* (PL517) are available from Jobcentres and Jobcentre Plus offices, or can be downloaded from the ACAS website (⌨ www.acas.org.uk).

Part-time Job Restrictions

Restrictions on part-time employment for an employer other than your regular employer may be included in your general conditions. Many British companies don't allow full-time employees to work part-time (i.e. moonlight) for another employer, particularly one in the same line of business. You may, however, be permitted to take a part-time teaching job or similar part-time employment (or you can write a book!).

Confidentiality & Changing Jobs

If you disclose any confidential company information, in the UK or overseas (particularly to competitors), you may be liable to instant dismissal and may also have legal action taken against you. You may not steal any confidential information (e.g. customer mailing lists) from an employer, but you may use any skills, knowledge and contacts acquired during his employ. If you make an invention while an employee, it remains your property unless you sell or licence it to your employer – provided the invention wasn't made as part of your 'normal duties' or you were specifically employed to invent things, e.g. in research and development.

You may not compete against a former employer if there's a valid, binding restraint clause in your contract of employment. Your contract may also contain a clause defining the sort of information that the employer considers confidential, such as customer and supplier relationships and details of business plans. If there's a confidentiality or restraint clause in your contract, which is unfair, e.g. it inhibits you from changing jobs, it is probably invalid in law and is unenforceable. If you're in doubt, consult a solicitor who's an expert in company law about your rights. If you're a key employee, you may have a legal binding contract preventing you from joining a competitor or starting a company in the same line of business as your employer and, in particular, enticing former colleagues to join your company. However, such a clause is usually valid for one year only.

Acceptance of Gifts

With the exception of those employed in the public sector, employees are normally permitted to accept gifts of a limited value from customers or suppliers, e.g. bottles of wine or spirits or other small gifts at Christmas. Generally, any gifts given and received openly and above board aren't considered a bribe or unlawful (although if you give your business to someone else in the following year, don't expect a 'bribe' of a bottle of wine next Christmas). You should declare any gifts received to your immediate superior, who decides what should be done with them. Most bosses pool all gifts and divide them among all employees.

Long Service Awards

Most large companies present their employees with long service awards after a number of years, e.g. 15, 20 or 25 years. These are usually in the form of a gift such as a watch or clock (so you can count the hours to your retirement), which are presented to individuals by senior management. Periods of absence on maternity leave usually count as continuous employment when calculating your length of service.

Retirement

Your general conditions may be valid only until the generally recognised British retirement age (there's no 'statutory retirement age'), which is based on the age at which people can receive the state retirement pension. This is currently 60 for women and 65 for men, but will be 65 for everyone from 10th April 2010. (Changes up to that point are being introduced gradually). If you wish to continue working after you've reached retirement age, you may need to negotiate a new contract of employment. If your employer has a compulsory retirement age, he isn't required to give you notice. However, it's illegal to have a lower **compulsory** retirement age for women than men or vice versa. Many companies present employees with a gift on reaching retirement age, the value of which usually depends on your number of years of service.

Discipline & Dismissal

Most large and medium size companies have comprehensive grievance and disciplinary procedures, which must usually be followed before an employee can be suspended or dismissed. Some employers have disciplinary procedures whereby employees can be suspended with or without pay, e.g. for breaches of contract. Employees may also be suspended (usually with pay) pending investigation into an alleged offence or impropriety. Disciplinary procedures usually include verbal and official written warnings. These procedures are to protect employees from unfair dismissal and to ensure that dismissed employees cannot (successfully) sue their employer. If you have a grievance or complaint against a colleague or your boss, there may be an official procedure to be followed to obtain redress. If an official grievance procedure exists, it's usually detailed in your general conditions.

Under normal circumstances, you cannot be fired in the first four weeks of an illness, and a woman is automatically regarded as unfairly dismissed if her employer does so because she's pregnant, has given birth or for any reason connected with her pregnancy and childbirth. Instant or summary dismissal without any right to notice or salary in lieu of notice is permissible only in exceptional circumstances, such as for acts of gross misconduct. These may include refusing to work (without a good reason); cheating or stealing from your employer; competing with your employer; insulting your employer or colleagues; assault on your employer or a colleague; or drunkenness during working hours on your employer's premises. You're entitled to written reasons for your dismissal and should ask to see them if they aren't provided voluntarily. They should, in any case, be provided within two weeks of the request. If you're 'forced' to resign your position, in law you're deemed to have been dismissed 'constructively' and can claim unfair dismissal (this may also apply if your duties and responsibilities are drastically downgraded and you're asked to do more menial tasks, which may be designed to force you to resign).

If you believe you've been unfairly dismissed, you can take your case to ACAS or the Equal Opportunities Commission. Protection against unfair dismissal includes a basic award for lost redundancy up to a maximum amount, and a compensatory award, which is the amount the tribunal considers appropriate for the loss suffered by the employee as a result of the dismissal. Unfair dismissal awards are limited to a maximum sum (currently £52,600) depending on an employee's age and length of service, whereas sex discrimination awards are unlimited. A special award may also be made where unfair dismissal was caused by an employee's membership or non-membership of a union, or where an employer ignored a tribunal's order of re-engagement. Many pamphlets on this and related topics can be downloaded from the DTI and ACAS websites (see page 48). Some of the most useful are *Unfairly Dismissed?* (PL712 Rev 18), *Rights to Notice and Reasons for Dismissal* (PL707), *Individual Rights of Employees* (PL716) and *Fair and Unfair Dismissal* (PL714).

Redundancy

The Redundancy Payments Scheme covers nearly all workers who are employed under a contract of employment, provided employees have at least two years' continuous service and meet the conditions outlined below. The main exceptions are those who have reached retirement age and continue to work, crown servants, and apprentices whose service ends at the end of their apprenticeship contract. You qualify for redundancy pay if you're dismissed wholly or mainly due to your job being phased out or when your employer wishes to reduce his workforce.

If you're made redundant, you're entitled to your normal notice period or pay in lieu of notice and are additionally entitled to redundancy pay. You're also usually entitled to reasonable time off work with pay to look for another job or arrange training. The amount of redundancy pay you receive depends on whether your employer pays the minimum amount required by law or more, either voluntarily or, for example, under pressure from trade unions. It may also be possible to take voluntary redundancy or early retirement and receive an early pension, e.g. in the case of ill health.

The Employment Protection (Consolidation) Act 1978 (as amended) states that an employee aged 18 to 65 (60 for women) who has worked continuously for 16 hours or more a week over a period of two years, or eight or more hours a week continuously for five years, is entitled to a statutory redundancy lump sum payment. The amount payable is based on a sliding scale depending on your age, length of service and salary. The older you are, the more redundancy pay you receive (pro rata). The basic payment is half a week's pay for each complete year of service after the age of 18 until age 22, one week for each year after the age of 22 until age 41, and one and a half weeks pay for each year after the age of 41 up to the age of 64.

After the age of 64 the total amount you receive is reduced by one twelfth for each complete month you're over 64. There's a limit on the amount of a week's pay that may be taken into account, which in 2007 was £310. It changes annually in line with the retail price index. The maximum amount payable currently is £9,300 (30 weeks at £310 per week) after 20 years' service – the maximum period of employment taken into account. You can expect to receive your statutory redundancy payment at about the time you leave your job and it's tax-free. However, additional redundancy payments you may receive from your employer may be taxable, although you should confirm the details of this with a tax office.

Many companies engage an 'outplacement' consultant to assist employees who are made redundant. This includes advice and counselling on future job prospects, job hunting, state benefits, retirement, retraining, setting up in business and financial advice for employees who receive large redundancy payments. Executives, managers and key personnel may have a clause in their contract whereby they receive a generous 'golden handshake' if they're made redundant, e.g. after a takeover. The receipt of a redundancy payment, irrespective of the amount, doesn't affect your eligibility to claim Jobseeker's Allowance.

For further information about redundancy payments, you can contact the Insolvency Service Redundancy Payments Helpline (☎ 0845-145 0004), pick up various pamphlets such as (PL808) *Redundancy Entitlement – Statutory Rights: a Guide for Employees*, (PL718) *Your Rights if Your Employer is Insolvent*, (PL699) *Transfer of Undertakings* and *Continuous Employment* and *A Week's Pay: Rules for Calculation* at Jobcentres or Jobcentre Plus offices or download them from the ACAS and DTI websites (see page 48).

References

In the UK, an employer isn't legally obliged to provide an employee with a written reference. If you leave an employer on good terms, he normally provides a written reference on request. If your employer refuses to give you a written reference or gives you a 'bad' reference, it's advisable to ask your immediate boss or a colleague for a written reference. In the UK, prospective employers usually contact your previous employer (or employers) directly for a reference, orally or written. This can be bad news for employees, as they have no idea what has been said about them and whether it was true or false. An employer is under no obligation (except perhaps morally) to provide a reference, but, if he does, he may not (legally) maliciously defame you although, should he do so, it's almost impossible to obtain legal redress.

Trade Union Membership

Trade unions went through a bad time in the '80s under the Conservatives and were largely legislated into being toothless tigers. Membership fell sharply by around 30 per cent and this process was exacerbated when entire industries disappeared and with them their old-established trade union traditions. The latter were not duplicated in the new world of low wages, unskilled jobs and insecurity. Falling membership, which occasionally reaches a temporary plateau, has characterised the scene ever since. According to the Labour Market Spotlight in 2006, 28.4 per cent of all employees were union members, far below the figures at the peak of membership in 1979.

Although the Labour party has been in power ten years, it shows no energetic signs of wanting to reverse this. However, it did pass the Fairness at Work Act 2000. Thanks to this, independent trade unions in organisations employing more than 20 workers now have the right to claim recognition for collective bargaining if they can show they enjoy majority support among the workforce through a ballot. Once recognised, they have rights to information and consultation and their officials can take time off to carry out their duties. The pay of one third of UK employees was affected by collective agreements in 2006.

By continental standards, this sounds utterly tame and yet seems an achievement when contrasted with the recent past. As a consequence of the Thatcher era, many companies are now non-union. Surprisingly, the majority of union members are now professionals, managers and service providers rather than manual workers, who often lack any protection at all. Industrial action taken by the lowest-paid workers, who often do the hardest and most unpleasant jobs, is rare and it's usually higher paid workers who can cause the maximum disruption who go on strike.

In the '60s and '70s, the unions were their own worst enemies and they succeeded in losing many jobs as a result of their restrictive practices, belligerence and bloody- mindedness by driving companies out of business (to say nothing of helping to drive the Labour party into the political wilderness). Anti-union legislation has actually helped strengthen the trade union movement in an odd way, by making it a model of democracy (unions must ballot members before undertaking any industrial action now and things no longer happen at the whim of a trade union boss).

Whether you're better off as a member of a trade union depends on the industry in which you're employed. In those in which they're recognised, employees' pay and conditions are decided by a process of collective bargaining between trade unions and employers.

Employers aren't allowed to discriminate against an employee in selection, promotion, transfer or training, and neither can he be dismissed because he belongs or wishes to belong to a trade union, even if many companies are non-union and still don't officially recognise any trade unions. (However some of their individual employees may be members). Legally, employees have the straightforward right to join or not join a union.

Many pamphlets are available from the websites of ACAS and the DTI, including (PL869) *Industrial Action and the Law.* Information about trade unions can be obtained from the Trade Unions Congress (TUC), Congress House, 22-28 Great Russell Street, London WC1B 3LS (☎ 020-7636 4030, 💻 www.tuc.org.uk).

3.

PERMITS & VISAS

Before making any plans to live or work in the UK, you must ensure that you have the appropriate entry documentation (e.g. a visa), as without it you aren't allowed into the country. If you're a national of a non European Economic Area (EEA) country (see page 24) you may need to obtain entry clearance. This applies to people who are intending to stay permanently, coming to the UK to work, or are nationals of countries whose citizens automatically require a visa to come to the UK just for a visit (for more on visa nationals see page 78). **If you're in any doubt as to whether you require clearance to enter the UK, enquire at a British Embassy, High Commission or other British Diplomatic Mission (collectively known as British Diplomatic Posts) overseas before making plans to travel to the UK.** Applications for entry clearance made in some countries can take some time to be processed owing to the high number of applications received.

The UK theoretically has strict laws regarding the entry of foreigners seeking political asylum or those who intend to look for work illegally, but in reality it appears that anyone can get into the country and do whatever they like (many illegal immigrants even manage to claim benefits for years before being rumbled). With the exception of those who aren't subject to immigration controls (e.g. EEA citizens and Commonwealth citizens with a parent born in the UK), the onus is on anyone coming to the UK to prove that you won't break the immigration laws. You must 'satisfy the immigration officer' that you qualify under the immigration rules, which may depend on your nationality and the economic situation in your home country. Immigration officials aren't required to prove that you may break the immigration laws and can refuse you entry on the grounds of suspicion only. If you're refused entry, you are 'removed' and sent back to your home country at your own expense (this isn't the same as deportation and doesn't automatically prevent your returning at a later date). You are given the reason in writing and may appeal, but only after your departure, if you don't have prior entry clearance (see page 75).

Nationals of some non-Commonwealth and non-EEA countries who have been given permission to remain in the UK for more than six months, or who have been allowed to work for more than three months, are required to register with the police (see page 109). **When applicable, this condition is stamped in your passport**, on entry or by the Immigration and Nationality Directorate (IND) of the Home Office, when granting an extension of stay. The Home Office (called the Interior Ministry in many countries) has the final decision on all matters relating to immigration.

Immigration is a complex subject and the information in this chapter is intended only as a general guide. You **shouldn't** base any decisions or actions on the information contained herein without confirming it with an official and reliable source, such as a British embassy. Permit infringements are taken seriously by the authorities and there are penalties for breaches of regulations, including fines and even deportation for flagrant abuses. The police and immigration authorities have the right to arrest anyone 'reasonably suspected' of being an illegal alien and can obtain search warrants to enter homes or places of employment. The penalties for harbouring illegal aliens are severe and prison sentences of up to seven years and heavy fines can be imposed on offenders.

Carriers (i.e. airlines and shipping lines) are fined £2,000 plus costs for each passenger they land who doesn't have valid documentation (especially visas). All vehicles, including private cars, are commonly searched for stowaways on entering the UK. Owners, hirers or drivers of vehicles in which clandestine entrants to the UK have hidden may similarly be liable to a penalty of up to £2,000 individually (or £4,000 collectively if more than one party is involved, i.e. a driver and his employer), for each illegal immigrant discovered, irrespective of whether they were aware of his presence.

The latest information about immigration and permits can be obtained from the Immigration and Nationality Directorate (which publishes leaflets and booklets regarding all immigration categories), local law centres, Citizens Advice Bureaux and community relations councils. The IND website (🖳 www.ind.homeoffice.gov.uk) provides comprehensive coverage of these matters and enables you to download application forms and their printed material in electronic form.

The address of the Immigration and Nationality Directorate (IND) is: Lunar House, 40 Wellesley Road, Croydon CR9 2BY. The Immigration and Nationality Enquiry Bureau (INEB) operates a telephone information service on ☎ 0870-606 7766, which deals with general enquiries about immigration rules and procedures, and queries about specific cases. Its lines are open from 9am to 4.45pm Monday to Thursday and from 9am until 4.30pm on Fridays. It frequently operates at full capacity and speaking to an official may involve a long wait. The busiest days are Monday, Tuesday and Wednesday. It's easier to get through towards the end of the week and in the afternoon. You can also use the following email address: ✉ ind publicenquiries@ind.homeoffice.gsi.gov.uk.

The organisation responsible for issuing visas and providing information about who needs one is UK Visas (a joint undertaking of the Foreign and Commonwealth Office and the Home Office), which is represented at British missions and embassies abroad, a complete list of which can be found at 🖳 www.fco.gov.uk. You should apply to your nearest British mission for a visa in the first instance. UK Visas can also be contacted by post at UK Visas, Foreign and Commonwealth Office, King Charles Street, London SW1A 2AH, or by telephone (☎ 020-7008 8438) between 9am and 5pm from Monday to Friday. The principal source of information for applicants is its website (🖳 www.ukvisas.gov.uk).

ENTRY CLEARANCE

With the exception of EEA nationals, other foreigners entering the UK may need entry clearance from the Home Office or a British Diplomatic Post in their country of residence, **before arrival in the UK. Entry clearance in the form of a visa or entry certificate also applies to returning residents who have been abroad for over two years.** Entry clearance is usually issued for a single entry, but may also allow multiple entries for a number of years, e.g. two (a fee is payable depending on the type of entry clearance issued).

Entry clearance is necessary to come to the UK for the following reasons:

● Settlement as the dependant of a UK resident ('settled' and 'settlement' being terms used to describe the situation of permanently resident foreigners living lawfully in the UK with no time limit on their stay);

- Residence as a person of independent means;

- To undertake employment;

- For business purposes;

- To accompany or rejoin anyone in the above categories as a dependant;

- To be united with a spouse;

- To enter as a fiancé(e) wishing for marriage and settlement;

- To exercise rights of access to a child resident in the UK;

- To visit for longer than six months;

- For any purpose in the case of nationals of a visa country (see page 78).

Unless there are special circumstances, you should always apply for entry clearance before arriving in the UK. It can involve one or more of the following documents:

- Visa (for visa nationals);

- Entry certificate (for non-visa Commonwealth citizens, also known as semi-visa nationals);

- Letter of consent (for a non-visa, non-Commonwealth citizen);

- Work permit.

People entering the UK for employment must usually have a work permit (see page 81) issued by Work Permits UK, a department of the Home Office. When applying for entry clearance, you must produce documentary evidence that you meet the requirements of the immigration rules covering the category in which you're applying. Evidence may include any of the following:

- A work permit sent to you by your prospective employer;

- A letter from a bona fide university, polytechnic, college or school, stating that you've been accepted on a full-time course of study and that you've paid your fees in full (or have been awarded a grant or scholarship);

- Evidence that your qualifications for a job or a course of study are genuine and satisfactory, e.g. certificates, diplomas and references;

- Evidence that you are able to support yourself and any dependants during your stay in the UK without recourse to public funds, e.g. a bank statement, letter from a bank or other evidence of financial support or, in the case of a student, a letter from a sponsor or scholarship agency. The term 'public funds' refers to the following state social security benefits (see page 336): Income Support;

Jobseeker's Allowance; Family Credit; Child Benefit; Housing and Council Tax Benefit; Housing and Homelessness Assistance; and any Disability Allowance.

● If your stay is for a short time only, you may be required to give an assurance that you will leave the UK at the end of that period.

Entry clearance is also required for any dependants you're bringing with you or who will join you in the UK. If applicable, you must prove that you're married and that you can support your dependants as well as yourself. Failure of your dependants to obtain entry clearance may mean that they are refused entry into the UK. When applying for entry clearance, you must complete forms requiring your first names (Christian or forenames), family name (surname) and date of birth. If these are written in a different order in your own culture, establish how they are written in English, and **always complete all forms in the same way**. This is particularly important for those whose language isn't written in Roman script (e.g. Arabic, Chinese or Russian).

If you're refused entry clearance, you're given the reason in writing and told whether or not you have a right of appeal and the time limit within which you must do this. **Always double check time limits**, as they're observed rigorously. **If you're unsuccessful in this, don't travel to the UK, as you will be refused entry.** Entry clearance doesn't guarantee you entry into the UK. Reasons for refusing entry to someone with entry clearance include deceiving the authorities to obtain entry clearance (e.g. an undisclosed criminal record); a change of circumstances since the entry clearance was granted; a decision by the authorities that your presence in the UK isn't conducive to the public good (someone likely to ferment trouble); or when medical reasons make it undesirable to admit you. **Anyone who arrives in the UK with entry clearance and is refused entry has the right of appeal** (see page 75), **and cannot be sent back until the appeal has been heard.** The time limit for appeals is 28 days. (It's shorter in asylum cases if appealing from within the UK – see page 95).

Anyone entering the UK may be referred to a medical inspector for an examination at their port of entry. In practice, this is carried out only if travellers come from places where contagious diseases are particularly prevalent or where outbreaks have recently occurred. Those who give medical treatment as the purpose of their visit or who appear to be in bad health are also more likely to be examined. Admission can be refused on medical grounds, but this does not apply in the case of returning residents.

Applicants for settlement as dependants from Commonwealth countries are required to have a medical examination before entry clearance is issued. The spouse and dependent children under 18 of a resident cannot be refused entry, but can be required to undergo necessary medical treatment in the UK. Au pairs (but not those from the EEA) are also required to obtain a medical certificate before arriving in the UK (including a chest x-ray), stating that they're in good health and free from contagious diseases. In all cases of correspondence or contact with British consular officials or the Home Office, ensure that you fully understand everything and seek help if you aren't absolutely certain.

Visas

Nationals of certain countries, officially called 'visa nationals', require a visa (an official stamp in their passport) to enter the UK, irrespective of the purpose of their visit, e.g. holiday, residence or employment. If you need a visa and arrive without one, you will be sent back to your home country at your own expense. Visitors' visas are issued for a maximum stay of six months and are never extended beyond this period. If you want to stay longer you must leave and apply for a new visa. Visa nationals aren't permitted to change their status.

In 2006, nationals of the following countries required a visa to enter the UK: Afghanistan, Albania, Algeria, Angola, Armenia, Azerbaijan, Bahrain, Bangladesh, Belarus, Benin, Bhutan, Bosnia-Herzegovina, Bulgaria, Burkina, Burma (Myanmar), Burundi, Cambodia, Cameroon, Cape Verde, Central African Republic, Chad, China, Columbia, Comoros, Congo (Democratic Republic of), Congo (Republic of), Croatia, Cuba, Djibouti, Dominican Republic, Ecuador, Egypt, Equatorial Guinea, Eritrea, Ethiopia, Fiji, Gabon, Gambia, Georgia, Ghana, Guinea, Guinea-Bissau, Guyana, Haiti, India, Indonesia, Iran, Iraq, Ivory Coast, Jamaica, Jordan, Kazakhstan, Kenya, Korea (North), Kyrgyzstan, Kuwait, Laos, Lebanon, Liberia, Libya, Macedonia, Madagascar, Mali, Mauritania, Moldova, Mongolia, Morocco, Mozambique, Nepal, Niger, Nigeria, Oman, Pakistan, Peru, the Palestinian Authority, Philippines, Qatar, Romania, Russia, Rwanda, Sao Tome e Principe, Saudi Arabia, Senegal, Serbia and Montenegro, Sierra Leone, Slovak Republic, Somalia, Sri Lanka, Sudan, Surinam, Syria, Taiwan, Tajikistan, Tanzania, Thailand, Togo, Tunisia, Turkey, Turkish Cyprus, Turkmenistan, Uganda, Ukraine, United Arab Emirates, Uzbekistan, Vatican City (service and emergency passports only), Vietnam, Yemen, Zambia and Zimbabwe.

If your 'leave to remain' expires while you're in the UK and you haven't applied for an extension, you're committing a criminal offence and could be fined up to £2,000, sent to prison, and/or recommended for deportation (see page 97). If you're deported, it's extremely difficult, if not impossible, for you to return to the UK.

If you're a visa national and planning a trip abroad, you should ensure that you have a multiple entry visa; otherwise you will require a new visa from a British Diplomatic Post. **Always check the situation before travelling.** You're liable to examination at the port of entry to confirm that you qualify for re-admission, and reports of people having difficulties at this point aren't unknown. Before leaving the UK, ensure that your passport doesn't need renewing and that your leave to remain won't expire within the next few months. If your leave to remain is due to expire within around two months of your planned return, you should renew it before leaving the UK. You should make your application in person, as a postal application usually takes some time to be processed.

If you don't have time to obtain a visa before leaving the UK, or your multiple-entry visa expires while you're abroad, you must apply for a new visa from a British Diplomatic Post before returning to the UK. For this you require the same documentation that was necessary to obtain your original entry clearance. On your return to the UK, you may be required to show evidence of your reason for coming to the UK and that you have sufficient funds to support yourself and any dependants (this also applies to non-visa nationals with limited leave to remain in the UK).

You may also need a visa to visit other countries if you're travelling from the UK and up-to-date information on this, and other travel requirements, is available from any travel agency or your country's embassy or consulate in the UK. Applications must be made in advance. Visas are usually valid for one to three months only, and they're often expensive. It can take weeks or even months to obtain a visa for some countries, particularly some African and Middle Eastern countries, during which time the embassy may retain your passport. There are companies in major cities that obtain visas for a fee.

New Visa Requirements

Since 13 November 2005 all non-visa nationals require entry clearance for all stays of more than six months. This requirement is applied to all nationalities previously exempt. If you are refused entry clearance as students for a stay of over six months you will be permitted to appeal against the decision. If you are coming for six months or less, and you are not a visa national, then it is not compulsory for you to apply for entry clearance before travelling to the UK (though it may well be in your best interest - in particular because there are only limited circumstances in which people without entry clearance are allowed to extend permission to be in the UK.

Entry Certificate

An entry certificate is required by non-visa nationals, such as Commonwealth citizens coming to work or settle in the UK. If you're a national of one of the countries listed below and are coming to the UK to work or settle, you must obtain special entry clearance in the form of an 'Entry Certificate' which, like a visa, consists of an official stamp in your passport. If you're refused entry to the UK for any reason, an entry certificate entitles you to an immediate right of appeal in the same way as a visa.

An entry certificate is issued by a British Diplomatic Post and is required by nationals of the following countries: Anguilla, Antigua, Ascension, Australia, Bahamas, Barbados, Belize, Bermuda, Botswana, Brunei, Canada, Cayman Islands, Cyprus, Dominica, Falklands, Gambia, Gilbert & Ellice Islands, Grenada, Grenadines, Kiribati, Leeward Islands, Lesotho, Malawi, Malaysia, Malta, Mauritius, Montserrat, Namibia, Nauru, New Hebrides, New Zealand, Papua New Guinea, St Helena, St Lucia, St Vincent, St Kitts & Nevis, Samoa, Seychelles, Sikkim, Singapore, Solomon Islands, Swaziland, Tonga, Trinidad & Tobago, Tristan da Cunha, Tuvalu, Vanuatu, Virgin Islands and Western Samoa.

Letter of Consent

A letter of consent is required by non-visa, non-Commonwealth citizens (of all countries that aren't listed above under **Visas & 'Visa Nationals'** or **Entry**

Certificate) wishing to enter the UK for the reasons stated below. A letter of consent is issued by a British Diplomatic Post abroad and is required by the following people:

- Spouse, children or other dependants of a person settled in the UK;

- Teachers or language assistants under approved exchange schemes, including their spouse and children under 18 years of age;

- Representatives of overseas media;

- Sole representatives of an overseas firm;

- Servants in a diplomatic mission or private household;

- Ministers of religion;

- Airport-based ground staff of an overseas airline, including their spouses and children under 18 years old;

- Investors;

- Writers, composers or artists;

- People setting up in business;

- People exercising rights of access to a child resident in the UK;

- A fiancé(e) seeking entry with a view to marriage and permanent settlement in the UK;

- Categories exceptionally allowed outside the rules;

- Commonwealth citizens, one of whose grandparents was born in the UK, taking or seeking employment or taking a working holiday.

If a person who requires a letter of consent arrives without one, he may be refused permission to enter the UK. Any non-visa national, both Commonwealth and non-Commonwealth, may apply for entry clearance when it isn't compulsory under the immigration laws, e.g. when coming to the UK to visit or study. If you fail to obtain entry clearance (when it's optional) you won't necessarily be refused entry, but you'll probably have more difficulty entering the UK if you arrive without it.

An application for a letter of consent should be made well in advance of your proposed date of travel and should be accompanied by the relevant documentary evidence. Where admission is sought as a dependant, evidence in the form of a birth and/or marriage certificate should be produced. If false representations are made or material facts concealed in order to obtain a letter of consent, or your circumstances have changed since it was issued so as to negate your claim to admission, you may be refused entry.

WORK & OTHER PERMITS

It's difficult to obtain entry clearance to work in the UK if you don't qualify under a permit-free category (see below), particularly if your prospective employer is located in an area of high unemployment. Normally, a work permit must be obtained by an employer for a named worker and is always issued for a specific job and for a specified period (the **Highly Skilled Migrant Programme** operates differently – see page 88). Permits are issued provided no other person who's already allowed to live and work in the UK can be found to do the job, which must be proven by providing copies of advertisements and explaining why any applicants (who don't require a work permit) weren't suitable.

Vacancies must be advertised in the local, national and European press, as well as in any appropriate trade and professional journals. The salary and conditions of employment offered must be equal to those prevailing for similar jobs; the qualifications and experience must be exactly what's required; and they must usually have been acquired outside the UK. Permits aren't issued to recruitment agencies intending to hire out the services of the worker in question to other parties. Employees should usually be aged between 23 and 54 (inclusive) and are normally expected to have an adequate knowledge of the English language. The lower age limit doesn't apply to sportsmen and sportswomen, and neither limit applies to artists and entertainers.

Applications for work permits are dealt with by Work Permits UK (☎ 0870 606 7766, ✉ wpcustomers@ind.homeoffice.gsi.gov.uk, 💻 www.workingintheuk.gov.uk). An employer must make an application no more than six months before the proposed entry of the person he wants to employ and no less than three months before that date. The necessary application form (WP1 for first applications) can be downloaded from the Work Permits UK website or ordered from its forms distribution centre (☎ 0870-521 0224).

After completion, the form must be sent, with documentary evidence of the applicant's qualifications and experience (including original references), the job description and evidence of advertising (plus full details of any replies received), to Work Permits (UK), PO Box 3468, Sheffield. Only forms obtained by post should be returned through the post and only forms obtained electronically should be returned as email. When an email application is made, the supporting documentation should be posted on separately. A work permit can be issued for up to five years.

(If the overseas worker is already living in the UK, the application must be made before their current permission to work runs out, otherwise they must stop working while the application is being considered. In this case, passports and police registration certificates must also be submitted with the application, where applicable). When an application has been approved for a Commonwealth citizen living in a Commonwealth country, the permit is sent to the prospective employee via the British government's representative there. For other countries, the permit is sent to the employer to forward to the prospective employee abroad. Work permits are issued to people in the following categories:

● Those holding recognised professional qualifications;

- Those holding qualifications equivalent to a UK degree;

- Highly qualified technicians with HND level qualifications relevant to the job they intend taking up in the UK;

- Those with HND level qualifications not strictly relevant to the job they intend taking up in the UK, plus one year of full-time work experience in that job;

- Those with three years experience of using specialist skills acquired through doing the type of job for which the permit is sought;

- Other key workers with a high or scarce qualification in an industry or occupation requiring expert knowledge or skills;

- Established entertainers, including self-employed entertainers coming to fulfil engagements (age limits don't apply);

- Sportsmen and sportswomen who meet the appropriate skills criteria; professional sportsmen and sportswomen taking part in competitions of international standing don't normally require permits; age limits don't apply;

- Those coming for a limited period of training or work experience (see page 91);

- People, whose employer does not have a commercial presence in the EU, coming to work in the UK on a service contract awarded to their employer abroad by a British-based organisation under the General Agreement on Trade in Services (GATS);

- Others, if, in the opinion of the Secretary of State, their employment is in the national interest.

Spouses and children under 18 wishing to accompany or join a work permit holder in the UK must obtain entry clearance from the nearest British Diplomatic Post to where they live, before travelling. Failure to do so may mean they're refused entry. A work permit holder must be able to provide accommodation and support his dependants without the use of public funds and must state this in writing. Permit holders aren't permanently restricted to the particular job for which their permit was issued, but are expected to remain in the same occupation. The consent of the authorities is required in order to change jobs.

A work permit is valid for entry into the UK within six months of its date of issue and is usually issued for a period of one year unless limited to a shorter period. Permits valid for one year can usually be extended on application to the Home Office. It's difficult to obtain permission to employ someone who's already in the UK, who came here for a reason other than employment, e.g. as a visitor or a student. First, the Home Office must decide whether his conditions of stay allow him to take employment or, if not, whether the conditions can be changed. Shortly before completing four years employment in the UK, work permit holders may apply to the Home Office for the removal of the time limit on their stay. This is called 'settlement'. When the time limit is removed, you may take any employment without reference to the authorities.

It's strictly forbidden for any non-EEA national to work in the UK without permission. If you're discovered working without a permit or permission, you're liable to deportation or prosecution, which could lead to a heavy fine or even imprisonment. If you have permission to remain in the UK (e.g. to study) this will probably be terminated. Certain categories of people can work full or part-time without a work permit, e.g. the wife of a work–permit holder, or, with certain restrictions, a student (see page 91), although permission is necessary in other cases. A number of leaflets concerning work permits are published by the authorities and are available from Jobcentres and Jobcentre Plus offices or can be downloaded from the Work Permits UK website (🖥 www.workpermits.gov.uk).

Permit-free Categories

The following people don't require a work permit:

- British nationals with the right of abode in the UK;

- Nationals of European Economic Area (EEA) countries and Switzerland, or their family dependants;

- Commonwealth citizens aged 17 to 30 on a working holiday and not intending to call on public funds, two years being the maximum period permitted as a working holidaymaker (see page 86);

- Participants in the UK Japan Youth Exchange scheme;

- Investors;

- Writers, composers and artists;

- Commonwealth citizens with a parent born in the UK. A 'Certificate of Entitlement to the Right of Abode' from a British Diplomatic Post is required before arrival;

- Commonwealth citizens with a grandparent born in the UK, the Channel Islands, the Isle of Man, the Republic of Ireland before independence on 31st March 1922, or aboard a British-registered ship or aircraft;

- Those who have such a connection through adoption (or natural parents if adopted) don't have this right of abode, but may obtain entry clearance to come to the UK. If so, they are admitted for a four-year period, after which they can apply for settlement (see page 97);

- Innovators and entrepreneurs;

- People setting up in business (see page 86). This includes self-employment and also covers barristers, solicitors and experts in overseas legal systems.

- Entertainers, provided they don't stay longer than six months and are making a personal appearance, attending a festival or performing for charity;

- Jewish Agency employees;

- Sportsmen and sportswomen coming for a specific event and not seeking to base themselves in the UK;

- Voluntary workers;

- Religious ministers, missionaries and members of religious orders. Members of religious orders teaching in an institution of their own order don't require a permit, but if they're otherwise engaged in teaching, a permit is required. The Unification Church (the 'Moonies') and the Church of Scientology aren't recognised as bona fide religions.

- Doctors and dentists coming to take up research or post-graduate training positions in hospitals. If they're coming to take up 'ordinary' posts, they require a work permit.

- Sole representatives of foreign companies in the UK;

- Representatives of overseas newspapers, news agencies and broadcasting organisations on long-term assignment to the UK;

- Servants (aged over 15) of private households or members of diplomatic missions;

- Employees of a foreign government or an international organisation of which the UK is a member;

- Teachers and language assistants under a scheme approved by the British authorities;

- Certain categories of seamen under contract to join a ship in British waters, the operational staff of foreign-owned airlines, or off-shore oil industry workers;

- Seasonal workers at agricultural camps under approved schemes, voluntary workers and au pairs. A seasonal or voluntary worker must have been given entry clearance specifically for that purpose; otherwise an 'employment prohibited' stamp (see page 105) also includes seasonal or voluntary work.

- Exchange students sponsored by BUNAC or the International Association for the Exchange of Students for Technical Experience (IAESTE) and, with certain restrictions, British-based foreign students.

Although people who qualify under the above categories don't require a work permit, they may still require entry clearance (unless they're EEA nationals).

EEA Nationals

If you're an EEA national, you can enter the UK in order to take up or seek employment, set up in business or become self-employed without a work permit. You can remain in the UK for as long as you wish without obtaining a residence permit or registering with the police. You may apply to the Immigration and Nationality Directorate (IND) for a residence permit (issued free of charge), but this isn't compulsory. Its purpose would be to initiate a process which could eventually lead to naturalisation. If any members of your household aren't EEA nationals, they should obtain EEA family member residence permits. They can do this before or after arrival in the UK, but, as the IND are currently dealing with high workloads, it's simpler and quicker to do it before travelling. Approach the nearest British diplomatic post. For any queries contact ✉ eea@visalondon.com.

Other British Nationals

In addition to British citizens with the right of abode in the UK, there are a number of British 'nationals' who don't have this right, termed 'other British nationals'. These people are citizens of British colonies, or former colonies, who were granted British citizenship in the days when it was the ambition of the British Empire to paint the whole atlas pink, and bestow upon everyone the 'honour' of British citizenship (see page 484). There are a number of categories:

- **British Dependent Territories Citizen (BDTC)** – Citizens of British colonies (e.g. Gibraltar) who have the right to citizenship of that country only, and who have been subject to British immigration law since 1962.

- **British National (Overseas)** – This is a category created so that Hong Kong residents, who aren't regarded as Chinese citizens under Chinese nationality law, wouldn't be formally stateless when their BDTC status (see above) ended on 1st July 1997. It doesn't affect their lack of immigration rights.

- **British Overseas Citizens** – People in former British colonies who were unable to gain citizenship of that country when independence was gained. These are mainly people of Indian and Chinese descent from East African countries, Malaysia and Singapore.

- **British Subjects** – Mainly people born in a princely state in India who weren't in India at the time of the passage of Indian independence and citizenship laws, and therefore didn't gain Indian citizenship.

- **British Protected People** – People from former colonies or territories previously under the protection of the UK, who were unable to gain new citizenship on independence.

Any British national (except a BDTC) who enters the UK legally, but for a temporary period, e.g. as a visitor, cannot, in practice, be deported, as he's effectively stateless and no other country would be under any obligation to receive him. A scheme called the 'special quota voucher' scheme allows 'other British nationals' to live in the UK, but only at a slow trickle rate. A British national (as defined above) who's granted permission to settle in the UK must obtain entry clearance issued by a British

Diplomatic Post before travelling. If he has dependants in the UK, he must show that he's able to support them without recourse to public funds.

Working Holidaymakers

The working holidaymaker scheme is an arrangement whereby (primarily) single people aged from 17 to 30 can come to the UK on an extended holiday for a maximum period of two years. To qualify you must be a Commonwealth, British Dependent Territories, British Overseas or British Nationals (Overseas) citizen. Married people can also use the scheme if both qualify for entry as working holidaymakers and they intend to holiday together. Couples mustn't have dependent children who are five or over or who will reach five years of age before they complete their holiday. There's no set amount of money you must bring with you, but the minimum in practice is enough for your return journey and at least the first month after arrival. You must be able to support yourself without recourse to public funds.

There are no longer as many restrictions on the type of employment you can take up over the two years. It can be almost any sort of work and it can be full-time or part-time. You can also now pursue a career or work as a professional (although professional sport and entertaining are excluded). Whatever work you do, you're expected to take a holiday for some part of your stay.

Any time spent outside the UK during the two-year period counts towards the maximum two years allowed in the country (from the date you were first given permission to enter the UK). After that, if an employer obtains a work permit on your behalf, you can remain for a further four years. (You become eligible to switch status by obtaining a work permit after 12 months). At the end of this period, you can apply for permanent settlement.

Entry clearance must be obtained from a British Diplomatic Post before travelling to the UK, as it isn't possible to arrive as a visitor and change your status to that of a working holidaymaker.

UK Japan Youth Exchange Scheme

This covers people aged 18 to 25 and operates in a similar way to the Working Holidaymaker scheme. There's an annual quota, and entry clearance can be obtained only from the British Embassy in Tokyo.

Self-employed People

If you wish to enter the UK to set up in business or self-employment and aren't an EEA national, you must obtain entry clearance (see page 75) in the form of a letter of consent (see page 79) specifically for that purpose, before arrival. To set up in business, you must show that you are investing a minimum of £200,000 of your own money and that your business will create new, paid, full-time employment for at least two people already resident in the UK. You must also show that there's a genuine need for your services and investment; that you will be occupied full-time in the running of the business; and that you will be able to support yourself and your dependants from the profits of the business without recourse to public funds. A business can take one of the following forms: sole trader, a partnership, or a UK registered company.

Self-employed lawyers intending to set up a new practice must simply bring sufficient funds to do so, unless joining an existing firm as a partner.

Some details of the above arrangements may differ for those business people coming from EU accession countries who have rights under agreements their home countries have made with the EU.

Incentives to set up in business are available to people from overseas on the same basis as they are to British nationals, including grants, training assistance and government factories for rent or lease. Financial assistance is available for manufacturing investment that's judged to be particularly beneficial to the British economy. British government and EEA financial incentives may be available for businesses established in areas where there's high unemployment or other economic problems (designated 'assisted areas'). A business person with the appropriate entry clearance may be accompanied by his spouse and any children under 18, who are initially admitted for one year provided that they also have entry clearance. Annual extensions are granted, as long as the immigration rules continue to be met and settlement is normally granted after four years' residence (see page 97).

If you don't qualify as a business person, a self-employed person with special talents or skills, e.g. an entertainer, artist, sportsman or sportswoman, or aren't covered by the Highly Skilled Migrant Programme (see page 88), it's difficult to obtain permission to enter the UK and work as a self-employed person. (See also **Self-employment** on page 37.)

Investors

A non-EEA national who has the sum of £1 million at his disposal, and who intends to live in the UK as his main home, can obtain permanent leave to remain. Entry clearance is required (see page 75). An investor must plan to invest at least £750,000 in British government bonds or in the share or loan capital of British companies. He may only be self-employed.

Sole Representatives

You must have been recruited abroad and represent a firm which has otherwise no presence in the UK. Your purpose must be to establish a registered branch or wholly-owned subsidiary of your company in the UK, and you must be employed full-time to represent it. You cannot be a majority shareholder in that company and must be able to maintain and house yourself and your dependants without recourse to public funds. Dependants can come with you, but need entry clearance before travelling.

Innovators

The Innovators Scheme, introduced in 2000, is intended to attract people with new and creative ideas who wish to set up businesses which, in the judgement of the authorities, will bring exceptional economic benefits to the UK. The focus is mainly, but not exclusively, on science, technology and e-commerce. You don't need a set amount of money to invest – someone else can provide the necessary capital – but you must create at least two full-time jobs in the UK, own at least five per cent of the company shares, and be able to support yourself and your dependants without recourse to public funds. The company must be registered in the UK. Permission to stay is initially granted for 24 months, and if requirements are met, can be extended at that stage up to another three years. Dependants can apply to come with you, but need entry clearance before travelling.

Highly Skilled Migrant Programme

People with skills which are in high demand in the UK may apply personally for a work permit under the terms of the Highly Skilled Migrant Programme (HSMP), and don't need a prior offer of employment. You can also apply if you're already in the UK on some other basis. A permit covers employment and self-employment and currently includes the following occupations: highway, transportation, structural, aircraft and railway engineers; actuaries; teachers; doctors, nurses and vets. Qualified General Practitioners (GP) fall into a priority category. Applicants are assessed on a points system covering their experience, qualifications, earning ability and whether they have a partner who has a degree or who has been previously employed in a graduate level job.

General enquires should be addressed to the Work Permits UK customer relations team on ☎ 0870 606 7766 or the British Embassy or High Commission in your own country. If successful, you will receive an official HSMP letter of approval with which you can then apply for entry clearance to come to the UK. Application forms can be downloaded from the Immigration and Nationality Directorate website or ordered by phone on ☎ 0114-259 1894. The address for postal contact is Customer Relations Team, Work Permits (UK), PO Box 3468, Sheffield.

Sectors Based Scheme for Low-skilled Migrants

This covers unskilled work in the food processing, hotel and catering industries. Employers may apply for work permits on behalf of workers aged 18 to 30, if they can show that they're unable to recruit locally. Quotas for such work permits are divided between European Union accession countries and others.

Science & Engineering Graduates Scheme

From Summer 2005, foreigners who have studied maths, science or engineering in the UK can work for 12 months in the country after completing their studies.

Spouses

The spouse of a non-EEA national with permission to live or work in the UK is granted entry clearance, provided the marriage is genuine, both partners intend to remain married and have actually met (the marriage cannot be arranged blind, as many are in Asian countries), and that they have somewhere to live and can support themselves without recourse to public funds. The spouse mustn't be under the age of 16. An application for entry clearance must be made to a British Diplomatic Post before travelling to the UK. The spouse of a non-EEA national entitled to work in the UK is also eligible to work there, although if he or she enters alone, their passport may be stamped to prohibit them from working. This can usually be changed on application to the Home Office. On arrival, the spouse is given permission to stay and work for 12 months. Towards the end of the 12-month period, provided the couple are still married and intend to live together, the spouse may apply to remain in the UK permanently. A parent of a child resident in the UK with access rights granted by a British court, can enter the UK provided he has entry clearance for this purpose.

Fiancé(e)s

The fiancé(e) of a non-EEA national settled in the UK, who wishes to enter for marriage and settlement, must obtain entry clearance in the form of a letter of consent (see page 79) from a British Diplomatic Post before travelling to the UK. Applicants must satisfy officials that a marriage will take place within a 'reasonably short time of their arrival in the UK' (usually six months) and that the 'primary purpose of marriage isn't to obtain entry or remain in the UK'. Both marriage partners must also intend to live together permanently and must have actually met. 'Marriages of convenience' to foreigners aren't illegal unless performed for money and, in any case, don't give foreigners the right to enter or remain in the UK. You must also show that you won't call on public funds and that you have access to funds and accommodation in the UK, without your having to work. Regulations are strictly enforced for men coming from the Indian subcontinent and for women from countries such as the Philippines and Thailand (where agencies operate a lucrative business providing wives for western men). People from other countries generally have fewer problems.

If you're permitted entry to the UK as a fiancé(e), you are initially granted entry for six months in order to get married, during which time you're forbidden to work. (If you enter the UK for a purpose other than marriage, e.g. as a tourist or student, and subsequently get married to someone who has permanent resident status in the UK, you must return home and apply to come back for settlement). You should ensure that your allotted period hasn't expired before you get married. After marriage you must write to the IND who require:

- Your passport;

- Your spouse's passport or birth certificate;

- Your marriage certificate;

- Evidence that you can support your spouse and provide accommodation;

- A letter requesting leave to remain in the UK as the spouse of a British citizen or of someone with permanent residence.

After marriage, you're initially permitted to stay for two years with no restrictions on working and after this time you're eligible to apply for settlement (see page 97). Foreigners with limited leave to remain in the UK who get married to a British or EEA national or a British resident, thus acquiring the right to remain in the UK, often find themselves subject to intense scrutiny by the immigration authorities. This is because an estimated 10,000 foreigners enter into marriages of convenience each year in order to remain in the UK ('professional' brides charge around £2,000 to £ 3,000 a time).

Children

Children under 18 (including natural children, step-children and adopted children) are granted permission to remain in the UK when both their parents are temporarily resident in the UK or have been granted permission to settle. An application for entry clearance for children must be made to a British Diplomatic Post before travelling to the UK. If one parent only is resident in the UK, he must show that he has sole responsibility for a child's upbringing or that serious or compelling family or other circumstances render their exclusion undesirable. In practice, it's usual for a child under 12 to be allowed to join a single parent, particularly the mother, in the UK. Children over 18 must usually qualify for entry clearance in their own right, although some consideration is given to unmarried daughters under 21 with no close relatives in their own country. Children must be maintained without recourse to public funds.

Relatives

Apart from EEA nationals, foreigners permanently resident in the UK may invite relatives who are abroad, other than a spouse or children under 18, to live with them in restricted circumstances. It's easiest in the case of the elderly. The widowed mother, grandmother, father or grandfather of a British resident may be granted such permission, provided he's over 65, or both parents, if one is over 65. A parent or grandparent over 65 who has remarried may be admitted if he or she cannot look to the spouse or children of that second marriage for support.

Other relations under 65 and over 18 are admitted only if the authorities deem that 'exceptional compassionate circumstances' exist. This is rare.

In all cases a British resident must be able to support and provide accommodation for his dependants without recourse to public funds. They must have been financially dependent on him or her for some time prior to coming to the UK, and must usually have no close relatives in their own country.

Part-time Employment

Generally, no distinction is made between full and part-time employment by the immigration authorities, and whether you can work at all in the UK generally depends on what has been stamped in your passport. Spouses are usually given initial permission to remain for one year, with no restrictions on employment and no requirement to obtain a work permit. Voluntary workers (see page 32) don't require a work permit, but unless a person is given entry clearance specifically for voluntary work, an 'employment prohibited' stamp (see page 105) applies.

Trainees & Work Experience

Under the Training and Work Experience Scheme (TWES), foreign nationals can work in the UK as trainees or gain practical work experience in a subject they've been studying in the UK or abroad. An employer must obtain a trainee or work experience permit and show how the training or work experience he offers is useful. Trainee positions are for a predetermined length of time and although permits are usually initially issued for one year, they may be extended for a maximum period of up to three years. The maximum period for work experience is normally one year, which in exceptional circumstances can be extended by a further year. Applications should be made at least eight weeks in advance of the anticipated start date. Although training and work experience are different categories, the application procedure is the same. The prospective employer must obtain form WP2 and guidance leaflet WP2 (notes) from Work Permits UK (for contact details see page 81). These contain sections to be completed by the employer and the prospective trainee.

The employer must confirm that the applicant intends to leave the UK after his training period, as anyone issued with a permit as a trainee or for work experience must do so. An overseas trainee or work experience applicant can bring his spouse and dependent children aged under 18 to the UK. After returning to his home country, a trainee is expected to put to use the skills learned for at least two years before an application (to return to the UK) under the main work permit scheme will be considered.

Students

Overseas students who are non-EEA nationals are permitted to enter the UK for the duration of a course, provided they've been accepted at a bona fide educational establishment and intend to leave the UK at the end of their course of study. Your course must be full or mostly full-time and must occupy a minimum of 15 hours a week during the daytime (9am to 5pm). You cannot combine a variety of part-time courses in order to make up the required 15 hours study per week, and evening courses don't qualify as full-time study. Your fees must have been paid in full and you must show that you can financially support yourself and, in the case of married students, your spouse and children under 18 (if accompanied by them), without recourse to public funds. You must prove that you're married by producing a marriage certificate. If your country of residence has strict foreign exchange controls, it's important to make arrangements for banking facilities in the UK or for money to be sent to you.

The spouse of a student and children under 18 aren't permitted to work unless you've been given leave to enter or remain in the UK for 12 months or more. If you haven't decided what or where you wish to study, it's possible to obtain entry clearance to enter the UK as a prospective student for up to six months, in order to find a college and enrol there. When you've arranged everything, you can then apply for an extension of your permit.

On arrival, you must have a letter from the college or school where you've been accepted as a student, stating your study hours, the length of your course and that you've paid (or can pay) your fees. If the immigration officer suspects that the course is merely a subterfuge to enable you to enter and remain in the UK, he can refuse you entry. The authorities may also check that you're attending classes. If you're permitted to enter the UK to study, you're usually granted permission to remain for the period of your course or at least one year, unless you're enrolled in a short course.

If you wish to extend your permission to remain, you must apply to the Home Office and provide the same documentary evidence that was necessary for your initial application. You must show that you're progressing naturally from one course to another and not spending an exceptional length of time on one course. If you're a visa national and wish to leave the UK (e.g. for a holiday) during your study period, you must apply for a re-entry visa before leaving. You must have a letter from your college or school stating that you are continuing with your studies on your return.

Students who have been granted leave to stay for more than six months and don't have a stamp in their passports prohibiting employment may take part-time work (evenings and weekends up to a maximum of 20 hours a week) or full-time holiday employment. They may also take placements which are part of a sandwich course. However, you shouldn't rely on finding part-time work in order to help pay for your course or living expenses, as this may be impossible in many parts of the UK. Some conditions related to working which were in force until recently have been lifted and you no longer need to obtain permission from your local Jobcentre or Jobcentre Plus office before earning some money. Nonetheless, restrictions still exist. As the consequences of breaking the law can be extreme and regulations change at regular intervals, **always check with your college welfare officer about the prevailing situation before taking a job**. You can also download guidance notes from the United Kingdom Council for Overseas Student Affairs (UKCOSA), the Council for International Education, at ⌨ www.ukcosa.org.uk, and the Department for Education and Skills booklet *International Students Working in the UK – What You Need to*

Know from 💻 www.dfespublications.gov.uk. As formerly, work you do mustn't interfere with your studies and you must receive the normal rate of pay. A student who works illegally in the UK, for example one who takes up a full-time job in term-time, risks prosecution or deportation.

If you're formally prohibited from working in the UK, you must first apply to the Home Office to have the prohibition lifted before your college can apply for permission to organise practical work experience.

Overseas students aren't permitted to work in the UK after completing their studies, unless there are exceptional circumstances, e.g. a student is highly qualified in a field of work where there's an acute shortage of skills. This is the case at the moment in electronics, engineering, technology and health-related areas. In addition to this, maths, science and engineering students have just been offered the chance to work in the UK for a year after graduation. Students who have studied in the UK may otherwise be permitted to gain a further qualification as a trainee or to gain work experience (see page 91).

While declaring that 'an intention to return' to their home countries is a condition of being allowed into the UK for student nurses, given the nursing shortage experienced by the National Health Service (NHS), some are in fact allowed to remain. Because nursing is currently on the official list of 'shortage occupations', it's relatively easy for a potential employer to arrange a work permit. For up-to-date details, student nurses should contact the Royal College of Nursing Immigration Advice Service, 20 Cavendish Square, London W1G 0RN (☎ 020-7647 3874, 💻 www.rcn.org.uk). They should do this **well before** their leave to remain in the UK expires.

Doctors and dentists who have studied in the UK may be granted an extension for postgraduate training, provided they have limited or full registration with the General Medical Council or General Dental Council. Extensions are granted for one year at a time up to a maximum of four years. Graduates may be eligible for a position as a postgraduate research assistant at the end of their course (e.g. to study for a PhD), although this is generally granted in exceptional circumstances only. Just as with nurses, many specialised areas of medicine and some of dentistry, are prominent on the official list of shortage occupations, increasing the possibilities of staying in the UK.

If you enter the UK as a visitor and aren't a visa national (see page 78), it may be possible to obtain permission to extend your stay in order to study, although the authorities may be suspicious that your real purpose in coming to the UK was to study (and not as a genuine visitor). A visa national who enters the UK as a visitor cannot obtain permission to study and must leave first and apply for a student visa in his home country. If you're unsure about anything regarding your status as a student, ask your student welfare officer or college principal, or contact UKCOSA (💻 www.ukcosa.org.uk), which is a registered charity established to promote the interests of overseas students in the UK and those working with them as teachers, advisors and in other capacities.

Prospective students and those planning to study for less than six months (and their dependants) have no right of appeal against refusal of entry clearance and refusal of leave to enter, although they receive a detailed explanation of why their application was refused and can make a second application.

Au Pairs

Unmarried people of either sex, aged from 17 to 27, are admitted as au pairs for a period (or aggregate period) of up to two years. (They can be 28 when their entry clearance is finalised as long as they were 27 when they applied for it.) They must have no dependants in the UK and must be nationals of a European Economic Area (EEA) country or Andorra, Bosnia-Herzegovina, Bulgaria, Croatia, Faroe Islands, Macedonia, Monaco, Romania, San Marino, or Turkey. Nationals of Bosnia-Herzegovina, Bulgaria, Croatia, Macedonia, Romania and Turkey must obtain a visa from a British Embassy or Consulate before travelling to the UK.

Full information is available on the Working in the UK website (🖳 www.workingintheuk.gov.uk). It's worth checking regularly as the rules change often.

People of Independent Means

Non-EEA nationals who wish to live, but not work, in the UK require entry clearance in the form of a letter of consent (see page 79) before arrival. To qualify you must be aged at least 60 and have under your control and disposal in the UK an income of not less than £25,000 a year. You must intend to make the UK your main home and be able to show that you're able to support and accommodate yourself and your dependants indefinitely, without working and without recourse to public funds. Your presence must be in the best interests of the UK or you must have close ties with the UK, e.g. close relatives, children attending school or periods of previous residence in the UK. If you're prohibited from working in the UK, this also applies to members of your family and any dependants. People of independent means are usually admitted for an initial period of one year and qualify for indefinite leave to remain after four years' continuous residence. Pensioners and students who are EEA nationals have the right of residence in any EEA country, provided they can prove they have sufficient income not to become a burden on the host country and have private health insurance.

Medical Treatment

A foreign national who wishes to enter the UK for medical treatment must satisfy the immigration officer that he has been accepted for consultation or treatment as a private patient, and that the latter is of finite duration. Evidence must be available that he can pay for it and support himself while undergoing it. He may also be medically examined on arrival before being permitted entry, and anyone suffering from a communicable (contagious) disease may be refused entry. An extension of the standard six months period allowed to visitors is possible if the visitor provides evidence from someone of NHS consultant rank, or who appears in the Specialist Register of the General Medical Council, that it's necessary. Visitors aren't permitted to enter or remain in the UK to receive treatment on the National Health Service.

Visitors

EEA nationals are free of restrictions. Non-EEA nationals can visit the UK for a period of up to six months, but entry clearance is still needed, as set out earlier on page 75. If in doubt about what you must do **contact a British Diplomatic Post beforehand to avoid possible problems after spending money on travel**. Although there's nothing to stop anyone leaving the UK for a few days after remaining for six months, and then returning for another six months, as soon as the authorities think that someone is spending more time in the UK than in their country of origin (or residence), or are really living in the UK, entry is refused.

The passports of visitors, who of course aren't entitled to work in the UK, are stamped with 'employment prohibited', and this is strictly enforced (see page 105).

Visitors may be required to convince immigration officers that they are staying for a short period only and won't attempt to find work in the UK. You may be asked to show proof that you can support yourself financially during your stay or that you have relatives or friends who can support you, and to show a return ticket or the money to buy one.

Immigration officers sometimes employ double standards and immigration advice agencies claim that many black and Asian visitors are refused admission, without proper account being taken of compassionate reasons why they should be permitted to remain. British residents can provide a letter of sponsorship for a visitor, explaining their relationship to the applicant, the purpose of the visit and where the visitor will be staying. This is primarily intended for those who plan to provide support and accommodation for a visitor, who wouldn't otherwise be able to support himself in the UK.

Visitors are usually given permission to stay for six months, even when planning a short visit only. If you're given permission to stay for less than six months on entry, you can apply to extend your stay up to a maximum of six months in total. If you want to establish temporary residence for longer than six months and believe you're eligible under the immigration rules, you should apply at a British Diplomatic Post before coming to the UK.

Frequent visitors (e.g. business people) can apply for a multiple-entry visitor's visa valid for up to five years. Non-EEA nationals may transact business during a visit, but unpaid employment and self-employment are forbidden in addition to paid employment and professional activity. Business visitors may attend trade fairs, conferences, short classroom training courses and meetings, provided such activities are essential for fact-finding purposes as recipients of services or briefings by British businesses.

Visitors have no right of appeal against refusal of entry clearance and refusal of leave to enter, although they can make a second application after receiving an explanation why their original application was refused.

Refugees

The only people who don't need to apply for refugee status on arrival in the UK are those whose status has already been decided abroad under the terms of the United Nations Refugee Convention.

Otherwise, to be granted refugee status in the UK, you must prove that you have 'a well-founded fear of persecution in your own country for reasons of race, religion, nationality, membership of a particular social group or political opinion'.

Since 2000, the provisions of the Human Rights Act have also come into play. This forbids the authorities from breaching a person's fundamental human rights, which means that if someone can show that return to the country from which they fled would do this, they must be offered protection.

People whom the Home Office believes would be in danger if they returned home, even if they don't fall into the above categories, may also be permitted to stay.

If you arrive in the UK seeking asylum, **you should apply for it immediately on arrival**. If you're already in the UK and political events in your home country make it impossible or dangerous for you to return there, you can also apply. Asylum seekers may be fingerprinted and in certain circumstances may be detained while their application is being decided.

If you don't receive a decision on your application within six months (there's usually a huge backlog of cases), you can apply for permission to work in the UK. While an application for asylum is pending, you're unable to travel abroad although, if you're granted asylum, you can apply for a United Nations Travel Document.

If your application is refused, you have a right of appeal. The Notice of Refusal which you receive is accompanied by a Notice of Appeal form, which **you must return within a ten-day time limit (28 days if you're outside the UK)**, if you wish to fight your case further. The Immigration Advisory Service helps you with this (see below). Should the Home Office believe you could have claimed asylum in a safe third country which you passed through on your way to the UK, it may try to remove you there to pursue your claim further. Some legal options remain to you, but taking professional advice is vital.

The number of people applying for asylum has risen dramatically over the past decade and the subject is now very much a political hot potato. As a consequence of this, proposals to change the law are a regular feature of public discussion, and over the lifetime of this edition of *Living and Working in Britain*, regulations will almost certainly be in state of flux.

According to the statistics available, the great majority of asylum applications are refused, and it's essential, especially if you intend to appeal, that you contact, as soon as possible, one of the organisations which help and advise asylum seekers. One of the principal ones is the Refugee Council whose main office in London is at 3 Bondway, London SW8 1SJ (☎ 020-7346 6700, 💻 www.refugeecouncil.org.uk). It also operates a One Stop Service centre at 240-250 Ferndale Road, London SW9 8BB (☎ 020-7346 6700). The Immigration Advisory Service (IAS) is another such organisation. Its London address is 2nd Floor, County House, 190 Great Dover Street, London SE1 4YB (☎ 020-7967 1200, 💻 www.iasuk.org). Telephone advice is available on Wednesday mornings between 10am and noon, or you can book an appointment to speak to an adviser. If you need urgent advice outside office hours on detention, deportation or removal, you can telephone ☎ 020-7378 9191 and leave a message on the answer machine. Don't forget to provide contact details. The IAS then does its best to ensure that an adviser returns your call on the next working day.

SETTLEMENT

Settlement is the name given to the status of permanent residence in the UK, which means you can stay in the UK indefinitely, without any restrictions on working or the need for a work permit. A foreigner married to a British citizen is granted settlement status after one year. Foreign nationals who have held a residence permit for four years and who have been in continuous employment, self-employment or business in the UK, can apply for settlement. If you've stayed in the UK legally for ten years and don't qualify under the normal rules, you can apply for settlement on the grounds of the length of your stay. In this case, the granting of settlement status depends on a number of factors, including whether you've established a way of life in the UK and have strong ties with the country; have been in trouble with the police or have a criminal record; have spent long periods abroad; and have strong family ties in the UK.

If you're a student, you should wait until the end of your studies before applying for settlement status. If you make an application for settlement as a student and are refused, you're unlikely to be permitted to extend your leave to remain as a student. This is because the Home Office takes an application for settlement as a sign that you don't intend to leave the UK when you've completed your studies. Settlement is also granted to the spouse of anyone who qualifies for settlement, provided both partners have been resident in the UK on the same temporary status for the same period.

A permanent resident can leave and enter the UK freely, as long as he doesn't remain out of the UK for more than two years at a time. Permanent residents who remain abroad for longer than two years, may still qualify to return to the UK as residents, for example if they have strong family ties there or have lived there most of their lives. In this case, an application for entry clearance must be made at a British Diplomatic Post. However, returning residents must make it clear that they're returning for the purpose of settlement. If they say that they're leaving again soon, they may be admitted as visitors only and will have great difficulty in regaining settlement status (so make it clear that you're returning home to stay). A settled foreign national can eventually apply for British citizenship (see page 484).

DEPORTATION

Any infringements concerning work permits, entry clearance, overstaying leave to remain and police registration are taken seriously by the authorities. If you break the immigration laws, the Home Secretary can issue a deportation order sending you back to your own country (at your own expense). The grounds for deportation include:

- Illegal entry into the UK;

- Failure to comply with your conditions of entry (e.g. working without a permit or official permission);

- Overstaying your leave to remain without obtaining an extension;

- Conviction of a criminal offence for a person over 17 (when deportation is recommended by the court);

- Your presence isn't considered to be in the public interest;

- Being the dependant of a deportee.

Anyone breaking the immigration law also faces a fine of up to £2,000 and up to six months imprisonment. In the present climate, these penalties may well be increased. If, in the opinion of the immigration authorities, someone entered the UK illegally or by deception, then he can be ejected from the country under a process called removal, without a court or appeal process. Police and immigration officers have the right to apprehend (without a warrant) anyone whom they 'reasonably suspect' to be in breach of the immigration law.

4.

ARRIVAL

On arrival in the UK to take up employment or residence, your first task is to battle your way through immigration and customs which, fortunately for most people, presents no problems. Non European Economic Area (EEA) nationals must complete a landing card on arrival in the UK. These are distributed on all international flights to the UK and are available from the information or purser's office on ships and ferries. For information regarding permits and visas see **Chapter 3**. British customs and immigration officials are usually polite and efficient, although they may occasionally be overzealous in their attempts to deter smugglers and illegal immigrants (so it pays to be **very** nice to them). You may find it more convenient to arrive in the UK on a weekday rather than during the weekend, when offices and banks are closed.

The UK isn't a signatory to the Schengen agreement (named after a Luxembourg village on the Moselle River where the agreement was signed), which came into effect on 1st January 1995 and introduced an open-borders policy between certain member countries. These are Austria, Belgium, Denmark, France, Finland, Germany, Greece, Italy, Luxembourg, the Netherlands, Portugal, Spain and Sweden. Iceland and Norway, although not EU members, enjoy associate status. The UK isn't a member and has no plans to join, because of declared fears of increased illegal immigration and cross-border crime, such as drug smuggling. Therefore, anyone arriving in the UK from a 'Schengen' country must go through the normal passport and immigration controls.

In addition to information about immigration and customs, this chapter contains checklists of tasks to be completed before, or soon after, arrival in the UK and when moving house, plus suggestions for finding local help and information.

IMMIGRATION

When you arrive in the UK, the first thing you must do is go through Passport Control, which is usually divided into two areas: 'European Union (EU)/EEA Nationals' and 'All Other Passports'. Make sure you join the right queue. Passport control is staffed by immigration officers who have the task of deciding whether you're subject to immigration control, and if so, whether or not you're entitled to enter the UK. You must satisfy the immigration officer that you're entitled to enter the UK under whatever category of the immigration rules you're applying to do so. Present your passport to the immigration officer with the following, as applicable:

- Entry clearance (visa, entry certificate or letter of consent);

- A work permit; (which may count as entry clearance in the case of some non-visa nationals, although this is being phased out over the next few years);

- A completed landing card (all non-EEA nationals);

- A letter from a bona fide educational establishment stating that you've been accepted on a full-time course of study;

- A letter stating you've been offered a position as an au pair, trainee or voluntary worker;

- Evidence that your qualifications for a job or a course of study are adequate, e.g. certificates or diplomas;

- Evidence that you're able to support yourself and any dependants during your stay without recourse to public funds, e.g. a bank statement or letter from a bank, or evidence of financial support such as cash, travellers cheques and credit cards;

- If your stay in the UK is for a short period only, you may need to give an assurance that you will leave at the end of that period.

If you leave the UK for any reason after your initial entry, e.g. for a holiday, you will be required to produce the same documents for re-admission. If you're entering the UK from a country other than an EEA member state, you may be required to have immunisation certificates. Check the requirements in advance at a British Diplomatic Post abroad before arriving in the UK.

The immigration officer may also decide to send you for a routine (and random) health check, before allowing you to enter the UK. After the health check, you must return to immigration to have your passport stamped. The UK has strict regulations regarding the entry of foreigners whose reason for seeking entry may be other than those stated. Generally, the onus is on anyone visiting the UK to prove that he's a genuine visitor and won't infringe the immigration laws. The immigration authorities aren't required to establish that you will violate the immigration laws and can refuse your entry on the grounds of suspicion only.

The treatment of foreigners by immigration officers varies, but some people complain of harassment and have trouble convincing officials that they're genuine visitors, e.g. people from Africa and the Indian subcontinent. Immigration officers are trained to assume that everyone who isn't an EEA national is trying to enter the UK illegally. Young people may also be liable to interrogation, particularly those travelling lightly and 'scruffily' dressed. It's advisable to carry international credit and charge cards, travellers cheques, return or onward travel tickets, student identity cards, or a letter from your employer or college stating that you're on holiday. Visitors arriving from 'exotic' regions (e.g. Africa, South America, the Caribbean, the Middle and Far East) may find themselves under close scrutiny from customs officials looking for drugs.

Be extremely careful how you answer seemingly innocent questions from the immigration authorities, as you could find yourself being refused entry if you give incriminating answers. Whatever the question, never imply that you may remain in the UK longer than the period permitted or for a purpose other than that for which you've been granted permission. For example, if you aren't permitted to work in the UK, you could be asked: "Would you like to work in the UK?" If you reply "Yes", even if you have no intention of doing so, you could be refused entry.

ENTRY REFUSAL

If you're refused entry into the UK, your legal position depends on whether or not you obtained entry clearance (see page 75) before arrival, as described below:

With Entry Clearance

If you're refused entry and have entry clearance (i.e. a visa, entry certificate, letter of consent or work permit), you cannot, in most cases, immediately be sent back to your home country, but are permitted to make an appeal (in the first instance to an independent adjudicator) and allowed to remain in the UK until it's been heard. However, there's no right of appeal in the case of people with visitor's visas, unless coming as 'family visitors' within the terms of the immigration rules, or as prospective or short-term students on a course of six months or less. You're given the reasons for refusal in writing and told how to make an appeal against the decision. There's a strict ten-day time limit within which your appeal must be returned and in the hands of the authorities. The address to which it must be sent is on the Notice of Appeal itself. (If returning it by post, always use the special delivery service.)

You should **immediately** contact the Immigration Advisory Service (IAS), who will help you make your appeal. The IAS is a registered charity specialising in this area and does not charge you. If you're a student, you can also contact the United Kingdom Council for Overseas Student Affairs (UKCOSA), 9–17 St Albans Place, London N1 0NX (☎ 020-7288 4330, 🖥 www.ukcosa.org.uk). They also operate an advice line on ☎ 020-7107 9922 between 1pm and 4pm, Mondays to Fridays.

The appeal process can take up to several months before a decision is made, although vigorous efforts are being made to reduce this time. If you entered the UK to work or study, you should continue with your plans, but it would be unwise to make any long-term commitments (such as paying for a long course of study or signing a long lease on a property), in case you lose your appeal and must leave the UK. Your action pending an appeal may depend on the advice you receive from the IAS (or other agencies), regarding the strength of your case and the likely outcome of your appeal.

Without Entry Clearance

If you have no entry clearance, you're asked to return to your home country immediately or given a short period of temporary admission (usually from 24 hours to a week, but sometimes more) until a final decision is made. If you aren't granted temporary admission, you may be held in a detention centre, e.g. at Heathrow airport, or you may be permitted to stay in private accommodation if you can reassure the authorities that you won't abscond. If you're granted temporary admission on this basis, you're given a date and time when you must report back to immigration. You must surrender your passport to the immigration officer and you must remain at the address which you've given him.

In either event, contact the Immigration Advisory Service (IAS) immediately, by telephoning the local representative (the IAS has representatives at all major international airports). Don't do anything until you've been advised by the IAS, who may be able to make a representation on your behalf to prevent your being deported. The period of temporary admission is to allow you time to provide the necessary evidence to support your case for entry into the UK. If, at the end of the period of temporary admission, you're unable (with the help of IAS or another agency) to provide the evidence required or you cannot convince immigration to allow you to stay, you should leave the UK voluntarily. If you refuse to leave voluntarily (or if you go into hiding), you're detained and forcibly removed, which will probably make it impossible for you to return to the UK in the future. If you leave voluntarily, there's no bar on re-entry, provided you can satisfy the immigration officials on your return. Contact anyone necessary before leaving. You can appeal against the refusal within 28 days, but only after you've returned to your home country.

PASSPORT STAMPS

If you're granted entry to the UK (officially called leave to remain), the immigration officer attaches a tamper-proof sticker to your passport, which indicates how long you may stay in the UK, whether you can work, and whether you're required to register with the police (see page 109). These stickers replace the old passport stamps which were easy to forge. Their meaning is self-explanatory. Your passport sticker is important and may be one of the following:

- Leave (permisssion) to enter for a specified purpose until a specified date. No recourse to public funds;

- Leave to enter for a specified purpose until a specified date. No recourse to public funds. Work (and any changes) must be authorised;

- Leave to enter for a specified purpose until a specified date. No work or recourse to public funds;

- Leave to enter for a specified purpose until a specified date to work in a specific position with certain conditions. Changes must be authorised. No recourse to public funds;

- Indefinite leave to enter the UK;

- Must register with the police within seven days;

- No longer required to register with the police.

If you enter the UK legally to work, live or study, you're usually given leave to remain for one year. Don't be concerned if you plan to stay longer, as you're able to extend this later, provided your circumstances remain the same. If you're unsure about the meaning of the sticker in your passport, contact the IAS (see address on page 104) for information and advice.

CUSTOMS

When you enter the UK to take up temporary or permanent residence, you can usually import your personal belongings duty and tax free. Any duty or tax due depends on where you came from, where you purchased the goods, how long you've owned them, and whether duty and tax has already been paid in another country. There are no restrictions on the importation of goods purchased tax and duty paid in another EU country, although there are limits for certain goods, e.g. tobacco, beer and wine (see page 467).

All ports and airports in the UK use a system of red and green 'channels'. Red means you have something to declare and green that you have nothing to declare (i.e. no more than the customs allowances, no goods to sell and no prohibited or restricted goods). If you're **certain** that you have nothing to declare, go through the 'green channel', otherwise go through the red channel. Customs officers make random checks on people going through the green channel and there are stiff penalties for smuggling.

If you're arriving by ferry with a motor vehicle, random checks can be rigorous – even to the point of dismantling the vehicle in search of undeclared or prohibited items!

A list of all items you're bringing in is useful, although the customs officer may still want to examine your belongings. If you need to pay duty or tax, it must be paid at the time the goods are brought into the country. Customs accept cash (sterling only); personal cheques supported by a cheque guarantee card; MasterCard, Visa and, at some ports and airports, Switch debit cards. If you're unable to pay on the spot, customs keep your belongings until you pay the sum due, which must be paid within the period noted on the back of your receipt. Postage or freight charges must be paid if you want the goods sent on to you.

Your belongings may be imported up to six months before, but no more than one year after your arrival, after transferring your residence. They mustn't be sold, lent, hired out, or otherwise disposed of in the UK (or elsewhere in the EU) within one year of their importation, without first obtaining customs authorisation.

If you're shipping your personal belongings (which includes anything for your family's personal use – such as clothing, cameras, television and stereo, furniture and other household goods) – unaccompanied to the UK, you must complete (and sign) customs form C3, obtainable from your shipping agent, HM Customs and Excise (see address below) or ⌨ www.hmce.gov.uk, and attach a detailed packing list. If you employ an international removal company, they handle the customs clearance and associated paperwork for you. Any items originally obtained in the UK or within the EU can be brought into the UK free of customs and excise duty or VAT, provided:

- Any customs duty, excise duty or VAT was paid and not refunded when they were exported from the UK (or the EU in the case of customs duty).

- They were in your private possession and use in the UK before they were exported.

- They haven't been altered abroad, other than necessary repairs.

- They're brought back within three years. (This is a condition which Customs & Excise normally waives if the previous three conditions have been met).

The personal belongings you're allowed to bring into the UK duty and tax free depend on your status, as shown below.

Visitors or Students Resident Abroad

If you're a visitor, you can bring your belongings to the UK free of duty and tax provided that:

- All belongings are brought in with you and are for your use alone.

- They're kept in the UK for no longer than twenty four months.

- You don't sell, lend, hire out, or otherwise dispose of them in the UK.

If you're unable to export your belongings when you leave the UK, you must apply to the nearest Customs and Excise Advice Centre for an extension.

In addition to the above, students attending a full-time course of study in the UK, can permanently import their clothing and household linen, study articles and household effects for furnishing their accommodation.

People Moving or Returning to the UK

If you're moving or returning to the UK (including British subjects) from outside the EU, you can import your belongings free of duty and tax provided you've lived at least 12 months outside the EU. Your possessions must have been used for at least six months outside the EU before being imported. Tax and duty must have been paid on all items being imported (this isn't applicable to diplomats, members of officially recognised international organisations, members of NATO or British forces and their spouses, and any civilian staff accompanying them). Articles must be for your personal use, must be declared to customs, and you mustn't sell, lend, hire out, or otherwise dispose of them in the UK (or elsewhere in the EU) within 12 months, without customs authorisation.

People with Second Homes in the UK

If you're setting up a second home in the UK, you can bring normal household furnishings and equipment with you free of duty and tax if you usually live in another EU country. If you've lived outside the EU for at least 12 months, you can import household furnishings and equipment for setting up a second home free of duty, but not free of added tax (VAT), which is levied at 17.5 per cent.

To qualify, you must either own or be renting a home in the UK for a minimum of two years, and your household furnishings and equipment must have been owned and used for at least six months. Articles must be for your personal use, must be declared to customs, and mustn't be sold, lent out, hired out, or otherwise disposed of in the UK (or elsewhere in the EU) within 24 months without authorisation from Customs and Excise. If furnishings and effects for a second home in the EU are imported unaccompanied, customs form C33 must be completed.

Further Information

Information regarding duty-free allowances (e.g. alcohol and tobacco) can be found on page 467; goods on which tax has been paid in the EU (page 477); the importation of vehicles (page 259); and the importation of pets and animals (page 501). Information concerning customs regulations is contained in a number of booklets, called Notices. They cover personal belongings, household effects, private motor vehicles and people moving to the UK after marriage (Notice 3); pleasure craft or boats (Notice 8); inherited goods and vehicles (Notice 368); antiques (Notice 362); and motor vehicles, boats or aircraft from elsewhere in the EU (Notice 728).

Copies of the notices listed above can be obtained from customs offices or downloaded from ⌨ www.hmce.gov.uk. The primary source of further information is the Customs and Excise national advice line ☎ 0845-010 9000 (or if telephoning from abroad ☎ +4420-8929 0152). Email and postal enquiry addresses for your local area can be found by using a search feature on the website. The principal address for written enquiries in London is HM Customs and Excise, Thomas Paine House, Angel Square, Torrens Street, London EC1V 1TA. Customs and Excise can also provide detailed information regarding the importation of special items.

Prohibited & Restricted Items

The following items are prohibited or restricted, although some may be imported with a special licence:

● Controlled drugs (e.g. opium, heroin, ecstasy, morphine, cocaine, cannabis, amphetamines, and LSD), explosives (including fireworks), firearms (including gas pistols, electric shock batons and similar weapons), flick knives and some martial arts weapons. The holder of a British firearm or shotgun certificate may import a weapon into England, Wales or Scotland. Customs instructs that such a person contact the national advice line **in advance**. It's illegal to own a handgun in the UK and the ownership of other guns has also been curtailed.

● Most animals and all birds, whether alive or dead (e.g. stuffed) and certain articles derived from protected species, including ivory, reptile leather, fur skins and goods made from them. **It's a criminal offence to attempt to smuggle an animal into the UK and it's almost always discovered.** Illegally imported animals are either exported immediately or destroyed and the owners are always prosecuted. They face (and invariably receive) a heavy fine (e.g. £500) and/or up to a year's imprisonment. The introduction of the Pet Travel Scheme (PETS) has made it both easier and cheaper to bring in some pets legally. For more information, contact the Pet Travel Scheme Helpline, Department for Environment, Food and Rural Affairs, Area 201, 1a Page Street, London SW1P 4PQ (☎ 0870-241 1710, 🖳 www.defra.gov.uk/animalh/quarantine/pets). (See also **Pets** on page 501).

- Pornographic material which isn't freely available in the UK.

- Meat, poultry and most of their products (whether cooked or not), including ham, bacon, sausage, paté, eggs and milk. Certain fish or fish eggs are also prohibited.

- Certain plants, seeds, vegetables, bulbs and fruits, although it's a complicated matter. The latest regulations can be obtained from the Department for Environment, Food and Rural Affairs, Plant Health Seeds Inspectorate, Room 334, Foss House, Kings Pool, York YO1 7PX (☎ 01904-455 174).

- Non-approved radio transmitters and cordless telephones.

If you're caught trying to smuggle any goods that aren't duty and tax free, customs may confiscate the goods, and if you hide them in your car, they can confiscate that as well! If you attempt to import prohibited items you may be liable to criminal charges or deportation.

POLICE REGISTRATION

Foreigners over 16 are required to register at their local police station within seven days of arrival if any of the following applies:

- They are nationals of Afghanistan, Algeria, Argentina, Armenia, Azerbaijan, Bahrain, Belarus, Bolivia, Brazil, China, Columbia, Cuba, Egypt, Georgia, Iran, Iraq, Israel, Jordan, Kazakhstan, Kuwait, Kyrgyzstan, Lebanon, Libya, Moldova, Morocco, North Korea, Oman, Palestine, Peru, Qatar, Russia, Saudi Arabia, Sudan, Syria, Tajikistan, Tunisia, Turkey, Turkmenistan, United Arab Emirates, Ukraine, Uzbekistan or Yemen or are stateless.

- They are a national of one of the above countries and have limited leave to stay in the UK for longer than six months for employment, or as au pairs, students, businessmen, self-employed people, investors, people of independent means or creative artists.

- They are a national of one of the above countries and weren't originally required to register, but have since been granted an extension of stay, which means that they will be in the UK for longer than six months.

- They are the spouse or child of a person who must register with the police.

- They are a national of any of the above countries given limited leave to remain, whom the immigration authorities suspect might not abide by their entry conditions.

Exceptions are seasonal workers at agricultural work camps, private servants of diplomatic households, clergymen, spouses of people settled in the UK, or those formally granted asylum.

When required, registration is indicated by the immigration stamp in your passport (see page 109). You must report to the police station nearest to where you're staying within seven days, even when you're staying in temporary accommodation. You need your passport, work permit if you have one, any letters from the Home Office or documents from the Overseas Visitors Record Office, two passport-size photographs (black and white or colour) and the fee, currently £34. In the greater London area, all residents must register at the Overseas Visitors Record Office, Brandon House, 180 Borough High Street, London SE1 1LH. The nearest underground station is 'Borough' and the information line is ☎ 020-7230 1208. Business hours are 9am to 4pm Mondays to Fridays and you should expect to wait for a long time (unless you're first in the queue).

Details, such as your name, address, occupation, nationality, marital status and the date your permission expires, are entered in a green booklet called a 'police registration certificate'. It's advisable to take a copy of your marriage and birth certificates with you. If the police registration certificate isn't given to you on the spot, you may need to surrender your passport, which is returned to you later with your certificate. Make a photocopy or a note of the certificate's number, date, and place of issue, in case you lose it (in which case the fee must be paid again). You should inform the authorities of any change in your situation within seven days, e.g. if you change your address or extend your leave to remain in the UK.

You're required to carry your police registration certificate with you at all times, but not your passport. It's advisable to take your police registration certificate with you when travelling abroad, as this makes re-entry into the UK easier. It should be surrendered to the Immigration Officer if you're travelling abroad for longer than two months. Unlike many other Europeans, Britons aren't legally required to prove their identity on demand by a policeman or other official.

COUNCIL TAX REGISTRATION

All residents or temporary residents of the UK are required to register with their local authority or council for council tax purposes soon after arrival in the UK, or after moving to a new home, either in the same council area or a new area.

EMBASSY & CONSULATE REGISTRATION

Nationals of some countries are required to register with their local embassy or consulate as soon as possible after arrival in the UK. Registration isn't usually mandatory, although most embassies like to keep a record of their nationals resident in the UK and it may help to expedite passport renewal or replacement. For a list of embassies and consulates see **Appendix A**.

FINDING HELP

One of the biggest difficulties facing new arrivals in the UK is how and where to obtain help with day-to-day problems. For example, finding a home, schools, insurance requirements and so on. This book was written in response to this need. However, in addition to the comprehensive information you will find here, you will also require detailed local information. How successful you are at finding help depends on your employer, the town or area where you live (e.g. those who live and work in the London area are much better served than those living in a rural village), your nationality and your English proficiency. Obtaining information isn't a problem, as there's a wealth of data available in the UK on every conceivable subject. The problem is sorting the truth from the half-truths, comparing the options available and making the right decisions. Much information naturally isn't intended for foreigners and their particular needs. You may find that your friends, colleagues and acquaintances can help, as they're often able to proffer advice based on their own experiences and mistakes. But beware! Although they mean well, you're likely to receive as much false and conflicting information as you are accurate (not always wrong, but possibly invalid for your particular area or situation).

Your local council offices, library, tourist information centre and Citizens Advice Bureau are excellent sources of reliable information on almost any subject (see page 497). Some large employers may have a department or staff whose job is to help new arrivals or they may contract this job out to a relocation consultant (see page 117). There are expatriate clubs and organisations for nationals of many countries in most areas, many of which provide detailed local information regarding all aspects of living in the UK, including housing costs, schools, names of doctors and dentists, shopping and much more. Clubs produce data sheets, booklets and newsletters, and organise a variety of social events, which may include day and evening classes ranging from local cooking to English-language classes. One of the best ways to get to know local people is to join a social club, of which there are hundreds in all areas of the UK (look under 'Clubs and Associations' in your local Yellow Pages).

Embassies and consulates usually provide information bulletin boards (jobs, accommodation, travel) and keep lists of social clubs for their nationals, and many businesses (e.g. banks and building societies) produce books and leaflets containing valuable information for newcomers. Local libraries and bookshops usually have books about their areas (see also **Appendix B**).

CHECKLISTS

Before Arrival

The following checklist contains a summary of the tasks that should (if possible) be completed before your arrival in the UK:

- Obtain a visa, if necessary, for all your family members (see **Chapter 3**). Obviously, this must be done before leaving for the UK.

- If possible, visit the UK before your move to compare communities and schools and arrange schooling for your children (see **Chapter 9**).

- Find temporary or permanent accommodation and buy a car. If you purchase a car in the UK, register it and arrange insurance (see pages 260 and 271).

- Arrange for shipment of your personal effects to the UK.

- Obtain an international credit or charge card, which will be invaluable during your first few months in the UK.

- Arrange health insurance for your family (see page 344). This is essential if you won't be covered by the National Health Service on your arrival in the UK (see page 307).

- Open a bank account in the UK and transfer funds (you can open an account with many British banks overseas). It's best to obtain some British currency before your arrival, as this saves you having to change money immediately.

- Obtain an international driver's licence, if necessary.

- Collect and update your personal records, including those relating to your family's medical, dental, educational (schools), insurance (e.g. car insurance), professional and employment history (including job references) and take them with you to the UK. Don't forget birth certificates, driver's licenses, marriage certificate, divorce papers, death certificate (if a widow or widower), educational diplomas and professional certificates, student identity cards, medical and dental records, bank account and credit card details, insurance policies and receipts for any valuables you're bringing with you. You also need the documents necessary to obtain a residence or work permit (see **Chapter 3**), plus certified copies, official translations and numerous passport-size photographs.

After Arrival

The following checklist contains a summary of tasks to be completed after arrival in the UK (if not done before):

- On arrival at a British airport or port, have your visa cancelled and passport stamped, as applicable.

- If you don't own a car, you may wish to rent one for a week or two until you buy one locally (see page 293). It's difficult to get around in rural areas without a car.

- Register for council tax at your local town hall (see page 110).

- Register with your local embassy or consulate (see page 110).

● Do the following within a few weeks of your arrival:

- Register with your local social security office (see page 336).

- Open an account at a local bank and give the details to your employer (see page 364).

- Arrange schooling for your children (see **Chapter 9**).

- Find a local doctor and dentist (see **Chapter 12**).

- Arrange whatever insurance is necessary (see **Chapter 13**), including health insurance (see page 344), car insurance (see page 271), home contents insurance (see page 349) and personal liability insurance (see page 352).

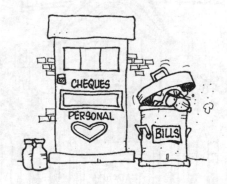

5.

ACCOMMODATION

In most regions, accommodation to buy and (to a lesser extent) to rent isn't too difficult to find, depending, of course, on what you're looking for and how much you can pay. There are, however, exceptions, e.g. London, where property at an affordable price is difficult to find unless you're a millionaire and rents (in relation to average salaries) can be astronomical. Particularly hard hit are those on low incomes; pensioners, the unemployed, single parents, students and the young. Accommodation usually accounts for around a quarter to a third of the average family's budget, but can rise to 40 or 50 per cent in high cost areas (or anywhere when interest rates are high).

Home ownership has increased steadily over the last 20 years thanks to easier access to mortgages, the previous (Conservative) government's encouragement to local authority tenants to buy their rented council homes, the relatively restricted rental market (and high rents), and the fact that property is an excellent investment and generally no more expensive than renting. The British have an obsession with property ownership (principal, second and investment homes) that's unparalleled in most other European countries, although home ownership is higher in Ireland, Italy, Greece, Luxembourg and Spain than in the UK, where it's around 70 per cent. It's slightly less in Portugal and Belgium and just 40 per cent in Germany.

Home ownership is, however, unevenly spread throughout the UK; it's only some 58 per cent in Greater London and 63 per cent in Scotland, compared with 73 per cent in Wales and 76 per cent in south-east England. The average age of first-time buyers in the UK has risen from 26 in '90s to around five years ago to 35 in 2007; it's now much harder for first-time buyers to get a foothold on the housing ladder owing to the high cost of property and the **very** high salary required to qualify for a mortgage. There are aroudn 2.3 people per household in the UK and over 30 per cent of households consist of one person only – up from 26.3 per cent in 1991. This trend (which is mirrored in France and other EU countries) is expected to continue, as most new homes are built for single occupation or large families in high income brackets. Four out of five people in the UK live in houses rather than flats (apartments).

Property prices have risen dramatically throughout the UK in recent years because of high demand and a shortage of homes for sale. Low interest rates have also given rise to rampant speculation, encouraged by the widespread availability of buy-to-let mortgages (20 years in existence in 2007 and responsible for much of the housing inflation). Predictions of a price collapse some years ago proved to be groundless and, although prices did fall marginally in some regions, they rose considerably in others. This goes to illustrate that the UK isn't one property market, but a collection of smaller ones that don't necessarily share the same characteristics.

As a rough rule of thumb, property values in the UK double every seven years, although in recent years prices in many areas have doubled in as little as three or four years. In the last decade values have increased by over 200 per cent in some towns and regions and most have seen rises of between 100 and 200 per cent. The lowest gains have been in Scotland and the north of England although, in recent years prices have risen dramatically in all areas thanks to second homeowners and investors.

In the last few decades, the UK property market has gone from boom to bust and back again and so far, predictions of a crash haven't come about (yet) with prices still rising. The forecast is for property to continue to increase in value by 5 to 10 per cent a year in most areas. Nevertheless, property remains one of the best long-term investments, particularly as the demand for homes far outstrips the supply, a situation that's expected to continue for some years. Much of south-east England, where demand is strongest, is heavily built up and those who live there are opposed to further development (now that they have their homes!), which will delay or restrict widespread development. However, in the long term, it has been estimated that one-fifth of the area of England will be built on by the year 2050.

RELOCATION CONSULTANTS

If you're fortunate enough to have your move to (or within) the UK paid for by your employer, it's likely he will arrange for a relocation consultant to handle the details. There are generally three types of relocation consultants in the UK: corporate relocation agents (whose clients are usually large companies), commercial property agents and home-search agents, who act for individuals. The larger relocation consultants may provide all three levels of service, while smaller companies may have just a few staff and offer a home-search service only. Companies that are members of the Confederation of British Industry (CBI) can use the CBI's relocation services.

Relocation consultants usually charge a registration (or administration) fee of £200 to £400, payable in advance. The fees charged by consultants vary widely and may range from around £500 a day for accompanied viewing of properties and other amenities. If finding a house is part of the service, a fee of 1 to 1.5 per cent of the purchase price is normal, with a minimum charge of around £1,000. (Usually only properties above a certain price level are considered to ensure an adequate return for the agent). To arrange the sale of an employee's house, provide a bridging loan, advise on mortgages, schools and insurance, and help a spouse find a job, a relocation consultant may charge a company £5,000 or more.

Home-search companies are becoming increasingly common and undertake to find the home of your dreams. This can save buyers considerable time, trouble and money, particularly if you have special or unusual requirements. Some specialise in finding exceptional residences costing upwards of £400,000. Sums saved by an expert negotiating the price on your behalf can be large. Buying property anywhere is usually a minefield, and buying it yourself in a foreign country and possibly an unknown culture can make you prey to unscrupulous sellers. Having someone aware of the local market, locations and pitfalls to do it for you is a big plus.

Finding accommodation for single people or couples without children can usually be accomplished in a week or two, depending on the area, while families usually take longer. You should allow at least two months between your initial visit and moving into a purchased property. Rented accommodation (see page 121) can usually be found in two to six weeks, depending on the location and your requirements. There are relocation consultants in all parts of the country, most of whom provide the services described below.

House Hunting

This is usually the main service provided by relocation consultants and includes rented and purchased properties. Services usually include locating a number of properties matching your requirements and specifications, and arranging a visit (or visits) to the UK to view them.

Negotiations

Consultants usually help and advise with all aspects of house rental or purchase and may conduct negotiations on your behalf, organise finance (including bridging loans), arrange surveys and insurance, organise your removal to the UK and even arrange quarantine for your pets (see page 501).

Schools

Consultants can usually provide a special report on local schools (state and private) for families with children. If required, the report can also include private boarding schools in the UK.

Local Information

Most consultants provide a comprehensive information package for a chosen area, including information about employment prospects, state and private health services, local schools (state and private), estate agents, shopping facilities, public transport, amenities and services, sports and social facilities, and communications.

Miscellaneous Services

Most consultants provide advice and support (particularly for non-working spouses) before and after a move, orientation visits for spouses, counselling services for domestic and personal problems, help in finding jobs for spouses and even marriage counselling services (moving to another country puts a lot of strain on relationships).

Although you may consider a relocation consultant's services expensive, particularly if you're footing the bill yourself, most companies and individuals consider it money well spent. You can find a relocation consultant through The Association of Relocation Professionals (ARP), PO Box 189, Diss, IP22 1PE (☎ 0870-073 7475, 🖳 www.relocationagents.com) or look in the yellow pages under Relocation Agents.

If you just wish to look at properties for rent or sale in a particular area, you can make appointments to view properties through estate agents in the area where you plan to live and arrange your own trip to the UK. However, you must make

absolutely certain that agents know exactly what you're looking for and obtain property lists in advance.

BUYING PROPERTY

Buying a house or apartment has traditionally been a good investment, although this was severely tested in the '90s, during much of which a property investment was anything but as safe as houses! However, most people still find buying preferable to renting. For a visitor, this depends on how long you're planning to stay and where you're planning to live. If staying less than two years, then you may be better off renting. For those staying longer, buying should be the better option, particularly as this is generally no more expensive than renting and you could make a nice profit.

Property has always been a good long-term investment and in the last few years it has out-performed the stock market and all forms of savings. Many homeowners dramatically increase the value of their family home by 'trading up' – that is, buying a bigger and more expensive home every few years. One of the reasons for the huge rise in property values in most regions in the last few years has been the realisation that owning property isn't just about having a roof over your head, but is an excellent long-term investment.

Prices

Apart from obvious things, such as size, quality and land area, the most important factor influencing the price of a house is its location. In January 2007, according to the official body, the Land Registry, a semi-detached house cost £134,000 in the north of England and £126,000 in Wales, compared with £213,000 in south-east England and £326,000 in London! A flat costing £125,000 in the north of England would set you back a massive £286,000 in London, and a terraced house selling for £79,000 in north-west England would cost £291,000 in London. In early 2007, the average price of a house in the UK was around £175,000 according to the Land Registry Index, which – as you can see from the above figures – is fairly meaningless, as regional variations are so great. As a general rule, prices in London and the south-east are never less than 50 per cent higher than the cheapest regions, and usually far more.

As with most things, higher-priced houses, e.g. over £400,000 (which outside London are usually termed executive or prestige homes by estate agents), generally provide much better value for money than cheaper houses, with a proportionately larger built area and plot of land, better build quality, and superior fixtures and fittings. Most semi-detached and detached houses have single or double garages included in the price.

There are few bargains when it comes to buying properties and, although you may possibly be able to negotiate a reduction of around 5 per cent (particularly if someone is looking for a quick sale in a buyer's market), there's usually a good reason if a property is substantially cheaper than other similar properties. You should generally be suspicious of a bargain. On the other hand, most sellers and estate agents price properties higher than the market price or the price they expect to receive, knowing that prospective buyers will try to drive the price down. So always haggle over the price (even if you think it's a bargain).

This is, in fact, one of the few occasions in the UK when you're expected to bargain over the price, although you should try to avoid insulting the owner by offering a derisory amount. Most house sales are part of a chain of sellers and buyers (around seven or eight isn't uncommon) and only one link needs to fail to jeopardise a whole series of sales. If you're a first-time buyer you may be eligible for special terms offered by many lenders (**Mortgages** on page 375).

Contracts

When buying property in England, Wales or Northern Ireland, prospective buyers make an offer subject to survey and contract. Either side can amend or withdraw from a sale at any time before the exchange of contracts (when a sale is legally binding). In a seller's market, gazumping (where a seller agrees to an offer from one prospective buyer and then sells to another for a higher amount) is rampant and **isn't illegal**. There are proposals to speed up the home buying process (from a few months to around four weeks), which would reduce the risk of gazumping, although many people believe that following the example of Scotland (see below) and many other countries is the only way to stamp it out altogether. On the other hand, in a buyer's market, a buyer may threaten to pull out at the last minute unless the seller reduces the price (called 'gazundering').

There's no gazumping in Scotland, as neither side can pull out once an offer has been made and accepted. In Scotland, when you wish to purchase a property, your solicitor contacts the seller's solicitor and notes your interest. Once the seller's solicitor has had sufficient interest, he usually fixes a closing date, by which time all offers must be submitted in writing. Once your offer in writing is accepted, it's legally binding and you cannot pull out. Therefore, it's vital that you have a survey done (and have the necessary finance) before making an offer in Scotland. The problem with this system is that each prospective buyer must have his own survey done, which some years ago prompted a proposed change in the law (yet to become reality), whereby the seller would be responsible for having a survey done before selling a property.

Information

There are numerous other books on the subject of buying a home, including *Buying, Selling and Letting Property* by your author David Hampshire (published by Survival Books). There are also many magazines published in the UK for homebuyers, including *What House (www.whathouse.co.uk)* and *What Mortgage (www.whatmortgage.co.uk)*, which contain the latest information about mortgages and house prices throughout the UK. All building societies and banks publish free booklets for homebuyers, most of which contain excellent (usually unbiased) advice.

You can use websites such Up My Street (💻 www.upmystreet.com), Proviser (💻 www.proviser.com) or Directgov (💻 www.direct.gov.uk) to check the facilities and property prices in a particular town or city suburb. There are also dozens of useful websites for prospective homeowners, including 💻 www.assertahome.com, 💻 www. findaproperty.com, 💻 www.fish4homes.co.uk, 💻 www.foxtons.co.uk, 💻 www.home-sale.co.uk, 💻 www.hot-property.co.uk, and 💻 www.houseweb.co.uk.

RENTED ACCOMMODATION

Rented accommodation is the answer for people who don't want the trouble, expense and restrictions involved in buying a house, or who are staying in the UK for one or two years only (when buying isn't usually practical). Unlike the situation in most European countries, there isn't a strong rental market in the UK as most families prefer to buy. According to figures issued in 2002, only 10 per cent of families lived in private rented accommodation in the UK which, although totalling some two million people, is much lower than on the continent.

There has traditionally been a chronic shortage of rental properties in many areas, particularly in London and other major cities, although this has eased in recent years with the explosion of buy-to-let mortgages. However, rental properties with three or more bedrooms (particularly detached houses) located in good areas are in short supply everywhere. Rental accommodation can be prohibitively expensive and the quality of properties often leaves much to be desired, particularly at the lower end of the market. You should be aware that renting accommodation is a jungle in the UK, which has one of the most unregulated letting markets in Western Europe (with little or no consumer protection against unscrupulous agents and landlords).

One of the reasons for the unpopularity of renting in the UK is that it has traditionally been relatively easy to obtain a 95 or even 100 per cent mortgage with repayments over 25 or 30 years. This means that it's usually cheaper or no more expensive to buy a home in the UK than it is to rent. According to research done by the Abbey National Building Society a few years ago, renting is around 35 per cent more expensive than buying a home over the long term! Owners can also make a tax-free profit (or a tax-free loss!) in a relatively short period, as no capital gains tax (see page 394) is payable on the profits from the sale of your principal home. Many people who cannot afford to pay a high mortgage often let a room (or rooms) to reduce the cost.

The Housing Act 1988 deregulated new lettings in the private sector. Since January 1989, new lettings have generally been of two kinds: an assured tenancy with a long-term security of tenure and an assured shorthold tenancy for a fixed period of at least six months (see **Rental Contract** on page 124). These changes were intended to encourage greater choice and competition in the rental market. Unlike many other countries, 95 per cent of rental properties in the UK are let furnished. The reason is historical, as until January 1989, landlords had much greater protection under the law if properties were let furnished, although this is no longer the case. The furniture and furnishings in many rental properties vary from fair to terrible, except for the rare luxury property (with an astronomical rent) that's let for a fixed term by owners who are spending a period abroad.

Rental property can usually be found in two to six weeks in most areas, with the exception of large houses (four or more bedrooms), which are rare and **very** expensive. Family accommodation in particular is in short supply in London, with the possible exception of luxury homes with enormous rents. Most people settle for something in the suburbs or country and commute to work. If you must travel into a city centre (particularly London) each day, you should be prepared to spend at least an hour or more travelling each way. Unfurnished houses and apartments are difficult to find anywhere and used to be rented on payment of a large fee (up to thousands of pounds), which was nominally for 'fixtures and fittings', but was in fact just a way of selling the tenancy (known as 'key money'). This is still practised, but rarer nowadays.

Most rented property is let through letting agencies or estate agents. They act on behalf of landlords, and yet many still charge tenants as well. This is illegal according to the Accommodation Agencies Act 1963, so fees you pay are termed pro forma as 'administration charges'. These are anything from £30 to £200 for taking up references, drawing up tenancy agreements and preparing an inventory. You must usually pay one month's rent in advance, depending on the type of property and the rental agreement, plus a deposit against damages equal to one or two months' rent. When you agree to rent a property, you're usually asked for a holding deposit of between £50 and £250 before an agreement is signed (this should go towards your rent, but is often simply an additional fee). Some letting agents (e.g. in London) charge an up-front fee of around £100 to house hunters with the promise of finding them accommodation, in return for which they simply supply a list of 'vacant' properties often just taken from newspapers. Some agents employ a wealth of scams and rip off the tenant and the landlord at every opportunity.

Agents usually have a number of properties available for immediate occupancy and lists are normally updated weekly. You should have no problem finding something suitable in most areas if you start looking at least four weeks before the date you wish to take occupancy. Most letting agents require a reference from your employer (or previous employer if you've been less than one year with your current one), and bank and credit references, or in the case of a company let, copies of audited accounts and status.

Your deposit should be put into a savings account in the names of the renter and the agent or landlord, although this is rare. If it isn't, and the letting agent goes bankrupt, you will lose your deposit. If possible, you should deal only with a member of the Association of Residential Letting Agents (ARLA) or the National Association of Estate Agents (NAEA), both of which insist that members have a bonding scheme or professional indemnity cover to safeguard rental income and deposits. However, agents are totally unregulated in the UK and you may have no option but to deal with 'cowboys'.

Further Information

Local Housing Aid or Advice Centres offer advice concerning finding somewhere to live and usually handle private and council house problems. Contact your local council for information. A Citizens Advice Bureau can also offer advice regarding the legal aspects of letting and a tenant's rights. In some towns and cities there are council-run housing aid centres, where you can obtain free advice on housing problems. There are also a number of useful books published detailing the legal rights and duties of landlords and tenants, including the *Which? Guide to Renting and Letting* by Peter Wilde and Paul Butt (Which? Books).

Rental Costs & Standards

Rental costs vary considerably depending on the size (number of bedrooms) and quality of a property, its age and the facilities provided. Not least, rents depend on the neighbourhood and the region, and are generally lowest in Scotland, Northern Ireland, Wales and the North of England, and highest in London and the south-east. Rents are also lower in rural than urban areas. As a general rule, the further a property is from a large city or town, public transport or other facilities, the cheaper it is. Rents are high, particularly when you consider that renting can cost more than buying a home in many areas. A rough guide to average monthly rents for furnished apartments and houses in the south-east (outside London and the M25 motorway) are shown in the table below:

No. of Bedrooms	Monthly Rent (£)
Bedsit/Studio	350 – 550
1	450 – 800
2	600 – 1,200
3	1,000 – 1,800
4	1,250 – 3,000+

The rents shown above are for good quality modern or renovated properties and don't include properties located in the central area of large towns, in major cities or in exclusive residential areas, for which the sky's the limit. In London, rents are at least 50 per cent higher than the minimum shown above, while in some remote country areas they may be lower. Rents for desirable houses with four or more bedrooms are £3,000 to £4,000 per month in many areas. It may be possible to find cheaper, older apartments and houses for rent, but they're rare, generally small and don't usually contain the conveniences that are standard in a modern home, e.g. no central heating or double glazing (heating in old houses can be highly eccentric). If you like a property, but think the rent is too high, try to negotiate a reduction or ask an agent to put your offer to the owner.

Kitchens normally contain an oven with a grill, refrigerator (small), fitted kitchen units, and occasionally a dishwasher and a separate freezer. Many houses don't have basements or utility rooms, so washing machines (usually provided) and dryers are located in the kitchen. Many houses have lofts and garages that are often used for storage. Most have baths and may also have a separate shower or an *en suite* shower or bathroom. Often shower attachments are run off a bath and don't have a separate pump (which means that the water trickles out). Bathrooms rarely contain a bidet. In general, British plumbing is better than that found in many countries (although Americans won't be impressed). Most houses and apartments have some form of central heating. An airing cupboard (linen closet) is common and usually contains the hot water boiler. Unfurnished apartments and houses usually have light fittings in all rooms, although there may be no bulbs or lampshades. Fitted wardrobes in bedrooms are rare and curtain rails aren't provided unless they're built-in. Most houses, whether furnished or unfurnished, are fully or partly carpeted.

Many rental properties are old houses, particularly in London and other large cities, that have been modernised and divided into apartments. At the bottom end of the market, many properties have dreadful furnishings, e.g. flowery wallpaper which may 'match' the equally awful three-piece suite, with sickly green carpets and brown bathroom suites (or vice versa). Up-market (i.e. expensive) property may, however, be furnished to a high standard. In furnished accommodation, you must usually provide your own bedding and linen, although crockery, kitchen utensils and most household appliances are usually provided. It may be possible to 'throw out' the owner's or landlord's tatty furniture and replace it with your own (but you may have to pay to move and store it).

Rental Contracts

When you find a suitable house or apartment to rent, you should insist on a written contract with the owner or agent, which is called a tenancy or rental agreement. Make sure that you obtain a rent book, which is used to record all payments you make. If you don't have a rent book, always pay by direct debit or cheque (when you should insist on a receipt). Your contract may include details of when your rent will be reviewed or increased, if applicable. When you wish to leave rented accommodation you must give at least one month's notice in writing, unless it's within the first six months of an assured shorthold tenancy (see below), in which case you must pay the rent to the end of the period. If your landlord wants you to leave, the notice he must give you depends on your agreement with him and whether your tenancy is covered by the law. It's a criminal offence for your landlord to harass you in any way in an attempt to drive you out. Under the Housing Act (1988), several kinds of rental agreement and tenancy (see below) were created, most of which provide tenants with fewer rights than previously and make evictions easier for landlords.

Assured Tenancy

An assured tenancy is a tenancy for an indefinite period and needn't be in writing. The landlord cannot live on the premises and, provided you pay the rent and take care of the property, you cannot be asked to leave. Your landlord must apply to a county court and must have a good reason to evict you, e.g. unpaid rent, damage to the property or its contents, or you must have otherwise broken your contract with him. However, if he offers you similar accommodation, needs the property for himself, or a mortgage lender needs vacant possession in order to sell it, a court may serve you with written notice to leave. The rent cannot be increased until one year after you first agreed the rent and, if you don't agree with the increase, you can ask the council's Rent Assessment Committee to set a fair rent.

Assured Shorthold Tenancy

An assured shorthold tenancy is a tenancy with a fixed time limit of not less than six months, for which a written rental agreement is necessary, stating clearly that it's an assured shorthold tenancy. You cannot terminate your agreement (or be evicted) during the first six months and, thereafter, you or your landlord must give two months' notice in writing to terminate the agreement. Under an assured shorthold tenancy you have the right in certain cases to ask the Rent Assessment Committee to set a fair rent.

No Agreement

If you don't have an agreement with your landlord, you're protected in law and have the same rights as an assured tenancy (see above) if your landlord doesn't live on the premises. Always try to obtain a tenancy agreement and retain evidence of all payments to your landlord. If, after taking up residence, you're offered a holiday let, licence agreement or tenancy with board and service, you should refuse and contact a Citizens Advice Bureau for advice. These agreements provide you with no security and few legal rights as a tenant.

Flat-sharers

The law regarding flat-sharing is more complicated and it's simpler when one person is the tenant and sub-lets to the others, which must be permitted by the tenant's agreement. It's possible for all sharers to be joint tenants with one tenancy agreement or individual tenants with individual tenancy agreements. Whatever the agreement, you should have only one rent book and pay the rent in a lump sum. It's usually the occupants' responsibility to replace flatmates who leave during the tenancy.

Deposits

Usually a deposit equal to one or two months' (the maximum permitted by law) rent must be paid for an assured shorthold tenancy. This should be repaid when you leave, provided there are no outstanding claims for rent, unpaid bills, damages or cleaning. Always check the contract to find out who holds the deposit and under what circumstances it will be returned, and obtain a receipt. Many agents and landlords go to almost any lengths to avoid repaying a deposit and tenants lose tens of thousands of pounds to unscrupulous landlords and letting agents who refuse to repay deposits when a lease has expired. Often a landlord makes a claim for 'professional' cleaning running into hundreds of pounds, even when you've left a place spotless. If the landlord fails to return your deposit you should threaten legal action and if this has no affect you should take him to the Small Claims Court (see page 497).

Don't sign a contract unless you're sure you fully understand all the small print. Ask one of your colleagues or friends for help, or obtain legal advice. British law (actually English or Scottish law) usually prevents you from signing away all your rights; nevertheless, it pays to be careful. If you have any questions regarding your rental agreement or problems with your landlord, you can contact your local Citizens Advice Bureau for advice (see page 497). They will check your rental agreement and advise you of your rights under the law.

UTILITIES

Utilities is the collective name given to electricity, gas and water companies (and usually also includes telephone companies). All the UK's utility companies have been privatised in the last couple of decades, quickly followed by increased prices and worse service. However, in recent years most people have been able to choose their electricity and gas supplier and the increased competition has led to lower prices. See **Electricity & Gas Bills** on page 132 for how to compare rates.

Electricity

The electricity supply in the UK is 240 volts (V) AC, with a frequency of 50 hertz (cycles). This is suitable for all electrical equipment with a rated power consumption of up to 3,000 watts. For equipment with a higher power consumption, a single 240V or 3-phase, 380 volts AC, 20 amp supply must be used (this is installed only in large houses with six to eight bedrooms or industrial premises). Power cuts are rare in most parts of the UK, although some areas experience more than their fair share. Electricity companies pay compensation for a power cut lasting longer than 24 hours, but nothing for cuts of less than 24 hours (which includes 99.9 per cent of cuts).

If you move into an old home, the electricity supply may have been disconnected by the previous electricity company, and in a brand new home you must also get the electricity connected. In the last few years householders have been able to choose their electricity company from among British Gas, Eastern Energy, EDF Energy/London Electricity, Northern Electric, Npower/Yorkshire Electricity, Norweb, Powergen, Scottish Hydro-Electric, Scottish Power/Manweb, Southern Electric, SWALEC, EDF/ South Western Electricity and United Utilities. However, names change quickly and mergers and takeovers are commonplace in the industry, so, by the time you read this, some may have changed. Some companies cover the whole country, while others cover certain regions only. To have the electricity connected or reconnected, you must choose an electricity company and complete a form. There's usually a charge for connection, and you should allow at least two days before it's completed. If you're in the UK for a short stay only, you may be asked for a security deposit or to obtain a guarantor (e.g. your employer). You must contact your electricity company to get a final reading when you vacate your home.

Power Rating

Electrical equipment rated at 110 volts AC (for example from the US) requires a converter or a step-down transformer to convert it to 240 volts AC, although some electrical appliances (e.g. electric razors and hair dryers) are fitted with a 110/240 volt switch. Check for the switch, which may be located inside the casing, and make sure it's switched to 240 volts **before** connecting it to the power supply. Converters can be used for heating appliances, but transformers, which are available from most electrical retailers, are required for motorised appliances (they can also be purchased second-hand). Total the wattage of the devices you intend to connect to a transformer and make sure its power rating **exceeds** this sum.

Generally, all small, high-wattage, electrical appliances, such as kettles, toasters, heaters and irons, need large transformers. Motors in large appliances such as cookers, refrigerators, washing machines, dryers and dishwashers, will need replacing or fitting with a large transformer. In most cases, it's simpler to buy new appliances in the UK, which are of good quality and reasonably priced, and sell them when you leave if you cannot take them with you. The dimensions of British cookers, microwave ovens, refrigerators, washing machines, dryers and dishwashers may differ from those in most other countries. All electrical goods purchased in the UK must conform to British safety standards. If you wish to buy electrical appliances, such as a cooker or refrigerator, you should shop around, as prices vary considerably (see **Household Appliances** on page 473). The British Electrotechnical Approvals Board (BEAB) label indicates that an electrical appliance has been tested for compliance with the appropriate safety standards by an independent approval organisation.

Frequency Rating

A problem with some electrical equipment is the frequency rating, which in some countries, e.g. the US, is designed to run at 60 Hertz (Hz) and not the UK's 50 Hz. Electrical equipment **without** a motor is generally unaffected by the drop in frequency to 50 Hz (except television sets, see page 186). Equipment with a motor may run, but with a 20 per cent drop in speed. However, automatic washing machines, cookers, electric clocks, record players and tape recorders are unusable in the UK if they aren't designed for 50 cycle operation. To find out, look at the label on the back of the equipment. If it says 50/60 Hz, it should be all right. If it says 60 Hz, you may try it anyway, but first ensure that the voltage is correct, as outlined above. If the equipment runs too slowly, seek advice from the manufacturer or the retailer. For example, you may be able to obtain a special pulley for a tape deck or turntable to compensate for the drop in speed. Transformers and motors of electrical devices designed to run at 60 Hz run hotter at 50 Hz, so make sure that equipment has sufficient space around it for cooling.

Fuses

Most apartments and all houses have their own fuse boxes. Fuses may be of three types: wire, cartridge fuses or circuit breakers. Older houses may have rewireable fuses, although these are rare nowadays. Cartridge fuses are found in few houses these days and are colour coded to signify their rating. Circuit breakers are usually fitted to modern houses (and houses that have been modernised). When a circuit is overloaded they trip to the 'off' position. When replacing or repairing fuses of any kind, if the same fuse continues to blow, contact an electrician – never attempt to use fuse wire or fit a fuse of a higher rating than specified, even as a temporary measure. When replacing fuses, don't rely on the blown fuse wire or fuse as a guide, as it may have been wrong. If you use an electric lawn-mower or power tools outside your home or in your garage, you should have a Residual Current Device (RCD) often known as a circuit breaker installed. This can detect current changes of as little as a thousandth of an amp and in the event of a fault (or the cable being cut), will disconnect the power in around 0.04 seconds.

Plugs

Irrespective of the country you've come from, all your plugs will require changing, or a lot of expensive adapters will be required. Modern British plugs have three rectangular pins (which are, of course, unique to the UK) and are fitted with fuses as follows:

Fuse Rating (Amps)	Colour	Use/Watts
1 (or 2)	Green	Shaver adapters (2-pin) only
2	White	Standard lamp
3	Red	Maximum 750W
5	Grey	750 to 1,250W
13	Brown	1,250 to 3,000W

All plugs in the UK are 'approved', e.g. shown by a BSI (British Standards Institute) or an ASTA-BEAB (Association of Short-circuit Testing Authorities/British Electrotechnical Approvals Board) symbol on them, which means they've passed an independent test before being offered for sale. Moulded plugs must be fitted to electrical appliances sold in the UK. Items such as audio and hi-fi equipment, electric blankets, radios, table lamps, soldering irons, televisions (some manufacturers recommend a 5-amp fuse) and slow cookers up to 720 watts, should be fitted with a three-amp fuse (red). Most other heavier domestic items (e.g. iron, kettle, toaster, vacuum cleaner, washing machine, electric fire, refrigerator, freezer, tumble or spin dryer, dishwasher, lawn mower) between 1,250 and 3,000 watts need a 13-amp fuse (brown). If you aren't sure what sort of fuse to use, consult the instructions provided with the apparatus. The fuse rating (amps) is calculated by dividing the wattage by the voltage (240). For maximum safety, electrical appliances should be turned off at the main wall point when not in use (the DOWN position is ON and the UP position is OFF).

Wiring

Some electrical appliances are earthed and have a three-core wire. The UK conforms to the standard European colour coding for wiring. The blue lead is neutral and connects to the left pin of the plug marked 'N'; the brown (or red) lead is the live lead and connects to the right (fused side) pin of the plug marked 'L'; if present, the green and yellow lead is the earth and connects to the centre (top) pin of the plug marked 'E'. Always make sure that a plug is correctly and securely wired, as bad wiring can prove fatal. Never use a two-pin plug with a three-core flex. If you have old wiring or sockets which accept round pin plugs, ask an electrician about the correct plugs and wiring to use. Leaflets about safety, plugs, fuses, and wiring are available from electricity companies.

Bulbs

Electric light bulbs were traditionally of the Edison type with a bayonet fitting, which is unique to the UK (the British pride themselves on being different). To insert a bulb you push it in and turn it clockwise around 5mm. However, nowadays bulbs (and lamps) with a screw fitting are also widely available. Bulbs manufactured for use in the US must never be used in the UK, as they will explode. Low-energy light bulbs are also available and are more expensive than ordinary bulbs, although they save money by their longer life and reduced energy consumption. Bulbs for non-standard electrical appliances (i.e. appliances not made for the British market) such as refrigerators, freezers and sewing machines, may not be available in the UK (so bring extras with you). Plug adapters for imported lamps and other electrical items may be difficult to find, so it's advisable to bring a number of adapters and extension leads with you, which can be fitted with British plugs.

Safety

Only a qualified electrician should install electrical wiring and fittings, particularly in connection with fuse boxes. You should use an electrical contractor who's approved by the National Inspection Council for Electrical Installation Contracting, Warwick House, Houghton Hall Park, Houghton Regis, Dunstable, Bedfordshire, LU5 5ZX

(☎ 01582-531000, consumer helpline ☎ 0870-013 0382, 💻 www.niceic.org.uk); a list is obtainable from your local electricity company's showroom. Always ask for a quotation for any work in advance and check the identity of anyone claiming to be an electricity employee (or any kind of serviceman) by asking to see an identity card and checking with his office. Most electricity companies carry out free visual checks of domestic installations. Special controls can be fitted to many appliances to make their use easier for the disabled and the blind or partially sighted (e.g. studded or braille controls).

Electricity is the most expensive method of central heating and can be up to 50 per cent dearer than other forms of central heating and hot water systems, particularly gas. To reduce bills and obtain the maximum benefit from your heating system, your home should be well insulated (see **Heating** on page 136). Cooking with electricity costs the average family up to three times as much as with gas. For further information and a wide range of electricity brochures, contact your local electricity company's showroom.

Complaints

If you have any complaints about your electricity bill or service, contact your local electricity company. If you don't receive satisfaction, contact Energywatch (3rd Floor, Artillery House, Artillery Row, London SW1P 1RT, ☎ 0845-906 0708, 💻 www. energywatch.org.uk), the electricity and gas consumer watchdog, which has seven regional offices. For information about bills, see **Electricity & Gas Bills** on page 132.

Gas

Mains gas is available in all but the remotest areas of the UK. However, you may find that some modern houses aren't connected to the mains gas supply. If you're looking for a rental property and want to cook by gas, make sure it already has a gas supply (some houses have an unused gas service pipe). If you move into a brand new home, you must have a meter installed in order to be connected to mains gas (there may be a charge for this depending on the gas company). In some remote areas without piped gas, homes may have a 'bottled gas' (e.g. Calor Gas) cooker. If you buy a house without a gas supply, you can usually arrange to have a gas pipeline installed from a nearby gas main. Generally it's connected free of charge if your home is within 25 metres of a gas main, otherwise a quotation is provided for the work. A higher standing charge is made for properties in remote areas.

Gas was previously supplied by British Gas throughout the UK as the monopoly supplier to some 19 million homes. Everyone in England, Scotland and Wales can choose from a variety of gas supply companies; depending on where you live, many may compete for your business, including Amerada, Beacon Gas, British Fuels, British Gas, Eastern Natural Gas, Norweb Energi, London Electricity, Midlands Gas, North Wales Gas, Northern Electric & Gas, ScottishPower, Southern Electric Gas, SWALEC Gas, York Gas and Yorkshire Electricity.

In 1998, almost all the new companies were cheaper than British Gas and some three million households had left it for one of its competitors; the number of customers deserting BG accelerated in the last few years when they proved to be much more expensive that their competitors after a spate of wholesale gas rises and they were forced to reduce their charges in 2007 to try to stop the rot. If your new home already has a gas supply, simply contact the company of your choice to have the gas supply reconnected or transferred to your name (there's a connection fee) and the meter read. (See **Electricity & Gas Bills** below for how to compare rates.) You must contact your gas company to get a final meter reading when you vacate a property.

Using gas is the cheapest method of central heating and water heating. It's estimated to be up to 50 per cent cheaper than other fuels, particularly if you have a high- efficiency condensing boiler. Gas companies may install gas central heating and delay payments for a period, e.g. six months. However, to reduce bills and obtain the maximum benefit from your heating system, your home must be well insulated (see **Heating** on page 136). Cooking with gas costs the average family around two-thirds less than with electricity. There's also a range of other gas appliances, including gas tumble dryers, which are cheaper to run than electric dryers. If you wish to purchase gas appliances, such as a gas cooker or a gas fire, you should shop around, as prices vary considerably (see **Household Appliances** on page 473).

Gas appliances, wherever purchased, can be fitted by independent gas fitters (who offer the fastest service) or your gas company. If you use an independent gas fitter, choose one who's registered with the Council for Registered Gas Installers (CORGI), 1 Elmwood, Chineham Park, Crockford Lane, Basingstoke RG24 8WG (☎ 0870-401 2200, 🖳 www.trustcorgi.com). Contact CORGI for the names of members in your area or ask your regional Energywatch office (see page 130). Special controls can be fitted to many appliances to make them easier to use by the disabled and the blind or partially sighted (studded or braille controls).

Gas central heating boilers, water heaters and fires should be checked annually, particularly open-flued water heaters, which are illegal in bathrooms (faulty gas appliances kill around 30 people a year and are fairly common in cheap rented accommodation). Free gas safety checks are carried out for those over 60, the disabled and those living alone who receive a state disability benefit. You can take out a service contract with your gas company, which includes an annual check of your gas central heating system, boiler and appliances. Without a service contract, a repair or routine service could involve you waiting anything from a few days to a few weeks. Private companies and engineers also maintain gas appliances and may be cheaper than gas companies. Always ask for a quotation for any work in advance and check the identity of anyone claiming to be a gas company employee (or any kind of serviceman) by asking to see an identity card and checking with his office.

Gas installations and appliances can leak and cause explosions or kill you while you sleep. If you suspect a gas leak, first check to see if a gas tap has been left on or a pilot light has gone out. If not, then there's probably a leak, in your home or in a nearby gas pipeline. Ring your local gas service centre (listed under Gas in the telephone directory) immediately and vacate the house as quickly as possible. Gas leaks are extremely rare and explosions caused by leaks even rarer (although often spectacular and therefore widely reported). Nevertheless, it pays to be careful. British natural gas has no natural smell (which is added as a safety precaution) and is non-poisonous. You can buy an electric-powered gas detector which activates an alarm when a gas leak is detected.

For further information and a wide range of gas brochures, contact your local gas company. If you have a complaint about your gas bill or service and you don't receive satisfaction from your gas company, you can contact Energywatch, the consumer watchdog (see page 130 and also **Heating** on page 136).

Electricity & Gas Bills

Electricity and gas companies usually levy a standing quarterly charge for supplying the service, reading meters and billing, which is added to your actual or estimated consumption. Most electricity and gas consumers use a credit meter, where you're billed in arrears for the electricity or gas used, and pay by direct debit (the cheapest and most convenient method), cash or cheque. Value added tax at 5 per cent is applicable to domestic electricity and gas bills.

Comparing Rates

You can make savings of around 10 per cent by choosing your supplier prudently. Many companies now provide electricity and gas and offer contracts for the supply of both fuels, often called a 'dual fuel' arrangement. This may result in a discount. Some companies guarantee prices for a number of years when you buy gas and electricity from them, although you may still be better off buying from separate companies. You can compare rates via Uswitch (🖳 www.uswitch.com) or the Energy Helpline (🖳 www.switchandgive.com). **You must compare rates, tariffs, standing charges and services carefully before changing your supplier.** The speed and efficiency with which companies organise transfers varies and some people have received bills from two suppliers simultaneously!

Electricity Charges

Electricity consumption is charged in units, one unit being equal to one kilowatt (1,000 watts) of electricity. Electricity companies offer a range of tariffs, some of which apply only to homes with night storage heaters and overnight immersion water heaters, when electricity is charged at a lower night tariff (for which a special meter may need to be installed). In addition to night storage and hot water heaters, economy periods can also be used to run washing machines, tumble dryers and dishwashers, e.g. with a timer.

Meter Reading

At least every second electricity or gas bill is an estimate (shown by an 'E' by the 'Present' meter reading), as meters are read every six months only. If nobody is at home when the meter reader calls; you can give the electricity or gas company the meter reading on the card provided or on the back of your bill; otherwise you receive an estimated bill until the next time the meter is read. Some houses have an outside meter box which can be read at any time by the meter reader. Electricity and gas companies are supposed to demand a meter reading if the meter hasn't been read for one year.

You should insist on actual rather than estimated meter readings in order to avoid overpaying or receiving unexpected 'catching-up' bills. In some cases, you may receive an actual bill after an estimated bill has been sent out. Always check bills, e.g. by checking against your meter reading, and question bills that are too high. If a bill is in dispute, pay the part that isn't in dispute, i.e. what you normally pay, and question the rest. If you receive an unusually large bill or aren't happy with the size of your bills (who is?), you can ask the electricity or gas board to check your meter. When moving house, you should give notice in writing in order to have a final meter reading.

Payment

Bills can be paid in a variety of ways, including by post (e.g. cheque); in cash, via a bank or building society credit transfer; by direct debit mandate; or at a post office. Customers who pay by direct debit receive a discount of up to 15 per cent. If you're a new customer without a previous payment record, you may be required to pay a deposit (e.g. £100) if you don't pay your bill by direct debit. If you pay your electricity or gas bill via a budget payment scheme, payments are estimated on your previous year's consumption. At the end of the year, what you've paid is compared to your actual consumption and you receive a rebate or a bill for the difference. Keep a record of all bills paid for future reference.

Disconnection

If you don't pay your bill, a warrant may be obtained from a judge or magistrate to cut off your supply. The electricity and gas industries publish a leaflet entitled *Paying Electricity and Gas Bills*, which tells you how to obtain help if you cannot pay a bill. All electricity and gas companies publish a *Code of Practice* on the payment of bills by domestic customers. Most pensioners are protected from disconnection during the winter months. Anyone who's in financial difficulty should contact their local electricity or gas company as soon as possible, who will try to come to an arrangement over any outstanding bills and may recommend a direct payment or pre-payment scheme.

If you're threatened with disconnection and cannot pay your bill, you should obtain immediate advice, e.g. from a Citizens Advice Bureau. If you're disconnected, you must wait two to three days to be reconnected after paying your bill along with a reconnection charge, and may be asked to pay a security deposit too. An electricity or gas company cannot disconnect you for non-payment of a bill that isn't for the supply of electricity or gas, e.g. a bill for a repair or other work.

The emergency free telephone number to call if you suspect a gas leak is ☎ **0800-111 999.**

Water

The water industry in England and Wales was privatised in 1989, when ten regional water companies were created to provide water and sewerage services (there are also a number of local water-only companies). You're unable to choose your water company (unlike electricity and gas companies), which have a monopoly in their area. Around 10 per cent of households in England and Wales have water meters. You're billed for the actual water used (plus a standing charge). For all other households, water and sewerage rates are based on the rateable value of a property (although rates were abolished in April 1990 and replaced by the council tax). In Scotland, fresh water is charged as an addition to the council tax (which includes sewerage) and in Northern Ireland, water and sewerage are paid as part of the domestic rates (there's no council tax).

Supply

The UK's climate has often fluctuated from one extreme to another in the past decade with floods in winter and droughts in summer. Because of a shortage of reservoirs, many areas of the UK (particularly in the south-east) experience an acute water shortage during prolonged periods without rain (e.g. around a week), resulting in water having to be rationed and the use of hosepipes and sprinklers and car washing banned. The ever-spiralling demand for water (which is expected to rise by 20 per cent by the year 2020) has also had an alarming affect on the UK's waterways and wildlife in the last decade.

Wastage & Conservation

The British are notoriously wasteful of water. There's very little conservation and few homes have water meters. The average garden sprinkler uses 200 gallons of water an hour, which is roughly enough to last a family of four for two days. Many people believe that the quickest way to reduce water shortages is to encourage people to conserve water and reduce wastage, e.g. by making water meters compulsory in all homes and charging consumers for the actual water used. (The bulk of the charges for water is, in fact, for maintaining the infrastructure and has nothing to do with the cost of the actual water). Water companies could also reduce wastage through leaks, estimated to amount to some 15 to 25 per cent of the total supply, and build more dams and reservoirs.

Water Meters

Water companies in England and Wales will, in future, be able to decide whether they charge a flat rate for all customers, or for the actual amount of water used, calculated by a water meter. Currently, you can have a water meter fitted voluntarily in England

and Wales, although this isn't possible in Scotland and Northern Ireland. Most industrial customers have water meters. The cost of having a water meter installed was formerly around £150, but is now borne by the water companies as a result of legislation. They're generally obliged to provide you with one if you wish, but they need not if it's too difficult or expensive. If you have a property with a high rateable value and low water consumption, you would probably benefit from having a meter installed. However, for most customers there's no incentive to install a meter, as it would result in higher bills. Most new houses are fitted with them.

Bills

Water companies include an annual standing charge of around £50 (for water and sewerage), which is the same for all properties, plus a variable charge based on the rateable value of your property, if you don't have a water meter. If you have a water meter installed, water is charged by the cubic metre. Bills, which usually include the cost of sewerage (except in Scotland), are sent out annually and can be paid in full, in two six-monthly payments or in ten instalments. In some areas, water and sewage are handled by separate companies and homeowners receive bills from each company. The steep rise in water bills since privatisation in 1989 is expected to continue over the coming years. The water companies and the regulators are currently in discussion about a series of major price increases. The cost of water varies widely depending on the local water authority concerned, but the average unmetered annual water and sewerage bill in 2007/2008 as projected by ofWAT, the water services regulation authority, was £325. The most expensive company in 2006/2007 was South-west Water, who charged £429.

Payment

Water bills can be paid by direct debit from a bank account (for which there's usually a rebate), which means that you aren't required to remember when they're due. If you don't pay your water bill, you receive a reminder ('Final Notice') and if this isn't paid immediately, the full amount usually becomes due. If you persistently failed to pay your bill, water companies could previously apply to a county court for permission to disconnect your supply, which happened to tens of thousands of households each year. However, it's now illegal to cut off the water supply to a home (which has led to even more non-payers)

Quality

The quality of tap water varies depending on the region. Although drinking water is among the cleanest and safest in the world, it doesn't measure up to EU standards in all areas. Water bills are scheduled to rise above inflation in the next few years to fund further improvements in drinking water quality. In recent years, there have been a number of scares about the poor quality of drinking water in some areas, some of which were a result of accidental contamination of the water supply. There are also concerns about the number and level of chemicals contained in water, particularly aluminium, lead (usually from old lead water pipes) and nitrates, although some (such as chlorine) are added as part of the water treatment process.

In some areas, homeowners have reported tap water infestations, such as freshwater shrimps or water fleas. Water companies are loth to admit liability for illness caused by the water supply, as the cost of compensation and cleaning-up can run into millions of pounds. If you have a tap connected to a garden hose, a washing machine or a dishwasher, or a shower with a flexible pipe over the bath, you must fit a non-return valve that stops pollution from dirty water siphoning back into the mains supply. A non-return valve can be plumbed in or you can buy one which screws directly onto a tap. If you're concerned about the quality of your tap water, contact your local water company or the Drinking Water Inspectorate, 55 Whitehall, london, SW1A 2EY (☎ 020-7082 8024).

Water in the UK is usually hard, particularly in the south-east, from a natural excess of magnesium and calcium compounds. Although hard water is generally good to drink, you need a copious supply of decalcification liquid to keep your kettle, iron and other apparatus and utensils clean. Water from some taps may be unsafe to drink, as it comes from storage tanks. Stainless steel pots and pans stain quickly when used to boil water, unless they're cleaned soon after use. Distilled water, or water melted from ice from your freezer, should be used in some electric steam irons. Tap and shower filters must be decalcified regularly.

Before moving into a new home, you should enquire where the main stopcock is, so that you can turn off the water supply in an emergency. If the water stops running for any reason, you should turn off the supply to prevent flooding from an open tap when the supply starts again. Contact your local water company if you have a problem reconnecting your water supply, as it could have been turned off by them.

If you need a plumber, e.g. as a result of a burst pipe, you may be able to get a recommendation or a list of names from your local water company, which may help prevent your being ripped off. When employing a plumber, always ask what the minimum call out charge is. The UK is famous for the eccentricity of its plumbing, although many burst pipes could be avoided by lagging (insulation) and leaving the central heating on during extremely cold weather when you're away from home.

Complaints

If you have a complaint which you cannot resolve with your water company, you should contact the Consumer Council for Water (1st Floor, Victoria Square House, Victoria Square, birmingham B2 4AJ, ☎ 0845-039 2837 ⌨ www.ccwater.org.uk), the consumer watchdog for the industry.

HEATING

Some 90 per cent of British homes have central heating (including all new homes) or storage heater systems, many of which also provide hot water. Central heating systems may be powered by oil, gas (the most common), electricity or solid fuel (e.g. coal or wood). Whatever form of heating you use, you should ensure that you have good insulation, including double glazing, cavity-wall insulation, external-wall insulation, floor insulation, draught-proofing, pipe lagging, and loft and hot water tank insulation, without which up to 60 per cent of heat goes straight through the walls and roof. Many companies advise and carry out home insulation, including gas and electricity companies, who produce a range of leaflets designed to help you reduce your heating and other energy bills.

The cost of heating your home varies depending on a number of factors, not least the fuel used, the size of your home and the length of time your heating is switched on. Most people in the UK switch their heating on for short periods only (using timer controls), e.g. for a few hours in the morning before the occupants go to work or school, and from around 4 or 5pm. when children or parents come home, until the family goes to bed. During the day and at night, many people turn the heating off. In order to reduce heating bills, many people selectively heat certain rooms only or parts of a house.

The cheapest method of central heating is gas, which is estimated to be up to 50 per cent cheaper than other forms of central heating and hot water systems, particularly if you have a high-efficiency condensing boiler. Many homes have storage heaters that store heat from electricity supplied at the cheaper off-peak rate overnight and release it to heat your home during the day. In an apartment block heated from a central system, radiators are usually individually metered, so you pay only for the heating used. If you wish to install heating in your home, you should use a company that's a member of the Heating and Ventilation Contractors Association (HVCA, ESCA House, 34 Palace Court, London W2 4JG , ☎ 020-7313 4900, 🖳 www.hvca.org.uk), which operates a guarantee scheme.

Reducing your energy consumption saves you money. For more information contact your gas or electricity company, Energywatch (see page 130), the Energy Saving Trust (☎ 0800 512 012, 🖳 www.est.org.uk) or the Energy Efficiency Advice Centre (☎ 0800-512 012). The National Energy Foundation (☎ 01908-665 577, 🖳 www.nef.org.uk) provides the names of energy surveyors in your area who will perform an energy survey for around £100.

Central heating dries the air and may cause your family to develop coughs. Those who find the dry air unpleasant can purchase a humidifier to add moisture to the air. Humidifiers that don't generate steam should be disinfected occasionally (to prevent diseases) with a special liquid available from chemists.

6.

POSTAL SERVICES

There's a post office in most towns and many villages in the UK and the organisation offers over 100 services, most of which are described in this chapter. The term 'post office' is used in the UK as a general term for three separate businesses: the Royal Mail, Post Office Counters Limited and Parcelforce. In addition, the former post office banking division, now Alliance & Leicester plc, still operates from post offices. For the sake of simplicity the term 'post office' has been used throughout this chapter to refer to all these services.

Inland post refers to post to addresses in Great Britain, Northern Ireland, the Channel Islands and the Isle of Man (although, oddly, the Channel Islands are considered an international destination by Parcelforce).

Of some 17,500 post offices, fewer than 600 are operated directly by the post office. The remainder are franchise offices or sub-post offices run on an agency basis by sub-postmasters and don't offer all the services provided by a main post office. Sub-post offices are often located in supermarkets, stationers and newsagents.

In addition to providing postal services, the post office acts as an agent for a number of government departments and local authorities (councils). For example, it sells television licences (they're sold nowhere else). The post office is also the largest chain of outlets for national lottery tickets, and provides bureau de change facilities in many branches (although you may need to order some foreign currencies) along with an international money transfer service in conjunction with Western Union International. It charges 1.5 per cent commission on the purchase of sterling travellers' cheques with a minimum fee of £3 (maximum £30), and none on those denominated in euros or dollars. This is lower than most banks (see **Foreign Currency** on page 359). The post office also buys and sells foreign currency free of commission.

Private sector couriers are permitted to handle only time-sensitive and valuable post, subject to a minimum fee of £1. The courier industry, particularly in London and other major cities, is growing rapidly and the UK is a major centre for international air courier traffic. Major companies include Federal Express, DHL, UPS and TNT, plus the post office Parcelforce service.

The post office produces a wealth of free brochures about postal rates and special services, most of which are available from any post office. It also has a helpline (☎ 0845-223 344) and an internet site (🖥 www.royalmail.com). The website is the best source of information about the numerous specialised services available to businesses. A guide called *Royal Mail – The Real Network* containing information about principal Royal Mail products and services, is available from post offices, along with a *Customer Charter* outlining the standards the organisation aims to meet.

If you have a complaint regarding any post office service, you should address it to Postwatch at Freepost Postwatch (☎ 0845-601 3265). Complaints about lost or damaged post must be made on form P58, *Enquiry about a missing or damaged letter or parcel*, which is available from any post office.

BUSINESS HOURS

Post office business hours are usually from 9am to 5.30pm, Mondays to Fridays, and from 9am to 12.30pm on Saturdays. In small towns and villages, there are sub-post offices (usually part of a general store) which provide most of the services offered by a main post office. Sub -post offices usually close for an hour at lunchtime, e.g. 1pm to 2pm, Mondays to Fridays, and generally also close on one afternoon a week, customarily Wednesday. Main post offices in major towns don't close at lunchtime. There are post offices at major international airports, some of which are open on Sundays and public holidays. In major cities, some post offices have extended opening hours, e.g. the Trafalgar Square branch in London, open from 8.30am to 6.30pm, Monday to Friday and 9am to 5.30pm on Saturdays. Plans are currently being made to allow sub-postmasters to open at times they consider most useful to their customers, so that in future opening hours will be more variable.

LETTER POST

The post office provides a choice of first and second class domestic post delivery. Postcards and standard letters weighing up to 60g cost 32p first class and 23p second class. Delivery targets are the next working day after collection for first class post and the third working day after collection for second class. Some 70 per cent of first class post is delivered the next day. It's unnecessary to mark post as first or second class, as any item which is posted with less than first class postage is automatically sent second class.

First and second class post is now dependant upon weight and size. Second class post cannot exceed 100g, but first class can. Once the sizing exceeds either 240mm length or 165mm width or 5mm thickness, first and second class post moves into the 'large letter' category. Packets can be posted second class within the length 353mm, width 250mm and 25mm thickness range, and up to 1000g in weight for £2.12. Standard parcel often works out cheaper than first class once the weight hits 1000g, but it does take three to five working days.

The cost of posting letters and postcards abroad is shown below. All international post is sent by air; there's no longer a surface post rate.

Item	Europe	Rest of the World
Surface Letter up to 20g	n/a	50p
Surface Letter up to 60g	n/a	72p
Surface Postcard	n/a	42p
Airmail Letter up to 10g	44p	50p
Airmail Letter up to 20g	44p	72p
Airmail Postcard	40p	50p

Destinations outside Europe are divided into two zones, World Zones 1 and 2, depending on distance from the UK. For airmail letters above 20g and surface letters above 60g, rates to these vary.

'Airletters' (pre-printed airmail letters) are available from post offices and stationers, and include postage, which is the same to all countries. They cost 42p each or £2.30 for a pack of six. Pictorial 'Airletters' are also available at £2.85 for a pack of 6 or 52p each.

Some items (e.g. newspapers and periodicals) must be registered with the post office. Call Royal Mail Customer Service on ☎ 0845-774 0740 if you need further details.

All domestic and international postal charges are listed in leaflets available from post offices. Any further information required can be obtained by writing to Royal Mail Customer Service, Freepost, RM1 1AA.

General Information

- Post boxes are red and are usually free-standing, but may be set into (or attached to) a wall. Main and sub-post offices have post boxes outside and most main post offices also have them inside. Collection times are shown on all post boxes. Post is usually collected several times a day from Mondays to Saturdays and once on Sundays from main post offices. Times are indicated by a yellow strip on the collection plate (or the location of the nearest Sunday collection box is shown). At main post offices there may be separate post boxes for local post (towns are often listed on the box), 2nd class, 1st class and foreign post, and pre-franked items. Sometimes there is also a special box for 'first day covers'. These are decorative envelopes used with commemorative stamps on their first day of issue.

- There's at least one delivery of post a day from Mondays to Saturdays in all areas. In many there are two (morning and early afternoon) from Mondays to Fridays. Post can also be collected from post offices. If you want a first class letter to reach its destination on the next working day, you must ensure you catch the latest recommended posting time.

- To ensure delivery the next day, first class post should be posted by 5pm for the local area or by 1pm for other parts of the UK excluding Northern Scotland.

- If you send a letter with insufficient postage , the addressee will be charged the shortage plus a surcharge of £1.The addressee must pay the difference between what has and what ought to have been paid plus a fee of 50p (which also applies to parcels). There's a surcharge of £1 on all unpaid or underpaid post from abroad, in addition to the amount of the underpayment. If the post office is unable to deliver a letter, it's returned to the sender with a sticker stating the reason why.

- Leaflets are published in September listing the latest posting dates for Christmas for international post (forces, surface and airmail).

- Airmail items, including letters for European destinations, should have a blue airmail label (available from post offices) affixed to the top left hand corner, or 'PAR AVION – BY AIR MAIL' written or stamped on them. Delivery of airmail letters takes an average of 2.2 days to Germany, 2.5 to Italy and Holland, and 2.7

to Spain. Airmail to destinations outside Europe usually takes five days. Surface mail to the rest of the world takes up to eight weeks. Underpaid airmail items may be sent by surface mail or incur a surcharge.

- You can receive post free of charge via selected post offices through the international *Poste Restante* service (where post is addressed to main post offices) for a maximum of three months. Post sent to a *Poste Restante* address is returned to the sender if it's unclaimed after 14 days, excluding special delivery and recorded items. Identification, e.g. a passport, is necessary for collection. To find your nearest relevant Post Office branch ring ☎ 0845-722 3344.

- If you want to pay for the cost of a reply to a letter which you send abroad, you can include an international reply coupon (60p each) with it. These are exchangeable at foreign post offices for postage stamps equivalent to the basic surface letter rate to the UK.

- Most post is sorted by machine. This is facilitated by the use of full and correct postal addresses (omitting all punctuation) with town, city or country names in capitals. Postcodes (zip codes) which allow addresses to be identified down to part of a street or in some cases even to an individual address, should never be omitted. The following format should be used:

> Reginald Percy Wilberforce-Smith
> 99A High Street
> Wombledon
> LONDON
> WO1 9XY

- If you don't know your postcode or want to find someone else's you can consult Postcode Directories at main post offices. Call ☎ 0906-302 1222 between 8am and 6pm (charged at 50p a minute), or check the post office's website (🖳 www.royalmail.com). You can also call ☎ 0845-711 1222, outside normal office hours, between 6pm and 8pm Monday to Friday, 9am to 5.30pm Saturdays and 9am to 2pm Sundays, at the much cheaper local rate. The post office prefers you to use United Kingdom (UK) in addresses, rather than Britain, Great Britain, England, Scotland, Wales or Northern Ireland. A Royal Mail approved *Postcode Atlas of Great Britain and Northern Ireland* (Collins) is available from bookshops. You should write your address on the back of post so that it can be returned to you if it's undelivered.

- Stamps can be purchased from vending machines located outside most post offices, in stores and shops, and at major tourist attractions. Books of six or twelve first or second class stamps are also sold at post offices and by over 40,000 shops (e.g. stationers, newsagents and general stores) throughout the UK. Books of stamps for international rate postage with airmail stickers are also available from post offices and other outlets. Stamps marked 1st or 2nd, but without a value, are valid indefinitely (even when prices change) for inland post up to 100g in weight (or in part payment for heavier items). They can also be used as full or part payment for items to European Union (EU) countries, but not to other international destinations. Similar stamps marked with an 'E' or 'Europe' are intended for items posted to European destinations weighing up to 20g or 40g respectively. Those marked 'worldwide' are for items weighing up to 40g posted to anywhere in the rest of the world.

- Like their counterparts elsewhere, the post office provides services for philatelists, including a mail order philatelic shop via the Royal Mail website, where stamps and stamp-related collectibles and first day covers can be ordered; and there are special postboxes in which to post the latter in main post offices, and brochures describing new issues of commemorative stamps. For more information, contact Royal Mail, Tallents House, 21 South Gyle Crescent, Edinburgh EH12 9PB (☎ 0845-764 1641). The Royal Mail website includes pages for young collectors under the heading 'Stamps for Kids'.

- There are reduced rates for post to and from members of HM Forces. Rates are listed in a *Sending Letters to HM Forces* leaflet available from post offices. Alternatively you can visit 🖥 www.royalmail.com/bfpo.

- Items specially produced or adapted for the blind can be posted first class to domestic addresses free. They can also be sent abroad by airmail or surface mail free, if they weigh less than 7kg. Speak to Royal Mail customer service about eligibility. Special 'Items for the Blind' labels (Reference number DP11), which enable you to make use of this concession, are available from the Royal National Institute for the Blind, 105 Judd Street, London WC1H 9NE (☎ 020-7388 1266). A box of 200 costs £4.99 plus VAT. The telephone number for ordering them is ☎ 0845-702 3153.

- If you're going to be away from your home for up to two months, you can have your post held by the post office and delivered on a day of your choice. The Keepsafe scheme costs £5.25 for 17 days, £8.40 for 24 days, £10.50 for 31 days and £15.75 for up to 66 days. A form is available from your local post office and a week's notice is required.

IMPORTANT, VALUABLE OR URGENT POST

The post office provides a number of services for the secure and quick delivery of important and urgent post to domestic and foreign addresses.

- A certificate of posting is available free on request at any post office counter. A number of items can be listed on one leaflet. A maximum of £28 (100 times the cost of first class postage) is payable in compensation for the loss or damage of ordinary letters or parcels, for which a certificate of posting has been obtained. Without this certificate the post office isn't liable to pay compensation. There's no compensation for money or jewellery sent by ordinary post.

- If you're sending money, jewellery, valuable documents or anything needing a guaranteed next day delivery within the UK, you should use special delivery next day. This costs £4.10 for items weighing up to 100g, and guarantees delivery by 1pm the next day (Mondays to Fridays) to addresses in England, Wales, Northern Ireland or populous areas of Scotland, and by 5.30pm to most of northern Scotland. In the case of remoter western and northern isles it's later still. There is also special delivery 9am, guaranteeing delivery by 9am. Rates are £8.95 (100g), £10.50 (500g), £12.20 (1kg) and £15.10(2kg). A form must be completed and a receipt is provided. A signature is collected on delivery, although not necessarily that of the addressee, and the time is noted. Confirmation of delivery is available by calling ☎ 0845-927 2100. If your item arrives later than the guaranteed delivery time you can contact Customer Service (☎ 0845-774 0740) and reclaim your fee. The maximum standard compensation for loss or damage is £500, but this can be increased to £1,000 for an additional fee of 45p or to £2,500 for an extra 90p.

- Consequential loss insurance can similarly be taken out. If delay, loss or damage to a special delivery item causes you expense beyond the cost of replacement, you then qualify for compensation ranging from £1,000 to £10,000. Fees start at £1.20, go up to £3.00 and are, of course, in addition to previously mentioned charges. Prepaid special delivery envelopes are available in three sizes for sending valuables through the post: C5 (16 x 23cm/£4.05), C4 (23 x 32.5cm/ £4.05) and C3 (34 x 44cm/£5.20).

- Recorded or signed-for delivery is available to domestic addresses for a fee of 68p, in addition to normal first or second class postage. You get proof of posting when handing in your item to the post office. After you enter the addressee's name and address on the 'recorded' slip, the bottom part is date stamped and returned to you as a receipt. It must be signed for on delivery, although the signatory needn't be the addressee. To check that it has been delivered phone ☎ 0845-927 2100, quoting your receipt number or visit the Royal Mail website where you can do this electronically. If you want a copy of the recipient's signature, call Customer Service and ask for proof of delivery. This costs an extra £2.20 and must be requested within 12 months of delivery. **The Royal Mail advises the public not to send valuables or money by recorded delivery.** If a recorded or special delivery item is lost or damaged, compensation is equal to 100 times the cost of first class postage.

- A similar accelerated service, Airsure, is available to fewer international destinations. It offers the advantage of being able to track your item's progress electronically right up to the point of delivery via Royal Mail's website. _It costs £4 in addition to standard postage and a prepaid C4 envelope valid for anywhere in the world and for contents weighing up to 300g costs £6. Airsure items aren't signed for on arrival.

- When speed isn't a priority, sending letters, small packets or printed papers to international destinations by the signed-for international service is another option. It costs £3.50 plus normal air or surface postage rates. This entitles you to compensation of up to £30 if lost or damaged and your item is tracked electronically until it leaves the UK. Royal Mail cannot supply a copy of the signature taken on delivery. For an extra fee of £1 you can qualify for additional compensation of up to £250 or £500, depending on the destination country.

Claims

Should you need to make a claim, it should be made within 12 months of posting. For lost or damaged post, you must complete a form (P58) available from any post office. A return address must be written on the back of all post sent by registered, special delivery or recorded mail.

PARCEL POST

The standard inland parcel service is operated by the Royal Mail and handles over 1 million parcels and packages every day, which are delivered within three to five working days to any address within the UK. There are restrictions on the size of parcels, depending on the service. Royal Mail parcel post includes the services detailed below.

Small Packets

An Airpack service is provided for sending small packages (such as videos, books, photographs, cassettes and clothes) weighing up to 500g. A padded envelope with a self-adhesive strip (including a customs form) is provided for a fee of £3.50 to Europe and £5.99 to the rest of the world. You may include a letter **only** if it relates to the contents of the packet.

Printed Papers

Unsealed commercial items (e.g. advertising material), non-personalised direct mail, calendars and literary items (e.g. books, newspapers and periodicals) up to 5kg in weight can be sent at a reduced 'Printed Paper' surface mail rate. Items should be marked 'Printed Papers', mustn't contain personal letters and taped messages, and must be packed so that they can be easily opened for examination or have a transparent window. Charges start at 85p for the first 100g.

Standard Parcel Delivery

This usually takes from three to five days to any address in the UK (including Saturday deliveries). The standard service for inland parcels costs £3.85 for up to

1kg, £5.31 up to 2kg, £7.70 up to 4kg, £8.74 up to 6kg, £9.97 up to 8kg, £10.70 up to 10kg and £12.46 for up to 20kg (the maximum permitted weight). Some post offices don't accept parcels weighing over 10kg. Compensation for loss or damage is limited to £28 per parcel, provided you complete a Certificate of Despatch when you send your parcel. Higher compensation is possible by paying a Compensation Fee of £1.00 (£100 compensation), £2.25 (£250 compensation) or £3.50 (£500 compensation). Domestic parcels can measure up to 1.5m in length and a total of 3m when length and girth are combined. Parcelforce provides inland express parcel delivery services and services to foreign destinations.

Next Day Services

There are a number of these in the UK, including Parcelforce by 9am, Parcelforce by 10am and Parcelforce by noon, all of which guarantee delivery by the time specified to all major UK business centres and to most of the rest of the UK and outlying areas soon after. Compensation for loss or damage of up to £150 is included in the price. This can be increased for an additional payment of 60p per £100 of cover, the ceiling being £2,500. Parcels must be signed for on arrival. The minimum fee for Parcelforce by 9am is £37.00 (up to 10kg plus £1.55 per extra kg) and for Parcelforce by noon it's £20.75 (up to 10kg plus £1.15 per extra kg). Parcelforce 24 and Parcelforce 48 provide a guaranteed next-day (£17.50 up to 10kg) or two-day delivery (£13.25 up to 10kg) to 95 per cent of all UK addresses. Their standard compensation rates are £250 and £150 respectively. Additional coverage costs the same as that for related services.

Parcelforce International Services

Parcelforce International Standard provides a parcel service to 239 countries and territories worldwide. This service (from £16.25 for parcels weighing up to 500g to selected continental EU countries) takes from three working days to Europe and from five working days to the rest of the world. The International Economy service (from £18 for parcels weighing up to 500g to Canada and the US) takes from ten working days to Europe to 20 working days to the rest of the world. There's no economy service to most western European countries and some other countries.

International Datapost

This is a guaranteed express international delivery service to 225 countries worldwide, usually up to a maximum weight of 30kg (or up to 20kg in some countries). Parcels sent via Datapost are delivered 'by noon' or 'by 5.30pm' to many destinations within Europe, although delivery takes longer to other destinations. Post can be handed in at post offices or collected from the sender's address. Costs start from £31.60 for parcels weighing up to 500g to the Republic of Ireland. There is a money-back guarantee in the event of late delivery.

Euro 48

This service offers guaranteed delivery in two working days to major European cities and to elsewhere in Europe in three or four working days, depending on the destination. Charges start at £22.30 for up to 500g to the Benelux countries.

Ireland 24

This service guarantees next day delivery from Northern Ireland to any destination in the Republic of Ireland and charges start at £17.50 for 500g.

General Information

The maximum international parcel weight varies from destination country to country, but is mostly 20kg or 30kg. Parcels over 10kg are accepted only at main post offices.

Further information about Parcelforce services is available from Parcelforce, PO Box 134, Leeds LS1 2UB (☎ 0870-850 1150, ✉ parcelforce@parcelforce.co.uk, 💻 www.parcelforce.com)

Customs Declaration

Parcels and small packets sent to international addresses outside the European Union (except Andorra, Gibraltar and the Vatican City) must be accompanied by a customs declaration label (CN22 for items of up to £270 in value and CN23 for goods valued at more than this). If an item being sent is of 'no commercial value' (NCV), you should write this on the customs form under 'value'. Forms are available from post offices.

Wrapping Parcels

A section entitled *Wrapping Up Well* in the booklet *Your Parcel, Our Parcel*, available from post offices, describes how to pack goods for sending through the post. When sending drawings, large photographs, paintings, or anything which will be damaged if bent, sandwich them between stiff cardboard. Cardboard boxes called Postpaks, padded ('Jiffy') bags and a range of 'pack & wrap' packaging materials are available from post offices and most department stores and stationers. Another detailed section in *Your Parcel, Our Parcel* entitled *Prohibited & Restricted Goods* lists what **cannot** be sent through the post. You can send quite large objects by parcel post, but it's advisable to enquire before packing a parcel of this kind whether or not it meets the requirements.

Christmas

Leaflets are published in September, listing the latest posting dates for Christmas for international economy parcels, which are roughly between 1st October (e.g. Australia) and 20th November, depending on the country (US around 23rd October).

POST COLLECTION

If the postman calls with post requiring a signature or payment when you aren't at home, he will leave a collection form. These items of post include recorded delivery, registered letters, surcharged items, special delivery/express, insured items, perishable goods or a parcel which is too bulky to be left. If you receive post from abroad on which customs duty or VAT is payable, this is collected by the post office (sums over £50 are collected only at main post offices). You can choose to collect an item which couldn't be delivered or you can complete the bottom part of the collection form and instruct the post office to:

- Allow someone else to collect it on your behalf (identity must be shown);
- Have it redelivered on a date of your choosing;
- Have it delivered to another address, e.g. a business or a neighbour.

Present the collection form at your local Letter Delivery Office, the address of which is printed on the form. Check the opening hours in advance, as some are open for collections only in the mornings, e.g. 8am to noon, Mondays to Fridays and 8am to 11am on Saturdays. Identification may be required and the address on it should be the same as that on the item to be collected. Post is retained for three weeks, with the exception of recorded delivery letters , which are retained for one week only.

You can have your post stored in a private box at most post offices for £53 a year (£43 for six months). Collection must usually be made during normal opening hours. You can also hire a private box for parcels at a Parcelforce delivery depot.

A private courier company **must** obtain a signature for all deliveries and if you aren't at home, they will leave a form asking you to contact them about redelivery.

CHANGE OF ADDRESS

Your post can be redirected to a new or temporary address in the UK for a charge of £6.90 for one month, £15.10 for three months, £34.90 for a year or double these charges to an address abroad. All letters are redirected to inland addresses by first class post (whether or not they were originally sent first class). Information about post redirection is available by calling ☎ 0845-774 0740. Parcelforce also operates a redirection service for parcels (☎ 0870-850 1150).

A Royal Mail Redirection Service form (P944), available from post offices, must be completed at least **five** working days before you wish redirection to begin (it can be completed up to three weeks in advance). The redirection can also be arranged by post or telephone and the fee paid by cash, cheque or giro transfer. If you require an extension, a further form P944 must be completed. Post can also be redirected from a Post Restante address, but usually for one month only.

If you receive post for the previous occupants of your home, or any post which comes through your letter box that isn't addressed to you, you have two legal options: you can send it on to the addressee by crossing out the address, writing the new or correct address and dropping it in a post box, without a stamp; should you not know the addressee's new address, you can cross out the address on the envelope, write 'Address Unknown' and simply post it. Throwing the post away is **illegal**.

POSTAL ORDERS

Postal orders are a convenient and safe way of sending small amounts of money by post to people who don't have cheque accounts. **You should never send cash through the post, within the UK or internationally, except by special delivery** (see page 144). Postal orders can be purchased for any amount up to £250. A fee is payable depending on the value: 45p for values up to £4.99, 85p for £5 - £9.99, and 8.75 per cent of the face value for £10 - £100. For £100 to the maximum value of £250 the fee is capped at £8.75. The post office prints the postal order with the payee's name, if required, and crossed or uncrossed (crossed must be paid into a bank account, uncrossed must be cashed at a post office).

Postal orders can be cashed in 47 (mostly Commonwealth) countries and UK dependencies worldwide, and are usually cheaper than sending an international cheque. For inland use, postal orders are an expensive way of paying your bills, particularly when a cheque drawn on most current accounts incurs no bank charges (provided you stay in credit). They should be used only when you or the recipient doesn't have a bank, building society or Girobank account.

NATIONAL SAVINGS ACCOUNTS

In addition to being an agent for Alliance & Leicester plc, the post office also operates National Savings, which manages a total of around 20 million accounts. This bank operates savings accounts **only** and doesn't provide lending facilities. (The post office also offer personal loans for £1,000 to £25,000 at competitive rates.) Customers are issued with a bank book in which all deposits and withdrawals are entered. There are two main types of account. The easy access savings account allows you to save in amounts of £10 or more and to withdraw up to £100 a day on demand. You must have a minimum of £100 in the account at all times, save in amounts of £10 or more and pay in by telephone, post or at the post office. There is a £300 withdrawal limit and interest rates are tiered and variable. A higher rate is paid to those who maintain a balance of at least £500, provided the account is open for a whole calendar year. Interest is paid annually at the end of the year and the first £70 of annual interest is tax-free (£140 for a joint account). Children over seven can open their own accounts.

The investment account is intended mainly for non-taxpayers, as it provides tax-free interest. Interest is paid annually at the end of the year. A month's notice must be given before making a withdrawal, but you can take out money on demand if you're prepared to bear a penalty equivalent to the previous 30 day's interest on the amount you withdraw. The minimum deposit is £20 and the maximum £100,000. Other National Savings investments include tax-free savings certificates (paying a fixed rate of interest or a lower fixed rate of interest combined with index-linking); taxable income and pensioners' bonds; and government stock (gilts).

National Savings Premium Bonds are a popular form of saving where 'interest' is paid in the form of cash prizes of up to £1 million, chosen by lottery (see page 419). For general information contact National Savings (☎ 0845-964 5000, 🖵 www.nsandi.com).

MISCELLANEOUS SERVICES

The post office provides a range of savings stamps (mostly used by pensioners, who buy them when drawing their pensions), designed to help people budget for their regular bills, including those for television license, road tax, telephone, council tax, water, electricity and gas. Stamps usually cost £5 each and are affixed to special cards.

7.

TELEPHONE

Nearly all homes in the UK have a fixed-line telephone and mobile phone use is among the highest in the world. You can make calls to anywhere in the UK and to most countries in the world without contacting the operator and, because telephone exchanges now operate digitally, a wide range of additional services such as call diversion and call waiting can be also accessed.

The cost of making telephone calls has gone down sharply in the last decade. (Even ET could afford to phone home now.) Long distance and international call charges in particular have fallen dramatically because of competition among the many indirect access providers who buy time from British Telecom (BT) or other companies to resell it to their own customers (see page 165).

The general emergency telephone number throughout the UK is ☎ 999 (see also **Emergency Numbers** on page 176).

TELEPHONE COMPANIES

The telephone system in the UK is dominated by British Telecom (BT), created and given a 25-year licence in 1984, when the state-owned monopoly was privatised. When the telecommunications market was opened to national and international competition in 1991, the UK stood at the forefront of technology in this sector, but other European countries, having subsequently liberalised their own telecoms industries, have now largely caught up. Well over 100 companies are licensed to operate telecoms services, and competition, although less intense than a few years ago, is still keen, so shopping around to compare rates could save you money.

Users can choose between BT, cable companies, a large number of indirect operators and one or two small radio-based organisations. Cable companies now offer convenient connections to over 50 per cent of homes, the major providers of services to consumers being Telewest and Virgin Media (formerly NTL), whose areas of coverage don't overlap. To find out if either operates in your area, check their websites (🖳 www.telewest.co.uk and 🖳 www.virginmedia.com) or look in your local telephone directory. Radio-based companies are restricted to remoter areas in which infrastructure does not exist for reasons of geography. Using the services of companies operating indirectly – in order to do so you first need a telephone line from a provider offering physical connections – you must dial a code before each number you call in the normal way.

The major companies which provide telephones and infrastructure, as well as the opportunity to make calls are BT, Telewest, Kingston, and Virgin Media. One of the largest indirect players is Onetel. Kingston offers attractive overall rates, but is active only in certain parts of the country, while Onetel is among the cheapest of the indirect companies, closely followed by British Gas and Tiscali. However, the savings you make by shopping around depend on how high your monthly bill is, when you make most calls, what sort of calls you make (e.g. local, national or international), and how frequently you call mobiles. Consult Uswitch (🖳 www.uswitch.com), which provides tariff calculations for numerous permutations of the possibilities, to find out which company offers the best deal. The increasing number and complexity of different schemes on offer, even from the same company, means that the cheapest option for you depends on how you use the telephone.

Most households still rent their telephone line from BT, but many additionally use indirect services for specific purposes, such as making international calls where saving money is usually possible. Occasionally, it's cheaper to switch company entirely if your pattern of telephone usage changes markedly. Where BT scores heavily is in reliability and being able to quickly put right anything which goes wrong. A significant consideration when choosing a telecoms company is whether it looks likely to stay in business for the foreseeable future. Smaller companies have come and gone with regularity over recent years, some going bankrupt and causing difficulties for their customers.

It should be noted that BT charges more for a local call than some other providers charge for a call to the US or Australia (as little as 2p per minute). If you make a lot of international calls, you should investigate the companies mentioned on page 165.

For information about providers, contact your local telecoms advisory service (see your local telephone directory) or the Telecommunications Users' Association, 57 London Road, Enfield, Middlesex EN2 6SW (☎ 0870-220 2073).

INSTALLATION & REGISTRATION

Before moving into a new home, check whether there's a telephone line and that the number of lines or telephone points is adequate (most new homes already have telephone lines and points in a number of rooms). If a property has a cable or other connection (see above), you could decide not to have a BT telephone line installed. If you move into an old house or apartment, a telephone line is probably already installed, although there won't be a telephone. If you're moving into accommodation without a telephone line, e.g. a new property, you must ask BT or one of the other infrastructure providers to install one.

BT's target for residential line installation is three working days, depending on the area and the particular exchange. The installation of a line where there wasn't one previously costs £124.99, alternatively, you can spread this connection charge with one initial payment of £27.49 followed by four subsequent quarterly payments of £27.49. This makes a total of £137.45 and includes an administration fee of £12.46. However to take over an existing line is free. If, unusually, a property still has an old-style telephone point (which cannot be unplugged), it should be replaced with a new-style 'linebox' or master socket. This can be done by BT only and it's illegal to do it yourself or get anyone other than a BT engineer to do it. Once you have a BT linebox or master socket, you can install as many additional sockets as you like, but you shouldn't connect more than four telephones to one telephone line. You can install additional sockets yourself by buying do-it-yourself (DIY) kits from BT or a DIY shop, or BT can install them for you (although their labour charges are astronomical). BT sells a wide range of extension kits, sockets and cords.

New residential subscribers, particularly tenants in rented property, may need to pay a deposit in rare instances when BT doubts their capacity to meet bills. BT will retain the deposit for a maximum of a year (provided bills are paid on time) and pay interest on it. You can appeal against this demand to your local district general manager. However, it's far more likely that new customers will be asked to agree to a maximum bill level, which eliminates this requirement. If this level is exceeded before the end of the quarter, BT contacts you to agree a course of action.

The procedure for having a telephone connected or installed is as follows:

1. Ring BT's customer service on (☎ 0800-800 150). They send you a form to complete.

2. Complete and return the form to the local district office address quoted on it.

3. If there's a deposit to pay, BT informs you and it must be paid before a line is installed or connected.

4. When BT has received your application (and deposit, if applicable), they schedule a date for the installation of your telephone line and notify you by post (you receive a 'job number'). If it's simply a matter of having an existing line reconnected, BT should be able to do this on or before the date requested.

5. Alternativly order via the web (💻 www.bt.com).

If you're moving to a new address in the same code area, it's usually possible to retain your existing number – check with British Telecom (☎ 0800-800 150).

CHOOSING A TELEPHONE

You aren't required to rent a telephone from BT and can instead purchase one from a wide range offered by the company and other retailers. The quarterly rental for a BT telephone is a minimum of £3.80, which means that in less than a year you will have paid the price of a basic telephone (the cheapest BT phone costs £11.99). The advantage of renting a BT telephone is that they fix it free of charge if it's faulty and you can change telephones as often as you wish. With an inexpensive purchased telephone, it's cheaper to throw it away and buy a new one than have it repaired. **Before buying a telephone it's wise to compare prices and features, which vary considerably.** All telephones used in the UK must be approved. This is indicated by a label with a green circle. Non-approved equipment is also available in the UK, but it's a criminal offence to use it, as it could damage the phone system. Always check that a telephone is approved for use.

Cordless telephones are popular and standard models can be operated up to 300m from their base unit. If you're thinking of buying a cordless telephone, remember that they rely on mains power and, therefore, are useless if there's a power failure. The European standard for cordless telephones, called Digital Enhanced Cordless Telecommunications (DECT), specifies a 300m range and a base unit that can drive up to six telephones. You may also consider a telephone with a built-in answering machine (see also **Call Minder** on page 161).

You can try the latest BT telephones at BT shops (see your local telephone directory) and other business communications equipment retailers, where advice and demonstrations are available. An illustrated catalogue of BT products is available on the shopping pages of their website (💻 www.bt.com) or you can phone (☎ 0800-800

150); literature is also available from BT shops. Compare telephones and equipment on sale in high street shops and, if possible, test before buying. If things go wrong, some retailers provide an unconditional money-back guarantee for a limited period.

For those with special needs, a variety of special telephones and attachments is available. If you live or work in a noisy environment, a headset can be purchased allowing hands-free operation. Special handsets are available for the blind (with a nodule on the figure 5) and extra large key pads for the partially sighted. Telephones fitted with a flashing light, loud ring, a built-in amplifier or an inductive coupler are available for the hard of hearing. BT publishes *Communications Solutions*, a guide for people who are disabled or elderly, which can be obtained by calling ☎ 150 or visiting your local BT sales office. If you need further information, you can also telephone BT's Age and Disability Action Unit (☎ 0800-919 591).

Finally, for those who dread receiving telephone bills, BT offers a range of payphones and cardphones, although they're **very** expensive. You can also arrange to have a telephone barred from making outgoing calls. (See also **Mobile Telephones & Pagers** on page 169.)

STANDARD TONES

Standard telephone tones (the sounds a telephones makes when not connected to a subscriber) are provided to indicate the progress of calls. Tones in the UK may be completely different from those used in other countries. There's sometimes a pause before you hear a tone, so hold on for a few seconds before replacing the receiver to allow the equipment time to connect your call. The following standard tones are used:

- **Dial Tone** – A continuous high-pitched hum, which is heard when you lift the receiver. This indicates that the telephone is connected to the network and you can start dialling.

- **Ringing Tone** – As standard, a repeated burr indicates that the dialled number is ringing. However, it's now possible, for a quarterly fee, to have personalised numbers on the same line, with individual tones which allow each user to identify whether the call is his.

- **Engaged Tone** – A single tone repeated at short intervals means that the dialled number is busy (engaged). An engaged tone sometimes means that the lines of the exchange you're dialling are engaged rather than the number you're calling. Try again after a short interval. Sometimes you hear a recorded message telling you that "All lines are busy, please try later."

- **Unobtainable** – A continuous steady tone means that you've dialled a number which isn't in use or is temporarily out of service. Check the code and number and dial again. If unsuccessful, check the number with directory enquiries; if the number is correct, check that it's in service by calling the operator. In some cases, you hear a recorded announcement, for example when an area code or number has been changed.

USING THE TELEPHONE

Using the telephone in the UK is much the same as in any other country, with a few British eccentricities thrown in for good measure. When dialling a number within your own exchange area, dial the number only, e.g. if you live in Toy Town and wish to dial another subscriber in Toy Town. When dialling anywhere else, you must dial the area code before the subscriber's number. Telephone numbers may be printed Toy Town 1234, 01567-1234 (as in this book), 01567 1234 or Toy Town (01567) 1234. The last is the recommended form, although rarely used! When the area name isn't shown, you may not know whether it's nearby or at the other end of the UK (although you can always ask the operator).

When dialling a British number from overseas, you must dial the international access code used in the country from which you're calling (e.g. 00), followed by the UK's international code (44), the area code **without** the first 0 (e.g. 1567 for Toy Town) and the subscriber's number. For Toy Town 1234, you would dial 00-44-1567-1234.

If you get a bad line, e.g. you're unable to hear the caller or the caller is unable to hear you, or a crossed line where you can hear voices in the background, the connection may improve if you redial the number.

Free Numbers

Free numbers, sometimes called 'freefone numbers' by BT, have the prefix 0800. They're usually provided by businesses which are trying to sell you something or, having sold you something, provide a free telephone support service. Some companies have a freefone name rather than a number, in which case you can telephone the operator (100) and ask for the freefone name.

Local & National Rate Numbers

Numbers with the prefix 0845 are charged at the local rate, irrespective of where you're calling from. Numbers with the prefix 0870 are charged at the national rate even when you're calling locally. Charges (which are around 4p and 8p per minute respectively) are the same whichever call provider you use.

Information & Entertainment

The use of premium rate information and entertainment numbers has been a feature of the past decade and includes numbers with the prefixes 0900, 0901, 0904, 0905, 09059, 0906, 0907, 0908 and 0909. The charge for premium rate numbers, which must be shown when they're listed or quoted, is 60 pence per minute with a maximum of £5 per call in the case of 0900, 0901 and 09059 numbers. Such numbers are huge money-spinners for the companies who make use of them, and are beloved by organisers of television (TV) and radio competitions which involve telephone calls to studios by members of the public (where they keep you on the line for as long as possible). Although the prizes concerned may look attractive, they cost nothing compared to the revenue generated by the telephone lines. **If you use these numbers frequently, you can go bankrupt!**

Information numbers offer a wide range of recordings on practically any subject. For example, you can hear a weather forecast, listen to your horoscope or obtain motoring information. Most such 'bulletins' last around three minutes and cost an absolute minimum of £4.50. Numbers beginning with 0909 offer services with an adult theme (such as sex chat lines) and can include live conversation.

Some people have received huge telephone bills, which include calls to national and international sex lines that they haven't made. It's extremely difficult to prove that you (or a family member) didn't make these calls, even if you can show that you were out of the country at the time! Although BT deny it, it's possible for someone to gain access to your line and to make calls at your expense. To prevent this happening you can use Call Barring (see page 161) to bar access to premium rate numbers or block international dialling from a private telephone.

If you have a complaint about information and entertainment numbers, you can contact the Independent Committee for the Supervision of Standards of Telephone Information Services (ICSTIS), Clove Building, 4 Maguire Street, London SE1 2NQ (☎ 0800-500 212 between 8.00am and 6.00pm weekdays).

Telephone Codes

It's important to know what kind of telephone (or even a pager) you're calling and what it's costing. A number's prefix tells you what type of number it is; for example 00 (international dialling), 01/02 (national area codes), 07 (mobiles, pagers and personal numbers), 08 (freefone and special rate services) and 09 (premium rate services).

The following (expensive) operator services are also available:

- **Alarm Call** – An alarm call costs £5.50, including value added tax (VAT). (It's cheaper to buy an alarm clock).

- **Reverse Charge Call** – A reverse charge, transferred or collect call, is where the person being called agrees to pay for the call. Useful when you have no change, the payphone won't accept your coins or when you're calling your mother-in-law.

All such domestic calls involve a charge of £4.00, including VAT for the services of the operator. Added to that are call charges which are levied at the normal rate. BT says there is no charge if you cannot be connected or the person called refuses the call. Calls can be made to BT numbers only. Some mobile networks have other more expensive arrangements and whether the call is accepted or not, a charge is made.

Line Faults

If you have a BT line, faults must be reported to BT: ☎ 151 for domestic user, ☎ 154 for business users. When you report your telephone out of order, ask for a reference number so that you can verify the number of days it's out of service, as you may be able to claim compensation. Standard coverage, which is included with the line rental, enables you to receive help between 8am and 5pm from Monday to Friday. If you pay an additional amount for Promptcare coverage, this can be extended to Saturday, and more still for Totalcare, 24 hours a day and Sunday too. Priority Fault Repair is available free, 24 hours a day every day for the disabled and elderly.

Faults should be repaired within two working days under the BT 'Customer Service Guarantee'. If this isn't achieved, BT pays a daily compensation rate up to a **maximum of £1,000** per line for residential customers (provided you can prove that you have lost money as a result of the fault). Most faults are fixed within one working day. To claim compensation, call 150 or write to the Claims Manager of the office which sends your telephone bill.

BT Chargecard

Direct-dialled calls and calls via an international operator can be made with a free BT Chargecard to over 130 countries and to the UK from over 100 countries using the BT Direct service. Direct-dialled BT Chargecard domestic calls cost 20p per minute at all times. There is a basic charge of 20p for the first minute after which price is calculated per second. If you call via the operator, there's an additional handling charge of £1.75 for all calls (even local ones). Calls from payphones are charged at BT public payphone rates (see page 167). BT Chargecards can be used to dial direct from any tone phone, which includes all BT payphones and most private phones, although they cannot be used from mobile phones.

When using a BT Chargecard from abroad, you may be charged an astronomical sum, e.g. over five times the cost of using a local payphone! To be more precise, rates range from 76p to £3.76 per minute. Calls are charged per minute or part minute with a one minute minimum charge. An operator's fee of £1.75 makes it even more expensive. However, BT says that if you must call the British operator to put a call through, you will not be charged this fee if you have tried to get through normally beforehand and failed. Chargecards are similarly expensive when making calls from the UK to other countries. Chargecards can also present security risks, in the UK and when used abroad. Although they offer convenience, it comes at a high price, which is fine, provided someone else is picking up the tab. For information about the BT Chargecard ☎ 0800-345 144.

BT Calling Features

The following services are available from BT to subscribers connected to a digital exchange; its competitors offer similar services.

- **Call Barring** – Call barring allows you to bar or block outgoing or international calls, or specific numbers such as premium rate services (see **Information & Entertainment Numbers** below). It costs £1.75 a month.

- **Caller Display** – Call display allows you to see the numbers of callers and decide whether you want to speak to them. Caller Display is free but you must have a suitable telephone.

    If you don't want your own number to be shown when you telephone other people, dial 141 before proceeding as usual. Customers can also block their number from ever being displayed by calling BT on ☎ 0800-800 150 or 150 and requesting this. When 141 is used or a customer has blocked their number permanently, the message 'number withheld' is displayed on caller display screens. This, of course, arouses a natural suspicion on the part of those called and many refuse to answer the telephone in these circumstances. Using the Choose to Refuse feature (see below), telephones can be set up to refuse such calls automatically. (If everybody withheld their number before dialling, the system would cease to function). Caller Display doesn't work with cable company lines or mobile phone calls.

- **Choose to Refuse** – Choose to refuse allows users to bar up to ten telephone numbers from which they don't wish to receive calls. This is free for the first month as a trial period but then costs £10.05 per quarter.

- **Anonymous Call Rejection** – Anonymous call rejection provides an automatic bar on anonymous calls to your number and is set up at the telephone exchange. It costs £12 per quarter.

- **Call Diversion** – Call diversion allows you to divert calls automatically from your own telephone to another telephone (in the UK or abroad) where you can be reached, e.g. from home to office or to a mobile phone. To divert calls, you dial *21*, the number to which you want calls to be diverted (code and subscriber's number), followed by #. To reset Call Diversion, dial #21#.

- **Call Minder** – Call minder is an answerphone service (at the local telephone exchange) which even takes messages while you're using the phone and answers two calls at once. It can record a total of 15 minutes or 30 messages. You dial 1571 to retrieve messages, when (if you have any new messages) you receive a recorded message telling you this when you pick up your telephone, e.g. "This is BT Call Minder . . . You have two messages. Please call to collect them." Message retrieval is free and messages can be retrieved from any tone telephone in the UK or abroad. Call Minder costs £7.50 monthly for one mail box.

- **Call Minder Extension** – The call minder externsion has the same features as Call Minder, but with the addition of up to six separate message boxes so that every member of a household can find what concerns them immediately. The use of box-specific personal identification numbers (PIN) ensures privacy. This costs £9 a month.

- **BT Answer 1571** – BT Answer 1571 records messages and makes you aware they're there by an irregular beeping the next time you lift the handset. It's free. You access messages by dialling 1571.

- **1571 Personal Greeting** – The 1571 personal greeting allows you to create your own greeting for callers and change it whenever you like. It costs a £1.50 a month.

- **1571 Message Alert** – The 1571 message alert makes you aware that you've missed a call, because you were on the telephone or internet, by ringing you as soon as the line becomes available. It costs £1.50 a month.

- **Call Return** – Call return allows you to find out the number of the last person to call you, whether you answered the telephone or not. You dial 1471 and a recorded announcement gives you the number. If you don't want your own number passed on in this way, you can dial 141 before any number you ring. To return the call of the last person to call you, dial 1474 and the number is dialled automatically. Call Return is a free service.

- **1471 Extra** – 1471 Extra allows you to access the date, time and number of the last five people to call you.

- **Call Waiting** – Call waiting tells you (via a beep on the line) if another call is trying to get through to you when you're already on the telephone and allows you to swap between the calls. It costs £1.50 monthly.

- **Reminder Call** – The reminder call function allows you to make alarm calls. To use it, you dial *55*, followed by the time required using the 24-hour clock, followed by #. For example to be called at 7am, dial *55*0700#.

- **Ring Back** – Ring back tells you the cost of calls. To use it, you dial *40*, the number you're calling, followed by #. When you hang up the exchange calls back and tells you how much the call cost.

- **Ring Me Free** – Ring me free allows someone to call you free of charge and bill the cost to your bill (so don't give the number to telephone salespeople). It costs 10p per use.

- **Three-way Calling** – Three-way calling allows you to hold a three-way conversation (one party can be abroad).

Call Diversion, 1471 Extra, Call Waiting, Reminder Call, Ring Back and Three-Way Calling are only available as part of a 'Feature Pack'. For more information ☎ 0800-800 150 or visit ▦ www.bt.com.

BT CALL RATES

BT remains by far the largest telephone company in the UK and, therefore, its call rates are listed here for comparison purposes. **This isn't meant as an endorsement of the company, which charges some of the country's highest rates.** The VAT rate of 17.5 per cent is applicable to line rental and calls, and is included in all rates shown, unless otherwise noted. For a large percentage of BT's customers, the line rental fee accounts for over half their bill.

BT has three charge rates for self-dialled, domestic calls from ordinary lines (not payphones or mobile phones), depending on the time and day. Daytime rate is in operation from 6am to 6pm, Mondays to Fridays; Evening and nighttime rate is from 6pm to 6am, Mondays to Fridays; and weekend rate is from 6am Saturday until 6am Monday. However, BT charges a minimum 3p set up fee for all calls whereas some companies offer national calls for less per minute at all times and are therefore cheaper during the day.

	Tariff/Cost per Minute (2007) Inclusive of VAT	
Type of Call*	Daytime	Evening/Night/Weekend
Local	3p	5.5p for up to one hour
National	3p	5.5p for up to one hour

* Local calls are calls made within your local call area, and national calls are calls made to numbers outside it. To clarify what constitutes your local area, consult your telephone directory.

Special Rates

BT and some other companies offer a complicated and confusing range of tariffs and discount schemes. It's difficult to calculate the value for money they offer but, when you do you find savings, they're usually modest and scarcely worth bothering about. BT publishes a leaflet entitled *UK Call Prices*, listing all its domestic call rates and their special tariffs include:

- **Light User Scheme** – If you make few calls and just want a telephone so people can call you, this is for you. Your bill for calls must be under £11.02 a quarter and you receive a rebate on your line rental of 9.5p for every 10p your call bill is below £22.03. BT makes no concessions for pensioners as, for example, telephone companies do in Belgium, France, Germany and Ireland.

- **Friends & Family** – BT customers can save 10 per cent on direct-dialled calls to ten nominated numbers (including one international and one mobile number) plus an extra 20 per cent to a 'best friend's' number. Friends & Family members can also receive a 10 per cent discount on five further international numbers by joining Friends & Family Overseas, which costs an additional £1 per quarter for customers who don't have BT Together.

- **BT Together Option 1** – For £11.00 per month line rental, you can make a local or national call during the daytime for 3p per minute, and an evening or weekend call for 5.5p for the first hour and then 1p a minute after that.

- **BT Together Option 2** – For £14.95 monthly line rental, you can make daytime calls for 3p a minute and calls of up to an hour in the evening and at the weekend free. If you go over the hour, you pay 1p a minute.

- **BT Together Option 3** – You pay £20.95 monthly line rental and you can make calls any time of up to an hour free.

- **Operator-connected Calls** – One of the more expensive people you can call is your local telephone operator. (It's often cheaper to visit someone personally by taxi than make a call via the operator). There is normally a 'handling charge' of £2.55, in addition to the cost of the call itself, which is charged in one minute blocks from private landline telephones and three minute blocks from payphones. **Calling in this fashion unnecessarily is inadvisable.** However, if a call has to be made via the operator because a dialled call has failed, the cost is roughly the same as a dialled call (although the minimum charge period is still three minutes).

BT TELEPHONE BILLS

You're billed every quarter (three months) by BT for your line rental, telephone rental (if applicable) and calls, when you're sent a blue telephone account plus a Statement. If applicable, the telephone connection fee is included in your first bill. BT provides all customers with itemised bills on request which include the number called, the date and time, the duration and the call cost. Customers can choose to have all calls itemised or some only. This information is also available via the internet (☎ www.bt.com).

BT telephone bills can be paid by budget account (to spread bills evenly over 12 months); quarterly direct debit; by post using the envelope provided; at your bank (complete the form provided) or at a post office. The best way for most people to pay their bill is monthly via a budget account or quarterly from an interest-bearing bank or building society account. With quarterly direct debit, your account is debited 14 days after you receive the bill. BT also offers a card on which you can collect 'stamps' from £2 plus (available from BT shops and post offices) to help spendthrifts save for their telephone bills. However, this pays no interest and, if you lose it, you've lost your money.

If you don't pay your bill within around 14 days of receipt, you receive a red Reminder of Payment, after which you have another 14 days in which to pay it. If you don't pay your bill within this period, your line is disconnected, usually without any further notification. You may, however, receive a further Important Notice reminder, which may give you a further few days to pay your bill, **but don't count on it**. If you're cut off, you may have to wait up to a week to have your line reconnected after paying your bill. You must also pay a reconnection fee (in your next bill) and may be required to pay a deposit against future bills. Elderly and disabled people can apply to be listed under a Protected Service Scheme, whereby they name someone who is told if a bill remains unpaid after a reminder. BT delay cutting off the service so that the named person can deal with it, which prevents, for example, someone returning from hospital to find that their telephone has been disconnected.

If you have a query about your account, call account enquiries on ☎ 150. If you feel that your bill is incorrect (e.g. too high) you shouldn't pay it, but should ask to have it checked by your local telephone manager. Unfortunately (despite thousands of cases that prove otherwise), BT believes that their billing system is infallible and it's almost impossible to prove that you didn't run up the bill or to get BT to admit that there's a fault in their system. BT doesn't, however, discriminate against the private telephone user and a large number of companies also complain that their bills are wrong. One investigation found that many companies were overcharged for calls and rental, as well as for equipment and engineering. We aren't talking about peanuts here: many companies have been overcharged by tens of thousands of pounds. (No wonder BT used to make such large profits!) If you don't have a fully itemised bill, it's almost impossible to prove that you didn't make calls charged to you.

If you're in dispute with BT over your bill (as many people seem to be at some time or other), you shouldn't be disconnected although, if only part of your bill is in dispute, **you should pay the part that isn't in dispute to avoid being cut off**. BT will disconnect a private customer who refuses to pay his bill indefinitely (companies with large bills usually receive better treatment). If you cannot obtain satisfaction from your local BT area manager (the telephone number is on your bill) or district general manager, you should contact the secretary of your national Advisory Committee (the address is listed in your telephone directory under Code of Practice for Consumers). Complaints about the telephone service are dealt with by the Office of Communications (Ofcom), Riverside House, 2a Southwark Bridge Road, London SE1 9HA (☎ 020-7981 3040 or visit 🖳 www.ofcom.org.uk). Ofcom has taken over from the Office of Telecommunications (Oftel) as regulator of broadcasting media, as well as telephone services. As a last resort you can go to legally-binding arbitration if your dispute is for less than £5,000.

INTERNATIONAL CALLS

All private telephones in the UK are on International Direct Dialling (IDD), allowing calls to be dialled direct to over 190 countries and reverse charge calls (collect) to be made to some 140 countries. To make an international call, dial 00, the country code, the area code without the first zero (with a few exceptions such as Italy) and the subscriber's number. Dial ☎ 155 for the international operator to make non-IDD calls, credit card calls, person-to-person and reverse charge calls (which aren't accepted by all countries). For international directory enquiries ☎ 118-505. The codes for the major cities of many countries are listed in telephone directories in section three International Information, including the time difference. (One sure way to upset most people is to call them at 3am).

BT charges for dialled international calls from ordinary lines are based on charge bands. In 2007 some standard evening/weekend rates (with BT were 10p per minute to Australia, 10p to France and Germany, 10p to Ireland, 7p to Japan, 46p to South Africa and 10p to the US. International charges are listed on the BT website (🖳 www.bt.com). **Rates are much higher during the daytime, Mondays to Fridays. Using an alternative company to BT, e.g. an indirect access company** (see below), can result in huge savings, even when comparing their standard charges with BT's lowest.

Indirect Access Companies

The cheapest companies for international calls are indirect access companies. Nowadays you simply dial a number to connect to the company's own lines or dial a code before dialling a number. They may offer low rates for all calls or just national and international calls. Some charge a subscription fee. Calls are charged at a flat rate 24 hours a day, seven days a week. Some companies allow you to make calls from any tone telephone (even abroad), while others restrict you to a single (e.g. home or office) number. Calls may be paid for with a credit or debit card, in advance, when you must buy a number of units, or by direct debit each month. Alternatively, you may be billed monthly in arrears.

Low-cost companies have devastated BT's erstwhile share of the international market, particularly with regard to transatlantic calls, which isn't surprising when you consider the savings that can be made. For example, Alpha Telecom (☎ 0800-279 6738, 💻 www.alphatelecom.com), charges a flat rate of 3p per minute to the Australia, Canada, France, Germany, Ireland, Japan, New Zealand and the US and 4p to South Africa (these rates aren't applicable to mobile phones or payphones). Compare these rates with BT's above. Isn't competition wonderful? Most other indirect access companies, such as Onetel (☎ 0845-308 1878, 💻 www.onetel.co.uk) Callmate (☎ 01274-301 600, 💻 www.callmate.com), Swiftcall (💻 www.swiftcall.co.uk) and TalkTalk (☎ 08000-049 7802, 💻 www.talktalk.co.uk), have similar rates to Onetel. It's possible to buy a box that you connect between your telephone and wall socket, which automatically routes long-distance and international calls via the cheapest carrier but, having located a carrier with rock bottom rates, such as one of the above, for the countries you call often, it's scarcely worth the bother nowadays.

Country Direct

Many European countries, including the UK, subscribe to a Country Direct service that allows you to call a special number giving you direct access to an operator in the country you're calling. The number varies according to the country from which you are making the call and you must establish this before you travel. The operator connects you to the number required and also accepts credit card or reverse charge calls. The number to dial is shown in telephone directories in the International Code section. You should be extremely wary of making international reverse charge calls to the UK using BT's UK Direct scheme, as you pay at least double the cost of using a local payphone. For information about countries served by the Country Direct service, call BT international directory enquiries (☎ 118 505) or the international operator (☎ 155), which is free.

International Calling Cards

You can obtain an international telephone calling card from telephone companies in many countries. It allows you to make calls from abroad and charge them to your telephone bill in your home country. American long-distance telephone companies (e.g. AT&T, MCI and Sprint) compete vigorously for overseas customers and all offer calling cards allowing foreign customers to bill international calls to a credit card. AT&T's service (☎ 0800-220 679 or visit 🖳 www.att.com), for example, allows you to make calls from almost any telephone in over 100 countries.

The benefits of international calling cards are that they're fee-free; calls can be made to or from most countries; can usually be made from any telephone, including hotel telephones; and are made via an English-speaking operator in the US (foreign-language operators are also available). Most important of all, call charges are often based on the 'callback' system and are charged at US rates (based on the cost between the US and the country you're calling from and to), which is usually much cheaper than calls made via local telephone companies. Some companies offer conference calling facilities that allow you to talk to a number of people in different countries at the same time. Other features may include a 'world office' facility that allows you to retrieve voice and fax messages, at any time, from anywhere in the world. If you do a lot of international travelling, it's advisable to have a number of cards, as the cheapest often depends on the countries you're calling from and to.

To find out more about international direct dialling, country codes, BT international services and related topics contact the BT international operator (☎ 155 or visit 🖳 www.bt.com).

PUBLIC TELEPHONES

Most public telephones (officially called 'payphones') permit International Direct Dialling (IDD), as well as domestic calls and calls made via the operator. Older ones are sterile grey 'vandal-proof' steel and glass booths containing push-button payphones, the really ancient red versions surviving only in some locations of historic interest. The latest payphones also offer internet, email and Short Message Service (SMS) texting facilities while video email telephones have already been on trial in London. Some humbler payphones aren't enclosed and offer little protection from the elements and surrounding noise (although if they remain in working order, most people are happy). A limited number offer more convenience for people with disabilities, and better wheelchair access. There are also private 'call shops' in major cities where you can usually make calls in more comfort.

Payphones are operated by BT and now chiefly accept credit cards – Visa, Visa Delta, MasterCard, Eurocard, American Express, Diners Club International and JCB – rather than coins. (There are 60,000 credit card kiosks, but prepaid phonecards are no longer in use). This eliminates theft because, of course, there is nothing in the phonebox to steal, and consequently it's easier to find one that works than in the past. BT claims that over 96 per cent of kiosks are in working order at any one time although, given the proliferation of mobile phones, the number is declining along with demand for them. Public payphones are to be found in all cities and towns; in public streets; inside and outside post offices and railway stations; and in hotels, pubs, restaurants, shops and other private and public buildings. If you're driving, finding a payphone is more difficult than in the past, but nowhere near as difficult as finding somewhere to park!

Emergency (999) calls are free from any payphone. If you need additional information dial ☎ 100 for the inland or ☎ 155 for the international operator. Calling from payphones, the BT domestic directory enquiry number is ☎ 118 500 (calls cost 23p per minute) or ☎ 118 505 for international enquiries (minimum charge of £1.50). Charges for dialled inland calls from payphones are calculated in units of 20p and cost a minmum of 40p; a 20p connection cost and minimum 1 minute at 20p per minute if you are using coins.

There is a £1.20 minimum charge when using a credit card and all inland calls in that event are charged at 20p a minute. Mobile numbers incur a £1.00 set up fee plus 64p per minute. Credit card international calls involve an additional £1 'setup' fee. Operator-connected calls from payphones cost far more than dialled calls and should be avoided, if at all possible.

Most payphones are push-button operated and accept all coins except for 1p, 2p and 5p (i.e. 10p to £2). You'll need at least £1 to make an international call with coins. Payphones should be avoided at all costs when making international calls, as the rates are prohibitive.

When using a payphone, partly used coins are lost, but wholly unused coins are returned when you hang up the receiver. Payphones also have a 'follow on call' button which is visible when you pick up the receiver. If you still have unused coins in credit, you can press this button and make another call using the remaining credit. If the display flashes, insert more coins until the flashing stops. It's advisable to insert relatively small coins unless you're calling long distance. Instructions for using payphones are as follows:

1. Lift the handset and wait for the dialling tone (a high pitched hum). If you don't hear a dialling tone, the telephone is out of order.

2. Insert the minimum call charge of 20p (or more for long distance calls) or a credit card. When you have inserted at least 20p, the credit display shows how much you have in credit and stops flashing. If you're using a credit card, you are instructed when to dial.

3. Dial the number required.

4. When your credit is exhausted, the credit display starts flashing again and a warning tone is given on the line. You have ten seconds in which to insert more coins before the call is disconnected.

5. Replace the handset and any completely unused coins are returned. If you still have credit for partly used coins, you can press the 'follow on call' button and make another call using the remaining credit. Otherwise, any credit is lost, so it pays not to insert too many 50p or £1 coins. If you're using a credit card, don't forget to take it with you.

If you have difficulties, call the operator on ☎ 100.

Private Payphones

Be wary of using private payphones, e.g. those located in pubs, restaurants, hotels, shopping centres and petrol stations. The charge rate for these is set by the owners, many of whom levy extortionate rates. The call charge should be displayed on all private payphones, although most don't. You should also avoid using hotel room telephones, where fees can be astronomical. Some hotels even charge a fee to connect guests to free (e.g. 0800) numbers used to make chargecard calls.

Credit Card Payphones in Taxis

A large number of London's licensed taxis, called taxifone cabs, are fitted with metered passenger payphones accepting all leading credit cards (taxifone cabs can be booked in advance). A BT chargecard can be used to make calls from payphones, but there's a high charge.

MOBILE TELEPHONES & PAGERS

Few countries in the world have as many mobile phone users as the UK. Practically anyone who wants one now owns one. Whereas they were once status symbols among yuppies and the young, they have now become just another everyday item. Mobiles are so widespread that many businesses (e.g. restaurants, cinemas, theatres, concert halls) ban them and some even use mobile phone jammers, which can detect and jam every handset within 100m. **In recent years, there has been widespread publicity regarding a possible health risk to users from the microwave radiation emitted by mobile phones.** Nothing has been reliably established as yet, but you can visit the Department of Health's official website on the subject to discover the facts (🖳 www.dh.gov.uk).

Mobile phone network providers include Vodafone, T-mobile, Orange, O2, and 3G. There are also a number of 'virtual' providers such as Virgin, Onetel and Sainsbury's who buy time from the major players and operate their own services. BT, having abandoned the mobile phone business a couple of years ago, is now returning with a new technology which uses its own landline network and bluetooth wireless connections in order to provide what is claimed will be a cheaper and more reliable service.

Details about areas of coverage are available on websites such as Mobile Shop (🖳 www.mobileshop.org/buyguide/coverage.htm). Coverage is most limited in the case of the newcomer 3G, but there's little discernible difference between the two major companies, O2 and Vodafone, although you should check out the reception in your local area, particularly if it's a remote rural district. Some companies have been criticised for the quality of reception offered in many parts of the country (and even worse customer service).

Subscribers can buy a GSM telephone, which can be used in many countries worldwide, including much of western Europe, Australia, Hong Kong, South Africa and parts of the Middle East. You must have a contract with a 'roaming' agreement if you wish to use your mobile abroad and should check the countries your service provider has contracts with.

Buying a mobile phone is an absolute minefield, as not only is there a variety of networks to choose from, but dozens of tariffs covering connection fees, monthly subscriptions, insurance and call charges. Before buying a mobile phone, shop around and compare telephone prices and features; installation and connection charges; rental charges; and, most importantly, charge rates. One way to do this is via Buy (🖳 www.buy.co.uk), which provides a mobile phone tariff calculator.

The cheapest telephones usually involve hefty running costs and tie in customers to long contracts with heavy penalties for breaking deals. An alternative to taking out a contract is to buy a 'pre-pay' or 'pay as you go' phone. You buy the telephone and then pay for line rental and call time separately. There's no contract, no monthly charge and no bill. Credit is entered onto your phone via your own phone card (similar in appearance to a credit card) when you buy the credit. Although they're extremely popular, pre-pay phones aren't cheap and high charges outweigh any advantages (although they're suitable for those who make few calls, but want to be able to receive them).

Telephones are sold by retail outlets such as BT shops, specialist dealers (e.g. Carphone Warehouse, The Link, and Phone City), department and chain stores (e.g. Dixons) and supermarkets, all of whom have arrangements with service providers or networks to sell airtime contracts along with telephones. Don't rely on always getting good or impartial advice from retail staff, some of whom know little or nothing about telephones and networks. Always deal with an independent company that sells a wide range of telephones and can connect you to any network.

Retailers advertise, almost daily, in magazines and newspapers, where a wide range of special offers is common and prices vary considerably. Telephones are even available free, if you're willing to sign a contract which ensures that retailers and network providers can recoup their costs and more through high line rental and call charges. Before buying a telephone, compare battery life, memory number capacity, weight, size and features which may include alphanumeric store, automatic call back, unanswered call store, mail box, call timer, minute minder, lock facility and call barring.

However, the network you connect to is far more important than the type of telephone you buy. The most important point is where you're going to use it, followed by when, how often and whether you will make mostly local or long distance and international calls. Don't be influenced by a cheap telephone when the real costs lie in high call and line rental charges.

Generally, the higher the connection and line rental charges, the lower the cost of calls. If you make a lot of calls, select a tariff with low call charges. Conversely, if you make few calls or need a phone mostly for incoming calls, choose a tariff with low monthly costs. The range of tariffs is primarily designed to confuse customers! Many users regret buying a mobile phone or at least the one that they bought or the network they signed up with. Once you sign a contract, you're usually stuck with the same telephone for at least 12 months. However you can, of course, transfer your mobile phone number between operators.

Costs

It's impossible to quote rates here, as there are too many options and they change too frequently (price wars regularly erupt when companies seek to increase or maintain their share of the market). **Mobile phones aren't a cheap option!** You can pay 25p, 40p or even 50p per minute for national peak time calls, and even 40p per minute for a local peak time call. This is typically **at the very least** more than three times BT peak time national rates (7.9p per minute) and ten times those charged by companies such as Onetel (2.5p per minute peak time national and local rate). The difference is even more dramatic when you compare the cost of international calls.

BT standard charges for calls to mobiles from fixed-line telephones have fallen in recent years and vary according to the network concerned. An example which broadly reflects the general situation would be 13p per minute (peak time rate), 8p per minute (evening rate) and 5p per minute (weekend rate) for connections to a mobile on the Vodafone or Orange networks.

According to a survey carried out by the magazine *Mobile Choice* and publicised by Ofcom, the average user sends eight SMS text messages a day, and the opportunity to 'text' is the main reason why 29 per cent of them acquired a mobile. The charge for this is important: the 10p per message charged by Vodafone and Orange (on a 'pay as you go' rate) seems typical.

Mobile phone companies have regularly been accused of overcharging customers most notably on a number of occasions by the industry regulator Ofcom. It has pointed out that British users pay around twice as much as other Europeans when travelling abroad and significantly higher prices in general. This criticism culminated in a European parliament decision in 2007 to bring in legislation to limit what companies can charge within the EU.

Car Phones

When buying a mobile phone for car use, you should choose one which provides hands-free use and on-hook dialling, i.e. where you don't need to hold the handset to use it. You can also get a phone with voice-activated dialling, where key words such as 'office' or 'home' will dial the appropriate number for you. You will be prosecuted for using a hand-held phone while driving as this has resulted in a number of fatal accidents.

Security

Theft of mobile phones is a huge problem and stolen mobile phones are usually reprogrammed (cloned) to make free calls abroad (although new phones are supposedly clone-proof). Mobile phones should never be left in cars. It's advisable to insure a phone for its real value because if it's stolen, you are billed for its replacement cost, not what you paid for it. All phones are provided with a unique serial number which allows their use to be blocked if they're stolen and phones can be programmed to stop users making certain calls, e.g. international calls.

Pagers

There are three main pager networks in the UK: BT, PageOne and Ascom (covering different parts of the country), plus those of all four mobile phone companies but, because of the ease with which SMS text messages can now be sent by mobile phone, these businesses are largely being allowed to wither on the vine. In countries such as Germany, the pager has already passed into history. The British government initially thought it would be able to auction off licences for the use of two-way paging, the latest technological development, but even when it decided to give them away it only had one taker, PageOne.

Pagers can be used as a 'cheap' alternative to mobile phones and can be used to receive messages rather than just as an alarm that instructs you to call a pre-designated number. Formerly, you had to return a call by phone but, if PageOne takes advantage of its licence, you will be able to send an answer. PageOne gives every indication of continuing to offer a pager service well into the future and would seem to be a prudent choice if you're looking around for one.

Before buying a mobile phone or pager, check the reviews and comparison tests in surveys conducted by *Which?* (see **Consumers' Association** on page 479), *What Cellphone?* and *W@MOB* magazines.

TELEGRAMS, TELEX & FAX

The old-fashioned telegram service has been defunct for some years, and BT's Telemessage service, which substituted for it, has now been reduced and restricted to business users. A company called TelegramsOnline (☎ 0800-190 190, 💻 www.telegramsonline.co.uk) has filled the ensuing gap and now provides a similar service to the general public. You can dictate messages over the telephone or send them via the internet to its bureau for delivery in the UK and abroad – messages can be sent as a fax, telex or radio telegram to a ship at sea. Their call centre is open 9.30am to 5pm from Mondays to Saturdays.

Special greetings formats for a variety of festive occasions can be used at no extra charge. International telegrams cost 96p per word. One word is classed as being one to ten characters, while longer words count as double. Festive formats aren't available.

Telex is the largest dedicated text message network in the world, with over 100,000 subscribers in the UK and over two million worldwide in over 200 countries. BT publishes *The Telex Book* containing a complete list of all British subscribers, available in paperback, hardback or on microfiche. Fax (or facsimile) is available to virtually all IDD destinations, but its popularity has suffered somewhat because of the ever more widespread use of email. Fax costs are billed in the same way as telephone calls and an A4 page is transmitted in around 60 seconds to almost anywhere in the world. BT publishes an annual official *UK Facsimile Directory* and provides international directories for over 50 countries. An order form for telex and fax directories is provided at the back of telephone directories.

Mobile phone and portable computer users can use a portable fax, which allows fax transmissions to be made from virtually anywhere in the UK. Integrated Services Digital Network (ISDN) lines allow you to send data, such as information held on computers, on a telephone line at high speed and virtually error-free, e.g. an A4 page takes around four seconds to send. Faxing and other office services are commonly available from high street bureaux specialising in this area. Shop around when buying a fax machine, as prices vary considerably. **Beware of bogus bills from publishers of international telex and fax directories, who send companies invoices for hundreds of pounds for unsolicited entries in trade and business directories.**

DIRECTORIES

British telephone subscribers, business and private, are listed in directories, each of which covers a local area, with businesses and private subscribers listed in separate sections. If you don't have the latest local edition when you move into a new home, you can get one free from your nearest BT phone shop. Those for adjacent areas can be obtained for £10 (☎ 0800-833 400). Private subscribers are usually listed under the name given when applying for a telephone, followed by their initials. If you want more than one entry in your local telephone book, e.g. when a husband and a wife both retain their family names or when two or more people share a telephone, there's a quarterly charge for each extra entry and a charge each time a new directory is published (approximately every 18 months). New directories are delivered to subscribers' homes. Each is divided into the following sections:

- **Section 1** – This covers numbers for use in emergencies, as well as those for BT information and services, call charge information and directory enquiries.

- **Section 2** – BT customer information and services, call charge information and directory enquiries, the BT code of practice, information about regulatory and advisory bodies, details of which directory covers which area and a map of your local area, as defined by BT for pricing purposes.

- **Section 3** – Local information such as address details for government offices, hospitals, the vehicle licensing office and museums along with national helplines, other information lines and points of contact for people with disabilities.

- **Section 4** – UK area codes and International country codes.

- **Section 5** – Business numbers and numbers for services offered to businesses.

- **Section 6** – Residential numbers.

Yellow Pages

In addition to subscriber directories, business listings called Yellow Pages are published and cover all regions of the UK. Yellow Pages are widely used and contain a local route planner and town maps, telephone information and national helplines. Subscribers are classified under a business or service heading (in alphabetical order), for the area covered by a directory. If you don't have the latest local Yellow Pages when you move into a new home, you can obtain a free copy from your local BT phone shop. Yellow Pages for areas other than your own cost £7.50 each plus pack and postage (paperback only) and can be ordered using the order form in any copy of Yellow Pages (or ☎ 0800-671 444). New Yellow Page directories are delivered to subscribers' homes. Yellow Pages are also available in public reference libraries and can be accessed free via the internet (💻 www.yell.co.uk).

Thomson Local Directories

These privately published directories are available for most of southern and central England and the most populous areas of northern England, Scotland and Wales (covering over 80 per cent of British households). They contain local community information (e.g. helplines, government departments, leisure, premium lines, maps and post office postcodes), a main directory of businesses and suppliers, and an alphabetical index of all local businesses. For a free copy, contact Thomson Directories, Thomson House, 296 Farnborough Road, Farnborough, Hants. GU14 7NU (☎ 01252-555 555, 💻 www.thomsondirectories.com). Directories are available for areas other than where you have a telephone.

Other Directories

Useful local telephone numbers are also listed in local monthly guides published by councils and chambers of commerce. BT publishes Business Pages for a number of regions, including London (☎ 0800-671444). There's also the **Talking Pages** (☎ 118 247), the classified telephone directory from Yellow Pages for businesses, shops and services throughout the UK, which costs 14p per minute (billed by the second) plus 49p connection charge. Telephone numbers can also be obtained over the internet (e.g. 💻 www.yell.co.uk).

Directory Enquiries

Calls to BT national directory enquiries (☎ 118 500) cost 42p per minute, billed by the second with an additional 24p standing charge per call. BT international directory enquiries (☎ 118 505) cost £1.50 per minute, billed in seconds with a £1.50 minimum charge. Use of the website service (💻 www.118500.com) is free. You can also access the free BT directory service on the BT website (💻 www.bt.com).

Other companies besides BT have recently been allowed to offer commercially-based operator enquiry services in the hope that competition would reduce costs to the public. Enquiry calls from blind or disabled people are free via BT but must be arranged in advance (☎ 0800-587 0195).

If you want directory enquiries to find a number for you, you must usually know the town or city of the person or business whose number you require. International numbers for most major cities in the world can also be obtained from directories in central reference libraries in major towns and cities, although you cannot rely on their always being up-to-date.

THE INTERNET

Charges for broadband and dial-up internet connection in the UK are among the lowest in Europe, which partly explains why half of all homes in the country are online. The best deals involve unlimited access anytime during the week, or access whenever you like during the evening and weekend for a set monthly fee. Broadband connection can now be had from around £10 per month (plus VAT) and you pay no more unless you download a considerable amount of data over the web.

A profusion of ISPs exist, some very big (Yahoo, Onetel, BT, Tiscali and AOL being among the most prominent names), and others very small, but seeming to offer better deals sometimes. There are two questions to bear in mind besides the cost when making a choice: will the ISP be around for very long (some go bust taking fees paid in advance with them); and how easy is it to log on? Sometimes small ones simply don't have sufficient capacity to allow very many of their customers to go online simultaneously. Ask around and get personal recommendations.

Broadband, which enables permanent connection to the internet and download times ten times faster than narrowband connections, is currently taking off in the UK with Ofcom estimating that one million Britons are likely to upgrade to it during the next 12 months. This is being encouraged by special offers, such as those from BT, Orange and others. Installation and a suitable modem are free. Prices for this service are diminishing and should continue to do so over the next few years.

There are many magazines for internet users in the UK, including *Net*, *Internet Magazine*, *Net Business*, *Internetworks* and *Web User*.

MOVING HOUSE OR LEAVING BRITAIN

When moving house or leaving the UK, you must notify your telephone company, preferably at least 14 days in advance (for BT, dial ☎ 0800-800 150). When moving house and remaining within the same code area, you should be able to retain your existing number. Don't forget to have the telephone line disconnected when moving house; otherwise the new owners or tenants will be able to make calls at your expense. **It's particularly important to notify a company well in advance if you're leaving the UK and want to get a deposit repaid.**

MALICIOUS CALLS

If you receive malicious or obscene telephone calls, BT gives the following advice:

1. Remain calm. Try not to encourage the caller with an emotional response; remember it's your telephone and you're in control.

2. Don't enter into any conversation. Simply place the handset down beside the telephone and ignore it for a few minutes before replacing it gently.

3. If the caller telephones repeatedly, don't say anything when you pick up the handset; a genuine caller will speak first.

4. If the calls are silent, don't attempt to coax the caller into speaking; just replace the handset gently if no one speaks.

5. Never provide any details about yourself or your family.

Tell your children not to give any information to strangers and that if anyone asks for their parents when they aren't at home, they should say that "you're unable to come to the telephone at the moment" (e.g. in the bath/shower), and **not** to tell callers that you aren't at home. If you need assistance in dealing with malicious calls or if you're receiving persistent malicious calls, ring BT (☎ 0800-666 700), this is a recorded advice line. If you have a phone suitable for Caller Display service this allows you to identify callers before answering the telephone. You can elect to use the Choose to Refuse or Anonymous Call Reject services and also speak to an adviser (☎ 0800-661 441); BT will eventually arrange for your calls to be intercepted. As a final resort, you can obtain a new unlisted number. BT publishes a leaflet entitled *Malicious Calls*. One rather drastic way to deter malicious callers is to blow a loud, piercing whistle down the telephone, but BT aren't very keen on this!

It's an offence to make malicious or nuisance calls in the UK (telephone salespeople please note). If you want to reduce the number of unsolicited sales calls you receive (who doesn't?), you can register with the Telephone Preference Service/TPS (☎ 0845-070 0707, 🖳 www.tpsonline.org.uk). After you register with the TPS, none of the Direct Marketing Association's 500 members should contact you, although this does not preclude calls from non-members or market research companies.

EMERGENCY NUMBERS

There's only one national emergency number in the UK, the 999 service, which is for police, fire and ambulance emergencies, plus coastguard, cave and mountain rescue services. Emergency 999 calls are free from all telephones, including payphones. When you ☎ 999, the operator asks you which emergency service you require ("Emergency, which service please?") and you are immediately switched through to that service. You must state clearly your name, location and give a brief description of the emergency. Some payphones are reserved for emergency 999 calls only, shown by a flashing message.

In addition to providing an emergency transport service for those in urgent need of medical attention, the ambulance service also deals with the victims of accidents such as drowning, asphyxiation (lack of oxygen), choking, electrocution, serious burns and hanging. In addition to attending fires, the fire service attends traffic accidents, natural and man-made disasters, and extricates people who are trapped (e.g. in a building). The fire brigade may charge for special services, such as supporting a house that's in danger of collapse as a result of subsidence (or rescuing a cat from a tree!). A new emergency code, 112, was introduced throughout the EU in 1992 to help foreign visitors and is used in addition to the existing 999 number.

The Samaritans provide a confidential counselling service in times of personal crisis. Local numbers are available in section one, Useful Information, of your telephone directory, along with numbers for other organisations offering free help and advice such as Alcoholics Anonymous. Local hospitals are also listed here. See also **Emergencies** on page 306 and **Counselling** on page 323.

SERVICE NUMBERS

The following BT service numbers are listed in Section Two of directories, where other local useful numbers are also given, and can be called from anywhere in the UK (except where noted):

Number	Service
0800-400 400	Business Sales and Customer Service (as 'Residential Customer Service' below)
100	Operator Services*
118 500	BT Inland Directory Enquiries
118 505	BT International Directory Enquiries
0800-800 150	Residential Customer Service (including sales, accounting, enquiries and general complaints)
0800-800 151	Residential Fault Reporting
0800-800 154	Business Fault Reporting
155	International Operator (non IDD, person-to-person, reverse charge and credit card calls)
0808-152 5252	Telemessages

* The operator makes calls which cannot be made by direct dialling, including those via BT's maritime services to people on board ships, and assists you if you're having difficulty making a call.

8.

TELEVISION & RADIO

Most British homes have at least one television (TV), over 60 per cent have more than one (25 per cent have three or more) and over 80 per cent have a video recorder – not simply to watch video tapes, but also to record their favourite TV programmes. Many additionally have CD/DVD players, and radio is also popular, with a wide variety of stations, including a plethora of independent broadcasters.

TELEVISION

Watching TV, referred to colloquially as the 'box' or 'telly', is the UK's most popular pastime (or a national epidemic, depending on how you view it). This antisocial disease has all but replaced all those boring things such as talking, listening to music, exercise, visiting people (particularly people without TVs), or generally doing anything which might exercise the brain or the body.

Many families have a TV in every room except the toilet, particularly in children's rooms where TVs (and computers) serve as tranquillisers for overactive kids. In households where TV reigns supreme, the box is far more influential with children than parents. Although television may well have killed off conversation, in deprived households with only one TV it does wonders for arguments (about which programme to watch). The average Briton is glued to the box for over 15 hours a week or 33 (24 hour) days a year (surprisingly, homes with cable and satellite TV watch little more than those receiving terrestrial TV only). Interactive TV services are the latest offering for couch potatoes and include home shopping and banking, educational programmes, computer games, and videos on demand.

While still producing a surfeit of nonsense (e.g. inane quiz shows and soaps; otherwise known as 'tabloid' TV) to cater for the TV junkies, British TV (and British-produced TV programmes) is generally recognised as the best, or least worst, in the world. British TV companies produce many excellent programmes, including documentaries, wildlife and nature programmes, serialised adaptations of novels, TV films, situation comedies, and variety shows, which are sold throughout the world. Other excellent programmes include current affairs, serious music, chat shows and sports coverage. Some three-quarters of Britons get their main information about the world from TV news, although the presentation is becoming more showbiz (newscasters are stars in their own right). Explicit sex is becoming commonplace and has led the Broadcasting Standards Council to try to ban gratuitous sex scenes.

Despite the generally high quality of TV programmes, the UK still has an active Campaign for Quality Television to keep TV companies on their toes. Competition between the British Broadcasting Corporation (BBC) (💻 www.bbc.co.uk), Independent Television (ITV) (💻 www.itv.com) and satellite TV companies is keen (particularly regarding sports coverage), although the UK experiences nothing like the US's ratings 'wars'.

BBC television has been broadcasting regularly since 1936 and introduced a second station (BBC Two) in 1964. The first regular commercial programmes began in London in 1955, followed by two more national commercial TV stations, Channel 4 (💻 www.channel4.com) in 1982 and Channel 5 (💻 www.five.tv) in 1997. In addition to the five national TV channels, there are also many cable and satellite channels, both of which have taken off in a big way in the last few years. Satellite TV is the only choice for those who want to watch foreign language TV.

Standards

The standards for TV reception in the UK aren't the same as in many other countries. TVs and video recorders manufactured for use in the US (NTSC Standard) and continental Europe won't function in the UK because of different transmission standards. Most European countries use the PAL B/G standard, except for France, which has its own standard called SECAM.

If you bring a TV to the UK from the US or the continent, you get a picture or sound, **but not both**. A TV can be converted to work in the UK, but it's usually not worth the trouble and expense. If you want a TV and video recorder (VCR) that works in the UK and other European countries (including France) and/or the US, you must buy a multi-standard model. Some multi-standard TVs also handle the North American NTSC standard and have an NTSC jack plug connection allowing you to play US videos.

Video

VCRs manufactured for non-British markets are unusable in the UK and recordings made for the North American market are unplayable in the UK (although NTSC standard video machines and TVs are useful for playing NTSC standard videos and video games in the UK). Video recordings made on a PAL VCR can usually be played back on any other PAL VCR with sound and vision. Most modern VCRs have a feature called 'Videoplus +' which allows you to record programmes simply by entering a 'Video Pluscode' (shown in most programme listings).

Stations

In most city and rural areas, five TV stations can be received: BBC One, BBC Two, ITV (independent television), Channel 4 and Channel 5. In areas where two ITV stations overlap, viewers can usually receive both stations. Under the Broadcasting Act 1990, the ITV channel was officially renamed Channel 3, thus allowing all channels to be referred to by a number. The BBC channels carry no advertising and are publicly funded through an annual TV Licence (see page 188), sales of *Radio Times*, and the trading activities of BBC Enterprises. With the exception of Wales, where many Welsh-language programmes are broadcast, and regional news broadcasts, BBC programmes are the same throughout the UK. All terrestrial TV stations broadcast for 24 hours a day, as do many satellite and cable stations. Programmes on BBC begin at odd times (e.g. 6.20, 8.05), depending on the length of programmes, as they aren't subject to commercial breaks. ITV programmes usually start on the hour or half hour. The terrestrial TV audience in the UK is fairly evenly divided between BBC and ITV.

BBC One

BBC One shows mainly general interest programmes, including light entertainment, a breakfast news and chat show, children's programmes, national and local news with weather reports, films (without commercial breaks; therefore ideal for video copies), popular series (including American and Australian soaps and other imported programmes), chat shows, current affairs, documentaries, comedy, plays, and live and recorded sport. BBC One has lost ground to ITV in recent years, particularly in news coverage, although its current affairs programmes, such as *Panorama*, are still among the best.

BBC Two

BBC Two caters more for minority interests and the intellectual or discriminating viewer, although it also shows general interest programmes. These include the Open University and schools programmes in the early mornings, documentaries, international films, travel and wildlife programmes, serious drama, foreign films with subtitles, art and history, rock and classical music (e.g. the BBC Proms concerts), live sports and hobby-oriented programmes (e.g. cookery and gardening). In *Newsnight*, BBC Two has the best daily in-depth current affairs and news programme. The launch of digital TV in 1998 heralded the introduction of three new digital BBC channels: BBC News 24, BBC Choice (the first new general channel from the BBC for 35 years) and BBC Learning (see also ▨ www.bbc.co.uk).

ITV

ITV companies are financed by the proceeds from advertising. There are 14 regional ITV companies covering the whole of the UK, as shown in the table below:

Name	Area
Anglia	East of England
Border	Northern England, Southern Scotland & Isle of Man
Carlton	London Weekdays
Central	East, West & South Midlands
Channel (CTV)	Channel Islands

Grampian	North of Scotland
Granada	North-west England
HTV West	Wales & West of England
LWT	London Weekend
Meridian	South & South-east England
Scottish	Central Scotland
Ulster	Northern Ireland
Westcountry	South-west England
Yorkshire-Tyne Tees	Yorkshire & North-east England

From 1st January 1993, the licence holders for each ITV region have been decided by a controversial sealed-bid system, the contract going to the highest bidder. Licences run for ten years.

In addition to the above stations, there's GMTV (💻 www.gm.tv), which is broadcast nationally on all ITV stations from 6 to 9.25am and includes news, information, current affairs and light entertainment. All programmes are in English with the exception of the occasional foreign film with subtitles, some Welsh language programmes on HTV (💻 www.htvwales.co.uk), and a few Gaelic broadcasts in Scotland. The ITV companies mostly produce their own programmes, but also buy them from abroad, particularly the ubiquitous American cops and robbers series and soaps.

ITV programmes are generally similar to those shown on BBC One and consist mainly of general interest and sports programmes, but with more soaps and game shows. Given a choice, most people prefer to watch programmes without commercial breaks. However, although they can be obtrusive, most commercials are shown between programmes and breaks aren't anything like as frequent as in the US. Watching a film can be a trial, but breaks are useful for toilet needs and making a cup of tea. ITV produces some excellent news and current affairs programmes, including *World in Action* and many superb documentaries and drama series. The ITV early news slot has moved from 5.40 to 6.30pm and been increased from 20 to 30 minutes.

Channel 4

Channel 4 started broadcasting in 1982 as an alternative commercial channel, catering primarily to minority interests and showing educational programmes. According to the terms of its charter, Channel 4 programmes must be complementary to those on ITV. It has a statutory duty to provide information, education and entertainment, and should cater for tastes and interests not normally provided on ITV. Programmes are similar to BBC Two (although not as highbrow) and include many excellent documentaries, travel programmes, art and music, foreign films and series with subtitles, current affairs, in-depth evening news (7pm), general interest series (often repeats of older series), and minority sports, some of which (such as American football) have established a large cult following. It has courted controversy in recent years by showing soft porn. In Wales, Channel 4 is the Welsh language channel, Wales S4C (Sianel 4 Cymru), which shows a majority of Welsh language programmes during peak viewing hours (6.30 to 10pm).

Channel 5

Channel 5, a new terrestrial general entertainment channel, went on air on 1st January 1997. It was initially available in around 75 per cent of homes, one in four of which required an extra aerial. Areas that don't receive Channel 5 include most of the south-east and south-west, parts of East Anglia and much of Northern Ireland, Scotland and Wales, because nearby existing TV transmitters would interfere with Channel 5 signals (although Channel 5 is available via cable and satellite).

Quality

The quality of programmes on British TV varies from terrible to excellent. The competition to buy foreign (e.g. American and Australian) programmes and exclusive rights to sporting events is fierce, particularly with the increased competition from satellite TV. This could result in TV companies producing more of their own programmes which, apart from being superior to much of the imported trivia, are also a lucrative export earner. The TV companies produce around 75 per cent of all programmes, a quarter of which are made by independent producers.

Complaints

If you wish to berate or praise the TV companies, they all welcome feedback from their viewers (particularly compliments). Letters to BBC Television should be addressed to BBC Information, PO Box 1922, Glasgow G2 3WT (☎ 0870-010 0222). You will find the address of your local ITV company in your telephone directory. If you have a complaint about a programme or advertisement, contact the Office of Communications (Ofcom), Riverside House, 2a Southwark Bridge Road, London SE1 9HA (☎ 0845-456 3000, 🖥 www.ofcom.org.uk) which is responsible for licensing and regulating all commercial (non-BBC) TV services in the UK including ITV, Channel 4, Channel 5, teletext, cable and satellite.

Television Sets

The price of a TV varies considerably depending on its make, screen size, features and, not least, the retailer (shop around). A 20in (51cm) colour TV with an FST (flatter squarer tube) screen, stereo sound (useful for stereo broadcasts, including satellite TV), remote control, Fastext and a SCART socket (a standard plug for making connections between televisions, videos and satellite receivers), costs between £250 and £350. A basic portable colour TV can be purchased for as little as £50, while a state-of-the-art 23in (59cm) colour TV with Fastext and Nicam digital stereo sound, costs from around £400. Nicam is a high quality, digital stereo sound system, developed by the BBC, ITV and the TV/video manufacturers and provides a dramatic improvement in TV sound, comparable to compact disc. Not everyone can receive Nicam sound, so check the availability in your area before buying a Nicam TV.

Widescreen digital TVs (with a built-in digital decoder) vary considerably in quality and cost from around £500, but will inevitably become cheaper as more models become available and demand increases. TV addicts can add Dolby surround sound (with a Dolby pro logic amp with a built-in decoder and separate speakers) and create cinema sound effects. If money is no object, you can buy a TV with a flat or plasma screen costing from around £1,000 to £2,000 for the smallest models. Other options include LaserDisc and Video CD (compact disc) systems, although these are expensive when compared with VHS video and a waste of money for most people. If you have a TV, VCR and a satellite receiver, you can buy a special remote control that operates all three.

Teletext

When buying a TV in the UK, you will find it advantageous to buy one with teletext (or 'fastext', an improved version), which, apart from allowing you to display forthcoming programme listings, also provides a wealth of useful and interesting information including news, weather, sport, travel, financial, consumer and entertainment. Two teletext information services are available: Ceefax (BBC) and Teletext (ITV). Both systems also provide subtitles for selected programmes for people with hearing problems. These are indicated in programme listings (usually by a star). Satellite stations also provide teletext services.

Buying Second-hand Televisions

There's an active market in second-hand TVs and videos (and most other things) in the UK so, should you wish to sell your old telly to buy one with all the latest bells and whistles (or because you're leaving the UK), you will have no problem. Second-hand colour TVs can be bought from retailers, rental companies and through advertisements in local newspapers from as little as £50. **Dealers are best avoided, as their prices are usually ridiculous.** Be wary of retailers who offer a derisory £50 for your old TV in part exchange for a new one. Not only is your old colour TV likely to be worth more than £50, the price of the new TV may also be uncompetitive.

Rental

TV rental is fairly common in the UK and is mostly offered by specialist national rental companies, e.g. Boxclever (Technology House, Ampthill Road, Bedford, MK42 9QQ, ☎ 0870-554 6563, 💻 www.boxclever.co.uk), although some local TV and radio shops also rent TVs. It's always cheaper to buy than rent a TV or video over a long period. Some people are tempted to rent by the ever-changing technology, although rental TVs are rarely the latest models and the minimum rental period is usually 12 or 18 months. Renting a TV is a habit carried over from the '50s and '60s, when few people could afford to buy a TV outright. **Today, renting hardly ever makes economic sense.**

Licence

An annual TV licence (£135.50 for colour, £45.50 for black and white) is required by all TV owners in the UK. Registered blind people are generously offered a reduction of 50% on production of the local authority's certificate for the blind. The fee is linked to the cost of living and is subject to a three-year agreement under the BBC's charter.

TV licences must be renewed annually and can be purchased from post offices or from TV Licensing, Bristol BS98 1TL (☎ 0870-241 6468, 💻 www.tvlicensing. co.uk). A Television Licence application form must be completed. The licence fee can also be paid by direct debit from a bank or building society account in one payment or in quarterly or monthly payments (which include a small premium). The post office operates a TV licence saving scheme, through the purchase of £1 TV licence stamps. If you're leaving the UK, you can obtain a refund on any unexpired three-month period of a TV licence by applying in writing to Customer Services at the address above.

A licence is required by anyone who has a TV or video (or has one installed), that can receive or record BBC, ITV, Channel 4, Channel 5, S4C, satellite or cable TV programmes. If a TV is used for video playback, as a computer monitor or to receive satellite TV only, the licence fee isn't payable. However, your TV must be incapable of receiving BBC and ITV channels, which can be done only by permanently disconnecting your TV aerial and tuner circuitry.

The licence fee covers any number of TVs (black & white or colour depending on the fee paid) owned by the licence holder, members of his family and domestic staff, at his main home. **The licence fee also covers a TV at a second home in the UK, provided that both TVs aren't used simultaneously.** If you've paid for a licence for a TV in a second home, you're entitled to a full refund.

Non-payment

Registration must be made within 14 days of installing a TV. The BBC use detector vans to check which homes have TVs and whether they've paid their licence fee. The BBC also runs advertisements to shame/frighten people into buying a licence. You can be heavily fined (up to £1,000) for not having a TV licence and, if you don't pay the fine, you can be imprisoned. Hundreds of people are fined or imprisoned each year for licence-fee default. An estimated 10 per cent of people in the mainland UK don't buy a licence. Shops selling or renting TVs must forward customers' names and addresses to the authorities.

Television Guides

TV programmes (terrestrial, satellite and cable) are listed in daily newspapers (Saturday newspapers also include Sunday programmes) and weekly guides such as *Radio Times* (published by the BBC), *TV Times*, *What's On TV* and *TV Plus*. Free TV guides are also provided with most daily and weekly newspapers. Regional ITV programme variations are shown in national newspapers, although not all newspapers list all satellite and cable programmes. Satellite television (see page 189) programme listings are published in yet more guides, including the *Satellite Times* and *Satellite TV*. Programmes can also be displayed via teletext. BBC radio programmes can also be displayed via BBC teletext.

Satellite Television

Although many people complain endlessly about the poor quality of TV in their home countries, many find they cannot live without it when abroad. Fortunately, the advent of satellite TV in the last decade means that most people can enjoy TV programmes in English and a variety of other languages almost anywhere in the world. The UK is well served by satellite TV, where a number of satellites are positioned carrying over 200 stations broadcasting in a variety of languages.

Astra

Although it wasn't the first in Europe (which was Eutelsat), the European satellite revolution really took off with the launch of the Astra 1A satellite in 1988. TV addicts are offered a huge choice of English and foreign-language stations, which can be received throughout most of the UK with a 60cm (or smaller) dish and receiver. The number of available channels is now 64 (or over 200 with digital TV). An added bonus is the availability of radio stations via satellite, including all the national BBC stations (see **Satellite Radio** on page 195).

Among the many English-language stations available on Astra are Sky One, Moviemax, Sky Premier, Sky Cinema, Film Four, Sky News, Sky Sports (including subscription events), UK Gold, Channel 5, Granada Plus, TNT, Eurosport, CNN, CNBC Europe, UK Style, UK Horizons, The Disney Channel and the Discovery Channel. Other stations broadcast in Dutch, German, Japanese, Swedish and various Indian languages. The signal from many stations is scrambled (the decoder is usually built into the receiver) and viewers must pay a monthly subscription fee to receive programmes. You can buy pirate decoders for some channels. The best served by clear (unscrambled) stations are Germans (most German stations on Astra are clear).

BSkyB Television

You must buy a Videocrypt decoder, an integral part of receivers, and pay a monthly subscription to receive all BSkyB (🖳 www.sky.com) or Sky stations except Sky News (which isn't scrambled). Various packages are available costing from around £12.50 to £38 a month for the premium package offering all movie channels plus Sky Sports. Subscribers are sent a coded 'smart' card (similar to a credit card), which must be inserted in the decoder to switch it on (cards are frequently changed to thwart counterfeiters). Sky subscribers receive a free copy of *Sky TV Guide* monthly.

Eutelsat

Eutelsat (owned by a consortium of national telephone operators) was the first company to introduce satellite TV to Europe (in 1983) and now runs a fleet of communications satellites carrying TV stations to over 50 million homes. Until 1995, they had broadcast primarily advertising-based, clear-access cable channels. Following the launch in March 1995 of their Hot Bird satellite, Eutelsat hoped to become a major competitor to Astra, although its channels are mostly non-English. The English-language stations on Eutelsat include Eurosport, Euronews, BBC World and CNBC Europe. Other channels broadcast in Arabic, French, German, Hungarian, Italian, Polish, Portuguese, Spanish and Turkish.

BBC Worldwide Television

Although intended for an international audience, it's possible to receive the BBC Worldwide TV stations, BBC Prime (general entertainment) and BBC World (24-hour news and information) in the UK via the Intelsat VI and Eutelsat II F1 satellites, respectively. BBC Prime is encrypted and requires a D2 Mac decoder and a smartcard (£75 plus VAT per year). BBC World is clear (unencrypted) and is financed by advertising revenue.

For more information and a programming guide, contact BBC Worldwide Television, Woodlands, 80 Wood Lane, London W12 0TT, UK (☎ 020-8433 2000, 🖳 www.bbcworldwide.com). The BBC publishes a monthly magazine, *BBC On Air*, giving comprehensive information about BBC Worldwide Television programmes. A programme guide is also listed on the internet (🖳 www.bbc.co.uk/schedules) and BBC World and BBC Prime have their own websites (🖳 www.bbcworld.com and www.bbcprime.com). When accessing them, you must enter the name of the country, so that the schedules appear in local time.

Equipment

A satellite receiver has a built-in Videocrypt decoder (and others such as Eurocrypt, Syster or SECAM, as required) and is capable of receiving satellite stereo radio. In addition to the standard dish provided free by BSkyB, you can buy a larger motorised dish (shop around as prices vary enormously) of up to 1.5m in size, which enables you to receive hundreds of stations in a multitude of languages from around the world. If you wish to receive satellite TV on two or more TVs, you can buy a system with two or more receptors. **When buying a system, ensure that it can receive programmes from all existing and planned satellites.**

Location

To receive programmes from any satellite, there must be no obstacles between the satellite and your dish, i.e. no trees, buildings or mountains (or anything else) must obstruct the signal, so check before renting or buying a home. Under current planning regulations, most householders are permitted to erect one satellite dish aerial without planning permission, provided it's no bigger than 90cm. Dishes can be mounted in a variety of unobtrusive positions. You may need planning permission to install a satellite dish or antenna on a house depending on its size, height, position, the location of the property, and whether or not a dish is already installed. If in doubt, contact your local council's planning department. Those living in conservation areas and in listed buildings are banned from erecting aerials on buildings (or may be required to mount them so they cannot be seen from public roads). In strong signal areas, it's possible to mount a dish indoors, provided there's a direct line to the satellite through a window or skylight.

Programme Guides

Many satellite stations provide teletext information, which includes programme schedules. Satellite programmes are also listed in most national daily newspapers, general TV magazines and satellite TV magazines such as *What Satellite and Digital TV*, available from newsagents or on subscription. The annual *World Radio and TV Handbook* by David G. Bobbett (Watson-Guptil Publications) contains information about and frequencies of all radio and TV stations worldwide.

Digital Television

Digital TV was launched on 1st October 1998 by BSkyB in the UK. The benefits include a superior picture, better (CD quality) sound, widescreen cinema format and access to many more stations. Digital TV also allows for interactive services, digital text and interactive TV.

To watch digital satellite TV, you require a Digibox and a (digital) Minidish, which is available free to UK subscribers (installation isn't included). Customers must sign up for a 12-month subscription and agree to have the connection via a phone line (to allow for future interactive services). **This occasionally causes problems with your telephone, resulting in massive phone bills – naturally BSkyB deny any responsibility.** In addition to the usual analogue channels (see above), digital TV offers BBC One, BBC Two, ITV, ITV2 and Channel 4, plus many other channels (a total of 200, with up to 500 possible). All major terrestrial stations are now available in digital and analogue; however, in order to receive digital terrestrial TV you need a separate decoder or an integrated TV (with a built-in decoder).

Cable Television

Cable television in the UK was originally confined to areas of poor reception (e.g. from natural geographical features or high-rise buildings) or where external aerials weren't permitted. However, there has been an explosion in cable TV in the last decade and it's the fastest-growing sector of the TV industry. Over ten million homes can now receive cable TV and there are around three million subscribers (although the UK still has a long way to go to match European countries such as Belgium, the Netherlands and Switzerland, where 90 per cent of the populations have access to cable TV).

The new broadband cable systems can carry up to 100 channels, including terrestrial broadcasts, satellite TV, channels delivered by videotape and local services. Most cable TV companies provide all the stations offered by satellite TV plus a few others (possibly including local cable TV companies such as Channel One in London). There's an initial connection fee of around £25 for cable TV, and a subscription of around £10 a month for the basic package, up to £35 a month for a package including all the premium channels. One of the main advantages is that most cable companies offer inexpensive telephone services, possibly including free local off-peak calls, which can save you enough on your telephone bill to pay for your cable TV. Digital TV is widely available and offers pay-per-view broadcasts, movies on demand, home shopping and access to the internet.

Cable TV is controlled by Ofcom (see page 186).

Video & DVD

There are numerous video and DVD hire shops in the UK, which reached (or exceeded) saturation point in the early '90s. The British video market is the second largest in the world after the US. The UK has the highest ownership of VCRs in Europe (around three-quarters of households). Many video shops are open until 8pm or even 10pm, seven days a week. To hire a video, you must usually be a member, for which shops require proof of your address and verification of your signature. If you're under 18, a parent is required to stand as a guarantor. Some video shops have a children's membership scheme with special deals for kids and cheap rental rates

▲ Cheltenham Spa, Gloucestershire
© Survival Books

▲ Bodiam Castle, E. Sussex
© Visit Britain (www.visitbritain.org)

▼ Burlington Arcade, Piccadilly, London
© Visit Britain (www.visitbritain.org)

© Survival Books

▼ Crummock Water, Cumbria
© Visit Britain (www.visitbritain.org)

▲ Bath, Avon
© Survival Books

◄ Winsford, Somerset
© Visit Britain (www.visitbritain.org)

▲ Edinburgh, Scotland
© Visit Britain (www.visitbritain.org)

▼ Bluegrass Festival, Tyrone, N. Ireland
© Visit Britain (www.visitbritain.org)

◄ Ben Nevis, Highlands, Scotland
© Visit Britain (www.visitbritain.org)

▲ Dunstanburgh Castle, Northumberland
© Visit Britain (www.visitbritain.org)

▲ Harpist, Harlech Castle, Wales
© Visit Britain (www.visitbritain.org)

▲ Farm, Lewes, East Sussex
© Visit Britain (www.visitbritain.org)

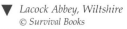

▼ Lacock Abbey, Wiltshire
© Survival Books

▲ Notting Hill Carnival, London
© Visit Britain (www.visitbritain.org)

Whitby, N. Yorkshire
© Visit Britain (www.visitbritain.org)

Guardsmen, London
© Visit Britain
(www.visitbritain.org)

Warwick Castle, Warwickshire
© Visit Britain (www.visitbritain.org)

Haver Castle Maze, Kent
© Visit Britain (www.visitbritain.org)

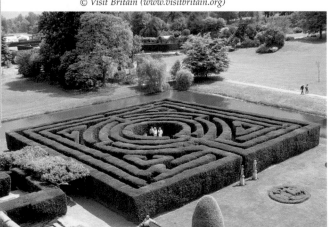

Palace of Westminster,
London. © Visit Britain
(www.visitbritain.org)

for children's films. Daily hire charges range from around £1.50 to £4, depending on the film rating (new top ten films are the most expensive) and the shop. There's usually no extra charge for weekend hire (e.g. Saturday to Monday), when a shop doesn't open on a Sunday.

Members are issued with a membership card, which must be shown when hiring videos. If you're late returning a film, you're charged an extra day's rental for each day overdue. If you lose or damage a film, you must usually pay for a replacement at retail price. Insurance against loss or damage is sometimes available for a one-time payment, e.g. £5. Videos can also be hired from public libraries, where the cost is usually 50p or £1 a night for films or fiction and £1 a week for non-fiction. Most video and DVD shops also sell second-hand films at reduced prices. Newly released videos usually cost around £15.99 and DVDs around £24.99 with similar proportionate differentials for older and cheaper subjects. HMV, Virgin and Woolworths have a wide selection of the latest videos and DVDs for sale and major supermarkets also stock a good range. Videos and DVDs can be bought, often at discount, by mail order from Mr Benson (🖳 www.bensons-world.co.uk) and Amazon (🖳 www.amazon.co.uk).

RADIO

Radio reception in the UK is excellent in most parts of the country, including stereo reception, which is clear in all but the most mountainous areas (although FM reception isn't always good in cars). The radio audience in the UK is almost equally split between the British Broadcasting Corporation (BBC) and commercial radio stations (although the BBC has been losing listeners to commercial stations at an alarming rate in recent years). Community and ethnic radio is also popular in many areas and a number of universities and colleges operate their own radio stations. In addition to the FM or VHF stereo wave band, medium wave (MW or AM) and long wave (LW) bands are in wide use throughout the UK. Shortwave (SW) band is useful for receiving foreign radio stations.

BBC

The BBC operates five network radio stations with easy to remember (if unimaginative) names: BBC Radio 1 (contemporary music, FM 97.6-99.8), BBC Radio 2 (entertainment, culture and music, FM 88-90.2), BBC Radio 3 (classical music, jazz, drama, discussions, documentaries and poetry, FM 90.2-92.4), BBC Radio 4 (conversation, comedy, drama, documentaries, magazine programmes, news, FM 92.4-94.6, LW 198), BBC Radio 5 Live (news, current affairs and sports, MW 693, 909) and around 40 English BBC local radio stations with some 10 million listeners. There's no advertising on BBC radio stations, although it's the main source of income for commercial radio stations. BBC radio is financed by the government and the revenue from TV licence fees, as no radio licence is necessary.

BBC radio programmes are published in national newspapers and Radios 1, 3 and 4 are broadcast in stereo on FM and in mono on AM. BBC radio programmes are also listed on the BBC TV teletext information service. If you have any difficulty locating the BBC's stations, send an SAE to the BBC Information, PO Box 1922, Glasgow G2 3WT (☎ 08700-100 222).

World Service

The BBC World Service broadcasts worldwide, in English and around 37 other languages, for over 770 hours a week. Although mainly intended for listeners outside the UK, the BBC World Service can be received loud and clear in most parts of England. The BBC World Service is the most famous and highly respected international radio service in the world, with regular listeners estimated at 120 million. The main aims are to provide unbiased news, project British opinion, and reflect British life, culture, and developments in science and industry.

News bulletins, current affairs, political commentaries and topical magazine programmes form the bulk of its output, supported by a comprehensive sports service, music, drama and general entertainment. Broadcasts in English (24 hours a day) are supplemented by programmes of special interest to Africa, Southern Asia and the Falklands Islands at peak listening times. For programme and frequency information write to BBC World Service, Bush House, Strand, London WC2B 4PH (☎ 020-7240 3456, 💻 www.bbc.co.uk/worldservice). General enquiries concerning BBC radio should be addressed to BBC Radio, Broadcasting House, Portland Place, London W1A 1AA (☎ 020-7580 4468, 💻 www.bbc.co.uk/radio). A BBC monthly magazine, *London Calling*, is available on subscription.

Commercial Radio

Commercial radio is hugely popular in the UK and is the UK's fastest-growing entertainment medium. Most cities can now receive at least five commercial stations (over ten in London). However, there are still only some 200 commercial radio stations in the whole of the UK, compared with around 1,000 in France and Italy, and over 9,000 in the US. The British are avid radio listeners and over 90 per cent of the population listen to the radio for 20 hours or more each week. Commercial radio is reported to have some 36 million listeners or almost 80 per cent of adults.

Stations vary from large national stations with vast budgets and millions of listeners to tiny local stations run by volunteers with just a few thousand listeners. Stations provide a comprehensive service of local news and information, music and other entertainment, education, consumer advice, traffic information and local events, and provide listeners with the chance to air their views, often through phone-in programmes. Advertising on commercial radio is limited to nine minutes an hour, but is usually less. The UK has three national commercial radio stations: Classic FM (💻 www.classicfm.com, FM 100-101.9) Virgin Radio (💻 www.virginradio.co.uk, popular music, FM 105.8, MW 1197, 1215) and Talk Sport (💻 www.talksport.net,

MW 1053, 1089), the UK's 24-hour, national, sports-talk commercial station. The UK's most popular commercial radio station is Capital Radio (💻 www.capitalradio group.com), which includes Capital FM (💻 www.capitalfm.com), Capital Gold (💻 www.capitalgold.com) and other regional radio stations, and is the world's largest metropolitan radio station with over 3 million listeners.

Digital Radio

Digital radio offers better sound quality, less interference and no frequency changing. It's available in around 90 per cent of the UK, although you need a special digital radio to receive it (it can also be received on a PC with a special digital card). All national BBC radio stations are broadcast digitally and new BBC digital radio programmes include BBC Radio 5 Live Sports Plus, BBC Parliament and BBC Xtra. Commercial radio has also gone digital with seven new national stations available only on digital. Digital One was awarded the franchise to launch a range of commercial radio channels and Classic FM (💻 www.classicfm.com), Virgin Radio and Talk Radio all broadcast digitally.

Satellite Radio

If you have satellite TV, you can also receive radio stations via your satellite link. For example, BBC Radio 1, 2, 3, 4 and 5, BBC World Service, Sky Radio, Virgin 1215 and many foreign (i.e. non-English) stations are broadcast via the Astra satellites. Satellite radio stations are listed in British satellite TV magazines such as *Satellite Times*. If you're interested in receiving radio stations from further afield, you should obtain a copy of the *World Radio TV Handbook* edited by Nicholas Hardyman (WRTH Publications).

9.

EDUCATION

British schools have a mixed reputation: while the quality of state education varies widely, universities and other higher education institutions have an excellent international reputation and educate tens of thousands of foreign students a year from all corners of the globe. Full-time education is compulsory in the UK for all children between the ages of 5 (4 in Northern Ireland) and 16, including the children of foreign nationals permanently or temporarily resident in the UK for a year or longer. No fees are payable in state schools, which are attended by over 90 per cent of pupils. The rest attend one of the 3200 private fee-paying schools, which include American, international and foreign schools. Some 80 per cent of pupils stay on at school after the age of 16 or go on to higher education. However, for those children entering secondary education in September 2007, the new compulsory age for schooling will mean they have to either be in school or on an approved training scheme until they are 18. From 2013, full-time paid employment will be against the law for under-18's.

Most state schools (primary and secondary) are co-educational (mixed) day schools, with the exception of a few secondary schools that accept boarders. Private schools include day and boarding schools and are mostly single-sex, although an increasing number of junior and some senior schools are co-educational. Admission to a state school for foreign children is dependent on the type and duration of the residence permit (see **Chapter 3**) granted to their parents. Your choice of state and private schools varies considerably depending on where you live.

One of the most important decisions facing newcomers to the UK is whether to send their children to a state or private school. In some areas, state schools equal the best private schools, while in others (particularly in neglected inner city areas) they lack resources and may achieve poor results. In general, girls achieve much better results than boys and immigrant children (e.g. from Asia) often do particularly well. The UK's education system has had a bad press in recent years and, according to many surveys, is falling behind the leading countries, particularly in mathematics (maths) and science. There's a dearth of vocational education and training in the UK, and general educational standards are inferior to those in many advanced industrial nations (e.g. Australia, Canada, Ireland, Japan and New Zealand). In 2006, the UK was ranked 12th in reading skills, 11th in Science and 19th in Maths out of 43 countries in the Organisation for Economic Co-operation and Development's (OECD) Programme for International Student Assessment (PISA) survey into the quality of primary and secondary education.

Many parents prefer to send their children to a private school, often making financial sacrifices to do so. Not so many years ago, private education was the preserve of the children of the nobility and the rich, although today around half of the parents of private school pupils were themselves educated at state schools. There has been a sharp increase in the number of children attending private schools in recent years, owing to the increasing affluence of the middle classes.

There's no legal obligation for parents in the UK to educate their children at school and they may educate them themselves or employ private tutors. Parents educating their children at home don't require a teaching qualification, although they must satisfy the local education authority that a child is receiving full-time education appropriate for his or her age, abilities and aptitudes (they check and may test your child).

FURTHER INFORMATION

The weekly *Times Educational Supplement* and *Scottish Education Supplement* (available from newsagents) contain up-to-the-minute news and opinion about education and schools in the UK, including management, governors, research and teaching posts. There are numerous books for parents faced with choosing a suitable state or private school, including the *Daily Telegraph Schools Guide* and the *Good Schools Guide*, both by John Clare. You can also consult an independent adviser such as Gabbitas Educational Consultants Ltd (126-130 Regent Street, London W1R 6EE, ☎ 020-7734 0161, ⌨ www.gabbitas.co.uk), who can provide advice and information on any aspect of education in the UK. There are many education-related internet sites, including Education UK (⌨ www.educationuk.org), the BBC (⌨ www.bbc.co.uk/learning) and Edubase (⌨ www.edubase.gov.uk). The Department for Education and Skills (DFES) has a very comprehensive website covering learning and career queries (⌨ www.dfes-uk.gov.uk).

An invaluable organisation for overseas students is the UK Council for Overseas Student Affairs (UKCOSA, 9-17 St Alban's Place, London N1 0NX, ☎ 020-7288 4330, ⌨ www.ukcosa.org.uk), which is a registered charity established in 1968 to promote the interests and meet the needs of overseas students in the UK and those working with them as teachers, advisors or in other capacities. The British Council (which has offices in around 80 countries) provides foreign students with information concerning all aspects of education in the UK.

In addition to a detailed look at state and private education, this chapter also contains information about higher and further education and language schools.

STATE OR PRIVATE SCHOOL?

If you're able to choose between state and private education, the following checklist will help you decide:

- How long are you planning to stay in the UK? If you're uncertain, then it's probably better to assume a long stay. Because of language and other integration problems, enrolling a child in a British school with a British syllabus (state or private) is only advisable for a minimum of one year, particularly for teenage children.

- The area in which you choose to live may affect your choice of local school(s). Although it's unnecessary to send your children to the state school nearest your home, you may have difficulty obtaining admission to a state school if you don't live within its catchment area.

- Do you know where you're going after the UK? This may be an important consideration with regard to your children's schooling. How old are your children and what age will they be when you plan to leave the UK? What future plans do you have for their education and in which country?

- What age are your children and how will they fit into a private school or the British state school system? The younger they are, the easier it is to place them in a suitable school.

- If your children aren't English-speaking, how do they view the thought of studying in English? Is teaching available in the UK in their mother tongue?

- Will your children require your help with their studies? Will you be able to help them, particularly with the English language?

- What are the school hours? What are the school holiday periods? How do the school hours and holidays influence your (and your spouse's) work and leisure activities?

- Is religion an important consideration in your choice of school? In British state schools, religion is usually taught as a compulsory subject. Parents may, however, request permission for their children not to attend. Some voluntary-aided schools are maintained by religious organisations and they may make stipulations as to religious observance. Religion is an issue in every area of life in Northern Ireland, where even primary education is divided along religious lines. Religion is also a contentious issue among certain ethnic groups, such as Muslims, who believe that education should be single-sex (particularly for girls).

- Do you want your children to attend a co-educational (mixed) school? State schools are usually co-educational.

- Should you send your children to a boarding school? If so, should it be in the UK or in another country?

- What are the secondary and further education prospects for your children in the UK or another country? Are British educational qualifications recognised in your home country or the country where you plan to live after leaving the UK?

- Does the school have a good academic record? All schools must provide exam pass rate statistics, e.g. GCSE (General Certificate of Secondary Education) and GCE (General Certificate of Education) A-levels, and a prospectus, which they may post to you.

- What are the facilities for art and science subjects, for example arts and crafts, music, computer studies (how many computers?), science, hobbies, drama, cookery and photography? Does the school have an extensive library of up-to-date books (a good library is usually an excellent sign)? These should be listed in a school's prospectus.

- How large are the classes? What is the teacher:pupil ratio?

Obtain the opinions and advice of others who have been faced with the same decisions and problems, and collect as much information from as many different sources as possible before making a decision. Speak to teachers and the parents of children attending schools on your shortlist. If possible, interview the headteacher before making a decision. Most parents find it's desirable to discuss the alternatives with their children before making a decision. (If it isn't already too late, you could always decide against children and save yourself a lot of trouble!)

Most Local Education Authorities (LEAs) provide schools for children with special educational needs, including those with emotional and behavioural difficulties, moderate and severe learning difficulties, communication problems, hearing or sight impairment, or physical disabilities (although these are being phased and all children included in mainstream schools). There are, however, few special teaching facilities in the UK for gifted children (see **Special Education** on page 214).

STATE SCHOOLS

The term 'state' is used here in preference to 'public' and refers to non fee-paying schools controlled by Local Education Authorities (LEAs) and funded from state taxes and local council tax revenue (officially called maintained schools). This is to prevent confusion with the term 'public school', used in the US (and Scotland) to refer to a state school, but which in England and Wales usually means a private fee-paying school. Private schools are officially referred to as independent schools in England and Wales.

If you live in a rural area, your LEA is one of the 39 English or eight Welsh county councils. In large cities, your LEA is the local borough council. All state schools have a governing body usually made up of a number of parent representatives and governors (appointed by the LEA), the headteacher and other serving teachers. In Scotland, education authorities must establish school boards (consisting of elected parents and staff members) to participate in the management and administration of schools. Most state schools have a Parents and Teachers Association (PTA).

Education Reforms

The state education system in England and Wales has been changing at a frenetic pace in the last few decades, which has led to a generation of curriculum chaos. Changes include the virtual abolition of the 11-plus examination (which was previously used to decide admission to higher secondary schools and which still exists in a few counties such as Buckinghamshire and Kent) and the introduction of non-selective comprehensive schools, where admission is irrespective of ability or aptitude. It's generally recognised that the introduction of comprehensive schools has raised the standard for the worst schools, while lowering the standards of some schools. Most state education is co-educational. In 1989 a new 'national curriculum' was introduced, which was revised in 1993.

The state school system in England and Wales has been going through a crisis for many years caused by a lack of funding, crumbling infrastructure (the school repair bill runs into many billions), and shortages of books (around a quarter of secondary schools are short of textbooks) and other equipment. Teacher morale is low, a result of low salaries (that have failed to keep pace with inflation), poor working conditions, a lack of professional recognition, stress, government interference and lack of consultation, cuts in education funding, and classroom disruption. Not surprisingly, this has led to a shortage of teachers (the state school system has some 10,000 teaching vacancies), particularly in maths and science, and the situation is deteriorating. There are also around 35,000 vacancies a day due to sickness, training or maternity leave, that are temporarily filled by private supply teachers at an estimated cost of £300 million a year.

In recent years, many schools have been forced to cut their teaching budgets, at a time when they should have been increasing them. Some schools have insufficient funds to buy books for the revised national curriculum and other essentials. (The UK spends less on books per pupil than most other EU countries). Some state schools, particularly primaries, rely on parents and charity fund raising to provide essential equipment (e.g. computers), books and stationery, carry out building repairs and in some cases even pay teachers' salaries. Parents may be asked to make donations (some schools ask parents for monthly 'fees') of £100 a year or more per child and business sponsorship also raises millions of pounds a year. Most schools have a 'school fund' to purchase equipment that schools cannot afford to buy out of their budgets. However, parents cannot be forced to pay for anything and all contributions are voluntary (many are for activities that take place wholly or mainly within school hours, e.g. school trips). It isn't always the best-funded schools or those with the best facilities that achieve the best exam results.

One of the most heated debates in the last few years has been over large class sizes, although this problem is being addressed by the government: class sizes are falling (and classes tend to become smaller as pupils get older). The UK's state schools have nearly twice as many pupils per teacher as many other European countries. Private schools are quick to point out that their small classes lead to more individual instruction and better results, which is supported by studies in other countries. There's often a huge variation between educational achievement in the same class and the UK doesn't have a system of holding back slow learners (e.g. for a year), as is widely employed in other European countries. However, many schools have reintroduced streaming, where pupils are taught in groups, according to their ability. There's no stigma attached to streaming, which simply recognises that children learn at different rates and some are brighter than others.

Standards

Illiteracy is a problem in the UK (where some two million people have no ability to read and write functionally) and the decline in reading, writing and arithmetic among children is causing increasing concern. The standard of reading and writing is often weak at primary level, especially in deprived urban areas where social problems are rife. In recent years, the gulf between the good and bad schools has widened (in state and private schools). In the worst schools, pupils have low expectations, lack ambition and aren't pushed to do their best. There can be a huge difference in examination results between schools, even those in the same area. Good schools are said to be getting better, while bad schools are getting worse (in recent years failing schools have been threatened with take-over 'hit' squads).

Types of School

There are two kinds of state school in the UK: county schools, and voluntary-aided and voluntary controlled schools, which are described below.

Foundation Schools

At Foundation Schools, the governing body employ the school's staff and have primary responsibility for admission arrangements. The school's land and buildings are owned by the governing body or a charitable foundation. Many of these schools were formerly grant-maintained schools which were phased out in 1999.

Voluntary-aided & Voluntary Controlled Schools

Voluntary-aided and voluntary controlled schools provide primary and secondary education, and are financially maintained by LEAs. The difference is that voluntary-aided school buildings are, in many cases, the responsibility of voluntary bodies (e.g. a church or a foundation). Schools with C of E (Church of England) or Catholic in their name may be aided schools. County schools are owned by LEAs and wholly funded by them. They're non-denominational (not church aided or supported) and provide primary and secondary education. LEAs also provide schools for children with special educational needs (see **Special Education** on page 214). State schools in England and Wales are usually classified as follows:

Type of School	Age Group
Nursery	Up to 5
Infant or First School	5 – 7 or 5 – 8
Junior or Middle	7 – 11 or 8 – 14
Primary	5 – 11
Secondary	11 – 18 or 12/13 – 18
Secondary Plus	11 – 16
Sixth Form College	16 – 19

In some parts of England and Wales, the transfer age from First to Middle school and from Middle to Secondary school is one year later than shown above (i.e. 8 and 12 respectively instead of 7 and 11). This is under review by some LEAs (although controversial), in order to come into line with the key stages of the national curriculum (see **Curriculum** on page 210) and make it easier for children to move to a school in another region (where applicable, information is published by county councils). In Scotland, the transfer to secondary schools is made at age 12.

Further Information: The Advisory Centre for Education (ACE) Ltd, 1C Aberdeen Studios, 22 Highbury Grove, London N5 2DQ (☎ 020-7704 3370, 💻 www. ace-ed.org.uk), provides information on all matters relating to state education and operates a telephone advice line from 2pm to 5pm Mondays to Fridays (☎ 0808-800 5793 in the UK, ☎ 020-7704 3397 from abroad). All county councils publish information and booklets for parents, as do most state schools.

Once you've made the decision to send your child to a state school, most experts advise that you stick to it for at least a year to give it a fair trial. It may take your child this long to adapt to the change of environment and the different curriculum, particularly if English isn't his mother tongue.

Choosing a State School

The quality of state schools, their teaching staff and the education they provide, varies considerably from region to region, LEA to LEA, and from school to school. If you want your children to have a good education, it's absolutely essential to get them into a good secondary school, even if it means moving house and changing your job. You have the right to express a preference for a particular state school and don't have to choose a school within your local LEA. However, priority is usually given to children with a family member already at a school, children with special family or medical circumstances, and to children living in a school's catchment area.

It's vital to research the best schools in a given area and to ensure that your child will be accepted at your chosen school, **before buying or renting a home**. Admission to most state schools is decided, largely, on the local catchment area; if you live outside a school's area, your child may not be admitted. Homes near the best state schools are at a premium and prices in many areas have risen because of high demand. A government-funded survey in 2002 revealed that house prices in areas with good schools are on average 10 per cent higher than other areas, a figure that rises to 21 per cent in London, the South-east and the North of England. Some parents are prepared to pay £50,000 extra in property prices in order to guarantee their children places at top primary schools! Some schools have been forced to reduce their catchment areas, thus excluding many children whose parents may have moved home specifically so that their offspring could attend a particular school. Children can be denied the right to attend a school simply because they live on the wrong side of a street.

Parental choice was a cornerstone of educational reforms in the '80s, although many believe it's a charade, as the money isn't available to fill the increased demand from parents for places at the best state schools. There are over one million surplus places in schools costing millions a year to maintain, while parents are fighting to get their children into the best schools. You can appeal against a refusal, as thousands of parents do each year, although most are unsuccessful. Many parents are dissatisfied with their child's school place. An LEA is obliged to provide transport or pay travelling expenses only when the nearest state school is over 3km (2mi) for under-8s or over 5km (3mi) for over-8s. You can apply to change schools if you or your child wishes, but given the possible disruption of your child's education, this shouldn't be undertaken lightly.

There has never been so much information available about schools as there is today. To help you choose an appropriate school, all primary and secondary schools are required to publish a prospectus giving details of educational, religious and social attitudes. A list of schools in a given area can be obtained from county or borough education offices in England and Wales (listed in telephone directories). Secondary schools are also required to publish full details of their GCSE and GCE A-level results (see **Examinations** on page 212). The government publishes school performance tables. There are many books written to help you compare different schools, including *The Sunday Times State Schools Book* (Bloomsbury), which details 500 of the best state schools throughout the country. *The Sunday Times* (and other newspapers) also publish education supplements to help parents choose a state (or private) school.

Admission

You should address enquiries about admission (enrolment) to state schools to the Chief Education Officer of the LEA or contact school secretaries or headteachers directly. If possible, enquiries should be made well in advance of taking up residence in a new area. All schools prefer children to start at the beginning of a term (see below). The school year in England and Wales normally begins in September and runs until July of the following year. In Scotland, it generally runs from mid-August to the end of June and in Northern Ireland from September to June. Most local councils publish information regarding school admissions and information is also available from the local Education Department.

Terms & School Hours

The school year is usually divided into three terms (autumn, spring and summer, a throwback to when children helped with the harvest), which are separated by 14 weeks holiday. The mid-term (or half-term) is usually marked by a one-week break. The typical term dates are as shown below, although the dates and the length of holidays vary depending on the school and the area:

Term	Dates (2007/2008)
Autumn	3rd September – 21st December
	(Half-term Holiday: 19th October or 29th October)
	(Christmas Holiday: 21st December – 7th January)
Spring	7th January – 4th April

	(Half-term Holiday: 15th – 25th February)
	(Easter Holiday: 4th April – 21st April)
Summer	21st April – 23rd July
	(Half-term Holiday: 23rd May – 2nd June)
	(Summer Holiday: 23rd July – early September)

Terms are a flexible length to accommodate the main public holidays. Most schools also close for staff training on certain days, which are listed in the school schedule. School holiday dates are published by schools well in advance, thus allowing plenty of time to schedule family holidays during official school holidays. Holidays shouldn't be taken during term time, although many parents ignore this and it isn't illegal. By law, parents are permitted to withdraw their children from school for up to two weeks a year without official permission.

However, it's unwise to take a child out of school, particularly when he should be taking examinations or during important course work assignments. The GCSE examinations (see page 212) are scheduled for late May and June, and if your child misses an exam you may have to pay the fee **and** will have to pay again for him to take it later. The school day in state schools is usually from 9am to noon and 1pm to 3.30pm or 4pm, Mondays to Fridays. Some (usually secondary) schools keep what are termed 'continental hours', starting at 8.30am and finishing at 2.30pm (with a short lunch break). There are no state school lessons on Saturdays.

Provisions & Uniforms

Most primary and secondary schools provide lunches (cafeteria self-service or buffet-style) for around £2.50 per day and parents are permitted to join their child for lunch in some schools. It may be necessary for pupils to order meals in advance and to book meals for a whole week, i.e. no meals on odd days. A child whose mother doesn't go out to work and who lives within walking or cycling distance of school, may go home for lunch. In Northern Ireland, a midday meal is provided for all primary school children who wish to have one. Most schools allow children to take a snack for morning break, e.g. biscuit, apple or crisps (chips), and milk is on sale in some schools. Free milk and lunches are provided for pupils whose parents receive Income Support (see **Social Security** on page 336) who may also be exempt from paying for travel and school outings. All secondary schools provide covered cycle racks for pupils who cycle to school. Primary school children usually need the following items:

● School bag or satchel, or a small bag or box for a packed lunch;

● A pencil case with pencils, etc. (not obligatory);

- Gym shoes (plimsolls), shorts, T-shirt and a towel for games and exercise periods;

- Sports bag for above (if satchel is too small).

Although most state schools have a school uniform, the rules about wearing them may vary. In some schools it's obligatory, in others not (rules may be more relaxed in infant and junior schools). Less well off parents, e.g. those claiming Income Support, can claim a uniform grant and some secondary schools may also help with the cost of uniforms. State schools went through a period in the '60s when school uniforms were unfashionable and were considered by educationalists to inhibit personality, in addition to being a burden on less well-off families (which is still the case).

In recent years, many state schools, particularly comprehensive schools, have reintroduced school uniforms in an attempt to instil in students a sense of identity, discipline and pride in their school. Those in favour of uniforms also argue that they enhance a school's reputation and, contrary to earlier belief, the children whose parents cannot afford good clothes don't stand out, as everyone wears the same.

Nursery & Pre-school

Attendance at a nursery school or kindergarten for children under five isn't compulsory. All children must start compulsory schooling in the term following their fifth birthday. A government scheme introduced in 1998 makes provision for part-time, 'early years' education for four-year olds from the term following their fourth birthday. Children are guaranteed three two-and-a-half hour sessions a week at a registered play scheme or school of the parents' choice, which is one of the lowest provisions of nursery education in Europe (in Belgium and France 95 per cent of children attend a nursery school). Children from three to five years old may be catered for in local state nursery schools, in nursery schools attached to primary schools or registered play schemes. However, the provision of state nursery schools by LEAs isn't mandatory, although LEAs must ensure that there are places at play schemes if there aren't enough state nursery schools. Admission to nursery education is usually on a first-come, first-served basis. Nursery schools have no catchment area and you can apply to any number of schools, although you must put your child down for entry as soon as possible. One advantage of putting your child down for entry at a state nursery school attached to a primary school is that you're usually ensured your child has a place at the primary school later.

The cost of private nursery school varies and is usually from £50 a week or £400 a term, although it can cost up to £5,000 a year. Some schools allow you to choose a number of morning or afternoon sessions, e.g. from £150 a term for two sessions a week, rising to around £400 a term for five full days a week. School hours vary, but may be from 9am to noon (morning session) and 12.15pm to 3.15pm (afternoon session). Children who attend nursery school all day usually require a packed lunch (a mid-morning snack and drink may be provided by the school). There are over 800 nursery schools in the UK using the world-famous Montessori method of teaching.

If you're unable to get your child accepted by a state-aided nursery school, you must pay for him to attend a private pre-school playgroup. These usually cost from £2.50 to £4 a session. Many playgroups accept children from age two, but stipulate that they must be toilet trained. Informal play facilities are provided by private nursery schools and playgroups, or may be organised by parents and voluntary bodies such as the Pre-School Learning Alliance (The Fitzpatrick Building, 188 York Way, London N7 9AD ☎ 020-7697 2500, 🖳 www.pre-school.org.uk), which provides places for some 800,000 under fives. To find out where the nursery schools and playgroups are in your area, get in touch with Childcare Link (☎ 0800–096 0296). Children attend between two and five weekly sessions of two and a half hours a day on average. Parents pay a fee each term and are encouraged to help in the running of the group. A playgroup doesn't generally provide education (just educational games) for under fives, although research has shown that children who attend nursery school are generally brighter and usually progress at a much faster rate than those who don't.

Nursery school is highly recommended, particularly if a child or its parents aren't of English mother tongue. After one or two years in nursery school, a child is integrated into the local community and is well prepared for primary school (particularly if English isn't spoken at home). A number of books are available for parents who wish to help their young children learn at home, which most educationalists agree gives children a flying start at school.

Primary School

Primary education in the UK begins at five years and in state schools is almost always co-educational (mixed boys and girls). Primary school consists mainly of first or infant schools for children aged five to seven (or eight), middle or junior schools for those aged 7 to 11 (or 8 to 12) and combined first and middle schools for both age groups. In addition, first schools in some parts of England cater for children aged from five to eight, nine or ten, and are the first stage of a three-tier school system: first, middle and secondary. Some primary schools also provide nursery classes for children aged five.

LEAs must provide a primary school place at the start of the term following a child's fifth birthday, although some admit children earlier. If a child attends a nursery class at a primary school, he usually moves up to the infants' class at the same school, although it isn't compulsory. Entry to a primary school isn't automatic and parents must apply to the head for a place. In England and Wales, the transfer to secondary schools is generally made at 11, while in Northern Ireland it can be 11 or 12. In Scotland, primary school lasts for seven years and pupils transfer to secondary school at the age of 12. In a few areas, children may take the 11-plus examination, which determines whether they go on to a grammar or high school, or to a secondary modern school (see **Examinations** on page 212).

Secondary School

Secondary schools are for children from 11 or 12 to 16 and for those who choose to stay on at school until age 18 (called 'sixth formers'). Most state secondary schools are co-educational, although there are many single-sex schools in Northern Ireland. Students are streamed in some secondary schools for academic subjects. The main types of secondary schools are as follows:

- **Middle Schools** – Although regarded as secondary schools, middle schools take children aged 8 or 9 who move on to senior comprehensive schools at 12 or 14.

- **Comprehensive Schools** – Admission is made without reference to ability or aptitude. Comprehensive schools provide a full range of courses for all levels of ability, from first to sixth year (from ages 11 to 18, although some cater for 11 to 16-year-olds only) and usually take students from the local catchment area. In some counties, all secondary schools are comprehensive.

- **Secondary Modern Schools** – Provide a general education with a practical bias for 11 to 16-year-olds who fail to gain acceptance at a grammar or high school. Like comprehensive schools, secondary modern schools cater for students from the local area.

- **Secondary Intermediate** – Northern Ireland only. Equivalent to a comprehensive school.

- **Secondary Grammar Schools** – Have a selective intake and provide an academic course for pupils aged from 11 to 16 or 18 years. In areas where the 11-plus examination is retained (see **Examinations** on page 212), entry to grammar school is for the 25 per cent or so who pass.

- **High Schools** – Are provided in some areas for those who pass their 11-plus exam, but aren't accepted at a grammar school.

- **Sixth Form Colleges** – Schools where 16-year-olds (e.g. from secondary modern schools) study for two years for GCE A-levels. It also takes students from comprehensive schools catering for 11 to 16-year-olds.

- **Technical Schools** – Provide an integrated vocational education (academic and technical) for students aged from 14 to 18. Schools take part in the Technical and Vocational Education Institute (TVEI) scheme, funded by the Manpower Services Commission (MSC).

- **City Technology Colleges** – Specialise in technological and scientific courses for children aged 11 to 18 (see below). City Technology Colleges are usually located in deprived parts of the UK.

Comprehensive schools are usually divided into five or seven year groups, with the first year having the youngest children, e.g. 11-year-olds. At the age of 16, students can take GCSE examinations (see **Examinations** on page 212) or leave school without taking any exams.

After taking their GCSEs, students can usually stay on at school for the sixth form (or transfer to a 6th form college) and spend a further two or three years studying for their A-level examinations, usually in order to qualify for a place at a university. They can also retake or take extra GCSEs or study for the B.Tech or GNVQ (General

National Vocational Qualification) exams at a 6th form college. Around 40 per cent of all students stay on at secondary school to take A-levels. The average pupil:teacher ratio in most state secondary schools is around 22, although class sizes are over 30 in some schools. Teaching time is from 22 to 26 hours in secondary schools, but may be increased to boost exam results.

City technology colleges are state-aided, independent of LEAs, and are a recent innovation in state education for 11 to 18-year-olds. Their aim is to widen the choice of secondary education in disadvantaged urban areas and to teach a broad curriculum with an emphasis on science, technology, business understanding and arts technologies. Although initially received with hostility and scepticism by the educational establishment, technology colleges have proved a huge success.

Curriculum

The Education Reform Act of 1988 established the progressive introduction of a national curriculum in primary and secondary schools, for the years of compulsory schooling from 5 to 16. This means that children in all parts of the England and Wales now receive the same basic education, which makes comparisons between how children are performing at different schools easier and facilitates transfers between schools. Before the national curriculum, headteachers (also called headmasters or headmistresses) in England and Wales were responsible for determining the curriculum in their schools in conjunction with LEAs and school governors.

The national curriculum (which has spawned a new language: 'curriculingo') was introduced over six years from autumn 1989 to summer 1995, ostensibly to bring the UK into line with Europe. It consists of eleven subjects which all children must study at school: English, mathematics, science, history, geography, information and communication technology (ICT), music, art and design, physical education (PE), design and technology (D&T) and a modern foreign language (in secondary schools from 11 years). English, mathematics and science are termed 'core' subjects, because they help children to study other subjects, and are compulsory up to GCSE level. Other subjects are termed 'foundation' subjects. The core subjects plus technology and a modern language are often referred to as the 'extended core'. In Wales, Welsh-speaking schools teach Welsh as a core subject and other schools in Wales teach Welsh as a foundation subject (although this has caused some dissension among English-speaking parents, when pupils are forced to learn Welsh against their parent's wishes). Religious education must be part of the curriculum and is decided locally. Parents can, however, decide whether their child takes part.

Schooling is divided into four 'key stages', which help parents know what their children are learning at various ages. Parents receive a report containing the results of Standard Assessment Tests (SATs) at the end of each key stage (at ages 7, 11, 14 and 16), based on national attainment targets. The key stages are:

Key Stage	Age	Year Groups (Classes)
1	5 – 7	1 & 2
2	7 – 11	3 – 6
3	12 – 14	7 – 9
4	14 – 16	10 & 11

In key stages 1 and 2, English, maths, science, information and communication technology (ICT), history, geography, art and design, music, design and technology (D&T) and PE are taught. In key stage 3, a modern foreign language and citizenship are added. In key stage 4, compulsory subjects are English, maths, science, ICT, D&T, PE, citizenship and a modern foreign language. Pupils must also study sex and religious education at all stages, although parents have the right to withdraw children from these lessons. In stage 3, children aged 11 to 14 should have 20 per cent of their timetable free for subjects other than the statutory requirements, increasing to 40 per cent in stage 4. Other subjects may be taught in addition to the national curriculum and religious education, and are decided by individual schools. All schools are required to publish information in their prospectus and the governing body's annual report about what's taught at the school. Children with special education needs also follow the national curriculum, where possible.

In Scotland, there's no set national curriculum and education authorities and individual headteachers decide what is taught. There are, however, national guidelines suggesting that the following subjects be taught between the ages of 5 and 14: English, mathematics, environmental studies (including science, social subjects, technology and health), expressive arts (including art, design, music, drama and physical education), and religious and moral education. These form the core area and are supplemented by other activities, which make up the elective area. Provision is made for teaching Gaelic in Gaelic-speaking areas. Standard tests are held in English and mathematics for 9 and 12-year-olds.

In Northern Ireland, there's a common curriculum for all schools with several areas of study, including: English; maths; science and technology; history and geography; creative and expressive area of study (art and design, music and physical education); religious education; and four educational cross-curricular themes (education for mutual understanding, cultural heritage, health education and information technology), which aren't separate subjects, but included within the other subjects. All secondary school pupils study a European language and the Irish language is available in Irish-speaking schools only. Secondary schools are known as Post-primary schools in Northern Ireland. There are also grammar schools and admission to these depends on the results of two Transfer tests examining pupils' knowledge in English, maths, science and technology.

The national curriculum has already been revised and is expected to be modified over the coming years to counter problem areas and to take into account the changing face of education and training. For further information contact the

Qualification and Curriculum Authority, 83 Piccadilly, London W1J 8QA (☎ 020-7509 5556, 💻 www.qca.org.uk).

Examinations

Before the introduction of comprehensive schools, the 11-plus examination was sat by all pupils in England and Wales at the age of around 11, and was the major turning point in a child's schooling. The major objection to the 11-plus was that it decided a child's future education at too young an age and left little room for late developers (very few children who failed the 11-plus made it into higher education). However, the 11-plus hasn't quite passed into history and it's still taken by primary school pupils in a few areas, where those who pass go on to a grammar or high school. Those that fail attend a secondary modern school. Places at advanced secondary schools are limited so, in addition to achieving the required 11-plus pass mark, pupils also require a recommendation from their headteacher. It's possible to transfer from a high school to a grammar school, but it's rare.

In England, Wales and Northern Ireland, the main examination usually taken at age 16 after five years of secondary education is the General Certificate of Secondary Education (GCSE). The General Certificate of Education Advanced (A) level may be taken after a further two years of study. In Scotland, the main examination is the Scottish Certificate of Education (SCE). SCE standard (ordinary) grade is taken after four years of secondary education and the SCE Higher grade (highers) after a further two years. Passes in the GCE A-level and SCE Higher grade exams are the basis for entry to further education, and are recognised by all British and European universities and most American colleges. In recent years, there has been a debate over whether GCSE and A-level standards are falling, although GCSE and A-level results remain the best guide to a school's teaching standards. The examinations held in England, Wales and Northern Ireland are described below.

General Certificate of Secondary Education

In 1988, the GCSE examination replaced the General Certificate of Education (GCE) Ordinary (O-level) and the Certificate of Secondary Education (CSE) examinations. The GCSE differs from its predecessors in that the syllabi are based on national criteria covering course objectives; content and assessment methods; differentiated assessment (i.e. different papers or questions for different ranges of ability) and grade-related criteria (i.e. grades awarded on absolute rather than relative performance). Coursework forms part of the assessment of GCSE results, depending on the subject and the examination board, and can vary from 30 per cent to as much as 70 per cent. When children reach the end of the third year of secondary education, they choose GCSE subjects with the help of teachers and parents (there's no restriction on entry to any examination).

Pupils sit their GCSEs at the age of 16 or earlier – e.g. if they're exceptionally gifted. Generally, five or six GCSE at grades A to C are required by children who intend to take A-levels and go on to higher education.

Advanced & Advanced Supplementary Levels

General Certificate of Education (GCE) Advanced level (A-level) examinations are usually taken during the two years after GCSE (at age 17 or 18) by those who wish to go on to higher education. In 2002, A-levels were changed somewhat in response to criticisms that standards had fallen (in recent years there has been a sharp rise in the number of A-level passes, particularly in top grades A and B, and many educationalists believe that exams and marking are deliberately being watered down in order to increase pass rates) and to encourage students to have greater flexibility in subjects. Students in their first year of A-levels can decide how many A-levels they wish to study. Each A-level has six units, which may be taken over two years (modular) or at the end of the two years (linear). Coursework may form part of the A-level units and there's a ceiling of 30 per cent coursework in most subjects. The first year of A-level study is known as 'AS' (see below) and the second year as 'A2'.

Advanced Supplementary level (AS-level) examinations may be taken during the first and second years of A-levels and consist of three units. An AS-level is graded as half an A-level and therefore two AS-level passes are usually accepted as the equivalent of one A-level pass. AS-level courses are intended to supplement and broaden A-level studies and examinations are graded A to E (as for A-level grades).

Advanced Education Awards (AEAs) were introduced by the government in 2002, to replace the old Scholarship levels (S-levels), although it's expected that AEAs will be taken by more students than the S-levels, which were somewhat elitist. AEAs aim to stretch the most able A-level students and to help differentiate between them, particularly in subjects where there's a high proportion of 'A' grades at A-level. At present AEAs are available in 16 A-level subjects (biology, chemistry, economics, English, French, geography, German, history, Irish, Latin, maths, physics, religious education, Spanish, Welsh and Welsh as a second language), which will be increased to 20 by 2005 with the introduction of business studies, computing, design and technology, and psychology.

Scotland has its own examination system, the Scottish Certificate of Education (SCE) standard (ordinary) and higher grade examinations. The standard grade (roughly equivalent to the GCSE) is taken at age 15 and the higher grade is usually taken at the age of 17 or 18. The Scottish Certificate of Sixth Year Studies (SCSYS) is a further qualification for pupils who stay on at school after passing the SCE higher grade. Some Scottish private schools set GCE A-levels as well as SCE higher grade.

The Certificate of Pre-vocational Education (CPVE) is a nationally-recognised award for 17-year-olds doing an extra year at school or college.

To gain acceptance to a university in the UK, a student usually requires at least two A-level passes (grades A to E). This is the minimum; to study some courses more passes and high grades are necessary, e.g. to study law and medicine, you usually require three A grade passes, while the requirement for some other courses may be two B grade passes and one C. If you receive an unexpectedly low grade in an exam, you can appeal to your school. There's a fee for most appeals, but if you're successful, the fee is returned. If you're going to appeal, do so as soon as possible, as an A-level course, a college or university place, or a job may rest on the outcome.

Special concessions are made for dyslexic children taking GCSE and A-level exams, which allow them to use an amanuensis or word processor to write answers and to have exam questions read out to them or recorded on tape.

SPECIAL EDUCATION

Special education is provided for children with moderate or severe learning difficulties (e.g. a hearing, speech, or sight impediment, a physical disability or autism) or a behavioural problem, which prevents or hinders them from attending a mainstream school for their age group. However, whenever possible, children with special education needs (SEN) are educated in mainstream schools, in order to give them the same education as other children. There are around 2,000 SEN schools in the UK (day and boarding schools), most of which are state schools, operated and financed by LEAs.

There are, however, too few special schools and it's estimated that around a third of pupils with special education needs are educated in mainstream schools (although there are often educational and social reasons for this). Some special schools are run privately by voluntary bodies, which may receive a grant from central government for capital expenditure and equipment. Day-to-day running costs are met by the LEAs for pupils placed in voluntary schools. Some private schools provide education wholly or mainly for children with special education needs. Most LEAs provide an educational psychological service for children with behavioural problems.

Some LEAs provide special teaching and facilities for gifted children (those with very high IQs), although there's little provision for young geniuses. In the past, the only avenue open to most parents was to pay for private tuition or apply for a private school scholarship. Mensa, the society for the super-intelligent, has established the Mensa Foundation for Gifted Children, which helps to develop the potential of gifted children through special schools and individual counselling. For information, write to Mensa, St John's House, St John's Square, Wolverhampton WV2 4AH (🖳 www.mensa.org.uk). It's important to choose the best possible school for a talented or gifted child.

The Advisory Centre for Education (ACE), 1C Aberdeen Studios, 22 Highbury Grove, London N5 2DQ (☎ 020-7354 8318, 🖳 www.ace-ed.org.uk) can answer questions and give advice on special education. Contact your local LEA for information about special schools in your area or write to the Department for Education and Skills (which publishes numerous booklets about special education downloadable from 🖳 www.dfes.gov.uk/sen) for a list of special schools throughout the UK. There are several books available for parents of children with special needs, including *Which? School for Special Needs* by Derek Bingham (John Catt Educational).

PRIVATE SCHOOLS

Private fee-paying schools are officially termed independent schools (although historically referred to as public schools) because they're independent of local or central government control. The UK is renowned for the quality and variety of its private schools, which include such world-famous schools as Charterhouse, Eton, Harrow, Roedean, Rugby, Westminster and Winchester. Many private schools, including many of the most famous names, are run as charitable foundations. Schools may be owned by an individual, an institution or a company and, although traditionally the preserve of the wealthy, they attract an increasing number of pupils from less privileged backgrounds.

Around 50 per cent of parents who choose a private education for their children were themselves educated in the state sector. There are some 2,300 private day and boarding schools in England and Wales, 150 in Scotland and around 15 in Northern Ireland, educating around 7 per cent of school age children. Schools take pupils from the ages of 2 to 19 and include boarding (from the age of 5) and day schools (some are both), single-sex and co-educational schools. Some schools cater for special education needs (see **Special Education** on page 214) and there are also private schools for gifted children in art, music, theatre or dance.

Among the private schools in the UK, are many which follow special or unorthodox methods of teaching, for example Montessori nursery schools and Rudolf Steiner schools. All private schools must meet certain minimum criteria and be registered with the Department of Education and Science. Although fee-paying, most private schools aren't run for private profit and all surplus income is reinvested in the running of schools. Private schools receive no grants from public funds and are owned and managed by special trusts. Most schools have a board of governors who look after the school and its finances. The headteacher is responsible to the governors, but usually has a free hand to choose staff and make day-to-day decisions.

Fees vary considerably depending on a variety of factors, including the age of pupils, the reputation and quality of the school, and its location (schools in the north of England are generally cheaper than those in the south). Day school fees vary from around £900 to £1,400 a term (three a year) for pre-preparatory schools, from £1,600 to £3,200 a term for junior preparatory schools and from £2,200 to £4,100 a term for senior day pupils. Boarding fees range from £3,700 to £6,500. Private schools for boys are generally more expensive than those for girls. Fees aren't all-inclusive and additional obligatory charges are made in addition to optional extra services. There are also commercial tutorial colleges or 'crammers', providing a one-term or one-year re-sit course for students who have failed one or more GCE A-levels. Fees are high and start at around £1,250 for a one-term, one A-level course, rising to as much as £10,000 for a one-year, three A-level course.

Private school fees tend to increase by an average of 5 to 10 per cent annually (unless you're rich or someone else is paying, start saving **before** you have any children). Many companies and banks specialise in insurance and investment policies for parents planning to send their children to private schools. Many senior and some junior schools provide scholarships for bright or talented pupils, which vary in value from full fees to a small proportion. Scholarships are awarded as a result of competitive examinations.

Private schools range from nursery (kindergarten) to large day and boarding schools, and from experimental schools to traditional institutions. A number of independent schools are also available for religious and ethnic minorities, for example schools for Muslims, where there's a strict code regarding the segregation of boys and girls. Most private schools are single-sex, almost equally split between boys' and girls' schools, but there are a number of mixed schools (co-educational) and a number of boys' schools admit girls to their sixth forms (by which time sex education is part of the curriculum). The different types of private school are shown in the table below:

Type of School	Age	Notes
All-through	2 – 18	Caters for all ages from nursery to senior or sixth form.
Pre-preparatory	2 – 7	Equivalent to LEA nursery and infant schools. Usually attached to junior schools.
Junior/Preparatory	7 – 11/13	Leads to admission to senior schools at 11+ or 13+ when the CEE (see below) is taken.
Senior	11 – 13/18	Sometimes has a lower school for pupils aged 11 to 13.
Sixth Form	16+	Many senior schools admit students at 16+, usually to study for GCE A-levels.

Most private junior schools (also called preparatory or prep schools) cater for boys from the age of 7 to 13 years, but some are for girls only and an increasing number are co-educational. Junior schools usually prepare pupils for the Common Entrance Examination (CEE) to senior private schools, which is a qualifying exam to test whether prospective pupils will be able to cope with the standard of academic work required. The CEE is set by the CEE board and is marked by the school which the pupil plans to attend. It's sat at 13 by boys and 11 to 13 by girls. Entrance to many schools is by an exam (e.g. the CEE), a report or assessment, or an interview. Most private schools provide a similar curriculum to state schools (see **Curriculum** on page 210) and set the English GCSE (see **Examinations** on page 212) and GCE A-level examinations. Some Scottish schools set the Scottish Certificate of Education (SCE) at standard (ordinary) and higher grades. Private school pupils can also take the International Baccalaureate (IB) examination, an internationally recognised university entrance qualification.

There are many advantages to private schools, not least their excellent academic record. According to one survey, pupils at private preparatory schools are nine times more likely to achieve 100 per cent passes in the national tests than those at state junior schools. Three out of four children gain five or more GCSE ordinary level passes, more than half gain two or more GCE A-levels and more than two-thirds gain one or more. Although private school pupils make up less than 10 per cent of the total, they take 35 per cent of the top GCE A-levels and provide over 25 per cent of university students, i.e. a student from a private school is almost four times as likely to go on to university as a student from a state school. Some private secondary schools have a near 100 per cent university acceptance rate and half of all 'Oxbridge' (Oxford and Cambridge universities) entrants are educated at private schools.

Don't assume, however, that all private schools are excellent or that they all offer a better education than state schools. In the last ten years, there has been a rapid expansion in private education, which some analysts believe has led to a reduction in standards in some schools. Some have expanded too fast and increased their class sizes considerably, particularly in areas of high demand, such as London and the south-east, and a number have been criticised by government ministers for their poor standards.

School uniforms are generally considered to be a mark of identity, pride and discipline in private schools (some 'public' schools, such as Eton, have a particularly eccentric mode of dress). Private schools provide a broad-based education (aimed at developing a pupil's character) and offer a varied approach to sport, music, drama, art and a wide choice of academic subjects. Their aim is usually the development of the child as an individual and the encouragement of his unique talents, which is made possible by small classes (an average of around 15 in senior schools and even less in many junior schools) that allow teachers to provide pupils with individually tailored lessons and tuition. Some private schools cater for special needs, including gifted children and slow learners or those who suffer from dyslexia, although the latter are usually better provided for in state schools. Private schools also cater for parents requiring a single-sex school (girls often progress faster without the distraction of the opposite sex), boarding facilities and those who wish their children to be educated in the customs of a particular religious belief.

Make applications to private schools as far in advance as possible (before conception for the best schools). Obviously, if you're coming from abroad, you won't usually be able to apply one or two years in advance, which is usually considered to be the best time to book a place. It isn't usually simply a matter of selecting a school and telling the head when you will be bringing little Cecil or Gertrude along. Although many nursery and junior schools accept pupils on a first-come, first-served basis, the best and most exclusive schools have waiting lists or a demanding selection procedure. Most popular schools, particularly day schools in the greater London area and other cities, have long waiting lists. Don't rely on enrolling your child in a particular school and neglect other alternatives, particularly if the chosen school has a rigorous entrance examination. When applying, you're usually requested to send previous school reports, exam results and records. Before enrolling your child in a private school, ensure that you understand the withdrawal conditions in the school contract.

Choosing a Private School

The following checklist is designed to help you choose an appropriate and reputable private school:

- Does the school have a good reputation? Does it belong to any recognised body for private schools such as the Incorporated Association of Preparatory Schools? How long has it been established? Is it financially stable?

- Do you plan to send your children to a junior or senior private school only, or both?

- Does the school have a good academic record? For example, what percentage of pupils obtain good examination passes or go on to good universities? What subjects do pupils do best in? All schools provide exam pass rate statistics. On the other hand, if your child isn't exceptionally bright, you may prefer to send him to a school with less academic pressure (some students find the educational demands very stressful in some schools).

- What does the curriculum include (a broad and well-balanced curriculum is best)? Ask to see a typical pupil timetable to check the ratio of academic to non-academic subjects. Check the number of free study periods and whether they're supervised.

- Do you wish to send your children to a single-sex or a co-educational school? Many children, particularly girls, make better progress without the distractions of the opposite sex (although their sex education may be neglected).

- Day or boarding school? If you're considering a day school, what are the school hours? Does the school provide transport for pupils to and from home? Many schools offer weekly boarding, allowing pupils to return home at weekends.

- How many children attend the school and what is the average class size? What is the ratio of teachers to pupils? Are pupil numbers increasing or decreasing? Check that class sizes are in fact what it says they are in the prospectus. Has the number of pupils increased dramatically in the last few years (which could be a good or a bad sign)?

- What are the qualification requirements for teachers? What nationality are the majority of teachers? What is the teacher turnover? A high teacher turnover is a bad sign and usually suggests under-paid teachers and poor working conditions.

- What extras are you required to pay? For example, optional lessons (e.g. music, dancing and sports), lunches, art supplies, sports equipment, school trips, telephone calls, clothing (most schools have obligatory uniforms, which can be **very** expensive), insurance, textbooks and stationery. Most schools charge parents for every little thing.

- Which countries do most students come from?

- Is religion an important consideration in your choice of school? What is the religious bias of the school, if any?

- Are special English classes provided for children whose English doesn't meet the required standard? Usually, if a child is under nine years of age, it doesn't matter if his English is weak. However, children over this age aren't usually accepted unless they can read English fluently (as printed in textbooks for their age). Some schools provide intensive English tuition for foreign students.

- If you've decided on a boarding school, what standard and type of accommodation is provided? What is the quality and variety of food provided? What is the dining room like? Does the school have a dietician?

- What languages does the school teach as obligatory or optional subjects? Does the school have a language laboratory?

- What is the student turnover?

- What are the school terms and holiday periods? Private school holidays are usually much longer than state schools, e.g. four weeks at Easter and Christmas and ten weeks in the summer. They often don't coincide with state school holiday periods.

- If you're considering a day school, what are the school hours?

- What are the withdrawal conditions, should you need or wish to remove your child? A term's notice is usual.

- What examinations are set? In which subjects? How do they fit in with future education plans?

- What sports instruction and facilities are provided?

- What are the facilities for art and science subjects, for example arts and crafts, music, computer studies (how many computers?), science, hobbies, drama, cookery and photography?

- What sort of outings and holidays does the school organise?

- What medical facilities does the school provide, e.g. infirmary, resident doctor or nurse? Is health and accident insurance included in the fees?

- What sort of discipline and punishments are imposed and are restrictions relaxed as children get older?

- What reports are provided for parents and how often? How much contact does the school have with parents?

- **Last, but not least, unless someone else is paying, what are the fees?**

Draw up a shortlist of possible schools and obtain a prospectus from each (some schools provide a video prospectus). If possible, obtain a copy of the school magazine. Before making a final choice, it's important to visit the schools on your shortlist during term time and talk to teachers and students. **Where possible, check the answers to the above questions in person and don't rely on a school's prospectus to provide the information.** If you're unhappy with the answers, look elsewhere. Having made your choice, keep a check on your child's progress, listen to his complaints and compare notes with other parents. If something doesn't seem right, try to establish whether the complaint is founded or not, and if it is, take action to have the problem resolved. Don't forget that you're paying a lot of money for your child's education and you should expect value for money. See also **State or Private School?** on page 199.

Further Information

There are a number of guides to private schools in the UK, including the The Independent Schools Guide (Gabbitas Educational Consultants), The Equitable Guide to Independent Schools (Trotman), which contains independent reports on over 520 private schools, and ISC Guide to Accredited Independent Schools, available free of charge from the Independent Schools Information Service (ISCIS), Grosvenor Gardens House, 35-37 Grosvenor Gardens, London SW1W 0BS? ☎ 020-7798 1500, ☐ www.iscis.uk.net), a guide to over 1,400 boarding and day schools in the UK and Ireland for boys and girls aged 2 to 19. ISCIS also organises an annual national exhibition of independent schools. Another excellent guide is the Independent Schools Yearbook edited by Judy Mott (A&C Black). It contains details of governing bodies, staff, admission, entrance examinations, scholarships and fees for major private secondary schools for boys and some preparatory schools. In addition to private schools that follow a largely British curriculum, there are also American, international and foreign-language private schools. See also **Nursery & Pre-school** on page 207.

HIGHER EDUCATION

Post-school education is generally divided into higher and further education. Higher education is usually defined as advanced courses of a standard higher than A-levels (see **Examinations** on page 212) or equivalent and usually refers only to first degree courses. Courses may be full-time, part-time or sandwich courses (nothing to do with food, but courses which combine periods of full-time study with full-time training and paid work in industry and commerce). Degree level courses are offered by 89 universities (48 old universities and 41 new universities which were formerly polytechnics), plus 15 Scottish central institutions and hundreds of Colleges of Higher Education (CHE), many of which provide teacher-training courses. The UK is internationally renowned for the excellence of its universities and other higher education establishments, which include the world-famous Oxford (12th century) and Cambridge (13th century) universities (collectively referred to as Oxbridge).

The age of admission to university is usually 18 (although they admit exceptional students at a younger age) and courses usually last for three years or four years. This is seen as a big advantage for foreign students from countries where courses often last much longer and results in British universities attracting almost 100,000 overseas students. There are also many American colleges in the UK, mainly in the London area. For information contact the Educational Advisory Service, The Fulbright Commission, Fulbright House, 62 Doughty Street, London WC1N 2JZ, ☎ 020-7404 6994, ☐ www.fulbright.co.uk).

In the last decade, there has been a boom in higher education and around 40 per cent of all school leavers now attend university. Since the early '80s, the number of undergraduates has almost doubled to 1.4 million and today's 18-year-olds have a 60 per cent chance of going to university, at some time in their lives. Many universities have lowered their entrance qualifications to attract more students and also because of falling standards among the UK's school leavers. In recent years, there has been a debate about the 'dumbing down' of higher education, as some universities accept students who failed their A-levels to fill empty places (universities face financial penalties if they don't enrol sufficient students). Some universities also 'mark up' students who fail their exams and many people believe that the standards of today's degrees have been watered down and are far lower than they were 20 or 30 years ago. Some analysts even believe that the UK's hallowed Oxford and Cambridge universities are falling below the standards set by some other countries, particularly the US.

Fees

British and European Union (EU) students must pay £1200 a year towards their tuition costs. Students whose parents earn less than £20,970 a year are exempt and there are also other special exemptions.

Student Loans

In the absence of grants, the government introduced a student loan scheme for maintenance, whereby students can take out interest-free loans. In 2007/8 loans varied from £2,620 (a student living at home not income assessed) to a maximum of £6,315 (for a student living away from home in London). From 2006 you have also been able to get a student loan for fees up to a maximum of £3,070, which is paid direct to your university or college on your behalf. A portion of a loan, currently 75 per cent, isn't available to all students with the remaining 25 per cent income assessed according to your family's income. Interest on the loan is linked to inflation.

Loans are repayable after the April following graduation, once your income is above the income threshold (£15,000). You pay 9 per cent of your income above the threshold; for example if your income is £19,000 a year, you would repay £30 a month (9 per cent of £4,000). Therefore, the amount you repay each month is directly related to your income. A free booklet entitled *Financial Support for Higher Education Students* is published by the Department for Education and Skills (⌨ www.dfes. gov.uk/studentsupport).

Students in financial difficulties may be entitled to non-repayable grants from the Access to Learning Fund, a one-stop, discretionary fund which has replaced Hardship Loans and Hardship Funds. Information is available from individual colleges and universities.

Grants

In addition to loans, students can apply for financial help from 'access funds' which colleges can distribute at their discretion to their most needy students. When you arrive at university, you are informed about student loans and the access fund by your college administration department or the student union. Banks also offer students interest-free overdrafts, although these should be treated with caution. An increasing number of companies and professional organisations (plus the military) sponsor higher education, in return for a number of years of service. Many students find it increasingly difficult to survive on their income and some are forced to choose their university not on course preference, but on where they can more easily survive on their meagre resources.

If you're starting at university or college you're eligible for a non-repayable Higher Education Grant of up to £1,000 a year, depending on your personal and household income; the maximum grant of £1,000 will be paid to people with an income of less than £16,340 in 2007/08.

EU Students

Grants covering fees and living expenses are also given to European Union (EU) nationals and their children working in the UK, and to officially recognised refugees and their children. EU nationals who are normally resident within the union area are eligible for grants (covering university fees only) on the same basis as British residents, but must pay their own living expenses. With the exception of these grants, authorities can give grants covering fees and living expenses only to students who have been resident in the UK (or the Channel Islands or Isle of Man) for the three years immediately before the first year of their course. The factors determining the size of a grant are complex, but depend largely on a student's financial resources and those of his parents.

Non-EU Students

Overseas students from outside the EU must pay the full cost of their courses and living expenses. This includes non-EU, EEA nationals unless they've been migrant workers in the UK or are the child or spouse of an EEA migrant worker. Fees for overseas students are as follows: Arts subjects from £6,250 to £7,650; Science subjects from £6,500 to £9,700; and clinical subjects from £9,960 to £18,000. There are, however, public and private scholarships and award schemes available to overseas students, particularly at postgraduate level. These are provided by the British government, the British Council, universities and individual colleges, and by a number of private trusts and professional bodies. Details of grants are available from around 80 British Council offices worldwide and from a comprehensive website (🖳 www.educationuk.org/scholarships). Even with a grant, you must be able to support yourself during your studies.

Young people aged 16 to 18 who have been admitted into the UK with their families or otherwise, may be permitted to continue their education at school or at a post-school establishment provided by LEAs. Fees may be payable and students must have an adequate knowledge of English and show evidence of suitable entry qualifications. A foreign national over 18 who wishes to study full-time in the UK on a course lasting longer than six months (and which leads to a professional or educational qualification) must provide evidence of his educational qualifications and his financial means. Evidence must be given to the educational establishment and to the immigration authorities (see page 102).

Cost of Living

The estimated annual living costs for students (excluding course fees) are around £730 a month in London and £585 in the provinces. Financial hardship has caused a big increase in student drop-outs in recent years, with one in eight students abandoning study for a job. Many universities have job clubs to help students supplement their income and around a third of students work their way through university. Overseas students studying in the UK for longer than six months are entitled to free health care from the National Health Service (see page 307). Students on shorter courses also benefit if their home country has a reciprocal health agreement with the UK; otherwise they should take out private health insurance.

Entrance Qualifications

The usual minimum qualification for entrance to a university is a mixture of GCE A-levels and AS-levels (see page 213) or SCE highers (set in Scotland). Generally, the better the university (or the better the reputation) and the more popular the course, the higher the entrance qualifications. Applicants usually need a minimum of two or three A-level passes and three GCSE passes (minimum grade C), including a foreign language and English and mathematics. The minimum entrance requirements are set by individual universities and colleges and vary considerably. The basic A-level entry requirement for most diploma courses is an A-level E grade and many colleges of higher education and universities accept students with a couple of A-level D grades. Universities and other institutions are usually flexible in their entrance requirements, particularly with regard to 'mature' students (anyone 21 or over) and those with qualifications other than A-levels. Some 20 per cent of university students are aged over 35.

Generally, overseas students' qualifications, which would admit them to a university in their own country, are taken into consideration. However, passes in particular GCSE or A-level subjects (or equivalent) may still be required. Whatever your qualifications, all applications are considered on their merits. Some universities have been forced to lower entrance requirements, particularly for science and engineering courses, due to a drop in GCE A-level standards (some have also extended engineering courses from three to four years). All foreign students require a thorough knowledge of English, which is usually examined unless a certificate is provided. British universities accept the International Baccalaureate (IB) certificate as an entrance qualification, but a US high school diploma isn't usually accepted. Contact individual universities for detailed information.

Courses

The university academic year runs from September or October to June or July and is divided into three terms of 8 to 10 weeks. Students study a main subject plus one or two subsidiary subjects and specialise in their main subject for the first one or two years. The main subject is often subdivided into parts, each taught by a different professor or lecturer, e.g. mathematics may be subdivided into pure, applied, geometry and algebra. In some universities, it's possible for students to design their own degree courses. Many students choose a sandwich course, which includes a year spent working in industry or commerce.

Fees

Although course fees are set by individual institutions, they may take into consideration government-recommended fee levels. For home students and students from EU countries, annual fees are set at three levels. EU students can obtain a booklet, *Investing in the Future: Help with Tuition Fees for European Union (EU) Students*.

Degrees

The most common degrees awarded are a Bachelor of Arts (BA) and a Bachelor of Science (BSc). Bachelor's degrees are given a classification, the highest of which is an 'honours' degree, which is awarded when the course included extra detail in the main subject. The highest pass is a first-class degree, which is quite rare. Second-class degrees classified as 2.1 (very good) and 2.2 (average) are usual, while a third-class degree is poor. The lowest classification is a 'pass'. Second degrees are usually a Master of Arts (MA) or a Master of Science (MSc), which are awarded to Bachelors for a one-year course in a subject other than their undergraduate subjects. Students who do post-graduate work in the same subject(s) as their undergraduate work, usually do a two-year Master of Philosophy (M-Phil) or a three-year Doctor of Philosophy (PhD) research programme. In some Scottish universities, a Masters degree is awarded as the first degree in arts subjects. Graduates who wish to qualify as teachers must do a four-year Bachelor of Education (BEd) degree course or a one-year post-graduate training course at a university or teacher training college (known as a Postgraduate Certificate of Education or PGCE).

Applications

To apply for a place at university, you should begin by writing to the Admissions Officer of selected universities, giving your personal details and asking for information. If you're encouraged by the reply, you must then apply formally. All applicants for entry to full-time, first degree (undergraduate) courses at British universities must be made to the Universities and Colleges Admissions Services (UCAS), PO Box 28, Cheltenham GL52 3LZ (☎ 0870-112 2211, 🖳 www.ucas.com), which publishes a handbook listing all universities, colleges and courses (over 100,000!). A useful book for university applicants is the *UCAS University and College Entrance Official Guide*.

Applicants can apply by post or online for a maximum of six courses (which may be at six different universities), for which there's a fee of around £15. The number of applicants per university place varies considerably from university to university. You would be wise not to make all your applications at universities where competition for places is at its fiercest (unless you're a genius). Most universities have between 10 and 15 applications per place available, with the most popular courses, including medicine, law, and arts courses such as English. The university year usually begins in October, so you should make your application in autumn of the year before you plan to start your course (e.g. apply in the autumn of 2007 for entry in October 2008). UCAS accepts applications from 1st September of the previous year and the closing date is 15th January (15th October for Oxford or Cambridge universities, where applicants apply direct to colleges and may need to take an entrance exam). Those with a number of offers must choose two by 15th May; otherwise they are deemed to have rejected all offers of a place.

Late Applications

Late applications are considered until June of the entrance year and a 'clearing' scheme operates up to September for late applications. When A-level results are announced in August each year, the quality newspapers (broadsheets) publish details of degree and Higher National Degree (HND) vacancies at university colleges for those who haven't yet attained a place. This is also intended to assist those who may have done better or worse than expected in their A-levels, and may wish to seek a place at a 'better' university or who no longer qualify for their original choice. Many colleges also advertise their courses in national newspapers, particularly in educational supplements. The electronic education network *Campus 2000* operates until 21st September each year and is the primary source of up-to-date vacancy details.

College Accommodation

The cost of accommodation is a major factor for many students when deciding which university to attend and an increasing number of students stay at home and study locally because of the rising costs. Following acceptance by a college or university, students are advised to apply for a place in a hall of residence ('in hall') or other college accommodation, such as self-catering houses and apartments. Such accommodation is limited to around one-third of all students, although most universities accommodate all first year students. Students should write as soon as possible after acceptance to accommodation or welfare officers, whose job is to help students find suitable accommodation (college and private). Some colleges guarantee accommodation to overseas students for the duration of their course. The cost of accommodation in halls of residence varies considerably and averages around £50 a week.

Private Accommodation

A large number of students rent privately-owned apartments or houses, that are shared with other students, although in many areas this kind of accommodation is difficult to find and expensive (from around £35 a week in the provinces up to £80 a week in London). Another alternative is to find lodgings (or digs) where you rent a room in a private house with meals included. The British Council may be able to help you find accommodation (the address of your local office can be obtained from British Diplomatic Posts abroad). If you're studying in London, contact the British Council Accommodation Unit (☎ 020-7930 8466). The British Council Information Centre (10 Spring Gardens, London SW1A 2BN, ☎ 020-7389 4548, 🖳 www.britishcouncil.org) provides information and advice on studying in the UK for overseas students. Their sister website, Education UK, also has excellent information on studying in the UK (🖳 www.educationuk.org).

Open University

In addition to the traditional universities (where students attend all lectures at the university), the UK also has an Open University (OU). It has no central campus and most study work is done at home. The OU is one of the biggest success stories of British education and, since its establishment in 1969, it has enrolled well over a million people. The Open University is, as the name suggests, open to all, irrespective of age, occupation, background or previous qualifications. There are no entry qualifications, no admission interview and no barriers of any kind, and courses are filled on a first-come, first-served principle. You must simply be 18 or over, resident in the UK and be willing to do a lot of hard work!

Open University students study at home in their spare time (some lectures are broadcast on BBC radio and TV, often starting as early as 6am). However, you aren't left to struggle along on your own: the OU has a network of 13 regional centres and over 250 study centres throughout the UK that are the bases for some 5,000 tutors and councillors whose job is to guide you through your studies. You also have the opportunity to meet fellow students at tutorials and residential summer schools. In addition to traditional degree courses, the OU offers short courses, self-contained study packs and post-graduate degrees. For further information contact the Central Enquiry Service, Open University, PO Box 197, Milton Keynes MK7 6BJ (☎ 0845-300 6090, 🖳 www.open.ac.uk).

Student Bodies

All universities have a huge variety of societies and clubs, many of which are organised by the students' union or council, which is the centre of social activities. Most college students' unions or councils in England and Wales are affiliated to the National Union of Students. There are also student union bodies in Scotland and Northern Ireland. Most universities have excellent sports facilities that may also be open to the public. Wherever you're studying, take at least six passport-size photographs for student identity cards, hall and travel cards.

Further Information

The Consumers' Association publishes a number of books for those planning to enter higher education, including *Making the Most of Higher Education* by Edith Rudinger, *Which? Subject?* and *Which? Career?* Other useful books include *The Student Book* by Klaus Boehm and Jenny Lees-Spalding (Trotman), which contains everything you need to know about how to get into and survive university, and *The Times Good University Guide* by John O'Leary (Times Books). The *School Leaver & Which Course* magazine is available at Careers Centres. UKCOSA (see page 199) provides a wealth of information for prospective foreign university students in the UK.

FURTHER EDUCATION

Further education generally embraces everything except first degree courses taken at universities and colleges of higher education, although the distinction between further and higher education (see page 220) is often blurred. Further education courses may be full or part-time and are provided at universities, colleges of technology, technical colleges (often referred to as 'tecs'), Colleges of Further Education (CFE), Adult and Community Colleges, and by numerous 'open learning' institutions. Each year, half a million students attend further education courses at universities alone, which are often of short duration and job-related, although courses may be full or part-time and may include summer semesters.

Qualifications that can be earned through further education include GCSE, GCE A-level, International Baccalaureate, BTEC (e.g. higher national certificate and diploma), SCOTVEC, City and Guilds, bachelors and masters degrees, MBA degrees, and a range of other nationally and internationally recognised certificates and diplomas. Qualifications for school-leavers include National Vocational Qualifications (NVQs) and General National Vocational Qualifications (GNVQs).

The Business and Technical Education Council (BTEC) organises over 250 courses, designed with the co-operation of major companies in various fields, available in colleges, training centres and companies. BTEC (SCOTVEC in Scotland) courses are a combination of academic and practical, and cover everything from computer studies to engineering, catering to travel and tourism. BTEC trains over 200,000 new students each year and offers three course levels leading to the BTEC first, BTEC national, and BTEC higher national certificates and diplomas.

Many further education courses are of the open learning variety (as provided by the Open University, see page 226) where students study mostly at home. Institutions include some 50 correspondence colleges which offer literally hundreds of academic, professional and vocational courses, and enrol many thousands of students each year. Most correspondence colleges are private commercial operations, although there are a few exceptions, including the National Extension College (NEC), which has no entry qualifications. NEC courses are generally acknowledged to be among the best in open learning and include GCSE, A-levels, general education, business skills, and personal development courses. For information contact NEC, Michael Young Centre, Purbeck Road, Cambridge CB2 8 HN (☎ 01223-400 321, 💻 www.nec.ac.uk).

Open learning courses in accounting, management, marketing, supervisory skills, small businesses, health and care, retailing, information technology, and engineering are run by the Open College (OC), which has regional offices in London, Manchester, Glasgow, Belfast and 80 local centres. The Open College of the Arts is an educational trust that caters for those wishing to develop their artistic abilities, but who wish or need to work from home. Courses include art and design, creative writing, drawing, painting, textiles, sculpture, garden design, photography, singing, the history of art, music and camcorders. For information write to the Open College of the Arts, Registration Department, Freepost SF10678, Barnsley S75 1BR (☎ 0800-731 2116, 💻 www.oca-uk.com).

Some institutions such as the Open University and Warwick University Business School offer distance learning Master of Business Administration (MBA) courses for those who cannot or don't wish to study on a full or part-time, locally taught basis. There are around 70 institutions offering MBA courses, which together accept some 15,000 students (many from overseas). The Open University alone enrols some 10,000 managers each year, making it the largest business education institute in the UK. Many other business schools offer MBA courses, covering subjects such as banking, business administration, communications, economics, European languages, information systems, management, marketing, public relations, and social and political studies. Fees for a full-time MBA are around £10,000 a year, although those at the London Business School are over £20,000 a year for two years (plus a further £10,000 a year in living costs).

The UK Basic Skills Unit, Commonwealth House, 1-19 New Oxford Street, London WC1A 1NU (☎ 020-7405 4017, 💻 www.basic-skills.co.uk) was established in 1980 and is the national unit in England and Wales for literacy, numeracy and related communication skills. It also has a limited, but important, role in the development of English for Speakers of Other Languages (ESOL). The unit publishes a wide range of information leaflets and booklets, including a comprehensive *Publications* catalogue. General information about adult education and training is available free in many towns and cities from educational guidance units (usually part of the public library service) and adult guidance agencies.

In London, many further education courses are listed in *Full-Time Floodlight, Part-Time Floodlight* and *Summertime Floodlight*, London's guide to April to August courses (published by Floodlight Publishing, 🖳 www.floodlight.co.uk).

LANGUAGE SCHOOLS

If you don't speak English fluently (or you wish to learn another language) you can enrol in a language course at one of over 5,000 language schools. Obtaining a working knowledge or becoming fluent in English while living in the UK is relatively easy, as you are constantly immersed in the English language and have the maximum opportunity to practise (the British aren't renowned for their proficiency in foreign languages). However, if you wish to speak or write English fluently, you must probably attend a language school or find a private tutor. Over 500,000 students come to the UK each year to learn English, 75 per cent from Western Europe, thus ensuring that English as a Foreign Language schools (over 1,000) are big business.

It's usually necessary to have a recognised qualification in English to be accepted at a college of higher or further education. In many areas, there's an ethnic minority language service providing information and counselling in a variety of languages. These organise a wide range of English classes, including home tuition, open learning and small classes, at beginner and intermediate levels.

There are English-language schools in all cities and large towns; however, the majority of schools, particularly those offering intensive courses, are to be found in the south. The largest concentration of schools is in London and the world-famous university towns of Oxford and Cambridge. There are also a large number of schools along the south coast of England, particularly in Brighton and Bournemouth. Edinburgh is the most popular location in Scotland.

You may find it advantageous to choose a school that's a member of Arels-Felco Ltd, the association of recognised English language-teaching establishments in the UK. Arels-Felco incorporates ARELS (Association of Recognised English Language Schools) and FELCO (Federation of English Language Course Organisations), and is a non-profit association whose members are recognised as efficient in the teaching of English as a foreign language by the British Council. Members must follow the association's regulations and code of conduct, which include high academic standards and rules governing the welfare of students. Some members of Arels-Felco are registered as non-profit educational trusts, which means value added tax (VAT) isn't payable on fees, and many members cater for the disabled, including blind, deaf and physically disabled students. Arels-Felco publishes an annual directory of members containing details of all courses, obtainable from Arels-Felco, 2 Pontypool Place, Valentine Place, London SE1 8QF (☎ 020-7242 3136). The British Council publishes *The Green List*, a listing of accredited schools, available online only from 🖳 www.britishcouncil.org.

Courses offered by schools that are members of Arels-Felco mainly fall into four categories: general English courses available all year round; courses for executives; junior (9+) holiday courses; and adult (16+) courses. Courses vary in length from one week to six months and cater for all ages from five (in special schools) through to senior citizens. The average class size is around 10 to 12, with 15 usually being the maximum. Most schools are equipped with computers, language laboratories, video studios, libraries and bookshops, and some even have their own restaurants and bars (to help loosen the tongue).

Most language schools offer a variety of classes depending on your current language ability, how many hours you wish to study a week, how much money you want to spend and how quickly you wish to learn. Full-time, part-time and evening courses are offered by many schools, and many also offer residential courses or selected accommodation with local families (highly recommended to accelerate learning). Courses that include accommodation (often half board, consisting of breakfast and an evening meal) usually offer excellent value for money. If you need to find your own accommodation, particularly in London, it can be difficult and expensive. Language classes generally fall into the following categories:

Category	Hours per Week
Compact	10 – 20
Intensive	20 – 30
Total immersion	30 – 40+

Most schools offer compact or intensive courses and also provide special English courses for businessmen, lawyers, journalists and doctors (among others), and a wide variety of examinations, all of which are recognised internationally. Course fees vary considerably and are usually calculated on a weekly basis. Fees depend on the number of hours of tuition per week, the type of course, and the location and reputation of the school. Expect to pay £150 to £350 a week for an intensive course providing 20 to 30 hours of language study per week. A compact course usually costs around £80 to £100 per week and half board accommodation around £80 to £90 a week extra (more in London). It's possible to enrol at a good school for an all-inclusive (tuition plus half-board accommodation) intensive course for as little as £200 per week. In London and other large cities, students in private accommodation may need to spend more time travelling to classes each day.

Total immersion or executive courses are provided by many schools and usually consist of private lessons for a minimum of 30 to 40 hours a week. Fees can run to £1,000 a week or more and not everyone is suited to learning at such a fast rate (or has the financial resources). Whatever language you're learning, don't expect to become fluent in a short period unless you have a particular flair for languages or already have a good command of a language. Unless you must learn a language quickly, it's better to space your lessons over a long period. Don't commit yourself to a long course of study (particularly an expensive one) before ensuring that it's the correct one. Most schools offer a free introductory lesson and free tests to help you find your appropriate level. Many language schools offer private and small group lessons. **It's important to choose the right course, particularly if you're studying**

English in order to continue with full-time education in the UK and must reach a minimum standard or gain a particular qualification.

Many language schools offer special English classes for *au pairs* costing from around £40 to over £150 a term, depending on the number of hours of tuition per week. Most courses for *au pairs* include around four hours study a week. The school year begins in the middle of September and ends in June, and some schools accept *au pairs* only in the September and January terms (*au pairs* arriving after Easter may find it difficult to obtain classes). There are usually no classes for *au pairs* over the summer holiday period (June to mid-September). Among the best value-for-money English courses are those run by state colleges under the control of Local Educational Authorities (LEAs), the Department for Education and Skills, or the Scottish Education Department.

Most colleges offer full-time, part-time and vacation English courses for overseas students throughout the year, with fees ranging from around £20 to £80 a week. Many courses are cheaper for EU nationals and may even be free during the daytime for those under 18. Colleges usually arrange accommodation for students. A booklet containing a list of colleges and their courses (including courses for English language teachers) is available from English UK, 56 Buckingham Gate, London SW1E 6AG (🖳 www.englishuk.com).

You may prefer to have private lessons, which are a quicker, but generally more expensive, way of learning a language. The main advantage of private lessons is that you learn at your own speed and aren't held back by slow learners or dragged along by the class genius. You can advertise for a teacher in local newspapers, on shopping centre or supermarket bulletin boards, university or school notice boards and through your or your spouse's employer. Your friends or colleagues may also be able to help you find a suitable private teacher. If you're living in the UK and speak reasonable English but need conversational practice, you might consider enrolling in a part-time course at an adult education institute.

Many British universities hold summer and other holiday courses for foreigners, e.g. Birmingham, London and Oxford. For a programme contact the Secretary, British Universities Summer Schools, University of Oxford, Department for Continuing Education, 1 Wellington Square, Oxford OX1 2JD (☎ 01865-270 360, 🖳 www.ox.ac.uk). The British Chamber of Commerce provides an English tuition advisory service in many countries and works closely with English schools, universities and other institutions. For information contact your local British embassy, consulate or high commission abroad. For an introduction to languages in the UK, see **Language** on page 44.

10.

PUBLIC TRANSPORT

Public transport services in the UK vary from region to region and town to town. In some areas, services are excellent and good value for money, while in others they're infrequent, slow and expensive. The UK has no unified general transport policy, particularly a long-term strategy that balances the needs of the public transport user against those of the motorist. Consequently, the UK has one of the most congested and ill-planned transport systems in Europe (exacerbated by the disastrous rail privatisation, which has driven even more people onto the roads). However, it isn't **always** essential to own a car in the UK, particularly if you live in a large town or city with adequate public transport (and where parking may be impossible, in any case). On the other hand, if you live in a remote village or a town away from the main train and bus routes, it's usually essential to have your own transport. Public transport is cheaper if you're able to take advantage of the wide range of discount, combination (e.g. rail, bus, underground and ferry), season and off-peak tickets available.

The UK's transport 'system' is heavily weighted in favour of road transport and the level of public transport subsidies in the UK is among the lowest in Europe, e.g. in the European Union few countries invest less per head of population on their railways. Despite more people using public transport in London than in any other European city (London has the world's largest rail and tube network), it has the most expensive public transport of any capital city in Europe, with fares around four times those of Rome and some 15 times more expensive than Budapest. The percentage of travellers using public transport is, not surprisingly, very low, with some 90 per cent of all journeys made by car.

The poor services and high cost of public transport have made a huge contribution to the heavy road congestion, with traffic levels in the south-east and other heavily populated areas approaching saturation point. Apart from the environmental damage caused by the ever increasing number of cars, road congestion costs businesses billions of pounds a year which, when added to the cost of road accidents, suggests a huge commercial benefit would be reaped from improved public transport. Many cities and counties promote the use of public transport instead of private cars, although trying to encourage people to travel by public transport has met with little success. One of the biggest problems facing the UK is that it's much cheaper to run a car than it is to use the railways. Most analysts believe the situation must be reversed if the UK isn't to suffer almost permanent gridlock in its major cities in the next decade or so.

Rising levels of traffic pollution are choking the UK's cities, where asthma and other bronchial complaints (which are aggravated by exhaust fumes) have increased hugely in recent years. Many experts believe the only answer is to pedestrianise town centres and severely limit traffic in towns and cities (as is done in many European countries), while at the same time investing heavily in non-polluting public transport systems. Although the UK killed off its trams (which in mainland Europe still perform an excellent role midway between a bus and a train) many years ago, a number of cities have introduced (or are planning to) new metro, light rail transit and supertram systems, and are banning cars from city centres. London has recently introduced a 'congestion charge' of £8 for vehicles using the central zone and this has already reduced traffic density and shortened journey times; it's likely that the zone to which the charge applies will soon be enlarged to include parts of west London.

A wealth of information is published by national and local public transport companies, local and county councils, and regional transport authorities, most of which provide a wide range of passes and fares for travellers. Many regions offer combined bus, train, underground (metro) and ferry passes, and offer special rates for children, students, young people, pensioners, families, the unemployed and those receiving social security benefits, in addition to off-peak travel reductions. Students can obtain an International Student Identity Card (ISIC), offering travel discounts in the UK and worldwide.

A guide to public transport (land, sea and air) for disabled people entitled *Door to Door* is available online from the Disabled Persons Transport Advisory Committee (🖳 www.dptac.gov.uk/door-to-door). Other useful books include, *Out and About*, a travel and transport guide for the elderly published by Age Concern, and the *Guide for the Disabled Traveller* (Automobile Association). If you find it difficult to use public transport, because of frailty or a disability, you should enquire whether your local council operates a 'dial-a-ride' or 'book-a-ride' service for residents. Free or reduced travel passes are available in most areas for senior citizens, the blind and the disabled, and many transport authorities publish information leaflets for disabled travellers.

Although primarily intended for tourists, *Getting About Britain*, is a useful guide to public transport services and fares for the independent traveller (🖳 www.getting aboutbritain.com). Public transport information is also available via the television teletext information service, via the internet (e.g. 🖳 www.bargainholidays.co.uk) and from TravelCall (☎ 08702-512264, 🖳 www.travelcallbreaks.co.uk), who claim to provide travellers with the cheapest, most direct and quickest routes for UK journeys.

TRAINS

The railway network in the UK is one of the most extensive in Europe with over 17,500km (11,000mi) of lines, some 2,500 stations and around 15,000 trains a day. The UK pioneered railways and the Stockton and Darlington Railway (1825) was the first public passenger railway in the world. In 1938, the UK set a world steam record of 126.5mph (203kph), although it now lags far behind its international competitors (incredibly, trains on many routes were actually faster 100 years ago!). It has been estimated that France (TGV), Germany (ICE), Italy (Pendolino) and Japan (Bullet Train) are up to 20 years ahead of the UK in high-speed train technology, with trains routinely running at speeds of up to 200mph (321kph) or faster.

British Railways was nationalised in 1947 and has been in almost continual decline ever since, owing to serious under-funding by a succession of governments. Over the years, cuts in funding have led to a reduction in the size of the rail network (which is expected to be reduced even further in future, as unprofitable lines are closed); a deterioration in the quality and frequency of services, massive increases in fares and a lack of investment in the infrastructure and rolling stock.

Privatisation

In an effort to reduce government subsidies and as part of its privatisation doctrine, one of the Conservative government's last acts in office was to privatise British Rail (completed in 1997) and passenger services are now operated by some 25 separate private companies. Other companies include those that lease locomotives and passenger carriages (rolling stock); freight service providers; infrastructure maintenance companies; and track renewal companies. In 2002, Railtrack, the company responsible for the tracks and infrastructure, went into liquidation and was taken over by Network Rail, a government-backed, non-profit company. Despite the privatisation, railway companies still receive government subsidies, although they've been reduced (while fares have rocketed).

Since privatisation, railway services have gone from bad to worse resulting in higher fares, fewer services, poor connections, increased train cancellations, late trains (punctuality is one of the biggest problems), too few seats (overcrowding is widespread), narrower seats, closed ticket offices, non-existent or unhelpful staff, poor or no catering on trains and a paucity of accurate information. **More importantly, there have been a number of fatal accidents in the last few years, often as a result of poor maintenance (now taken over by Network Rail staff), which has deterred many people from travelling by rail.** Not surprisingly there's widespread public dissatisfaction, which results in over one million complaints a year! In fact, most observers believe that privatised rail services are even worse than official figures reveal and that the UK now has the worst (and most expensive) railways in Western Europe.

Trains are expensive and even if you're able to take advantage of special tickets, excursion fares, family reductions and holiday package deals, they're still usually dearer than buses (or private cars) over long distances. The harsh reality (accepted by every other western European country) is that it's impossible to run a comprehensive, quality rail service at a price people are willing to pay (or can afford) without huge public subsidies. Although services are expected to improve in the long term, most analysts believe that without increased state subsidies (or re-nationalisation) the only certain thing about the UK's rail service is that fares will continue to increase and services be reduced.

Types of Train

Most trains consist of first (shown by a '1' on windows) and standard class carriages. Services categorised as suburban or local are trains that stop at most stations along their route, many provided by modern Sprinter and Super Sprinter class trains, with push-button operated or automatic doors. Long-distance trains are termed express and InterCity, and stop at major towns only. Express services are provided by new 158 (158kph/98mph) class trains in some areas. InterCity 125 trains, so named after their maximum speed of 125mph (201kph), are the world's fastest diesel trains and operate on most InterCity services. New InterCity 225 (225kph/140mph) trains have been introduced on major routes.

All InterCity 125 and 225 trains are air-conditioned, have a buffet car in standard class and a restaurant car in first class, although the food has been criticised for its poor quality and high cost. During rush hours (before 9.30am and from 4 to 7pm), trains are frequent on most routes, although it's best to avoid travelling then, as trains are packed and fares are at their peak. Although travelling by train may not always compare favourably on paper with air travel, it's often quicker when you add the time required to get to and from town centres and airports. Many towns and cities are served by half-hour or hourly services.

First Class

InterCity Pullman is the name given to the fastest first class and executive class services between London and major business centres in England and Wales. Executive tickets include a first class ticket, seat reservations, 24-hour parking, vouchers for a meal or refreshments on the train, and central zone tube tickets for London arrivals. Executive passengers can purchase vouchers for breakfast, lunch and dinner, which are served at your seat. Pullman lounges are available for all full fare first class or executive passengers at London's Euston and King's Cross stations, plus Edinburgh, Glasgow Central, Leeds and Newcastle stations, where telephones, photocopiers, televisions and meeting rooms are provided.

Steam & Holiday Trains

Although the major operators no longer operate steam trains, the UK is still a mecca for steam fans and private railway steam trains provide scheduled services in many parts of the country. Steam fans should obtain a copy of the yearbook of the Association of Railway Preservation Societies, *Railways Restored* by Ian Allan, which is a guide to over 100 steam lines, museums and static railway exhibits throughout the UK (many are operated by volunteers and provide limited scheduled services for tourists and railway enthusiasts). Many railway magazines (e.g. *Steam Railway*) are published in the UK and leaflets about steam trains and services are available from tourist information centres.

Trains can be hired for the day in most parts of the UK and some companies operate special day and longer trips for train enthusiasts in Pullman-style, first class, saloon coaches, many including travel on narrow-gauge railways. The ultimate (and the world's most expensive) nostalgic rail journey in the UK is on the *Royal Scotsman*. You can also book a trip on the famous Orient Express from London to Venice, which is one of the world's most popular train trips. If you're planning a holiday in the UK travelling by train, it will pay you to visit a travel agent, who will provide you with comprehensive rail information and a detailed itinerary at no extra cost.

General Information

● Many main railway stations offer a choice of restaurants and snack bars, although the standard of food often leaves much to be desired.

- Food and drink machines are provided at many stations.

- Some old trains have doors with no handle on the inside. To open the door from the inside you must open the window and turn the handle on the outside.

- It's prohibited to open the windows of air-conditioned carriages or put your feet on seats.

- Many large railway stations provide wash, shower and brush-up facilities, including hair dryers. Some also provide nappy (diaper) changing rooms. Most main line stations charge 10p to use a toilet.

- Most main stations have instant passport-size photograph machines.

- Public payphones (which accept credit and debit cards) are available on InterCity and express train services.

- There are car parks at most railway stations, where fees usually range from around £2 to £3 a day (some stations also have free car parks, while others are free at weekends). Season tickets are also available. There's a high incidence of car theft (and the theft of articles from cars) at station car parks, so don't leave anything in your car and take precautions against theft (see **Car Theft** on page 287).

- Some London railway stations, e.g. Victoria, have banks with extended opening hours.

- Accommodation for smokers on trains is extremely limited and sometimes non-existent. There are fines for those caught smoking in non-smoking areas.

- Railway companies often carry out engineering work affecting services, particularly at weekends. You're advised to check with local information offices before travelling. Planned engineering work may be detailed in timetables and train delays are also listed on television teletext services.

- Toilets are provided on trains on all but the shortest distance services (but shouldn't be used when a train is in a station).

- Travel insurance for rail passengers is available from main line stations.

- Luggage can be sent unaccompanied and can be insured. Many stations and airports have luggage lockers, left luggage offices and luggage trolleys (although they're often difficult to find). When using a luggage locker, insert the correct money to release the key. Note the number of the locker (on the key) in case you lose the key. Railway porters are available at large stations.

- Bicycles can be sent between any two stations using local services, i.e. excluding express and InterCity services.

- It's possible to hire a car from all major stations (e.g. Hertz executive connections or rail-drive services) and, if you book 24 hours in advance, a car can be arranged to meet you at around 100 major stations at any time of the day or night. Cars can also be hired on the spot from some stations and left at other mainline stations. To make a Hertz InterCity reservation, contact your local travel agent or InterCity Business Travel Service.

- Wheelchairs for disabled passengers are provided at major railway stations, and most trains have special facilities for the storage of wheelchairs, including all InterCity services.

Tickets

Railway operators offer a bewildering range of tickets depending on a variety of considerations, such as the day and time of day you're travelling, when you will be returning and how often you travel. The private railway companies operate diverse services ranging from local rural lines to major cross-country routes, many offering few standard services and tickets. Therefore, with the exception of national InterCity services, some rail passes and tickets may be available only in certain regions, although most provide similar services. Ticket staff are supposed to provide you with the cheapest ticket available for your journey, although overcharging is commonplace (if less widespread than previously). Always double or treble check ticket prices before buying a ticket for a long-distance journey involving a number of railway companies.

There are two classes of travel on most routes, first and standard (or second) class. First class fares are around 50 per cent more expensive than standard class, which is used by the vast majority of travellers. Only single, day return and season tickets are issued for first class travel. One Day Travelcard (valid only after a certain time of day, e.g. 9.30am) and AwayBreak tickets are issued for standard class travel only, but the holders of Network cards may purchase first class supplement tickets that are valid for the day on which the ticket is dated. At weekends and on public holidays you can upgrade a standard ticket to first class on all InterCity trains on payment of a supplement.

Children aged 5 to 15 pay half the adult fare (except for Apex, SuperApex and shuttle advance InterCity tickets, where no child fare is available) and children under five travel free (subject to a maximum of two children per fare-paying adult). All tickets and passes are described in leaflets available from any station.

A ticket must usually be purchased from a ticket office or machine before boarding a train. If a station is unstaffed, a ticket may be obtained from the conductor on the train (if there is one) or you must pay at your destination. In many areas, local public transport tickets can also be purchased at post offices, ticket agencies, travel agents and corner shops. At many stations there are ticket machines, although these sell tickets to a limited number of local destinations only. There are various types of machines, but you usually select your destination from those listed, select the ticket type required and then insert the amount displayed. Machines usually accept all coins from 5p to £1, plus £5, £10 and £20 notes. There are also machines selling 'permit to travel' tickets (for a nominal fee) indicating the boarding station and the time. You give the permit to the ticket inspector on the train or the ticket collector at your destination, and must pay the difference between the permit's cost and the fare.

Fare Evasion

Fare evasion is rife and costs around £50 million annually, particularly at undermanned stations. Ticket inspectors check tickets on many trains and staff carry out undercover operations to detect persistent fare evaders, who face heavy fines and possibly a prison sentence. In 1990, on-the-spot fines of £10 were introduced in some areas although, if you're discovered travelling without a valid ticket, you're normally required to pay only the full or correct fare for your journey. Fare-dodgers who don't pay their fines may be blacklisted and reported to credit agencies. If you're discovered travelling in first class with a standard ticket, you must pay the full first class fare, not just the fare difference. You must usually show your ticket (or surrender an expired ticket) to a ticket collector at your destination station.

Bookings

Seats can be reserved on all InterCity trains (Apex tickets include free reservations). If you're travelling in a group, you can make up to four reservations together for the same fee. InterCity bookings are free on some services or included in the fare. Seats can be reserved from two months in advance and up to two hours before a train departs (or from 4pm the previous day for early morning trains). InterCity seats can be booked from over 300 stations nationwide or from an appointed travel agent. When booking, you should indicate any preferences, such as smoking or non-smoking, window or aisle seat, or facing or back to the direction of travel.

A ticket doesn't guarantee you a seat – in fact during rush hours you're lucky to get one – and it's advisable to reserve seats on long journeys, particularly when travelling during holiday periods or at weekends. Don't sit in a seat with a 'reserved' sign on it (unless it's yours). Special seats are reserved for the disabled on most trains. Tickets can be ordered by telephone and paid for with an Access, American Express, Switch or Visa card.

Eurostar Passenger Services

The opening of the Channel tunnel in 1994 gave the UK a direct rail connection with the continental rail system, with the introduction of the Eurostar train service to Brussels and Paris. This threatens to drag the UK's railways screaming and kicking into the 21st century, although passengers had to wait until October 2003 for high-speed trains on the British part of the journey. Since the start of Eurostar services, an estimated 25 per cent of business travellers have switched from air to rail for journeys between London and Brussels and Paris. However, many have switched back to air travel, as Eurostar is more expensive than budget flights and, if you don't travel in first class, it's also cramped and uncomfortable.

Eurostar trains run from London Waterloo International to Paris and Brussels at speeds of up to 185mph, taking around 2 hours 35 minutes to Paris. Later in 2007 St. Pancras International will become Eurostar's new London home and create a high-speed link to the Continent from the heart of the City. Meals in first class are complementary (i.e. you've already paid for them in the price of your ticket), although the food leaves much to be desired. There are a range of special fares (including discovery special, weekend return, Apex weekend, pass holder (for holders of international rail passes), senior return, youths (under 26) and groups. For reservations ☎ 08705-186 186 or 🖳 www.eurostar.com. See also **Eurotunnel** on page 246.

UNDERGROUND TRAINS

The London underground railway system (or 'tube', as it's known locally) celebrated its centenary in 1990 and is internationally famous, ranking alongside the Paris metro and the New York subway. London's tube network covers the largest area of any underground rail system, with 391km (242mi) of track, of which around 171km (106mi) is underground, and 267 stations. The tube runs to all areas of central and greater London, connecting with all London mainline stations, and provides the quickest way to get around London.

Like the rail network, the tube has also been embroiled in a public/private ownership debate, between the government (who wants to bring in private investment and part-ownership) and London's mayor, who wants it to remain entirely public-owned and funded. While the arguments rage, the lack of investment has led to a deterioration in the infrastructure, which has resulted in a number of accidents and derailments of trains, and the suspension of services for urgent engineering work.

The tube operates from 5 or 5.30am until around 12.30am (a notice of first and last trains is displayed at each station). If possible, you should try to avoid travelling during the rush hours, e.g. around 8 to 10am and 4.30 to 6.30pm, when passengers are packed in like sardines (when travelling with children or friends, hang on to them, as it's easy to become separated in the crush). Platforms are reached from street level by lifts, stairs or, in central London, by escalators. When travelling on an escalator, you should stand on the right (or on the same side as everyone else). After a fatal fire at King's Cross underground station, **no smoking is permitted anywhere within the tube system**. To plan your journey, check the maps showing the zones and stations displayed at all stations, or obtain a free Tube Map from any underground or London railway station.

The tube has 12 lines (excluding the Docklands Light Railway), each with a different name and colour (e.g. the Central line is red, the Circle line is yellow). New lines have been built in recent years (e.g. the East London line) and existing lines (e.g. the Jubilee line) are being extended. Where lines cross **and** where there's an interchange station, it's shown on maps by a circle. Check the line(s) you need to reach your destination and where you must change before starting a journey. Once on board a train, you can follow your progress on the map displayed in each carriage above the seats or at the ends of carriages (make sure you're travelling in the right direction!). Underground trains stop at all stations (apart from a few that operate during rush hours only) and the doors open and shut automatically.

The London underground system is divided into areas, called zones, central London being designated zone one. New underground fares were introduced in

January 2007 - for example, travel within zones 1-6 currently costs £4.00 per adult ticket (cash single fare), though children travel for less. You can also buy an Oyster Card, a cheaper and more convenient 'electronic' ticket, or a Travelcard (see below). Travel which excludes zone one has cheaper fares. Tickets can usually be purchased at all underground stations and you should always buy a ticket before you start your journey, and keep it for inspection and collection at your destination. Children under five travel free and those aged 5 to 15 travel at reduced rates, which are often less than half (around 40 per cent) of the adult fare. Children need a Child Rate Photocard (available from station ticket offices, London Travel Information Centres and selected newsagents on production of a passport size photograph and proof of age) for travelcards valid seven days or longer, and 14 and 15-year-olds need a Child Rate Photocard to purchase any child rate ticket. Photocards are issued free of charge.

Tickets are available from ticket machines, which accept all coins from 5p to £1 and £5 notes (some accept credit cards), and from ticket offices. Often there are long queues at ticket offices, so **always** keep some change handy for machines or buy a season ticket. If you must pay an excess fare, a special window is provided at some central London stations, otherwise you must pay the ticket inspector. Machines are also installed in over 2,000 newsagents throughout London to dispense Travelcards, bus passes and London Transport cards.

To gain access to platforms at most central London stations, a ticket must be inserted in an automatic gate. Don't forget to retrieve your ticket. If the gate 'eats' your ticket or doesn't open, a 'seek assistance' message is displayed (ask a ticket inspector for help). Magnets, such as those fitted to some handbags, can destroy the magnetic information stripe on tickets, causing them to be rejected by automatic ticket gates. Take care, particularly if you have a season ticket. Rail tickets that include tube travel can also be used in these gates. You're subject to an on-the-spot fine for travelling without a valid ticket.

A London Travelcard is available which includes tube travel, most London buses (including some Green Line buses, but excluding Airbuses and Night Buses), most National Railway services and the Docklands Light Railway (which is actually part of the tube system). Travelcards are based on a six-zone system. They can be bought from tube station ticket offices (one-day cards are available from some machines) and from rail stations within the tube network. A limited range of cards can also be purchased from some bus garages, selected newsagents and travel agents. Travelcards are valid for one day, a weekend, a week, a month or any period up to one year. A photocard is required (see above) for seven-day, one-month and annual travelcards. Tickets can be purchased via the internet (💻 www.ticket-on-line.co.uk).

Travel information for the tube and London buses is available via ☎ 020-7222 1234 (24 hours) or 💻 www.tfl.gov.uk. Access & Mobility, Transport for London, Windsor House, 42–50 Victoria Street, London SW1H 0TL (☎ 020-7941 4500, 💻 www.tfl.gov.uk) publishes a leaflet entitled *Access to the Underground* for elderly and disabled passengers.

There are other underground urban railway networks in Glasgow, Liverpool, Manchester and Tyne and Wear (Newcastle). The latter is a modern light rapid transit (LRT) system 56km (35mi) in length with over 40 stations. Many other cities have plans for LRT or supertram systems, although they could be cancelled because of lack of funds.

BUSES

In the UK, there are two main types of bus service: town and city services and long-distance, often referred to as coaches. Each region has its own local bus companies providing local town and country services. In large towns and cities, most bus services start and terminate at a central bus station and it can be confusing trying to find the right connection. If you need assistance, ask at the bus station information office. Most bus companies provide free timetables and route maps, and many local district and county councils publish a comprehensive booklet of timetables and maps (possibly for a small fee) for all bus services operating within their boundaries. In many cities night bus services are in operation. Timetables are also posted at major bus stops.

National long-distance bus services are listed in *Getting About Britain* distributed by Visit Britain (see **Tourist Information** on page 403). Local bus companies organise special day trips and outings throughout the UK, plus European tours. Check that a holiday bus company is a member of the bonded Bus and Coach Council, which pays compensation should a member be unable to meet its commitments. London Transport bus information is listed on the television teletext service. See also **Timetables & Maps** on page 248.

The deregulation of bus services in 1986 allowed any bus company to operate on any route, and led to cut-throat competition and many companies going out of business. In the last decade, the largest operators have swallowed up many of their competitors (amid numerous claims of dirty tricks) and on many routes have established a monopoly or near monopoly.

Long-distance Buses

A number of companies provide long-distance bus services. The major operator is National Express (NE) which provides a nationwide service in England, Wales and Scotland (where services are operated in conjunction with its sister company Caledonian Express Stagecoach). Some local bus companies operate express bus services (which make a limited number of stops) within their area, e.g. London Transport's Green Line Coach service. Bus companies also operate sightseeing trips throughout the UK.

National Express serves over 1,400 major towns and cities nationwide (daily with the exception of Christmas Day) and carries over 11 million passengers more than a billion miles a year. It operates a fast and reasonably-priced hourly service to the most popular destinations. Express buses are the cheapest form of long-distance travel within the UK and, although journeys take up to twice as long as trains, fares are often 50 per cent lower. National Express coaches arrive and depart from Victoria Coach Station (☎ 020-7730 3466 for information) in London, which is a 10-minute walk from Victoria railway station.

Tickets can be purchased in advance at around 2,000 National Express agents (most travel agents) throughout the UK or from departure points. Assured reservations can be made for a small fee at least one day in advance and are recommended at busy times, on overnight services, when boarding at a suburban point, or when it's important that you travel at a particular time. Access or Visa card bookings are accepted and must be made at least five days in advance if the tickets are to be posted to you. Journeys may be broken, but tickets must be officially endorsed at the start of each journey. Information and tickets can be purchased via phone (☎ 08705-808 080 or ☎ 0990-808 080 for credit/debit card bookings) and credit card bookings can also be made via the internet (🖥 www.gobycoach.com). You're requested to limit yourself to one suitcase on National Express buses (plus hand luggage), although this isn't obligatory. Smoking is permitted on single-decker buses at the rear of the bus and on double-deckers at the rear of the upper deck only.

International bus services are also available and include Eurolines, Supabus, Hoverspeed and Transline services, with regular buses to around 200 destinations in Europe. Most international services operate from London Victoria Coach Station, although some operate directly from the provinces. International services usually have domestic nationwide connections.

Airbus, Airlink and Flightline bus services are provided at all international airports, including inter-airport bus services. Airbus services operate from London Euston and Victoria stations to Heathrow airport. All international and regional airports have bus services to local cities and towns. Some local bus companies provide saver cards for the young, e.g. those under 24, offering discounts of around 50 per cent for travel after 9am. Many other reduced fare tickets are available, including cheap day returns, season tickets, rover tickets and family tickets.

Rural & City Buses

Most counties and regions are served by one or more local bus companies (e.g. London and its suburbs are served by London Transport), which often operate single and double-decker buses (including London's world-famous red buses). In many towns and cities, bus companies also use mini-buses. Services usually operate from around 6am to midnight and in major cities there's a also a night bus service, e.g. London has an excellent night bus service (with slightly higher fares than day buses) operating from 11pm to 6am. Like national bus companies, local bus companies organise local, national and international day trips and tours with pick-up points in local towns and villages. Buses are often slow during the day due to traffic congestion, particularly in major towns and cities, and it's often quicker to take a train or, in London (and a few other cities), the tube (see **Underground Trains** on page 241). In rural areas, buses run infrequently, rarely to where you want to go and they usually follow a circuitous route that takes in the surrounding villages and towns. A direct journey taking, say, 15 minutes by car can easily take an hour or two by bus!

Buses throughout the UK are usually denoted by a route number, which is shown at bus stops and on buses. The destination of a bus is also shown on the front and sometimes also on the side or back (so you can see which bus you've just missed). Always check the route number and direction of a bus before boarding. If in doubt, ask someone. There are compulsory stops (called 'fare' stops) and request stops, where you must hail a bus by raising your hand if you want it to stop. When you want to get off a bus at a request stop, you must signal the driver by pressing a button or pulling a cord inside the bus, which activates a buzzer or bell in the driver's cab. Make sure you give the driver adequate time to stop and don't ring the bell at the lat minute just as you're approaching your stop. You usually get off a bus via the middle or back doors.

Most buses are one-person operated, where you show your ticket or pay the driver when you get on. On some double-decker buses, tickets are purchased from a conductor on the bus. Keep your ticket, as it may be inspected at any time during your journey. Fares in London and some other cities are based on a zone system, as for London tube trains. In London, in addition to standard double-decker buses, Red Arrow single-decker buses operate frequent services between major railway stations in central London. On Red Arrow buses, a flat rate fare is charged for adults and children, which is inserted in a machine (no ticket is issued). Have the exact fare ready when boarding or buy a Travelcard (see **Underground Trains** on page 241) or bus pass valid for the central fare zone. A Travelcard includes travel on most London buses, the London tube, south-east railways and the Docklands Light Railway. London Transport publishes extensive bus guides (including maps) for all areas and operates a 24-hour information service (☎ 020-7222 1234, 💻 www. tfl.gov.uk).

Most bus companies charge reduced rates (usually half fare or less) for children aged 5 to 15 and those under five travel free if they aren't occupying a seat (although some bus companies may limit the number of free children per adult). There's usually no charge for dogs, which are carried at the discretion of the driver or conductor (if the bus is already carrying a dog, they may refuse, although guide dogs are usually accepted). You're usually charged an additional full fare for non-collapsible baby carriages and prams. Senior citizens (over 60) and blind and disabled people may be entitled to free or half fare travel in certain areas, but usually require a permit from the local district or borough council. Most bus companies provide bus pass or season tickets on most routes (weekly, monthly or annual), both point-to-point and unrestricted, for which a photocard is usually required. In some areas a 'Sunday Rider' or 'rambler' ticket provides unlimited Sunday travel on most local bus services (Sunday timetables are provided). Bus services on unprofitable routes are often subsidised by local councils and run as a public service, e.g. early morning commuter and hospital services.

From Mondays to Saturdays, services usually run at the same times each day. On Sundays and public holidays a restricted service is usually in operation, with the exception of Christmas and Boxing Days, when no services are normally provided. All buses have an official seating capacity and allow a certain number of passengers to stand when all seats are occupied, shown on a notice displayed in vehicles. Anything left on a bus can be reclaimed from the offices of the bus company (the largest have their own lost property offices). There may be a small charge for the return of property, depending on its value. If you find an article of lost property on a bus, you're required by law to hand it to the driver or conductor.

In central London, a special service for disabled passengers uses small buses equipped with wheelchair lifts to connect Paddington, Euston, King's Cross, and Waterloo stations and the Heathrow/Victoria bus link. Free or subsidised door-to-door bus services are provided for the blind and disabled in most areas. Bus timetables (free or for a nominal fee) are provided by all bus companies and are available from transport companies and public libraries. (See also **Timetables & Maps** on page 248.)

FERRIES & EUROTUNNEL

Regular car and passenger ferry services operate all year round, within the British Isles and to continental ports in Belgium, France, Germany, Holland, Iceland, Spain and various Scandinavian countries. The proportion of passengers travelling to and from the UK by sea has reduced considerably since the early '60s, given the reduced cost of air travel and competition from Eurotunnel (see below). The major ferry companies operating international services are P&O (which also operates as P&O Stena Line on some routes) and Brittany Ferries, which dominates the routes in the western Channel (Caen, Cherbourg, Roscoff and St Malo) with around 40 per cent of the market. Hoverspeed operates a hovercraft service from Dover to Calais and catamaran (Seacat) services on the same route plus Folkestone to Boulogne and Dover to Ostend. A larger Hoverspeed superseacat service operates from Newhaven to Dieppe.

Some ferry services operate during the summer months only, e.g. May to September, and the frequency of services varies from dozens a day on the busiest Dover-Calais route during the summer peak period, to one a week on longer routes. Services are less frequent during the winter months, when bad weather can also cause cancellations. Most Channel ferry services employ large super ferries with a capacity of up to 1,800 to 2,000 passengers and 700 cars. Ferries carry all vehicles, while hovercraft take all vehicles except HGVs, large trucks and buses. All operators except Hoverspeed offer night services, which may be cheaper. Berths, single cabins and pullman seats are usually available, and most ships have a restaurant, self-service cafeteria, a children's play area and shops. Generally, the longer the route, the better and wider the range of facilities provided, which often makes it worthwhile considering alternative routes to the Dover-Calais crossing. Although Dover-Calais is the shortest route and offers the most crossings, longer passages are generally less crowded and more relaxing, and fares are often lower.

On longer routes, most ships provide hairdressing, fast-photo developing, pools, saunas, live entertainment, cinemas and discos. Most ferries have a range of shops, which are huge money-spinners and the reason ferry companies offer such low winter fares (ferry companies make up to 50 per cent of their profits from on-board sales). Most ferries offer day cabins with en suite facilities, which provide somewhere to leave luggage, shower and change, or just have a nap. When travelling on a cross-Channel ferry with your car, remember to take any items required during the crossing with you, as you aren't allowed access to the car decks during journeys. Many ships cater for children and mothers, and have play areas, baby-feeding and changing rooms. All major ferry operators offer a business class (e.g. P&O's club class) typically costing an extra £7 to £10 per person, per trip. It includes a quieter lounge; free tea, coffee and newspapers; and fax, photocopier and other facilities. Ferry companies also provide ship-to-shore telephone, telex, fax (shore only), and photocopiers on ships and at ports.

It isn't always necessary to make a booking, although it's advisable when travelling during the summer peak period, particularly on a Friday or Saturday (and when you require a berth on an overnight service). Like air travel, ferry services are sometimes subject to delays due to strikes, out of service ferries, or simply the large number of passengers. If possible, it's best to avoid travelling during peak times. Check-in times depend on the particular crossing and are from 20 to 60 minutes for motorists and from 20 to 45 minutes for foot passengers. Comprehensive free timetables and guides are published by shipping companies and are available from travel agents (although it's **much** quicker to book direct).

Fares

Peak fares are high, e.g. a standard Dover-Calais return with P&O (🖳 www. poferries.com) for a vehicle up to 5m in length costs around £260 (£140 single), including the driver and one passenger. This drops to around £120 for a five-day return during the cheapest period. If you want a single ticket only, it may be cheaper to take advantage of a special offer and throw away the return ticket. Ferry companies offer a range of fares, including standard single and return fares, Apex fares, and 5 and 10-day returns. Children under four years old travel free and those aged from 4 to 14 travel for half fare. Students may be entitled to a small discount during off-peak periods. Bicycles are transported free on most services.

Whenever you travel, always check for special offers. Last-minute tickets can be purchased at up to 50 per cent discount from 'bucket' shops. P&O shareholders who own at least £600 worth of P&O concessionary stock receive a 50 per cent discount on Dover-Calais and Felixstowe-Zeebrugge crossings, and 40 per cent off Portsmouth-Cherbourg, Portsmouth-Le Havre and Portsmouth-Bilbao crossings. Some ferry lines have clubs for frequent travellers, e.g. the Brittany Ferries French and Spanish Property Owners Clubs (☎ 08703-665 7333, 🖳 www.brittanyferries.co.uk), offering savings of up to 30 per cent on single and standard return fares. The Eurodrive Travel Club (☎ 0870-442 2440, 🖳 www.eurodrive.co.uk) claims to be able to obtain the cheapest rate for any ferry company.

Day Trips

A huge boost to ferry companies in the low winter season in recent years has been the explosion of low-cost shopping trips to Calais and Boulogne. However, this is having a detrimental affect on summer crossings, as many people balk at paying £300 for a summer crossing when a winter trip costs as little as £25 return for a car and £1 for foot passengers! Most special offers are usually by coupon only, which are available in most daily newspapers during the winter (off-peak) season. Half of those who make return crossings from Dover to Calais are simply making day trips or one-night stays.

British Isles

Within the UK there are regular ferry services to the Isle of Wight, i.e. Portsmouth to Fishbourne and Ryde, Southsea to Ryde and from Lymington to Yarmouth. Car ferry services operate from England to Douglas (Isle of Man) from Heysham, Fleetwood and Liverpool. From Douglas there are regular services to Belfast and Dublin. Regular services operate from the west of Scotland to the Western Isles and to the Orkney and Shetland Isle from the north and east of Scotland. Regular ferry services to the Channel Islands are operated from Poole, Torquay and Weymouth throughout the year. Services to Ireland operate between Stranraer-Larne, Fishguard-Rosslare, Holyhead-Dun Loghaire (for Dublin) and Swansea-Cork.

Eurotunnel

Eurotunnel (💻 www.eurotunnel.com), previously known as Le Shuttle, started operating its shuttle car train service from Folkestone (access to the Eurotunnel terminal is via the M20 motorway, junction 11a) to Coquelles, near Calais, in 1995. The train runs at 15-minute intervals during peak periods, taking just 35 minutes. One of the advantages (in addition to the short travel time) of Eurotunnel is that you can remain in your car isolated from drunken soccer fans and screaming kids. Fares are similar to ferries, e.g. a peak (summer) club class return costs around £340 and an off-peak (January to March) return £170, for a vehicle and all passengers. It's advisable to book (☎ 08705-353 535, 💻 www.eurotunnel.com), although bookings are for a particular day, not a particular train or time, so you may have to wait for one or two trains to depart before being able to board. Don't expect to get a place in summer on the 'turn up and go' service, particularly on Fridays, Saturdays and Sundays. Demand is lighter on services from France to the UK, when bookings may be unnecessary. Trains carry all 'vehicles', including bicycles, motorcycles, cars, trucks, buses, caravans and motorhomes. Vehicles carrying gas are banned.

TIMETABLES & MAPS

All British public transport companies produce comprehensive national and local timetables, route maps and guides, although with the UK's often chaotic road traffic conditions and the railways' innumerable delays and cancellations, you would be wise to confirm times before travelling. A national timetable is published, although InterCity and local timetables stand a better chance of being accurate, as they're published more frequently. Most public transport services run frequently, particularly during rush hours. At major airports and railway stations, arrivals and departures are shown on electronic boards and visual display units. Bus timetables may be for individual routes, all routes operated by a particular company, or all routes serving a city, town or region. Bus timetables, which include all local bus company services, are often published by local or county councils and are available free (or for a nominal price) from bus companies, libraries and tourist information centres. Many county councils publish excellent public transport guides and maps (available from libraries, tourist centres, newsagents and council offices), which include all bus, rail and ferry transport services operating within the county.

National Rail publishes the *Great Britain Passenger Railway Timetable*, although it's largely a work of fiction (and in 1999 was printed with 35 days in March and 34 in April – not a good sign!). In some areas, combined timetables and guides are published, including all local bus, rail, metro (underground) and ferry services. In Wales, timetables and guides are published in English and Welsh. In London, the number for general rail enquiries is ☎ 08457-484 950 and for London Transport it's ☎ 020-7222 1234. London has 11 mainline rail stations serving different parts of the UK. Trains don't travel across London, therefore if your rail journey takes you via London, you must change to your onward station (via tube, bus or taxi). For National Rail enquiries call ☎ 08457-484 950.

TAXIS

Taxis are usually plentiful except when it's raining, you have lots of luggage or you're late for an appointment. There are two kinds of taxis, licensed taxis or cabs (abbreviation of cabriolet) and private hire cars or minicabs. All taxis must be licensed by the local municipal or borough council and have a registered licence number. Minicabs don't always need to be licensed, although most are. The main difference from the passenger's point of view, is that taxis can be hailed in the street and minicabs can be booked only by telephone. In addition to taxi services, many taxi and minicab companies operate private hire (e.g. weddings, sightseeing), chauffeur and courier services, and provide contract and account services, e.g. to take children to and from school. Many taxi and minicab companies provide a 24-hour service with radio-controlled cars.

Taxis aren't particularly expensive in the UK and are cheaper than in many other European countries. London taxis (officially called Hackney Carriages) cover an area of around 1,580km^2 (610mi^2). Each cab has a licence number plate and the driver (cabby) wears a badge bearing his driver number. There's a minimum charge of around £2.20 for the first 335.8m or 72.2 seconds, plus 20p for each additional 167.9m or 36.1 seconds (a lot of time is spent stuck in traffic); and once the fare is or exceeds £13.40, there is a charge of 20p for each additional 117.7 m or 25.3 seconds, or part thereof. There are extra charges for additional passengers, luggage, and surcharges for evenings between 8pm and midnight, nights, weekends and public holidays. The fare from London-Heathrow airport (served by London cabs) to central London is around £40 - £70, for a 30-60 minutes journey. There are also business class cabs in London with more luxurious seats, soundproofing and a telephone (and higher rates than standard cabs). In rural areas, taxis charge around £3 a mile (1.6km). Taxi drivers expect a tip of around 10 per cent of the fare, although it isn't obligatory.

If fares have recently been increased and the meter hasn't been adjusted to the new rates, an 'additional fares' list is displayed inside the cab. Recommended fares for a number of destinations may be published in information booklets, e.g. the *Guide to Heathrow Airport* published by the British Airports Authority (BAA). Licensed taxis can ply for hire anywhere within their fare area and can be hailed on the streets, hired from taxi ranks (special waiting places for taxis), railway stations, airports and hotels, or can be ordered by telephone.

Minicabs

Minicabs usually have no meters although, if they do have a meter and are licensed by the local council, it must be set to the rates fixed by the council. If a minicab has no meter, **you must agree the fare in advance when booking and confirm it before starting your journey**. Minicabs cannot be hailed in the street and it's illegal for them to tout for business (although they do, particularly late at night). Licensed taxis and minicabs must be insured for 'hire and reward', which means the driver is insured to carry fare-paying passengers. If a minicab is unlicensed, it's unlikely to be insured for hire and reward. There are no licensing requirements for minicabs in London, which means that minicabs may not be insured to carry fare-paying passengers. Local minicab companies can be found in the yellow pages.

Don't use the services of private car drivers (always without meters) who may approach you at airport terminals or railway stations, as they're 'pirate' taxis and aren't licensed to ply for hire and aren't insured to carry paying passengers.

When travelling with large objects, mention it in advance when booking by telephone. New 'London-style' black cabs are designed to take wheelchairs and are common in London and other major cities (when booking by telephone specifically ask for a wheelchair taxi, if required). In some areas, there are low-fare schemes for the elderly and disabled, using tokens or vouchers issued by local councils. In most London boroughs, a Taxicard scheme is provided for disabled residents who cannot use buses and trains. Information about low-fare or Taxicard schemes can be obtained from local councils. In some areas, women are advised not to travel by minicab alone at night (ask the local police for advice).

Complaints

Complaints about service or hire charges can be made to the local taxi or minicab licensing office (if licensed). Complaints about London cabs can be made to the Public Carriage Office, 15 Penton Street, London N1 9PU (☎ 08456-027 000, 🖳 www.tfl.gov.uk). Make a note of the taxi's licence number, the driver's badge number, and the date and time of the incident. If you think you've been overcharged, obtain a receipt.

AIRLINE SERVICES

The airline business is extremely competitive in the UK and fares are now similar to North American and the lowest of any European country (the UK is the main crossroad for the world's long-haul airlines). In addition to the lowest scheduled fares, charter flights are available to most European destinations throughout the year for a fraction of scheduled airline fares. British Airways (BA) is the UK's national airline and is the western world's largest airline with flights to over 150 international destinations. BA is part of the Oneworld alliance that includes American Airlines, Canadian Airlines, Cathay Pacific, Finnair, Iberia and Qantas. Although it's been one of the world's most profitable airlines, BA has made a loss in recent years with increased competition from budget airlines and a reduction in the number of business and first class passengers. BA no longer operates Concorde supersonic aircraft, which were taken out of service in autumn 2003.

The main British intercontinental opposition to BA comes from Virgin Atlantic, which is consistently rated as one of the best airlines in the world, e.g. by readers of *Business Traveller* magazine. Virgin has pioneered new customer values and its first an businss class services includes an on-board bar and lounge, a choice of three meals, individual seatback screens with a choice of on-demand films and seats that convert into full-length 'beds'. British Midland, the UK's second largest airline, has an excellent reputation for its standards of service and low fares, on domestic and international routes, and is regularly voted the UK's top domestic carrier.

Domestic air services are provided between British international and provincial airports by a number of airlines, including Air UK, British Airways, British Midland, Brymon Airways, Capital Airlines, FlyBE and GB Airways (a BA franchise partner), most of which offer reduced off-peak and standby fares.

Like hotels, most airlines deliberately overbook as an insurance against passengers not turning up or who cancel at the last minute. The European Union has agreed a compensation scheme under which airlines are required to pay passengers denied boarding due to over-booking ('bumped' passengers), although compensation levels are strictly limited. BA, which claims 99 per cent of its flights are trouble-free, bumps around 10,000 passengers a year, although it at least pays some compensation (which is more than most airlines). **You should check-in at least two hours before an intercontinental flight and at least one hour before a European flight – if you arrive late you may get bumped.**

Allow time for traffic delays, accidents and security checks, and check with airlines for up-to-date flight information. Catching a plane in the UK (apart from a domestic shuttle flight) **isn't** the same as catching a bus. If you're flying to the continent during a public holiday period or at any time during the summer (particularly on a charter flight), you should be prepared for a delay. However, flight times are also getting longer owing to congestion.

Useful publications for frequent air travellers include the Official Airline Guides (OAG) Worldwide *Pocket Flight Guide*, *The Complete Sky Traveller* by David Beaty (Methuen) and *The Round the World Air Guide* by Katie Wood and George McDonald (Fontana). Frequent fliers may wish to obtain a copy of the *Official Frequent Flyer Guidebook* (Airpress).

Airports

There are over 100 licensed civil airports in the UK, including many international airports, the most important of which are London-Heathrow, London-Gatwick,

Manchester, Glasgow, Birmingham, Luton, Edinburgh, Belfast, Aberdeen, Newcastle, East Midlands and London-Stansted (all handling over one million passengers a year). Many regional airports also operate a limited number of international flights (excluding flights to Ireland, which are widespread), including Bristol, Cardiff, Humberside, Leeds-Bradford, London-City, Lydd, Norwich, Southend and Teeside. Regional airports often have bargain fares to popular European destinations. A number of smaller airports operate scheduled domestic flights to regional and international airports.

National Express (see **Long-distance Buses** on page 243) provides scheduled bus services to Heathrow, Gatwick, Manchester and Birmingham international airports from major cities. They also provide airport-to-airport services between these airports and Luton for passengers with inter-connecting flights. Major airports have direct rail and/or bus connections to local rail stations. Short and long-term parking is available at most airports, although it's expensive (cheaper off-airport parking is usually available).

London's Heathrow airport is the world's busiest international airport, handling over 50 million passengers a year (Terminal 1 alone handles 20 million passengers a year), which is expected to increase to over 80 million by 2016. Heathrow has four terminals (and is planning a fifth) and handles mostly scheduled flights. London's Gatwick airport handles over 25 million passengers a year, although it has only one runway (although an additional runway is under consideration) and just two terminals. It's used extensively by charter airlines. Heathrow and Gatwick have excellent bus and rail connections to central London, the provinces and other British airports. Heathrow can also be reached by tube and via the high-speed Heathrow Express direct rail connection from Paddington station, taking just 15 minutes. Many of the UK's regional airlines are denied landing rights at Heathrow and Gatwick, and passengers are often forced to fly via the continent to pick up an international flight or must get to these airports by rail or road.

Flight information is available direct from airports and via the television teletext service. Thomas Cook publishes a comprehensive *Airports Guide – Europe*, containing detailed information about 75 major airports in Europe, including public transport serving airports.

Fares

Air fares to and from the UK are among the cheapest in the world. Transatlantic fares can be much lower these days thanks to greater competition between BA and Virgin (and other American carriers). BA and Virgin routinely match each others prices and, along with other airlines such as Ryanair (an Irish airline based in Dublin, but operating widely in the UK) and Easyjet, 'give away' thousands of tickets on certain routes during special promotions. Stiff competition from US airlines has also shaken up the transatlantic fare structure. The low 'shoulder' period from Christmas to Easter is best for transatlantic bargains (prices rise sharply again in the spring), when fares are cut by up to 50 per cent.

Deregulation in 1997 led to a spate of new low-cost airlines such as Easyjet (🖳 www.easyjet.co.uk), Ryanair (🖳 www.ryanair.com) and BMI Baby (🖳 www.bmi

baby.com), which have hit the profits of the major airlines and cemented the UK's position as Europe's low-cost, air travel hub. Always book online for the lowest fares (often you have no option). Budget airlines offer a no-frills service (most operate without tickets) and undercut other airlines by charging for seats only – meals, drinks (even tea and coffee), entertainment (films, headphones) and even baggage must be paid for separately. The biggest problem facing airlines trying to gain access to a new route is the allocation of takeoff and landing slots during peak times, which are jealously guarded by major airlines (which is why new airlines must operate from smaller, less popular airports).

Most airlines provide a vast range of tickets depending on when you want to fly, how many nights you want to stay, how much notice you give, and whether you fly on a fixed (pre-booked) flight or an open ticket. Business tickets may range from standard, business return, day return, Eurobudget and Eurobudget return. (Children under 12 usually travel at 33 to 50 per cent of the adult fare – although there are no discounts on some routes – and have the same luggage allowance as adults.)

If you've ever wondered why airlines spend so much time and money wooing business travellers, it's because a business class seat produces up to **seven** times the profit generated by an economy class seat. BA has high business class fares on some routes, particularly on routes where there's little competition, and the difference in price between economy and business fares is much greater in the UK than in most other European countries. This may explain why many companies have cut the cost of their travel budgets in recent years by ordering executives to travel economy and use budget airlines.

Many airlines also offer discounts for youths, students and senior citizens. **If you're planning a trip abroad during school holidays, book well in advance, especially if you're going to a popular destination, e.g. Paris or New York.**

Whatever your destination, it pays to shop around for the best deal (one of the best is a round-the-world ticket from around £1,300 allowing up to 15 stops). The day of the week and the departure times of flights vary considerably between airlines and you can often save money by taking an off-peak or night flight. All airlines publish six-monthly or annual timetables. It's advisable to contact a travel agent that can provide you with comprehensive travel information, a detailed itinerary and all tickets at no extra cost. Also compare fares from a number of travel agents. However, you should be aware that some of the low-cost flights and holidays advertised by travel agents are limited offers, restricted to certain dates and often include hidden extras. Keep in mind also that fares on public transport to outlying (non-Heathrow) airports can cost between £10 and £18 one way.

Always make sure you fully understand any ticket restrictions. It pays to be wary of tickets offered by bucket shops (outlets which sell cheap airline tickets) and anyone who's not an International Air Transport Association (IATA) travel agent, as there's a lucrative trade in forged tickets. To find a cheap flight, check the classified advertisements in daily and Sunday newspapers (e.g. *The Sunday Times* and *Observer*) and entertainment magazines, such as London's *Time Out*. The best deals for students are usually offered by STA Travel and Campus Travel. It's best to book holiday flights with a company with an Air Travel Organisers' Licence (ATOL) issued by the Civil Aviation Authority, as ATOL pays compensation should a member be unable to meet its commitments (☎ 020-7453 6427/6430 for information). Holidays booked through a member of the Association of British Travel Agents (ABTA) are also covered by a bond system (☎ 020-7637 2444).

Luggage

The size, weight and number of items of hand luggage vary according to the airline and the class of your ticket (most airlines allow first and business class passengers extra hand luggage). The luggage allowance on flights from the UK is usually 15kg for charter flights, 20kg for economy class, and 30kg for business and first class passengers.

All additional bags should be checked in at the airline check-in desk for carriage in the aircraft hold – obtain a check-in stub as, without it, you cannot claim for compensation if it's lost or stolen. On flights to and within the US, around 10 per cent of hold luggage is opened for security checks and if cases are locked they're broken open, therefore it pays you not to lock bags when travelling there. **Keep any valuables in your hand luggage and make sure your luggage is fully insured.**

Prohibited items and substances are listed in airport and airline information leaflets and guides, including *Can I Take It? Dangerous Articles in Baggage* and *Cabin Baggage* available from BA offices and appointed travel agents. You may not carry any sharp items in hand luggage, including tweezers, nail files and clippers, and scissors (can you attack an airhostess with a pair of nail clippers?). If in doubt, ask the airline with which you're travelling. Don't pack electronic equipment such as personal computers and cameras in your hold luggage, but keep them in your hand luggage. If you have a portable computer, it's wise to have it checked by hand, as data could be erased or corrupted by powerful X-ray machines. Passengers are requested not to leave their luggage unattended at any time at British airports, as it may be stolen or taken away by security staff.

11.

MOTORING

British roads are among the most crowded in Europe. The south-east of England is the most congested region in Europe and, in Western Europe, only Italy has more vehicles per mile than the UK. The most significant increase in the last two decades has been in the number of women drivers, which doubled between 1975 and 1993. However, the UK has a relatively low level of car ownership compared with some other European countries. Traffic density in the major cities and towns is particularly high and results in frequent traffic jams.

During rush hours, from around 7.30 to 9.30am and 4.30 to 6.30pm Mondays to Fridays, the traffic flow is painfully slow in many areas, particularly on busy motorways, e.g. anywhere on the M25 London orbital motorway, on the M1, M3 and M4 motorways into and out of London, and in and around most major cities. Most town centres are chaotic during rush hours, particularly central London, where the average traffic speed is around 10mph (it takes as long to cross most city centres in a car as it did 200 years ago in a horse and cart!). Journey times have doubled in the last ten years and the UK's motorists spend an average of around five days a year in jams, which are estimated to cost British industry billions of pounds annually.

Central London has introduced a congestion charge to counteract this problem. It operates from 7am to 6pm on Mondays to Fridays (excluding bank holidays) and costs £8 a day if paid by midnight the day before travelling and £10 if paid by midnight the day after travelling. The area of central London affected is clearly marked by signs and cameras read car number plates and check them against a database, therefore there's no need for a physical ticket or pass of any sort. The charge can be paid at any of the following: at selected shops, petrol stations and car parks; by post; by telephone; by SMS text message from your mobile phone; at BT Internet kiosks; or online (🖥 www.cclondon.com). The fine for non payment is £100 which is reduced to £50 if paid within 14 days.

Traffic jams are also created throughout the UK by the pervasive road works, particularly in towns and on motorways – plastic traffic cones are a common sight on the motorway. (New legislation is to be introduced to reduce the frequency and length of disruptions caused by road works). Traffic jams have spawned a number of navigation gadgets to warn drivers of hold-ups in order that they may avoid them. Outside rush hours and towns, car travel is often trouble-free and you may even come across a motorist with a smile (rather than a scowl) on his face, although you may need to travel as far as North Wales or Scotland to see him.

The UK's road network suffers from the lack of investment in the railways, which has resulted in millions of tonnes of freight thundering through towns and villages, destroying roads and buildings, and polluting the environment. A greater investment in off-road public transport would also cut the number of private vehicles on roads, particularly in cities. Successive British governments have responded piecemeal to the UK's transport problems and have failed to strike a balance between investment in roads and public transport. Most motorists would like to see more investment in public transport to ease road congestion (and get all the **other** motorists off the roads).

Planners are finding it impossible to build enough roads to cater for the expected rise in traffic (the number of cars is set to double in the next 25 years). The newest motorways (such as the M25 orbital motorway around London) are already hopelessly overcrowded because road planners badly underestimated the density of traffic and built too few lanes. The M25 (opened in 1986) was designed to handle 80,000 vehicles per day and already it averages around double this, rising to over 200,000 on some sections. Road-widening schemes are underway on many main roads, which simply add to the traffic problems (at least in the short term).

One of the biggest problems created by road traffic is pollution (including noise pollution) which is strangling London and many other cities, where levels are already well above international health limits on hot days. An intense public debate is under way about the best way to take the UK's transport system into the 21st century. Many experts believe that drastic measures are needed to curb car use by banning most traffic from city centres, while at the same time providing inexpensive, frequent and fast public transport between and within cities. There are already plans to ban cars from busy towns on days of heavy pollution, when asthmatics, bronchitis sufferers and the elderly are particularly at risk. There are also proposals to keep traffic out of villages and away from beauty spots, in an attempt to stop traffic pollution destroying them.

There are around 3,500 deaths a year on British roads and over 300,000 injuries. These figures, although unacceptably high, are among the lowest casualties of any developed country (it's difficult to have an accident when you're stuck in a traffic jam). A quarter of deaths in road accidents involve drivers under the age of 25 (who hold 10 per cent of licences) and thousands of young drivers and their passengers are maimed for life each year. The UK has no additional speed restrictions for young and inexperienced drivers, who can also drive high-performance cars immediately after passing their driving tests. Women drivers have half as many accidents as men, but usually cover fewer miles.

Traffic information is available from motoring organisations (see page 294) and via the television teletext service. The Automobile Association's Roadwatch telephone information service provides the latest information on the state of the motorways (☎ 0900-340 1100 – calls cost 60p per minute) and main trunk roads throughout the UK. The AA also provides a wealth of other telephone information, including Weatherwatch, road works, motoring law, hints and advice, new and used car information, and touring information (for general information ☎ 0870-600 0371).

VEHICLE IMPORTATION

If you plan to import a motor vehicle or motorcycle, either temporarily or permanently, first make sure that you're aware of the latest regulations. Obtain a copy of Notice 3 (*Bringing your Belongings and Private Motor Vehicle to the United Kingdom From Outside the European Union*) or PI1 (*Permanent Import of Motor Vehicles into Great Britain*) from Her Majesty's Customs and Excise, Thomas Paine House, Angel Square, Torrens Street, London EC1V 1TA (☎ 0845-010 9000, 🖳 www.hmce.gov.uk). You must complete customs form C104F if you're importing your private vehicle for no more than six months in a 12-month period. If you're setting up home in the UK, you must complete form C104A. Forms are available from shipping agents or from the above address. Information is also available from motoring organisations (see page 294). The regulations also apply to the importation of boats and aircraft.

You should check whether you're able to register and licence a particular vehicle in the UK and whether it can, if necessary, be modified to comply with British standards of construction, i.e. receive National Type Approval. Check with the manufacturer's export department, the British importers or the vehicle licensing authority in the UK that the vehicle you're planning to import meets the latest regulations. For further information, obtain a copy of leaflet P11 from HM Customs and Excise at the above address. If you wish to import a car (except as a visitor), inform the customs staff on arrival in the UK. Whether you're required to pay import duty and car tax depends on how long you've owned the car and how long you've lived abroad. Duty is 10 per cent on cars, 8 per cent on motorcycles below 250cc and 6 per cent on those above 250cc, plus value added tax (VAT) at 17.5 per cent. There's a reduced rate of duty for vehicles imported from some countries.

A vehicle purchased abroad duty and tax-free may be imported and used in the UK only by a diplomat, a member of an officially recognised international organisation, a member of NATO or British forces or the civilian staff accompanying them. Importing some exotic foreign cars (most American cars) isn't advisable, as you may have problems with servicing and spares; and, if it's a monster, manoeuvring and parking on the UK's narrow roads can be difficult or impossible. All cars registered in the UK over three years old must undergo an annual serviceability test (see **Test Certificate** on page 266).

VEHICLE REGISTRATION

A vehicle registration document (V5) shows the registered keeper (the person who keeps the vehicle on public roads and not necessarily the legal owner) of a vehicle. It gives the keeper's name and address, the registration mark (number) and other details about the vehicle. A new registration document must be issued each time there's a change in the details printed on it, e.g. a change in the address of the keeper.

When you import a vehicle into the UK (either free of tax and duty or when duty and tax have been paid on importation) you're given a Customs and Excise clearance form C&E 386. You also receive a Department for Transport notice PI1 *Permanent Import of Motor Vehicles into Great Britain* and leaflet V277, explaining the legal requirements you must satisfy in order to register a vehicle in the UK. Leaflet V100 contains notes about registering and licensing a motor vehicle and leaflet V355 tells you what you need to know about registering and licensing motor vehicles that haven't previously been registered in the UK. Both are available from post offices. If you wish to import a vehicle permanently, after bringing it into the UK temporarily (e.g. as a visitor), you must contact your nearest Customs and Excise office. If you import a car on arrival or at a later date, you require the following documents:

- The invoice, receipt or bill of sale or transfer for the vehicle, made out in your name;

- The foreign registration document (either full or temporary) for the vehicle, made out in your name;

- A green card or international insurance certificate, made out in your name;

- If you've owned the vehicle longer than six months and wish to import it free of duty and tax, you require proof of how long you've owned it.

When you've received customs clearance, you're given form C&E 386, which you must take to the nearest Vehicle Registration Office (VRO) to get your vehicle registered and licensed. You also need the following documents:

- A British insurance certificate or cover note (see **Car Insurance** on page 271). A foreign insurance certificate, with or without a green card, isn't valid for a car registered in the UK and kept by someone resident in the UK. You can drive on foreign registration plates with valid foreign insurance until you've applied for British registration. If your foreign insurance isn't valid in the UK, you must obtain temporary insurance through an office of the Automobile Association (AA) or the Royal Automobile Club (RAC) (see **Motoring Organisations** on page 294) at your port of arrival or, if this isn't possible, you must visit a local insurance office before driving in the UK.

- A current British test certificate (see page 266) if your vehicle is over three years old or a declaration of exemption. If your vehicle isn't old enough to require testing or is exempt, you need an exemption certificate.

- The road tax fee (see page 272) for 6 or 12 months. The VRO provides you with the tax disc on payment of the fee (cheques are accepted).

- If the vehicle was previously registered in Germany, the VRO wants to see evidence that the German number plates have been invalidated. Ask at a VRO for information.

- A completed form V55/5 (*Application for a First Licence for a Motor Vehicle and Declaration for Registration*), available from a post office or VRO.

The VRO allocates you a registration number (corresponding to the year of manufacture of your vehicle) which you take to a garage to have British registration plates made and fitted to your vehicle. When the plates have been fitted, you must display your road tax disc inside your car windscreen (see page 272). Your vehicle registration document (V5) is sent to you direct by the Driver and Vehicle Licensing Agency (DVLA) a few weeks later. If your vehicle has been admitted without duty and tax being paid, the vehicle registration document is endorsed with the words 'Customs Restricted Until (date)'. This can be exchanged for a standard registration document when you've paid the duty or tax or after the one-year restriction period has expired. A useful website dedicated to the subject is Car Importing (🖳 www. carimporting.co.uk).

If you buy a new car from a garage in the UK, they apply for a registration number on your behalf and fit registration plates. When you buy a used vehicle in the UK, you should always be given the registration document. However, the document doesn't prove legal ownership and you should satisfy yourself that the seller either owns the vehicle or is entitled to offer it for sale. You should ask to see a bill of sale in the seller's name or other evidence, such as a hire purchase discharge document. **If you have any doubts about the ownership of a vehicle, you shouldn't buy it: for example, if you're buying privately and the address on the registration document doesn't tally with the seller's address.**

When you buy a used vehicle, you must complete the back of the registration document ('Notification of Changes') and send it to the DVLA.

New British registration numbers are released twice a year by the Department for Transport, when a new two-digit year identifier is issued. Thus you can (usually) tell the age of a car from its registration number, which normally remains with it throughout its life. From 1999, there have been two number plate changes a year on 1st March and 1st September (introduced to eliminate the August rush when changes were made once a year). It's absolutely vital for some people to be seen driving a car with the latest registration, which leads to a mad scramble for new cars in March and September each year (although this isn't simply snob appeal, as the registration of a second-hand car affects its resale price).

If you want to give someone who has everything a present, you could consider buying him a personalised registration number. The ultimate 'one-upmanship' is to have your initials or name on your car number plate. Most of the best numbers (A1, RU12, FU2) were snapped up years ago and are virtually priceless, but there are still hundreds for sale each week in publications such as *The Sunday Times*, *Exchange & Mart* and car magazines. A number of companies enjoy a lucrative business selling registration numbers, which can cost thousands of pounds even for the most obscure numbers (the prices are ludicrous to the uninitiated). Numbers are also sold by auction. When you change cars (or buy a new number), you can have the registration number transferred to your new car.

The DVLA (which issues licence numbers) also cashes in on this profitable business and allows motorists to create their own number when registering a new vehicle, for a hefty fee. Call the DVLA enquiry line (☎ 0870-240 0010, 🖥 www.dvla.gov.uk) for information. It is optional for motorists to display the euro symbol on number plates - you can still drive in Europe with the oval 'GB' sticker on your vehicle.

BUYING A CAR

After years of decline, the British car industry is now relatively profitable, although most major manufacturers are foreign-owned (American, French, German or Japanese). Most British cars exist in niche markets such as Aston Martin, Morgan and TVR. Cars are more expensive in the UK than in many other European countries, although you can obtain a discount off the list (book) price of most new cars. Whether you're buying a new or second-hand car, it's worthwhile considering a diesel-engined vehicle. Although diesel fuel is around the same price as unleaded petrol in the UK, diesels are cheaper to run (e.g. 35 to 40 per cent better fuel consumption) and have a much longer engine life.

Car sales are covered by the Misrepresentation of Goods Act 1967, which means that a seller cannot lawfully make false claims. If you buy from a dealer, you're additionally covered by the Sale of Goods Act 1979, which says a car must be of 'merchantable' quality and good for the purpose intended. *Which?* magazine (see **Consumers' Association** on page 479) publishes an annual *Which? Car* edition containing independent information on best buys, performance, comfort, convenience, reliability, trouble spots, running costs, safety, recalls, and new and second-hand prices. New and used car reports are available from the AA's Car Buyer's Guide (☎ 0870-600 0376).

New Cars

Making comparisons between new car prices in different countries is often difficult because of fluctuating exchange rates and the different levels of standard equipment. These may include electric windows and mirrors, central locking, electric sun roof, alloy wheels, stereo radio/cassette/CD, power steering, ABS, air bags, automatic transmission, leather or power seats, cruise control and air conditioning. Some manufacturers include many of these items as standard equipment, while others charge dearly for them as 'optional extras'. A catalytic converter is fitted as standard equipment to all petrol-engined cars sold in the UK. Paying for expensive optional extras on many cars is unlikely to increase the car's value when you sell it, although many cars are easier to sell with options such as power steering, central locking and electric windows. Capital depreciation is a greater threat than rust to a new car owner, as a car's value can drop by as much as 60 per cent within three to four years.

The manufacturer's list price includes the wholesale price, the dealer's profit, car tax and 17.5 per cent VAT on all these items. In addition, you must usually pay for delivery (average £450), number plates (e.g. £25), a tank of petrol, floor mats, mud flaps and road tax (see page 272). Delivery charges have increased considerably in recent years and are a rip-off used to hike car prices (and are exclusive to motor vehicles). They can vary considerably for the same car, depending on the supplier. When comparing prices, ask dealers for the on-the-road price, including delivery and the other charges listed above.

Another important aspect of buying a new car is the warranty period, during which major parts are insured against replacement. Many manufacturers now provide extended warranties of up to four years with unlimited mileage and most others offer an extended warranty for an annual fee (usually with a mileage limit). Some manufacturers offer three years (or longer) unlimited mileage or a limit of 96,000km (60,000mi). If you do a high annual mileage and change your car every two or three years, you would be well advised to buy a car with an extended warranty or pay for extra cover. However, warranties usually contain a range of get-out clauses for manufacturers.

Shop around and compare prices, discounts and incentives from a number of dealers. There has been a slump in sales to private buyers (rather than fleet sales) in recent years, which means that buyers can usually get a good deal. Free insurance, servicing and petrol are just some of the added incentives offered in recent years. You can often get a good bargain by buying an old model that has been, or is due to be, replaced by a new model. When new registration numbers are issued (see **Vehicle Registration** on page 260), it's a good time to buy a new car with the previous year's registration number, which may be sold for thousands of pounds below the list price.

Finance Deals

Dealers offer a range of finance deals that may be a better option than paying cash, particularly if you're offered a one or two-year, no-interest deal. However, most require deposits of up to 50 per cent. A plethora of deals is on offer and seven out of ten cars are bought on a leasing or hire purchase scheme. One such deal is called the 50-50 scheme, where you pay 50 per cent and drive for two years, after which you either pay the balance or hand the car back to the dealer and walk away. The most popular deals are personal contract plans (a combination of hire purchase and rental) which are offered by car manufacturers and some banks, and account for one in five of all car sales.

Although not as cheap as no-interest finance packages, deposits on personal contracts are lower at 20 to 30 per cent. After deducting the deposit, the manufacturer deducts the Minimum Guaranteed Future Value (MGFV) that he expects the car to be worth in two or three years' time when the contract expires. The balance is divided into 24 or 36 equal monthly repayments and interest is charged on the MGFV and the amount outstanding. At the end of the two or three-year period, the customer can pay the MGFV or simply return the car to the dealer.

You can reject a new car if it's faulty, but you have only a few days or weeks in which to do so. If you buy a real 'lemon' you can have it inspected by one of the motoring organisations (see page 294) or a member of the Institute of Automotive Engineers (☎ 01543-266 906), which usually provide irrefutable, independent evidence in the event of a legal battle with the manufacturer.

You may save money buying a car abroad, although prices have fallen considerably in the UK in the last few years and it's generally no longer worthwhile for the relatively small savings.

Used Cars

Used cars can be excellent value for money, particularly low mileage cars less than one year old, where the savings on the new price can be as high as 25 per cent. The minute a new car leaves the showroom, it's usually worth 10 per cent less than the purchase price. Some models depreciate much faster than others and often represent excellent second-hand bargains. If you intend to buy a used car, whether privately or from a garage, check that:

● It has a test certificate, if applicable (see page 266) and that its condition matches its declared age.

● It hasn't been involved in a major accident and suffered structural damage. If in any doubt, obtain a declaration that it's accident-free, which should be in writing.

- It's in good mechanical condition. Check the bodywork in daylight, preferably with an expert (if you aren't one yourself).

- The import tax and duty have been paid if it's an imported model. The registration document of a vehicle imported without tax and duty being paid, is annotated with 'Customs Restricted Until (date)'.

- It hasn't been stolen or is subject to a leasing or hire purchase contract, in which case the original owner or lender can legally demand it back. Thousands of cars are sold each year before they're paid for. If in doubt, check with the Hire Purchase Information (HPI) register through a Citizens Advice Bureau.

- The official service record book have been completed and stamped, and that routine servicing has been carried out regularly by an authorised dealer (mandatory for a manufacturer's warranty to be valid). It's best to buy a car with a full service history (fsh), that should also verify the mileage (see 'clocking' below).

- The price roughly corresponds to that shown in guides to used car prices (see below).

- A written guarantee or warranty is provided (see below). The manufacturer's warranty is usually transferable to subsequent owners.

If you're buying a car from a dealer who's a member of the Society of Motor Manufacturers and Traders (SMMT), the Motor Agents Association (MAA), the Vehicle Builders and Repairers Association (VBRA) or the Scottish Motor Trade Association (SMTA), extra protection may be afforded (but don't count on it). Most garages provide a warranty on used cars, e.g. 3 to 12 months (unless it's covered by a manufacturer's warranty), although you should check what it includes and more importantly, what's **excluded**. You may be able to purchase an additional one to three years warranty, depending on the age and make of the car. The best warranties are supported by the manufacturer.

Most experts recommend that you don't buy a used car that you couldn't afford to run from new, although you could forego fully comprehensive insurance on an inexpensive vehicle. The higher the new price of a car, generally, the more it costs to repair and service. Many cars have **very** expensive parts that may need replacing, including catalyst-equipped exhausts, ABS systems, engine control units, automatic gearboxes, electronically-controlled heaters, nose and tail fairings, power-steering racks, dashboard electronics and power accessories. The more electronic gadgets a car has, the more there is to go wrong (the cost and fitting of replacement parts would deter many people from buying certain cars).

You can get a guide to the value of most second-hand cars from motoring magazines such as *What Car?*, *Motorists Guide* and *Parker's Car Price Guide*, all of which are published monthly. Always do your own research in your area by comparing prices at dealers, in local papers (and free car magazines) and in the national press, e.g. *Exchange & Mart* and the *Auto Trader*. Many private sellers are willing to take a considerable drop and dealers also usually haggle over the price. The average annual mileage for a car in the UK is around 12,000mi (19,311km) a year and cars with high mileage (e.g. 20,000mi/32,186km a year) can usually be bought for substantially less than the average price. An innovation in recent years has been the car 'supermarket' (e.g. CarLand, 🖥 www.carland.com), selling nearly-new or used models, mainly ex-fleet or ex-lease.

You must be extremely careful when buying a used car, whether from a garage or privately. Sellers use many ploys such as 'clocking' (winding back the mileometer); false test certificates (most likely on older cars); and any number of ruses to hide major faults such as accident damage, rust or imminent engine failure. It's advisable to check a car's history before buying it to ensure that it hasn't been written off (e.g. a 'cut and shut', where two 'good' halves are cut and welded together making a death trap), stolen, disguised or the number plates changed. This costs around £25 and can be done by the AA's Data Check (☎ 0800-056 8040) which maintains a register. Cars written-off in road accidents are also substituted by stolen cars, so it's advisable to check that the vehicle identification number matches the registration number. The mileage can usually be verified by buying a car with a full service history (fsh). **Complaints about second-hand car purchases regularly outnumber all other consumer complaints!**

You have a certain amount of protection in law, whether buying from a dealer or privately, although legally you're better off buying from a dealer. The Automobile Association (see **Motoring Organisations** on page 294) publishes a booklet entitled *The Law about Buying and Selling a Car*. For people who know little about cars, the Office of Fair Trading publishes a booklet entitled *Used Cars*, which includes tips about buying, service and repair. If you buy a 'lemon' (a dud), you should take legal advice to find out whether you have a valid complaint.

Always check a car carefully (particularly the tyres, which may be illegal) and take it for a test drive. It's advisable to obtain an independent inspector's report from one of the motoring organisations (see page 294) before buying, although this may not be possible with a private sale, when a decision must often be made on the spot. Keep a copy of any advertisements which include a description and note any claims made by the seller. **Beware of dealers claiming to be private sellers (which is illegal). If the seller's name and address isn't the same as that in the vehicle registration document, you should be suspicious (it could also be stolen).**

In addition to buying a car from a dealer or privately, you can also buy a car from car auctions throughout the UK. These are, however, generally for the experienced buyer and the trade, who buy around 90 per cent of all cars sold at auction. ADT Auctions, one of the largest in the UK, produces a booklet for would-be buyers and sellers, available from any of their auction centres (see yellow pages).

TEST CERTIFICATE

All vehicles (cars, motorcycles, motor caravans, light goods and dual-purpose) that are over three years old must have an annual Department for Transport (DfT) test. This was previously called the Ministry of Transport test or 'MOT' and the name has stuck. Passenger-carrying vehicles with more than eight seats and taxis (excluding private hire cars) must be tested after they're one year old and there are also separate rules for goods vehicles over 1,525kg (30cwt), about which information can be obtained from a VRO.

Tests are performed by officially approved test centres, including local authorities and most large garages, many of which will test your car while you wait (although you may need to make a booking). Some garages do tests seven days a week and even provide a free collection and delivery service. The test usually takes 20 to 30 minutes, depending on the condition and cleanliness of your car, and includes all lights, steering and suspension, brakes (including the handbrake), tyres and wheels, seat belts and general items such as windscreen washers and wipers, horn, exhaust system and silencer, exhaust emission and vehicle structure (e.g. soundness of the bodywork). Tyres require 1.6mm of tread over 75 per cent of their width. The test has been made more stringent over the years and it's now difficult to get an old car to pass.

Recently certification has been computerised and all records are held on a central computer. The official (maximum) cost of the test is around £50, although some garages charge less. When your car passes the test, you're given a Test Certificate (VT20), if it fails, you are given an advisory list of the defects which must be corrected. If the tester completes the 'Warning' (section D) part of the test report, you're allowed only to drive it home, to a garage for repairs or to another testing station after repair. You can appeal against a test failure by completing form VT17 (available from any testing station) and sending it to the local Department for Transport office with the appeal fee, within 14 days of failure.

You can have your car tested anytime, for example if you want to sell it. However, if it fails the test, even when it isn't due, you're unable to drive it until it has passed. It's an offence to use a vehicle on public roads without a valid test certificate. You're permitted only to drive it to a testing station where you've pre-booked a test. Without a test certificate, you cannot renew your road tax (see page 272). If you lose your test certificate, you can get a duplicate from the testing station which carried out the test, provided you have the serial number or the approximate date of issue.

It's unwise to buy a vehicle without a recent test certificate, even at a bargain price (which should make you even more suspicious), as many old cars fail their test. The standard of testing is variable, owing mainly to a wide variation in the interpretation of test standards. It's unlikely that two testing stations will find the same faults on an old car, e.g. one over five years old. Even buying a car with a new test certificate doesn't guarantee that it's in good condition (it has been estimated that some 50,000 test certificates are altered or completed fraudulently each year). It's easy for someone to obtain a false test certificate and many testers lose their licences each year for issuing false certificates. **A valid test certificate should never be taken as a guarantee of a car's roadworthiness, particularly as many aspects of a car's operation aren't tested, e.g. engine and gearbox.** Many garages fail cars for no apparent reason (other than to generate work for themselves!) and pass others that should have been failed. Over half of all vehicles are tested incorrectly.

If you're buying a car privately without a guarantee, you would be well advised to have an independent inspection carried out by one of the motoring organisations (see page 272). If you ask a garage (or anyone) to do a pre-test check on your car, don't ask them to repair it to test standard to get it through the test, as this could result in unnecessary expense. Ask them to take it for the test to find out what (if anything) needs fixing. Essential repairs recommended by a garage may not be the same as those officially required after a test. An MOT handbook on mechanical safety for cars and light vans, entitled *How Safe Is Your Car?*, is issued by the Vehicle Inspectorate. Police carry out roadworthiness spot checks on vehicles. **If your vehicle is found to be unroadworthy, the fact that you have a valid test certificate is irrelevant.**

SELLING A CAR

The main points to note when selling a car are:

- A potential buyer cannot test drive your car unless he's covered by your or his own insurance. You're responsible if someone drives your car with your permission without valid insurance.

- It's illegal to sell a car in an unroadworthy condition, unless you're selling it as a non-runner without a test certificate (see above). Never describe a car as being in a better condition than it is; if it's subsequently found to have any faults, you could be liable to reimburse the buyer or pay for repairs.

- Inform your insurance company. Either cancel your insurance or transfer it to a new car. If you cancel your insurance, even for a short period, this may affect your no-claims discount when you take out insurance on a new car. When you sell a car, you're required to notify the motor vehicle registration office by completing the appropriate part of the vehicle registration papers (see page 260). The new owner of the car must also register his ownership with them (this is intended as a cross-check of ownership).

- If you're selling your car privately, you should insist on cash. It's usually a formality for the buyer to accompany you to your bank and make a cash transfer on the spot. There are confidence tricksters who will, given half a chance, happily give you a dud cheque and drive off with your car. Be wary of banker's drafts and building society cheques, which, although as good as cash, may be counterfeit or stolen (some crooks try to pass them over a public holiday period when the banks are closed). If someone insists on paying by cheque, you should never allow them to take your car until the cheque has cleared. Don't allow a dealer or car auctioneer to take your car until a cheque has cleared, as cheques sometimes bounce after companies have ceased trading.

- Include in the receipt that you're selling the car in its present condition (as seen) without a guarantee, the price paid and the car's mileometer reading. The new owner may ask for a declaration in writing that the car is accident-free, which applies to major accidents that have caused structural damage and not slight knocks.

- You can advertise a car for sale in local newspapers, on free local notice boards, in the Saturday or Sunday editions of national newspapers, and in many motoring newspapers and magazines. Among the best market places are *Exchange & Mart* and *Auto Trader*. The best place to advertise a car depends on the make and value of the car. Cheap cars are probably best sold in local newspapers, while expensive and collectors' cars are often advertised in the motoring press and in the broadsheet Sunday newspapers, such as *The Sunday Times*. Buyers usually travel a long way to view a car that appears good value for money (if nobody telephones, you will know why).

DRIVING LICENCE

The minimum age for driving in the UK is 17 for a motor car (up to 3.5 tonnes laden) or motorcycle over 50cc and 16 for a motorcycle (moped) up to 50cc, an invalid carriage and certain other vehicles. For commercial vehicles up to 7.5 tonnes laden, the minimum age is 18 and for heavy goods vehicles (HGV), it's 21. Driving licences are issued for certain categories of vehicles, e.g. category A is for a motorcycle, B is for a car, C is for a truck and D is for a bus. Holders of a full foreign driving licence or an international driving permit may drive in the UK for one year.

If you hold a licence from a European Economic Area (EEA) member state or a licence issued in Australia, Barbados, British Virgin Islands, Cyprus, Gibraltar, Hong Kong, Japan, Kenya, Malta, New Zealand, Singapore, Switzerland or Zimbabwe, you can obtain a British driving licence in your first year in the UK, without taking a driving test. **If you don't apply during your first year, you aren't permitted to drive after this period until you've passed a driving test.** If you hold a licence issued by a country that isn't listed above, you must take a driving test during your first year in the UK. If you don't pass the driving test during your first year, you must apply for a provisional licence and drive under restricted conditions (e.g. with a qualified driver) until you've passed your test.

Some foreign licences (for example those printed in Arabic or Japanese) must be translated into English or an international driving permit must be obtained before arrival. To apply for a British driving licence, you must obtain an application form (D1) and form D100 (which explains what you need to know about driver licensing) from any post office. An eye test certificate isn't required, although you must be able to read a number plate at 67 feet (20.5m) in daylight, with glasses or contact lenses, if necessary (you're tested). British licences now contain a photograph and come in two parts; a plastic, credit-card size identity card and a paper licence (old paper-only licences can be exchanged for a photocard licence). Complete form D1 and send it to the DVLA with the appropriate postcode (shown on the form) and the following:

- Your foreign driving licence and, if applicable, an international driving permit, which are returned to you;

- A permanent address in the UK;

- A cheque or postal order for the fee (not cash or banknotes).

Your British driving licence is sent to you around one week later and is valid until age 70. Don't forget to sign it. After the age of 70, it must be renewed every three years, provided you remain fit to drive. However, you must declare any health problems which might make you unfit to drive **at any time** and not just when applying for a licence. An international driving permit is required if you intend to drive in some countries. This may vary depending on which driving licence(s) you hold. Check with one of the motoring organisations (see page 294).

An international driving licence, valid for one year only, is obtainable from these organisations for £4, either in person or by post. You must provide a passport-size photograph and the fee and complete a form giving details of your British, Northern Ireland or British Forces Germany (BFG) driving licence. Holders of a British or foreign car driving licence can ride a motorcycle of up to 125cc in the UK without obtaining a special licence. For motorcycles over 125cc, you must have a motorcycle licence (see **Motorcycles** on page 282). Foreign licences issued by EU member states and certain other countries, can be exchanged for a British licence within five years of becoming resident in the UK.

If you change your permanent address within the UK, you must notify the DVLA as soon as possible by completing the section on the back of your British licence and returning it to the address shown. A new licence is issued free of charge (if you have an old-style paper licence, you receive a photocard licence). You can be fined a maximum of £50 if you fail to notify the DVLA of a change of address. A new licence is issued for the following reasons:

- You wish to exchange an old-style paper licence for a photocard licence;

- Your licence has been lost, stolen, destroyed or defaced;

- To receive a clean licence after the expiry of endorsements (see below);

- To add or remove provisional motorcycle group D or add new groups to a full licence;

- To obtain a new licence after a period of disqualification;

- To exchange a Northern Ireland licence for a UK licence.

A provisional licence is exchanged free for a full licence after passing a driving test. A policeman can ask to see your driving licence at any time and you must either produce it immediately or take it personally to a police station (named by you) within seven days. Driving without a licence or while disqualified attracts a heavy penalty. Court convictions for many motoring offences result in an 'endorsement' of your licence, which means you're given a number of penalty points. Most offences 'earn' a fixed number of penalty points (e.g. speeding usually merits three penalty points), but some are at a court's discretion. If you want to request a court hearing for a fixed penalty offence, you must usually do so within 28 days. If you don't pay a fine within the set period it may be increased dramatically. Some offences cannot be dealt with under the fixed penalty system and you must appear in court.

If you total 12 or more penalty points within three years, you're automatically disqualified from driving for a minimum of six months. If you already have points on your licence and a new offence would bring your points total to 12 or more, you must appear in court (as only a court can disqualify you from driving). If you've been disqualified in the past three years, you usually lose your licence for a minimum of one year (two previous disqualifications normally lead to a two-year ban). You can be disqualified for a single offence, such as drunken or reckless driving, which can also result in a prison sentence where injury or death resulted. If you drive while disqualified, you can receive a prison sentence and have your car confiscated.

The length of time endorsements remain on a driving licence depends on the offence, e.g. it's 11 years from the date of conviction for offences involving drunken driving and four years for all other offences from the date of the offence or the date of the conviction. You can apply for the removal of a penalty point endorsement after three years from the date of the offence. You can also apply for a disqualification of four years or longer to be lifted after a minimum period of two years. You must apply for a new licence (using form D1) after a period of disqualification. Further information about driving licences can be obtained from Customer Enquiries (Drivers) Group, DVLA, Sandringham Park, Swansea SA7 0EE (☎ 0870-240 0009, 🖳 www.dvla.gov.uk).

CAR INSURANCE

There are three categories of car insurance available in the UK, as described below.

Third Party

This is the minimum cover available, which includes insurance against claims for injury to other people caused by your passengers. Third party insurance provides the minimum legal cover in all EU countries plus the Czech Republic, Hungary, Norway, the Slovak Republic and Switzerland without a green card. Not all insurance companies offer third party car insurance.

Third Party, Fire & Theft

Third party, fire and theft (TPF&T) includes loss or damage caused to your car and anything fitted to it by fire, lightning, explosion, theft or attempted theft. It usually includes broken glass.

Comprehensive

Comprehensive covers all the risks listed under the two categories above, plus damage to your own car, theft of contents (usually limited to £100 or £150), broken glass (e.g. windscreen replacement), personal accident benefits and medical expenses (e.g. £100 or £200). It also usually includes damage from natural hazards, e.g. storm damage. Extra cover may be offered free or for an additional fee and may include the cost of hiring a car if yours is involved in an accident or stolen; legal assistance; no-claims discount protection; and extra cover for a car stereo or phone.

Windscreen damage, mostly due to stones thrown up by other vehicles, results in around 1.5 million claims a year. Comprehensive insurance may also cover you against loss when your car is in a garage for service or repair. Check a policy for any restrictions: for example, you may not be covered against theft if your car isn't garaged and locked overnight. Most lenders usually insist on comprehensive insurance for leasing, contract hire, hire purchase and loan agreements.

Any insurance policy can include other people to drive your car (either individually named or any driver). Comprehensive insurance generally covers you only for third party when you're driving a car that doesn't belong to you. Separate passenger insurance is usually unnecessary as passengers are automatically covered by all British motor insurance policies (people are injured in around 40 per cent of all accidents, yet two out of three don't bother to make a claim). Personal accident, medical expenses, clothing and personal effects cover are usually included in comprehensive policies. Around two-thirds of British motorists have fully comprehensive insurance.

Green Card

British motor insurance doesn't include a free green card (which extends cover to the countries listed under **Third Party** above). This is usually available for a maximum period (e.g. three months a year) and is expensive. However, it isn't necessary to have a green card when driving in Western Europe although, without one, you're covered only for the minimum third party insurance required by law.

ROAD TAX

Road tax (officially called 'vehicle excise duty' or 'vehicle licence') is required for all cars. Vehicles registered before March 2001 are taxed according to their engine size: vehicles with engines of less than 1,550cc are taxed at £115 per year and those with engines of 1,550cc and over at £180 per year. However, vehicles registered after March 2001 are taxed according to the number of grams of carbon dioxide (CO_2) their engines emit per kilometre driven, as shown in the table below. Emission levels are related to the size of a car's engine as well as to the type of fuel, and since March 2006 cars are divided into seven 'bands' according to engine size.

Band	CO_2 Emission (g/km)	Tax for 12 Months/6 Months (£) Diesel	Petrol	Other Fuel
A	Up to 100	-	-	-
B	101 – 120	35	35	15
C	121 – 150	115/63.25	115/63.25	95/52.25

D	151 – 165	140/77	140/77	120/66
E	166 – 185	165/90.75	165/90.75	145/79.75
F	Over 185	205/112.75	205/112.75	190/104.50
G	Over 225	300/165	300/165	285/156.75

Motorcycles are taxed according to engine size: those under 150cc at £15 per year, those between 151 and 400cc at £30, those between 401 and 600cc at £47 and those with larger engines at £64 (£35.20 six months). Three-wheeled motorcycles over 150cc are taxed at £64 (£35.25 six months)

Road tax is usually paid at a post office, where forms and information leaflets are available (spendthrifts can purchase £5 stamps to help save for their road tax). If you're registering a vehicle for the first time, it's possible to license it for part of a month plus 6 or 12 months. To obtain your road tax disc, you must complete a Vehicle Licence Application Form (V10). Notes about registering and licensing a vehicle are contained in leaflet V100 (a separate licence and form is required for a heavy goods vehicle). Take your completed form V10 to any post office with your vehicle registration document or a completed form V62 (see **Vehicle Registration** on page 260); a valid insurance certificate or cover note (see **Car Insurance** on page 260); a valid test certificate, if applicable (see page 266); a disabled exemption certificate, if applicable; and the payment (e.g. cash or cheque).

Alternatively you can tax your car online at www.dvla.gov.uk if you are the registered keeper of the vehicle and your name, address and any changes you have made to your vehicle have been updated on DVLA records. The easy to use service will take you step by step through the process. An electronic check will be made to confirm that you have the necessary insurance, vehicle test (MOT) and entitlement to disability exemption (if appropriate). A tax disc and receipt for payment will be sent to you through the post within five working days.

To tax your vehicle on line you'll need the following:

- the 16 digit reference number printed in the yellow box on the front of your renewal reminder or the 11 digit reference number found on the front of your Vehicle Registration Certificate and your vehicle registration number;

- a debit or credit card, (there is a £2.50 service charge on credit card transactions);

- a vehicle test certificate (you must have been issued with a new style certificate to use the service);

- insurance, which will be checked on the Motor Insurance Database run by the Motor Insurers Information Centre (you cannot use the service if you have recently changed your Insurance Company);

- Entitlement to disability exemption (if applicable).

You can also apply by phone (☎ 0870-850 4444 or textphone/minicom ☎ 0870-850 4445). Some applications must be made at a Vehicle Registration Office (VRO), which are listed in leaflet V100. After paying your road tax, you receive a tax disc showing the registration number and the date to which duty has been paid. This must be displayed on the inside of the windscreen of your car on the left-hand side (top or bottom). It's usually inserted in a plastic holder available from garages and motor accessory shops.

Road tax cannot be transferred from one vehicle to another, although you can obtain a refund for each whole month it still has to run, e.g. when you sell a car or take it off the road. To do this, you must remove the tax disc and take it with a completed form V14 (available from post offices) to any VRO or send it to Refund Section, DVLA, Swansea SA99 1AL. You should apply for an exchange tax disc if the taxation class of your vehicle changes, e.g. if you convert a car into a truck or motor caravan, or if you buy a vehicle with a licence which doesn't cover your use of the vehicle. If your tax disc has been lost, stolen, destroyed or spoilt in any way (e.g. the figures cannot be read), you can obtain a duplicate licence for a small fee. Complete form V20 and send it to a VRO.

In recent years, there has been a clampdown on tax evaders. If a vehicle has been taxed since 1st January 1998, it must have a current tax disc or you must file a Statutory Off Road Notification (SORN) with the DVLA. If you use or keep a vehicle on a public road that isn't taxed, you're subject to a mimium fine of £1,000 plus you will need to buy a tax disc and pay any arrears owing since the vehicle was last taxed plus a £80 penalty. If you fail to file a SORN, the fine is also £1,000 and, if you make a SORN declaration when a car is being used or kept on a road, it could cost you £5,000 or two years in prison. You may also find your vehicle wheelclamped by a DVLA wheelclamping agent, in which case you will have to pay a release fee and produce a valid tax disc or pay a surety fee.

GENERAL ROAD RULES

The following general road rules and tips may help you adjust to driving in the UK:

- Among the many strange habits of the British is that of driving on the left-hand side of the road. If you're used to driving on the right it may be helpful to have a reminder (e.g. 'think left!') on your car's dashboard. Take extra care when pulling out of junctions, one-way streets and at roundabouts. Remember to look first to the **right** when crossing the road and drivers of left-hand cars should make sure that headlights are dipped to the left when driving at night.

- If you're unused to driving on the left, you should be prepared for some disorientation, although most people have few problems adjusting to it. Some drivers have a real fear of driving on the 'wrong' side of the road. If this applies to you, the International Drivers Service (☎ 020-8570 9190) specialises in teaching foreigners how to survive on British roads. The traffic system, density and speed of traffic are all also completely alien to many foreigners, particularly Americans.

- All motorists are advised to carry a warning triangle, although it isn't mandatory. If you have an accident or a breakdown (see **Accidents** on page 284), you should signal this by switching on your hazard warning lights. If you have a warning triangle, it must be placed at the edge of the road, at least 50m behind the car on secondary roads and at least 150m on motorways.

- There's no priority to the right (or left) on British roads (unlike, for example, the continental priority to the right). At all crossroads and junctions, there's either an octagonal stop sign with a solid white line on road or a triangular give way sign (dotted white line on road), where a secondary road meets a major road. 'Stop' or 'give way' may also be painted on the road surface. You must stop completely at a stop sign (all four wheels must come to rest), before pulling out on to a major road, even if you can see that no traffic is approaching. At a give way sign, you aren't required to stop, but must give priority to traffic already on the major road.

- The different types of traffic signs can usually be distinguished by their shape and colour as follows:

  - Warning signs are mostly triangular with **red** borders;

  - Signs within circles with a **red** border are mostly prohibitive;

  - Signs within **blue** circles, but no red border give positive instructions;

  - Direction signs are mostly rectangular and are distinguished by their background colour; **blue** for motorway signs, **green** for primary routes and **white** for secondary routes. Local direction signs often have blue borders with a white background. Signs with brown backgrounds are used to direct motorists to tourist attractions. All signs are shown in a booklet entitled *Know Your Traffic Signs* (see below).

- On roundabouts (traffic circles), vehicles already on the roundabout (coming from your right) have priority over those entering it. There are many roundabouts in the UK, which, although they're a bit of a free-for-all, speed up traffic considerably and are usually preferable to traffic lights, particularly outside rush hours (although some busy roundabouts also have traffic lights). Some roundabouts have a filter lane, reserved for traffic turning left. **Traffic flows clockwise round roundabouts** and not anti-clockwise as in countries where traffic drives on the right. You should signal as you approach the exit you wish to take. In addition to large roundabouts, there are also mini-roundabouts, indicated by a round blue sign. Roundabouts are particularly useful for making a U-turn when you discover that you're travelling in the wrong direction.

- On country roads, sharp bends are shown by signs and the severity (tightness) of a bend is indicated by white arrows on a black background (or vice versa); the more arrows, the tighter the bend (so **slow** down).

- For all adults (14 years and over) the wearing of front and rear seat belts is compulsory and the driver is responsible for ensuring children under 14 use the correct seat belts or child restraints. Seat belts or restraints must be appropriate for the age and weight of a child which the law puts ito the following categories; Children up to 3 years old and Children aged 3 and above, until they reach EITHER their 12th birthday OR 135cm in height who must use the correct child seat. Children over 1.35m (4ft 5in) in height, or who are 12 or 13 years old can use adult seat belts. Child seats are designed for various weights of child. As a general guide:

– Baby seats are for babies weighing up to 13kgs (birth to 9-12 months) or until they can support their own head. They face backwards and are fitted into the front or rear of the car with a seat belt. They should never be used in the front where the front seat is protected with a frontal airbag.

– Child car seats are for children weighing between 20 to 40lb (9 to 18kg), aged nine months to about four years, and have their own straps. They face forwards and are usually fitted in the back seat of a car with a seat belt.

– Booster seats and booster cushions are for children weighing 33 to 80lb (15 to 36 kg), aged around 4 years and upwards. They are designed to raise them so they can use an adult seat belt safely across both their chest and lower abdomen.

Special harnesses and belts are also available for the disabled. All belts, seats, harnesses and restraints **must be correctly fitted and adjusted, without which they may be useless.** Some child car seats have fatal flaws and many cars have seat belt straps that are too short for rear-facing baby seats. It's estimated that some two-thirds of child seats are wrongly fitted. The RAC (☎ 08705-722 722) has a safety video entitled *There's No Excuse!* If all available restraints in a car are in use, children may travel unrestrained (although this is extremely unwise).

It's estimated that seat belts would prevent 75 per cent of the deaths and 90 per cent of the injuries to those involved in accidents. Lap belts fitted in the centre rear seat of many cars are dangerous and should be replaced. In addition to the risk of death or injury, you can be fined £50 for ignoring the seat belt laws. It's the driver's responsibility to ensure that passengers are properly fastened. If you're exempt from wearing a seat belt for medical reasons, a safety belt exemption certificate is required from your doctor. The ultimate protection is supposed to be afforded by airbags, although a number of deaths have been blamed on them in recent years.

● Don't drive in lanes reserved for buses and taxis, unless necessary to avoid a stationary vehicle or obstruction, and give priority to authorised users. Bus lanes are indicated by road markings and signs indicate the period of operation, which is usually during rush hours only (although some lanes are in use 24 hours a day), and which vehicles are permitted to use them. Bus drivers get irate if you illegally drive in their lane and you can be fined for doing so.

● Headlights must be used at night on all roads except unrestricted roads with street lamps not more than 185m (200 yards) apart and subject to a speed limit of 30mph. You must use your headlamps or front fog lamps at any time when visibility is generally reduced to less than 100m. It's legal to drive on parking (side) lights on roads with street lighting (although they do little to help you see or be seen). **Headlight flashing has a different meaning in different countries.** In some, it means "after you", while in others it means "get out of my way". In the UK, headlamp flashing has no legal status apart from warning another driver of your presence, although it's usually used to give priority to another vehicle, e.g. when a car is waiting to exit from a junction. Hazard warning lights (all indicators operating simultaneously) are used to warn other drivers of an obstruction, e.g. an accident or a traffic jam on a motorway (using them when parking illegally has no legal significance unless you've broken down).

- Front fog or spot lights must be fitted in pairs at a regulation height. Rear fog lamps should be used only when visibility is seriously reduced, i.e. to less than 100m, and shouldn't be used when it's just dark or raining. Unfortunately, many British drivers don't know what fog lamps are for and use them when visibility is good, but don't use them (or any lights) in fog.

- The sequence of traffic lights is red, red + amber (yellow), green, amber and back to red. Red + amber is a warning to get ready to go, but you mustn't start moving until the light changes to green. Amber means stop at the stop line. You may proceed only if the amber light appears after you've crossed the stop line or when stopping might cause an accident. A green filter light may be shown in addition to the full lamp signals, which means you may drive in the direction shown by the arrow, irrespective of other lights showing.

  You may notice that many traffic lights have an uncanny habit of changing to green when you approach them, particularly during off-peak hours. This isn't magic: around half of the UK's traffic signals are vehicle-activated, where sensors between 40 and 150m from the lights (depending on the speed limit) are set into the road and change the light to green unless other traffic already has priority. Signals stay at green for a minimum of seven seconds, although it can be as long as one minute.

- At many traffic lights, cameras are installed to detect motorists driving through red lights (you receive notification around one month later and must **prove** that you weren't driving to avoid prosecution). Traffic lights are placed on the left side of the road at junctions and may also be duplicated opposite.

- Always approach pedestrian crossings with caution and don't park or overtake another vehicle on the approach to a crossing, marked by a double line of studs or zigzag lines. At pelican (pedestrian) crossings, a flashing amber light follows the red light, to warn you to give way to pedestrians before proceeding. **Pedestrians have the legal right of way once they've stepped on to a crossing without traffic lights and you must stop. Motorists who don't stop are liable to heavy penalties.** Where a road crosses a public footpath, e.g. when entering or emerging from property or a car park bordering a road, you **must** give way to pedestrians.

- The UK lacks a rule of the road which compels slow-moving vehicles (such as tractors or cars towing caravans) to pull over to allow other traffic to overtake. The AA states that a driver towing a caravan who sees more than six vehicles following him, should pull over and let them pass, but it isn't compulsory. Worse still, timid drivers who never overtake anything unless it's stationary, bunch up behind slow moving vehicles, thus ensuring that nobody can overtake without having to pass a whole stream of traffic (or forcing a gap).

● Fines can be exacted for a wide range of motoring offences, although on-the-spot fines aren't imposed. Convictions for most motoring offences means an 'endorsement' of your licence, which results in penalty points being imposed (see **Driving Licence** on page 269). Serious offences, such as dangerous or drunken driving involving injury or death to others, can result in a prison sentence.

● Many motorists seem to have an aversion to driving in the left-hand lane on a three-lane motorway, which in effect reduces the motorway to two lanes. It's illegal to overtake on an inside lane unless traffic is being channelled in a different direction. Motorists must indicate before overtaking **and** when moving back into an inside lane after overtaking, e.g. on a dual carriageway or motorway. Learner drivers, pedestrians, cyclists and mopeds aren't permitted on motorways.

● White lines mark the separation of traffic lanes. A solid single line or two solid lines means no overtaking in either direction. A solid line to the left of the centre line, i.e. on your side of the road, means that overtaking is prohibited in your direction. You may overtake only when there's a single broken line in the middle of the road or double lines with a broken line on your side of the road. If you drive a left-hand drive car, take extra care when overtaking (the most dangerous manoeuvre in motoring) and when turning right. It's wise to have a special overtaking mirror fitted to your car.

● The edges of motorways and A-roads are often marked with a white line with a ribbed surface, which warns you through tyre sound and vibration when you drive too close to the edge of the road.

● In the UK, there are three main kinds of automatic railway crossings: automatic half-barrier level crossings, automatic open crossings and open level crossings without gates or barriers. Always approach a railway level crossing slowly and **stop**:

   – As soon as the amber light is on and the audible alarm sounds followed by flashing red warning lights (half-barrier level crossings and automatic open crossings);

   – As soon as the barrier or half-barrier starts to fall (if applicable) or the gates start to close;

   – In any case when a train approaches.

Many automatic and manual crossings have a telephone to contact the signalman in an emergency or to ask for advice or information. In remote areas, open level crossings have no gates, barriers, attendant or traffic lights. Some level crossings have gates, but no attendant or red lights. If there's a telephone, contact the signalman to check that it's okay to cross; otherwise, provided a train isn't coming, open the gates wide and cross as quickly as possible. Close the gates after crossing. **Crossings without gates must be approached with extreme caution (including pedestrian railway crossings).**

- Be particularly wary of cyclists, moped riders and motorcyclists. It isn't always easy to see them, particularly when they're hidden by your car's blind spots or when cyclists are riding at night without lights. **When overtaking, always give them a wide berth.** If you knock them off their bikes, you may have a difficult time convincing the police that it wasn't your fault; far better to avoid them (and the police). Drive slowly near schools and be wary of children getting on or off buses.

- A 'GB' nationality plate (sticker) must be affixed to the rear of a British- registered car when motoring abroad. Drivers of foreign-registered cars in the UK must have the appropriate nationality plate affixed to the rear of their car (not an assortment). Yellow headlights, which in the past were fitted to all vehicles in France, are illegal in the UK (except for visitors) and should be converted.

- If you need spectacles or contact lenses to read a number plate 79.4mm high at a distance of 20.5m (67ft) in good daylight, then you must always wear them when motoring. It's advisable to carry a spare pair of glasses or contact lenses in your car.

- A new law was introduced on 1st December 2003 prohibiting the use of mobile phones while driving (or even stationary with the engine running), unless it's a hands-free phone in a cradle (using headphones and a microphone is legal, provided the phone is in a cradle). Using a phone when driving is one of the most common and hazardous driving habits in the UK and has been calculated to increase the risk of an accident by some 400 per cent (even hands-free phones are considered to be unsafe, as they distract the driver's attention). New legislation to increase the penalty for using a hand-held phone whilst driving came into force in February 2007. The fine increased to £60 and three penalty points on your licence. Penalty points can mean higher insurance costs. If you get six points within two years of passing your test, your licence will be revoked and you will need to re-sit the test. If the case goes to court, you could risk a maximum fine of £1,000, which rises to £2,500 for the driver of a bus, coach, or heavy goods vehicle

- A booklet published by the Department for Transport entitled *The Highway Code* (The Stationery Office) contains advice for all road users, including motorists, motorcyclists and pedestrians. It's available for 99p from bookshops, British motoring organisations and on the internet (💻 www.highwaycode.gov.uk) and is essential reading. Although *The Highway Code* shows many commonly used road signs, a comprehensive explanation is given in a booklet entitled *Know Your Traffic Signs*, available at most bookshops for £3. A free booklet entitled *On the Road in Great Britain* (in English, French, German, Italian and Spanish) is published by the Department for Transport and is available from British motoring organisations, travel agents and government offices.

BRITISH DRIVERS

Like motorists in all countries, the British have their own idiosyncrasies and customs. In general, Britons have a reputation for being good drivers, and most are courteous. Unlike many other Europeans, they're usually happy to give way to a driver waiting to enter the flow of traffic or change lanes. However, tempers are rising on the UK's overcrowded streets and road rage ('invented' in California, where drivers blow their tops and attack or drive into other motorists) is becoming more common. It's often provoked by tailgating, headlight flashing, obscene gestures, obstruction and verbal abuse, so be careful how you behave when driving. Although British drivers are generally law-abiding (except with regard to speed limits), a recent survey found that millions would drive on the wrong side of the law if they thought they could get away with it.

Many drivers are afraid of motorways and have little idea how to drive on them; common faults include poor lane discipline, undertakers (motorists who overtake on the inside), driving too fast in poor conditions (e.g. fog and heavy rain), and driving much too close to the vehicle in front. Many motorists drive too close and have no idea of safe stopping distances. *The Highway Code* (see **General Road Rules** on page 274) states that the safe stopping distance (including thinking distance, the time it takes for drivers to react) is 75ft (23m) at 30mph/50kph, 175ft (53m) at 50mph/80kph and 315ft (96m) at 70mph/113kph.

These stopping distances are on dry roads, for cars with good brakes and tyres, in good visibility with an alert driver (if you're half asleep and driving an old banger on a wet or icy road, you had better not exceed 10mph; otherwise you will never stop in an emergency). Although these distances may appear generous, many other countries recommend longer stopping distances. If further proof is needed of how dangerous and widespread tailgating is, simply witness the statistics on the number of 'concertina' (multiple car) accidents in the UK, particularly on motorways in bad weather conditions. As a safety precaution, try to leave a at least a three car length gap between your car and the vehicle in front. This isn't just to allow you more time to stop, should the vehicles in front decide to get together, but also to give a tailgater more time to stop. **The closer the car behind you, the further you should be from the vehicle in front.** Motorway police criticise motorists for driving too close, too fast and for not looking far enough ahead.

One thing most foreigners immediately notice when driving in the UK is the speed at which most people drive, which is often 50 per cent above the prevailing speed limit. The exception to this rule is the ubiquitous 'Sunday driver', so-called because he rarely drives on any other day of the week and is never actually going anywhere, but just enjoying the scenery (hence his maximum 20mph speed). You will also notice that many motorists are reluctant to use their lights in poor visibility or until it's completely dark at night; even then, they may use parking lights only in areas with street lighting. Sometimes it's just as well that people fail to use their headlights, as many are badly adjusted and dazzle oncoming drivers (it's hard to believe they're ever checked during the annual serviceability test).

One of the biggest problems when motoring in towns and most residential areas, is the vast number of cars parked (legally or illegally) on roads, so that you have to stop because your side of the road is completely blocked or because oncoming traffic isn't keeping far enough over to its side of the road to allow you sufficient room to pass. Parked cars are also particularly hazardous when pulling out of busy junctions. (many more of which should have roundabouts).

Take it easy when driving in winter. Although heavy snow is rare, particularly in the south, the UK has a lot of fog and ice, which make driving extremely hazardous (it also gets dark at around 4pm or even earlier in the north). Black ice is also common and is the most dangerous sort, because it cannot be seen. When road conditions are bad, allow two to three times longer than usual to reach your destination.

BRITISH ROADS

There are some 362,000km (225,000mi) of roads in the UK, including around 3,100km (1,950mi) of motorways. In general, the quality of British roads is excellent, although some main roads and motorways are in a poor condition through being constantly chewed up by juggernauts and the heavy volume of traffic. Poor road design and shoddy workmanship have added to road problems and cost the British taxpayer millions of pounds each year. Many suburban roads are full of potholes, particularly in London where some councils cannot afford to repair them. Roads in all areas are often badly repaired after being constantly dug up by utility companies (telephone, electricity, gas, water, cable television) and local councils. It's estimated that some 600,000 holes are dug each year in London's roads alone, around double the national average.

Speed 'bumps', known as 'sleeping policemen', are a common sight, particularly in residential areas, near schools, on private roads, in university grounds and in car parks. They're designed to slow traffic (or wreck your suspension) and are sometimes indicated by warning signs as, if you fail to slow down, it's possible to turn your car over. (People have been killed after hitting speed bumps at high speed).

The UK has a smaller motorway network than many other western European countries. The controversial M6 toll road, currently bypassing Birmingham, may be joined by a much longer toll road on the M6, linking Birmingham to Manchester. It's impossible to introduce toll booths as used on the continent and vehicles would be fitted with a transponder which would communicate with toll-charging gantries installed on motorways. Motorists would receive a monthly bill. Tolls are expected to create havoc on other roads, as motorists desert motorways for A and B roads.

The Severn Bridge was privatised in 1991 and there are now two separate bridges. There's a toll charge of £5.10 for cars when crossing westwards only (crossing eastwards doesn't incure a charge). Another significant toll area is the Dartford Crossing, which is an integral part of the M25 orbital motorway around London (although not in fact a motorway) and crosses the Thames to the east of the capital. Travel north is by tunnel, south by bridge and the toll for cars is either direction is £1.

Motorway travel in the UK is generally fast, although it's often slowed to a crawl by road works and the ubiquitous contra-flow, where two-way traffic occupies a single carriageway. However, despite their high traffic density, motorways are the UK's safest roads, accounting for just 3 per cent of all casualties. Casualties on town and rural roads are proportionately very much higher. By the year 2020, traffic on motorways is set to rise by between 50 and 100 per cent (there are already numerous bottlenecks during rush hours and even all day on some sections).

Emergency SOS telephones are located on motorways, where arrows on marker posts at the roadside indicate the direction of the nearest telephone. The hard shoulder on motorways is for emergencies only and **you mustn't stop there simply to have a rest** (for which you can be fined). The hard shoulder is a dangerous place to stop and many fatal accidents on motorways involve vehicles stopped there.

TRAFFIC POLICE

Police must have a reason to stop motorists in the UK, e.g. erratic driving or a defective bulb, although they can usually find a pretext if they want to stop you. Police cars sometimes display messages to motorists behind them via a panel inside their rear windscreen, e.g. 'Seatbelt', 'Reduce Your Speed', 'Do Not Pass', 'Accident Ahead' or 'Follow Me'. Undercover police also wear plain clothes and drive unidentified cars. If someone in plain clothes stops you, wait for identification to be shown before unlocking your car door or winding down your window. Never antagonise a police officer or make any smart cracks, as this is the fast lane to prosecution. If you remain courteous you may be let off with a caution. If you think you haven't committed an offence and wish to contest it in a court of law, don't accept a fixed penalty notice, but ask for a full charge to be brought against you.

You aren't required by law to carry your car or motorcycle papers when motoring in the UK. However, if you're stopped by the police (for any reason) while driving, they may ask to see the following:

- Driving licence (British if held);

- Vehicle registration document (log book);

- Test certificate (see page 266);

- Insurance certificate (or an international motor insurance certificate, if you drive a foreign-registered car).

If you don't have your papers with you when stopped by the police, you must take them personally to a police station (named by you), usually within seven days. They mustn't be sent by post.

MOTORCYCLES

Motorcycling is popular in the UK, both as a means of transport and as a pastime (scooters and motorcycles have become fashionable again in recent years), with over one million motorcyclists. In recent years, motorcycle accidents have been greatly reduced by the compulsory wearing of helmets, better bikes and protective riding gear, better training and defensive riding by bikers. In general, laws that apply to cars also apply to motorcycles. However, there are a few special points that apply to motorcyclists in particular:

- A moped can be ridden at the age of 16 with a provisional licence (see **Driving Licence** on page 269). A moped is defined as a 'motorised cycle' with an engine of not more than 50cc. Anything larger is classified as a motorcycle. The maximum legal speed a moped can be ridden is 30mph (50kph).

- A full motorcycle licence can be obtained at the age of 17 after passing a test.

- British standard (or equivalent) approved crash helmets are compulsory for both riders and passengers.

- It's illegal for a motorcycle rider with a provisional licence to carry a pillion passenger (unless the pillion passenger holds a full motorcycle licence). To carry a pillion passenger, a motorcycle must be fitted with a dual seat and footrests.

- You must use dipped headlights, day or night.

- You must have valid third party insurance.

- You cannot ride a motorcycle over 250cc until you've held a full motorcycle licence for two years.

Motorists with a full motor car licence (British or foreign) may ride a motorcycle (up to 125cc) without passing a test or obtaining a special licence. Unlike a motorcyclist with only a provisional licence, it isn't compulsory for a qualified motorist to take a test for a moped. An 'L' (learner) plate must, however, be displayed.

Insurance for motorcycles is high and similar to that for cars (see **Car Insurance** on page 271). The cost of insurance depends on your age (riders under 25 pay **much** more), type and cubic capacity of your motorcycle, and the length of time you've held a licence. No-claims discounts are lower than for cars (the maximum is 20 or 25 per cent only) and policies usually carry an excess.

Since July 1996, all learner riders throughout the EU have had to follow a course of training designed to take them safely through stages to a full licence. After an initial compulsory basic course, riders receive a provisional licence that allows them to ride bikes up to 12bhp for two years. After taking a test, they're limited to machines up to 33bhp for a further two years. 'Mature' riders aged 21 or over can qualify to ride larger bikes after accelerated training.

An MOT handbook on motorcycle safety entitled *How Safe Is Your Motorcycle?* is produced by the Vehicle Inspectorate and the Home Office publishes a leaflet *Put the Brakes on Bike Theft* (available from police stations and libraries). Essential reading for all bikers is *Sorry Mate, I Didn't See You* by Tim Monaghan (Crown Publications).

ACCIDENTS

The UK has a lower accident rate than most other European countries, although the death toll is still unacceptably high. It's generally recognised by the police and other experts that the majority of accidents could be avoided by improving driving standards (including less speed and less alcohol consumption by motorists), and the eradication of accident black spots through the redesign of roads and junctions. One of the most common causes of accidents, particularly on motorways, is that drivers fall asleep. If you feel tired, you should stop and rest immediately, as it's almost impossible to drive through it. You're recommended to take a break, even just to stretch your legs and get some fresh air, **at least** every two hours. Sleeping at the wheel is such a serious problem that, in future, cars may be fitted with 'driver fatigue' alarm. However, motorways are the UK's safest roads and 75 per cent of all road deaths happen on urban roads, which carry only 40 per cent of all traffic. Motorways carry 15 per cent and account for 6 per cent of road deaths.

If you're involved in (or cause) a car accident that results in injury to a person or a large animal (dog, horse, cattle, ass, mule, sheep, pig or goat) that isn't in your vehicle, or cause damage to any vehicle or property (apart from your own), the procedure is as follows:

1. Stop immediately. If possible move your car off the road and keep your passengers and yourself off the road. If you have an accident (or a breakdown) on a motorway, don't stay in your vehicle whatever the weather (even if parked on the hard shoulder), as there's a danger that another vehicle will run into you (a surprising one in eight of all motorway deaths occur on the hard shoulder).

   Wait on the embankment or nearby land (this also applies to stopping on other fast roads). Failing to stop after an accident or failure to give particulars or report to the police are potentially two seperate serious offences, for which there is a maximum fine of £5,000 and a licence endorsement of five to ten penalty points for each

2. Warn other drivers of any obstruction by switching on your hazard warning lights (particularly on motorways) or by placing a warning triangle at the edge of the road, at least 50m behind your car on secondary roads and 150m on a motorway. If necessary, for example when the road is partly or totally blocked, turn on your car's dipped headlights and direct traffic around the hazard. In bad visibility, at night or in a blind spot, try to warn oncoming traffic of the danger, e.g. with a torch, or by waving a warning triangle up and down.

3. If anyone is injured, immediately ☎ 999 for an ambulance, the fire brigade (if someone is trapped or oil or chemicals are spilled) or the police. If an ambulance is called, the police come automatically. Emergency telephones are provided on motorways. Give first aid only if you're qualified to do so. Don't move an injured person unless absolutely necessary to save him from further injury and don't leave him alone except to telephone for an ambulance. Cover him with a blanket or coat to keep him warm.

4. You must call the police if there are any injuries, damage to property of a third party whom you cannot contact, or the road is blocked. If you think someone else involved in an accident is drunk or has otherwise broken the law (e.g. their vehicle is unroadworthy), you should call the police. The police normally breathalyse everyone involved in an accident, as a matter of routine. The police may refuse to attend an accident scene if nobody has been injured. Calling the police to the scene of an accident may result in someone being fined for a driving offence. In all cases, you mustn't say anything which could be interpreted as an admission of guilt, even if you're as guilty as hell. Admitting responsibility for an accident, either verbally or in writing can release your insurance company from responsibility under your policy. In other words, you must say nothing (not even 'sorry') or only that your insurance company will deal with any claims. Let the police and insurance companies decide who was at fault.

5. If you or any other driver(s) involved decide to call the police, don't move your vehicle or allow other vehicles to be moved. If it's necessary to move vehicles to unblock the road, mark the positions of their wheels with chalk and measure the distance between vehicles. Take photographs of the accident scene if a camera is available (a throwaway camera kept in your car is preferable to using a mobile phone camera as the later can be modified digitally at a later date) or make a drawing showing the positions of all vehicles involved before moving them.

6. Check immediately whether there are any witnesses to the accident and take their names and addresses, particularly noting those who support your version of what happened. Write down the registration numbers of all vehicles involved (or possible witnesses) and their drivers' and owners' names, addresses and insurance details. Note also the identification numbers of any police present. You must (by law) give anyone with reasonable grounds for requiring them (e.g. the owner of damaged property) your name and insurance details, and the vehicle owner's name and address (if different).

7. If you're unable to give your insurance details to anyone who has reasonable grounds for requiring them, you must report the accident in person to a police station within 24 hours. If you've caused material damage, you must inform the owner of the damaged property as soon as possible. If you cannot reach him, report the accident to a police station within 24 hours (this also applies to damage caused to other vehicles when parking). It's often advisable to report any accident involving another vehicle within 24 hours to avoid any repercussions later. If you have an accident involving a domestic animal (except a cat) and are unable to find the owner, it must also be reported to the police. This also applies to certain wild animals, e.g. deer. Make sure your visit is officially recorded by the police officer on duty and that you receive signed verification of your report.

8. If you're detained by the police, you aren't required to make a statement, even if they ask for one. If you do make a statement, don't sign it unless you're certain that you understand and agree with every word.

9. Lastly, you should report all accidents to your insurance company in writing as soon as possible, even if you don't plan to make a claim (but reserve your right to make a claim later). Your insurance company will ask you to complete an accident report form, which you should return as soon as possible (don't forget to sign it).

Many insurers will handle a claim for you; otherwise you must write to the other driver's insurance company yourself, giving details of your claim (but inform your insurance company). If your car is involved in an accident and the other driver isn't insured or cannot be traced, you may be able to claim from a legal expenses scheme operated by the Motor Insurers' Bureau (MIB) and financed by insurance companies (☎ 01908-830 001, 💻 www.mib.org.uk). The fund doesn't cover hit-and-run accidents where the driver cannot be traced and claims are limited to a maximum of £100,000. The Royal Society for the Prevention of Accidents (RoSPA), Edgbaston Park, 353 Bristol Road, Birmingham B5 7ST (☎ 0121-248 2000, 💻 www.rospa.com) and the Department for Transport publish various leaflets concerning car and motorcycle safety.

DRINKING & DRIVING

As you're no doubt well aware, drinking and driving make a dangerous cocktail. Around a tenth of all injury accidents (and over 500 deaths a year) result from driving with excess alcohol in the blood, and around 20 per cent of drivers and motorcyclists killed in accidents have alcohol levels above the legal limit. On Friday and Saturday nights between 10pm and 4am, around two-thirds of drivers and riders killed are over the legal alcohol limit. In the UK, you're no longer considered fit to drive when your breath contains 35 micrograms of alcohol per 100ml or your blood contains 80mg of alcohol per 100ml (or 107mg per 100ml of urine).

For someone of average body weight, the recognised maximum they can drink and still remain under the limit is two pints of average strength beer or its equivalent. Anything more than two small beers or even a glass of wine may be too much for someone of slim build or someone unused to alcohol. Random breath tests aren't permitted. However, the police can stop any car under any pretext (e.g. to check that it isn't stolen) and ask the driver to take a breath test (particularly around Christmas and the New Year, when there's a crackdown on drunken driving). This involves simply blowing into a device which turns red if you fail the test. It's an offence to refuse to take a breath test, for which the penalty is the same as failing the test.

If you fail the breathalyser test, you're taken to a police station and are given a further test on a special analyser after around 20 minutes. If you're still over the limit, you have the right to request a blood or urine test, which may also be requested by the police. The police and most people choose blood tests. If a test wasn't requested by the police, you must pay a fee if you're found to be over the limit. Samples of blood or urine are put into separate containers, one of which is sealed and given to you for private analysis (should you so wish). You can still be over the legal limit the morning after a heavy night's drinking. You can also be disqualified for driving while under the influence of drugs (cannabis smoked days before a test can show up in specimens and can result in a disqualification for driving while under the influence of drugs). You can also be convicted of being drunk if you're 'in charge of a vehicle' even though you aren't actually driving it. This carries the same penalties as drunken driving.

If you're convicted of drunken driving, you lose your licence for a mandatory 12 month period, receive a heavy fine (maximum £5,000) and/or 6 months imprisonment. You can even be imprisoned for up to ten years if you cause an injury or death. Second offenders within a period of ten years are disqualified for three years. Drunken drivers must pay much higher insurance premiums after disqualification. Convicted drivers can take a hard-hitting course to get their licence back sooner (an idea borrowed from the US). Courses last for 20 to 30 hours, spread over five or six sessions and cost between £50 and £200. This can result in reductions of up to 25 per cent in the period of disqualification and a discount of up to 40 per cent on the heavy insurance bills faced after a ban.

If you have an accident while under the influence of alcohol it could be expensive. Your car, accident and health insurance could all be nullified. This means you must pay your own (and any third party's) car repairs, medical expenses and other damages.

CAR THEFT

Over 370,000 cars are stolen each year in the UK, which has the highest (per capita) number of stolen cars in Europe. Car crime is a huge and profitable business, costing billions of pounds a year and representing around a third of all reported crime. It's estimated that some 70 per cent of stolen cars are broken up and sold for spares, while the rest are given a false identity and sold (many are exported to the Middle and Far East). One car in ten becomes a victim of 'autocrime' in England and Wales, and if you regularly park your car in a city street, you have a one in four chance of having it or its contents stolen. Having your car stolen means more than just taking a taxi home. It may mean weeks of delay sorting out insurance; extra time and expense travelling to work; possible loss of personal (maybe irreplaceable) possessions; and loss of your insurance no-claims discount. It may also involve hiring a solicitor or going to court to re-claim your car after it has been sold by the thief (if a car is stolen and sold, it can be a nightmare getting it back).

If you drive a new or valuable car, it's wise to have it fitted with an alarm, an engine immobiliser (preferably of the rolling code variety with a transponder arming key) or other anti-theft device (such as a tracker) , and to use a visible deterrent such as a steering or gear lock. This is particularly important if you own a car that's desirable to car thieves, which includes most new sports and executive cars, that are often stolen by professional crooks to order (although the most vulnerable cars are GTI hatchbacks which are often stolen and wrecked by joyriders – a British phenomenon). A reflection of the high rate of stolen cars is that it's standard practice for many new cars to be fitted with dead locks and sophisticated alarm systems (some cars such as the Jaguar XJ are, according to experts, virtually theft-proof). Professional thieves now steal cars by towing them or removing them on trailers rather than cracking security devices. Needless to say, if you're driving anything other than a worthless wreck, you should have theft insurance (which includes your stereo and belongings).

Don't take unnecessary risks and always lock your car, engage your steering lock and completely close all windows (but don't leave pets in an unventilated car). Never leave your keys in the ignition, not even in your driveway or when filling up at a petrol station. Put any valuables (including clothes) in the boot or out of sight and don't leave your vehicle documents in the car or any form of identification. If possible, avoid parking in commuter and long-term car parks (e.g. at airports and railway stations), which are favourite hunting grounds for car thieves. When parking overnight or when it's dark, park in a well-lit area, which helps deter car thieves.

Car theft has spawned a huge car security business in the (losing) battle to prevent or deter car thieves. Shops offer a multitude of car alarms, engine immobilisers, steering and gear stick locks, personal wheel clamps, systems for window etching with the car registration number, locking wheel nuts and petrol caps, and removable/coded stereo systems (a favourite target of thieves). A good security system won't prevent someone breaking into your car (which usually takes a professional a matter of seconds) or prevent its being stolen. What it does do is to make it more difficult and may prompt a thief to look for an easier target. If you plan to buy an expensive stereo system, buy one with a removable unit or control panel/fascia (which you can pop in a pocket), but never forget to remove it, even when stopping for a few minutes (although thieves sometimes steal the back box, leaving you with a useless fascia). Finally, insure your car stereo for its full replacement value. If all else fails, buy a Reliant three-wheeler, as no self-respecting crook would touch it! For complete peace of mind, particularly in London, you're better off using public transport.

The best (and most expensive) security for a valuable car is a tracking device, such as Securicor Trakbak and Tracker Network, that's triggered by concealed motion detectors. The vehicle's movements are tracked by radio or satellite and the police are automatically notified and recover over 90 per cent of vehicles. Some systems can immobilise a vehicle while it's on the move (which might not be such a good idea!). Many insurance companies offer a discount on comprehensive insurance (e.g. 20 per cent) when you have a tracking system fitted.

A lot of information is available on car security, including *How to Buy a Car and Keep it* and *Keep Your Car Secure* published by the Home Office Crime Prevention Unit. If your car is stolen, report it to the police and your insurance company as soon as possible. Don't, however, expect the police to find it or even take any interest in your loss. Further information about car crime prevention can be obtained from your local police station or from the Home Office Public Relations Branch, Room 157, 50 Queen Anne's Gate, London SW1H 9AT.

FUEL

Fuel, priced in litres, varies considerably in cost, according to local competition, the state of the world oil market and whether war has broken out in the Middle East. In 2007, the price was around 94p a litre for premium unleaded and around 99p for lead replacement and super unleaded (leaded petrol is available only from a limited number of suppliers – see 🖳 www.leadedpetrol.co.uk). Diesel fuel is available from most garages and costs 96p, around the same price as premium unleaded – or up to double the price in other EU countries! After sharp tax increases in recent years, the UK now has the most expensive petrol in Europe.

The price of fuel varies little, although savings may be made by buying from supermarkets, which have around 20 per cent of the market. Shop around for the best buy, as prices can vary. It's cheaper in England than other parts of the UK, although some towns with a lot of passing trade (e.g. Dover) are expensive. Prices must be displayed. As one observer commented, a sign of the increasing crime rate in the UK is that every time you stop for petrol you get mugged by a ruthless gang of criminals (the oil companies **and** the government). Some oil companies provide stamps or saving points, which can be exchanged for gifts, although most motorists would prefer cheaper fuel. The cleanest fuels of all are compressed natural gas (CNG) and liquefied petroleum gas (LPG). Most petrol engines can be converted to use both petrol and CNG/LPG (and can be switched between them). However, its availability is limited. For a list of outlets contact the LP Gas Association, Pavilion 16, Headlands Business Park, Salisbury Road, Ringwood, Hants. BH24 3PB (☎ 01425-461 612).

Most petrol stations are open from 8am to 10pm and on motorways they're usually open 24 hours. It's no problem finding a petrol station, as all towns usually have at least one. Signs on motorways indicate the distance to the next petrol station. When paying in self-service petrol stations, you simply tell the cashier your pump number (most pumps don't issue receipts). Outside normal business hours, some petrol stations have automatic pumps accepting £5 or £10 notes.

Most garages provide air (there may be a nominal charge of 10p or you may be given a token if you buy petrol), use of a car vacuum cleaner (fee around 10p) and a car wash (£2 to £6, depending on the type of wash chosen). Beware of car washes with wheels, which can be trapped under body parts and wreck them (e.g. spoilers). Most petrol stations also have a shop selling a wide range of motoring accessories and other goods. In fact, the main business of many petrol stations isn't selling fuel, on which profit margins are minimal (except for the government!). Today's petrol stations are more like convenience stores and sell a wide range of confectionery, snacks, drinks (even beer, wine and spirits), pizzas, newspapers and magazines, and take in dry-cleaning (some even have cafés or their own bakery).

SPEED LIMITS

The following speed limits are in force for cars and motorcycles throughout the UK, unless traffic signs show otherwise:

Type of Road	Speed Limit
Motorways and dual-carriageways	70mph (113kph)
Unrestricted single carriageway roads	60mph (97kph)
Built-up areas (towns)	30mph (48kph)*

* Applies to all traffic on all roads with street lighting unless otherwise indicated by a sign.

Speed limits are marked in miles per hour, not kilometres. When towing a caravan or trailer, speed limits on all roads (except those in built-up and residential areas) are reduced by 10mph (16kph). Cars towing caravans aren't permitted to use the outside (overtaking) lane of a three-lane motorway at any time. Speed limits for buses, coaches and goods vehicles not exceeding 7.5 tonnes are the same as when towing, except that the permitted speed limit on motorways is 70mph. Heavy goods vehicles (exceeding 7.5 tonnes) are permitted to travel at 40mph on single carriageways, 50mph on dual carriageways and 60mph on motorways.

You're forbidden to drive in the fast lane on motorways, unless you're overtaking, and you can be fined for doing so. Special speed limits on motorways are shown by illuminated signs and flashing lights, but aren't usually compulsory. You can be prosecuted for driving too slowly on a motorway.

Speed cameras (both fixed and mobile) are in widespread use throughout the country. They're allegedly mainly used to reduce traffic speed and therefore accidents, although this is disputed by motoring organisations, who maintain that they're simply a way of increasing revenue. There are very few cameras on the country's most dangerous stretches of roads and, since police forces have been able to retain the fines, cameras have sprouted throughout the country. Over 1 million motorists a year are prosecuted for speeding, resulting in fines of over £millions a year. The good news is that the use of speed camera alert systems isn't illegal and they're widely sold and used; however, the best models (such as Cyclops) which use a Global Positioning Satellite (GPS) speedometer to detect cameras, cost over £350. There's also an annual fee (around £50) to update the system.

There's a maximum fine of £1,000 for speeding and 3-6 penalty points although the usual fine in magistrates courts is around £50. Speeding fines usually depend on an offender's previous convictions and the speed above the limit. There's no consistency in the punishment meted out to speeding drivers and the size of the fine and the length of a ban often depends on your legal representation, your position and standing in the community, and the leniency or otherwise of the magistrate. Average fines vary from as low as £30 to over £150 in different parts of the UK. Fines for speeding vary from a fixed penalty of £40 for marginal speeding (e.g. up to 15mph above the limit), to hundreds of pounds for speeding of 30mph or more above the limit, when you're almost certainly prosecuted in court and may be disqualified from driving for a period.

If you're stopped for marginal speeding, you have the choice of paying a fixed penalty or going to court. If you go to court and lose, your fine is likely to be higher and you must also pay costs (so make sure you have a good case). Usually, you're permitted to drive 10 per cent over the limit to allow for speedometer error. So, if you're clocked at 33mph in a 30mph zone, or 66mph in a 60mph zone, you won't usually be prosecuted for speeding. In addition to fines, driving licences are 'endorsed' for most motoring offences, using a points system. A fixed penalty for speeding carries three penalty points (see **Driving Licence** on page 269).

Despite prosecutions and fines, speeding is common in the UK and many motorists have a complete disregard for speed limits, particularly on motorways, where they're rarely enforced. A large number of people consistently drive at over 100mph. It's estimated that two-thirds of drivers exceed urban speed limits and over 50 per cent of cars on motorways exceed 70mph. Needless to say, excessive speed is a contributory factor in many accidents, but just one among many, not the major cause. However, a pedestrian is almost ten times more likely to die as a result of an impact from a car driven at 40mph than one driven at 20mph.

In some areas (e.g. residential estates, private roads, school and university grounds, and car parks) there are speed bumps, known as 'sleeping policemen', designed to slow traffic. These are sometimes indicated by warning signs and, if you fail to slow down, it's possible to damage your suspension or even turn your car over.

GARAGES & SERVICING

Garages are generally open from 8am to 6.30pm and usually close for lunch between noon and 1pm. Servicing and repairs at main dealers are expensive (particularly in major towns) and the cost of labour is usually around £30 to £40 an hour. Smaller garages are usually cheaper, although the quality of work is variable and it's best to choose one that has been personally recommended. Ask your friends and colleagues if they can recommend a garage close to your home or work place. However, if anything goes wrong (and it often does), you have a better chance of redress with a main dealer or a garage that's a member of a trade association (such as the Retail Motor Industry Federation or the Scottish Motor Trade Association) or approved by one of the motoring organisations (see page 294). When a car is under warranty, it must usually be serviced by an approved dealer in order not to invalidate the warranty. The date or mileage at which services are due may be calculated from the previous service, and not according to the standard periods and mileage indicated in the service record. Check in advance. Most main dealers have 'set price' published fees for regular services and certain repairs. Many garages, including most main dealers, provide a free replacement car while yours is being serviced, although you must book it in advance and arrange for comprehensive insurance. Some garages collect your car from your home or office and deliver it after the service, or drop you off at a station or local town and pick you up to collect your car.

Always obtain a number of quotations for major mechanical work or body repairs and tell the garage if an accident repair is to be paid for privately, as many increase the price when an insurance company is paying. Quotations for accident repairs usually vary wildly and some garages include the replacement of unnecessary parts. Always get a second opinion if you're quoted a high price for a repair, e.g. by simply ringing an approved dealer. High-tech systems are often replaced needlessly, often in ignorance rather than deliberately. Poor workmanship and overcharging by garages are the biggest concerns for motorists in the UK. Always instruct a garage what to do in writing and, for anything other than a standard service, get a written estimate that includes labour, parts and VAT. Ask the garage to contact you (give them a telephone number) and obtain approval before doing anything that isn't listed or if the cost is likely to exceed the original estimate. **Large official dealers typically charge around £50 an hour for servicing and you can usually save two-thirds or more by having your car serviced in Belgium or France (and enjoy a 'free' day out).**

If you must buy spare parts, you can save 50 per cent or more by buying them from a specialist company advertising in the motoring press or in weekly magazines such as *Exchange & Mart*. Wherever you buy parts, beware of cheap, supposedly branded parts, which can prove fatal (the UK is a prime target for counterfeiters, as motorists often go for the cheapest parts). You should never buy second-hand tyres, many of which fail to meet legal standards and are liable to suffer blow-outs and to cause serious accidents. Always make sure that your tyres are correctly inflated, as they're the most crucial part of your car with regard to safety.

Check how a bill is to be paid and make sure there's no misunderstanding about the collection time and date. If the car isn't ready, the garage should supply you with a replacement car free of charge. Always obtain a bill listing all work completed, showing parts and labour costs. A garage must use reasonable care and skill when servicing your car. This includes car washes, and tyre and exhaust replacement companies, Department for Transport testers or anyone else who does work on your car. If your car is damaged in any way while it's in a garage's care, they're liable: a sign disclaiming liability isn't legal.

The motor trade business in the UK has the same poor reputation as in most other countries, although admittedly only a relatively small percentage of garages are real rogues (which is no consolation if you fall victim to one of them). In checks carried out after servicing, many jobs are found not to have been done properly or indeed at all, and the percentage of complete and satisfactory services is often as low as 10 or 20 per cent. Probably every experienced motorist in the UK has had unsatisfactory service from a garage at some time or another. Women are particularly vulnerable to crooked garages and mechanics, who routinely charge women two-thirds more than men for the same work. A garage is usually entitled to keep your car until you've paid the bill, even if the work was done badly, and you must pay the bill and try to obtain satisfaction afterwards.

Free legal advice can be obtained from a Consumer Advice Centre (CAC) or a Trading Standards (or Consumer Protection) Department. British motoring organisations operate a free legal advice service for members and if you have a major problem it may be worthwhile getting them to carry out an independent inspection of your car (see **Motoring Organisations** on page 294). If a garage is a dealer, you can complain to the manufacturer or importer, although some manufacturers seem to prefer bad publicity rather than ensure that customers are satisfied. If the garage is a member of a trade association or is approved by the AA or RAC (see page 294), you can make a complaint to them.

Although you're covered by law against shoddy workmanship and overcharging, trying to obtain redress through the courts is a long and arduous business, with no guarantee of success. It's often not worth the time and effort unless the sum involved runs into hundreds or thousands of pounds. Not surprisingly many motorists do their own servicing.

ROAD MAPS

The UK's roads are designated by letters that define the type of road, followed by a route number. Motorways (coloured blue on maps) have the prefix 'M' followed by a low number such as M1, M2, M3 or M25. Trunk roads link principal towns and cities, as well as taking in more remote parts of the country. They're coloured red on maps and have the prefix 'A', e.g. A1 or A2. The higher the number, the more minor the trunk road. Minor or secondary roads, many of which are prefixed with the letter 'B', link small towns and villages, and are coloured brown or yellow on maps. In Wales, town and route signs are in English and Welsh. There are a vast number of road maps available, from local town maps to road atlases for the whole of the British Isles. The following road maps are among the best available:

- Geographers' A-Z Map Co. Ltd produces an excellent range of street atlases, street plans, town maps, and road and county maps for all areas of the UK, many containing a comprehensive index of every street.

- The AA and RAC motoring organisations (see page 294) and the Ordnance Survey produce a variety of comprehensive maps, including the AA *Big Road Atlas Britain*. Other good large-scale maps (around 3mi/5km to the inch) are the *Ordnance Survey Motoring Atlas*, *Collins Road Atlas Britain* and *Philip's Motoring Atlas Britain*.

- Local town maps are often available from libraries and tourist information centres, including touring maps such as the AA county series of 'day drives'. Detailed town maps are usually available from local bookshops and newsagents.

- Good free maps are available from tourist information centres, libraries and car hire companies.

CAR HIRE

There are four multinational car hire (which is usually preferred to 'car rental') companies in the UK (Avis, Budget, Europcar and Hertz), plus a number of large independents, e.g. British Car Rental, Godfrey Davis, Kenning Car Rental, Practical and Swan National. All have offices in towns throughout the country and at most major international airports (open from around 6.30am to 11pm). Most major companies provide one-way hire, which means you can hire a car at one branch and leave it at another (for an extra charge). When hiring from a national company, check whether you're being quoted the national or local rate (which is cheaper). The national rate is usually charged when hiring in major cities or at airports and should be avoided unless someone else is paying. Always check what's included in the rental charge, as what appears to be an expensive quote could turn out to be the cheapest.

Cars can also be hired from many garages and local car hire offices in most towns, which often charge much lower rates than the nationals. Look in local newspapers and under *Car Hire* in the yellow pages. Shop around for the best buy, as the car hire business is extremely competitive. However, you should be aware of cowboy companies who offer 'hire cars from hell'. Many cars offered by local companies, particularly in tourist areas, are unroadworthy and could put your life at risk. Be particularly careful if hiring an older car (cars from major hire companies aren't more than three years old and are usually less than one year old), as it could be in a dangerous condition. If you're offered an old car or a car with high mileage, it's probably wise to reject it (unless the company is in the business of renting cheap wrecks). If you hire a car in an unroadworthy condition, you're responsible if you're stopped by the police or cause an accident.

All national hire companies offer fly-drive deals on flights to or within the UK, which must be booked in advance. You can also hire a car from major railway stations and leave it at another station or delivery point. Providing you book 24 hours in advance, a car can be waiting to meet you at the station at any time of day or night. Cars can also be hired on the spot from some stations from Hertz and other hire companies. Hertz (and other companies) charge their highest rate for fly-drive and executive connection services. Special rates are available when combined with British Rail InterCity weekend or longer trips. Rental costs vary considerably between rental companies, particularly over longer periods (weekly and monthly rates are lower). Rates are inclusive of unlimited mileage, collision damage waiver insurance, personal accident, baggage insurance and VAT. Rental cars usually mustn't be driven outside the UK unless prior arrangement is made with the rental company and continental insurance (a green card) obtained.

To hire a car in the UK, you require a full British, European or international driving licence, which must have been held for a minimum of one year (or two years if under 23). If you hold a British licence with an endorsement for driving without due care and attention (or worse), you may be refused car hire, although an endorsement for speeding is usually permitted. You may be asked for some form of identification in addition to your driving licence. The minimum age is usually between 18 and 23, although those aged 18 to 21 must normally provide their own fully comprehensive insurance or purchase collision damage waiver (CDW) insurance at a special (high) rate. Drivers under 21 are usually restricted in their choice of cars and some hire companies insist on a higher minimum age (e.g. 25) for some categories of cars.

You must usually be aged 23 to 25 to hire a minibus or motor caravan (the maximum age for hiring a car may be 70 or 75). A minimum deposit of £50 to £75 (or equal to the total hire charge) is usually required if you don't pay by credit card (national car rental companies also have their own credit cards) and may be much higher if you don't take out CDW insurance. Cheques must be supported by a guarantee card. When paying by credit card, check that you aren't charged for erroneous extras or for something for which you've already paid, e.g. petrol. In fact, paying by credit card usually means that you give the hire company a 'continuous authority' (or blank cheque) to debit your card account.

Vans and pick-ups are available from major rental companies by the hour, half-day or day, or from smaller local companies (which once again, are cheaper). You can also hire a motor caravan, a caravan or trailer, or a minibus from a number of companies (prices vary with the season). In addition to self-drive car hire, in many cities you can hire a car with a chauffeur for business or sightseeing. The British Tourist Authority publishes an annual *Vehicle Hire* directory.

MOTORING ORGANISATIONS

There are five national motoring organisations in the UK: the Automobile Association/AA (☎ 0870-085 2721, 💻 www.theaa.com), Britannia Rescue (☎ 0800-591 563, 💻 www.britanniarescue.com), Green Flag National Breakdown (☎ 0845-

246 1557, 🖳 www.greenflag.co.uk), Mondial Assistance (☎ 020-8681 2525, 🖳 www. mondial-assistance-group.co.uk) and the Royal Automobile Club/RAC (☎ 08705-722 722, 🖳 www.rac.co.uk). By far the largest organisation is the AA, followed by the RAC and Green Flag. All organisations offer continental cover as an option and a sixth company, Europ Assistance (☎ 0870-737 5720, 🖳 www.europ-assistance.com), offers continental cover only. Other companies also offer breakdown cover through contractors. There are few essential differences between the services provided by British motoring organisations, although membership costs vary. Free gifts and discounts are usually offered to new members.

All organisations offer a range of membership levels (e.g. individual, couple and family) and different levels of service which may include roadside assistance, relay (get you home), 72-hour European breakdown cover, home start and relay plus (which provides a free replacement car for up to 48 hours). Some organisations cover the car (for any driver), while others cover the driver (in any car). Organisations charge from around £40 a year for recovery only, up to over £200 for the premium service, which includes European recovery. Direct Line Rescue (☎ 0845-246 8702) recently introduced a new roadside-rescue service (using a network of 1,500 contractors), which undercuts the rates charged by motoring organisations, and some insurance companies offer membership of a motoring organisation for a low fee, e.g. from £35 a year. Most organisations offer inducements to new members such as free mobile phones, free or reduced-cost MOT tests, free safety checks and 50 per cent off windscreen replacements.

All motoring organisations waive the enrolment fee (if applicable) or give a discount when you pay by direct debit (from a current account) or continuous payment via a credit card. Associate membership is usually available and applies to your spouse (or partner) and dependent children under the age of 25 up to a maximum of three people. Some organisations provide personal cover for an extra charge, so that you and your spouse can drive any car. Most organisations charge an extra fee for older cars (e.g. those over seven or ten years old). If you use the breakdown service a large number of times (e.g. ten) during a year, you may find that your premium is increased dramatically or you're expelled from the organisation (they prefer members who never use their services).

Although a relative newcomer compared with the AA and RAC, Green Flag National Breakdown deserves a special mention and is highly rated for its customer care, not just against other motoring organisations, but against all comers. It guarantees that all customers will be seen within one hour of reporting a problem (an average 35-minute wait is claimed) and pays a £10 penalty if it fails. Green Flag offers a continental European service for an additional £16.

Members of British motoring organisations who break down anywhere in the UK can call their organisation by phoning a 24-hour service telephone number for assistance. Keep your membership card in your car and quote your membership number when calling for help. Most organisations have reciprocal arrangements with motoring organisations in other European countries. Non-members can also get assistance, but it can be expensive (although you may be able to join on the spot and save the fee). Emergency SOS roadside telephones are provided on motorways, connected to police control rooms. Beware of having your car repaired after it's towed away by a garage 'approved' by a motoring organisation. **Always get a quotation first and make sure it's competitive.**

Some motoring organisations will carry out an independent inspection of a car, for example before buying a second-hand car. It usually takes around a week to arrange an inspection, which can be carried out at your home or office. The fee depends on the organisation and the make and model of car.

PARKING

Parking in most cities and towns is often a problem, particularly on Saturdays when everyone's doing their shopping. On-street parking is a particular problem and most roads without parking meters or bays have restricted or prohibited parking. Despite the fact that the average car spends 95 per cent of its life parked, half the cars in a city centre during peak hours are looking for a parking space. In residential areas, most homes either have limited or no off-road parking; this means that, when driving in residential areas, you must usually weave in and out of parked cars, which often entirely block one side of the road. British companies don't usually provide employees (except directors) with parking facilities in large cities and towns, so check in advance whether parking is available at your workplace (if it isn't, it could be very expensive). Outside cities and towns, parking is usually available at offices and factories.

Parking Restrictions

On-road parking (waiting) restrictions are indicated by yellow lines at the edge of roads, usually accompanied by a sign indicating when parking is prohibited, e.g. 'Mon-Sat 8am-6.30pm' or 'At any time'. If no days are indicated on the sign, restrictions are in force every day, including public holidays and Sundays. Yellow signs indicate a continuous waiting prohibition and also detail times when parking is illegal. Blue signs indicate limited waiting periods. Yellow lines give a guide to the restrictions in force, but the signs must always be consulted. The following road markings are in use in most towns:

Road Marking	Prohibitions
White zigzag line	No parking or stopping at any time (often located next to or studded area a zebra crossing)
Double yellow lines	No parking at most or all times (it may be possible to park on double yellow lines during some periods, but if you're in doubt, don't)
Single yellow line	No parking for at least eight hours between 7am and 7pm on four or more days of the week
Broken yellow line	Restricted parking shown by a sign

Double red lines indicate a red route, which came into operation in London in 1991 to speed up traffic. On red routes, you aren't permitted to stop between the hours of 8am and 7pm (or as indicated by a sign) Mondays to Fridays, except for loading. Special parking bays are marked in red, where parking is strictly limited, e.g. for loading or delivering between 10am and 4pm only. If you park illegally on a red route, your car will be towed away in double quick time.

Loading restrictions are shown by one, two or three short yellow lines marked diagonally on the kerb and a sign. For more information consult *The Highway Code* (see **General Road Rules** on page 274). In most towns, there are public and private off-road car parks, indicated by a sign showing a white 'P' on a blue background. Parking in local authority car parks usually costs from around 20p for a half-hour or an hour. Parking in short-term car parks may become progressively more expensive the longer you stay and can cost as much as £5 for over five hours parking. However, parking is generally cheaper (per hour) the longer you park, up to a maximum of around nine hours. It's often cheaper to drive to a convenient British Rail (BR) station, where parking costs from £2 to £3 a day and take a train into town. Weekly, monthly and annual season tickets are usually available at railway and London Underground stations and some private car parks.

Parking in public car parks and at meters may be free on Sundays and public holidays (check the notice **before** buying a ticket). In many areas there are 'park and ride' parking areas, where parking and/or public transport into the local town or city may be free (particularly at Christmas time). Some supermarkets without their own car parks offer parking refunds to customers. Many councils produce car park maps, showing all local parking areas, available free from council offices, libraries and tourist information centres. Temporary car parks are provided in the weeks before Christmas in many towns and cities. When parking in any official parking area, ensure that you're parked within a marked bay, otherwise you can receive a parking ticket.

Multi-storey Car Parks

The method of payment in multi-storey car parks varies. On entering most private car parks, you collect a ticket from an automatic dispenser (you may need to press a button) and pay either before collecting your car (at a cash desk or in a machine, which may accept both coins and banknotes), or in an automatic machine at the exit (keep some coins handy). Some machines don't issue you with a ticket with which to exit the car park, and after paying you must exchange your ticket at a special kiosk for yet another ticket. If you've already paid, you insert your ticket in the slot of the exit machine (in the direction shown by the arrow on the ticket).

Other multi-storey car parks (usually operated by local councils) are pay-and-display (see below), where you must decide in advance how many hours parking you require and buy a ticket from a machine for this period. If you park in a multi-storey car park, make a note of the level and space number where you park your car (it can take a long time to find your car if you have no idea where to start looking). Speed bumps are common in multi-storey car parks. Many private car parks offer season tickets, e.g. NCP. British car parks, particularly multi-storey car parks, are designed for toy cars and have tiny parking bays where cars must be parked at right angles (why can't we learn from the Americans and park our cars at an angle?).

Parking Meters

With a parking meter, the maximum permitted parking period varies from 30 minutes to two hours. Meter-feeding is illegal. You must vacate the parking space when the meter time expires, even if it was under the maximum time allowed, and you may not move to another meter in the same group. Meters normally accept a combination of 5p to 20p coins, and are usually in use from 7am to 7pm, Mondays to Fridays, and from 7am to 6pm on Saturdays (check meters to be certain). Meters at railway stations and airports may be in use 24 hours a day. Don't park at meters which are suspended, as you can be towed away. If you remain at a meter beyond the excess charge period, you're liable for a fixed penalty (which is usually £20) handed out by a police officer or a traffic warden. Parking meters are being phased out and replaced by pay-and-display parking areas.

Pay & Display

These are parking areas where you must buy a parking ticket from a machine and display it in your windscreen. It may have an adhesive backing, which you can peel off and use to stick the ticket on the inside of your windscreen or a car window. Parking costs 20p or 30p an hour, in most towns, and machines usually accept all coins from 5p to £1. When you've inserted sufficient coins for the period required, press the button to receive your ticket. Pay-and-display parking areas usually operate from 7am to 7pm, excluding Sundays and public holidays. A new pre-paid parking scheme (called Easypark) is in operation in some towns. Motorists buy a card costing from £3 to £125 (gold card), which is used to pay for parking in special machines (a bit like using a phone card). Cards are sold at post offices, shops, garages and council offices. In some towns, a 'scratch and display' parking scheme has been introduced, where motorists buy vouchers and scratch off panels to show the month, day, date and time of arrival (and display the voucher in their window).

Parking Fines

The fine for illegal parking depends on where you park. There's usually a fixed penalty ticket of £30 for parking illegally on a yellow line. Parking in a dangerous position, or on the zigzag lines near a pedestrian crossing, results in a higher fine, e.g. a £60 fixed penalty and three points on your driving licence (see page 269). Penalties for non-payment or overstaying your time in a permitted parking area (e.g. at a parking meter or in a pay-and-display area) are set by local authorities, when you receive a yellow ticket.

In some cities, you shouldn't even think about parking illegally on a yellow line, as your car will be towed away in the blink of an eye. You must then pay a towing fee of around £100 plus a fixed penalty. A car pound doesn't release your car until you've paid and accepts only cash or a guaranteed cheque. All car pounds charge a daily storage fee after the first 24 hours of around £10 to £20 per day. You cannot be towed away from a pay-and-display area or a parking meter (unless the parking bay is suspended).

Illegal parking is a serious problem in central London and has led some boroughs to employ private contractors to control parking. In London and other major cities, parking permits are issued to local residents, allowing them to park in reserved 'residents only' spaces. If you park there without a permit, you will get a ticket. Some three million parking tickets are issued each year in London. If a car is parked in a dangerous position or is causing an obstruction, it can be removed and impounded by the police. This results in a fee of around £80 to get it released plus a fixed penalty fine.

Clamping

In central London and an increasing number of other cities and towns, illegal parking can result in your car being 'clamped', where a large metal device is clamped on to one of the wheels of your car, thus preventing your driving it away. Thousands of cars are clamped each week in London alone and many are towed away. To free your car from this heinous (but very effective) device, you must go to the clamping station listed on your ticket, pay an unclamping fee plus a fixed penalty fine, and return to your vehicle and await the truck to come and unclamp your car (which usually takes around four hours). If you don't remove your car within a certain period, you can be clamped a second time. In certain cases, your car may be seized by bailiffs and sold at auction (at well below it's value) to pay a fine. There's a new Parking Appeals Service in London (☎ 020-7747 4700, 🖳 www.parkingandtrafficappeals.gov.uk).

Cars parked at meters aren't usually clamped unless the parking bay is suspended, the meter was 'fed' with coins, or the car has stayed two hours beyond the period paid. Owners of private car parks or private land can also clamp a car parked illegally and can set their own charge to remove clamps (e.g. £100 or more). It's inadvisable to park on private land, particularly where there's a 'clamping' sign, as illegal clamping is widespread throughout the UK. Many 'cowboy' clamping companies clamp and tow away cars that are legally parked and charge up to £250 a time, if they can get away with it. Whether parking restrictions exist or not, when parking on a road, be careful where you park, as you can be prosecuted for parking in a dangerous position and could also cause an accident.

If your parked car contributes to an accident, you may also have to pay damages. Take care in car parks, as accidents often occur there and may not be covered by your car insurance. Parking on pedestrian footpaths is illegal everywhere. Parking in towns with your hazard warning lights on makes no difference if you're parked illegally. Wherever you drive, keep a plentiful supply of coins handy for parking and pay-and-display meters.

12.

HEALTH

The UK is renowned for its National Health Service (NHS), which provides health care to all British citizens and most foreign residents. The standard of training, dedication and medical skills of British doctors and nursing staff is among the highest in the world, and British medical science is in the vanguard of many of the world's major medical advances (many pioneering operations are performed in the UK). Emergency medical services are generally excellent. Many foreigners visit the UK each year for private medical treatment and Harley Street in London is internationally recognised as having some of the world's pre-eminent (and most expensive) specialists, encompassing every conceivable ailment. The infant mortality rate is around 6 per 1,000 births (an all-time low), while the average life expectancy is around 75 for men and 80 for women. The main causes of death are circulatory diseases (including heart attacks and strokes) and cancer. Nearly half of all British men and more than a quarter of women who die between the ages of 45 and 55 do so as a result of heart and circulatory disease, in which the UK is a world leader. However, the total number of smokers is reducing, although it remains the greatest preventable cause of illness and death, and is responsible for over 100,000 deaths and 30 million lost working days each year. Around 30 per cent of Britons smoke, including many more women (particularly young women) than men.

Alcohol abuse is an increasing problem, although drunkenness (lager louts) is more of a social problem than a serious health problem (unlike alcoholism). According to the Mental Health Foundation, around six million people (one in ten) suffer from mental illness. Stress is an increasing problem and an estimated 250 million working hours are lost annually due to stress-related absences. (More people are also turning to anti-depressants to cope with life).

As you've probably already realised, the British aren't exactly the healthiest of people, a fact largely attributed to their high sugar and fat diet and generally bad eating habits, followed closely by excess alcohol, smoking and general sloth (armchair sport is much more popular than working up a sweat). Some doctors even prescribe exercise classes on the NHS for those who are overweight. The NHS organises a number of health education schemes, including campaigns to promote awareness of the dangers of heart disease, smoking, drugs and AIDS. However, preventive medicine has a low priority.

Air pollution caused by sunshine and high temperatures (increasingly common in the UK) is an increasing concern, not just in the cities, but in rural areas, where asthmatics, bronchitis sufferers and the elderly are particularly at risk. Levels of air pollution are already well above safe health limits on hot days and in cities signs of asthma are found in some 20 per cent of children. Hay fever sufferers can obtain the daily pollen count between March and July from weather broadcasts and daily newspapers. Noise pollution is also a problem and many people's lives are ruined by noisy neighbours (incessant noise causes chronic illnesses and drives people to commit murder and suicide). The UK has a high incidence of skin cancer due to over-exposure to the sun and the maximum exposure time for the fair-skinned is now included in television (TV) weather forecasts on hot days.

Private clinics are common and do a profitable business in abortions and cosmetic surgery (among other things). If your nose, ears or *derrière* are too big, or you would love to fill a full D cup, just nip down to your local specialist who will tuck those unwanted bits out of sight (or make others more prominent) as fast as you can say £3,000. If you're contemplating cosmetic surgery, it's worthwhile doing your homework on the internet or getting a personal recommendation or two, as there are lots of cut-price cowboys in the business.

The UK also has many private health farms, where inmates pay a queen's ransom for the privilege of being locked away from temptation (e.g. alcohol, cream cakes, chocolate and sweets) for a week or two.

Residential and nursing homes are also an important part of the private health sector (although not all are private). Long-term health care is an increasing problem in the UK, where local councils can no longer afford to provide free care for those who need it and the elderly may be evicted from residential care because social security payments are failing to keep up with the increasing fees. Local authority social services and voluntary organisations provide invaluable help and advice to the most vulnerable members of the community, including the elderly, disabled and children in need of care.

INFORMATION

For a quick and confidential answer to health problems, you could try calling one of the many helplines that have sprung up in recent years, including NHS Direct where medical staff are available to answer any health queries (☎ 0845-4647, ⌨ www. nhsdirect.nhs.uk). The website also provides comprehensive health information, including an online health encyclopedia. The service has proved extremely popular and there are concerns that it will become saturated before long. Other services providing information on a wide variety of health topics include Primecare (☎ 01707-286 800, ⌨ www.primecare.uk.net) and Healthline, run by BUPA (☎ 0900-920 9200, ⌨ www.bupa.co.uk). Helpline calls are usually charged at local call rates (see **Information & Entertainment** on page 158). There are also many internet sites where medical advice is available (one of the best British sites is ⌨ www. healthworks.co.uk). Telephone information, although approved by medical experts, should never be used as a substitute for consulting your family doctor and internet 'doctors' and medical advice must be used with extreme caution.

The Medical Advisory Service (☎ 020-8995 8503) provides a general helpline and a free telephone helpline for men from 7pm to 9pm (there's generally less information available to men, who are often ignorant of health matters). 'Do-it-yourself' doctors may also be interested in the British Medical Association (BMA) *Complete Family Health* (Dorling Kindersley), a comprehensive family medical book which, although expensive at around £35, is highly recommended. Other useful books include *Which? Medicine, Women's Health* and *Men's Health*, all published by Which? Books (⌨ www.which.net), who also publish a bimonthly magazine, *Which? Way to Health* (see **Consumers' Association** on page 479). The College of Health publishes numerous booklets (⌨ www.collegeofhealth.org.uk) and the Department of Health (Richmond House, 79 Whitehall, London SW1A 2NL, ☎ 020-7210 4850, ⌨ www.dh.gov.uk) publishes information on a wide range of topics (a catalogue is available), many of which are available free from chemists, clinics and doctors' surgeries.

Finally, you can carry a Donor Card, available from chemists, libraries, doctors' surgeries and supermarkets. A move is afoot to reverse the current situation so that you must carry a card if you **don't** want to donate your organs. If the thought of donating your organs is more than you're prepared to contemplate, perhaps you're willing to donate a pint of blood twice a year. If you're over 18 and under 60 and in good health, the National Blood Service would like to hear from you (☎ 0845-771 1711, 🖳 www.blood.co.uk).

You can safely drink the water in the UK, but wine tastes much better (and in moderation, it even does you good!).

EMERGENCIES

The action to take in a medical emergency depends on the degree of urgency. If you're unsure who to call, ask the telephone operator (☎ 100) or call your local police station. They tell you whom to contact or even call the appropriate service for you. Always give the age of the patient and, if possible, specify the type of emergency. **Keep a record of the telephone numbers of your doctor, local hospitals and clinics, ambulance service, first aid, poison control, dentist and other emergency services next to your telephone.**

● In minor emergencies or for medical advice, you should telephone your family doctor. Failing this, you can ask the operator (☎ 100) for the telephone number of a local doctor or hospital (or consult your telephone directory). Some hospitals have minor injuries units, emergency units, and accident and emergency departments (it's advisable to check where they are in advance and the quickest route from your home). Police stations keep a list of doctors' and chemists' private telephone numbers, in case of emergency. In some cities and regions, there are private 24-hour doctor services making house calls, but check the cost before using them.

● ☎ 999 for an ambulance, **but in emergencies only**. Most ambulances are equipped with cardiac, oxygen and other emergency equipment. Health authorities can make a charge when an ambulance is called to an emergency, although this is unlikely. The cost of a private ambulance is usually covered by a private health insurance policy. The UK doesn't have a national air ambulance service, although there are emergency helicopter services in some cities (e.g. London) and the Royal Air Force operates a rescue service in remote inland and coastal areas.

● If you're physically able, you can go to the Accident, Casualty or Emergency department of an NHS general hospital, many of which provide a 24-hour service. Check in advance which local hospitals are equipped to deal with emergencies and the quickest route from your home. This information may be of vital importance in the event of an emergency, when a delay could mean the difference between life and death. Emergency cases, irrespective of nationality and ability to pay, are **never** turned away and treatment is free for everybody (including visitors), except when hospitalisation for longer than one night is necessary. (If you're a national of a country with a reciprocal health agreement with the UK, treatment is free). In some cities, e.g. London, there are private walk-in clinics open around 12 hours a day, providing emergency treatment for medical and dental accidents and minor ailments.

● If you have a dental problem, telephone your own dentist or, if it's out of normal surgery hours, call your own or another dentist providing an emergency service (listed in yellow pages). Some dental and general hospitals provide a free emergency service. A dentist isn't obliged to treat anyone, even in an emergency.

If you have a rare blood group or a medical problem which cannot easily be seen or recognised, e.g. a heart condition, diabetes, a severe allergy or epilepsy, you may be interested in Medic-Alert. Medic-Alert members wear an internationally-recognised emblem on their wrists or around their necks. On the back of your emblem is engraved your medical problem, membership number and a telephone number. When you're unable to speak for yourself, doctors, police or anyone providing aid can obtain immediate vital medical information from anywhere in the world by phoning a 24-hour emergency number. Medic-Alert is a non-profit registered charity and life membership is included in the cost of the bracelet or necklace plus an annual fee. For more information contact the Medic-Alert Foundation, 1 Bridge Wharf, 156 Caledonian Road, London N1 9UU (☎ 020-7833 3034, 💻 www.medicalert.co.uk).

NATIONAL HEALTH SERVICE

The pride of the British welfare system is (or was) the National Health Service (NHS), established in 1948 to ensure that everyone had equal access to medical care. The NHS includes services provided by family doctors, specialists, hospitals, dentists, chemists, opticians, community health services (e.g. the district nursing and health visitor services), the ambulance service, and maternity and child health care. Originally, all NHS medical treatment was free, the service being funded entirely from general taxation and National Insurance contributions.

However, as the costs of treatment and medicines have increased, part has been passed on to patients via supplementary charges. While hospital treatment, the ambulance service and consultations with doctors remain free, many patients must now pay fixed charges for prescriptions, dental treatment, sight tests and NHS glasses, although charges are usually well below the actual cost. Family doctors, called General Practitioners (GPs), still make free house calls. Community health workers and district nurses visit people at home who are convalescent, bedridden or have newborn babies.

The NHS is run by Regional Health Authorities, District Health Authorities (corresponding approximately to local authority boundaries), Family Practitioner Committees and Special Health Authorities. If you want to find the name of your District Health Authority, inquire at your local library or ask a doctor's receptionist. Often, health service boundaries aren't the same as those of the local council area. For information about how to register with an NHS family doctor (GP), see **Doctors** on page 309. The quality of service you receive from the NHS depends very much on where you live, as waiting lists for specialist appointments and hospital beds vary from area to area. Patients of **Fundholding GPs** (see page 310) often have shorter waits, as GPs can shop around for the shortest queues.

The NHS provides free or subsidised medical treatment to everyone with the right of abode in the UK and to anyone who, at the time of treatment, has been a resident for the previous year. Exceptions to the one-year qualifying rule include European Union (EU) nationals; refugees or those with 'exceptional leave to remain' in the UK; students on a course of over six months; foreign nationals coming to take up permanent residence in the UK; certain groups of sailors or off-shore workers; non-EU recipients of British war disablement pensions; overseas crown servants; British pensioners living abroad; NATO personnel stationed in the UK; prisoners; anyone with a permit to work in the UK; and the spouse and children of the above.

Nationals of countries with reciprocal health agreements with the UK also receive free or subsidised medical treatment, including European Economic Area (EEA) nationals and citizens of Anguilla, Australia, Austria, Barbados, British Virgin Islands, Bulgaria, Channel Islands, Czech Republic, Falkland Islands, Gibraltar, Hungary, Iceland, Isle of Man, Malta, Montserrat, New Zealand, Norway, Poland, Romania, Russia, Slovak Republic, St Helena, Switzerland, Turks and Caicos Islands, and states comprising the former USSR and Yugoslavia. Exemption from charges for nationals of the above countries is generally limited to emergency or urgent treatment (e.g. for a communicable disease) required during a visit to the UK.

Anyone who doesn't qualify under one of the above categories, must pay for all medical treatment received, although minor medical and dental emergencies may be treated free of charge, e.g. emergency treatment at a hospital outpatients department as a result of an accident (or patients admitted to hospital for no longer than one night). **If you aren't covered by the NHS, you should take out private health insurance** (see **Health Insurance** on page 344), **as medical treatment in the UK can be very expensive, with the cost of an operation and hospitalisation running into thousands of pounds.**

PRIVATE HEALTH TREATMENT

Private health treatment functions within the NHS and independently of it. Private patients can choose to pay for treatment in most NHS hospitals and all NHS consultants are permitted to treat private patients in addition to their NHS patients (some have been accused of neglecting their NHS patients for lucrative private work). In addition to specialist appointments and hospital treatment, people commonly use private health treatment to obtain second opinions, private health checks or screening and for complementary medicine. Around seven million people have private health insurance of some kind and around 25 per cent of all operations are performed privately. If you must see a GP or specialist privately, you (or your insurance company) must pay the full fee, which is usually left to the doctor's discretion. You should expect to pay around £40 or more for a routine visit to a GP.

Most patients who receive private health treatment are insured with provident associations, such as BUPA and AXA PPP, which pay for specialist and hospital treatment only, and don't include routine visits to doctors and dentists (which are covered by the NHS). The overriding reason most people have private health insurance is to circumvent the interminable NHS waiting lists for non-emergency specialist appointments and hospital treatment. Private patients are free to choose their own specialist and hospital, and are usually accommodated in a private, hotel-style room with a radio, telephone, colour TV, en suite bathroom and room service. Private health insurance is often paid for by employers.

Although some health checks and scans are available on demand under the NHS or with private health insurance, many aren't (including the most expensive). Comprehensive health checks or health screening can be performed at private clinics throughout the UK, costing from around £250 to £350. Complementary (or alternative) medicine is popular and is chosen by some five million patients a year although, with the exception of certain fields such as acupuncture, chiropractics, homeopathy and osteopathy, it isn't usually covered by the NHS or private health insurance.

Always make sure that a 'doctor' or medical practitioner is qualified to provide the treatment you require, as (surprisingly) anyone can call himself a doctor in the UK. When selecting a private specialist or clinic, you should be extremely cautious and choose only someone who has been recommended by a doctor or clinic you can trust. It's sometimes advisable to obtain a second opinion, particularly if you're diagnosed as having a serious illness or require a major operation (but don't expect your doctor or specialist to approve). According to some reports, unnecessary operations are becoming increasingly common. Private patients don't have the same protection as NHS patients, although complaints about treatment that's paid for by a private health insurance policy may be taken up by your insurance company. As a last resort you can complain to the General Medical Council, providing the medical practitioner is a qualified doctor.

With the deterioration of the NHS and its ever-increasing waiting lists, you're strongly advised to consider taking out private health insurance, which ensures you receive the medical treatment you need, when you need it. However, the quality of private treatment isn't better than that provided by the NHS and you shouldn't assume that, because a doctor (or any other medical practitioner) is in private practice, he's more competent than his NHS counterpart. In fact, often you see the same specialist or are treated by the same surgeon on the NHS and privately. For information about private health insurance, see **Health Insurance** on page 344.

DOCTORS

There are excellent family doctors, generally referred to as General Practitioners (GPs), in all areas of the UK. The best way to find a doctor, whether as an NHS or a private patient, is to ask your colleagues, friends or neighbours if they can recommend someone. Alternatively you can consult a list of GPs for your Health District in your Community Health Council (CHC) office or contact your local Family Health Services Authority (FHSA). FHSAs publish lists of doctors, dentists, chemists and opticians in their areas. These are available at libraries, post offices, tourist information offices, police stations and Citizens Advice Bureaux. You can also look up doctors in the Medical Directory available in public reference libraries. If you're a student, some colleges have their own student health centre where you should register. GPs or family doctors are listed under *Doctors* (Medical Practitioners) in yellow pages.

Surgery hours vary, but are typically from 8.30am to 6 or 7pm, Mondays to Fridays, with early closing one day a week, e.g. 5 or 5.30pm on Fridays (evening surgeries may also be held on one or two evenings a week). Emergency surgeries may be held on Saturday mornings, e.g. from 8.30am to 11.30am or noon. Most doctors' surgeries have answering machines outside surgery hours, when a recorded message informs you of the name of the doctor on call (or deputising service) and his telephone number.

NHS Doctors

NHS doctors are contracted by their local FHSA to look after a number of patients (average around 2,000) who make up their list. In Scotland, the contract is with the Health Board and in Northern Ireland with the Central Services Agency. Doctors are paid by the NHS according to the number of NHS registered patients on their list and an NHS doctor can refuse to register you as a patient if he has no vacancies. If you're looking for an NHS doctor, you must live within a doctor's catchment area. If you have trouble getting on to an NHS doctor's list, contact your local FHSA which has a duty to find you a doctor. If you're living in a district for less than three months or have no permanent home, you can apply to any doctor in the district to be accepted as a temporary resident for up to three months. After this period, you must register with the doctor as a permanent patient or you may register with another doctor. An NHS doctor must give 'immediate necessary treatment' for up to 14 days to anyone without a doctor living in their area, until the patient has been accepted by a doctor as a permanent or temporary resident.

Fundholding GPs

Under the NHS reforms instituted in 1991, the government created fundholding GPs, where GPs manage their own budgets and can shop around and buy services for their patients direct from hospitals and other health service providers. Over 40 per cent of doctors are GP fundholders. Non-fundholding GPs must rely on their district health authority (DHA) for health services and cannot refer patients to hospitals of their choice. Fundholding GPs usually provide a wider range of services and their patients experience shorter waits to see specialists and for hospital beds, as GPs can shop around for the shortest queues. This has created a two-tier health system with patients of non-fundholders being disadvantaged. However, because fundholding GPs tend to spend more time on administration, they spend less time with their patients than non-fundholding GPs. Even so, generally you're much better off with a fundholding GP.

Group Practices

Around 80 per cent of GPs work in a partnership or group practice, around 25 per cent in health centres, providing a range of medical and nursing services. Health centres may have facilities for immunisation, cervical smears, health education (well person clinic), family planning, speech therapy, chiropody, hearing tests, physiotherapy and remedial exercises. Many also include dental, ophthalmic, hospital outpatient and social work support. Most health centres or large surgeries have district nurses, health visitors, midwives and clinical psychologists in attendance at fixed times. If your doctor is part of a partnership or group practice, when he's absent you're automatically treated by a partner or another doctor (unless you wish to wait until your doctor returns).

Choosing a Doctor

It's advisable to enquire in advance (e.g. by asking the receptionist) whether a doctor has the 'qualifications' you require, for example:

● Is he or she of the right sex?

● Is he easily reached by public transport, if necessary?

● Is it a group practice? This may be preferable to an individual practice, where you may be required to see a locum (replacement) doctor when your doctor is absent (in a group practice, doctors cover for each other outside surgery hours).

● Does the practice run ante-natal, family planning, well woman (or well person), diabetic or other clinics?

● What are the surgery hours (Saturday and evening surgeries may be held)?

● What is the procedure for home visits?

● Does the doctor practise preventive or complementary medicine?

● Does the doctor prescribe contraception?

● If you're a private patient, what's the cost?

All NHS GPs must produce practice guides for all patients, containing the names of doctors, times of surgeries and any special services provided, such as ante-natal, family planning, well woman or diabetic clinics. It's often advisable to meet a prospective doctor before deciding whether to register with him. When you've found a suitable NHS doctor who will accept you, you must register with him by completing part A of your medical card and giving it to his receptionist. If you don't have an NHS medical card, you must complete a form provided by the GP which he sends to the local FHSA (which sends you a medical card within a few weeks of registration).

Appointments & House Calls

Most doctors operate an appointment system, where you must make an appointment in advance. You cannot just turn up during surgery hours and expect to be seen. If you're an urgent case (but not an emergency), your doctor usually sees you immediately, but you should still telephone in advance. Surgeries are often very busy and you may have to wait well past your appointment time to see a doctor. NHS doctors make free house calls and emergency visits outside surgery hours (at their discretion), when patients are bedridden or unable to visit their surgery. In the UK, a doctor is responsible for his patients 24 hours a day and, when he's unavailable, must make alternative arrangements, through his partners in a group practice, a voluntary rota between individual doctors or a commercial deputising service. When you call your GP outside normal hours, he's unlikely to attend you personally at home. Most GPs use an outside medical service which exists to provide house calls and an 'after hours' service.

Changing Doctors

An NHS patient can change doctors, providing he can find a new doctor who will accept him. (A doctor can refuse to accept a patient or remove anyone from his list without giving a reason). Be careful what reason you give for wanting to change doctors, as doctors tend to be wary of accepting a patient who has had a 'disagreement' with a colleague. One 'legitimate' reason for changing doctors is that you wish to be treated by a doctor of the opposite sex to your present one (it's hard luck if all doctors in your area are of the same sex). Under new reforms, it's easier to change doctors: you don't need to inform your old doctor and can just visit a new doctor's surgery and ask to be registered.

Your doctor is able to give advice or provide information on any aspect of health or medical after-care, including preventive medicine, blood donations, home medical equipment and special counselling. If you're an NHS patient, he should also be able to advise you about the range of medical benefits provided under the NHS, including maternity care, contraceptive help and psychiatric treatment. NHS patients must always be referred to a specialist, e.g. an eye specialist, gynaecologist or orthopaedic surgeon, by a GP.

If you would like a second opinion on any health matter, you may ask to see a specialist although, unless it's a serious matter, your doctor will probably refuse to refer you. If your doctor refuses, you won't be able to obtain a second opinion from another NHS doctor unless you change doctors. The only other possibility is to consult another doctor or specialist as a private patient. Patients who have a foreign (i.e. not British) private health insurance policy may be free to make appointments directly with specialists. **In many cases where a second opinion is sought, the second doctor doesn't confirm the first doctor's diagnosis.** GPs often drop patients who ask questions and almost 100,000 are removed from GP lists each year. Some GPs don't like answering medical questions, or patients who question or refuse treatment or ask for a second opinion – you're simply supposed to do as you're told!

Complaints

If you have a complaint against your NHS GP, you should, in the first instance, contact your local FHSA, usually within eight weeks of the event. If you need help to make a complaint, you can ask your Community Health Council or a Citizens Advice Bureau (CAB). In the event of serious professional misconduct, your complaint is passed to the General Medical Council. Family doctor booklets are published by the British Medical Association (BMA) and are available from doctors' surgeries, clinics and chemists or direct from the BMA.

Medicentres

An innovation in recent years has been the introduction of private drop-in medicentres around London, where doctors and nurses are on hand for consultations and to perform tests, screening, health checks, vaccinations and minor treatment. Medicentres are a walk-in service designed to fit around your schedule – there's no need to be registered and you don't require an appointment. Medicentres are located in the high street, e.g. in branches of Boots, and in shopping centres. Patients pay £59 for a consultation and membership deals from £195 a year are available. For more information ☎ 0870-600 0870 (🖥 www.medicentre.co.uk).

MEDICINES

Medicines and drugs are obtained from a chemist (or pharmacy), most of which provide free advice regarding minor ailments and suggest appropriate medicines. There are three categories of drugs and medicines: those that can be prescribed only by a doctor (via an official form called a prescription) and purchased from a chemist; medicines that can be sold only under the supervision of a pharmacist; and general-sale list medicines (such as aspirin and paracetamol) that can be sold in outlets such as petrol stations and supermarkets. Some drugs and medicines requiring a doctor's prescription in the UK are sold freely in other countries, although other drugs are freely available in the UK that are controlled elsewhere. (Increasing numbers of previously restricted drugs are now available over the counter).

At least one chemist is open in most towns during evenings and on Sundays for the emergency dispensing of medicines and drugs. In major cities, at least one chemist may be open until midnight or later every day of the week. A rota is posted on the doors of chemists and published in local newspapers and guides. If you require medicine urgently when all chemists are closed, you should contact your GP or local police station. Requests for repeat prescriptions may be accepted by your doctor by post or telephone. If you have regular repeat prescriptions, you can have a pharmacy pick up your prescription from your doctor, which can then be collected from the pharmacy. Many pharmacists use a computer to keep information about the health problems and medicines of regular customers.

Anyone living one mile from a chemist is entitled to obtain prescriptions from a dispensing doctor (who's permitted to dispense drugs and appliances). If he doesn't have them in stock, he writes a prescription (in a secret language decipherable only by doctors and pharmacists). In some rural areas, patients who live over a mile from a pharmacist are permitted to collect their drugs from their GP. Some medicines aren't recognised by the NHS, in which case your doctor usually informs you and may offer to prescribe an alternative. If you insist on having the unrecognised medicine, you must usually pay for it yourself.

To obtain medicines prescribed by a doctor, simply take your prescription form to any chemist. Your prescription may be filled immediately if it's available off the shelf, or you may be asked to wait or come back later. NHS prescriptions for medicines are charged at a fixed rate of £6.85 (they cost just 20p in 1979!) per item, although four out of five prescriptions are free. The average cost of prescription drugs would be around £10 if they were bought over the counter, but many would cost much less than the prescription charge if they were freely available. It may be possible to get your GP to write a private prescription, although many doctors won't do this, as they would be in breach of their terms and conditions of service with the NHS. Those with comprehensive private (e.g. foreign) health insurance may be able to reclaim the cost of prescriptions from their insurance company.

Some medicines prescribed by a doctor (e.g. certain pain killers) can be replaced by substitute medicines that can be purchased over the counter for less than the prescription charge. Boots, the UK's largest chain of chemists with over 1,300 stores, is often the cheapest place to buy non-prescription drugs (many own brand). An expected end to price-fixing on medicines will allow supermarkets to slash the price of common drugs.

Many people qualify for free prescriptions (e.g. prescriptions for hospital outpatients and day patients), including children under 16; students under 19 in full-time education; pensioners (men over 65, women over 60); expectant mothers and those who have had a baby in the last year; those with certain medical conditions, e.g. diabetes or epilepsy, or a permanent disability which prevents them getting around without help; and people on low incomes receiving state benefits. With the exception of children under 16 and pensioners, all those entitled to free prescriptions must apply for an exemption certificate or a refund.

When you're exempt, you must complete and sign the declaration on the back of the prescription form. Ask your district health authority where and how to apply. Claim form AGI is available from local social security offices, hospitals, dentists and opticians. Those who aren't exempt, but need frequent prescriptions can reduce the cost by purchasing a prepayment certificate 'season ticket', which covers all charges for a fixed period. Prepayment certificates cost £34.65 for four months (you save money if you have more than four prescriptions) and £95.30 for a year (you save if you have more than 12 prescriptions). You can order by telephone (☎ 0845-850 0030) or online (🖳 www.ppa.org.uk). Leaflet HC12 contains information about prescription charges and is available from your local social security office or from 🖳 www.dh.gov.uk/publications.

Most chemists also sell non-prescription medicines and drugs, toiletries, cosmetics, health foods and cleaning supplies. Some chemists, such as Boots, may have departments selling anything from records and books to electrical and photographic equipment and kitchen appliances (in addition to those items mentioned above). Boots also sell a range of health care equipment. A health food shop sells health foods, diet foods, homeopathic medicines and eternal-life-virility-youth pills and elixirs, which are quite popular (even though their claims are usually in the realms of fantasy). Growing fears about the side-effects of drugs have led to a huge growth in complementary medicine in the last decade, although the UK is still way behind many other EU countries, particularly France and Germany.

Always use, store and dispose of unwanted medicines and poisons safely, e.g. by returning them to a pharmacist or dispensing doctor, and never leave them where children can get their hands on them.

HOSPITALS & CLINICS

Most British towns have a hospital or clinic, signposted by the international hospital sign of a white 'H' on a blue background. There are many kinds of hospitals, including community hospitals, district hospitals, teaching hospitals and cottage hospitals. Major hospitals are called general hospitals and provide treatment and diagnosis for in-patients, day patients and outpatients. Most have a maternity department; infectious diseases unit; psychiatric and geriatric facilities; rehabilitation and convalescent units; and cater for all forms of specialised treatment.

Some general hospitals are designated teaching hospitals and combine treatment with medical training and research work. In addition to general hospitals, there are specialist hospitals for children, the mentally ill, the disabled, the elderly and infirm, and for the treatment of specific complaints or illnesses. There are also dental hospitals. Only major hospitals have an accident or emergency department. Many NHS hospitals have sports injury clinics, although you must usually be referred by your GP, and some have minor injuries units. Cottage hospitals, as the name implies, are small local units, often caring for the elderly and infirm. In many areas, there are NHS Well Woman Clinics, where women can obtain medical check-ups and cervical smear tests, and NHS Family Planning Clinics. You can be referred to these clinics by your GP or you can refer yourself. You can also refer yourself to an NHS Sexually Transmitted Diseases (STD) or venereal disease (VD) clinic for an examination.

Since 1991, NHS hospitals have been able to opt out of local health authority control in favour of self-governing status and a grant from central government (NHS 'trust' status). In recent years, NHS hospitals have been rated in performance tables, although these have been condemned by the BMA as unfair and misleading, and shouldn't be taken as anything but a rough guide. Small hospitals are generally rated higher than large city hospitals; district hospitals generally outperform specialist teaching hospitals (where there are longer waiting times, more cancelled operations and delayed appointments are more frequent) in patient care.

Private Hospitals & Clinics

In addition to NHS hospitals, there are private hospitals and clinics in all areas, many providing only specialist services (e.g. health checks and sports injuries) and which usually don't cater for accidents or emergencies (or anyone without private health insurance or a large bank balance). Some provident associations (e.g. BUPA and AXA PPP, see **Health Insurance** on page 344) operate their own hospitals and clinics throughout the UK. Private patients are provided with single rooms equipped with all the comforts of home, including radio, TV, telephone, en suite bathroom and room service (a visitor can usually enjoy a meal with a patient in the privacy of his room). A single room with en suite bathroom in a private hospital costs from around £200 to £300 per day. A day bed may cost from around £25 an hour or £200 per day.

If you don't have health insurance or are a visitor to the UK, you may be asked to pay a (large) deposit in advance, particularly if there's any doubt that you will survive the ordeal (most private hospitals accept credit and charge cards). Many private hospitals also provide fixed-price surgery, subject to an examination by a consultant surgeon. Some hospitals offer interest-free loans to pay hospital bills (e.g. a 10 per cent deposit with the rest payable over 12 months). This is one solution for those who cannot afford health insurance and don't want to wait. However, make sure that you aren't being overcharged, as you can often have an operation cheaper elsewhere in the UK or even abroad (e.g. in France) and possibly save thousands of pounds.

According to Action for Victims of Medical Accidents (AVMA), there are higher health risks in private hospitals than in NHS hospitals, and there may be less emergency equipment and fewer experienced staff. You have almost no protection in law when you're treated at a private clinic or hospital compared with your rights as an NHS hospital patient. When things go wrong (as they occasionally do), you're usually better off in an NHS hospital.

Choice of Hospital

Except for emergencies, you may be admitted or referred to an NHS hospital or clinic for treatment only after consultation with a GP or a consultant (or from an NHS clinic such as a family planning or well woman clinic). Patients with private health insurance may be treated at the hospital of their choice, depending on their level of insurance cover. NHS patients can ask to be treated at a particular hospital or to be referred to a particular consultant, but have no right to have their request met. If your GP isn't an NHS fundholder (**Doctors** on page 309), you're admitted to a hospital under the control of your local health authority, unless special surgery or treatment is necessary that's unavailable locally. Patients of fundholding GPs may be admitted to any NHS hospital. In an emergency, you are treated at the nearest hospital. Children are usually admitted to a special children's general ward or a children's hospital well stocked with games, toys, books and other children.

Accommodation

NHS hospital accommodation is in wards of various sizes, e.g. 12 beds, some of which are mixed. Many NHS hospitals have private rooms (known as 'pay beds') and under NHS reforms, they're permitted to charge for extras such as a single room with a telephone, a TV or a wider choice of meals. In most NHS hospitals, you choose the meals you would like the day before and provision is made for vegetarian and other diets. Some wards have dining room tables for those sufficiently mobile and most have day rooms for mobile patients. The service, facilities and standards of NHS hospitals vary considerably depending on the area. The best compare favourably with private hospitals (apart from a possible lack of modern conveniences). On the other hand, some NHS hospitals are dingy and depressing, and are perhaps the last place on earth you would wish to be when you're ill. Hospital stays for the same complaint or operation vary considerably (e.g. by up to double the period) depending on the hospital and the surgeon. If possible, you should choose your surgeon carefully, as some have insufficient experience or skills, particularly when it comes to using the latest techniques, such as keyhole surgery. Many new treatments aren't properly evaluated for their effectiveness and unnecessary – and even harmful – operations aren't uncommon. Needless tests and X-rays are estimated to cost the NHS over £20 million a year. NHS hospital patients receive free medicines and appliances. Medicines given to out-patients or day patients at a hospital are also free, but medicines prescribed to be taken at home must be paid for (in the same way as all prescriptions), unless you're entitled to free prescriptions.

Visiting Hours

Visiting hours vary depending on whether you're in a private or a general ward (no prizes for guessing which patients have the most generous visiting hours), although some NHS hospital general wards have liberal visiting hours. In a private hospital or clinic, there may be no restrictions on visiting hours. Parents of children in hospital may have unrestricted visiting hours and many hospitals provide a bed for a child's parent to stay overnight.

Complaints

Hospitals usually have a specially appointed officer to deal with complaints. If you don't receive satisfaction, you should contact your FHSA or the general manager of the local health authority as soon as possible. If you're an NHS patient, you can ultimately complain to the health service commissioner. Ask your Community Health Council or a Citizens Advice Bureau for advice and information.

CHILDBIRTH

Childbirth usually takes place in a hospital, where a stay of two days is usual. If you wish to have a child at home, you must find a doctor or midwife (see below) who's willing to attend you, although it's generally impossible for the birth of a first child. Some doctors are opposed to home births, particularly in cases where there could be complications and when specialists and special facilities (e.g. incubators) may be required. You can also choose to hire a private midwife (a nurse specialising in delivering babies), who attends you at home throughout and after your pregnancy.

For hospital births, you can usually decide (with the help of your GP or midwife) the hospital where you wish to have your baby. You aren't required to use the hospital suggested by your GP, but should book a hospital bed as early as possible. Your GP also refers you to an obstetrician. Find out as much as possible about local hospital methods and policies on childbirth, directly or from friends or neighbours, before booking a bed. The policy regarding a father's attendance at a birth varies depending on the hospital. A husband doesn't have the right to be present with his wife during labour or childbirth (which is at the consultant's discretion), although some doctors expect fathers to attend. If the presence of your husband is important to you, you should check that it's permitted at the hospital where you plan to have your baby and any other rules that may be in force.

Midwives are responsible for educating and supporting women and their families during the childbearing period. Midwives can advise women before they become pregnant, in addition to providing moral, physical and emotional support throughout a pregnancy and after the birth. Your midwife may also advise on parent education and ante-natal classes for mothers. After giving birth, mothers are attended at home by their midwife for the first ten days or so, after which they see a health visitor and their GP to monitor their child's health and development.

Information

There are many organisations providing information about family planning and support in pregnancy and childbirth, including the FPA, formerly known as the Family Planning Association, 2-12 Pentonville Road, London N1 9FP (☎ 0845-122 8690, 🖥 www.fpa.org.uk) and the National Childbirth Trust, Alexandra House, Oldham Terrace, Acton, London W3 6NH (☎ 0870-044 8707, 🖥 www.nctpregnancyand-babycare.com). For general information about benefits and other help during pregnancy and when your baby is born, contact the government agency Child Support (☎ 08457-133 133, 🖥 www.csa.gov.uk). An interesting book for mothers-to-be is *The New Pregnancy and Childbirth: Choices and Challenges* by Sheila Kitzinger (Dorling Kindersley).

DENTISTS

The UK's annual consumption of over 750,000 tonnes of sweets (over 13kg per person) ensures that dentists (and sweet manufacturers) remain financially healthy. Despite the efforts of dentists to promote preventive dentistry, millions of Britons never go near a dentist (mostly out of fear) unless they're dying from toothache. Fortunately, when you need help there are excellent dentists in all areas. The best way to find a good dentist, whether as an NHS or a private patient, is to ask your colleagues, friends or neighbours (particularly those with perfect teeth) if they can recommend someone. Dentists are listed under *Dental Surgeons* in yellow pages and are permitted to advertise any special services they provide, such as private and NHS patients, emergency or 24-hour answering service, dental hygienist, and evening or weekend surgeries. Around 50 per cent of dentists hold an evening surgery one day a week or open on Saturday mornings. There are mobile dentists in some regions.

In some areas, community dental clinics or health centres provide a dental service for children, expectant and nursing mothers, and disabled adults. Some hospitals provide a free emergency service, e.g. on Sundays and public holidays. Dental hospitals (e.g. in London) provide a free emergency service on most days. Many family dentists are qualified to perform special treatment, e.g. periodontal work, although you must usually see a specialist. False teeth (dentures) are made by a dental technician and prescribed and fitted by dentists. Most dental technicians carry out emergency repairs on dentures (see yellow pages).

The cost of dental treatment has risen considerably in recent years and it pays to keep your mouth shut during dental check-ups, which are recommended every six months. However, dental care isn't particularly expensive in the UK compared with many other western countries. Fees vary considerably, depending on the area and the dentist, e.g. from £15.90 to £35 for a check-up, from £15.90 to £30 for scaling and polishing, and from £20 to £43.60 for an X-ray and a small (amalgam) filling.

NHS Treatment

In 1990, a new NHS contract was drawn up between the NHS and the British Dental Association, which caused many dentists to leave the NHS and accept only adult private work, rather than accept the fees and conditions imposed by the NHS. Since 1992, over one million people have been de-registered as NHS patients, many opting to go private. Less than half of all dentists accept new non-exempt NHS patients. The quality of work performed under the NHS often isn't as good as that provided under private treatment, because dentists often use inferior materials owing to cost restraints and have less time to treat patients (NHS dentists may treat up to 60 patients a day).

NHS patients are asked to sign a form and give their NHS number (or show a medical card) before beginning treatment. You must sign the form again when treatment has been completed to acknowledge that you've had the treatment listed. Don't sign it a second time before your course of treatment is complete. Many dentists treat NHS and private patients and don't have a list of NHS registered patients like GPs. A dentist who accepts NHS patients may have a quota and, if it's full, he may offer to treat you only as a private patient. Consult your FHSA if you have trouble finding an NHS dentist. **If you want to have treatment as an NHS patient, you must make this clear to the dentist's receptionist when registering.**

You should take your NHS medical card to the dentist when you have your initial examination. Each time you visit a dentist, whether the same dentist or another one, you must re-confirm that you will be treated as an NHS patient. NHS dental patients aren't required to live within a certain catchment area and can change dentists whenever they like. Once you're registered as an NHS patient, a dentist cannot refuse to treat you and essential work is always completed under the NHS when clinically necessary. As at April 2007, there are three bands of NHS treatment charges - £15.90, £43.60 and £194.00, covering the cost of examination, diagnosis, preventive advice and various treatments, respectively. There's a standard NHS charge of £15.90 for a dental check-up. There's no extra charge for stopping bleeding, denture repairs, home visits or opening a surgery in an emergency (although you must pay for treatment as usual).

A list of dental charges and exemptions is published by the NHS and is available from them or your FHSA. Exemptions include children and young people in full-time education; the over-60s; expectant mothers and those who have had a baby in the last year; and those on low incomes receiving state benefits. NHS patients who aren't under 18, or receiving unemployment or supplementary benefits, must usually pay a proportion of their dental treatment and for the whole cost of cosmetic treatment, e.g. bridges and crowns.

Dentists may ask for payment in advance and NHS dentists must receive prior permission from the Dental Estimates Board (DEB) before certain expensive work can be undertaken. If you miss a dental appointment without giving 24 hours notice, your dentist may charge you a standard fee. Of course, had you turned up on time, your dentist would probably have kept you waiting. If a dentist sees you as an emergency NHS patient outside normal surgery hours, he isn't permitted to make an extra charge. In some areas, an emergency dental service is operated by the local health authority. A dentist isn't obliged to treat someone who isn't a patient, even in an emergency.

Unnecessary Treatment

According to a report by the General Dentist Practitioners Association (GDPA), a number of dentists remove or fill teeth unnecessarily. Always try to obtain an accurate, preferably written, quotation before beginning a course of treatment. Few dentists are willing to quote an exact fee for work, and often a 'rough estimate' is only a fraction of the final bill. If you have regular check-ups and usually have little or no treatment, you should be suspicious if a new dentist suggests that you need a lot of fillings or extractions. In this case, you should obtain a second opinion before going ahead (however, two dentists rarely agree on exactly the same treatment).

Complaints

If you have a complaint concerning dental treatment completed under the NHS, you should write to your local FHSA within six months of the end of the course of treatment. For complaints regarding private treatment, you must contact the General Dental Council, 37 Wimpole Street, London W1G 8DQ (☎ 020-7887 3800, 💻 www.gdc-uk.org). The British Dental Association (☎ 020-7935 0875, 💻 www.bda-dentistry.org.uk) provides a list of dentists in your area, but (wisely) doesn't handle complaints. For information about **Dental Insurance** see page 346.

OPTICIANS

As with dentists, there's no need to register with an optician. You simply go to the one of your choice, although it's advisable to ask your colleagues, friends or neighbours if they can recommend someone. Opticians are listed under *Opticians - Dispensing* or *Opticians - Ophthalmic* (optometrists) in yellow pages and may advertise their services, such as contact lenses or an emergency repair service. Opticians (like spectacles) come in many shapes and sizes.

Your sight can be tested only by a registered ophthalmic optician (or optometrist) or an ophthalmic medical practitioner. Most high street opticians are dispensing opticians (who make up spectacles) and ophthalmic opticians, who test eyesight, prescribe glasses and diagnose eye diseases. An eye specialist may be an ophthalmic medical practitioner (a doctor who treats eye diseases and also tests eyesight and prescribes lenses), an ophthalmologist (a senior specialist or eye surgeon) or an orthoptist (an ophthalmologist who treats children's eye problems). If you must see an eye specialist, you must usually be referred by your GP.

The optometrist business is competitive and unless someone is highly recommended, you should shop around for the best deal. Recent years have seen a flood of 'chain store' opticians such as Vision Express (and those in Boots) opening in high streets and shopping centres. Prices for spectacles and contact lenses vary considerably, so it's wise to compare costs (although make sure you're comparing like with like) before committing yourself to a large bill, particularly for contact lenses. The prices charged for most services (spectacle frames, lenses, hard and soft contact lenses) are often cheaper in the UK than elsewhere in Europe, although higher than North America.

Spectacles

The prices of spectacle frames vary considerably (e.g. from around £20 to over £200 for designer frames) depending on the quality, style and origin (and the optician). The costs of spectacle lenses also vary widely (e.g. £50 to £300) depending on the strength and complexity of your prescription, and whether you choose a tint or special lenses. Most people should expect to pay between £100 and £150 for frames and lenses. Special offers are common such as 'buy a new pair of glasses and get a second pair of prescription sunglasses free'. Some opticians offer free spectacles for a child when a parent buys a new pair of glasses. Always carefully compare offer prices and consider whether you really need (or want) what's offered, e.g. will you actually use a free pair of prescription sunglasses?

Ready-made reading glasses are available from chemists (e.g. Boots) and other shops without a sight test or prescription, at a fraction of the cost of a prescription pair, e.g. £10 to £20. They're also available from opticians, but are more expensive. Wherever you buy your spectacles, take advantage of any guarantee, after-sales service or insurance arrangements for repairs or replacements. Most opticians offer insurance against accidental damage, e.g. £20 a year for lenses and £10 for frames. If you're sold defective glasses or contact lenses, you have rights under the law relating to the sale of goods.

Contact Lenses

Soft contact lenses are available in major cities from around £40 or £50, although the more usual price is £80 to £140, depending on the optician and the brand of lenses. You can insure contact lenses against loss or damage for around £25 a year. Disposable (one-day) and extended-wear (e.g. one or three months) contact lenses are widely available, although most medical experts believe extended-wear lenses should be approached with extreme caution. **Obtain advice from a doctor or eye specialist before buying them.** One-day contact lenses cost around £1 a day.

Sight Tests

If you aren't entitled to a free sight test under the NHS, you must have the test as a private patient, which usually costs between £17 and £30. Some opticians offer a special low price (or even free tests) for pensioners. Sight tests are valid for two years, although you should be aware that your eyesight can change considerably during this time. You don't need to buy your spectacles (lenses or frames) or contact lenses from the optician who tests your sight, irrespective of whether you're an NHS or private patient, and you have the right to a copy of any prescription resulting from an NHS or private sight test.

Certain people receive free sight tests under the NHS, including children under 16, full-time students under 19, registered blind or partially sighted people, those diagnosed as diabetic or glaucoma sufferers, and people on low incomes receiving state benefits. NHS leaflet HC11, explains who's entitled to free sight tests and NHS vouchers for glasses, and is available from social security offices, NHS family doctors and opticians.

Laser Surgery

In the last few years, laser surgery to correct short-sighted vision has become increasingly popular. It's heavily promoted by laser surgery clinics, which are unregulated and don't need any special qualifications or registration, and costs between around £500 and £1,000 per eye. There are conflicting reports about its effectiveness, particularly for those with severe short-sight, who are generally considered poor candidates. Some eye specialists warn against having it done, as it can cause permanent eye damage in certain cases, although it also achieves some remarkable results. **However, the long-term effects are unknown and it should be treated with caution.**

Complaints

If you have a complaint regarding your optician, which you're unable to resolve, you should write to the Association of Optometrists, Consumer Complaints Service, 61 Southwark Street, London SE1 0HL (☎ 020-7261 9661, 💻 www.assoc-optometrists.org) or, for dispensing opticians, the Association of British Dispensing Opticians, 199 Gloucester Terrace, London W2 6LD (☎ 020-7298 5100, 💻 www.abdo.org.uk). Help the Aged (207-221 Pentonville Road, London N1 9UZ, ☎ 020-7278 1114, 💻 www.helptheaged.org.uk) collects unwanted spectacles, which they distribute to the elderly in Africa and Asia.

COUNSELLING

Counselling and assistance for health and social problems is available within the NHS, and from thousands of local community groups and volunteer organisations, ranging from national associations to small local groups (including self-help groups). Local authorities provide social workers to advise and support those who need help within their communities. If you need to find help locally, you can contact your local authority, local voluntary services or a Citizens Advice Bureau (see page 497). Many colleges and educational establishments provide a counselling service for students, and hospital casualty departments have a psychiatrist on call 24 hours a day. Problems for which help is available are numerous and include drug rehabilitation; alcoholism (e.g. Alcoholics Anonymous); gambling; dieting (e.g. Weight Watchers); smoking; attempted suicide and psychiatric problems; homosexual and lesbian-related problems; youth problems; battered children and women; marriage and relationship counselling (e.g. Relate); and rape.

Trained counsellors provide advice and help for sufferers of various diseases (e.g. multiple sclerosis and muscular dystrophy) and the disabled (e.g. the blind and deaf). They also help very sick and terminally ill patients (e.g. cancer, leukaemia and AIDS sufferers) and their families to come to terms with their situation. A number of voluntary organisations and local authorities run refuges for battered wives (and their children) or maltreated children, whose conditions have become intolerable (some provide 24-hour emergency telephone numbers). If you, or a member of your family, are the victims of a violent crime, the police put you in touch with a local victim support scheme.

In times of need, there's nearly always someone to turn to and all services are strictly confidential. In major towns, counselling may be available in your own language if you don't speak English. If you need help desperately, someone speaking your language can usually be found. The Samaritans provide a strictly confidential telephone counselling service in periods of personal crisis, for the lonely, desperate and suicidal through over 175 branches throughout the UK and Ireland (see your telephone directory or ask the operator for your local phone number). Children can call Childline (☎ 0800-1111), which answers around 10,000 calls a day.

DRUG & ALCOHOL ABUSE

Drug abuse is a serious problem in the UK, where drug addiction has increased almost tenfold in the last two decades and areas of some cities are being slowly turned into no-go areas by the drug trade. Despite a major campaign of education for the young, and increased vigilance by police and customs officers to reduce the supply of drugs from abroad (particularly heroin, cocaine and crack), record levels of drugs are still being imported into the UK. Soft drugs such as cannabis are treated more leniently in most areas and many people found in possession of a small amount are unlikely to be prosecuted (although it's still illegal). Many people believe that the authorities are fighting a losing battle against the drug barons and that universal prohibition has increased consumption. There have even been calls to legalise drugs which, although taken seriously by some professionals, are rejected outright by the authorities.

The drug problem is also of increasing concern to those in the fight against AIDS (see **Sexually Transmitted Diseases** on page 325), as the sharing of needles among drug addicts (many of whom are also homosexuals) is a major cause of the spread of AIDS. Many cities operate a needle exchange scheme for drug addicts. Glue sniffing is a big problem among the young in certain areas. It's illegal to sell certain solvents (e.g. glue, lighter fuel) to children under 18 while knowing or having reason to believe they're to be used for intoxication.

Some NHS hospitals have special drug treatment units, where treatment is usually on an outpatient basis, although in-treatment may be provided when necessary. Doctors have a duty to notify the authorities of any patient they consider to be addicted to a controlled drug. Many voluntary organisations provide drug advice and rehabilitation services, including residential facilities. There are dozens of voluntary groups in all areas of the UK providing counselling, advice and support for drug users and their relatives and friends (see your local telephone directory or yellow pages). If you can afford to pay for private treatment, a number of private clinics and hospitals specialise in treating people for drug, alcohol and chemical abuse and other health problems. For help and advice, contact the National Drugs Helpline (☎ 0800-776 600).

Alcohol Abuse

Apart from the direct or indirect loss of life, alcohol abuse costs British industry over £1 billion a year in lost production due to absenteeism. It's estimated that some 7 million Britons have a drink problem, many of whom are unaware of it. The consumption of alcohol is also a serious problem among children. A national alcohol helpline known as Drinkline (☎ 0800-917 8282) operates from 9am to 11pm Mondays to Fridays, to advise those concerned about their own or someone else's drinking, and Alcoholics Anonymous has groups in all areas (see your telephone directory).

Smoking

As in most countries, smoking contributes to a huge loss of life and working days, although the number of smokers has steadily decreased over the last 15 years, from some 45 per cent in 1975 to less than 30 per cent in 1999. However, smoking among teenagers is increasing and there have been calls to curb or ban the advertising of tobacco products, particularly advertisements targeted at the young. In recent years, there has been increasing concern about 'passive smoking' (where non-smokers involuntarily inhale the smoke generated by smokers), although the issue is nothing like as heated as in the US (where anyone who smokes in a public place is liable to be fined). However, smoking is banned in many public places and on most public transport, and from 1st July 2007 has been prohibited in all enclosed public spaces such as pubs, restaurants and private clubs.

The cost of cigarettes in the UK is among the most expensive in the EU and the government collects around £10 billion in tobacco tax from the £13 billion spent annually on cigarettes and tobacco. High tobacco taxes are allegedly intended to curb consumption. Employers estimate that they get 20 per cent less work from employees who are unable to smoke in the workplace and some pay smokers less in an effort to encourage them to quit. Smoking-related illness accounts for 50 million lost working days a year and bosses are also worried about claims for passive smoking from non-smokers.

Action on Smoking and Health (ASH), 102 Clifton Street, London EC2A 4HW (☎ 020-7739 5902, 🖳 www.ash.org.uk), provides advice on giving up smoking and information on smoking and the rights of non-smokers. There are also non-smoking clinics and self-help groups throughout the UK to help those wishing to stop smoking. Contact your local health authority for information. ASH provides numerous free publications, most of which are downloadable from the website.

SEXUALLY TRANSMITTED DISEASES

Like most western countries, the UK has its fair share of sexually-transmitted diseases, including the deadly Acquired Immune Deficiency Syndrome (AIDS). The furore over AIDS has died down in the past few years, and many fear that this will cause those most at risk to be lulled into a false sense of security. The explosion of AIDS predicted by many 'experts' hasn't materialised, particularly among the heterosexual population, although the number of heterosexual cases is increasing. **To date, there's no cure for AIDS (over 10,000 people have died from it in the UK).**

The spread of AIDS is accelerated by the sharing of needles by drug addicts, among whom AIDS is rampant (many heroin addicts are infected with the HIV virus). In an effort to reduce needle sharing among HIV-positive drug addicts, syringe exchange centres have been set up throughout England (☎ 0800-567 123 for 24-hour information), and in some cities free syringe vending machines have been provided. The spread of AIDS is also accelerated by prostitutes, many of whom are also drug addicts.

Prostitution is illegal; therefore it's impossible to effect any control over the spread of sexually transmitted diseases by prostitutes. The best protection against AIDS is for men to wear a condom, although they're not foolproof (against AIDS or pregnancy) and the only real protection is abstinence. Condoms are on sale at chemists, some supermarkets, men's hairdressers, and vending machines in public toilets in pubs and other places. They're also available free from family planning clinics.

Many hospitals have clinics for sexually transmitted diseases or you can refer yourself to a Sexually Transmitted Diseases (STD) or VD clinic. Both provide free tests, treatment and advice. All cases of AIDS and HIV-positive blood tests must be reported to local health authorities (patients' names remain anonymous). If you would like to talk to someone in confidence about AIDS, there are many organisations and self-help groups providing information, advice and help in all areas, including the National AIDS Helpline (☎ 0800-567 123). Other organisations are listed in telephone directories. The NHS, health authorities, councils and many organisations (including those listed above) publish free information about AIDS.

BIRTHS & DEATHS

Births and deaths must be reported to your local Registrar of Births, Deaths and Marriages (look in your local telephone directory).

Births

In recent years the British birth has fallen to its lowest level for 150 years, despite the fact that the UK has the highest rate of teenage pregnancies in Europe. Either parent can register a birth by simply going to the registrar within six weeks of a birth and giving the child's details (no proof of birth is necessary). Both parents must report to the registrar if they aren't married, i.e. the child is illegitimate, if they both want their details to be included on the birth certificate; otherwise the mother registers the birth and only her details are listed. A birth is usually registered in the area where the baby was born, but can be done through another office. Births and deaths of foreigners in the UK may need to be reported to a consulate or embassy, for example to obtain a national birth certificate and passport for a child, or to register a death in the deceased's country of birth.

Deaths

When someone dies, a medical certificate must be completed by a doctor and taken to the registrar (see above) within five days. If someone dies suddenly, accidentally, during an operation, in unusual circumstances, or the cause of death is unknown, the doctor notifies the police and/or the coroner, who decides whether a postmortem is necessary to determine the cause of death. The registrar needs to know the personal details of the deceased, including his date and place of birth and death, details of a marriage (if applicable), and whether he was receiving a state pension or any welfare benefits. The registrar then issues a death certificate and the 'notification of disposal', which authorises the funeral to take place.

The death certificate must be given to a funeral director (or undertaker) to arrange the burial or cremation (or alternatively he arranges for the body to be shipped to another country for burial). If you wish to remove a body from England or Wales, permission must be obtained from a coroner at least four days before the date of shipment. You may wish to announce a death in a local or national newspaper, giving the date, time and place of the funeral, and your wishes regarding flowers or contributions to a charity or research. The traditional dress for a Christian funeral is black or dark dress.

Cost

Funerals are expensive (many think they're a rip-off), partly as a result of many family and small funeral businesses being gobbled up by large national and international companies, which have grabbed a large slice of the market. With some 650,000 deaths in the UK each year, it's big business and the increase in the cost of dying in the last few decades has exceeded the increase in the cost of living. In the last ten years, the cost has doubled to around £2,000 (£2,600 in London). You can save money by having a body cremated rather than buried, although the cost is still high at around £1,350. You can pay in advance for your funeral through a variety of pay-now-die-later schemes, with price and service guaranteed, although there are no legal safeguards and the prepaid funeral trade is ripe for fraud, mismanagement and over-selling (a number of funeral plans have gone bust in recent years). Pre-paid funeral schemes cost between £1,000 and £2,000 and have been taken out by some 250,000 people (although this is expected to increase tenfold in the next few years).

As the cost of traditional burials increases, alternative burials are becoming increasingly popular (you can even take a body to a crematorium yourself). The Natural Death Centre (☎ 0871-288 2098, 🖥 www.naturaldeath.org.uk) can provide information about cheap, 'green' funerals. There's a shortage of burial space in the UK and graves may soon have to be recycled (as already happens in many other countries). You can also choose to be buried in your own garden, although this can reduce the value of your property by up to 50 per cent! If you want to have a body buried abroad or have someone who died abroad buried in the UK, the body must probably be transported by air, which can be **very** expensive.

A cheaper solution, and one that many think socially responsible, is to leave your body to science. Teaching hospitals, always short of material for their students to work on, normally arrange collection at their own expense, and pay for a cremation later. Your doctor can supply details of arrangements for your area.

In the event of the death of a resident of the UK, all interested parties must be notified. You need a number of copies of the death certificate, e.g. for the will, pension claims, insurance companies and financial institutions. If you must obtain a copy of a birth, marriage or death certificate, the cheapest way is to apply to the registrar in the area where it was registered. Alternatively you can apply to the General Register Office, Trafalgar Road, Southport PR8 2HH (☎ 0845-603 7788, ✉ certificate.services@ons.gsi.gov.uk) and pay a search fee.

Information

The government agency, The Pension Service gives advice (💻 www.the pensionservice.gov.uk). The Inland Revenue (taxman) has a telephone helpline for inheritance information (☎ 0845-302 0900) and publishes a leaflet *What To Do About Tax When Someone Dies* (IR45). Help the Aged (207-221 Pentonville Road, London N1 9UZ, ☎ 020-7278 1114, 💻 www.helptheaged.org.uk) publishes a free booklet entitled *Bereavement*. Cruse Bereavement Care can also provide comprehensive help and advice (126 Sheen Road, Richmond upon Thames, London TW9 1UR, ☎ 0844-477 9400, ☎ www.crusebereavementcare.org.uk). Other useful books include *What to Do When Someone Dies* by Paul Harris (Which? Books) and *Through Grief* by Elizabeth Collick (Darton, Longman and Todd). (See also **Wills** on page 395.)

13.

<u>INSURANCE</u>

In the UK, you can insure practically anything, from your car to your camera, the loss of your livelihood to your life. You can also insure against most eventualities, such as rain on your parade or village fete, or the possibility of twins (or sextuplets) or missing your holiday. For particularly unusual requests, you may be required to obtain a quote from Lloyd's of London, the last resort for unusual insurance needs, not only within the UK, but also internationally. If you earn your livelihood courtesy of a particular part of your anatomy, e.g. your voice, legs, teeth or posterior, you can also insure it against damage or decline. However, if an insurance requirement is particularly unusual or risky, you may find premiums prohibitively high and restrictions may be placed on what you can and cannot do.

The UK is renowned as a nation of gamblers, which is reflected in the relatively low levels of insurance, not only for such basic requirements as loss of income or life insurance, but also insurance for homes and their contents. After serious flooding caused millions of pounds' worth of damage in recent years, it was revealed that as many as half of all households in some areas had no building or home contents insurance or were under-insured. Many people tend to rely on state 'insurance' provisions, which come under the heading of Social Security. These include sickness and unemployment benefits, income support (for families on low incomes) and state pensions. Social security usually provides for the most basic needs only and those who are reduced to relying on it often exist below the poverty line.

It isn't necessary to spend half your income insuring yourself against every eventuality from the common cold to a day off work, but it's important to be covered against any event which could precipitate a major financial disaster. **As with everything to do with finance, it's important to shop around when buying insurance. It bears repeating – always shop around when buying or renewing insurance!** Simply picking up a few brochures from insurance brokers or making a few telephone calls can save you a lot of money (enough to pay for this book many times over).

If you're coming to the UK from abroad, you would be wise to ensure that your family has full health insurance during the period between leaving your last country of residence and your arrival here. This is particularly important if you're covered by a company health insurance policy terminating on the day you leave your present employment. If possible, it's better to continue with your present health insurance policy, particularly if you have existing health problems which may not be covered by a new policy. If you aren't covered by the National Health Service (see page 307), it's important to have private health insurance.

There are just two cases in the UK when insurance for individuals is compulsory: buildings insurance if you have a mortgage (because your lender will insist on it) and third party motor insurance, which is required by law. You may also need compulsory third party and accident insurance for high-risk sports such as hang-gliding, mountaineering and parachuting. Voluntary insurance includes pensions, accident, income protection, health, home contents, personal liability, legal expenses, dental, travel, motor breakdown and life insurance.

If you want to make a claim against a third party or a third party is claiming against you, you would be wise to seek legal advice for anything other than a minor claim. British law is likely to be different from that in your home country or your previous country of residence, and you should never assume that it's the same.

INSURANCE COMPANIES

Insurance is big business in the UK and there are numerous insurance companies to choose from, many providing a wide range of insurance services, while others specialise in certain fields only. You can buy insurance from many sources, including traditional insurance companies selling through their own salesmen or independent brokers, direct insurance companies (selling direct to the public), banks and other financial institutions, post offices, motoring organisations, and department and chain stores. Policies offered by banks are generally the most expensive and don't offer the best cover. The major insurance companies have offices or agents (brokers) throughout the UK, including most large towns. Many brokers provide a free analysis of your family's insurance needs.

Brokers

If you choose a broker, you should use one who's independent and sells policies from a wide range of insurance companies. Many brokers or agents are tied to a particular insurance company and sell policies only from that company. (This includes most banks and building societies). A broker should research the whole market and take into account your individual requirements, why you're investing (if applicable), the various companies' performance records, what you can afford and the type of policy that's best for you. He mustn't offer you a policy because it pays him the highest commission – which, incidentally, you should ask him about (particularly regarding life insurance), as he's obliged to tell you. It's also worthwhile trying internet brokers such as Screentrade (🖳 www.screentrade.com), who usually provide very competitive quotes. (Most major insurance companies also have websites).

Direct Insurance

In recent years, direct marketing and direct response insurance companies (bypassing brokers) have resulted in huge savings for consumers, particularly for car, buildings and home contents insurance. Direct marketing companies provide quotations over the telephone and often you aren't even required to complete a proposal form. Compare premiums from a number of direct sales insurance companies, e.g. Direct Line (🖳 http://uk.directline.com), Churchill (🖳 www.churchill.com) and Eagle Star (🖳 www.zurichinsurance.co.uk) with the best offers from brokers **before** choosing a policy.

Shop Around

When buying insurance, you should shop till you drop and then shop around some more! Premiums vary considerably (e.g. by 100 to 300 per cent), although you must ensure that you're comparing similar policies and that some important benefits haven't been omitted. The less expensive companies may be stricter when it comes to claims and may take longer to settle them. The general wisdom is that it's better to pay for independent insurance advice than to accept 'free' advice, which is often more expensive in the long run. You should obtain a number of quotations for each insurance need and shouldn't assume that your existing insurance company is the best choice for a new insurance requirement. Buy only the insurance that you **want** and **need** and ensure that you can afford the payments (and that your cover is protected when you're sick or unemployed). Don't sign a contract until you've had time to think it over.

Claims

Although insurance companies are keen to take your money, most aren't nearly so happy to settle claims. Some insurance companies practically treat customers as criminals when they make a claim. Fraud is estimated to cost the insurance industry some £20 million per week (according to the BBC in October 2003) and staff may be trained automatically to assume that claims are fraudulent. If you need to make a claim, don't send original bills or documents to your insurance company unless it's absolutely necessary (you can always send a certified copy). Keep copies of all bills, documents and correspondence, and send letters by recorded or registered post, so that your insurance company cannot deny receipt.

Don't bank a cheque received in settlement of a claim if you think it's insufficient, as you may be deemed to have accepted it as full and final settlement. Don't accept the first offer made, as most insurance companies try to get away with making a low settlement. (If an insurer pays what you claimed without a quibble, you probably claimed too little!) When dealing with insurance companies, perseverance often pays. Insurers are increasingly refusing to pay up on the flimsiest of pretexts, as they know that many people won't pursue their cases, even when they have a valid claim. Don't give up on a claim if you're sure you have a good case, but persist until you've exhausted every avenue. Some insurance companies provide a 24-hour help line for policyholders in case of emergencies.

Complaints

Regrettably, you cannot insure yourself against being uninsured or sue your insurance broker for giving you bad advice. However, if you buy insurance through a registered insurance broker and discover that your insurance premiums haven't been paid or that you've been sold the wrong policy, you should be able to obtain compensation through the broker's compulsory professional indemnity insurance (insurance for insurance for insurance). This insurance pays out if, as a result of a broker's error, you discover you aren't insured. Members of the Association of British Insurers (🖳 www.abi.org.uk) have similar (but less comprehensive) cover, although you have greater protection if you buy from a registered broker or direct from an insurance company. In recent years, the financial ombudsman (see below) has received more complaints than at any time since the service was established over 20 years ago. However, only around a third of cases dealt with by the ombudsman end in success for policyholders.

Lately, British insurance companies (and their representatives) have plummeted in public esteem after being involved in a number of scandals and dubious practices. These include the mis-selling of pensions and annuities; levying exorbitant commissions and charges; refusing to pay out on legitimate claims by bending the rules and exploiting 'small print' loopholes (some insurance companies go to extraordinary lengths not to pay claims); 'churning' (the dubious buying and selling of policies to generate commissions); offering fraudulent advice; overcharging on buildings and other insurance; and handing over 'surplus assets' to shareholders rather than to policyholders. **Misrepresentation or even outright fraud on the part of insurance companies and agents isn't uncommon.**

Disputes

Most financial fields have their own independent arbitrator, called an ombudsman, whose job is to mediate between companies and individuals in dispute, but only when a company's internal complaints procedures have been exhausted. There are ombudsmen for disputes involving insurance companies, banks, building societies and investments. If you decide to go to arbitration with an ombudsman, his decision is usually binding on all parties. There's a maze of insurance associations, ombudsmen and regulators. The Financial Ombudsman Service, South Quay Plaza, 183 Marsh Wall, London E14 9SR (☎ 0845-080 1800, 💻 www.financial-ombudsman.org.uk) deals with most insurance complaints or can tell you whom to contact. The Association of British Insurers (ABI), 51 Gresham Street, London EC2V 7HQ (☎ 020-7600 3333), publishes a number of free leaflets regarding insurance matters and also handles complaints regarding policies issued by member companies. You can also ask your insurance company or broker for guidance or contact a Citizens Advice Bureau (see page 497).

INSURANCE CONTRACTS

Read all insurance contracts before signing them. If you don't understand everything, ask a friend or colleague to 'translate' it or take legal advice. If a policy has pages of legal jargon and gobbledegook in very small print, you have a right to be suspicious: it's common practice nowadays to be as brief as possible and write clearly and concisely in language which doesn't require a legal degree. Always check any exclusions or conditions and have them explained if you don't understand them. New European Union (EU) directives on unfair terms and legal-speak in consumer contracts may curb the insurance companies' discretion to increase future charges as they wish. At present, there's no requirement for insurers to notify policyholders about increases or how they affect the final pay-out (e.g. of a with-profits policy). Take care how you answer questions in an insurance proposal form as, even if you mistakenly provide false information, an insurance company can refuse to pay out when you make a claim.

Long-term life insurance and pension plans are designed so that it's almost impossible to work out how much you're being charged in fees. Since 1st January 1995, insurance companies have been required to reveal to customers how much is taken from pension and insurance premiums for commission, administration and management expenses (plus providing specific illustrations of the maturity and surrender values for policies from July 1995). However, these rules apply only to endowment policies, personal pensions, and term assurance paying out benefits after the age of 70. If you have ordinary term insurance (e.g. to cover a mortgage), permanent health insurance, critical illness cover, unit trusts, mortgage payment protection or an independent savings account (ISA), a salesman doesn't have to reveal the costs of the policy. Commission on a life policy amounts to around 20 per cent of the first year's premiums. Some direct insurers such as Virgin Direct (🖳 http://uk.virginmoney.com) charge no commission on premiums, which has forced others to follow suit. There's a government tax of 5 per cent on insurance premiums, rising to 17.5 per cent for travel insurance and some insurance for vehicles and domestic and electrical appliances. Most long-term insurance is exempted from a premium tax.

Most insurance policies run for a calendar year from the date on which you take out a policy. All insurance policy premiums should be paid punctually, as late payment can affect your benefits or a claim although, if this is so, it should be noted in your policy. **Before signing any insurance contract you should shop around and take a day or two to think it over. Never sign on the spot, as you may regret it later. With some insurance contracts, e.g. life insurance and pension annuities, you have a 'cooling off' period of up to 14 days, during which you can cancel a policy without penalty.**

SOCIAL SECURITY

Social Security is the name given to the state benefits paid to residents of the UK, e.g. unemployment and sickness benefits, maternity pay, income support and family benefit. Social Security is an insatiable monster, costing an estimated £120 billion per year according to HM Treasury and payments have grown by over two-thirds in the last 15 years. Some benefits are dependent on your National Insurance contributions (see page 338); others on your circumstances, income or savings, while some have no preconditions. Benefit dependency has soared in recent years and the government is now trying to rein in the cost (many experts now believe that the benefit system is unworkable and should be replaced rather than reformed). Almost one-third of the population receives some form of state benefit, including over two million people (a three-fold increase between the early '80s and late '90s) who receive incapacity benefit and severe disablement allowance for being unable to work (the qualifying 'test' is a farce).

It's estimated that as many as one million people don't claim the Social Security benefits to which they're entitled; therefore it's important to know your rights. On the other hand, many thousands of people receive Social Security payments in error and many more make fraudulent claims. An estimated over five million national insurance numbers are bogus and may be used by fraudsters to claim Social Security benefits at a cost of up to £4 billion per year. Benefit errors are estimated to total some four million per year (most concerning income support) and claimants are just as likely to be overpaid as underpaid. If you're turned down for Social Security or receive less than you think you're entitled to, you should challenge the payment and take independent advice, e.g. from your local Citizens Advice Bureau .

It isn't necessary to be a British citizen to claim Social Security and some foreigners move to the UK purely to take advantage of the system. Social Security payments can be made in cash from any post office or can be paid directly into a bank, building society or post office account. Social Security benefits and national insurance contributions are reviewed annually and increased in line with the retail price index (RPI). Increases are paid from 6th April, which is the start of the tax year.

Leaflets

Leaflets are published for all Social Security benefits and are available from Social Security offices and (usually a limited number) from post offices, job centres and council offices. Leaflets include *Which Benefit* (FB2), which includes details of all Social Security benefits and lists all available leaflets, and *Social Security Benefit Rates* (NI196), which lists the latest benefit rates, earnings rules and national insurance contribution rates. Other general leaflets include *Bringing up Children?* (FB27) and the *Young People's Guide to Social Security* (FB23).

Information

General information can be obtained by calling the Benefit Enquiry Line (☎ 0800-882 200). In addition to English, some leaflets are also available in other languages, including Arabic, Bengali, Chinese, Greek, Gujarati, Hindi, Punjabi, Somali, Turkish, Urdu and Vietnamese. Telephone information is also available in other languages. Information about Social Security can be obtained from your local Citizens Advice Bureau (CAB), Welfare Rights Office, Consumer Advice Centre or Legal Advice (or Law) Centre. Your local council may also provide a telephone advice service.

Detailed information about all Social Security benefits is contained in the *National Welfare Benefits Handbook* (income related benefits) and the *Rights Guide to Non-means-tested Social Security Benefits*, both available from the Child Poverty Action Group, 94 White Lion Street, London N1 9PF (☎ 020-7837 7979). *Your Rights* by Sally West is a guide to benefits for older people, published by Age Concern England, Astral House, 1268 London Road, London SW16 4ER (☎ 0800-009 966) and available from most bookshops. Help the Aged, 207-221 Pentonville Road, London N1 9UZ (☎ 020-7278 1114) publishes a number of leaflets for the aged, including *Can I Claim It?*

Appeals

If you disagree with a decision regarding a claim for Social Security, you usually have the right of appeal (see leaflet GL24 *How to Appeal*). You must appeal in writing to your local Social Security office or Unemployment Benefit office (if applicable), usually within three months of a decision. Some appeals must be made within 28 days, so make sure you check.

Going Abroad

With the exception of pensions, benefits are paid only to those resident in the UK, although you can leave the UK for a limited period and still qualify for certain benefits. The UK currently has bilateral agreements with all European Economic Area (EEA) countries plus Australia, Barbados, Bermuda, Canada, Cyprus, Israel, Jamaica, Jersey, Guernsey, Malta, Mauritius, New Zealand, the Philippines, Switzerland, Turkey, the US, and Yugoslavia and its former republics.

National Insurance

National insurance (NI), called social security in most countries, is mandatory for most working people in the UK aged from 16 to the state pension age of 65. NI contributions entitle you to state benefits such as the Retirement Pension, Unemployment Benefit, Sickness Benefit, Maternity Allowance, Widow's Benefits and Invalidity Benefit. You qualify for these benefits only if you've already paid (or have been credited with) enough of the right class of contributions at the right time.

When you arrive in the UK, you must apply for a national insurance number from your local Department for Work and Pensions (DWP) office, which may take six to eight weeks to be allocated. You receive a plastic NI number card with your personal number on it, which usually remains the same all your life. You must give your NI number to your employer if you're an employee, or to your local Social Security office if you're self-employed, so that your NI contribution record can be kept up to date.

Your contributions and those of your employer depend on your income and status, e.g. employee or self-employed. NI contributions are calculated as a percentage of your salary and are paid on earnings between £100 (lower earnings limit) and £670 per week (upper earnings limit), in the tax year 2007/2008. You don't pay NI contributions if you earn less than the lower earnings limit and on earnings above the upper limit you pay the much reduced rate of one per cent. NI rates are normally increased in April at the start of each tax year and sometimes change during the tax year.

If you're over 65, you aren't required to pay NI contributions, whether or not you've retired from work, although if you continue to work as an employee, your employer must still pay contributions for you. Your level of NI payments depends on whether your employer's pension scheme (see **Company Pension Fund** on page

60) is contracted in or out of the State Earnings Related Pension Scheme (SERPS). There are five classes of NI contributions.

Class 1

Class 1 contributions are for employees earning between £91 and £610 per week. The employee and employer contribute and, providing your NI contributions are up to date, you qualify for most state benefits. On earnings above £610 per week, a rate of one per cent applies. Employers' contributions vary depending on an employee's earnings. Your NI contribution card is stamped by your employer. If you go abroad, e.g. to work, you can continue to pay class 1 contributions voluntarily for one year, after which you can pay class 3 contributions (see below) in order to maintain your payment record and qualify for a full retirement pension.

Class 1A

Class 1A contributions are for employers who provide their employees with a car or petrol for private use. The employer pays Class 1A contributions, not the employee.

Class 2

Class 2 contributions are for self-employed people (men under 65, women under 60) whose earnings are more than £4,215 per year. Your contribution is £2.20 per week which entitles you to claim all state benefits except Unemployment Benefit, compensation for industrial injuries, Statutory Sick Pay and Statutory Maternity Pay. Your contributions go towards any SERPS entitlement in your pension. If your profits are above a certain amount, you may need to pay profit-related Class 4 contributions (see below) in addition to Class 2 contributions. Payment can be made by buying NI stamps from a post office or via a direct debit from a bank, building society or post office account.

Class 3

Class 3 contributions are voluntary contributions for anyone without a full record of NI contributions or who isn't liable to pay Class 1 or Class 2 contributions, e.g. someone working abroad, a self-employed person with low profits, or someone who stopped working voluntarily. Class 3 contributions can also be paid if you've been excluded from Class 2 contributions. Class 3 allows you to make voluntary payments, at a flat rate of £7.15 per week, at any time during the six years following a break in payments (after which it's too late). By filling the gaps in your NI contributions, you can protect your retirement pension or widow's benefits. Payment can be via a lump sum in addition to those methods listed under Class 2 above.

Class 4

Class 4 contributions are also for the self-employed. In addition to Class 2 contributions, you must pay a further eight per cent of any profits between £5225 and £34,840 per year (2007/08). Class 4 contributions are assessed and collected by the Inland Revenue when you pay income tax on your profits. You receive tax relief on these contributions.

If you aren't working for certain reasons, you receive NI credits, which means that your NI contribution record is unbroken during the non-working period; these include the following:

- You're claiming Unemployment, Sickness, Maternity or Invalidity Benefit or Statutory Sick Pay.

- You're in full-time education.

- You're on an approved training course, e.g. youth training.

- You're aged 60 to 64 and not working, e.g. you retired early.

If you're at home looking after children and claiming Child Benefit, or looking after a sick, disabled or elderly person (without invalid care allowance), you may qualify for Home Responsibilities Protection. This helps you to keep your pension rights, even though you aren't paying NI contributions or receiving credits. See leaflet NP27A, *Looking After Someone at Home? How to Protect your Pension*.

The UK has a reciprocal arrangement with around 30 countries, including all EU member states, allowing social security contributions paid in one country to be taken into account under the social security schemes of another country. If you live in the UK for a short period only, you may be exempt from paying NI contributions, particularly if your home country has a bilateral agreement with the UK. To qualify, you must usually have been transferred to the UK by your employer for a short period only and must remain covered by your home country's social security scheme. Information can be obtained from the Overseas Pension Service (☎ 0191-218 7777).

If you retire to a country with which the UK doesn't have an agreement, you must arrange with the DWP to receive your pension abroad. Under agreements with Australia, Canada, New Zealand and Norway, the level of pension is frozen when you leave the UK and you won't receive annual increases based on the retail price index. Employees of international organisations and diplomatic missions are usually exempt from paying NI contributions.

PENSIONS

Everyone who pays national insurance (see above) is entitled to a state retirement pension, although for most people this barely provides sufficient income to pay for their basic needs, let alone maintain their standard of living in retirement. The value of the state pension has fallen considerably in real terms in the last few decades, and many pensioners live in poverty. Most people make far too little provision for retirement and are in for a rude shock when they retire: some 80 per cent of people don't save enough for their retirement. Most people should double their pension payments in order to retire on a good salary and you must pay even more into your fund if you want to retire early at age 50 or 55 on a decent income.

Falling gilt yields (on which annuities are based) in recent years have also hit retirement incomes. As a result, most insurance companies have been affected by pension guarantees made when gilt yields were high, which are costing insurers some £10 billion. An increasing number of people have been taking early retirement, either voluntarily or after having been made redundant. This means that unless you have a large private income or pots of money, it's imperative to have a company or private pension to secure your future after retirement.

Most people who have the opportunity join a company pension fund or, provided that they can afford it, take out a personal pension plan. You receive tax relief on all pension contributions at the highest rate paid on your earned income and can pay contributions into a personal pension fund net of income tax. The gains on investments from a pension are tax-free, but your pension on retirement is taxable as earned income. **It's worth noting that no other form of savings provides more tax breaks than a pension, e.g. free of income and capital gains tax, although most pension funds have performed very badly in recent years.** Many have shortfalls (or 'black holes') from falling stock markets and are worth around a third less than they should be. This has led many employers to close their final salary pension schemes, forcing workers to rely on less generous schemes where the investment risk is borne entirely by the employee. Such is the dissatisfaction with private pensions, that increasing numbers of people are buying residential property to fund their retirement rather than having a pension plan.

The investment fund accrued by your pension must be invested in an annuity to pay your pension in your retirement years. When you retire, you have the right to shop around for the best annuity you can find from **any** insurance company. Many people fall into the trap of opting for an annuity recommended by their insurance company, which often costs them thousands or even tens of thousands of pounds. Retirees can now buy annuities at different times during their retirement up to the age of 75, when they must buy a conventional annuity. For information, consult an annuity specialist or Annuity Direct (☎ 0500-506 575). If you retire abroad, British pensions are paid gross, but you must obtain a declaration from the foreign country's taxation authorities that you're a resident there for tax purposes and are taxed on your worldwide income there (see also **Double Taxation Agreements** on page 383).

DIY Pensions

You can save thousands of pounds with a do-it-yourself (DIY) pension by cutting out the middleman and choosing your own investments and there's little or no commission to pay. The savings on pension payments of just £100 per month can be almost £1,000 in the first year alone. A number of companies offer execution-only services, including Best Invest (☎ 020-7189 9999), Chartwell Investment

Management (☎ 01225-448 732), Lansdown Pensions Direct (☎ 0117-988 9956) and TQ Direct (☎ 01204-405 556).

Information

Before making any decisions regarding your pension, you should thoroughly investigate the various options available and take professional advice, e.g. from a member of the Society of Pension Consultants, St Bartholomew's House, 92 Fleet Street, London EC4Y 1DG (☎ 020-7353 1688, 💻 www.spc.uk.com) or the Association of Consulting Actuaries, Warnford Court, 29 Throgmorton Street, London EC2N 2AT (☎ 020-7374 4594, 💻 www.aca.org.uk). There are many publications dedicated to pensions in the UK, including *Your Pension* magazine and *The Which? Guide to Pensions* by Jonquil Love (Which? Books). Bear in mind that pensions are the most expensive, mis-sold, misunderstood, poorly performing financial product you can buy (and the one most people need most of all).

ACCIDENT INSURANCE

Accident insurance, although uncommon in the UK, is available from a number of companies. It includes lump-sum payouts in the event of death or permanent disability (e.g. £100,000 to £250,000) or hospitalisation as the result of an accident, and usually provides hospital (e.g. £50 to £125 per day) and convalescence benefits (e.g. £200 per week) after a minimum period in hospital. The cost of accident insurance is usually between £7.50 and £25 per month depending on the number of people insured and the cover provided. You may be able to choose higher cash payments by increasing your premium. Accident insurance can often be combined with permanent health insurance (see below). Occupational accident insurance is compulsory and is paid by your employer. It covers accidents or illness at work and may also cover accidents that occur when travelling to and from work or when travelling on company business.

PERMANENT HEALTH INSURANCE

Permanent health insurance (PHI) is designed to provide you with a weekly or monthly income when you're unable to work because of sickness or injury. Most employees have three possible sources of income when they're unable to work: Statutory Sick Pay (SSP) or Occupational Sick Pay (OSP) paid by their employer and Incapacity Benefit paid by the DWP. Your right to OSP depends on your employment contract (see **Contract of Employment** on page 53). Around 50 per cent of small companies with fewer than ten employees and some 55 per cent of all private sector firms have an OSP scheme.

An OSP scheme pays an employee's salary for a limited number of weeks only, depending on his length of service, for example:

Period of Service	No. of Weeks' Salary
Less than 13 weeks	0
13 weeks – 2 years	8
2 years – 5 years	10
5 years – 10 years	15
Over 10 years	26

PHI Policies

To ensure an adequate income when you're unable to work, you should take out a permanent health insurance (PHI) policy, also called income replacement insurance, which guarantees you a fixed amount each week (you decide how much) in the event of illness, injury or invalidity. A permanent health insurance policy (which shouldn't be confused with private health insurance, see page 344), pays you a fixed amount each month or a percentage of your salary if you're ill for a long period or permanently disabled in an accident. This type of policy is common among the self-employed and is also provided by employers with an OSP scheme. However, only some 15 per cent of the population have PHI insurance, on their own account or through their employer. You're around 15 times more likely to be off work for six months or longer than you are to die before the age of 65!

PHI policies typically pay up to 75 per cent of your gross annual earnings (up to a maximum salary of around £50,000), although you can insure a smaller proportion of your salary to reduce the premiums. The longer you wait for the income protection insurance to pay out, the lower your monthly premium. Usually, you can choose when the payments start, e.g. four weeks, three months or six months, or even one or two years after an accident or the onset of an illness. For example, your company may pay your salary for up to six months of an illness or after an accident, in which case you can choose to defer payments from your PHI policy for this period. Some policies pay benefits for a limited period only, e.g. up to a maximum of five years, while others continue payments until you return to work or retire. **You should avoid a policy that defines disability as the inability to do any job!**

The longer the period for which you require cover, the higher your monthly premium. Premiums also depend on your health record, age, salary, sex, job (high or low risk) and whether you smoke. Premiums and benefits may be index-linked. The younger you are, the lower your premiums, although women tend to pay more than men on average (because of a worse claims record). Depending on your age and type of job, some insurance companies may require you to have a medical examination or obtain a report from your family doctor. If you take out income protection insurance, policy payments are tax-free for the financial year in which you fall sick and the following year. If your employer provides the insurance, all income is taxable.

HEALTH INSURANCE

The National Health Service (NHS) provides free or subsidised medical treatment to all British subjects with the right of abode in the UK and to anyone who, at the time of treatment, has been a resident for the previous year (there are exemptions for certain groups). For further information about the NHS see page 307. Anyone living or working in the UK who isn't eligible for treatment under the NHS should take out a private health insurance policy (also referred to as private medical insurance or PMI).

This section deals exclusively with private health insurance, which is available from non-profit provident associations (e.g. BUPA, 🖳 www.bupa.co.uk, AXA PPP, 🖳 www.axappphealthcare.co.uk, and WPA, 🖳 www.wpa.org.uk) and various other sources, including general insurance companies, banks, building societies and motoring organisations. Many schemes offered by banks and other financial institutions are provided through the British United Provident Association (BUPA) or the Private Patients Plan Ltd (AXA PPP), although terms, benefits and premiums usually vary. Permanent health insurance is another name for income protection insurance (see page 342) and shouldn't be confused with private health insurance.

The number of people with private health insurance increased from around 1.5 million in 1966 to some 6.5 million in 1998 (around 12 per cent of the population), half of whose premiums are paid by employers. The remainder is split between those who pay their own premiums and those who share them with their employers. In the early 21st century, however, the number of individuals willing to pay for private health insurance out of their own pocket is falling, because of the high premiums. Private health care is restricted mainly to the middle to upper income brackets. The best advertisement for private health insurance is the eternal NHS waiting lists for non-emergency operations. NHS waiting list numbers have dropped from a high of 1.3 million in 1998 to just over 860,000 in 2006, but they remain extraordinarily high.

There's no tax relief on private health insurance premiums, despite the fact that they save the NHS billions per year. Private health insurance isn't usually intended to replace NHS treatment, but to complement it. Most health insurance policies fall into two main categories: those providing immediate, private specialist or hospital treatment (e.g. BUPA, AXA PPP and WPA) and so-called 'budget' or 'waiting-list' policies, where you're treated as a private patient when waiting lists exceed a certain period. Under waiting-list policies, if you cannot obtain an appointment with an NHS specialist or an NHS hospital admission within a certain period (e.g. six weeks), you can do so as a private patient.

Most health insurance policies have an annual limit on the amount they pay out for each policyholder, which may be anywhere between £5,000 and £1 million. They usually include consultations with specialists; hospital accommodation and nursing; operations or other treatment (e.g. physiotherapy, radiotherapy, chemotherapy); physicians', surgeons' and anaesthetists' fees; all drugs, X-rays and dressings while in hospital; home nursing; and a daily cash allowance when hospitalised under the NHS.

You cannot normally take out private health care to cover or obtain treatment for an existing or previous medical condition and there's usually a qualifying period of around three months before you can make a claim. For example, if you need a hernia operation, for which there are currently long NHS waiting lists, you cannot obtain private health cover to jump the queue. Your only solution, other than waiting your turn under the NHS, is to have private treatment and pay for it yourself. A vasectomy, for example, costs around £400 and a routine knee replacement between £7,000 and £10,000. In fact, if you have serious health problems, you must pay extra for insurance or may be refused cover altogether.

The cost of private health insurance depends on your age and the state of your health. There are maximum age limits for taking out health insurance with some insurers, e.g. 65 for BUPA, although age limits may be higher if you're willing to accept some restrictions. Some companies have special policies for those aged over 50 or 55. There are generally no restrictions on continuing membership, irrespective of age. Treatment of any medical condition for which you've already received medical attention or were aware existed in the five years before the start date of the policy, may not be covered. Existing health problems may be covered after two years' membership, if no further medical attention has been required. Some group policies do, however, include cover for existing or previous health problems. Other exclusions are listed in the policy rules.

The cost of health insurance has increased at double the rate of inflation in recent years. One of the reasons is that BUPA and AXA PPP have a stranglehold on private healthcare in the UK (they also own many hospitals) and other companies find it difficult to gain a foothold in the market. The cost varies considerably depending on the insurance company and whether you have fully comprehensive health insurance or a 'waiting-list' policy. The cost of insurance also depends on the hospital in which you're treated (the more expensive hospitals cost around twice as much as the cheapest). Should you choose to have treatment outside the hospitals covered by your insurance policy (which may be severely restricted), you may have to pay the whole cost of treatment yourself.

Standard policies may offer three scales (usually designated A, B and C) of hospital treatment which may include London NHS teaching hospitals (A, high scale), provincial NHS teaching hospitals (B, medium scale) and provincial non-teaching hospitals (C, low scale). Accommodation is usually in a private room, but in some hospitals it may be in a twin or four-bed ward. Premiums range from a few pounds per week for a budget plan offering limited benefits up to hundreds per month for a comprehensive policy with a major insurance company. Comprehensive top-of-the-range cover costs from £50 per month for a single person and from around £140 for a family (some companies offer lower premiums, but have a compulsory annual excess of £500 or £1,000).

Always shop around and compare premiums and levels of cover from a number of insurers (over 60 plans are available from around 30 companies). Take care to find the right policy for your family, as benefits vary widely and many people waste money on policies that are useless to them. The major companies include BUPA, AXA PPP, Norwich Union and WPA, which together have around 80 per cent of the market. Budget policies are better than nothing (particularly to bypass NHS waiting lists), but aren't usually such good value as standard policies. A no-claims discount is usually available, which means you can save up to 50 per cent on the 'standard' rate, and some companies offer discounts for non-smokers. You may also have the option of paying an excess (deductible) in order to reduce costs, e.g. the first £150 of a claim.

Premiums must usually be paid by direct debit, monthly, quarterly or annually. If you don't pay annually, there's usually an extra charge, e.g. five per cent. Premiums are usually reviewed annually and increased in line with (or above) inflation. Premiums usually increase with age, but won't generally be increased as a result of the number of claims you've made (unless you change insurance companies, so take care). Your policy cannot be cancelled through ill health. You don't usually require a medical examination to take out private health insurance, but must complete a medical questionnaire. Depending on your age and health record, your family doctor may be required to provide a medical report.

It's also possible to take out an international health insurance policy, which may be of interest to those living in the UK temporarily or those who work in different countries. Some policies offer members a range of premiums from budget to comprehensive cover. Policies offer at least two fee scales, one covering the whole world, including North America and the other, excluding North America. Most policies include a full refund of hospital, ambulance, home nursing (usually for a short period), outpatient, emergency dental treatment and repatriation charges. Policies include an annual overall claims limit, e.g. from £100,000 to £1,000,000 (the higher the better, particularly for North America).

Some comprehensive policies provide a fixed amount for general medical costs (including routine doctors' visits) and optional dental, optical and maternity expenses. Premiums range from around £700 to over £2,500 per year, depending on your age, level of cover and the areas covered (if North America is covered, premiums are much higher). If you don't require permanent international health insurance, you should consider a policy which provides limited or optional cover when you're abroad. All bills, particularly those received for treatment outside the UK, must include precise details of treatment received. Terms such as 'Dental Treatment' or 'Consultation' are insufficient. It's also helpful if bills are written in English (although impossible in many countries).

When changing employers or leaving the UK, you should ensure that you have continuous medical insurance. For example, if you and your family are covered by a company health scheme, your insurance probably ceases after your last official day of employment. If you're leaving the UK, you must cancel a British health insurance policy in writing if you aren't a member of a company health scheme. **If you're planning to change your health insurance company, you should ensure that no important benefits are lost. When changing health insurance companies, it's recommended that you inform your old insurance company, if you have any outstanding bills for which they're liable.**

DENTAL INSURANCE

Dental treatment that isn't covered by the NHS isn't usually included in private health insurance policies, although it's often available as an extra. Specialist dental policies have boomed since the '90s and have been boosted by the ever-diminishing number of dentists that accept NHS patients (fewer than half). Plans provided by BUPA and Denplan (a subsidiary of AXA PPP) have an average premium of around £15 per month. Patients must be 'dentally fit' (if you have 'bad' teeth, you won't be accepted) and are graded according to the condition of their teeth. Insurance doesn't usually cover expensive items such as crowns, bridges and dentures.

You can also obtain dental insurance (usually optionally) under some foreign health insurance policies or a worldwide health scheme. Emergency dental treatment and treatment required as the result of an accident may, however, be covered by a standard health insurance policy or an accident policy. If in doubt, contact your health or accident insurance company. For details of dental treatment covered by the National Health Service (see page 307). **If you have healthy teeth and rarely pay for more than an annual check-up and a visit to a hygienist, dental insurance offers poor value.**

BUILDINGS INSURANCE

For most people, buying a home is the biggest financial investment they will ever make. When buying a home, you're usually responsible for insuring it before you even move in. If you take out a mortgage to buy a property, your lender usually insists that your home (including most permanent structures on your property) has buildings insurance from the time you exchange contracts and are legally the owner. If you buy the leasehold of an apartment, your buildings insurance is arranged by the owner of the freehold. Even when not required by a lender, you would be extremely unwise not to have buildings insurance.

Buildings insurance usually includes loss or damage caused by fire; theft; riot or malicious acts; water leakage from pipes or tanks; oil leakage from central heating systems; flood, storm and lightning; explosion or aircraft impact; vehicles or animals; earthquake, subsidence, landslip or heave; falling trees or aerials; and cover for temporary homelessness, e.g. up to £5,000. Some insurance companies also provide optional cover to include trees and shrubs damaged maliciously or by storms. There may be an excess, e.g. from £25 or £50 (sometimes more), for some claims, which is intended to deter people from making small claims. Buildings insurance should be renewed each year and insurance companies are continually updating their policies, so you must take care that a policy still provides the cover required when you receive a renewal notice.

Lenders fix the initial level of cover when you first apply for a mortgage and usually offer to arrange the insurance for you, but you're normally free to make your own arrangements. If you change your buildings insurance from your lender to another insurer, you may be charged a transfer fee (e.g. £25) and an 'administration' fee to encourage you **not** to change. If you arrange your own buildings insurance, your lender will insist that the level of cover is sufficient. Most people take the easy option and arrange insurance through their mortgage lender. This is generally the most expensive option. Some direct insurance companies guarantee to cut buildings insurance costs for the majority of homeowners insured through banks and building societies.

The amount for which your home must be insured isn't the current market value, but the cost of rebuilding it, should it be totally destroyed. This varies depending on the type of property and the area. For example, an inexpensive terraced house in the north of England could cost twice its market value to rebuild whereas a more expensive detached property in the south of England may cost a lot less than its market value to rebuild, given the high value of land. There's generally no deduction for wear and tear and the cost of redecoration is usually met in full. Buildings insurance doesn't cover structural faults that existed when you took out the policy, which is why it's important to have a full structural survey done when buying a property.

Many people pay far too much for their buildings insurance, as many insurance companies have greatly over-estimated the cost of rebuilding. In many cases, building costs were calculated using the Royal Institute of Chartered Surveyors (RICS, ⌨ www.ricsfirms.com) Rebuilding Costs Index rather than the correct Tender Price Index, which takes into account actual building prices. The RICS produces a table to calculate the cost of rebuilding your home, which should be used when assessing the cost. If you're in doubt, check how the rebuilding cost of your home was calculated and whether it's correct.

Most lenders provide index-linked buildings insurance, where premiums are linked to inflation and building costs (premiums are usually added to your monthly mortgage payments). It is, however, your responsibility to ensure that your level of cover is adequate, particularly if you carry out improvements or extensions which substantially increase the value of your home. All lenders provide information and free advice. If your level of cover is too low, an insurance company is within its rights to reduce the amount it pays out when a claim is made, in which case you may find you cannot afford to have your house rebuilt or repaired, should disaster strike.

The cost of buildings insurance varies according to the insurer, the type of building and the area, and is calculated per £1,000 of insurance, e.g. from £1.25 per £1,000 of cover per year in an inexpensive area to between £ 2.50 to £4 (or over £4 in London) in more expensive areas. Therefore, insurance on a property costing £100,000 to rebuild usually costs from £125 to £400 per year. In recent years, increased competition, particularly from direct insurers, has helped to moderate premium increases. Shop around, as many people can reduce their premiums by half. (But don't believe the advertising blurb, as some companies that claim to save you money actually charge more).

Insurance for 'non-standard' homes, such as those with thatched roofs, timber construction, holiday homes, period properties and listed buildings, is usually much higher. Owners of houses vulnerable to subsidence (e.g. those built on clay) and those living in flood-prone areas (whose numbers are increasing, as more residential housing is built on flood plains and weather changes increase the risk of flooding) are likely to pay much higher premiums. The highest level of cover usually includes damage to glass (e.g. windows and patio doors) and porcelain (e.g. baths, washbasins and WCs), although you may have to pay extra for accidental damage, e.g. when your son blasts a cricket ball through the patio window. Always ask your insurer what **isn't** covered and what it costs to include it (if required).

It's estimated that over a million people pay too much for their insurance cover, because their insurers have wrongly assumed that they're at risk from subsidence. (Even when your home isn't at risk from subsidence, it's difficult to find a policy that excludes it). Subsidence is a risk primarily in east and south England, exacerbated by a series of warm, dry years beginning in the '90s.

Premiums can usually be paid monthly (although there may be an extra charge) or annually. Some home insurance policies charge an excess (e.g. £50 or £100) for each claim, while others have an excess for certain claims only, e.g. subsidence or landslip, which is usually £1,000 or £2,000.

Many insurance companies provide emergency telephone numbers for policyholders requiring urgent advice. Should you need to make emergency repairs, e.g. to weather-proof a roof after a storm or other natural disaster, most insurance companies allow work up to a certain limit (e.g. £1,000) to be carried out without an estimate or approval from the insurance company, but check first. If you let your house (or part of it) or you intend leaving it unoccupied for a period of 30 days or longer, you must usually inform your insurance company. A booklet entitled *Buildings Insurance for Home Owners*, including a valuation table, is available from the Association of British Insurers (🖥 www.abi.org.uk, see address on page 335).

Buildings insurance is often combined with home contents insurance (see below), when it may be termed household insurance, although it's often cheaper to buy buildings and home contents insurance separately.

HOME CONTENTS INSURANCE

Home contents insurance (also called house insurance) is recommended for anyone who doesn't live in an empty house. Burglary and house-breaking are a major problem (particularly in cities) and there's a burglary every minute somewhere. A 2003 report commissioned by *The Sunday Times* studied actual (as opposed to government) crime figures. It showed that the UK suffers some of the highest burglary rates in the world. A British home is almost twice as likely to be burgled as one in the US and three times more likely than a home in France.

Although there's a lot you can do to prevent someone breaking into your home, it's often impossible or prohibitively expensive to make your home burglar-proof without turning it into a fortress. However, you can ensure that you have adequate contents insurance and that your most precious possessions are locked in a safe or safety deposit box.

Types of Policy

A basic home contents policy covers your belongings against the same sort of 'natural disasters' as buildings insurance (see page 347). You can optionally insure against accidental damage and all risks. A basic contents policy doesn't usually include such items as credit cards (and their fraudulent use), cash, musical instruments, jewellery (and other valuables), antiques, paintings, sports equipment and bicycles, for which you must normally take out extra cover. You can usually insure your property for its second-hand value (indemnity) or its full replacement value (new for old). This covers everything except clothes and linen (for which wear and tear is assessed) at the new cost price. Replacement value is the most popular form of contents insurance. It's best to take out an index-linked policy, where the level of cover is automatically increased by a percentage or fixed amount each year.

A basic policy doesn't usually cover accidental damage (caused by you or members of your family to your own property) or your home freezer contents (in the event of a breakdown or power failure). A basic policy may include replacement locks, garden contents, personal liability insurance (see below), loss of oil and metered water, and temporary accommodation. If not included, these can usually be covered optionally. Some policies include legal expenses cover (e.g. up to £50,000) for disputes with neighbours, shops, suppliers, employers and anyone who provides you with a service. Most contents policies include public liability cover up to £1 million. Items such as computers and mobile phones may need to be listed as named items on your policy, and equipment used for business isn't usually covered (or may be covered only for a prohibitive extra payment). If you have friends or lodgers in your home, their personal property won't usually be covered by your policy.

Premiums

Premiums depend largely on where you live and your insurer. All insurance companies assess the risk by location based on your postcode. **Check before buying a home, as the difference between low and high-risk areas can be as much as 500 per cent!** The difference between premiums charged by companies for the same property can also vary by as much as 200 per cent. Annual premiums are usually calculated per £1,000 of cover and range from around £3 to £4 in a low-risk area to between £12 and £20 in a high-risk area, sometimes more. Although many homeowners in high-risk areas would be willing to forego theft insurance, insurance companies are unwilling to offer this, because premiums would be substantially reduced if theft was omitted (theft is a convenient excuse to load premiums). Your premiums are also higher if you live in a flood-prone area.

As with buildings insurance, it's important to shop around for the lowest premiums, which vary considerably depending on the insurer. If you're already insured, you may find that you can save money by changing insurers, particularly if you're insured through a bank or building society, which are usually the most expensive. However, watch out for penalties when switching insurers.

Combining your home contents insurance with your buildings insurance (see page 349) may save you money, although it's often cheaper to buy separate insurance. However, it can be advantageous to have your buildings and contents insurance with the same insurer, as this avoids disputes over which company should pay for which item, as could arise if you have a fire or flood affecting your home and its contents. Those aged over 50 or 55 (and possibly first-time homeowners) are offered discounts or special rates by some companies (e.g. Saga, 💻 www.saga.co.uk, who specialise in insurance for people over 50). Some companies also provide special policies for students in college accommodation or lodgings (ask an insurance broker).

Security

Most insurers offer no-claims discounts or discounts for homes with burglar alarms, high security locks, neighbourhood watch schemes and smoke detectors. In high-risk areas, good security is a condition of insurance. Beware of the small print in policies, particularly those regarding security, which insurers often use to avoid paying claims. You forfeit all rights under your policy if you leave doors or windows open (or the keys under a mat or flower pot), particularly if you've claimed a discount due to your 'Fort Knox' security. If there are no signs of forced entry, e.g. a broken window, you may be unable to claim for a theft. You should inform your insurer of any changes that may affect your policy, e.g. a storm blows away a wall of your house. If you're going to leave your house empty for a long period, e.g. a month or longer, you should inform your insurer.

Sum-insured or Bedroom-rated?

There are two ways to insure your possessions: 'sum-insured' (where you calculate the cover you need and the insurer works out the premium based on the cover required) and 'bedroom-rated' policies (where you pay a set premium based on the number of bedrooms). Take care that you don't under-insure your house contents (including anything rented such as a television (TV) or video recorder) and that you periodically reassess their value and adjust your premium accordingly (half of all homeowners are thought to underestimate the value of their home contents). Your contents should include everything that isn't part of the fixtures and fittings and which you could take with you if you were moving house. If you under-insure your contents, your claim may be reduced by the percentage by which you're under-insured.

With a bedroom-rated policy, the insurance company cannot scale down a claim because of under-insurance; however, you're usually better off calculating the value of the contents to be insured. Some companies have economy, standard and deluxe rates for contents valued, for example, from £10,000 to £40,000. You can take out a special policy if you have high-value contents, which may be cheaper than a standard contents policy. However, this usually requires a valuation costing around £300 and therefore isn't worthwhile unless your home contents are worth over £50,000. **Always list all previous burglaries on the proposal form, even if nothing was stolen.**

Worldwide Cover

An 'all risks' (also termed a worldwide or extra cover) policy is offered by most insurance companies as an extension to a home contents policy. With this type of policy, your personal possessions (such as jewellery, watches and cameras) are covered against accidental loss or damage outside your home, anywhere in the world. Usually each item valued above a minimum sum, e.g. £250 to £1,000 must be declared in writing (it's wise to take photographs of your valuables and to keep a record of the make and serial numbers of valuable items). The cost is between £12 and £35 per year for each £1,000 covered, depending on where you live.

Claims

Some insurers provide a 24-hour emergency helpline for policyholders and emergency assistance for repairs for domestic emergencies, such as a blocked drain or electrical failure, up to a maximum limit (e.g. £200) for each claim. Take care when completing a claims form, as insurers have tightened up on claims and few people receive a full settlement. Many insurers have an excess of from £25 to £75 on claims. If you make a claim, you must usually wait months for it to be settled. Generally, the larger the claim, the longer you have to wait for your money, although in an emergency, most companies make an interim payment. If you aren't satisfied with the amount offered, don't accept it and try to negotiate a higher figure. If you still cannot reach agreement on the amount, you can contact the financial ombudsman for independent arbitration.

PERSONAL LIABILITY INSURANCE

Although common on the continent of Europe and in North America (where people sue each other for millions at the drop of a hat), personal or legal liability insurance is unusual in the UK. However, home contents policies (see above) usually include personal liability insurance up to £1 million and it's usually included in a travel policy (see below). Personal liability insurance covers individuals and members of their families against compensation for accidental damage, injury or death caused to third parties or their property. It usually covers anything from spilling wine on your neighbour's Persian carpet to your dog or child biting someone.

HOLIDAY & TRAVEL INSURANCE

Holiday and travel insurance is recommended for all who don't wish to risk having their holiday or travel ruined by financial problems or to arrive home broke. As you probably know, anything can and often does go wrong with a holiday, sometimes before you even get started (particularly when you don't have insurance). The following information applies equally to residents and non-residents, whether they're travelling to or from the UK or within the UK. Nobody should visit the UK without travel (and health) insurance!

Travel insurance is available from many sources, including the Post Office, travel agents, insurance companies and agents, banks, automobile clubs and transport companies (airline, rail, ferry and bus). Package holiday companies and tour operators offer insurance policies, some of which are compulsory, too expensive and don't provide adequate cover. You can also buy 24-hour accident and flight insurance at major airports, although it's expensive and doesn't offer the best cover. Before taking out travel insurance, carefully consider the range and level of cover you require and compare policies.

Short-term holiday and travel insurance policies should include cover for holiday cancellation or interruption; missed flights; departure delay at the start and end of a holiday (a common occurrence); delayed, lost or damaged baggage; personal effects and money; medical expenses and accidents (including evacuation home); flight insurance; personal liability and legal expenses and default or bankruptcy insurance, e.g. against a tour operator or airline going broke.

The cost of travel insurance varies considerably, depending on where you buy it, how long you intend to stay in the UK and your age. Generally, the longer the period covered, the cheaper the daily cost, although the maximum period covered is usually limited, e.g. six months. With some policies, an excess must be paid for each claim. As a rough guide, travel insurance for the UK (and most other European countries) costs from around £20 for one week, £35 for two weeks and £70 for a month for a family of four (two adults and two children under 16). Premiums may be higher for those aged over 65 or 70.

If you must make a claim, you should provide as much documentary evidence as possible to support it. Travel insurance companies gladly take your money, but they aren't always so keen to pay claims and you may have to persevere before they pay up. Always be persistent and make a claim irrespective of any small print, as this may be unreasonable and therefore invalid in law. Insurance companies usually require you to obtain a written report and report a loss (or any incident for which you intend to make a claim) to the local police or carriers within 24 hours. Failure to do so may mean that a claim won't be considered.

Health Cover

Medical expenses are an important aspect of travel insurance and you shouldn't rely on insurance provided by reciprocal health arrangements (see **National Health Service** on page 307), charge and credit card companies, household policies or private medical insurance (unless it's an international policy), none of which usually provide adequate cover. However, you should take advantage of what they offer. The minimum medical insurance recommended by experts is around £280,000 in the UK and the rest of Europe, and £1 million for the rest of the world (many policies have limits of between £1.5million to £5.25 million). If applicable, check whether pregnancy-related claims are covered and whether there are any restrictions for those over a certain age, e.g. 65 or 70 (travel insurance is becoming increasingly expensive for those aged over 65).

Always check any exclusion clauses in contracts by obtaining a copy of the full policy document, as not all relevant information is included in an insurance leaflet. High-risk sports and pursuits should be specifically covered and listed in a policy (there's usually an additional premium). Special winter sports policies are available, which are more expensive than normal holiday insurance ('dangerous' sports are excluded from most standard policies). Third-party liability cover should be £2 million for North America and £1 million for the rest of the world. This doesn't cover you when you're using a car or other mechanically-propelled vehicle.

Annual Policies

For people who travel abroad frequently, whether on business or pleasure, an annual travel policy usually provides the best value, but carefully check exactly what it includes. Many insurance companies offer annual travel policies for a premium of around £70 for an individual (the equivalent of around three months insurance with a standard travel insurance policy). Trailfinders (☎ 0845-058 5858, 💻 www.trail finders.com) and other companies also offer competitive deals for two individuals. For example, an annual policy for travel within Europe costs around £100 for two people, allowing individual trips of up to 45 days. Worldwide annual policies, allowing individual trips of up to 70 days, cost around £150 for two people. Some insurance companies also offer an 'emergency travel policy' for holiday homeowners who must travel abroad at short notice to inspect a property, e.g. after a severe storm.

The cost of an annual policy may depend on the area covered, e.g. Europe, worldwide (excluding North America) and worldwide (including North America), although it doesn't usually cover travel within your country of residence. There's also a limit on the number of trips a year and the duration of each trip, e.g. 90 or 120 days.

MOTOR BREAKDOWN INSURANCE

Breakdown insurance for cars and motorcycles, when travelling within the UK and in most European countries, is available from British motoring organisations (see **Motoring Organisations** on page 294). Travel insurance for motoring holidays is also available from travel agents, banks and building societies.

14.

FINANCE

Competition for your money has never been fiercer and, in addition to many British and foreign banks, financial services are provided by building societies, investment brokers, insurance companies, the post office and even large chain stores, supermarkets and service organisations. London is the most important financial market in Europe and the third most important in the world after Tokyo and New York. Deductions from gross salary, including income tax, social security and other benefit contributions, total an average of around 30 per cent (overall the tax burden has increased in recent years when direct and indirect taxes are taken into account). However, taxes (particularly income tax) are still lower in the UK than in many other European countries. The cost of living has been steadily rising in recent years and the UK is now one of the most expensive countries in Europe in which to live and London one of the most expensive cities in the world.

The UK is a credit-financed society (in recent years, debt has doubled, while savings have halved) and companies queue up to lend you money or give you credit – although they're more circumspect than they were in the '80s when they would lend to anyone. Credit and assorted other plastic cards have largely replaced 'real' money and now account for over 75 per cent of all retail purchases. Britons owe over £16 billion on credit cards and almost five per cent of cardholders owe £5,000 or more. Your financial standing is usually decided by the number of cards you have, which include credit cards, cash cards, debit cards, cheque guarantee cards, charge cards, store cards and affinity cards. British banks are following the US's example and are trying to introduce a cashless society: in future to be cardless may equate to being creditless.

The UK has been one of the least regulated financial service industries in the western world, in the sense that there are few controls over interest rates and charges, although recently-created regulatory bodies should tighten things up. Currently, however, anyone can set himself up as an investment expert and charge whatever fees and interest he wishes. The UK has been described as the financial rip-off centre of Europe and it's estimated that finance companies overcharge small investors by over £500 million per year. Personal finance is a jungle and there are plenty of predators about just waiting to get their hands on your loot. Always shop around for financial services and never sign a contract unless you know exactly what the costs and implications are. Although bankers, financiers and brokers don't like to make too fine a point of it, they aren't doing business with you because they like you, but simply to get their hands on your pile of chips. It's up to you to make sure that their share is kept to a minimum and that you receive the best possible value for your money. **When dealing with financial 'experts', bear in mind that while making mistakes is easy, fouling up completely requires professional help!**

When you arrive in the UK to take up residence or employment, make sure you have sufficient cash, credit cards, luncheon vouchers, coffee machine tokens, silver dollars, gold sovereigns and diamonds to last at least until your first pay day, which may be some time after your arrival. Don't, however, carry a lot of cash. During this period you will find that a credit card or two is useful. Among the many British eccentricities is the government's financial tax 'year', that runs from 6th April to 5th April of the following year. There are numerous books and magazines published to help you manage your finances, including *The Penguin Guide to Personal Finance* by Alison Mitchell (Penguin) and the *Moneywise Family Finance Guide* (Clark Publishing). The Consumers' Association (see page 479) publishes a number of excellent financial books, including *450 Money Questions Answered, Getting the Best Deal for Your Money, Which? Way to Save and Invest, Finance Your Future* and *How to Buy, Sell and Own Shares*. Personal finance magazines include *Personal Finance, Money Observer, What Investment* and *Moneywise*. Personal finance information (including the best loan and mortgage interest rates) is published in the financial pages of the Saturday and Sunday editions of national newspapers, and is also available via the television teletext information service and on the internet. For information regarding pensions, see page 340.

The figures and information contained in this chapter are based on current law and Inland Revenue practice, which are subject to change (frequently).

BRITISH CURRENCY

As you're probably aware, the British unit of currency is the pound sterling, which is currently very strong, sterling's early 2007 rise above US$2.00 is a consequence of sterling strength which the population hopes will limit the need for interest rates to be raised.

The British pound has a number of colloquial names, including quid and smacker. Fiver (£5) and tenner (£10) are also commonly used. The pound is divided into 100 pence and British coins are minted in 1p and 2p (bronze); 5p, 10p, 20p and 50p (cupro-nickel); and one (nickel-brass) and two (bronze outer rim, cupro-nickel centre) pounds. The 20p and 50p coins are seven-sided; all other coins are round. Smaller, lighter coins have been introduced in recent years, although British coins are still heavier than those in many other countries. Banknotes are printed in denominations of £5, £10, £20 and £50 pounds; the higher the denomination, the larger the note (it's best to avoid £50 notes, as many people seem to think they're homemade). Forgery is a problem in most western countries and there are a 'significant number' of forged notes in circulation, so be on your guard if someone insists on paying a large bill in cash (the £20 note was redesigned again early in 2007 to thwart counterfeiters).

If you believe that banks have a licence to print money, with respect to Scottish and Northern Irish banks, you would be absolutely correct. Shopkeepers and traders don't legally need to accept notes issued by Scottish and Northern Irish banks (which include a £1 note, replaced by a coin in England and Wales, and a £100 note), even in Scotland and Northern Ireland. Scottish banknotes are naturally accepted without question in Scotland, but understandably they aren't so well received in the rest of the UK. Don't take Scottish or Northern Irish banknotes abroad, as you will receive a much lower exchange rate than for Bank of England banknotes (that's if anyone accept them at all). The Channel Islands and the Isle of Man have some local coins and notes, but the monetary system is the same as in the rest of the UK.

FOREIGN CURRENCY

The UK has no currency restrictions and you may bring in or take out as much money as you wish, in practically any currency. The major British banks change most foreign bank notes (but not coins), but usually give a better exchange rate for travellers' cheques than for bank notes (although travellers' cheques have been rendered obsolete by debit and cash cards according to most travel experts). In addition to banks, many travel agents, hotels and shops in major cities change or accept foreign currency, but usually at a less favourable exchange rate than banks. There are currency exchange machines at some international airports where you can change a range of foreign currencies for sterling.

Buying & Selling Currency

When buying or selling foreign currency, beware of excessive charges. Apart from differences in exchange rates, which are posted by all banks and *bureaux de change*, there may be a significant difference in charges. Most high street banks and building societies charge 1 or 2 per cent commission with a minimum charge of £2 or £2.50 (some, such as Nationwide, have scrapped commission charges). All banks and building societies buy and sell foreign currency, although not all stock foreign currency and you must often order it two or three days in advance. You can also buy and sell foreign currency at main post offices, although you must order currency at sub-post offices 24 hours in advance. Post offices charge 1 per cent commission on currency exchange (with a minimum fee of £2.50) and accept payment by credit card.

Exchange Rates

It pays to shop around for the best exchange rates (the worst rates are offered by high street banks), particularly if you're changing a lot of money (it's possible to bargain over rates in some establishments). Most banks have a spread of up to 8 per cent between their buying and selling rates for foreign currencies. The sterling exchange rate against most European and major international currencies is listed in banks and the quality daily newspapers. **Don't change money at hotels or the ubiquitous independent *Bureaux de Change* in London and other cities, unless you have no choice or money to burn, as they levy high charges or offer poor exchange rates.**

Cash Transfers

If you have money transferred to the UK by banker's draft or a letter of credit, bear in mind that it may take up to two weeks to be cleared. You can also have money sent to you by international money order (MoneyGram) via a post office, a cashier's cheque or telegraphic transfer, e.g. via Western Union (the quickest, safest and most expensive method). You usually need your passport to collect money transferred from abroad or to cash a banker's draft (or other credit note). If you're sending money abroad, it's best to send it in the local currency so that the recipient won't have to pay conversion charges. Some countries have foreign exchange controls limiting the amount of money that can be sent abroad. Insured post is the only safe way to send cash, as the insured value is refunded if the money is lost or stolen.

Postal orders can be sent to Commonwealth countries and a Girobank post office transfer can be made to most countries (usually free when transferring money to a Girobank holder). Postcheques (Girobank customers only) can be sent to certain countries. You can also send money direct from your bank to another bank via an interbank transfer. Most banks have a minimum service charge for international transfers, which generally makes it expensive, particularly for small sums. Overseas banks also take a cut, usually a percentage (e.g. 1 or 2 per cent) of the amount transferred. **When travelling anywhere don't rely on one source of funds only.**

CREDIT RATING

Whether you're able to get credit (or how much) usually depends on your credit rating, which is becoming increasingly important in today's financial world. Most financial institutions use credit scoring and a credit reference agency report to find out whether you're creditworthy. If you're newly arrived in the UK, a lender may use an agency in your previous country of residence. If you're refused credit, you can ask why and can demand (on payment of a £2 fee) to see the credit agency's file on you (they cannot refuse), which must be supplied within 40 days. You can obtain a copy of your credit file by writing to Experian, Consumer Help Service, PO Box 8000, Nottingham NG80 7WF or checking with Equifax (💻 www.econsumer.equifax.co.uk); to be safe it's advisable to check with both agencies. Individuals can also check the credit rating of a company or person with whom they're planning to do business.

In many cases, files are found to contain false information or information about unpaid debts belonging to family, friends or neighbours, or because a person shared an address with someone. If the information in your file is incorrect, you have the right to demand that an agency removes the false information or corrects it, which should be done within 28 days. You must show that information was registered in error, that your defence wasn't considered (perhaps through being abroad at the time), or that the amount owed was paid in full within a month of a county court judgment. If an agency doesn't correct false information, you can appeal to the Information Commissioner's Office, Wycliffe House, Water Lane, Wilmslow, Cheshire SK9 5AF (☎ 01625-545 745). Write giving full particulars of the incorrect information and the date you sent a correction to an agency.

Banks and other financial institutions usually have a credit scoring system, based on information received from credit reference agencies. If you have a bad credit rating, it's almost impossible to obtain credit. Your credit score depends on many factors, such as your age and occupation, marital status, how long you've held your current job, whether you're a homeowner, where you live, whether you're on the electoral roll, whether you have a telephone and your credit track record. However, if you're able to provide collateral (i.e. security, such as a property), for example for a bank loan, people will fall over themselves to lend you money (particularly those who charge extortionate interest rates). Finally, if you're refused credit, try looking on the bright side: without credit you cannot run up any debts.

The Office of Fair Trading (☎ 08457-224 499) publishes a leaflet entitled *No Credit* and the CCN Group (Consumer Help Service, CCN Group, PO Box 40, Notts. NG7 2SS, ☎ 0115-976 8747) publishes a free leaflet entitled *Helping You to Understand Your Credit File*.

BANKS & BUILDING SOCIETIES

The major British banks with branches in most towns throughout the UK (termed 'high street' banks) include the National Westminster (🖥 www.natwest.com), Barclays (🖥 www.barclays.co.uk), Lloyds TSB (🖥 www.lloydstsb.com), HSBC (🖥 www.hsbc.co.uk) and the Abbey (🖥 www.abbey.com). Other major banks with branches in large towns are the Bank of Scotland (part of HBOS Group, 🖥 www.bankofscotland.co.uk), the Royal Bank of Scotland (🖥 www.rbs.co.uk) and the Co-operative Bank (🖥 www.co-operativebank.co.uk). There are also telephone banks (including First Direct, 🖥 www.firstdirect.com) that don't have branches and are 'open' 24 hours per day. For the wealthy, there are many private banks (mainly portfolio management) and foreign banks abound in major cities (there are over 500 foreign banks in the City of London alone). Most banks have websites and many offer online banking, a rapidly growing area. In recent years, there has been a flood of new-style 'banks' such as Virgin Direct, supermarkets and shops such as Marks and Spencer, who have shaken up the traditional high street banks with their innovative accounts and services.

Banks provide free banking for personal customers who remain in credit, pay interest on account balances and offer a range of financial services (although they usually **aren't** the best place to buy insurance or pensions). If you do a lot of travelling abroad, you may find the comprehensive range of services offered by the high street banks advantageous. In a small country town or village, there's usually a sub-post office, but not usually a bank. Many services provided by banks are also provided by Building Societies (see below).

The relationship between the major banks and their customers has deteriorated in the last decade. During the recession, banks dramatically increased their charges to personal and business customers to recoup their losses on bad loans to developing countries. Few people have a good word to say about their banks, which are widely perceived to be profit-hungry, impersonal and definitely not customer-friendly. Complaints against banks have risen greatly in recent years. Banks made record profits (running into billions of pounds) in the '90s and early 2000s, which has served only to further annoy customers. Many think their banks are ripping them off: for example, it can take four days to transfer cash from one account to another over the internet, a transaction that should be instantaneous. Often the worst place to buy financial products is from a major high street bank; building societies usually offer better deals.

Not surprisingly, banks aren't exactly happy with their poor public image and most have been busy trying to improve customer relations by introducing codes of conduct and payments for mistakes or poor service. Many people could save money by changing their banks. You shouldn't allow loyalty to prevent you from switching banks as, when times are hard, your bank won't hesitate to withdraw your safety net (during the recession, banks were directly responsible for the failure of hundreds of small businesses through arbitrarily withdrawing or refusing overdrafts and loans).

Building Societies

Building societies date back to 1775 and were originally established to cater for people saving to buy a home. Savers would deposit 5 or 10 per cent of the cost of a home with the building society, which then lent them the balance. A building society would rarely lend to anyone who wasn't a regular saver, although this changed many years ago. In 1987, the regulations governing institutions offering financial services were changed and, as a result, banks and building societies now compete head-on for customers. There has been a wave of mergers and takeovers in recent years, and the number of societies has fallen dramatically. Many building societies have converted to banks (called de-mutualisation) in recent years, offering account holders large cash incentives as an inducement to vote in favour of such moves. Many people (known as carpetbaggers) have taken advantage of these pay-outs by opening accounts at a number of building societies.

Nowadays, building societies offer practically all the services provided by banks, including current and savings accounts, cheque guarantee cards, cash cards, personal loans, credit cards, insurance and travel services. In an effort to woo customers away from banks, many building societies produce special brochures and 'transfer packs' (even containing pre-printed 'letters') detailing exactly how to transfer your account. Building societies don't all offer the same services, types of accounts or rates of interest (those offering the best interest rates are often the smaller societies). If you're looking for a long-term investment, the number of branches may not be of importance and members of all building societies can use cash dispensers at other building society branches via the Link system.

Deposit Protection

All banks, including branches and subsidiaries of foreign banks accepting sterling deposits in the UK, must be licensed by the Bank of England and contribute to the Deposit Protection Fund (DPF) which guarantees that 90 per cent of deposits up to £20,000 will be repaid if a bank goes bust. Because of the limit, it's worthwhile spreading your investments around several banks and financial institutions.

Complaints

Banks are very slow to rectify mistakes or to resolve disputes and rarely accept responsibility, even when clearly in the wrong. It has been estimated (based on actual proven cases) that banks routinely overcharge small business customers by hundreds of millions of pounds every year. If your bank makes a mess of your account and causes you to lose money and spend time resolving it, you're quite within your rights to claim financial compensation for your time and trouble, in addition to any financial loss. However, banks typically stall complaints for up to six years and simply use their financial muscle to wear down customers (some banks fight every case in the courts). If you have a complaint against a British bank and have exhausted the bank's complaints procedure, you can apply for independent arbitration to the Financial Ombudsman Service, South Quay Plaza, 183 Marsh Wall, London E14 9SR (☎ 0845-080 1800).

If you have a complaint against a building society and have exhausted its complaints procedure, you can apply for independent arbitration to the Financial Ombudsman Service (☎ 0845-080 1800). Deposits in British building society accounts are protected by a similar compensation scheme to that for banks, under which you're guaranteed to receive 90 per cent of your investment (up to a maximum of £20,000) if it goes bust.

Business Hours

Normal bank opening hours are from 9 or 9.30am until 3.30 or 4pm (some are open until 5.30pm) Mondays to Fridays, with no shutdown over the lunch period in cities and most towns. Most branches are open late one day per week until between 5.30 or 6pm (it varies according to the bank and its location) and many open on Saturdays, e.g. from 9.30am until 12.30pm (some are open until 3.30pm). Most banks in Scotland and all banks in Northern Ireland close for an hour at lunchtime. Building societies are generally open from 9am to 5pm, Mondays to Fridays, and from 9am to noon on Saturdays. *Bureaux de change* have longer opening hours, including Saturdays and Sundays in tourist areas and large cities, but should be used in dire circumstances only, owing to their high commission and/or poor exchange rates. When banks are closed, you can change money at post offices, which are usually open from 9am to 5.30pm, Mondays to Fridays, and from 9am to 12.30pm on Saturdays. All banks are closed on public holidays which are generally called bank holidays.

Most banks at major airports are open from 6.30 or 7am to 11 or 11.30pm, seven days per week, and some airports, e.g. London's Gatwick and Heathrow airports, have 24-hour banks. Some banks at London railway stations also have extended opening hours (e.g. those at Victoria). Most banks, building societies and main post offices have 24-hour cash dispensers/machines (officially called Automatic Teller Machines/ATMs) at branches for cash withdrawals, deposits and checking account balances. Cash machines are also located in some supermarkets and other large stores.

Opening an Account

If you're planning to work in the UK and will be paid monthly, one of your first acts should be to open a current (or cheque) account with a bank, building society or the Girobank (post office), in common with over 80 per cent of the British working population. Your salary is usually paid directly into your account by your employer (many insist that your salary is paid into an account) and your salary statement is sent to your home address or given to you at work.

On arrival in the UK, you may need to wait up to two months for your first pay cheque. Although this is unusual, you should check with your employer, who may (if necessary) give you a salary advance. Employees who are paid weekly are often paid in cash, in which case it's up to you whether you open a bank or building society account (although it's difficult to survive without one nowadays). Many people have at least two accounts, a current account for their out-of-pocket expenses and day-to-day transactions, and a savings account for long-term savings (or money put aside for a rainy day). Many people have bank and building society accounts. Before opening an account, compare bank charges, interest rates (e.g. on credit cards) and other services offered by a number of banks. **If you're planning to buy a home with a mortgage, one of the best accounts is an all-in-one account or mortgage current account** (see **Mortgages** on page 375).

To open an account, you simply go to the bank or building society of your choice and tell them you're living in the UK and wish to open an account. You will be asked for proof of identity, e.g. usually a passport or driving licence, plus proof of address in the form of a utility bill. Foreign residents may be required to provide a reference from their employer or a foreign bank. Many banks provide new account holders with a free cash card wallet, cheque book cover and statement file. After opening an account, don't forget to give the details to your employer (if you want to get paid). The facilities you should expect from a current account include a cheque book; a paying-in book; a cheque guarantee card (preferably £100 or £250); interest paid on credit balances; no charges or fees when in credit; a free cash card and lots of cash machines; a free debit card; monthly statements; an automatic authorised overdraft facility; and the availability of credit cards. Most of these are standard.

With a current account you receive a cheque book (usually containing 30 cheques) and a cash card (see page 368). A cheque guarantee card is usually provided on request and guarantees cheques up to £50, £100 or £250. When using a cheque guarantee card, the card number must be written on the back of the cheque. Most businesses won't accept a cheque without a guarantee card. A cheque book usually also contains paying-in slips (at the back), with which you can make payments into your account. You also receive a separate paying-in book.

Most people pay their bills from their current account, by standing order or by cheque. Bank statements are usually issued monthly (optionally quarterly). Interest may be paid on deposits (usually quarterly) and an overdraft facility may be provided. Most banks don't levy any charges on a current account, provided that you stay in credit. However, if you overdraw your account without a prior arrangement with your bank, you may be billed for bank charges on all transactions for the accounting period (usually three months).

Cheques

Cheques are usually crossed, which normally takes the form of two parallel lines across the face of the cheque. A crossed cheque theoretically provides additional security, because it can be paid only into a bank account and cannot be cashed by a bank. Banks don't recommend uncrossed cheques, although some supply them. To obtain cash from a bank, write the cheque in your own name or write 'cash' alongside 'Pay' (but never send a cheque made out to cash through the post). If you make a mistake when writing a cheque, you can change it, but the correction must be initialled.

Take great care when sending cheques through the post, particularly for large amounts, as cheques can be stolen and paid into another account, from which the money is quickly withdrawn. Crooks often steal post from post offices and pay cheques into their own accounts. They simply use the name of the payee, but their own account number and banks don't check that the payee and account number tally. This makes a mockery of the safety of cheques! Cheque fraud is rising and the British Bankers' Association recommends not paying bills through the post. Cheques usually take three to five days to clear (some banks make customers wait up to ten days for clearance), although some banks have scrapped the cheque-clearing period on payments and credit cheques of up to £1,000.

Cheque Safeguards

There are a number of ways to safeguard your cheques, one of which is to add the words 'account payee only' to the crossing, in between the two parallel lines (most banks now only issue cheques with this pre-printed). Although this has no legal significance, it means that your bank should only credit the account of the named payee and they would be considered negligent if they credited an 'account payee only' cheque to the wrong account. If sending cheques through the post, make sure you use registered mail or a courier that records delivery.

Claims

If a cheque is converted, cashed, negotiated or transferred unlawfully, your bank will probably take refuge behind the law and refuse to accept any responsibility (unless you have billions on deposit). However, if the amount or other details on a cheque are changed and your bank pays out, it cannot make you liable for the forgery. If you're a victim of fraud and believe your bank or building society was negligent, you should demand compensation. If it isn't offered, you should take your case to the banking ombudsman (see page 363).

Charges

All banks make a charge for 'bounced' cheques. If you accidentally go into the red for a few days and are charged bank charges for a full month or three months, a complaint to your bank manager in writing, if necessary, threatening to transfer your account elsewhere, may get you a reduction (if not, you can always carry out your threat). Most banks and building societies have a long list of service charges for current accounts. However, provided you stay in credit, it's still possible to avoid paying charges by shopping around. If you're thinking of changing bank (or building society), check carefully whether you will lose any important benefits such as a credit card (with a high spending limit) or a preferential loan or overdraft facility.

High-interest Cheque Accounts

Most banks and building societies offer high-interest cheque accounts for customers who maintain a minimum balance, e.g. £1,000. These accounts offer a range of benefits, including a cheap overdraft facility and a £250 cheque guarantee card. Some current accounts pay variable rates of interest depending on the account balance. Interest on high-interest accounts may be paid monthly and there's usually no transaction or monthly fees. If you don't need instant access to large sums of cash, you're better off with a Savings Account (see page 367). **It's never wise to keep a lot of cash in an account with a cash card, as fraudulent withdrawals aren't unknown!**

It would appear that many people have money to throw away, as they keep quite large sums in accounts that pay no interest or minimal interest only, e.g. 0.5 per cent. Naturally, banks don't go out of their way to explain to customers the most advantageous accounts for their money, or indeed even explain about account fees or charges (which helps boost their profits by millions each year). Even modest balances in an interest-earning account can earn enough to ward off inflation. If you never overdraw on your current account and aren't being paid interest, you're making a free loan to your bank (something they most certainly **won't** do for you).

SAVINGS ACCOUNTS

All banks and building societies provide a wide range of savings accounts, also called deposit, term deposit or high-interest accounts, most of which are intended for short or medium-term savings rather than long-term growth. When opening an account, the most important considerations are how much money you wish to save (which may be a lump sum or a monthly amount), how quickly you need access to it in an emergency and whether you're a taxpayer.

Before committing your money to a long-term savings account or investment, shop around, not just among banks and building societies, but also other financial institutions. Interest rates, conditions and fees vary, so take them into account. Banks and building societies often introduce new types of accounts paying increased rates of interest, **but they don't usually notify existing customers of this (some even forbid staff to tell customers about accounts paying higher interest).** The interest rates on obsolete accounts are often less than 0.5 per cent on balances of £500 to £25,000 (no wonder they make large profits!). It's estimated that billions of pounds are languishing in obsolete accounts earning derisory amounts of interest. Interest rates are forever changing (increasing or decreasing in line with the official bank lending rate) and it may not pay you to tie your money up for a long period. When there's a cut in the base rate, most banks cut savings interest rates long before they cut their lending rates. In 2003, savings rates on instant access accounts hit historically low levels.

Most banks and building societies have two basic types of account: instant access and notice accounts. Instant access accounts, as the name implies, allow you instant access to your money. There's usually a minimum balance, although this may be as low as £100. Interest rates usually depend on the account balance, e.g. £100, £1,000, £3,000 or £10,000. With a notice account, you're required to give notice before you make a withdrawal, usually between 30 and 90 days. Notice accounts pay marginally higher rates of interest. If there's any chance that you will need immediate access to your money, you should keep it in an instant access account (the extra interest on the best 90-day accounts is usually only around 0.5 to 1 per cent more than on the best instant access accounts). Interest is paid quarterly, half-yearly or yearly.

You may find a high-interest cheque account useful, as it offers all the usual facilities of a current account, plus high interest depending on the account balance (which must usually be a minimum of £1,000). There are also high-yield bonds and investment accounts for large deposits, e.g. £10,000, provided that you can tie your money up for a long period (at least one year). A monthly income account requires you to invest a lump sum (usually over £1,000) on which you receive a high rate of interest paid monthly. Building societies also offer monthly income accounts and accounts for those who wish to save a regular amount each month. Regular savings accounts usually pay a higher rate of interest, but you may have limited access to your money, e.g. one withdrawal every six months. Taxpayers looking for a long-term investment are usually better off investing in an Individual Savings Account (ISA).

Interest on accounts is paid tax-free (gross) to non-taxpayers, e.g. married women who aren't working, retirees, children and non-residents. Non-taxpayers must complete a form to confirm their tax status; otherwise interest is paid net of basic rate income tax, which can be reclaimed by non-taxpayers. A leaflet entitled *Can you stop paying tax on your bank and building society interest?* (IR110) is available from tax offices. Higher-rate taxpayers are required to declare their interest income on their income tax return. Savings can also be deposited in offshore bank accounts, where interest is paid gross although, if you're a British resident, interest may be taxable.

The best savings interest rates are published in Saturday and Sunday newspapers such as *The Times* and *The Sunday Times*, and in financial magazines such as *Personal Finance*, *Money Observer*, *What Investment* and *Moneywise*. Information is also available via the television teletext information service and on the internet. *Which?* magazine (see **Consumers' Association** on page 479) also offers invaluable advice and surveys.

CASH & DEBIT CARDS

One of the most important innovations in banking in the last 20 years has been the introduction of cash (or cashpoint) and debit cards, which are routinely issued to current account holders.

Cash Cards

A cash card allows you to withdraw money from cash machines (ATMs), 24 hours per day (or 6am to midnight), seven days per week. The freedom from bank queues, banking hours and bank tellers provided by cash cards is very convenient, and you should think twice before opening an account with a bank or building society which doesn't provide cash machines locally (although most small institutions have agreements with other banks or building societies so that you can use their ATMs). Most people prefer to use cash machines rather than make over-the-counter withdrawals.

All banks and building societies issue cash cards, which can be used to withdraw up to £1,000 per day (although a maximum of £250 is more usual) from any of the participating bank's or building society's cash machines (provided that you have the money in your account) or those belonging to the same network. The main networks are Visa, Plus, Cirrus and Link. All major banks have networks of over 5,000 machines. Most banks and building societies allow free withdrawals from machines belonging to the same network, although most levy a 'handling' fee (e.g. 1.5 to 2.25 per cent) for a cash withdrawal from a cash machine belonging to a bank outside their network. However, some building societies, such as Nationwide, don't levy these fees.

Other services offered by banks and building societies via cash machines include mini-statements (usually the last five transactions), account balances, the paying of bills (via a bank giro), deposits, transfers between accounts, cheque book and statement ordering, and the facility to change your personal identification number (PIN), used to validate ATM transactions. These services are usually available only via cash machines located at branches of your own bank.

When your application for a card is approved, your card and PIN are sent under separate cover (for security reasons). If you don't have a secure post box (i.e. a private address or personal post box), you should collect your PIN from your bank. Cards aren't usually sent by registered post. For extra security, some banks activate cards only after customers have reported their safe arrival. **If you receive an unwanted card, cut it up and return it to your bank or building society with instructions to cancel it.** For security reasons, you should **destroy your PIN as soon as you've remembered it and should never write it down (not even coded).**

Although it's relatively rare, cash machines do go wrong and occasionally give the wrong amount of cash, make mistakes on receipts, and 'phantom withdrawals' can turn up on your bank statement. You should obtain a receipt for withdrawals and check them against your statement. If you have a problem with a machine, make a note of its location, the date and time, and exactly what happened. Notify your bank as soon as possible. However, you have only a slim chance of convincing your bank that their 'infallible' machine has made a mistake. The financial services ombudsman investigates more complaints about cash machines than anything else. Don't keep a lot of money in an account for which you have a cash card and **never** have a cash card for a savings account with a large balance. Don't use a cash dispenser in a 'high risk' area at night, as muggings sometimes occur.

If you lose your cash card, you must notify the issuing bank or building society immediately by telephone and confirm it in writing within seven days. Your liability is limited to £50, provided that you aren't negligent, e.g. by writing your PIN where somebody can find it.

Debit Cards

Most cash cards are also debit cards belonging to the 'Switch' or 'Delta' networks. Debit cards are accepted by most retailers and mail-order businesses and have largely replaced cheques. There's no limit to the amount you can pay with a debit card, provided that you have the money in your account or have a pre-arranged overdraft. Debit cards have certain advantages over cheques, one of which is that they eliminate the need for cheque-guarantee limits. Many retailers, e.g. supermarkets, allow customers to obtain up to £50 in cash, known as 'cash-back', when paying a bill with a debit card. Most cash and debit cards can also be used as cheque guarantee cards and can be used abroad, e.g. Visa or MasterCard debit cards, to obtain cash and buy goods and services. They aren't, however, credit cards and you can draw only on funds in your account. There's usually a charge for obtaining cash abroad.

Chip & PIN Cards

New Chip and PIN cards were introduced in October 2003 and offer a higher level of security. When paying for goods with your Chip and PIN card, you now have to enter a four-digit PIN (the same as the PIN you use at the ATM) instead of giving the retailer a paper signature.

Old cards still work on the signature system (as do overseas credit cards), but they are being phased out rapidly.

CHARGE & CREDIT CARDS

The British love plastic money and the UK is one of the most credit-oriented societies in the world. However, banks love them even more, as interest rates on unpaid balances are the highest in Europe. British-based companies offer some 1,500 different brands of plastic – enough to burst the seams of even the fattest of wallets. It has been calculated that, if the over 30 million plastic cards in the UK were laid end to end, they would stretch from the doors of the Bank of England to the shores of Africa. British retail outlets, whatever their size, usually accept credit and charge cards, generally referred to collectively as credit cards.

The main difference between charge and credit cards is that, with a charge card, you defer paying the bill for a few weeks or months, but you **must** pay the total balance outstanding when it's due (otherwise a penalty payment is payable); whereas a credit card allows you to spread your repayments over a period. Credit cards are much more popular than charge cards, both with cardholders and businesses. Credit and charge cards may be issued as ordinary, gold and platinum cards, with different credit and benefit levels. Always sign a card as soon as you receive it. Cards can be used to purchase goods by post or over the telephone or internet, in the UK and abroad, although goods should be sent only to the cardholder's address. Always check that a credit card slip is made out for the correct amount before signing it.

Charge Cards

A charge card allows you to charge the cost of goods and services to a card company and they include American Express (Amex), Diners Club, Eurocard and the Thomas Cook Corporate card. You can also obtain cash via cash machines, although the fee is high. With most charge cards, there's a high spending limit or possibly none at all. Holders of charge cards pay an annual fee to the card company (e.g. Amex and Diners Club fees are £37.50), which may be waived for the first year for new customers. Diners Club also has an enrolment fee of £20. In general, charge cards are issued to high earners only (£20,000 may be the minimum, although the level tends to be lower than formerly, to attract more customers) or those with a high 'net worth'.

Many companies provide their own charge cards for customers, e.g. department and chain stores, petrol companies, British Telecom, car hire companies and airlines.

One of the major advantages of international charge cards is that, if they're lost or stolen, they can usually be replaced at short notice when you're travelling, e.g. within 24 hours, in some countries. Apart from the on-the-spot replacement of lost cards, you will find that charge cards offer few advantages over credit cards (see below), most of which, e.g. Visa or MasterCard, are more widely accepted, in the UK and worldwide. They're also cheaper and more convenient to use.

Credit Cards

Credit cards are issued by most financial institutions, including all banks and building societies, plus a range of other businesses such as car manufacturers, newspapers and travel agents. Visa is the most widely accepted credit card and is issued by most banks, closely followed by MasterCard. Some issuers allow you to choose between MasterCard and Visa or to have both. With the waning popularity of charge cards, American Express introduced a credit card in 1995. Credit cards are definitely not for long-term borrowers although, if you borrow less than £1,000 and pay it off within one year, it's generally cheaper than a loan.

Costs & Interest Rates

Banks compete fiercely for credit card customers, on interest rates and the supplementary services attached to cards. You can apply for a credit card at any bank or building society and it may not be necessary to be a customer. Most charge an annual card fee of between £10 and £12. A number of cards can be issued for one account (a second card is usually issued free). When choosing a card, bear in mind that a free card with no annual fee may have a high interest rate (which is fine if you plan to pay off the balance each month). Interest rates vary considerably from around 10 to 20 per cent, sometimes more, i.e. they're very high, and rarely reduced, even when general interest rates fall. Some banks offer lending tiers, where the higher the balance, the lower the interest rate charged. The best cards are those with no annual fee and a low interest rate, usually restricted to homeowners and/or those with an excellent credit rating. The best credit and store card interest rates are published in the Saturday edition of newspapers such as *The Times* and *The Daily Telegraph*.

Benefits

You should also compare the benefits offered by card issuers, which may include cash discounts on travel bookings; holiday discounts; foreign currency ordering; helplines; air miles; discounts on new cars; points schemes; reduced hotel and car hire rates; free accident travel insurance; and free insurance on goods purchased with cards. Some cards, called affinity cards, have ties with registered charities, where a charity (or a number of charities) benefits with each new card issued and each time a card is used.

Credit Limit

The credit limit for most cardholders starts at around £1,000, although some card issuers allow you to choose your spending limit up to £5,000. Increasing your credit limit is usually a formality, provided that your credit rating is good and you pay your bills on time. When changing card companies, check that you're able to keep your previous credit limit and that you don't lose any important benefits. Many card companies allow existing cardholders to transfer their card balance when switching cards.

Cash Withdrawals

MasterCard and Visa can be used to obtain cash from cash machines in the UK and abroad. You need a PIN to withdraw cash. When you use your card to obtain cash, there's a handling charge and/or commission, e.g. from 1.5 to 2.25 per cent or a minimum of £1.50. There's a daily limit on cash withdrawals in the UK and abroad, e.g. between £200 and £500. There are also hidden charges in currency conversion of from 0.5 to 2.75 per cent. Interest is usually charged on cash withdrawals from the date they're made.

Bills

MasterCard and Visa require you to repay a minimum of £5 or 5 per cent of the balance each month, whichever is higher. If you pay off the full amount outstanding, you aren't charged interest and receive up to seven weeks' free credit. Some credit card issuers offer protection insurance, which covers payments in case of sickness, accident or unemployment (check exactly what's covered), which is worth considering. Protection insurance premiums are calculated according to your account balance and are added to your card payments each month.

Legal Protection

Under the Consumer Credit Act 1974, when you pay for goods or services with plastic you have legal rights against the credit card company as well as the supplier for goods valued from £100 to £30,000 (including bankruptcy of a supplier). Most credit card users can also claim compensation from their credit card company when they buy faulty goods or services abroad. However, not all card issuers are party to this agreement, so check. Claims must usually be made within 90 or 120 days. **If you have a legitimate complaint, you shouldn't pay the bill until you've received satisfaction.**

Lost or Stolen Cards

Over 5,000 credit cards are lost or stolen every day. If you lose a credit card or have it stolen, report it immediately to the police and the issuing office, and confirm the loss in writing as soon as possible.

Insurance

You can insure all your credit, cash and cheque cards for around £12 per year with a number of credit card protection companies, e.g. Sentinel and the Card Protection Plan (☎ 0870-608 1529, 💻 www.cpp.co.uk). If you lose any of your cards, you simply telephone a 24-hour number and the insurance company contacts your card issuers for you. When a signed credit card is lost or stolen, your liability is limited to £50 before notification and nothing after notification (provided that you weren't negligent).

Foreign Cards

Many foreigners can obtain an international charge or credit card in a country other than the UK and be billed in the currency of that country (or retain existing international cards). You may, however, find it more convenient and cheaper to be billed in sterling, rather than a foreign currency, e.g. US$. Where you must wait for the bill from outside the UK, payments may vary due to exchange rate fluctuations and bills may arrive after the 'payment due date'.

Store Cards

Most major department and chain stores issue their own account credit cards, e.g. Marks & Spencer, Debenhams and John Lewis, and some stores don't accept any credit cards but their own, although this practice is declining. Interest rates are quoted monthly and are usually **very** high, e.g. up to double what you pay with a MasterCard or Barclaycard.

Even if you don't like plastic money and shun any form of credit, credit cards do have their uses. For example, no deposits on hire cars (which may only accept payment by credit card), no pre-paying hotel bills, safety and security, and above all, convenience. However, in the wrong hands they're a disaster and should be shunned by spendthrifts.

LOANS

It pays to shop around when you want a loan, as many borrowers pay too much interest on their loans. Interest rates for borrowers are relatively high (even though base rates have been historically low) and vary considerably depending on the lender, the amount, the period of the loan and, most importantly, whether the loan is secured or unsecured. A secured loan is cheaper, for which you must offer collateral as a guarantee against defaulting on the repayments, e.g. a life insurance policy (75 to 90 per cent of the surrender value is usual) or a property. However, you should beware of loans where your home is used as security, as if you fail to repay it, you can lose your home (if you have spare equity in a home, re-mortgaging may be the best way to raise money). If you want a loan to buy a new car, the best deals are usually provided by motor manufacturers. **If you're planning to buy a home with a mortgage, one of the best accounts is a an all-in-one account or a mortgage current account (see Mortgages on page 375), which allows you to borrow at the same rate as your mortgage interest rate.**

The rate of interest charged on loans is quoted as a flat rate or the Annual Percentage Rate (APR), which is the true rate of interest and includes all charges (e.g. documentation fees or maintenance charges). APR is usually just under double the flat rate. All interest rates on goods must, by law, quote the APR figure, so you're able instantly to compare rates. Most personal loans offer a fixed rate of interest throughout the term of the loan. Beware of loans with a variable rate of interest ('APR var.'), as the interest rate could rise and you may be unable to meet the repayments (or your loan repayments could be extended). Some loan repayments are delayed for six months, although you should be aware that low-start interest or deferred loan repayments ultimately cost you much more than ordinary loans.

Always shop around and compare APRs for personal loans from a number of financial institutions, as they vary considerably. It isn't always necessary to have an account with a bank or building society to obtain a loan from them. If you're able to offer security for a loan or can get someone to stand as a guarantor, you're usually eligible for a lower interest rate (with an APR up to 10 per cent lower than an unsecured loan). However, you should be wary of acting as a guarantor for someone else's debts without some sort of security (or at least being prepared for the worst). Anyone providing a loan or mortgage where your home is security must state in their advertising and documentation that 'your home is at risk if you don't keep up repayments on a mortgage or other loan secured on it.'

Borrowing from private loan companies (moneylenders), as advertised in newspapers, is expensive (very high interest rates, plus fees and commission). Use them only as an absolute last resort when **all** other avenues have been exhausted and the loan is a matter of life and death. The UK is a loan shark's paradise and there's little control over interest rates. One loan shark in Glasgow was found to be charging 30p in the £1 each week! Extortionate deals like this are in fact illegal, although there's no legal definition of extortionate and loans with around 50 per cent APR have been judged legal. In general, the more desperate your financial situation, the more suspicious you should be of anyone who's willing to lend you money.

The best personal (unsecured) and secured (by second mortgage) loan rates are published in the Saturday editions of newspapers such as *The Times* and *The Daily Telegraph*.

MORTGAGES

Mortgages are available from a huge number of lenders, including building societies, high street and foreign banks (including offshore banks), direct lenders, finance houses and credit companies, insurance companies, developers, local authorities and even employers. The UK has a fiercely competitive mortgage business with around 150 lenders offering over 3,000 different mortgage products vying for your business. There are over 11 million mortgages in the UK, worth a staggering £750 billion in 2003 – equal to the annual take home pay of the entire country! The average loan of a first-time buyer is over £90,000 and for someone moving up the property ladder is over £100,000.

Mortgage rates were their lowest for 50 years a few years ago but have now steadily increased as the Bank of England attempts to control spending and reduce inflation. However, by shopping around for the best rate you can still knock 1 or 2 per cent off the standard interest rate for several years, pay off some of your loan without charge or switch to another lender for a better deal. Surveys consistently show that homeowners are losing out on potential savings of £billions a year by failing to switch to more competitive home loans. Overpaying on your mortgage in order to pay it off early saves you tens of thousands of pounds in interest and is recommended when the interest paid on savings is low.

In England, Wales and Northern Ireland, you can apply for a mortgage after an offer on a property is accepted. **In Scotland you must apply for a mortgage and have it approved before making an offer on a property.** If the offer is successful, it's legally binding and you're contractually obliged to complete the purchase, which isn't the case in the rest of the UK.

A voluntary Mortgage Code for lenders was introduced in the '90s which sets standards of good mortgage advisory practice and provides safeguards for clients. Details are contained in a booklet (published in large print, audio and braille formats), available from lenders or from the Council of Mortgage Lenders, 3 Savile Row,

London W1S 3PB (☎ 020-7437 0075 for recorded information, 💻 www.cml.org.uk). However, the code has been criticised as too vague and is broken by many lenders.

Income

Three factors determine whether you can obtain a mortgage and its size: income, credit history and the property itself (lenders won't lend on a ruin). If you're an employee in steady employment, you should have no problem obtaining a mortgage, although whether it's enough to buy the home you want is another matter entirely.

You can usually borrow up to 3.75 times your gross (pre-tax) salary or 2.75 times the joint income of a couple. For example, if you earn £30,000 per year and your wife £25,000, you would qualify for a £151,250 mortgage (2.75 x £55,000). However, lenders are flexible and some lend 3.25 times your salary plus the salary of a partner, while others lend much more to those with good career prospects (e.g. graduates). Some lenders lend selcted borrowers up to five or even ten times their annual salary! The amount you can borrow also depends on how large a deposit you can put down. Up to four people can legally share the ownership of a property (although most lenders allow a maximum of three co-owners), when the incomes of all co-owners are taken into account.

Most lenders give you a conditional decision over the telephone and provide a written 'mortgage promise' that you can show sellers to prove that you're a serious buyer. If you're refused a mortgage, you can ask the Council of Mortgage Lenders (see above) for advice.

Self-certification Mortgages

Self-certification mortgages are targeted at the self-employed (a huge market, which includes some three million people) and allow borrowers to estimate their earnings rather than provide proof of income. Borrowers can obtain a mortgage of between 75 and 85 per cent of the value of a property. The rates offered to high-risk borrowers are typically around 2 per cent above the standard rates for new customers. Brokers may push self-certification mortgages to the self-employed, as they earn higher commission.

Loan-to-value

The loan-to-value (LTV) ratio is the size of the mortgage as a percentage of the price or value of a property. A £180,000 mortgage on a house worth £200,000 has an LTV ratio of 90 per cent. Most borrowers can obtain 90 to 95 per cent mortgages and some lenders offer 100 per cent mortgages (some lenders even offer up to 125 per cent mortgages!). The larger the deposit you can pay (as a percentage of the value), the larger the mortgage you can obtain and the wider the choice of mortgages and deals available.

Mortgage Indemnity Guarantee

If you borrow more than a certain loan-to-value ratio, which varies according to the lender, you must usually have a mortgage indemnity guarantee (MIG) – also called a high lending fee, mortgage risk fee or maximum advance premium. This is to protect the lender in the event that you're unable to repay the loan and the lender is forced to repossess a property. Many lenders insist on an MIG if you borrow over 90 per cent (it can be lower) of the value of a property. However, a number of lenders don't levy MIGs, including HSBC, the Nationwide Building Society, the Co-Operative Bank and Northern Rock, although they may charge a higher interest rate when the loan-to-value ratio is over 90 per cent.

Where applicable, the difference between the LTV and the MIG threshold is the amount on which you must pay MIG, which typically costs around £2,000 on a £100,000 loan. The interest rate charged for MIG varies and it can be paid up-front or added to the mortgage (some lenders allow you to pay it over a few years without interest). If you add it to the mortgage, the MIG premium is likely to cost you three times as much over 25 years and if you pay off the mortgage early you don't receive a refund of a portion of the MIG.

Interest Rates

You can generally choose between fixed and variable rate mortgages. An important aspect of a mortgage is how interest is calculated, which may be daily, monthly or annually. Daily is the best method for borrowers as, when you make payments (or overpayments), they take effect immediately. With a repayment mortgage, payments include part interest and part capital repayments, and when interest is calculated annually the outstanding debt doesn't decrease daily or even monthly, but once per year. This results in your paying interest on money you've already repaid!

Fixed Rate

Fixed loans for up to 25 years are rare in the UK (unlike in Europe and the US) and aren't popular with borrowers or lenders. A few years ago (with falling rates) fixed rate loans were at a record low, although now they are rising again many market analysts are recommending fixed rate loans to avoid being caught out by future interest rate rises. Those on tight budgets who cannot afford an increase in their mortgage repayments are better off with a fixed rate mortgage, where the interest rate is fixed for a number of years (e.g. from one year to the whole mortgage term) no matter what happens to the base rate in the meantime. The longer the fixed rate period, the lower the interest rate offered. If interest rates go down, you may find yourself paying more than the current rate, but at least you know exactly what you must pay each month.

To judge whether a fixed rate mortgage is worthwhile, you must estimate in which direction interest rates are heading – a difficult feat that even the so-called experts cannot manage. The standard fixed rate is usually around 1.5 per cent above the base rate. Building societies typically offer standard fixed rate mortgages that are around half a percentage point below high street banks. If you have a fixed rate for a pre-set period, there are high penalties for switching lenders during this period. The interest rate returns to the standard variable rate (SVR) after the fixed rate period.

Variable Rate

Most property buyers choose a variable rate mortgage, where the interest rate goes up and down depending on the base rate. Theoretically, when the base rate (set by the Bank of England) changes, the variable rate should rise or fall by the same percentage. However, when the base rate falls many lenders don't pass on cuts (or the whole amount) to borrowers, ostensibly to protect savers, because when mortgage rates are cut the interest paid to savers must also be reduced.

You can be locked into a fixed rate deal that costs much more than the current variable interest rate and there may also be other restrictions such as early repayment penalties and no capital repayments during the period of a limited fixed, discounted or capped rate of interest. The best deals are offered to new borrowers and often have a maximum loan of £200,000 or £250,000, which excludes 'wealthy' buyers and existing borrowers. Lenders cannot require you to buy expensive buildings and contents insurance from them, but will insist that you have buildings insurance and will require evidence.

Repayment Mortgages

Repayment mortgages account for some 80 per cent of all mortgages in the UK. They're so called because you repay the original loan and interest over the period of the mortgage, similar to most personal loans. Your monthly payment includes interest (mostly interest at the start) and capital (mostly capital towards the end of the term) payments. As interest rates rise and fall, your repayments go up or down, but assuming a constant interest rate, your payments would remain the same for the period of the loan. One advantage is that the term of the loan can be extended if you have trouble meeting your monthly repayments.

One disadvantage of a repayment mortgage is that you don't have a life policy and you must therefore take out a 'mortgage protection' policy to ensure that your loan is paid off if you die. This policy isn't expensive, as it pays off the mortgage only if you die before the term of the loan is completed (and both the term and amount owed decrease over time). For the majority of people, a repayment mortgage together with adequate life insurance is the best choice, as it's the only loan that guarantees to pay off your mortgage by the end of the term (provided you maintain the stipulated payments).

Interest-only Mortgages

Interest-only mortgages account for around one in five of all mortgages – you take out a mortgage loan in the normal way and pay interest as usual. However, instead of agreeing to repay the loan at a fixed date in the future, the loan simply stays in existence until you (not the lender) decide to repay it, which could be anytime from six months to 60 years. Interest-only loans are good for single people with no dependants, heavily-mortgaged families, those whose earnings fluctuate, people who expect to receive an inheritance and those whose salary is likely to rise substantially in the future.

It isn't necessary to have an insurance policy to repay the loan should you die, but it's recommended if others are dependent on your income. Most lenders lend only from 50 to 75 per cent of a property's value on an interest-only mortgage **without** a linked investment. For most people, it's essential to make provision for repaying the capital sum at the end of the original mortgage term, which can be done with an investment (such as an ISA), endowment or pension mortgage (see below). An Individual Savings Account (ISA) can be invested in cash, stocks or life insurance, and the pay-out is tax-free. However, owing to the high charges and poor performance of these products in recent years, particularly endowments, interest-only mortgages are no longer so popular. They're favoured by the majority of buy-to-let investors and are a good way to get on to the housing ladder, as your repayments are lower, although you can store up problems for the future.

Endowment Mortgages

With an endowment mortgage you pay interest over the length of the loan. You also take out an endowment life insurance policy, which should provide a large enough lump sum to pay off the mortgage at the end of the term, usually 25 years. Your monthly mortgage payments are made up of an interest payment and an insurance (endowment) payment. The policy also carries life insurance, which ensures that, if you die, the mortgage is paid off in full and any money left over is paid to your estate. The loan and endowment are separate and you can obtain them from different sources. You should obtain independent advice and try to find a lender with a low interest rate and an insurance company with a good track record.

Like all endowment policies, you could be left with a tax-free sum at the end of the term after your loan has been paid off, although there are no guarantees. In recent years, some endowments have been worth less than the holders paid in, even after ten years! **Consequently, in recent years mortgage advisers have advised most borrowers to avoid endowment mortgages like the plague!**

The best independent advice is found in surveys carried out by publications, such as *Which?* magazine (see **Appendix A**), which accept no advertisements, and daily newspapers. The best variable, fixed rate and discount mortgage rates are shown on TV teletext services, published in daily and Sunday newspapers such as *The Sunday Times*, *The Sunday Telegraph*, *The Observer* and *The Independent on Sunday*, and are listed in monthly mortgage magazines such as *What Mortgage* (🖥 www.what mortgageonline.co.uk), *Mortgage Magazine* and *Home Buyer & Mortgage Adviser*.

For more information about mortgages, see our sister publication, ***Buying, Selling & Letting Property*** (Survival Books).

COUNCIL TAX

The council tax replaced the reviled poll tax (or community charge) in 1993, which itself replaced property rates in 1989 in Scotland and 1990 in England and Wales. The council tax is a local tax levied by local councils on residents to pay for such things as education, police, roads, waste disposal, libraries and community services (see **Local Government** on page 493). Each council fixes its own tax rate, based on the number of residents and how much money they need to finance their services.

The amount payable depends on the value of your home, relative to others in your area, as rated by your local council (not necessarily the market value). Properties in England, Scotland and Wales (there's no council tax in Northern Ireland) are divided into the following bands:

Value Band	England	Scotland	Wales
A	Up to £40,000	Up to £27,000	Up to £30,000
B	£40,001 – £52,000	£27,001 – £35,000	£30,001 – £39,000
C	£52,001 – £68,000	£35,001 – £45,000	£39,001 – £51,000
D	£68,001 – £88,000	£45,001 – £58,000	£51,001 – £66,000
E	£88,001 – £120,000	£58,001 – £80,000	£66,001 – £90,000
F	£120,001 – £160,000	£80,001 – £106,000	£90,001 – £120,000
G	£160,001 – £320,000	£106,001 – £212,000	£120,001 – £240,000
H	Over £320,000	Over £212,000	Over £240,000

The tax payable varies considerably depending on the borough or county where you live. Wales has more areas with low bills than England or Scotland, and rural charges tend to be lower than urban ones. But low city charges aren't unheard of, even in London. In recent years, council tax rates have spiralled throughout Britain and many people receive bills of £1,000 to £2,000 even for relatively low value properties.

The tax includes payments for the county, borough or district council; the local police, fire and civil defence authorities; and possibly a 'special expenses' payment in certain areas. It can usually be paid by direct debit from a bank or building society account, by post with a personal cheque, in person at council offices, by credit card, or at a bank or post office. Payment can be made as a lump sum (for which a reduction may be offered) or in ten instalments per year, from April to January (12 instalments in Scotland). In recent years, taxes have increased as a result of inadequate funding from central government and many councils have been forced to cut services to meet their budgets. Average bills have almost doubled since the tax was introduced in 1993.

The full council tax assumes that two adults are living permanently in the dwelling. If only one adult lives in a dwelling (as their main home), the bill is reduced by 25 per cent. If a dwelling isn't a main home, e.g. it's unoccupied or is a second home, the bill is usually reduced by 10-50 per cent. Exempt dwellings include those that are unfurnished (exempt for up to six months); undergoing structural alteration or major repair (exempt for up to six months after completion); are left empty for specific reasons (e.g. the occupier is in hospital, a nursing home or prison, or is a student); or are occupied only by people under 18 years of age.

Certain people aren't counted when calculating the number of adults resident in a dwelling, e.g. full-time students and 18 and 19-year-olds who have just left school. If you, or someone who lives with you, has special needs arising from a disability, you may be entitled to a reduction in your council tax bill. Those receiving income support (see page 336) usually pay no council tax and others on low incomes have their bills reduced. You can appeal against the assessed value of your property and any errors due to exemption, benefits or discounts.

All those who are liable for council tax must register with their local council when they take up residence in a new area, and are liable to pay council tax from their first day of residence. A register is maintained by councils, containing the names and addresses of all people registered for council tax, which is open to public examination. If you don't want your name and address to appear on the register, e.g. for fear of physical violence, you can apply for anonymous registration. New arrivals in the UK must register with their local council after taking up residence or after moving house. When moving to a new county or borough, you may be entitled to a refund of a portion of your council tax.

VALUE ADDED TAX

Value Added Tax (VAT) is payable at a standard rate of 17.5 per cent on all goods and services, with the exception of domestic fuels, women's sanitary protection products, children's car seats and cycle helmets, on which the rate is 5 per cent. The following goods and services are zero-rated:

- Most food (but not catering, which includes meals in restaurants, cafés and hot take-away food and drink);

- Sales and long leases of new buildings; construction of most new buildings (but not work to existing buildings);

- Young children's clothing and footwear;

- Books and newspapers;

- Mobile homes and house boats;

- Dispensing of prescriptions and the supply of many aids for disabled people;

- Export of goods;

- Domestic supplies of water and sewerage;

- Public transport of passengers.

Certain business transactions are exempt from VAT (not the same as zero-rated). Exempt supplies include most sales, leases and lettings of land and buildings; insurance; betting, gaming and lotteries; the provision of credit; certain education and training; and the services of doctors, dentists and opticians.

If you're self-employed and your annual turnover (not just profits) is more than £56,000 annually, you must be registered for VAT. A business which makes exempt supplies only cannot register for VAT, but a company making zero-rated supplies can. An individual is registered for VAT, not a business, and registration covers **all** the business activities of the registered person. The prices of some goods, e.g. computers and other business equipment, are advertised or quoted exclusive of VAT (although almost all other advertised prices are inclusive of VAT). The VAT you're charged on goods and services that you use in setting up your business can be reclaimed, subject to certain conditions.

There are stiff penalties for those who fail to register for VAT or who make a false declaration. A wrong declaration can result in a 30 per cent penalty (even for accidental errors) plus interest on all underpayments. There are also penalties for making late returns, which must be made quarterly (this may be extended to annually for traders with an annual turnover under the £56,000 threshold). If you're in any doubt as to your registration or VAT declarations, you should contact your local VAT office, the address of which is in your local telephone directory under *Customs and Excise*. Many VAT publications and leaflets are published, including *Should I be Registered for VAT?* and *The VAT Guide*, copies of which are sent to you when you register. All VAT publications are available on request from VAT offices. It's the declared aim of the European Union (EU) eventually to have just one universal rate of VAT for the whole union, although this will take some time to accomplish.

INCOME TAX

It's hardly surprising that the British don't always see eye to eye with the French. After all it was because of Napoleon that income tax was introduced in 1799 (the 'good' news is that it was introduced as a temporary measure only and may be rescinded at any time). Another Frenchman, William the Conqueror, was to blame for the introduction of the budget.

Domicile

Your liability for British taxes depends on where you're domiciled and whether you're a British resident. Your domicile is the country which you regard as your natural and permanent home. A person can be resident in more than one country, but at any given time he can be domiciled in one only. To be regarded as resident in the UK for a given tax year (the 5th April to the 4th April of the following year and not a calendar year), you must normally be physically present there for at least part of that year. You will always be regarded as resident in the UK with respect to income tax, if you spend six months (183 days) or more there in any one year (whether in one continuous period or during a number of visits). A resident in the UK may be classified as 'resident' or 'ordinarily resident'. Ordinarily resident is broadly equivalent to being habitually resident, i.e. a person who's resident in the UK year after year is ordinarily resident there. A person may be resident, but not ordinarily resident, in the UK for a given tax year, e.g. he could normally live outside the UK but visit the UK for six months or more in that year. Alternatively, he may be ordinarily resident in the UK, but not resident for a given tax year, e.g. he usually lives in the UK, but goes abroad for a long holiday and doesn't set foot in the UK during that year. Each tax year is looked at as a whole and a person can be classified only as resident or non-resident for a particular tax year and not, for example, resident for part of the year and non-resident for the remainder.

If you're a new permanent resident in the UK (i.e. someone not ordinarily resident), you're considered resident only from the time of your arrival (the same rule applies to anyone leaving the UK for permanent residence abroad, who becomes not ordinarily resident in the UK from the time he left). If you're classified as a resident, you're liable to British income tax on all income arising from a source in the UK. If you're a British resident **and** domiciled in the UK, you're liable for taxation in the UK on your worldwide income, including capital gains tax. A booklet (IR20) entitled *Residents and Non-residents – Liability to Tax in the United Kingdom* explains the rules outlined above.

Double Taxation Agreements

The UK has double taxation agreements with around 80 countries, which despite the name, are to prevent your paying double taxes and **not** to ensure that you pay twice. Under double taxation treaties, certain categories of people are exempt from paying British tax. If part of your income is taxed abroad in a country with a double taxation treaty with the UK, you won't need to pay British tax on that income. If you're a British citizen living abroad, you won't usually be liable for British tax provided that your absence from the UK covers a complete tax year and you **don't**:

● Remain in the UK for 183 days or more in any tax year;

● Have accommodation available in the UK and don't make any visits to the UK, no matter how short, unless you're employed full-time abroad;

● Visit the UK for a total of more than three months per year in four or more consecutive years.

You may also be liable for taxes in your home country. Citizens of most countries are exempt from paying taxes in their home country when they spend a minimum period abroad, e.g. one year. It's usually your responsibility to familiarise yourself with the latest tax procedures in your home country or country of domicile. If you're in doubt about your tax liability in your home country, contact your embassy or consulate. It's possible for some foreigners to live legally in the UK without paying British tax. To qualify you must reside in the UK for less than 183 days in a calendar year or your salary must be paid and taxed by your employer in another country with a double taxation treaty (see above) with the UK. For information about double taxation agreements, refer to *Double Taxation Relief* (IR6), available from tax offices.

Tax Rates

The UK has three income tax rates after a tax free allowance of £5,035 (2007/08). The first £1,960 of taxable income is taxed at the lower rate of 10 per cent. Taxable income from £1,961 to £30,500 is taxed at 22 per cent, known as the basic rate of tax. The higher rate tax of 40 per cent is the highest rate of tax on earned income in the UK and is payable on taxable income above £30,500 per year. The rate of income tax payable in the UK is among the lowest in Europe. Your taxable income is your income after all allowances and deductions have been made from your gross income (from all sources).

Like everything in the UK, there's a two-tier tax system, first class for the self-employed and a second class system, called PAYE (Pay As You Earn), for employees. The self-employed pay their tax in arrears (as all employees do in many European countries), whereas an employee's income tax is deducted at source weekly or monthly from his salary by his employer. Although the Inland Revenue (IR) may give individuals a hard time when it comes to paying their tax bills, British companies withhold billions from the tax authorities each year over disputed corporation tax bills, plus billions more contested by the self-employed and those owing capital gains tax.

Tax Evasion

Tax evasion is illegal and is a criminal offence, for which you can be heavily fined or even sent to prison. Nevertheless, there's a flourishing black economy which the Inland Revenue estimates amounts to around £10 billion per year in unpaid tax on undeclared income. The IR has tightened up its ability to collect tax and catch tax dodgers in recent years and carries out investigations into tens of thousands of 'suspicious' tax returns each year (it has 12 months from the date you file a return to launch an enquiry). In most cases where taxpayers owe money, the outcome is settled out of court with taxpayers making a full disclosure and a monetary settlement.

▲ Lake District, Cumbria
© Visit Britain (www.visitbritain.org)

▲ Loch Awe, Strathclyde, Scotland
© Visit Britain (www.visitbritain.org)

▲ Liverpool, Merseyside
© Visit Britain (www.visitbritain.org)

▼ Llangollen, Wales
© Visit Britain (www.visitbritain.org)

▲ Letbury, Hereford & Worcestershire
© Visit Britain (www.visitbritain.org)

◀ *Trebah Gardens, Cornwall*
  © *Visit Britain (www.visitbritain.org)*

▲ *Portbradden, Co. Antrim, N. Ireland*
  © *Visit Britain (www.visitbritain.org)*

▼ *Piper, Glasgow, Scotland*
  © *Visit Britain (www.visitbritain.org)*

▲ *Caernarfon Castle, Gwynedd, Wales*
  © *Visit Britain (www.visitbritain.org)*

▼ *Millennium Bridge, Gateshead, Tyne & Wear*
  © *Visit Britain (www.visitbritain.org)*

▲ *The Seven Sisters, Seaford, E. Sussex*
© *Visit Britain (www.visitbritain.org)*

▼ *Rugby, Cardiff, Wales*
© *Visit Britain (www.visitbritain.org)*

▲ *Potter, Burlaston, Staffordshire*
© *Visit Britain (www.visitbritain.org)*

▲ *Blackpool, Lancashire*
© *Visit Britain (www.visitbritain.org)*

▶

Rothsay, Strathclyde, Scotland
© *Visit Britain (www.visitbritain.org)*

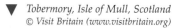

Polperro, Cornwall
© Visit Britain (www.visitbritain.org)

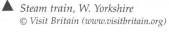

Steam train, W. Yorkshire
© Visit Britain (www.visitbritain.org)

Torquay, Devon
© Visit Britain (www.visitbritain.org)

Science Centre, Glasgow, Scotland
© Visit Britain (www.visitbritain.org)

Tobermory, Isle of Mull, Scotland
© Visit Britain (www.visitbritain.org)

Tax Avoidance

Tax avoidance, i.e. legally paying as little tax as possible, if necessary by finding and exploiting loopholes in the tax laws, is a different matter altogether (from tax evasion). It's practised by most companies, wealthy individuals and self-employed people, although the opportunities for anyone paying direct or PAYE tax are strictly limited. Unfortunately, there are few (legal) ways an individual paying PAYE tax can reduce his income tax bill, although it's possible to appeal against your PAYE coding notice or anything connected with your tax affairs that you believe is incorrect. Whether you're self-employed or an employee, you should ensure that you don't pay any more tax than is necessary.

Accountants

If your tax affairs are complicated or you're unable to understand your own finances (like the majority of people), you should consider employing an accountant to deal with your tax affairs (most high street banks also provide a personal tax service). This probably applies to most self-employed people, but very few who are on PAYE. However, don't just pick an accountant by sticking a pin in the yellow pages, but ask your friends, colleagues or business associates if they can recommend someone. If you're self-employed, you should choose an accountant who deals with people in your line of business and who knows exactly what you can (and cannot) claim.

Substantial tax savings can be made with regard to pensions, independent taxation, and trusts to avoid capital gains and inheritance tax. Some tax avoidance schemes apply only to the very rich, as the cost of using them is prohibitive to anyone else. As soon as the Inland Revenue closes one loophole, tax accountants find another one. Accountants' fees vary from £50 to £150 per hour, so ask in advance what the rates are (they're highest in London). You can reduce your accountant's fees considerably by keeping itemised records of all your business expenses (preferably on computer), rather than handing him a pile of invoices and receipts. However, a good accountant usually saves you more than he charges in fees.

Tax Changes

Changes in direct or indirect taxation are generally announced in the main Budget Statement in March each year. Changes to income tax come into effect in the following tax year (from 5th April to 4th April), although amendments can be made at any time and some tax changes don't come into effect until a year later. Taxes and allowances quoted in this section largely refer to the 2007/2008 tax year (ending on 5th April 2008).

Information

There are many books published about how to reduce your income tax bill, including the *Daily Mail Income Tax Guide* and the *Daily Telegraph Guide to Income Tax*. The Consumers' Association publishes an annual *Tax Saving Guide* which isn't sold by newsagents or bookshops, but is free to subscribers of *Which?* magazine (see **Consumers' Association** page 479), plus an annual guide entitled *Which? Way To Save Tax*. A tax guide written especially for the elderly is *Your Tax and Savings* by John Burke, available from Age Concern England. The Inland Revenue publishes a huge number of leaflets on every conceivable tax subject, all of which are listed in a leaflet entitled *Catalogue of leaflets and booklets*. Copies of tax leaflets can be ordered by telephone from tax offices and tax enquiry centres (TECs), which are usually open from 10am to 4pm. If you have a home or business computer, a number of tax computer programs are available such as *QuickTax* (Intuit) and *TaxCalc* (Which? Books), designed to make it easier to calculate and check your income tax payments.

Finally, never trust the taxman to take only what he should or to allow you the correct allowances and deductions. While the IR won't cheat you deliberately, it isn't uncommon for them to make mistakes. If you pay PAYE tax, make sure that your tax code is correct (see below) and never hesitate to dispute a tax bill with which you disagree. It's estimated that Britons pay some £5 billion in unnecessary tax each year (mostly on income) and that savers and investors waste millions by not taking advantage of tax concessions.

Independent Taxation

Under independent taxation, spouses are allocated their own tax allowances and privacy in their dealings with the Inland Revenue. Each partner has his or her own tax bill and needn't tell the other what they earn or how much tax they pay (not that most people would dream of telling fibs about their income to their spouses). A couple usually needs to work together to make the most of independent taxation. Before the introduction of independent taxation (April 1990), a wife didn't pay her own tax on savings and investments, even if a couple opted for separate taxation, and her husband was responsible for the tax bill on her investments.

Married couples can reduce their tax bill by switching savings and assets between them. If one partner isn't working, it's important to put any savings in the non-working partner's name in an account or investment that pays interest gross, and which allows the interest to be offset against the tax allowance. Despite the savings to be made, many couples are slow to take advantage of tax rules. In addition to a personal allowance, married couples born before 6th April 1935, also receive a married couple's allowance, usually claimed by the male partner. The downside of independent taxation is the extra work involved in completing two tax returns and the extra cost if an accountant is employed. The Inland Revenue publishes many leaflets about independent taxation and most banks and building societies offer free advice (alternatively you can discuss it with your accountant).

Pay As You Earn

Income tax is collected by the Inland Revenue (IR). All employees pay direct income tax or Pay As You Earn (PAYE) income tax, which is deducted from gross salaries at source by employers. PAYE isn't a separate tax, but simply the name given to the system of direct (income) taxation. Any additional income, whether tax is deducted at source or not, must be declared to the Inland Revenue. This may include part-time employment or income from investments or savings. PAYE tax applies to all income tax which is payable on earnings to which the scheme relates and includes tax at the lower, basic and higher rates.

Some employers may not deduct PAYE tax from an employee's earnings, particularly in the case of casual or part-time employees, and where the distinction between employee and self-employed is blurred. This is illegal and a hazardous practice for employers, who are responsible for deducting all their employees' income tax at source, unless a person is categorised as self-employed by the tax office. Tax on Unemployment Benefit and other Social Security benefits, such as Maternity Pay and Statutory Sick Pay, also comes within the PAYE scheme. The PAYE scheme is disadvantageous to many employees, who would be entitled to claim larger and more allowances if they were classified as self-employed, and would also have the benefit of paying their tax in arrears.

PAYE Tax Code

The level of tax for those taxed under the PAYE system is denoted by a tax code. A notice of coding, Form P2 (T), is sent out in January or February for the next tax year starting in April, to employers and employees (although not everyone receives one each year). When you receive a new code, your notice of coding shows how the calculations have been made. You should check that the deductions, allowances and the total are correct. You don't receive a notice every year, but your current tax code is always given on your pay or wage slip (which you get when you receive your weekly or monthly salary). Your pay slip also shows your gross pay (your salary without any deductions) to date and the amount of tax you've paid to date.

If your circumstances change you should tell the Inland Revenue. They send you a new income tax return to complete (see below) or simply change your tax code. You must inform the IR of any changes in your tax status, e.g. marriage, a dependent relative, divorce or separation, which entitles you to an additional allowance, or a change in your income (maybe from a part-time job) or company benefits (e.g. a company car). It's in your interest to do this as, should the Inland Revenue find out later, you won't only be liable for any tax owed plus interest, but can also be fined up to 100 per cent of the amount of unpaid tax.

Your tax code is also printed on your P45, a certificate given to you when you leave your employment and which should be given to a new employer when you start a new job. Your P45 shows your PAYE code, your total earnings and how much tax you've paid since the start of the current tax year. If you're unemployed after leaving a job and are eligible to claim Jobseeker's Allowance, you must give your P45 to the benefit office when registering for Unemployment Benefit. When you find a job, the benefit office gives you a P45 for your new employer. If you don't have a P45 when starting a job, e.g. for your first job from school or after arriving in the UK from abroad, you should ask your new employer for a P15 *Notice of Coding* form. Complete this form and ask your employer to send it to the IR, who then gives you a tax code (you can send it yourself if you want to keep the information private). Your employer also completes a P46 form (stating your salary) to notify the Inland Revenue that you're employed by him, which you will be asked to sign. If you don't have a P45 on starting a job, your employer taxes you under a special system called an emergency code. If you pay too much tax, it's repaid by your employer in your next pay cheque as soon as he receives your PAYE tax code.

Your tax code is made up of a series of numbers (usually three) and a letter, e.g. 645H. The numbers are the total allowances minus the last digit, e.g. allowances of £6457 become code number 645. A code of 0 (zero) applies when you have two or more jobs and your allowances have already been used to calculate the code number for your main employment. Some codes don't have a number or have numbers that don't stand for allowances, e.g. BR or DO. The letter tells the Inland Revenue your tax status:

Code	Meaning
BR	Tax is deducted at the basic rate
DO	Tax is deducted at a higher rate
Y	You're aged 75 or over and have the full personal allowance
K	Deductions from your free-of-tax pay, such as taxable state benefits, exceed your personal allowances
L	Entitlement to the basic personal allowance (for those aged under 65)
NT	No tax is to be deducted
OT	You receive no allowances after adjustments, and tax is deducted at the lower, basic and higher rates depending on your income
P	Entitlement to the personal allowance for those aged 65 to 74
T	Someone who doesn't fall within the above categories (e.g. no allowance due to other employment) or someone whose code should end in L, P or V, but doesn't want an employer to know his or her status
V	Someone who's entitled to the personal and married couple's allowance for those aged 65 to 74

If you have the letter L, P or V after your tax number, your employer can alter your tax when allowances are changed by a budget. If you have a T code and allowances are changed by the budget, the IR must work out your code again and inform you and your employer. Codes BR and DO are affected only if the tax rates or bands change. The tax code is used by your employer to calculate the amount of income tax to be deducted from your salary. If it's wrong, tell the Inland Revenue. Never assume that your tax code is correct, but check it yourself or ask an accountant or tax expert to check it for you. If you have any questions about tax, contact any tax office or tax enquiry centre. Around April, you should receive a form P60 showing how much tax you've paid in the previous tax year. You should check it and keep it in a safe place, as you may be asked to produce it at a later date.

There are a number of forms with which to reclaim tax or to ensure you don't pay tax unnecessarily: Form P50 is used to reclaim tax, e.g. when you return to work after a period of not working during which you didn't claim Unemployment Benefit; Form P187 is used to reclaim tax if you have no P45; Form R40(S) is used to reclaim tax if you think you've paid too much (for whatever reason). Students should complete Form P38(S) when they start a holiday job and think their total taxable income for the whole tax year is likely to be **less** than the basic personal allowance. This ensures you don't pay tax on your holiday earnings or that it's refunded.

Self-employed

One person in eight in the UK is self-employed, as a 'sole trader' or in partnership with others. You're generally much better off if you're self-employed, as you can claim more in the way of expenses than employees (paying PAYE tax). Another advantage for the self-employed is the delay between making profits and paying tax on them. To be treated as self-employed, you must convince your tax office that you're genuinely self-employed and in business for yourself. The definition of self-employed is much the same as in most countries and includes:

- Working freelance for a number of clients;

- Supplying your own tools or equipment;

- Risking your own money in a business;

- Having the final say in how the business is run;

- Using your home as your office;

- Responsibility for meeting losses as well as taking profits;

- The freedom to hire other people on your own terms;

- Correcting unsatisfactory work in your own time at your own expense;

- Paying your own expenses and charging an overall fee for your services.

To check whether you're entitled to be self-employed, contact your local Inland Revenue office (see also leaflet IR56 *Employed or Self-employed*).

If you're self-employed, as well as tax, you pay class two national insurance contributions (see page 338) and must also pay class four contributions at 8 per cent on profits between £5,225 and £34,840 per year (2007/08), payable at the same time as your income tax. The following list is a guide to the deductions you can make from your gross income when calculating your taxable profits:

- National insurance contributions, accident insurance, health insurance and unemployment insurance;

- Premiums for life insurance, endowment and private pensions;

- Business expenses, e.g. car expenses (including travel to and from your place of work), outside or subsidised meals (not free meals), employment-related education and books, and accountant's fees;

- Standard allowances are permitted for many items without proof of expenditure. Personal allowances vary depending on individual circumstances, e.g. single or married, divorced or widowed, and the number of children or dependants;

- Interest charges on loans, overdrafts and leasing contracts;

- Telephone, electricity and office expenses;

- Capital allowances for equipment, e.g. computers, office equipment and car;

- Certain donations to recognised charities.

You shouldn't hesitate to claim for anything that you believe is a legitimate business deduction. The IR deletes them if they don't agree, but what they never do is allow you a deduction that you're entitled to and have forgotten to claim. The Inland Revenue publishes a number of leaflets for the self-employed, including *Starting in Business* (IR28). **If you're self-employed, you will almost certainly find it pays to hire an accountant to complete your tax return.**

Allowances

Before you're liable for income tax, you're allowed to earn a certain amount of income tax-free. If you earn below your taxable limit, you aren't liable for tax. Everyone has a tax-free personal allowance and a married couple is entitled to an additional married couple's allowance, both of which are increased for those aged 65 and over (even more for the over-75s). Under independent taxation for married couples (see page 386), each partner is wholly responsible for his or her own tax affairs, including income and capital gains tax. The tax-free allowances for the 2007/2008 tax year are described below.

Personal Allowance

All residents in the UK who have an income from any source, e.g. salary, pension, interest on savings or dividends from investment are entitled to a personal allowance to set against his taxable income, which depends on your age as follows:

Age	Allowance (£)
Under 65	5,225
65 – 74*	6,285
Over 74*	7,690

* Pensioners whose annual income exceeds £18,300 have their allowance reduced by £1 for every £2 of income above this level, until they reach the basic allowance.

Married Couple's Allowance

A married couple's allowance is granted in addition to personal allowances. The married couple's allowance can be split between spouses or allocated entirely to either spouse. The higher age allowance is paid when either partner qualifies. The married couple's allowance depends on age as follows: £6,065 at 10% - if either you or your spouse or civil partner was born before 6 April 1935 but aged under 75 (so the allowance is worth up to £606.50 off your tax bill). £6,135 at 10% - if either you or your spouse or civil partner is aged 75 or more (so it is worth up to £613.50 off your tax bill).

Initially the married couple's allowance is set against the husband's income. Although it's called the married couple's allowance, if the husband doesn't work (e.g. he's a house-husband) and the wife does, then the married couple's allowance can be claimed by her. However, if the husband receives Unemployment Benefit, a pension or any taxable income, it must be set against his allowance first. Anything left over can be transferred to his wife. In the first year of marriage, the husband receives one twelfth of the married couple's allowance for each month he's been married. You must inform your local tax office when you get married in order to claim the allowance. If two people live together as a couple without getting married, they're taxed as two single people and don't receive the married couple's allowance. If a couple is separated or divorced, they're able to claim the allowance for the tax year in which they permanently separate.

Other Allowances

Additional tax credits (introduced in 2003/04) can be claimed by anyone bringing up children (under the age of 16 or in full-time education) on their own, irrespective of whether they're single (unmarried), divorced, separated or widowed; for further details see (www.inlandrevenue.gov.uk/rates/taxcredits.htm). There's a blind person's relief of £1,730 for registered blind people in 2007/08.

Income Tax Returns

If you're self-employed or a higher-rate taxpayer, you should be sent a tax return annually, although if you pay your income tax through PAYE and your tax affairs are fairly simple, you will rarely receive one. If you think you're paying too much tax, inform your tax office. Similarly, if you aren't paying tax on part of your earnings, it's up to you to inform the tax office. If you don't receive a return (or all the forms required) and need one, it's your responsibility to request it (☎ 0845-900 0404).

Self-assessment

A self-assessment system was introduced in 1997 and was the biggest tax reform for 50 years. Under the old system, the Inland Revenue issued estimated assessments which could then be challenged by individual taxpayers. Self-assessment embraces some nine million self-employed people, company directors and taxpayers with substantial investment income or complex tax affairs, who must calculate their own tax liability. In theory, it's a simpler method of calculating tax, although there are hidden complexities and harsh penalties for late filing, and reservations have been expressed about the IR forcing people to become tax 'experts'. Many reports indicate that the first few years of self-assessment have been chaotic, to say the least, with many people wrongly fined and over one million people sent incorrect bills.

Schedule

The self-assessment schedule for the tax year 2007/08 is as follows:

6th April 2007	A tax return or notice to complete a tax return (SA316) is sent to all people who get a tax return each year.
31st July 2007	A second automatic penalty of £100 is charged for people whose return was due back by 31st January 2007, but who haven't sent it in. Some people make 'payments on account', normally one-half of the previous year's tax liability. The payments are due on 31st January in the tax year and 31st July of the following tax year. If you need to make a second payment, this is the date by which it should be paid.
30th September 2007	You must send your 2007/08 tax return by this date if you want the Inland Revenue to calculate your tax for you. You must send in your 2007/08 return in by this date if you want the revenue to collect your tax (below £2,000) through next year's PAYE code.
31st January 2008	If you were sent a tax return by 31st October 2007, this is the deadline for sending back completed forms for the 2007/08 tax return.

| 1st February 2008 | If you were sent a tax return by 31st October 2007 you face a penalty of £100 if it isn't received back by the Inland Revenue by this date. |
| 6th April 2008 | A tax return or notice to complete a tax return is sent out to all people who get a tax return each year. |

Completing the Return

Under self-assessment, all taxpayers receive the same standard return which covers savings, investments, state benefits and pensions, in addition to allowances and reliefs that you wish to claim. You may receive additional forms depending on your sources of income, e.g. those in a partnership. The return is supplied with explanatory notes, but some people have a lot of trouble understanding the system. If you need help with your tax form or are unclear about a specific point, you can call the self-assessment helpline (☎ 0845-900 0444). Always keep a copy of your tax form and anything else you send to your tax office. This will be vital if your tax form gets lost in the post or there are any queries later. **Don't forget to sign the return!** All tax records should be retained for five years from the latest date by which the tax return is to be filed.

Late Filing

There are heavy fines for late filing and late payers under the self-assessment scheme. If you miss the deadline for filing your tax return by a single day you must pay an automatic £100 fine (incurred by hundreds of thousands of people each year). Failure to return the tax form by the end of February means a five per cent surcharge is levied on the tax owed. If you send in your return after the 31st July (i.e. over six months late) you must pay a further £100 fine, and a delay of 12 months incurs a penalty of up to 100 per cent of the tax payable, plus a discretionary charge of £60 per day until your return is filed. You must also pay interest on unpaid tax bills. You can appeal against a penalty for filing a late return.

Payment on Account

If you're self-employed or receive rental or investment income without having tax deducted at source, you must pay income tax on account. Two payments must be paid on account of tax due, one by 31st January (the same day as filing your return) and the other by 31st July, each amounting to half of your liability for the previous year (excluding tax deducted at source, e.g. on PAYE income). A third balancing payment (or refund if you've overpaid) is made by the following 31st January.

Late Payment

Late payment of tax incurs interest charges at a floating rate decided by the Treasury. A delay of 28 days adds a five per cent surcharge and a delay of six months a further five per cent (total ten per cent). Interest on surcharges are due within 30 days of their imposition.

CAPITAL GAINS TAX

Capital Gains Tax (CGT) is applicable whenever you sell or otherwise dispose of (e.g. lease, exchange or lose) an asset which, broadly speaking, is anything you own. Anything you sell, from a second home to shares or antiques, which reaps profits above £9,200 per year (2007/08) is liable to CGT, payable at 10, 20 or 40 per cent, depending on your highest rate of income tax (companies pay corporation tax at their normal rate). CGT liability must be included in your income tax return. You don't have to pay CGT on your car; your main home; household goods and possessions worth less than GBP 6,000 when you sell them; National Savings certificates; premium bonds; betting winnings; most life insurance policies; government securities; and personal injury compensation.

If an asset disposed of was acquired **before** 31st March 1982, no capital gains tax is usually payable. The value of assets purchased and disposed of after this date are adjusted for the increase in the retail price index (RPI) between 31st March 1982 and the date of disposal. If the asset was acquired **after** 31st March 1992, then its cost is adjusted for the increase in the RPI between the date of acquisition and its disposal. The adjusted cost is then deducted from the net sales proceeds to arrive at the gain or loss. This calculation is termed the indexation allowance (RPI tables are provided to make calculation easy). To complicate matters further, from 6th April 1998 a new taper relief system was introduced and applies to assets purchased from this date. This works by reducing the tax payable on a gain depending on how long you've owned it. You must own a non-business asset for at least three years and a business asset for at least one year before taper relief reduces your tax bill. The percentage of capital gains payable on a non-business asset reduces to 95 per cent after three years and a maximum of 60 per cent after ten or more years. For further details, see 🖳 www.inlandrevenue.gov.uk/rates/cgt.htm.

If you have two homes, living part of the year in one and part in another, you must choose which is your main residence for capital gains tax purposes. It's best to choose the one on which you think you will make the largest profit as your main home. You should inform the tax office within two years of buying a second home (otherwise the Inland Revenue may decide which property is your main home), although you can change your mind at any time by informing your tax office. Your choice of main residence for capital gains tax purposes shouldn't affect your choice for council tax purposes (see page 380).

Under independent taxation, husbands and wives each have an annual capital gains exemption of £9,200 (total £18,400) and it isn't possible for one spouse's losses to be set against the other's gains. Capital gains tax is payable on overseas investments only when the money is brought back into the UK. The Inland Revenue publishes a number of leaflets about capital gains tax. If you're liable for CGT, you should obtain advice from an accountant, as you may be able to reduce your tax liability.

INHERITANCE TAX

In the UK, inheritance tax (IHT) of 40 per cent is payable on any bequests above £300,000 (2007/08) when left to anyone other than your spouse or a registered charity). The tax-free threshold is usually increased annually and is likely to be much higher when you die (but then so will the value of your estate). The best way to reduce your IHT liability is to simply give some of your money away to family or friends or to a deserving cause, so long as it doesn't adversely affect your standard of living. Your liability to inheritance tax can be avoided by judicious financial planning and transferring assets, which is one of the most effective forms of tax planning. One way to avoid IHT is with a trust or an insurance policy, which pays the tax liability (with your children or grandchildren as beneficiaries), although you must live for seven years after setting it up.

You're permitted to give away up to £3,000 per year, which can be carried over for one year. Small gifts up to £250 don't count and you can give £250 to as many people as you wish in one year. Any taxable gifts over £250 made in the previous seven years are included in your estate, although the amount of tax payable is reduced according to a sliding scale. A gift given seven years before death incurs no inheritance tax and relief and from 20 to 80 per cent is given on gifts made between three and seven years before death. Inheritance tax is payable in full on gifts made within three years of death. Tax payable on lifetime gifts (other than those that fall under the seven-year rule) is 20 per cent. You can also make a one-time gift to a non-domiciled spouse of up to £55,000.

Those liable for inheritance tax must submit an account to the IR detailing the assets they've inherited and their value within 12 months of receiving them. There's a fine of £100 for anyone who makes a late declaration and much higher fines for providing fraudulent or incorrect information.

Inheritance tax is a complicated subject and depends on whether you're domiciled in the UK (defined in Inland Revenue leaflet IHT1). Before making any gifts or transfer of property or any bequests in your will (see below), it's vital to obtain legal advice from a solicitor who specialises in inheritance tax. There are a number of useful books, including *The Which? Guide to Giving and Inheriting* by Jonquil Lowe (Which? Books).

WILLS

It's an unfortunate fact of life, but you're unable to take your worldly goods with you when you take your final bow (even if you have plans to come back in a later life), so it's better to leave them to someone or something you love, rather than to the Inland Revenue or leave a mess which everyone will fight over (unless that's your intention!). Surprisingly, over two-thirds of Britons die intestate, i.e. without making a will, which means that the inflexible laws of intestacy dictate how the estate is divided. It's estimated that over £750 million in inheritance tax could be avoided if more people planned their taxes and made wills. Most married people imagine that when they die, everything they own will automatically be inherited by their partner. **This isn't true**.

A surviving spouse is entitled to as much as half of a house and any other property, plus between £125,000 and £200,000 of the spouse's cash, depending on whether there are any children. If you have no children, then a share of your estate passes to your parents (if they're alive) or other relatives. Under the laws of intestacy, common law spouses have no legal rights. The biggest problem of leaving no will is the delay in winding up your estate (while perhaps searching for a will), which can cause considerable hardship and distress at an already stressful time. When someone dies, an estate's assets cannot be touched until inheritance tax (see above) has been paid and probate (the official proving of a will) has been granted. You usually require probate for estates worth more than £5,000, although you can exclude assets (e.g. a home) owned as 'joint tenants' from this sum.

All adults should make a will irrespective of how large or small their assets. If your circumstances change dramatically, for example you get married, you must make a new will, as marriage automatically revokes any existing wills under English law (similarly, divorce means that gifts in a will to an ex-spouse are invalid). Husband and wife should make separate wills. Similarly, if you separate or are divorced, you should consider making a new will (but make sure you have only one valid will). A new bequest or a change can be made to an existing will through a document called a 'codicil'. You should check your will every few years to make sure it still fits your wishes and circumstances (your assets may also increase dramatically in value).

If you're a foreign national and don't want your estate to be subject to British law, you may be eligible to state in your will that it's to be interpreted under the law of another country. To avoid being subject to British death duty and inheritance laws, you must establish your country of domicile in another country. Domicile in the UK is defined in Inland Revenue leaflet IHT1 and information is also given in a booklet (IR20) entitled *Residents and Non-residents – Liability to tax in the United Kingdom* (see also **Income Tax** on page 382). If you don't specify in your will that the law of another country applies to your estate, then British law will apply. If your estate comes under British law, your dependants will be subject to British inheritance laws and tax. Inheritance law is slightly different in Scotland from in the rest of the UK, where part of the estate must be left to any children and where you can hand-write your own will, called a holograph, which doesn't need to be witnessed.

Many people make tax-free bequests to charities in their wills, which is why charities are so keen for you to make a will. One of the best reasons for leaving money to charity is to cut the taxman out of your will or at least reduce his share. Once you've accepted that you're mortal (the one statistic you can rely on is that 100 per cent of all human beings eventually die), you will find that making a will isn't a complicated or lengthy process. You can draw up your own will (which may be better than none), but it's wise to obtain legal advice from a bank or solicitor who will draw up a simple will for around £75 for a single person, or up to £125 for a couple (fees vary considerably and you should shop around). Some banks will draw up wills only if they're made executors of the estate (see below) and should therefore be avoided. Many wills are drawn up incorrectly by solicitors, so you may be better off doing it yourself!

For those who would rather do it themselves, a simple will form can be purchased from stationers for around 50p, which also provides some guidance on writing your will. However, bear in mind that a will must be written in a tax-efficient manner and that lawyers have a field day sorting out homemade wills. You must have two witnesses (to your signature, not the contents of the will) who cannot be beneficiaries or your spouse. If you wish, you can list all your 'valuables' and who's to get what (the list can be kept separate from the will and changed without altering the will itself).

You also need someone to act as the executor (or personal representative) of your estate, which can be particularly costly for modest estates. Your bank, building society, solicitor (the least expensive, but far from cheap), or other professional will usually act as the executor, although this should be avoided if at all possible, as the fees can be astronomical. Banks' fees are based on a percentage of the estate and work out at around £500 or more per hour! **It's best to make your beneficiaries the executors and then they can instruct a solicitor after your death if they need legal assistance.** Keep a copy of your will in a safe place (e.g. a bank) and another copy with your solicitor or the executors of your estate. You should keep information regarding bank accounts and insurance policies with your will(s), but don't forget to tell someone where they are!

There are a number of books on wills, including *Wills and Probate* and *What to do when Someone Dies* (Which? Books). Many charities also produce free guides in the hope that you will leave them a bequest.

COST OF LIVING

No doubt you would like to know how far your pounds will stretch and how much money (if any) you will have left after paying your bills. The UK has a high cost of living and high rates of duty, on everything from petrol to tobacco and alcohol to cars, make it one of the world's most expensive places to live. British consumers pay more for food and most consumer goods than people in most other major countries. While direct taxes are relatively low, indirect taxes are high. In 2006, the UK had one of the highest costs of living in the world according to figures from Employment Conditions Abroad. London is now the world's second most expensive city with only Tokyo being more expensive, according to a survey by Mercer Human Resources Consulting.

The UK's inflation rate is based on the RPI, which gives an indication of how prices have risen (or fallen) over the past year. The prices of around 600 'indicator' items are collected on a single day in the middle of the month (a total of around 130,000 prices are collected for the 600 items in the RPI basket). The UK's inflation rate in March 2007 rose to 3.1 per cent.

However, on the plus side, the UK's standard of living has soared in recent years and, compared with most other European Union countries, British workers take home a larger proportion of their pay after tax and Social Security. The gap between rich and poor is the largest since records began in 1886, and state pensioners are unable to afford basic comforts such as a healthy diet, a car and an annual holiday. There's a huge gap between the wealthy south of England and the poor north of England, Scotland and Northern Ireland, although the gap was narrowed by the recession in the early '90s. In contrast, the middle classes have never been better off than in recent years and the super rich go on spending sprees buying holiday homes, cruises, yachts, power boats, luxury cars and private aircraft.

It's difficult to calculate an average cost of living, as it depends on each individual's particular circumstances and lifestyle. What is important to most people is how much money they can save (or spend) each month. Your food bill naturally depends on what you eat and is usually around 50 per cent higher than in the US, and up to 25 per cent higher than in other Western European countries. Approximately £250 should be sufficient to feed two adults for a month in most areas (excluding alcohol, fillet steak and caviar). Even in the most expensive areas (i.e. London), the cost of living needn't be astronomical. If you shop wisely, compare prices and services before buying and don't live too extravagantly, you may be pleasantly surprised at how little you can live on. It's also possible to save a considerable sum by shopping for alcohol and other products in France, buying your car in Europe, and shopping overseas by post and via the internet (see **Buying Overseas** on page 477).

A list of the approximate **minimum** monthly major expenses for an average person or family in a typical provincial town are shown in the table below. **These are necessarily 'ball park' figures only and depend on your lifestyle, extravagance or frugality and where you live (almost everyone will agree that they're too low or too high!).** When calculating your cost of living, deduct the appropriate percentage for income tax (see page 382), national insurance (see page 338) and pensions from your gross salary.

MONTHLY COSTS (£)			
ITEM	**Single**	**Couple**	**Family of Four**
Housing (1)	400	600	800
Food	150	300	450
Utilities (2)	100	150	200
Leisure (3)	150	200	300
Car/travel (4)	150	150	200
Insurance (5)	50	75	100
Clothing	150	250	400
Council Tax (6)	60	100	100
TOTAL	**£1,210**	**£1,825**	**£2,550**

1. Rent or mortgage on a modern apartment or semi-detached house in an 'average' provincial suburb. The amount for a single person is for a bedsit or sharing accommodation (a young man is assumed!). Other costs are for a two (couple) or three-bedroom property (couple with two children). They don't include council or other subsidised housing.

2. Includes electricity, gas, water and telephone, plus heating bills.

3. Includes all entertainment, sports and holiday expenses, plus TV licence, newspapers and magazines (which could of course be much higher than the figures given).

4. Includes running costs for an average family car, plus third party insurance, road tax, petrol and servicing, but not depreciation or credit costs.

5. Includes all 'voluntary' insurance, excluding car insurance.

6. This is a guesstimate only, as council tax is based on a property's value.

15.

LEISURE

Tourism is one of the UK's largest and most profitable industries, employing over 2m people directly or indirectly and earning over £87 billion in 2006. The UK was the world's seventh leading tourist destination and received over 32 million overseas visitors in the same year. Figures were higher before the events of 9/11, but are now gradually rising again. The diversity of leisure opportunities in the UK is enormous and London provides more cultural activities than any other city in the world (some foreigners believe that the UK is a giant theme park). Whatever your favourite leisure interests, you will find them represented in abundance. There's a profusion of art galleries, museums, gardens, stately homes, zoos, sports facilities, sporting events, children's entertainment, cinemas, theatres, dance and music events, gambling locales, pubs, restaurants and much more.

The country has many aspects ranging from picturesque country towns and villages to bustling modern cities, all exuding a sense of history to be found in few other countries, and people are drawn to it for many reasons: its rich traditions, quality of live entertainment (particularly in London) and lively arts scene feature prominently. Nowhere provides a more varied and vibrant nightlife for the young (and young at heart) than London, which is besieged by the youth of the world. It's also home to some of the world's best (and most expensive) hotels and restaurants.

However, don't make the mistake of visiting only London and neglecting the UK's magnificent provincial cities and countryside, where a wealth of historic sites and spectacular natural beauty await you – including fishing villages, national parks, Scottish moors, castles, wild heathland, country inns, charming villages, bleak and rugged mountains, ancient cathedrals, sandy beaches, broads and marshlands. Whether you're a country or city lover, there's something for you in the UK. It's a small country so, no matter where you live, you can regard most of it as your playground. Good road and rail connections ensure that a huge area is accessible for day excursions and practically anywhere is within reach for a weekend trip, particularly if you travel by air. The cost of air travel from the UK to most European countries is reasonable by European standards and is becoming ever cheaper thanks to low-fare airlines; continental weekend breaks are feasible to most destinations, but watch out for airport taxes, which are rising.

In most cities, there are magazines and newspapers devoted to entertainment, e.g. *Time Out* and *What's On in London*. *Time Out* magazine also publishes the *Time Out London Visitors' Guide*. Arts and entertainment programmes published at varying frequencies and events information are available from tourist offices in all major centres. Many councils also publish maps and brochures pinpointing local places of interest and leisure facilities. Youth organisations and centres organise a range of activities for young people and children during school holidays, which are often subsidised by local authorities.

Many councils publish free directories listing local sports clubs, leisure facilities, arts and community centres, and opportunities for countryside and outdoor activities. They almost invariably also contain useful information for disabled people. A good source of general tourist information is *In Britain*, the official bimonthly magazine of Visit Britain (formerly the British Tourist Authority), which contains comprehensive listings of forthcoming events nationwide. Visit Britain also publishes a brochure entitled *Forthcoming Events* and provides similar information on its website (⌨ www. visitbritain.com). If you wish, it will send you a monthly email newsletter customised to reflect your interests. Other magazines of interest are *This England* and *The Scots Magazine*, plus an array of county magazines. Public transport companies publish maps and information leaflets for travellers and most local newspapers include events and entertainment pages. Such information can also be obtained from the television teletext information service and numerous websites.

The main aim of this chapter (and indeed the of the whole book) is to provide information that isn't found in standard guide books of which there are literally hundreds. Some of the best include the *Michelin Green Guide to Britain*, *Baedeker's Britain* and *Fodor's Britain* (see **Appendix B** for a list).

Tourists and day-trippers should take care not to become victims of rip-off prices in tourist areas (particularly in central London) and attractions. If prices aren't displayed, always ask the price before ordering or buying anything, and check the service charge and other extras in restaurants. For information about sports facilities, see **Chapter 16**.

TOURIST INFORMATION

There are Tourist Information Centres (TICs) in all major towns and ports, and at principal railway stations and airports; staff can provide you with a wealth of information and book you a hotel room. Centres are signposted by the National Tourist Information sign of a red 'i' on a white background and are often housed in public libraries. A search facility on the Visit Britain website (🖳 www.visitbritain.com) brings up the contact details for any of them – just enter the location – and a printed list is available from Visit Britain, Thames Tower, Black's Road, Hammersmith, London W6 9EL (☎ 020-8846 9000), which has also offices in some 20 countries.

TICs have no standard opening hours although 9.30 or 10am to 5 or 5.30pm, Mondays to Saturdays (when they may close an hour earlier) is usual. Later closing times and Sunday opening may operate in summer. In smaller towns, centres may close for lunch, e.g. from 1 to 2pm. Some close from September to Easter or open mornings only in winter, e.g. from November to March. Many rural TICs close from 24th December to 1st January inclusive. Always telephone to check opening hours in advance. An answerphone service often provides this information when centres are closed.

As well as the services mentioned, TICs provide local and regional guides and public transport information; act as box offices for local theatre and concert halls; take bookings for local and city tours, excursions, guided walks and congresses; and arrange car hire or guide services. Most centres will book you a room in any other town which also has a TIC providing the 'Book-a-Bed-Ahead' service (for which a fee is charged).

In addition to local TICs, the Britain and London Visitor Centre (1 Regent Street, London SW1Y 4XT) provides similar services for the entire UK. These include, in addition to those mentioned, the booking of sightseeing trips and theatre tickets; a *bureau de change* and London's most comprehensive British travel bookshop, stocking over 1,000 different maps and travel guides. Masses of leaflets and brochures covering all areas of the UK, many of which are published by the Scottish, Welsh, Northern Irish and English regional tourist boards, including local events diaries, are also available. You can book a room anywhere in the UK here. Whatever you want to know about travel locally or nationally, the Britain and London Travel Centre will tell you or give you contact details of someone else who can help. Opening hours are 9.30am to 6.30pm Mondays, 9am to 6.30pm Tuesdays to Fridays and 10am to 4pm on Saturdays and Sundays. Saturday opening is extended from mid-May to September and is 9am to 5pm. This is a walk-in operation only and does not take telephone calls.

You may also be interested in the services of VisitLondon, formerly the London Tourist Board (☎ 020-7932 2020, ⌨ uk.visitlondon.com), which offers a competitive hotel booking service online and by telephone (☎ 08456-443 010). It's also a prime source of information about the capital.

London Marketing is a commercial organisation offering a similar service (☎ 020-7437 4370, ⌨ www.londontown.com) and runs an information kiosk in Leicester Square, which is open from 8am to 11pm. You can also use 450 British Telecom telephone boxes with internet connections to use London Marketing's services, without paying for the connection. Look for kiosks marked 'London Town.com – Kiosk Edition'. Among the options immediately facing you on the screen are hotels, tickets, events, maps, and tours. The same organisation also provides a freephone telephone number (☎ 0800-566 366) which connects you with an adviser who can answer your queries.

HOTELS

British hotels range from international five-star luxury establishments, castles and converted stately homes to budget hotels and guesthouses, and quality can vary widely. Don't judge the situation in the rest of the UK by the standards and rates prevailing in London, where demand outstrips supply, allowing even the worst hotels to charge exorbitant rates (and where the best such as the Savoy and Claridges charge astronomical prices). If you're planning to stay in London, always book in advance and spend as much as you can afford if you want a half-decent hotel (which costs over £90 a night). If you don't need to be in the middle of town, out of town hotels (except those at Heathrow airport, which charge London rates) offer better value for money.

British hotels are among Europe's most expensive and often offer a poor standard of accommodation. A survey conducted by the Department of National Heritage some years ago found that they were the most expensive and worst value for money in Europe and that around a quarter of all visitors were dissatisfied with their accommodation. Little has changed since then. Inexpensive hotels (e.g. around £40 a night) are particularly hard to find and budget travellers must usually settle for bed and breakfast (B&B) accommodation (see page 407), rather than a 'proper' hotel.

The tourist board, motoring organisations and well-known guidebooks use varying hotel grading systems. Visit Britain has its own 'star' and 'diamond' system covering over 16,000 hotels, motels, guesthouses, inns, bed & breakfast houses and farmhouses throughout the UK, but excluding Northern Ireland. (The diamond system relates to B&Bs, inns and farmhouses). The standards required and facilities needed to earn from one to five stars reflect the international hotel rating system. Visit Britain-rated hotels are listed in a searchable database on the Visit Britain internet site. It also publishes a series of *Where to Stay* guides for England in its other capacity as the English Tourist Board.

Hotels may also be rated according to other classification systems, such as those of Michelin, Les Routiers, the Automobile Association and Royal Automobile Club (see **Motoring Organisations** on page 294). The AA and the RAC (among others), all charge establishments for the privilege of being included in their listings. Therefore the fact that a hotel isn't recommended **isn't** an indication that it doesn't meet the quality criteria.

Rates vary depending on the location, season and amenities provided, as well as the quality of accommodation offered, but the following table can be used as a **rough** guide:

Rating	Price Range
Listed	£35 – 45
1	£45 – 65
2	£65 – 85
3	£85 – 120
4	£120 – 160
5	£160 – 300+

Budget hotels in London can cost from £40 to £65 per person, per night, although the average hotel price is from £80 to £150; outside London the average hotel price is from £60 to £100. The average price of a single room in a four-star hotel in London is £160 to £200. The prices quoted above are per person for two people sharing a double room with bath (prices are usually quoted per room and not per person). Many hotels charge a punitive single room supplement (up to 50 per cent) for a single occupant of a double room. Always check whether the price quoted includes value added tax (VAT) which, at 17.5 per cent, can make quite a difference. Watch out for expensive extras such as telephone charges, breakfast and menu mark-ups. A deposit may be required when booking. Once you've confirmed bookings, you're liable to pay the full bill even if you cancel.

During off-peak periods and at weekends, you can usually haggle over room rates, particularly late at night at large hotels (which frequently have reduced rates, but often won't tell you unless you ask). Bargains can also be found via the internet (try the Hotel Reservations Network at 🖳 www.bookhotel.com and sites such as 🖳 www.lastminute.co.uk for London and other cities). Charges are usually reduced for children sharing their parent's room and many hotels have family rooms.

Many hotels offer reduced weekend rates (which is two nights – Friday and Saturday), particularly during off-peak periods. Dinner, bed and breakfast are usually included in this arrangement. Some hotels also offer a similar arrangement restricted to the off-season for stays of five nights or longer. Others reduce rates for senior citizens and children. Those catering mainly for foreign students often offer weekly full-board rates and many provide Christmas and New Year festivities programmes with tariffs which include accommodation and all meals. Most hotels with restaurants offer half-board (breakfast and evening meal) or full-board (breakfast, lunch and evening meal) at advantageous rates.

An English cooked breakfast when included in the price, or available for an extra charge, is sometimes served 'buffet style' (self-service), and consists of fruit juice, cereal, a hot main course of grilled bacon, eggs, sausages and tomatoes ('heart attack on a plate'), toast and marmalade or jam, and coffee or tea.

Most top class hotels provide air-conditioned rooms with tea and coffee making facilities; room service; radio and colour television (TV), maybe with an in-house video film service and satellite TV; en suite bathroom or shower; telephone (often direct dial); mini-bar; hair dryer; and a trouser press. Some provide no-smoking rooms and rooms for the disabled. Many offer a choice of restaurants and bars; secretarial, business and conference facilities; a health and leisure centre with swimming pool, a gymnasium, solarium, sauna, Jacuzzi; sports facilities; theatre booking agencies; hairdressing salons and a range of shops.

Because of the high price of British accommodation, foreign chains of budget hotels have arrived and have been expanding over the past decade. They follow a two-star format and provide reasonable accommodation cheaply. Most prominent is Travelodge (☎ 08701-911 600, 🖳 www.travelodge.co.uk) in whose hostelries two adults and two children can stay for a flat rate of around £45 a night including VAT (possibly less with special offers). This includes en suite bathroom, TV, radio and tea-making facilities. Breakfast can be ordered and eaten in your room for an additional £4.45 and there's also usually a restaurant (although nothing too grand) in the building or nearby. Rooms with facilities for the disabled are also available. You may bring your dog for £5 extra.

Travelodge's 280 hostelries aren't only located near motorways and A roads, but increasingly also in city centres and near tourist attractions. A searchable database of Travelodges is on the website along with a button to click if you would like to be sent a printed list. Travelodges are open seven days a week from 7am to 10pm and accept Switch, Visa, MasterCard, American Express and Diner's Club cards. You can cancel a booking by telephone before 4pm on the arranged day of arrival.

Most people should be able to find something to suit their budget and tastes, but when an international convention or a business fair is taking place, or you're in a popular locale, you should book well in advance, particularly for a top hotel.

All hotels, motels, inns and guesthouses with four bedrooms or more (including self-catering accommodation) must display a notice showing their minimum and maximum overnight charges. Prices shown must include any service charge and may include VAT, although it must be indicated whether or not these are included (if VAT isn't included, it must be shown separately). If meals are provided with accommodation, it must be made clear and, where prices aren't standard for all rooms, then the price range can be shown.

Information

Apart from the wealth of information encompassing all standards of accommodation provided on its website, Visit Britain also publishes the *Where to Stay* series of guides which includes *Hotels & Guesthouses* and *Farmhouses, Bed & Breakfast, Inns & Hostels*. These only cover England.

General hotel guides include *The Good Hotel Guide* (Ebury Press), the *AA Hotel Guide*, the *Which? Guide to Good Hotels*, the RAC's *Hotel Guide,* the *AA Britain and Ireland Hotel Guide* and *Recommended Hotels in Great Britain.*

Many kinds of accommodation are also rated by regional tourist boards according to their accessibility for wheelchair users and others who have difficulty walking. Information and advice about accommodation for physically disabled people is available from Visit Britain and the Holiday Care Service, The Hawkind Suite, Enham Place, Andover, SP11 6JS (☎ 08451-249 971, 💻 www.holidaycare.org.uk). The latter is a registered charity.

BED & BREAKFAST

Bed and breakfast (B&B) accommodation consists of a room in a private house, country pub, farmhouse or even on a university campus, and is found throughout the UK from cities to remote hamlets. B&B accommodation is more informal than a hotel and provides an opportunity to meet the British in their own homes. Many ordinary homes providing B&B accommodation indicate this with a *Bed & Breakfast* sign outside or in the window. Guest house accommodation is similar in price and standard to B&B, but is usually available only in towns.

Although it's advisable to book in advance for public holiday weekends or at any time in London, it's usually unnecessary, particularly if you're touring and need a room for one or two nights only. If you're a smoker, you should check in advance whether smoking is permitted. If you don't book in advance, you have more freedom to go where you please, but you should bear in mind that some B&Bs have a minimum stay of two or three nights. When booking in advance, confirm your arrival time to ensure that your hosts are at home. If you're staying for more than one night, you may be expected to vacate your room for most of the day and to leave by noon (or earlier) on your last day.

Like hotel accommodation, B&B standards vary greatly from a basic single room sharing a bathroom to a luxury double room with *en suite* bathroom (possibly in a country house). Many B&Bs are graded by regional tourist boards using Visit Britain's diamond classification system (see above) and room rates range from around £25 to £50 per person, per night outside London (excluding country houses), and to £30 to £50 in London. Rates in country houses tend to mirror those of hotels. B&B accommodation is the cheapest form of accommodation for tourists or travellers who don't want to stay in one place for more than a few days. If you require temporary accommodation for a week or longer there may be a reduced rate. The cheapest rooms don't contain a television and sometimes may not include towels, in which case they're usually available for a small fee. Many B&B hotels provide tea and coffee-making facilities in all rooms. Note that B&B establishments and cheap hotels aren't usually very warm in winter. As the name suggests, bed and breakfast always includes breakfast (usually a full cooked English breakfast, see above). Many B&Bs also offer an optional evening meal (dinner) at a reasonable price, which must usually be ordered in advance. Some B&Bs won't accept children and many don't cater for the disabled.

Farmhouse B&Bs are an interesting alternative for those who want a change from towns. Visit Britain publishes on its website a list of agencies representing individuals offering home-stay accommodation in which you're treated more like a guest of the family than a customer and may be invited to take part in family activities. Guest houses, found mainly in seaside towns and other tourist centres, are similar to B&Bs, but cater more for visitors wishing to stay for a week or two rather than a few nights. Rates range from around £30 to £60 per person per night, outside London and usually include half-board.

Tourist Information Centres provide a wide range of brochures and guides containing information about bed and breakfast accommodation throughout the UK, including a series of B&B touring maps. The most comprehensive guide to B&Bs is *The Good Bed & Breakfast Guide* by Elsie Dillard & Susan Causin (Which? Books), listing over 1,000 B&Bs. Other B&B guides, including *Bed and Breakfast Guest Accommodation in England* (English Tourism Council), *The Best Bed and Breakfast – England, Scotland and Wales* (UKHM Publishing), the *AA Bed & Breakfast Guide,* Alastair Sawday's *Special Places to Stay in Britain*. B&B accommodation can be booked through a number of agencies, including Bed & Breakfast (GB), PO Box 47085, London, SW18 9AB (☎ 0871-781 0834, ✉ bookings@bedbreak.com), Wolsey Lodges Ltd, 9 Market Place, Hadley, Ipswich, Suffolk IP7 5DL (☎ 01473-822 058) and London Homestead Services, Maida Vale, London (☎ 020-7286 5115). See also the books listed under **Hotels** on page 404. The Visit Britain website (🖳 www.visitbritain.com) includes a searchable database of bed and breakfast accommodation, and a list of agencies representing a number of hosts.

SELF-CATERING

Self-catering cottages, bungalows, apartments (flats), houseboats, houses, chalets and mobile holiday homes are available for rent in holiday areas and popular cities. An apartment is often a good choice for a family, as it's much cheaper than a hotel room (particularly in London), provides more privacy and freedom, and allows you to prepare your own meals as and when you please. Standards, while generally high are variable, and paying a high price doesn't always guarantee a well furnished or well appointed apartment (although most look wonderful in brochures). Many self-catering establishments are classified by regional tourist boards using the Visit Britain system.

Studios (bedsits) are available in London from around £200 per week or £50 per night, per person. The cost of an apartment in London for four people ranges from around £500 to £2,000 per week. There's no low season and rates are usually the same throughout the year (elsewhere rates vary depending on the season). In London and other cities, student hostels are available from around £18 a night in shared dormitories with cooking facilities. Rooms are also available in private homes with cooking facilities, which are provided in the room or in a shared kitchen.

The weekly rent of a country cottage varies considerably from around £250 to £1,000 per week for four people, depending on its location, size, amenities available and the season. If you want to try something different you can hire a canal boat (or choose a hotel boat), where all you need to do is sit back and enjoy the passing scenery along some of the UK's 3,220km (2,000mi) of canals (and the canal-side pubs). No previous boating experience is necessary. Hire costs vary from around £280 to £750 per week for four people, depending on the size and class of boat and the season. For information about holiday hire boats, contact British Waterways, Willow Grange, Church Road, Watford, WD17 4QA (☎ 01923-201 120, ⌨ www.britishwaterways.co.uk and for more holiday oriented material ⌨ www.waterscape.com).

Before booking any self-catering accommodation you should check the holiday changeover dates and times; what's included in the rent (e.g. cleaning, linen); whether cots or high chairs are provided or pets are allowed; if a garden or parking place is provided; and what sort of access there is to public transport. Self-catering accommodation is usually let on a weekly basis from Saturday to Saturday, often for a minimum of one or two weeks.

Many useful fact sheets and booklets are available from Tourist Information Centres with titles such as *Apartments in London*, usually providing information pertaining to a local area, while the official guide to *Self-Catering Holiday Homes in England* (English Tourism Council) contains hundreds of graded cottages, bungalows, apartments, houses and chalets throughout the country. Other books for self-caterers include the *The Good Holiday Cottage Guide* (Swallow Press) and *Self-Catering Holidays in Britain* (FHG Publications). The National Trust (see **Gardens, Stately Homes, Parks & Zoos** on page 412) also provides a list of holiday homes and cottages for rent, while self-catering accommodation, including cottages, is advertised in magazines and national newspapers such as *The Sunday Times*, *The Observer* and *Dalton's Weekly*.

YOUTH HOSTELS

For those travelling on a tight budget, one way to stretch limited financial resources is to stay in a youth hostel, which may vary from a castle to a cottage, a hunting lodge to a stately home. There are over 290 youth hostels in the UK, including around 60 in Scotland run by the Scottish Youth Hostel Association (SYHA). Many open all year round. Membership is open to all, although the permitted minimum age of children accompanied by an adult is generally five, or 14 when unaccompanied. (In 70 hostels, which are suitable, children under three may accompany their parent/s.) Children aged between 5 and 15 are given free membership when their parents (or a single parent) are members. There are currently more than 230,000 members of the Youth Hostel Association.

Youth hostels provide separate dormitories (8 to 16 beds) for males and females, and duvets (or blankets), pillows and a short sleeping bag are available if required. Many youth hostels have small dormitories (four to six beds) that can be used by families and some have a self-contained family annexe or special family rooms (with their own kitchen, living room and bathroom), where you can come and go at any time of the day. Family or group accommodation must be booked by telephoning before 10am or after 5pm, or using the website reservation facility (⌨ www.yha.org.uk). It isn't necessary for single people to book, but it's often advisable, to avoid disappointment.

Most hostels also provide hot showers, central heating, laundry facilities, and small shops selling souvenirs and foodstuffs. Usually, hostels are closed during the day from 10am to 5pm (except for family units) and close for the night at 11pm. Guests must remain quiet until 7am and alcohol isn't permitted on the premises. You're usually expected to help with simple chores, such as sweeping the floor and washing up.

Self-catering kitchens are provided at all permanent hostels, many of which also provide a cheap restaurant. Overnight rates in England and Wales vary depending on the hostel, which is graded on a scale from 1 to 9 (9 is London). Prices range from £5 to £10 per night for under 18s (and up to £30 in London) and from £10 to £14 per night for adults (up to £28 in London). Rates are sometimes higher in July and August. Hostels in Scotland are graded from one to three and rates are similar to those in England and Wales.

All guests must be members of their national Youth Hostelling Association or an association affiliated to the International Youth Hostel Federation (IYHF). Individual membership of the YHA costs £7 a year for those under 18, £14 for adults, £28 for families (includes both parents and all children under 18) and £14 for a one-parent family. Life membership costs £210. Membership fees of the SYHA (Scotland) and HINI (Northern Ireland) are slightly lower than for the YHA. Associations organise a wide variety of action and adventure holidays lasting from a few days to a few weeks, during which you can participate in many sports and adventurous pastimes such as abseiling, rock-climbing or parachuting. Local YHA groups organise regular social evenings and weekend activities.

For further information about youth hostels in England and Wales, contact the YHA National Office, Trevelyan House, Dimple Road, Matlock, Derbyshire DE4 3YH (☎ 01629-592 600). For information about Scottish youth hostels, contact the Scottish Youth Hostel Association, 7 Glebe Crescent, Stirling FK8 2JA (☎ 01786-891 400, ⌨ www.syha.org.uk). Hostelling International Northern Ireland is at 22 Donegall Road, Belfast BT12 5JN (☎ 028-9032 4733, ⌨ www.hini.org.uk). All YHAs publish handbooks and accommodation guides, and excellent maps (usually free) showing hostel locations, giving opening dates and describing facilities. A *YHA Accommodation Guide* is available from bookshops and the organisation publishes a quarterly magazine, *Go Guide*, which is free to members.

If you're interested in international youth hostelling and staying at some of the 6,000 youth hostels around the world, check the international travel links on the YHA website (⌨ www.yha.org.uk) for organised programmes.

CARAVANS & CAMPING

The UK has around 3,500 licensed caravan (trailer), chalet and camping parks, 2,600 of which are graded under a quality scheme operated by the British Holiday and Home Parks Association (⌨ www.bhhpa.com) and the National Caravan Council (⌨

www.nationalcaravan.co.uk) in co-operation with local tourist boards. The system used is similar to that for rating hotels, but with as much emphasis on quality as the number of facilities provided. A database of these inspected sites can be found at 🖳 www.ukparks.com. In addition to the main caravan parks, the Camping and Caravanning Club maintains a list of over 1,260 certificated locations, which are generally small and secluded camps often located in the grounds of a house or farm. Permission is required to camp anywhere outside official sites.

The cost of parking a touring caravan is from around £8 to £12 a night or from around £8 to £10 for motor caravans, depending on their length and the particular caravan park. The cost of pitching a tent at a camping site is usually from £5 to £8 a night, again depending on the tent size and the site. Many caravan parks also have static caravans that can be hired for £100 to £450 a week, depending on the size, amenities and number of berths required. In addition to buying your own caravan, which costs anything from £5,500 to £25,000 depending on its size (e.g. two to six-berths), build quality and fittings, you can also hire touring caravans in all areas.

Whether you own or hire a caravan, ensure that it's roadworthy, as over half are found to have faults in police spot checks. Campers must have a Federation Internationale de Camping et de Caravanning (FICC) camping carnet, which covers them for £100,000 against third party risks. It can be purchased for £4.75 from camping and caravanning organisations. A similar card is available from the Caravan Club under a slightly different name – the international camping card – and at a slightly higher price.

The AA publishes Camping & Caravanning in Britain and Ireland and Visit Britain's Where to Stay series of guides includes Camping & Caravan Parks in Britain, listing over 700 parks throughout the country. Other books on the subject are Camping Caravanning Britain by George Gurney (Mirador) and International Camping and Caravanning Guide to Great Britain 2004 by Dudley Scarff (CMP). Some English regional tourist boards also publish touring caravan and camping guides for their areas. A number of magazines for caravanners, motor caravanners and outdoorsmen are published in the UK, including Practical Caravan, Motor Caravan and Trail.

Various organisations for caravanners and motor caravanners exist, among them Camping and Caravanning Club, Greenfields House, Westwood Way, Coventry CV4 8JH (☎ 0845-130 7631, 🖳 www.campingandcaravanningclub.co.uk), the Motor Caravanners' Club Ltd, Freepost (TK 1292), Twickenham TW2 5BR, (☎ 020-8893 3883, 🖳 www.motorcaravanners.eu) and the National Caravan Council Ltd, Catherine House, Victoria Road, Aldershot, Hampshire GU11 1SS (☎ 01252-318 251, 🖳 www.nationalcaravan.co.uk).

MUSEUMS & ART GALLERIES

The UK has numerous museums and art galleries, including housing some of the most important collections to be found anywhere in the world (the British have been looting and pillaging for centuries to fill them.) London is home to the UK's most celebrated collections and admission to most of them is free (a great British tradition).

This also applies to commercial art galleries. However, charges are still made for 'special' exhibitions, usually of a temporary nature.

London institutions which charge, have fees of around £4 to £7.50 (average around £6 for adults) and £1 to £3 for children (usually under the age of 16); students usually receive a reduction on production of a student identity card. Such museums and art galleries sometimes offer free admission one day a week or offer annual family season tickets. Leading museums and galleries are open seven days a week (including most public holidays) from around 10am to 5 or 6pm, Mondays to Saturdays, and 2 or 2.30pm to 6pm on Sundays. Opening times vary, so check in advance, particularly when planning to visit the smaller London and provincial museums and galleries, some of which open on only a few days a week. Many museums and galleries provide reductions for disabled people and some have wheelchair access.

In addition to the great national collections, there are also many excellent smaller museums, galleries and displays in stately homes and National Trust properties, throughout the UK, many of which are well worth a visit. Most councils publish free directories of local arts organisations, and provide information about activities. Art lovers may be interested in *Insight Museums and Galleries of London* by Clare Peel (Insight Guides).

GARDENS, STATELY HOMES, PARKS & ZOOS

Lists of gardens, stately homes, castles, theme parks, zoos, botanical gardens and national parks are available from tourist offices or are to be found in any good guide book, and touring by car is the best way to see them. Most are open throughout the year, although many have reduced opening hours from October to March.

The National Trust (NT) is a privately-funded charitable organisation that looks after over 300 historic buildings and 612,000 acres of countryside in England, Wales and Northern Ireland. Many gardens, landscaped parks, and prehistoric and Roman sites, are also in its care. You can become a member for £32.50 a year or £58.50 a year for a family (including all children aged under 18). Membership provides free access to all NT buildings and sites. The NT issues a free handbook to every new member and you can hear about new developments and events for families and children by signing up for a free email newsletter. There are also over 200 local associations and centres throughout the UK organising a range of activities, details of which can be found in a searchable directory on their website (🖳 www.nationaltrust.org.uk); for further information write to the National Trust (Membership Department, PO Box 39, Warrington WA5 7WD, ☎ 0870-458 4000). You can also join at any National Trust property and have your entrance fee refunded. The National Trust for Scotland is a separate organisation (Wemyss House, 28 Charlotte Square, Edinburgh EH2 4ET, ☎ 0131-243 9300, 🖳 www.nts.org.uk).

English Heritage has broadly similar aims and membership costs £34 a year for adults. This enables you to visit 400 English Heritage properties without further charge. You also receive a property guidebook, maps, an events diary, a quarterly magazine and free entry to special events. For information contact English Heritage, Customer Service Department, PO Box 569, Swindon SN2 2YP (☎ 0870-333 1181, 💻 www.english-heritage.org.uk). If you're a keen horticulturist, you may be interested in joining the Royal Horticultural Society (80 Vincent Square, London SW1P 2PE, ☎ 020-7834 4333, 💻 www.rhs.org.uk). Membership starts at £44 and entitles you to free entry to many beautiful gardens and a range of other benefits.

The UK has a number of internationally acclaimed zoos, including London and Whipsnade (50km/30mi north of London), but there are also others throughout the UK (e.g. Bristol, Chester, Edinburgh, Glasgow and Manchester) plus a number of safari parks (e.g. Longleat) where animals roam free. (Remember to keep your car windows closed). Zoos are open most days of the year (some close only on Christmas Day) and admission is from around £5 (children from around £3).

The country also has almost 100 theme parks which are very popular (around 100 million visitors annually) and are an excellent place for a special (i.e. expensive) day out for the children. The most popular include Alton Towers (Staffordshire), Pleasureland (Southport), Thorpe Park (Surrey), Chessington World of Adventures (Surrey), Pleasure Island (Lincolnshire) and Legoland (Windsor, Berkshire).

CINEMAS

There has been a cinema renaissance in the last two decades, following a decline in the '60s and '70s, when many cinemas were turned into shops, bingo halls and even places of worship. Today around 2,600 separate screens are in operation and cinemas are thriving. Attendances have more than doubled in the last ten years. The mainstream cinema scene is dominated by the major chains such as MGM and Odeon. In the last decade, many multiplexes have been built (often in new out-of-town leisure and shopping complexes) each with ten or more screens, Dolby or THX surround sound, and offering comfortable, extra-wide seats with ample leg-room in air-conditioned auditoriums. Free parking, cafés, restaurants, bars and games rooms may also be available.

London has numerous cinemas (around 100 in inner London alone) showing not only the latest films, but many classics and foreign-language films, usually screened with their original soundtracks and subtitles. However, many London cinemas have small screens. Ticket prices range from around £3 for children's matinees in provincial cinemas up to around £16 (average £7 to £12) for first-run films in London's West End. Most cinemas offer reductions (usually half price or less) for children and pensioners, although you should check in advance, as some reductions apply only to certain performances. Many cinemas have a reduced price day, usually Mondays, when admittance for afternoon shows is cheaper. (Discounts, on the other hand, may be available on any afternoon). Many modern cinemas have facilities for the disabled.

All films on general release are given a classification by the British Board of Film Censors (shown below) which denotes any age restrictions:

Classification	Age Restriction
U	None
PG	Parental guidance advised
12a	No one under 12 admitted unless accompanied by an adult
15	No one under 15 admitted
18	No one under 18 admitted

Children (or adults) who look younger than their years may be asked for proof of their age, e.g. a school identity card, student card or driving licence, for admittance to age-restricted performances. Most cinemas accept telephone bookings (major credit cards accepted) and tickets can usually be purchased in advance. There may be an additional fee when booking by credit card, e.g. 50p to £1 a ticket. Tickets may, however, be sold only on the day of the performance. Booked seats are usually held until 30 minutes before a performance begins.

There are private film clubs in the major cities and local film societies in all areas, and a number of magazines for film buffs are published. In London, *Time Out* and *What's On* provide comprehensive film reviews and list all London cinema programmes and performance times. National and local papers publish cinema programmes (mostly London ones in the former) and most also review the latest films.

THEATRE, OPERA & BALLET

The UK is world-renowned for the quality and variety of its theatre, opera and ballet companies, and London has the world's most vibrant theatre scene with over 150 commercial and subsidised venues, including around 50 in the West End. Between five and ten new major productions open to the paying public each week on average, and a much greater number when smaller and fringe venues are taken into account.

Major auditoriums include the Royal National Theatre (South Bank), the Barbican Centre, the Royal Opera House (Covent Garden), and the Royal Court Theatre embraces modern drama; classical plays; comedy; musicals; revue and variety; children's shows and pantomime; opera and operetta; ballet and dance. London's fringe theatre is lively and extensive, and provides an excellent training ground for new companies and playwrights. Many venues nationwide support youth theatres, and people of all ages who see themselves as budding Laurence Oliviers or Katherine Hepburns can audition for local amateur dramatics societies. The theatre is well patronised throughout the country and is one of the delights of living in the UK, particularly if your home is within easy reach of London.

Excellent theatre and musical entertainment isn't confined to London. Many provincial towns also have acclaimed theatres, concert halls and arts centres attracting international stars (and they charge only a fraction of London's West End prices). The arts are subsidised by the Arts Council which, among other things, funds a repertory company touring programme that ensures the arts reach areas without permanent theatres.

The cost of tickets for most London musicals and plays ranges from around £14 to £45 and from £10 to £35 for provincial theatres.

Opera, along with ballet, is largely patronised by only a small minority of the middle and upper classes. Ticket prices for performances at the Royal Opera House in Covent Garden partly explain why: a seat in the orchestra stalls costs around £150, while a seat offering a reasonable view costs in excess of £60. A limited number of bargain 'slip' seats with a very restricted view can be bought for as little as £11, but this probably has as more to do with the public relations of an institution which has been subsidised by the National Lottery to the tune of £70 million, than anything else. Prices vary with the production and the section of the theatre concerned and tickets at the top end of the price spectrum are markedly cheaper for ballet rather than opera performances.

Provincial ballet and opera tickets also cost far less, e.g. those for the English National Ballet on tour are between £10 and £55, while seeing the Glyndebourne Touring Opera costs between £21 and £49. Scotland and Wales have their own national opera companies, admission to whose performances is reasonably priced.

Dance performances in general tend to be relatively less expensive than opera. In addition to classical ballet, dance companies are popular and numerous throughout the UK, specialising in everything from contemporary dance to traditional forms from all corners of the globe.

Tickets for ballet, opera and musicals are in heavy demand, so you should apply well in advance. Some London musicals are solidly booked for months in advance, with many tickets being purchased by overseas tour operators selling theatre package tours. British ticket agencies also have representatives in many countries, allowing purchases to be made abroad. Most theatres accept credit card telephone bookings. Non-credit card telephone bookings are usually honoured for a number of days (e.g. three) unless booked on the day of the performance, when they're kept until around an hour before the performance is due to begin. Postal bookings with payment by cheque or credit card can also be made (but give alternative dates if possible). (Many theatres also ask for a first class stamped addressed envelope). You can, of course, buy tickets personally beforehand at theatre box offices. Most London box offices are open from around 10am on performance days; however, in the case of West End shows, it's advisable, even then, to telephone in advance and make a reservation before collecting your ticket, just to enhance your chances of success.

Discounts are usually available for groups (size varies) and school parties. Concessions (reduced price tickets) are often available for families, senior citizens (60+), young people (age varies from under 18 to 14-30 year-olds), students and the unemployed (students must show student identification and the unemployed a UB40 form.). Concession tickets may be 'standby' only, which means they've been left over and are sold cheaply a few hours before a performance. Among venues which do this is the Royal National Theatre. You can buy a subscription to a season of performances at many theatres and obtain a large discount, e.g. 30 to 40 per cent.

It's advisable to purchase tickets directly from the venue, because ticket agencies charge a booking fee ranging from 15 to 25 per cent of the face value (similar to ticket touts, in fact). Before buying tickets from any secondary source, you should check the official box office price first (printed on the ticket) so that you know exactly how much commission you're being asked to pay. Most ticket agencies don't actually have any tickets, but simply ring the box office, which you might just as well do yourself. If you desperately want to see a show and cannot wait, you may be able to buy tickets from ticket 'touts', although you may be asked for two or three times a ticket's face value.

The exception to the foregoing advice is the Society of London Theatre's Ticket Booth in London's Leicester Square, which sells tickets for West End shows at half-price on the day of performance. There's an additional administrative charge of £2.50. Cash, credit and debit cards are accepted, but not cheques or travellers cheques. Seats are sold 'from the top of the pile' with no choice about where you sit, but they're generally in the orchestra stalls and provide a good or excellent view. The booth is open from 10am to 7pm, Monday to Saturday, and noon to 3.00pm on Sunday.

Always check performance times with the box office or in a newspaper or entertainment magazine. If you're late for a live performance, you may have to wait until the interval before being permitted to take your seat, although it may be possible to watch the show on a TV monitor. There are usually evening performances from Mondays to Saturdays and often a matinee performance on one weekday, usually a Wednesday or Thursday, and Saturday. There are no performances on Sundays (even actors and actresses are entitled to a day off!).

Most theatres have a number of spaces for wheelchairs, induction loops for the hard of hearing, and toilets for wheelchair users (but mention any special needs when booking). Some theatres produce braille programmes and brochures and most allow entrance to guide dogs for the blind. Some theatres have signed performances for the deaf and hard of hearing, but usually only on certain dates, so check first. Restaurants and/or bars are a feature of almost all of them, and some London and most provincial theatres have private or public car parks nearby. If you wish to have a drink or a cup of coffee during the interval, it's best to order it in advance before the show starts and avoid the crush. Many of the points mentioned above concerning theatre facilities and tickets, also apply to concert halls and tickets (see below).

Free programmes covering London or provincial theatres are available from Tourist Information Centres, and two very comprehensive sites providing the same information and more on the internet (🖳 www.officiallondontheatre.co.uk and 🖳 www. londontheatre.co.uk). On the former, you can sign up for a weekly email bulletin to keep right up to date with what is happening. Most British newspapers contain reviews of London and provincial shows, particularly broadsheet daily and Sunday newspapers which have their own theatre critics. London's entertainment magazines *What's On* (mainstream, conservative) and *Time Out* (progressive, more for the younger reader) carry comprehensive reviews and details of all London's shows, as does the Evening Standard's weekly *ES* magazine. Websites of interest include 💻 www.shakespeares.globe.org., www.nationaltheatre.org.uk and www.theatrenet.com.

Keen theatregoers living in Hertfordshire and Buckinghamshire can join Encore for Theatregoers, Pound Orchard, Peggs Lane, Aylesbury, Buckinghamshire, HP22 5HX (☎ 01296-630 112), which organises trips to regional and West End theatres and concert venues.

CONCERTS

Classical concerts are staged regularly throughout the UK by British and international performers and celebrated international festivals cover orchestral, choral, opera, jazz, folk, rock and world music. London's unrivalled concentration and variety of music venues, and its four major orchestras, the London Symphony Orchestra (LSO), the London Philharmonic Orchestra (LPO), the Royal Philharmonic Orchestra (RPO) and the Philharmonia, make it the music capital of the world. Acclaimed provincial orchestras include those in Birmingham, Manchester and Bournemouth, along with the BBC National Orchestra. One of the most famous classical music seasons is 'the Proms' (promenade concerts), performed at the Royal Albert Hall, and culminating in the celebrated 'Last Night of the Proms' concert which is televised internationally.

Most major cathedrals take part in a summer festival of music performed by the London Festival Orchestra. Provincial professional and amateur orchestras and ensembles perform individual and subscription series of concerts, tickets for which are reasonably priced. Tickets are usually available for a whole season of classical performances or a selection of them, interest-free payment for which can sometimes be made by direct debit and spread over a period, e.g. six months. In summer, free open-air concerts are staged in public parks by orchestras and bands throughout the country.

Local music societies or music clubs regularly organise concerts and recitals, for which members (or 'friends') receive priority bookings; reduced seat prices; savings on meals, holidays and special events; a free mailing list; and may even take part in programme planning. Tickets usually range from around £5 to £15. You can become a member or friend of a music society, orchestra or theatre for as little as £10 a year. Free lunchtime organ and choral concerts are performed in cathedrals and churches throughout the year, and free outdoor concerts are staged in summer (a collection is usually made to help meet expenses). Look for announcements in your local newspapers or enquire at your nearest TIC.

In addition to classical and choral music, just about every other kind of music is performed regularly somewhere in the UK. This includes brass and steel band music, country & western, folk, heavy metal, hip hop, house, jazz, indie, medieval, reggae, rock, rhythm and blues and soul music to mention just a selection. Fans of certain kinds of music, e.g. folk or jazz, can find specialist clubs in most cities, usually with low membership fees. The UK is a world leader in the popular music industry, and

London is again the centre of attraction, with more 'gigs' in one night than most provincial cities stage in a month. These range from pub sessions to those of mega rock stars who fill Wembley stadium.

Concert ticket prices are generally lower than in many other western countries, although the prices for superstars can be astronomical. They cost from £5 to £70 depending on who's performing and the venue, with smaller more local ones offering discounts for students and usually increasing prices on Fridays and Saturdays.

For potential music-makers, a wide range of amateur musical groups exists, including orchestras, marching bands, choral societies and even barbershop singers, most of which are constantly on the lookout for new talent. Free music is also provided by an army of buskers, many of whom are excellent (and most of whom are illegal).

Many publications are dedicated to the popular music industry, most prominently the *New Musical Express*. Classical music magazines have burgeoned in recent years and include *Classical Music, Gramophone,* and *Early Music Today*. The London entertainment magazines *Time Out*, and *What's On* provide comprehensive music reviews and list all concerts in the London area. Free music newspapers and magazines are also available in some areas. Information about provincial concerts is available from local TICs and libraries. Among the many websites of interest are the London Symphony Orchestra (💻 www.lso.co.uk), London Net (💻 www.london net.co.uk – all kinds of music, including a free email magazine), Folk and Roots (💻 www.folkandroots.co.uk – folk music) and London Organ (💻 www.london organ.co.uk) for organ recitals in and around London. Many of the points listed under **Theatre, Opera & Ballet** on page 414 concerning theatre facilities and tickets also apply to concert halls and tickets.

SOCIAL CLUBS

Numerous social and other clubs exist, including Rotary clubs, workingmen's clubs, business clubs, church groups, Conservative clubs, the Freemasons, international friendship clubs, Kiwani clubs, Labour clubs, Lion and Lioness clubs, Royal Antediluvian Order of Buffaloes (RAOB) clubs, Round Table clubs, ex-servicemen's clubs, sports clubs and women's clubs. Expatriates from a wide array of countries also have their own organisations in major cities and elsewhere; ask at your embassy for information. Prominent among them are American Men's and Women's clubs. The many famous, exclusive and very upper crust men's clubs in London principally exist to enable members to escape from their wives.

Clubs exist almost everywhere focussing on pastimes such as chess, bridge, whist, art, music, theatre, photography, cinema and local history. If you want to integrate into your local community, one of the best ways is to join one or more of them. In major cities, there are also singles clubs, some of which operate nationally and organise a comprehensive range of activities throughout the week. If you're retired, you may find your council publishes a programme of recreational activities for your age group. Most publish calendars of sports and social events, and information about local groups and associations is displayed in libraries.

DANCE CLUBS & NIGHTCLUBS

There are dance clubs and nightclubs in all major centres, open until 2 or 4am, with entrance fees ranging between £5 and £25, which sometimes includes a 'free' drink, drinks being usually expensive. Admission may be cheaper if you arrive early (before the real action starts). London has one of the most cosmopolitan nightlife scenes to be found anywhere, with venues to suit every taste in music, fashion and atmosphere. A huge variety of gay clubs also exists in London, information about which is available from gay publications such as the *Pink Paper,* free in bars and cafés.

It's common to charge a fee for membership (which may be only temporary) in the admission price, although this sometimes requires being sponsored by at least two members and waiting a few days until it becomes valid. However, some clubs admit visitors accompanied by a member. The dress code is usually smart casual, which excludes jeans, leather, T-shirts and trainers, although in some establishments this may represent the ideal style (fashion usually dictates, depending on the venue). Some up-market establishments admit couples only. Only clubs with a music or dancing licence can sell alcohol after 11pm. All-night clubbing was legalised in 1990, but around 3am alcohol gives way to fruit juices, or black coffee.

'Alternative' comedy provides cheap and exciting entertainment and is popular in London (which has more comedy clubs than any other city in the world) and many provincial cities. Observational, spontaneous and surrealist comedians vie with impressionists and sketch teams nightly for the limelight. Admission is around £5 to £15, there's usually a reduction for students and the unemployed, and the club circuit is becoming ever larger.

GAMBLING

Gambling is one of the UK's favourite pastimes (sometimes it's an occupation) and embraces horse and greyhound racing; the football pools; sweepstakes; the National Lottery; bingo halls; casinos; slot machine (or amusement) arcades; card games; raffles; betting on the results of general elections, public appointments, football matches or other sports events; and forecasting the names of royal babies or ocean liners. You can bet on almost anything, although one bookmaker refused to quote on the date of the end of the world (the punter wanted to pay with a post-dated cheque!).

National Lottery

Launched in 1994, the lottery is operated by Camelot, for whom it has proved a licence to print money. It's the UK's answer to the state lotteries staged by European countries and most US states (the previous national lottery in the UK was suspended in 1826 when the operator absconded with the takings). While initially a tremendous success, it has recently declined in popularity. Tickets cost £1 each and jackpots can be £20 million or more when 'rolled over' for a few weeks. (This happens when no one has chosen the six main numbers in the draw and the prize money is added to that of the following week, thus allowing a bigger jackpot to build up). Your chance of landing the jackpot is 14 million to one against (there's a much greater likelihood you will be struck dead by lightning tomorrow), although this doesn't prevent a majority of Britons playing regularly.

You must be aged 16 or over to play (although many younger children get around this). Tickets can be bought from corner shops, newsagents, supermarkets, petrol stations and post offices, all which display the National Lottery symbol of a smiling hand with crossed fingers. This must be done by 7.30pm on Saturdays to be included in the Saturday draw. All you need do is choose six numbers between 1 and 49 (you need three out of six to win a prize). Don't lose your ticket, as it's the only proof that you're a winner. The draw on Saturday evenings is shown live on BBC television. Winning numbers are broadcast on radio and television, published in national newspapers and displayed by National Lottery retailers. Prizes must be claimed within 180 days after the winning draw. Don't be fooled by unofficial overseas agents for the National Lottery who charge far more than the face value for each £1 ticket! If you wish to take part while abroad, you can buy a subscription ticket for six months or one year direct from the organisers (💻 www.national-lottery.co.uk).

The lottery was ostensibly created to provide money for 'good causes', including sports, the arts, the National Lottery Charities Board and the National Heritage Memorial Fund. Of the proceeds, under 30 per cent of turnover goes to 'good causes' and another 12 per cent to the government in tax. Donations to charities have fallen considerably since the lottery began and many face serious cash shortfalls in the next few years. Scratch cards with instant prizes of up to £50,000 – which have been likened to fruit machines and are highly addictive – and a second weekly draw on Wednesday evenings were introduced later, and exacerbated this situation. Lottery addicts have swamped Gamblers Anonymous since its inception, and disputes over prize money have caused marriages to break up and friends to fall out. Sadly, one man even shot himself after failing to buy a ticket in a week in which the set of numbers he invariably used would have won him the jackpot prize.

Betting Shops

Some of the UK's 10,000 or more turf accountants (usually called betting shops or bookies, short for bookmakers) will be found in just about any town in the country. These were legalised in the '60s to allow off-course betting on horse and greyhound races. Traditionally, their turnover increases in difficult economic times when many Britons turn to gambling for relief, but they, along with all other sectors of the gambling industry, have been hard hit by the National Lottery in recent years. You can also bet on horse and greyhound races by post or telephone, while on-course tote betting is also popular. A racing results service is provided on the teletext information service on ITV4.

Football Pools

Until the National Lottery was launched, the football pools were the UK's biggest weekly 'flutter' with a weekly turnover of £900 million, and participants can still win huge cash prizes by forecasting (i.e. guessing) the results of football matches. The treble chance is the most popular bet, involving punters guessing which matches will be score draws (matches which end in a draw with each team scoring at least one goal) and prizes can run to around £2 million. Many millions of people, within the UK and around the world, have a weekly bet on the pools. If you don't want to fill out a coupon every week, you can arrange a standing order always using the same numbers.

Casinos

London is one of the world's most celebrated gambling centres among the seriously rich and it comes as no surprise to discover that it's home to over 25 of the UK's some 120 casinos (only France has more in Europe). Its casinos have a turnover of well over £2.2 billion a year. Turnover is much smaller in provincial casinos, where gamblers generally play more often, but for smaller stakes. Casino staff are prohibited by law from taking tips, so that if you give one it ends up in the pockets of the management or is returned. The strict rules under which British casinos now operate are criticised by some as archaic, when computer gambling (via credit card) is available on the internet 24-hours a day (although how you can guarantee getting your winnings is another matter).

Premium Bonds

Premium Bonds aren't an investment, as no interest is paid. They're similar to a ticket in a lottery, except that you cannot lose your original investment and can cash in your bonds at any time, at face value. The 'possible' premium is in a monthly draw (made by ERNIE, the Premium Bonds computer), which offers prizes ranging from £50 to £1 million (around 250,000 prizes totalling up to £20 million a month). You must invest a minimum of £100 at any one time, purchases must be in multiples of £10 (e.g. £110, £120), and the maximum holding is £30,000. Bonds can be purchased at any post office, by post or online (🖳 www.nsandi.com) and are entered into the next draw after purchase. Results are announced in the national press and are available at main post offices (including a list of unclaimed prizes).

Other

Other forms of popular gambling are bingo (casinos for housewives, where around five million have a weekly flutter in 1,000 commercial bingo clubs), slot-machine arcades (the poor man's Las Vegas) and sweepstakes (the most popular of which is the Irish Sweepstake). If you have a gambling problem, Gamblers Anonymous (PO Box 5382, London W1A 6SA, ☎ 020-7384 3040) may be able to help (but unfortunately they cannot provide you with a stake).

PUBS

The UK is noted for its pubs (an abbreviation of public houses), which are a British tradition going back to Roman and Saxon times (drunkenness isn't a new phenomenon – the British have been sots for millennia), when inns were established to meet the needs of travellers. A pub is one of the most welcoming places in the UK (particularly on a freezing winter's night when many have inviting open log fires) and represents the heart of local communities.

According to research by Datamonitor, every Briton over 15 drank an average of 240 pints of beer in 2006, although of course in reality some drank noticeably more than others. This compares with the 336 pints drunk by each Czech, whose country topped the international beer consumption league, and the Australian average of a mere 182 pints per head. Statistically, the average British male spent £1,144 on beer in the same year. Despite heavy marketing, the British have proved resistant to the scourge of mineral water, drinking far less than the European average. (It's interesting to note that despite the UK's reputation as a nation of drunks, the country has more teetotallers – people who don't drink alcohol – than any other European country).

According to licensing statistics, there were over 82,000 pubs in the UK in 2006, and every town and many villages have at least one, although the tendency for rural pubs to close down is continuing. A pub is the local meeting place for business and pleasure and, if you arrange to meet a stranger anywhere in the UK, it's invariably at a pub (even in an unfamiliar town you can always find a pub). However, in recent years they've been under increasing pressure, with margins on beer cut to the bone and falling sales (beer consumption is declining), and few pubs could survive without serving food. The new laws banning smoking in pubs comes into force on July 1st 2007 throughout England and Wales (following earlier bans in the Republic of Ireland, Northern Ireland and Scotland).

There are excellent pubs in most cities, towns and country areas, many occupying beautifully restored historic buildings. Frequently, many have fascinating names which date back centuries, although the modern 'theme' pubs currently popular may change their themes and therefore their names every few months.

Most traditional pubs have two bars: a 'posh' bar called a 'lounge', 'saloon' or 'private' bar, and a public bar for the riff-raff and those in dirty working clothes (who aren't usually allowed into lounge bars). The public bar is usually where the darts board, slot machines and other games are to be found. Many modern pubs have only a single large lounge bar. Some pubs have a jukebox and pubs with a young clientele often play continuous loud pop music (which can be a nightmare) or feature discotheques and live rock bands on a number of nights each week (places to avoid if you want a quiet drink). Karaoke is popular in many pubs, where frustrated would-be pop stars get up on stage and perform their favourite songs (taped backing music and words are provided).

Most pubs provide reasonably priced hot and cold food at lunchtimes (usually self-service from the bar) and some have excellent à la carte restaurants in the evenings. An increasing number serve decent wines and imaginative meals with change from £15 (but, alas, still far too few). However, the quality of food is extremely variable, so ask around. Country pubs usually offer the best value for money. Pub restaurants operate in the same way as any others and credit cards are usually accepted. Lunch is usually served between noon to 2pm and dinner from 7pm to 9.30pm.

Many pubs also provide accommodation. Traditionally these were called inns, although nowadays they're usually referred to as hotels or pub hotels. Many pubs also have an off-licence, which is a small room from which they sell alcohol for consumption off the premises (off-licences are shops that sell alcohol and which are governed by special licensing hours).

British pubs serve a multitude of beers and alcoholic beverages, from continental lagers to traditional British ales, with a total of over 1,000 brands. In the last few decades, there has been a revival in traditional or 'real ales', brewed from fresh barley, hops and oats. The British produce the widest range of beers in the world, including many draught beers (on tap) drawn from casks or kegs, such as the ever popular bitter, stout (e.g. Guinness), mild and a wide variety of continental lagers (many brewed in the UK under licence). In addition to draught beers, numerous bottled and canned beers are also available, including brown ale (Newcastle is the most famous brand name), pale ale, light ale and many more.

Although the UK pays lip service to the metric system, beer is still sold in pints (568ml) and not litres (a small beer is half a pint). Wine is sold by the glass (there's no law regarding the quantity) and spirits by one-sixth of a gill (24ml) in England and Wales (in Scotland and Northern Ireland they're larger). One big difference between the UK and other countries is that in the UK you always order drinks and bar food at the bar and pay in cash when you order. You cannot 'run a tab' and pay when you leave (or when you fall off your chair), as is common on the continent. Receipts aren't usually given unless you ask for one (which would be considered very unusual in any other establishment).

Some British pubs are owned by brewery conglomerates and therefore sell beer produced only by their owners. Most, however, are now owned by operating chains, and even those still brewery-owned must, by law, offer 'guest beers'. If you want a pub with a wide selection of the best beers, choose a free house, which is a pub with no brewery ties and therefore free to sell whatever beer it chooses (which usually means the pick of the most popular brands). Most pubs sell an average of around 20 different draught and bottled beers. A large variety of spirits, cocktails and a (usually limited) selection of wines is also available. Pubs also sell non-alcoholic soft drinks and usually tea and coffee.

On public holidays, such as Christmas Day, Boxing Day and New Year's Eve, pubs are often granted an extended licence until midnight or 1am. (Although Christmas Day closing is becoming more prevalent). The new 24 hour licensing law allows Britain's pubs, clubs, bars, supermarkets and service stations to apply for the new longer opening licenses. Critics of the new law fear the extension of the licensing hours will create a breed of drunken yobs bringing havoc to quiet residential areas. In contrast, some areas of Wales and on some Scottish islands, pubs are closed on Sundays. Bars in restaurants, hotels and other buildings, are generally governed by the same licensing laws as pubs, except when a special licence has been granted. Pub landlords have the right to refuse to admit or serve a customer and cannot by law serve anyone who's drunk.

Many traditional games are played in pubs, including darts, bar billiards, pool, skittles (nine pins), dominoes, and cards. Pinball and similar machines may also feature. You aren't permitted to play games for money, as gambling is illegal in pubs.

The legal age for buying and consuming alcohol in a pub is 18, although children over 14 are admitted at the discretion of the landlord and can consume non-alcoholic drinks. Children under 14 are admitted to beer gardens, family rooms, pub restaurants and an increasing number of pub lounges. Pubs can apply for a 'children's certificate' until 9pm or 9.30pm to allow children to join their parents in the bar for a meal.

The law with regard to driving and drinking is strict (see **Drinking & Driving** on page 286) and the police are particularly active over Christmas and the New Year. If you have more than a couple of drinks, you would be well advised to hitch a ride with a sober friend or use public transport. Most pubs sell a variety of low-alcohol beers and wines and a wide choice of non-alcoholic drinks, including coffee.

Wine bars can be found in most cities and towns and have become increasingly popular in recent years. Most wine bars serve food, and the atmosphere usually resembles that of a smart restaurant, rather than a pub.

Books of interest to pub buffs – including those who like to eat before getting drunk and rolling into bed – are *Great Food Pubs* (Ebury), *Time Out's Eating and Drinking in Great Britain and Ireland*, *The Which? Guide to Country Pubs*, Roger Protz's *Britain's Best 500 Pubs*, *The AA Pub Guide*, and *Pubs for Families* (CAMRA). No serious beer drinker should ever be without the CAMRA *Good Beer Guide* and *The Good Pub Guide* (Ebury Press), edited by Alisdair Aird, which contains details of over 5,000 pubs (a L-O-N-G pub crawl), including the type of food served, its quality and price, atmosphere, service, facilities for children and much more. For dog lovers there's *Dog Friendly Pubs, Hotels and B&B's* (Ebury).

RESTAURANTS & CAFES

The standard of restaurants varies widely, probably more so than anywhere else in the world. Most foreigners are familiar with the infamous (and previously well-deserved) image of a UK full of 'greasy spoon' establishments (specialising in fried food and overcooked vegetables), which are still lingering on in major cities and tourist areas. However, those who believe that time spent in the UK means bringing your own food supply or facing starvation (or food poisoning), are in for a pleasant surprise. True, there are many thriving restaurants, cafés and fast food establishments whose fare would be condemned as unfit for human consumption in more discriminating countries. However, a revolution has occurred in the last decade or so and there's now also a plethora of excellent restaurants offering a quality and variety of culinary delights hardly bettered anywhere in the world. In fact, top class restaurants are usually excellent and sometimes outstanding. You need only to open the pages of the latest Michelin red guides to realise that British food doesn't always live up (or down) to its dreadful reputation. On the negative side, prices for good food are often astronomical (wine is also **very** expensive) and even modest food can be costly.

Despite being synonymous with junk food, 'fast' or 'take-away' (take out) food **can** be very good, and comes in amazing variety. Most take-away establishments accept telephone orders and an increasing number make home deliveries (e.g. pizzas). And more Chinese and Indian restaurants providing a take-away service now offer deliveries. (There may be no reduction for a take-away meal, but you save on VAT). A take-away and free delivery service is becoming generally more commonplace among restaurants offering national cuisines. An exception are shops selling the traditional British take-away meal of fried fish and chips, the quality of which is variable (i.e. often terrible). You must usually go out of your way to find a good fish and chip shop, although it's well worth the effort.

Self-service restaurants and cafés are also commonplace in towns. Many should be avoided like the plague (although they're inexpensive, the food can be terrible and the coffee's even worse). Cyber cafés, where you can access the internet, and American-style coffee shops, such as Starbucks and the Seattle Coffee Co, have blossomed in profusion over the past decade. Some fast food and 'cheap' restaurants in tourist areas are a rip-off, particularly in London, and motorway service stations have a well-earned reputation for everything that's worst about British food (although standards are improving).

The best bets for those wishing to eat well and cheaply are British pubs (pub grub or bar food, is usually served at lunchtime only, e.g. noon to 2pm) and ethnic restaurants, particularly Chinese, Indian, Greek or Turkish and Italian ones, where the standard of food, although not uniform, is usually high and a meal costs around £10 to £18 a head (without wine). A medium-priced restaurant sets you back around £30 to £50 a head. Some restaurants, particularly those in hotels, provide separate vegetarian and diabetic menus (some even provide healthy low-fat meals). Jewish kosher restaurants are also fairly common in major centres. In some areas, you may find restaurant clubs, where two people can eat for the price of one. Ask at local restaurants if there's one in your area.

London is now one of the world's great eating capitals, rivalling Paris and New York for quality and ethnic variety, although not good value. For its residents, the *Time Out London Eating and Drinking Guide* is invaluable, listing over 1,500 restaurants, cafés and bars. When you do find really good food, it's often outrageously expensive (it's far cheaper to eat out in France, Italy, Portugal or Spain). Paying £90 to £150 (or more) a head for a meal isn't unusual if you want the very best, although many people think the prices charged by top restaurants are unjustified. The UK still has a lot to learn from the continent about good food that doesn't cost the earth.

Most restaurants are licensed to serve alcohol, but only with meals. The cost of wine can also be astronomical, with a mark-up of 200 per cent plus VAT. Many restaurants charge up to three times the shop price for branded wine or offer cheap plonk in make-believe, own-label bottles or in carafes (restaurant wines are usually rendered as obscure as possible so that customers won't realise the mark-up they're paying). Champagne is the biggest rip-off of all, with customers being charged £50 or £60 or more (or £10 a glass) for the privilege of drinking it in a restaurant. Unfortunately 'bring your own' (BYO) restaurants are almost unheard of in the UK (where are all the enterprising Aussies?).

Many restaurants offer 'tourist' or set-price menus at lunch time (usually from noon to 2pm), which include a choice of meals, maybe with soup and sometimes a dessert, from around £12. Some offer half-portions for children or have a children's menu. McDonalds (the American chain of hamburger restaurants) has branches in most towns and often organises special events and children's parties. Children of all ages are usually admitted to licensed restaurants, although few restaurants cater particularly for children (without their own credit cards). Cafés in the UK, unlike those in most continent countries, aren't licensed to sell alcohol.

Many department stores, galleries and museums have excellent value-for-money restaurants, often providing breakfast and lunch menus. Cheap meals are also provided by the YWCA and YMCA, the YHA, community centres and leisure centres. It's advisable to make a reservation for more expensive or popular restaurants, particularly for lunch, on Friday and Saturday evenings and at anytime for parties of four or more people. Most restaurants close on one or two days a week (opening times are usually posted outside). Because restaurants may serve alcohol outside licensing hours provided it's served with food, many get particularly busy after 11pm when the drunks are thrown out of the pubs (it's amazing the number of people who eat dinner in the early hours of the morning). Restaurants are often open until the early hours, particularly in cities such as London where you can eat until 3am or later.

All restaurants and cafés are obliged by law to display their tariffs where customers can see them before entering. If an establishment has an extensive *à la carte* menu, the prices of a representative selection of food and drink currently available must be displayed, in addition to any *table d'hôte* menu. All service or cover charges must also be clearly stated and prices shown must be **inclusive** of VAT. If a restaurant attempts to include any charges that aren't listed on the menu (which is a common practice in tourist areas), you should refuse to pay.

If you have a complaint regarding anything stated (or not stated) in a menu, or there's a big difference between what's stated and what you're served or charged, you can make a complaint to your local Trading Standards Officer. Your best bet is to reach a compromise with the manager or owner and negotiate a reduction to take into account your complaint. You can legally refuse to pay for anything inedible and insist on leaving, but should leave your name and address (and show proof of identity). If you do this, the management cannot prevent you leaving or call the police, as you've committed no offence.

Many restaurants and hotel bills include a service charge (around 10 per cent), designed to reduce tipping (and increase profits). Most British people still feel obliged to leave a tip of around 10 to 15 per cent, a practice which is encouraged or even expected in many establishments (most employees would find it difficult to survive on their meagre salaries without tips).

There are plenty of good restaurant guides published in the UK. However many (like most hotel guides) charge restaurants for entry, including *Les Routiers*, the AA and the RAC, which has led people to question their impartiality. Even motorway service stations (renowned for their awful food) are included in *Les Routiers*! Among those that don't charge for inclusion are the *Michelin Red Guide, Harden's London Restaurants and Harden's UK Restaurants* (Harden Ltd), the *Good Food Guide* (Which? Books) and the *Which? Pub Guide*.

LIBRARIES

The UK has one of the best public library services in the world (although it has suffered in the last decade, as local authorities have been forced to economise and reduce their budgets), and public libraries are found in all centres of any size. Residents in rural areas without a local library are often provided with a mobile service. Public libraries are run by county and borough councils and around a third of residents are registered users (one hopes the rest are book buyers). Anyone who lives, works or studies in the UK can join their local library free of charge, on production of proof of identity (e.g. a medical card or driving licence) and their current address, although children under 15 or 16 must usually be sponsored by a parent or guardian. Library members can borrow books from any library within their borough or county, and also elicit details and schedules regarding mobile services. When you join a library, you're usually given a computer membership card with which you can borrow up to eight to ten books (fewer in some libraries) at a time, for a period of three or four weeks.

At the end of the period, you may renew the loan of a book (in person or by telephone or post) for a further three or four weeks, provided nobody else has asked for it. Renewals may be repeated a set number of times before the book must be returned. If books aren't returned by the due date (stamped in the front of the book or written in if you renew by telephone), you must pay a small fine. Fines may not be levied on children or pensioners (although some councils have ended these concessions). Occasionally libraries have a moratorium on fines on overdue books, so that lenders can return them without financial loss.

Library opening times vary, but are usually around 9.30 or 10am to 5.30 or 6pm. There may be late opening (e.g. until 7 or 8pm) on a few days a week and earlier closing on one or two other days (e.g. 4 or 5pm), as well as a half-day (usually, but not always, on a Wednesday) when closing is at 1pm. Some libraries may close on one or more days a week (e.g. Mondays or Wednesdays) and all are open on Saturdays, e.g. 9.30am to 4pm. Where there's a demand, as in some London boroughs, they also open on Sundays, usually between 11am and 4pm. (In some places, council budget cutbacks have reduced opening hours drastically). Most libraries have computerised catalogues which can be used by borrowers to locate any book held in stock by the county library service. You can normally log on to these on the internet. Books can be requested from other libraries within the county or borough, for which a small fee is usually charged.

In addition to lending books, local libraries also provide reference sections where you will find encyclopedias, dictionaries, trade directories, Stationery Office publications, atlases, maps, telephone directories and any number of other reference works. Many also have computers connected to the internet, which can be booked free for periods of up to two hours. Nearly all include copies of local and national newspapers and magazines in their reading rooms. All this makes libraries the best source of local and general information on almost any subject. Stocks of books in large type for those with poor eyesight as well as free 'talking books' (on cassette) for blind and partially-sighted readers are also normally available.

16.

SPORTS

Sports facilities are generally excellent throughout the UK, whether you're a novice or an experienced competitor. Among the most popular sports are soccer (football), rugby (union and league rules), cricket, athletics, fishing, snooker, horse racing, motor racing, golf, archery, hiking, cycling, squash, badminton, tennis, swimming and skiing, an large number of which were British inventions. Most water (sailing, windsurfing, waterskiing, canoeing, yachting) and aerial sports (hang-gliding, parachuting, ballooning, gliding, light aircraft flying) also enjoy a keen following. A good general website for sports information is 24 Hours Sport (💻 www.24 hoursport.co.uk).

The leisure industry is big business and new sports facilities and complexes, including golf clubs, yacht marinas, indoor tennis clubs, dry-slope ski centres, health and fitness clubs and country clubs are sprouting up in all areas. They're all part of a huge growth market which is expected to gain even greater momentum in the coming years, as more people retire early and have more time for leisure and sport (ironically, many people won't be able to afford to retire at all). Many sports owe their popularity (and fortunes) to television (TV) and the increased TV coverage (and competition for TV rights) generated by the proliferation of cable and satellite TV stations. Professional and amateur sports have benefited hugely in recent years from the increase in the commercial sponsorship of individual events, teams, and league competitions.

The vast majority of sports facilities are 'pay-as-you-play', which means you don't need to join a club or enrol in a course to use them, although there are also many private clubs you can join by paying an annual membership fee. Participation in most sports is inexpensive and most towns have a community sports or leisure centre, financed and run by the council. District, borough and county councils publish free directories of clubs in their area and regional sports councils provide information about local activities. Most higher educational establishments and many large companies provide extensive sports facilities for students or employees, usually for a nominal fee, and many state schools have extensive sports facilities (which may be open to the public during evenings, weekends and holiday periods). Some organisations such as the YMCA and YWCA allow members to use their sports facilities at any time, on payment of a weekly, monthly or annual fee, and many clubs have cheap rates for those under 18 or students.

In contrast to the extensive and often excellent sports facilities for competitors, facilities for spectators often leave more to be desired. It's only in the last decade that major soccer stadia have left a primitive past behind in which most spectators were expected to stand on the 'terraces', with no protection from the cold and rain. Following a number of tragedies, soccer clubs were obliged (for safety reasons) to convert these to all-seat stadia, many of which are among Europe's best.

Despite the excellent sports facilities and the estimate that over 25 million people over the age of 13 regularly participate in sport and exercise, around half the population takes none at all (apart from strolling to the local pub and staggering back). Participation in many sports is the reserve of an elite group with everyone else relegated to the role of spectators (or TV couch potatoes). Sports participation for the young isn't helped by the government, which spent years trying to reduce the amount of time devoted to it in state schools. Lottery money certainly helped the English Institute of Sport (💻 www.eis2win.co.uk), which now has a web of centres around the country, but it seems more dedicated to producing winners than spreading the ethos of the game for the game's sake.

Perhaps the inert majority have been listening to the statisticians, who estimate that you're up to 17 times more likely to drop dead playing sport than reading a book, although if you exercise regularly you're actually 20 times less likely to drop dead so early. Sports injuries are estimated to cost the economy some 7.5m lost working days a year, most occurring in rugby, soccer, hockey, cricket and martial arts. If you injure yourself, there are sports injury clinics in most towns and sports physiotherapists in most sports centres. In addition to sports with an obvious element of danger (such as most aerial sports and mountaineering), many other sports (including most winter sports, power boat racing, waterski jumping, show-jumping and pot-holing) may not be covered by your health, accident or life insurance policies. Always check in advance and take out special insurance where necessary.

Sports results are given on the television teletext information service and published widely in daily newspapers. The Sunday broadsheet newspapers provide comprehensive cover and a nationwide results service (particularly for soccer and rugby). Numerous magazines are published for all sports, from angling to yachting, most of which are available (or can be ordered) from any newsagent. For information about sports facilities, contact Sports England, Third Floor, Victoria House, Bloomsbury Square, London WC1B 4SE (☎ 0845-850 8508, 🖳 www.sportengland. org). The Central Council of Physical Recreation (CCPR), Francis House, Francis Street, London SW1P 1DE (☎ 020-7976 3901, 🖳 www.ccpr.org.uk) is the national association of governing bodies of sport and recreation in the UK. The names and addresses of sports associations and federations can be obtained from Sports England or the CCPR.

AERIAL SPORTS

Most aerial sports have a wide following, particularly gliding, hang-gliding, paragliding, hot-air ballooning and microlighting. The main thing most aerial sports enthusiasts have in common is madness and money, both of which are usually required in abundance to fulfil man's ultimate ambition, although there are a number of inexpensive options available. One of these is hang-gliding, which has become increasingly popular in recent years with hang-gliding schools in all regions. Paragliding is one of the cheapest and easiest ways to 'fly', and entails launching yourself off a steep mountain slope with a paraglider or being tow-launched by a vehicle. When you've gained enough height, you release the tow and float off on your own. Although generally safer than hang-gliding, paragliding can be dangerous or even lethal in the wrong hands. Paragliders must complete an approved course of instruction lasting around four days, after which (if you survive) you receive an F1 'licence' that allows you to purchase a paraglider and fly when supervised by an experienced pilot. Paragliding equipment costs from around £750 second-hand to £4,000 new. It's as well to bear in mind that every landing is a 'controlled crash' and have insurance to cover all eventualities.

Hot-air ballooning has a small, but dedicated, band of (wealthy) followers, the most famous of whom is Richard Branson (the owner of the Virgin group of companies). Participation is generally limited to the wealthy because of the high cost of a balloon, although the sport has never enjoyed greater popularity. To buy a balloon costs anything from £13,000 to £60,000, plus over £100 an hour to fly it and over £1,000 annual insurance (it's the only form of transport more expensive and less reliable than the UK's railways). A flight in a balloon costs around £100 and is a marvellous experience, although there's no guarantee of distance or duration, as flights are dependent on wind conditions and the skill of your pilot (not to mention a safe landing).

Aircraft and gliders (sailplanes) can be hired with or without an instructor (provided you have a pilot's licence) from most small airfields. A new plane can cost anything from £50,000 to £100,000, although shared-ownership schemes are bringing the joys of flying to a much wider audience. There are many gliding clubs and parachuting and free-fall parachuting (sky-diving) flights or jumps can be made from most private airfields.

Microlights and ultralights (a go-cart with a hang glider on top and a motorised tricycle below) are an excellent alternative to 'real' aircraft as they can be assembled and disassembled quickly, are easily transported and cheap to run. They are designed to carry a maximum of two people and can be stored in a garage. Most machines are strong and safe, and the sport has a good safety record. It's one of the cheapest and most enjoyable ways of experiencing real flying, costing from around £5,000 for a second-hand machine up to £30,000 for a new top-of-the-range craft. Fliers require a private pilot's licence that costs up to £10,000 in tuition fees and normally takes up to six months and 40 hours of instruction to obtain, including classroom training and written examinations. (It's cheaper and quicker to learn to fly in the US, where costs are lower and the weather is better.)

Most aerial sports and private aviation are specifically excluded from many insurance policies, including, for example, health insurance and mortgage life insurance policies. Before taking up any aerial sport, you should ensure you have adequate health and accident insurance, that you have sufficient life insurance and that your affairs are in order. Why not take up fishing instead? A nice, sensible, **safe** sport (not that the fish would agree).

CRICKET

Cricket is a peculiarly English sport which usually takes foreigners some time to understand. (Many British people don't understand the finer points, including your author). If you don't know the difference between a stump and a bail, or an over and a wicket, you may as well skip this bit, as any attempt to explain would take around 100 pages and almost certainly end in failure. The first-class cricket season in England runs from April to September, when the main competition is for the Frizzel County Championships, competed for by 18 county teams organised into two divisions. Matches are played over four days, and many of them are drawn, owing to the vagaries of English weather. In addition to the County Championship, county teams also compete in the ECB National Cricket League, where limited-over matches are played in one day, and in two one-day knockout competitions: the Twenty20 Cup and the Cheltenham & Gloucester Trophy (the final of which is played at Lord's, the home of English cricket). In addition to the first-class County Championship, there's a Minor Counties Championship (Eastern and Western Divisions), a Second XI Championship and a multitude of local village teams, school teams, university teams, pub teams and women's teams, who compete at all levels throughout England. Scotland and Ireland also have cricket teams, although they (wisely) don't take the game seriously. There's an England ladies cricket team (who have been doing well lately, but have a hard job getting misogynists to take them seriously) and the game is played at all levels by women and girls throughout the UK. For those who wish to play with a straighter bat or brush up on their googly technique, there are cricket schools and coaching courses in many areas.

Cricket is played at international level (called test matches) by a number of Commonwealth countries, including Australia, India, New Zealand, Pakistan, South Africa, Sri Lanka, the West Indies and Zimbabwe. During the English cricket season, the England cricket team is usually engaged (i.e. getting beaten) in one or two minor series of international matches (three tests) or a major series (five or six tests). If you think four days (county matches) is a long time for a single match to last, a test match lasts five days, usually with a rest day after two or three days' play. One-day internationals are also played. The England cricket team also conducts overseas tours during the English winter, when it plays a series of test matches. The old enemy (in cricketing terms) are the Aussies (Australians), with whom England compete every few years for the Ashes (which aren't human, but the burnt remains of an old cricket bail from the early days of international cricket). A world cup knockout competition also takes place at regular intervals. The largest cricket website in the world is Wisden's (⌨ www.cricinfo.com), which is huge, while that of the England and Wales Cricket Board (⌨ www.edb.co.uk) is equally indispensable.

CYCLING

Cycling isn't as popular in the UK as on the continent and not much more than 2.3 per cent of journeys are made by bicycle in the UK compared to an average of 18 per cent in Denmark and 27 per cent in Holland. However, around 1.5 million cycles are sold each year (over a third bought to replace stolen machines!), which adds up to an awful lot of cyclists. It's estimated that in 2006 4.6 billion kilometres were cycled in the UK. Most people buy cycles for shopping or getting around towns, rather than cycling purely for pleasure, exercise or sport (e.g. touring or racing). Competitive cycling embraces road and track racing, cycle speedway, time-trialling, cross-country racing, touring, bicycle polo and bicycle moto-cross.

A wide range of cycles is available to suit all pockets and needs, ranging from a very basic shopping bike costing around £100 to a professional racing bike costing thousands. In between these extremes are commuter or town bikes, touring bikes, mountain bikes, BMX bikes, tricycles, tandems and bicycles with folding frames. Before buying a bike, carefully consider your needs, both now and in the future, obtain expert advice (e.g. from a specialist cycle store) and shop around for the best deal. Make sure you purchase a bike with the correct frame size. Mountain bikes have become increasingly popular in recent years and cost from around £150 up to £4,000 (expect to pay around £200 to £300 for an adequate bike).

Bicycles can also be hired by the day or week from cycle shops in cities and tourist areas; costs vary considerably, but are usually from around £5 to £10 a day depending on the type of bike (town, touring or mountain) and the area. Tandems, tricycles and folding bikes can also be hired in some areas. There may be lower rates for children and for weekly rental. Ask at local Tourist Information Centres or check the local yellow pages. Make sure a hired bicycle is insured against theft or damage.

Apart from travel to work or into town, cycling is an excellent way to explore the countryside at your leisure and get some fresh air and exercise at the same time. However, fresh air is in short supply in the UK's polluted cities, where many cyclists wear face-masks as protection against traffic emissions (although, according to medical experts, they offer little or no protection against carbon monoxide). The growing popularity of cycling in recent years has led to an increase in the number of accidents with motor vehicles. It's important never to underestimate the dangers of cycling (particularly for children) on the UK's overcrowded roads. British motorists don't respect cyclists as much as their counterparts in most continental countries and cyclists in the UK are ten times more likely to be involved in an accident than those in (for example) Denmark. Helmets are essential attire, particularly for children, as is reflective clothing and bright (preferably flashing) lights at night.

There are now large numbers of cycle paths all around towns in the Uk, a decision made in 1995 gave the go-ahead to build a national network of 8,000km (5,000mi) of dedicated cycling paths at a cost of £42.5m, partly funded by the National Lottery 'Millennium Fund'. Radical measures have been put forward to promote cycling in an effort to reduce traffic congestion and pollution on the roads. Some towns and cities plan to solve (or ease) their traffic problems by introducing cycle priority routes, including traffic light priority, lock-up parking and even changing rooms for wet cyclists.

If you're interested in joining a cycling club, your local library should have information about local clubs or you can contact the British Cycling Federation, National Cycling Centre, Stuart Street, Manchester M11 4DQ (☎ 0870-871 2000, 🖳 www.britishcycling.org.uk). Keen cyclists may be interested in joining the Cyclists Touring Club (CTC), Parklands, Railton Rd, Guildford, Surrey GU2 9JX (☎ 0870-873 0060, 🖳 www.ctc.org.uk), which is the UK's national cyclists' association with over 200 local groups throughout the UK. The CTC actively campaigns for the rights and safety of cyclists on the road and publishes an excellent free booklet, *Positive Cycling*. Membership includes free third party insurance, legal aid, technical advice, touring information and a bimonthly magazine. The CTC also operates a bicycle insurance scheme.

An interesting book for those who live in the London area is *On Your Bike*, published by the London Cycling Campaign, 2 Newhams Row, London, SE1 3UZ (☎ 020-7234 9319, 🖳 www.lcc.org.uk). Other useful books include *Richard's New Bicycle Book* by Richard Ballantine (Pan), which is a guide to choosing and using a bicycle (and can be bought at the Bicycling Bookshop – see below) and *Complete Bike Book* by Chris Sidwells (Dorling Kindersley). Ordnance Survey publishes a series of excellent *Cycle Tours*. Local cycling guides and maps are published by councils, conservation and cycling groups in many areas, who also publish safety booklets and brochures for children. Around 15 magazines are published for cyclists, including *Cycling Plus*, *Cycling Weekly*, *Cycle Sport* and *Mountain Biking UK*. The

Bicycling Bookshop (⌨ www.pennyfarthingworldtour.com) has a vast array of books on the subject, new and old.

BMX

Rinks and specially designed circuits are provided in many towns for BMX cycles (acrobatics on a bicycle). Children can start at around seven, but participants of all ages should be protected against falls with crash helmets and elbow and knee pads. It's difficult to hire equipment, as it's too easily stolen, although BMX bikes can usually be hired. The cost of using purpose-built facilities is around £2 to £5 (including the hire of a bike) or nearer £1, if you provide your own bike.

FISHING

Fishing (or angling) facilities are superb and fishing is the biggest participant sport in the country, with over 4 million anglers (the numbers are rising each decade). There are a huge variety of well-stocked waters and some of the best salmon and trout (brown, sea and rainbow) fishing in the world. In addition to the many rivers and lakes (or lochs in Scotland), trout fishing is possible at over 160 reservoirs. Scotland is world-famous for its salmon fishing (and its scotch).

There are three types of fishing in the UK: sea, game and coarse fishing. Sea fishing is simply fishing in the open sea, while game fishing takes place at specially constructed fisheries stocked with trout or salmon. Coarse fishing is the most popular form of fishing and is common in designated rivers or man-made waters for many species of fish, including bream, carp, perch, pike and tench. Coarse fishermen use live bait such as maggots and worms, and none of the fish caught are killed, but are returned to the water (after being weighed and recorded in the case of competitions). The close season, which is the period when fishing isn't permitted, varies for different species of fish and between the various River Authorities who are responsible for recreational fishing. **Always check when the close season is before fishing anywhere in the UK.**

In England and Wales, you must obtain a fishing permit (called a rod licence), which is issued by the National Rivers Authority. You can also buy it online from ⌨ www.environment-agency.gov.uk. A non-migratory trout and coarse fish licence for the full 2007/8 season costs £24.50 for an adult and £5.00 for a child. A one-day licence costs £3.25. An adult's salmon and sea trout licence costs £66.50 and a child's £33.25. The charge for a one-day licence in this case is £7.00. Licences are also obtainable from fishing tackle suppliers, hotels and post offices in most areas and online from the Environment Agency (see website above). Once you've obtained a rod licence, you must obtain permission to fish from the owner of the water, which usually entails paying a membership fee or buying a ticket (a day permit costs around £2 or £3 a day in some areas). In some ponds or lakes, fishing may be free. Deep-sea and coastal fishing are free, apart from sea trout and salmon fishing, which is by licence only. For information on river fishing, contact the information officer of the appropriate National Rivers Authority. In some areas, 24-hour recorded telephone information is provided about fishing conditions and river levels, and fishing platforms are provided for disabled anglers. Ask at Tourist Information Centres for more details.

Rod licences aren't required in Scotland, although written permission must be obtained from the water's owner to fish for salmon or sea trout or to fish in freshwater for other fish. Each district in Scotland has its own close season for salmon fishing, which is generally from the end of August to the end of February. Information regarding permits can be obtained from local Tourist Information Centres. In Northern Ireland, a licence is required for each rod for game fishing and this is issued by the Foyle Fisheries Commission or the Fisheries Conservancy Board, depending on the area. Permission to fish is also required from the owner of the water, which usually means taking out short-term membership of a local fishing organisation or buying a ticket.

When sea fishing from the shore (e.g. from rocks), be careful where you position yourself, as in some areas it's possible to be swept out to sea and drowned.

You should be wary of eating fish caught in some of the UK's rivers, as the level of pollution could be harmful to your health, to say nothing of what it does to the poor fish – if they could talk, they might plead with you not to throw them back! However, it isn't all bad news and many estuaries and rivers (such as the Thames) have been cleaned up in recent years and wildlife is returning, some of which hasn't been seen for decades.

Visit Britain publishes an annual booklet, *Game Fishing Holidays*, containing an introduction to game fishing, a list of hotels and inns with private fishing, fisheries and fishing holiday organisers. No fewer than 25 monthly or bimonthly magazines for anglers are published.

FOOTBALL

Soccer (or Association Football as it's officially called) is the UK's national spectator and participation sport. All major British cities have a professional or semi-professional soccer team and most towns and villages have a number of amateur clubs (well over 40,000 in total) catering for all ages and standards. Most professional clubs and leagues are sponsored and professional players wear the name of their sponsor on their shirts. The league season in the UK officially runs from August to May (although professional soccer seems to be expanding continually in one way or another, with competitions such as the international UEFA Cup in the summer). There's no mid-season winter break, as in many other European countries, although many clubs would like one (British soccer players are **real** men and play in all weather conditions).

Most matches are played on Saturdays, although some clubs play regularly on Friday evenings and there are Tuesday, Wednesday, Sunday afternoon and Monday evening Barclaycard Premiership and Nationwide Football League matches most weeks, which are televised live on Sky TV. It isn't necessary to buy a ticket in advance for most matches, although Premiership games, local derbies (matches between neighbouring clubs) and cup matches are usually 'all-ticket', meaning tickets must be purchased in advance. The thriving market for tickets which are acquired and sold on at a fat profit is testimony to demand far exceeding supply.

In England, the Football Association (FA) runs the world's oldest league competition (instituted in 1888) and now consists of three divisions with a total of 72 clubs (24 in each division). At the top is the FA Premier League, with the top 20 clubs and below this is the Football league, with three divisions of 24 clubs. The three worst-performing Premiership clubs face relegation to the First Division each season, and three First Division teams are promoted in their place. The Premiership has created a huge gulf between its top clubs and those in the lower leagues. Relegation from the Premiership can cost a club over £20 million in lost revenue from TV, sponsorship, advertising and ticket sales (and precipitate the loss of a club's best players).

In Scotland, a Premier division was established in 1975/76 to improve competition and increase gate receipts by restricting the league to the top ten clubs, who play each other four times a season (a total of 36 matches).

The cost of tickets in England has risen at well over double the rate of inflation in recent years to fund expensive new all-seat stadia and they now average around £40 for Premiership games. Season tickets are even more expensive and English Premiership fans pay from around £500 to £1,000 or up to four times more than their continental counterparts. The high price of tickets does not deter supporters and many premier league clubs sell out every home game. However, the top clubs are pricing many traditional working class fans out of the game. Football in England (and to a lesser extent Scotland) is now **big** business, highlighted by US tycoon Malcolm Glazer's take over of Manchester United for £790m in June 2005 (they won the league in 2007 against all the odds, so maybe it wasn't such a bad deal).

Thanks to the millions pumped into soccer by sponsors and TV companies in recent years, top British clubs now compete with the richest Italian and Spanish clubs for the best foreign players. British football has been revitalised over the past decade by this, although it has had a detrimental affect on the development of up and coming home-grown stars (some Premiership teams regularly field only one or two English players). It's often cheaper to buy top-class players abroad than in the UK and many clubs have resorted to doing this, as prices in the UK have skyrocketed. Transfer fees of £5 million or £10 million are commonplace and top players command fees in excess of £30 million. This has also put severe pressure on clubs' wage bills: salaries have gone through the roof since the Bosman ruling removed transfer fees for players who have reached the end of their contracts. Many clubs (often without huge resources) spend tens of millions of pounds on wages in an attempt to remain in the Premiership. Premiership salaries are typically £20,000 to £30,000 a week, but many players receive over double this and world class players earn over £100,000 a week (in contrast, many players in lower divisions earn around £500 a week).

England has a number of other semi-professional leagues, including the Vauxhall Conference League, from which teams can be elected to the English Football League division three. The Scottish League has three divisions, each with ten clubs. Northern Ireland has the semi-professional Irish League and Wales the amateur Welsh League (although three Welsh teams, Cardiff, Swansea City and Wrexham, play professional football in the English Nationwide League).

In addition to national league football, the UK also has a number of national cup competitions. In England, the main knockout competition is the FA Cup, instituted in 1871 and open to amateur clubs, the final of which is usually played at Wembley Stadium. From 2007 the final returned to the new Wembley Stadium in north London. Cup final tickets cost from £50 to £95 but can easily go for around £1,000 or more a pair on the black market. Other national cup competitions in England are the League Cup (or currently the Carling Cup after its present sponsor), in which all league clubs take part, and various other competitions for professional teams in the lower divisions of the Nationwide Football League.

The FA Community Shield is competed for in an annual match between the FA Premier League champions and the FA Cup winners on the weekend before the start of the English football season. It's currently played at Cardiff's Millennium Stadium while Wembley Stadium is being redeveloped. In Scotland, teams compete for the Scottish FA Cup and the Scottish League Cup, which opens the Scottish football season. There are also cup competitions in Northern Ireland and Wales. British clubs also participate in European cup competitions, including the Champions League (for national league winners and other top–placed teams) and the UEFA Cup for top–placed teams that don't qualify for the Champions League, and domestic cup winners.

The English football league is among the most competitive in the world and even matches between teams from the top and bottom of divisions are usually keenly contested. English teams have had considerable success in Europe over the last few decades, despite the fact that top English clubs usually play many more matches than clubs in other European countries. The points scoring system in the English league differs from that in most countries, three points being awarded for a win (instead of two) in order to discourage negative defensive football at away matches (it works). However, other countries have adopted this points system in recent years.

Controversial changes to the rules governing foul tackles in the last decade have tended to make the role of referees far more prominent. How they interpret the rules determines the course of the game and this can vary widely. Although generally of a high standard, some referees seem to play by their own rules and a few appear bent on ruining the sport by booking (yellow card) and sending off (red card) players for trivial offences. British referees are generally much harsher than those in other European countries. Players who 'take a dive' in the penalty area can expect little mercy – if it happened in Italy or Spain there would be nobody except the goalkeepers on the field after ten minutes!

There are dozens of websites devoted to football, but two which are useful for orientation are the BBC's (⌨ www.bbc.co.uk/football) and the Scottish Premiership website (⌨ www.scotprem.com).

GOLF

There are over three million golfers and around 2,000 courses, including private and practice courses, in the UK. Golf was the country's fastest-growing sport in the '80s, but was over-developed as a consequence, and golf courses built during that period (around 600) have been struggling to survive. Scotland, where golf originated in the 15th century, has many of the UK's most beautiful courses (including links courses) and boasts no fewer than seven world-famous championship locales. In the UK, there are public (municipal) and private courses, and although golf is a relatively expensive sport, you don't have to be a millionaire to play (unless you spend all day at the 19th hole). No membership is required to play on a public golf course, although it's advisable to book in advance. In some areas, there are few public courses – or indeed none at all – but private clubs may allow visitors to play, although only during weekdays, and provided that they're members of a club elsewhere and can produce a handicap certificate.

It isn't necessary to purchase a set of clubs, as they can be hired for around £7 for 18 holes. Second-hand beginner's sets of clubs can be purchased for as little as £50, while new sets start at around £230. Green fees (the cost of a round) are reasonable at most public golf clubs, averaging around £5 to £10 per round (18 holes), although fees at top private courses are from between £30 and £50 a day. Fees are usually increased by around 20 to 25 per cent at weekends and on public holidays. Green fees are reduced for nine-hole courses and many municipal courses allow juniors (under- 18s) to play at a cheap rate. Fees may be reduced in winter.

The top private golf clubs are often extremely difficult to join and expensive (there's huge snob appeal attached to belonging to a fashionable club). However, membership at most clubs is available from around £200 to £3,000 a year. Private clubs usually have strict dress rules and don't allow jeans or T-shirts on the course (players are also requested to observe golf etiquette and not to strike their opponents or dig holes in the greens). Many private golf clubs are part of a larger country club or hotel sports complex, the facilities of which may include a luxury hotel, restaurant, bar, tennis, squash, swimming pool, snooker and clay pigeon shooting.

Many golf clubs have golf nets and covered driving ranges, and most also have professionals (instructors) to help reduce the number of balls you lose. (Beware of courses with lots of water which have a voracious appetite for golf balls). Driving ranges are also provided in most areas with all-weather floodlit bays, practice bunkers and putting greens. The big advantage of a driving range (apart from the reasonable cost of £2 or £3 for a basket of 50 balls) is that you don't need to go and find your balls in the undergrowth or buy new ones when they land in the water.

Crazy golf, approach golf, pitch and putt and putting greens are available in most areas for those who set their sights a little lower than winning The Open. They're often features of public parks.

Visit Britain publishes an annual booklet, *Golfing Holidays*, containing a list of golf events in the UK, hotels and inns offering golfing facilities, and golf holiday organisers. Numerous golf books are published, including the *Sunday Telegraph Golf Course Guide to Britain and Ireland, Pocket Golf Rules* by Jonathan Vickers (Harper Collins), *Britain's 100 Extraordinary Golf Holes* by Geoff Harvey and Vanessa Strowger (Aesculus Press), *The AA Golf Course Guide 2004* and *The Thinking Man's Guide to Golf* by Colin Montgomerie (Orion). Excellent websites include 🖥 www.golf-uk.co.uk, www.golfingguides.net and www.golf.co.uk.

GYMNASIA & HEALTH CLUBS

There are gymnasia and health and fitness clubs in most towns, where sadists are employed and masochists go to torture themselves. Working out is popular and many companies provide their own health and leisure centres or pay for corporate membership for staff. In addition to many private clubs, most public sports and leisure centres have tonnes of expensive bone-jarring, muscle-wrenching apparatus, designed to get you into shape or kill you in the attempt. Middle-aged 'fatties' shouldn't attempt to get fit in five minutes (after all it took years of dedicated sloth and over-eating to put on all that weight), as overexertion can result in serious sports injuries. A good gymnasium or health club will ensure this doesn't happen and carries out a physical assessment, including a blood pressure test, fat distribution measurements and heart rate checks. In your pursuit of the body beautiful, it pays to give the intensive care unit (or mortuary) a wide berth.

Most sports and leisure centres (see page 450) have a health and fitness club or circuit training and exercise rooms, where supervised weight training sessions are held (single sex and mixed). Non-supervised users may require a special card to show that they're competent users (that body-destroying equipment is no joke). Membership of a public club isn't usually necessary, although membership may confer preferential booking facilities and the free use of equipment at certain times. Some sports and leisure centres charge an annual membership fee of around £50 or more (e.g. in London). Peak use of the fitness room is around £5 an hour or per session on a casual basis and there's often a lower charge during off-peak times (usually 9am to 5pm, Mondays to Fridays).

Charges can often be reduced by purchasing a book of tickets (e.g. ten sessions). Many sports and leisure centres also provide a huge variety of exercise classes, including t'ai chi, high impact (energetic) and low impact (gentle) aerobics classes (e.g. callanetics), yoga, aqua-aerobics (in the swimming pool) and various dance routines. Some centres hold dance and exercise classes for all ages and levels of fitness (from beginners to superpeople), during the daytime (including weekends) and evenings. Always check the class standard before enrolling.

Private health and fitness clubs are popping up overnight in all areas in what is a huge growth market. The cost of membership of a private club varies considerably, depending on the area, the facilities provided and the local competition. It's generally around £300 a year for a single person, although this can be reduced by up to a third by taking advantage of off-peak reductions (usually before 5pm, Mondays to Fridays). Casual attendance (if permitted) usually costs between £5 and £10 a session. Some clubs offer reduced rates for husband and wife or family membership. Charges seem to be falling in some areas where an inordinate number of people joined up primarily because it was a prevailing fad, and then eventually got fed up with all the grunting and groaning. Clubs are usually open seven days a week from 7 or 8am until around 10pm. On Saturdays and Sundays, some clubs may be open only from around 9am to 1pm.

All clubs provide a free trial and assessment and produce personal training programmes for members. Many private health and fitness clubs organise aerobics and keep-fit classes, have a sauna, solarium, Jacuzzi, and steam bath, and provide massage and aromatherapy. Many top class hotels have health clubs and swimming pools that are usually open to the general public, although access to facilities may be restricted to residents at certain times.

HIKING

Whether you call it walking, rambling, hiking or orienteering, getting from A to B for fun and pleasure (as opposed to not being able to afford a bus or train ticket) is extremely popular and is the most common form of exercise (what's more it's free!). In England and Wales, there's a total network of over 220,000km (137,000mi) of public footpaths, bridleways (paths fit for riders, but not vehicles) and byways, which is more than in any other country in the world. Many paths have been joined together to form continuous well-marked, long-distance routes or national trails, as they're known in England and Wales (the longest is 600mi/1000km). In Scotland, the law differs for the moment (see below), although walkers there generally have an absolute right of access to uncultivated land, unless there's proven danger to walkers or wildlife.

Public rights of way grew up as part of the ancient communications system in use long before any form of transport was invented, and landowners must, by law, give walkers the right of passage across their land, which is fine in theory. Recent campaigns by walkers have led to clashes with landowners and farmers, some of whom will go to any lengths to deny walkers access to their land. The government reluctantly decided that the Country Landowners Association and its 50,000 members (who are estimated to own over half of the countryside in England and Wales) would never allow access to their land voluntarily, and passed the Countryside and Rights of Way Act 2000.

In addition to the thousands of miles of public footpaths, there are 14 national parks in England and Wales which were established to protect the UK's finest landscapes from rabid developers and provide people with the opportunity to use and enjoy the open countryside. The land within the national parks remains largely in private ownership and visitors should walk only where access is permitted and should respect the lives and work of those who live there. There are no national parks in Scotland (the whole country is practically a national park) but it has 40 National Scenic Areas occupying one eighth of the country and offering some of the most beautiful and unspoilt walking in Europe.

Hiking paths are signposted (or waymarked as it's called in 'hiking talk') by signs showing the destination and sometimes the distance. In England and Wales, national trails are waymarked with an acorn symbol. In Scotland, long-distance footpaths are waymarked by a thistle symbol. The footpaths and rights of way in the UK are often poorly signposted (signposts are often deliberately destroyed by landowners) and, away from national trails, part of your time may be spent searching for the path. When following a path you should look out for waymarks and use a map (see below). In England and Wales, paths are often signposted where they join roads, but many footpaths or tracks may be indicated only by arrows (yellow for footpaths, blue for bridleways and red for byways) or by special markers if the path is used as a recreational route. A map is essential when using trails without waymarks.

Orienteering is popular and is a combination of hiking and a treasure hunt or competitive navigation on foot. It isn't necessary to be super fit and the only equipment that's required (in addition to suitable walking attire) is a detailed map and compass. For information contact the British Orienteering Federation, 8a Stancliffe

Houe, Whitworth Road, Darley Dale, Matlock, Derbyshire DE4 2HJ (☎ 01629-734 042, 🖳 www.britishorienteering.org.uk). If you're interested in joining a walking club contact the Ramblers Association, 2nd Floor, Camelford House, 87-90 Albert Embankment, London SE1 7TW (☎ 020-7339 8500, 🖳 www.ramblers.org.uk). It promotes rambling, protects rights of way, campaigns for access to open country and defends the beauty of the countryside against those who would destroy it for financial gain. It has over 300 local groups throughout the UK and members receive a quarterly magazine, a yearbook, equipment discounts, free membership of their local ramblers group and the opportunity to participate in numerous walks with experienced guides.

General information about walking is provided in a Visit Britain leaflet entitled *Walking in Britain*, which also contains a list of companies which organise guided walking holidays. An excellent book for keen walkers is *The Good Walks Guide* by Tim Locke (Which? Books). In many towns and country areas, guided local walks are conducted throughout the year (which may be part of a comprehensive programme of walks), ranging from sightseeing tours of towns to walks around local beauty spots, for which there may be a small fee. Walks are usually graded, e.g. easy, moderate or strenuous, and dogs can usually be taken unless otherwise stated. Ask for information at Tourist Information Centres or local libraries.

MOTORSPORTS

Motor racing has a huge following and embraces everything from Formula One (F1) grand prix to stock car racing. Among the many classifications of motor racing in the UK are Formulas One, Two and Three; Formula 3000; sports car and Formula Ford racing; rallying; hill-climbing; historic sports car racing; competitions among special one-make series (such as TVR, Renault 5, Mazda MX-5 and Honda CRX, to name but a few); autocross; go-karting; and bantam racing for kids. The most famous motor racing venues in the UK are Brands Hatch and Silverstone, host to the British Grand Prix, which is part of the F1 World Motor Racing Championship. This is one of the UK's most expensive sporting events, with tickets costing hundreds of pounds. Regular race meetings are also held at Caldwell Park, Castle Combe, Donington Park, Oulton Park, Snetterton and Thruxton Park. National hot rod, saloon, stock car and banger racing also arouse enthusiasm among the young (which sometimes involves practice on public roads). Meetings are held on most Saturdays during the main season, which runs from April to October at stadia throughout the UK.

Motorcycle racing is almost as popular and includes grand prix racing at 125cc, 250cc, 350cc, 500cc levels and superbikes over 1,000cc. The Isle of Man Tourist Trophy circuit is the UK's most famous (or infamous) which, because it's on public roads around the island, lacks the safety features (and the fast-acting emergency services) found at purpose-built circuits. This has led to the deaths of many riders over the years. Other forms of motorcycling with a large following are sidecar and speedway racing, scrambling and moto-cross. Speedway is held at stadia around the UK from March to August. There are a number of magazines dedicated to motor sports in the UK and lots of websites, including 🖥 www.fia.com, 🖥 www.passport2sport.co.uk and 🖥 www.motorsport.co.uk.

RACKET SPORTS

There are excellent facilities for most racket sports, particularly badminton, squash, racketball and tennis. There are two main types of racket sport centres: public leisure centres and private clubs. Many have around six squash courts (also used for racketball) and six badminton courts. Some have indoor tennis courts, although these aren't usually permanently available, as halls are used for other sports. There are also private clubs for most racket sports, particularly squash and tennis. Court fees are reasonable although annual membership fees may be high. Some private clubs are highly exclusive and it's difficult to join unless you have excellent connections, pots of money or are very famous. If you're an advanced player, you may find the level of competition is higher at private clubs than at community leisure centres. Racket sport leagues and competitions are also organised by many companies and schools, and some of the latter have their own courts.

Tennis

Despite the popularity of tennis as a spectator sport (particularly Wimbledon), actually **playing** tennis isn't so popular, largely because it isn't much fun in the cold and rain. Indoor tennis courts are relatively scarce and prohibitively expensive, and are a necessity in the depths of a British winter. More indoor courts are, however, being built all the time. The cost of hiring an indoor tennis court at a sports centre (if possible) is from £10 to £20 an hour, depending on the time of day (short tennis on a reduced size court can also be played in some sports centres). Most local councils and some private sports centres provide a number of outdoor hard and grass courts (clay courts aren't common), which can be hired for £2 to £5 an hour (adults) or from around £1 or £2 an hour for under-16s. Some centres have outdoor courts with artificial surfaces which can be used in all weathers and some parks and most sports centres have floodlit outdoor courts. There may be a nominal membership fee of around £5 to use some municipal courts.

If you're a serious tennis player you may be interested in joining a private club. Costs vary, but can be high, e.g. a £150 enrolment fee plus a £300 annual subscription (or a monthly fee of around £25) for single membership of an exclusive tennis club, with indoor and outdoor courts. Many private clubs also have gymnasia and swimming pools that can be used by members for an increased payment. Special rates are usually available for couples and families. Sports centres and private clubs usually have coaches available for private or group lessons. National, county and local tennis competitions are held at all levels for both sexes. The official website of the Lawn Tennis Association is 🖥 www.lta.org.uk.

Squash

Squash (or more correctly squash rackets) has been declining in popularity since its heyday in the '80s, but is still widely played and there's an abundance of courts in sports centres and private squash clubs in all areas. England has a larger number of players and courts than any other country in the world and boasts the current world no. 1 player, Peter Nicol (who recently 'defected' from his native Scotland!). Private clubs usually cater exclusively for squash, and clubs combining squash and tennis (or some other sport) are rare. Many private squash clubs have a resident coach, providing individual and group lessons.

The cost of hiring a court in a sports centre is from around £5 to £7 for a 40 or 45 minute session or £6 to £10 for an hour. Off-peak (before 5pm) fees may be around £3 or £4 for 45 minutes (students and the unemployed are entitled to use council facilities for half price during off-peak hours in some areas). Annual membership of a private squash club varies from around £50 to £120 a year; off-peak, family and junior membership may also be available. Court fees are usually around the same or a little lower than for municipal courts, although there may be an extra charge for guests.

Racketball, an 'easy' version of squash, is played on a squash court and rackets and balls can be hired from most squash clubs.

Squash is an energetic sport and you should think twice about taking it up in middle age, particularly if you're unfit, have high blood pressure or a heart or respiratory problem. Around 50 per cent of all sports deaths in the UK occur on squash courts! Players of any age should get fit to play squash and shouldn't play squash to become fit. Doctors recommend that players don't take a sauna after a squash game, which can be dangerous, as it increases the heart rate and body temperature. Tennis or badminton are better choices for the middle-aged as they aren't as frenetic as squash, although singles badminton can be a hard slog. Useful websites are 🖳 www.squashplayer.co.uk and 🖳 www.englandsquash.com.

Badminton

Badminton, with an estimated 2.5 million players, is more popular than tennis. Most badminton facilities are provided by public sports and community centres, and private clubs are rare. The cost of hiring a badminton court in a sports centre is around £5 to £8 an hour or around £4 an hour at off-peak times.

Court costs for all racket sports are usually cheaper before 5pm during the week and after 5pm at weekends, although lunch-time periods may be charged at peak rates for some sports, e.g. squash. Courts in public sports and leisure centres can be booked up to two weeks in advance, while private clubs may allow bookings to be made further in advance. You must usually cancel a booked court 24 or 48 hours in advance; otherwise you must pay for it if it isn't re-booked. Rackets, shoes and towels can usually be hired (or purchased) from public sports centres and private clubs. Most centres and clubs organise internal leagues, ladders and knockout competitions, and also participate in local and national league and cup competitions.

For information from the sport's governing body in England see 🖳 www. badmintonengland.co.uk.

Table Tennis

Table tennis is popular and is played as a serious competitive sport and as a pastime in social and youth clubs. Most sports centres have a number of table tennis tables for hire for as little as £2 an hour and bats can be hired for a small fee. If you want to play seriously there are clubs in most areas. Costs vary, but it's an inexpensive sport with little equipment necessary.

Many private sports clubs hold residential coaching holidays throughout the year. Visit Britain publishes a leaflet about residential badminton, squash, table tennis and tennis holidays in the UK, and information can also be obtained from travel agents and Tourist Information Centres. To find the racket clubs in your local area, look in the yellow pages, enquire at your local library or contact the appropriate national association.

ROCK-CLIMBING & CAVING

Those who find walking a bit tame might like to try abseiling, rock-climbing, mountaineering, caving or pot-holing (subterranean mountaineering). The UK has a distinguished record in international mountain climbing and few mountains in the world haven't been climbed at some time by British mountaineers, often for the first time. If you're an inexperienced climber you would be well advised to join a climbing club (over 300 are affiliated to the British Mountaineering Council) before heading for the hills. There are climbing schools in all the main climbing areas and many local clubs have special indoor training apparatus (e.g. a climbing wall) for aspiring mountaineers. Some sports and leisure centres also provide facilities for climbing training.

A number of climbers, cavers and pot-holers are killed each year in the UK (mostly in Scotland), many of whom are inexperienced and reckless. Many more owe their survival to teams who risk their own lives to rescue them. **It's extremely foolish, not to mention highly dangerous, to venture off into the hills (or holes) without an experienced guide, proper preparation, excellent physical condition, sufficient training and the appropriate equipment. It's also essential to tell someone where you're going and when you expect to return.**

Mountain, fell or hill-walking shouldn't be confused with 'ordinary' hiking (see page 443), as it's generally done at much higher altitudes and in more difficult terrain, and should be attempted only with a qualified guide. It can be dangerous for the untrained or inexperienced and should be approached with much the same degree of caution and preparation as climbing. The Royal Air Force provides a helicopter rescue service for those who get lost or stuck on mountains. A good map is vital for those who venture into remote areas. Ordnance Survey maps, available in 1:25 and

1:50 scales, are highly recommended and are available from bookshops, newsagents and leisure shops.

Many adventure holiday companies provide tailor-made vacations for climbers or cavers, including equipment, tuition, transport and accommodation. For information ask Visit Britain or Tourist Information Centres. For information about climbing in the UK, contact the British Mountaineering Council, 177-179 Burton Road, Manchester M20 2BB (☎ 0870-010 4878, 💻 www.thebmc.co.uk).

RUGBY

There are two separate codes of rugby (or rugby football) in the UK, rugby union and rugby league. The main difference between the codes is that rugby union (which used to be strictly amateur) is played with teams of 15 players and rugby league, which is played by amateurs and professionals, has 13 players to a team (two less to pay). However, after a momentous decision by the International Rugby Football Board in 1995, rugby union became a professional sport. This was brought about mainly because rugby union was in danger of losing its best players to new rival professional organisations (and to rugby league) and the fact that many countries (the UK excepted) had been secretly paying their top union stars for years anyway.

Rugby union is played in all regions of the UK and has a wider following than rugby league, with the top ten clubs in England playing in the Zurich Premiership (💻 www.zurichrugby.co.uk). Since 1995, club rugby's administrators have been over-optimistic about the game's capacity to increase its base of supporters and therefore income, and consequently clubs have lurched from crisis to crisis. Paying players has turned out to be not quite so simple as imagined. Falling attendances at some clubs have exacerbated this funding crisis. Below the Zurich Premiership is National Division One from which there's promotion for the winners to thePremiership. This is followed by the National Leagues and the geographically based Powergen Leagues. The English Clubs Rugby Union Championship is the national club competition, with most matches being played on Saturdays. The Celtic League involves clubs from Ireland, Wales and Scotland and the Scottish-Welsh League includes only clubs from the latter two.

England, Scotland, Wales and Ireland compete each year for the rugby union Triple Crown. The home nations also compete with France and Italy for the International Championship. The ultimate achievement is the Grand Slam, which is when a team wins all its championship matches. The annual England versus Scotland fixture is contested for the Calcutta Cup. Rugby union is also played internationally at the highest level by Australia (the Wallabies), New Zealand (the All Blacks) and South Africa (the Springboks) and at a lower level by many other nations (such as Argentina, Fiji, Romania and Western Samoa). Every four years, the Rugby World Cup is staged in a different rugby-playing country.

Rugby league is played professionally in the UK, mainly by teams in the north of England who compete in the Super League and Challenge Cup, the final of which is played at Millenium Stadium in Cardiff while Wembley Stadium is being redeveloped. There are also many amateur rugby league teams for players of all ages, including a number of teams in the London area dominated by Australian expatriates. Rugby league is played internationally by Great Britain, Australia, New Zealand, France and Papua New Guinea. Most towns, schools and universities have rugby teams competing in local league and cup competitions, in one or both rugby codes.

Rugby, like football, has spawned a profusion of websites, among which are 🖳 www.ukrugbyguide.co.uk, which contains links to innumerable other sites, and 🖳 www.rfu.com, the site of the Rugby Union.

SKIING

Skiing is a popular sport with the British, despite the fact that there are only a few ski resorts in the British Isles (in Scotland), and these could never hope to cater adequately for the country's 2 million skiers. Scottish ski centres include Aonach Mor, Cairngorms (Aviemore), Glencoe, Glenshee and Lecht. However, for most British skiers, skiing in Scotland is of little interest and isn't a viable alternative to a skiing holiday in the Alps or North America. In comparison with the Alps, Scotland suffers from a lack of atmosphere, and skiing conditions early in the season are unpredictable, with storms and strong winds often causing lifts to be closed and badly affecting the state of the snow. The best time to ski in Scotland is generally late in the season, from March to May.

The British, however, have made up for their lack of snow (and mountains) with dry-slope skiing. There are 76 such centres in the UK (more than in any other country), catering for over 300,000 skiers a year. You will find a list of them on 🖳 www.natives.co.uk/whatsnew/dryski.htm. As well as being an excellent training ground for the 'real thing', dry-slope skiing has become a popular sport in its own right. Most centres have a ski racing team and dry-slope competitions are held regularly throughout the year. Learning to ski on a dry-slope can save you time and money when you arrive in a winter resort, and also helps experienced skiers find their ski-legs before arriving. A dry-slope consists of around $2,000m^2$ of ski-matting, usually with separate areas for beginners and advanced skiers. The maximum descent of 'pistes' is around 500m, although most are 200m to 300m. Poma or button ski tows (or even a chair lift) are usually provided and floodlights light up evening skiing in winter. Most centres are council-run or commercial ventures, although a few have been built by enthusiasts themselves.

You should use your own ski boots (they can also be hired) and wear old clothes, as the matting can damage expensive ski suits. Gloves are usually compulsory. Don't use good skis, as they don't take kindly to the artificial surface and make sure that the bindings of hired skis are adjusted to your weight and ability. Equipment hire is usually included in the hourly rate, which varies considerably. Many centres offer weekly and season tickets, which are usually good value for money. It's best to ski at quiet times, as centres can get extremely crowded at weekends, particularly towards Christmas when everyone is keen to get in a bit of practice before heading off to the Alps. Tuition is provided at all levels for adults and children, although off-piste skiing is frowned upon! A three-hour course costs from around £45 to £65, depending on the centre.

Skiing can also be practised indoors on a new type of artificial snow, which genuinely feels like the real thing. There are three such centres offering this at the moment: the Snozone in Milton Keynes, Buckinghamshire, close to London; the Snowdome in Tamworth, Staffordshire, in the Midlands; and Xscape in Castleford, Yorkshire. Remember that, in contrast to dry slopes, these places get really cold – the temperature is never more than -3°C and with the wind-chill factor when skiing it can feel like -15°C, so wrap up well. Prices are around £20-25 for an adult for one hour of recreational skiing after 8pm and £15-20 for a child. Skiers at a loose end in the summer might also like to try grass skiing, which is quite popular.

If you're looking for a book about learning or improving your skiing, the Sunday Times book *We Learned to Ski* (Collins) is an excellent choice for all standards. A number of ski magazines are published in the UK. The Daily Mail International Ski Show is held at Earls Court in November, where all the latest equipment and clothing can be seen.

SNOOKER & BILLIARDS

Snooker is a highly popular sport and most large towns boast at least one snooker or billiards club. Many hotels, bars and sports clubs also have snooker tables. Snooker clubs, most of which have bars and many also restaurants, often open from around 10am to midnight daily. In the last few decades, the popularity of snooker has increased tremendously, owing mainly to the success of televised championships. These have transformed what was once a minority pastime with a seedy image into a successful national sport with a huge following. (It's estimated that over 8 million people play the game in the UK). Professional competitions are now held throughout the world and top players are millionaire celebrities. Snooker is played increasingly by women, professionally as well as for fun, and they make up a large part of TV audiences.

Billiards, however, is waning in popularity, although it still arouses considerable interest elsewhere in the world. American pool is also played fairly widely, although it's very much the poor cousin of snooker and to a lesser extent billiards. A game called 8-ball, commonly played in pubs, with teams competing in local leagues, is also held in affection along with bar billiards.

SPORTS & LEISURE CENTRES

Most towns have a community sports or leisure centre (also called recreation centres), usually run and financed by the local council. Some cities and towns also have modern commercial sports centres, which, although more expensive than municipal centres, offer unrivalled sports facilities (and some charge minimal membership fees). A huge range of sports and activities are catered for, including badminton, basketball, netball, swimming and diving, squash, indoor soccer (five-a-side), rollerskating, BMX bikes, gymnastics, yoga, weight training, table tennis, tennis, racketball, aerobics, cricket, climbing, canoeing (in the swimming pool), archery, bowls, hockey, trampolining, martial arts and snooker. Councils publish a wealth of information about local sports and leisure centres.

Some centres have ice rinks and dry-slope skiing facilities, while most have one or more (e.g. main and learning) indoor swimming pools, squash courts (usually around six), badminton courts, sports halls (which are available for hire), general activity and fitness rooms, and a games room. Sports shoes with light-coloured soles which don't leave marks should be worn for all indoor activities. Many sports centres have a health and beauty salon, that may include a sauna, Turkish bath (or steam room), Jacuzzi, solarium, spa bath, massage and a beauty treatment room.

Centres usually provide meeting rooms, nursery facilities, a sports shop (usually with a racket re-stringing service), a reasonably-priced restaurant or café, and a licensed bar. All centres provide parking, which is often free. In addition to sports activities, some centres (usually called recreation centres) also organise a range of non-sporting leisure activities, e.g. art, bingo, bridge, chess, dancing, music, photography, Scrabble and whist.

Sports and leisure centres are usually open seven days a week from around 9am to 11pm, although some smaller centres use school sports facilities and are available only from early evening (e.g. 5pm) Mondays to Fridays and at weekends. Many close on public holidays and over the Christmas and New Year period, when leaflets listing opening hours are provided. Membership, for which there's usually a nominal fee of around £10 a year, may be necessary, although this may be required only if you want to book courts or equipment (usually one or two weeks in advance). Non-members may need to pay in advance when booking facilities (notice of cancellation is usually 24 or 48 hours).

In some centres, particularly in London and other major cities, annual membership costs from £10 to £60 a year and may be higher for non-residents. Season tickets, block bookings and subscriptions are usually available for some facilities. Most centres charge spectators an entrance fee of around 50p and all have reduced rates for children (or juniors), at around half the adult rates. They also have daytime off-peak rates (usually before 5pm) for most facilities. Some commercial sports centres offer a day pass (e.g. £10 for adults, £5 for children) that allows you to sample as many sports or health sessions as you wish (e.g. between 7am and 5pm). Many centres also organise sports sessions or clubs for the middle-aged (50+) at reduced rates and others organise women-only activities. Membership and hire fees may be reduced for under 18s, senior citizens, the disabled and the unemployed.

All sports and leisure centres run clubs and have club nights for a variety of sports. They also organise leagues, tournaments, ladders, knockout competitions and special events. Membership of a club may reduce court fees and entitle members to free or almost free participation on club nights. Most centres run fitness training and sports courses throughout the year (junior and adult), and also offer individual and group coaching. Equipment can be hired for a number of sports, including squash and badminton rackets and table tennis bats.

Holiday sports sessions and play schemes are held during school holidays (e.g. summer) and at weekends, and most centres organise special sports and games parties for children on request. All centres have changing rooms and showers. Theft from changing rooms isn't uncommon and you should take **all** your belongings and clothes with you or lock them in a storage locker. Most centres allow the use of storage lockers free of charge, usually on payment of a returnable deposit.

SWIMMING

There are public heated indoor and outdoor swimming pools in most towns, many located in leisure centres (see page 450). You can also swim at numerous beaches. British beaches have for long had a doubtful reputation as far as cleanliness is concerned, but they're definitely improving. A survey in 2001 by the Marine Conservation Society established that a third of them met the very highest standards while 11 per cent failed to meet minimum water quality standards. Sixty more beaches than were monitored during the previous survey passed the test. Details are given in the M.C.S.'s *Good Beach Guide* (🖳 www.goodbeachguide.co.uk), which includes surveys of over 800 beaches. Those which failed were often polluted by sewage, it must be added. There are even aturist and no-smoking beaches in some resorts.

The temperature of indoor pools is generally maintained at 23 to 30°C (74 to 80°F). Many centres have a main pool and a teaching pool, often with a waterslide (jet slide, water chute), flumes, wave machine, whirlpool or waterfall -great fun for kids, young and old. Some centres provide diving boards at certain times and paddling pools for toddlers. Many also have sunbeds, saunas, solaria and Jacuzzis. Separate sessions are arranged for various groups and ages, focussing on early morning swimming, lane swimming, diving, senior citizens, mums and babies, over 25s, school holidays and aqua-aerobics. Aqua-natal sessions for expectant or post-natal mothers are also a possibility.

Pools are usually very busy at weekends and on public holidays and it's best to go during the week if you can. If you're going along for a general swim, check in advance whether the pool has been booked for a special session. The cost is usually from £2 to £3 for adults and £1 to £2 for juniors under 16 and senior citizens. There are generally reduced rates for family groups. Most centres provide annual season tickets, for around £70 to £120 a year, allowing you to swim at any time. Often swimming season tickets can be combined with another sport, e.g. squash. Some swimming sessions are reserved for members of a leisure centre and some public pools provide closed weekly sessions for naturists and those who cannot afford bathing costumes.

Before entrusting your children to the care of some swimming pools, you should check the safety standards, as they vary considerably and some are unsafe (public pools must have adequate lifeguard cover). This also applies to beaches, many of which fail to meet basic safety standards owing to a lack of emergency equipment, lifeguards and warning flags. Most leisure centres provide swimming lessons (all levels from beginner to fish) and run 'improver' and life-saving courses. Swimming courses for children are usually held during term times or at weekends.

WATERSPORTS

All watersports, including sailing, windsurfing, waterskiing, rowing, power-boating, canoeing, surfing and subaquatic sports are popular in the UK – which is hardly surprising considering it's surrounded by water and has hundreds of inland lakes and rivers where such sports can be enjoyed. Boats and equipment can be hired at coastal resorts, lakes and rivers, and instruction is available for most watersports in holiday areas. Jet and surf skis can also be hired more frequently nowadays. For more information visit 🖳 www.britishwatersports.co.uk.

Rowing

There are around 500 rowing clubs in the UK and over 300 regattas, the most famous of which is the Henley Regatta. The University Boat Race (inaugurated in 1836), between eight-oared crews from Cambridge and Oxford universities, at Easter, is the most famous rowing race in the world (it's shown live on TV). Canoeing for children is sometimes taught in indoor swimming pools in winter. Budding canoeists must be able to swim 50 metres before being admitted to a canoe club and the wearing of life jackets is compulsory (see 🖳 www.ara-rowing.org).

Surfing, Windsurfing, Waterskiing & Sub-aqua

Wetsuits are almost mandatory for surfing, windsurfing, waterskiing and sub aquatic sports even during the summer months (the water is freezing in and around the UK at almost any time of the year). They can be hired in areas where there's a demand. Surfing is popular and is centered at Newquay in Cornwall, which has staged a number of world-class events. Pollution is one of the biggest problems for water sports enthusiasts off the UK's coastline, and ear infections and stomach complaints are common among surfers. Scuba diving is another popular sport. Participants must pass a medical examination and undergo an approved training course to obtain the PADI open water diving certificate. Courses are run at many swimming pools and cost from around £230 to £300. Equipment can cost hundreds or even thousands of pounds, although second-hand equipment is available. The season runs from April to September, and the best areas in the British Isles are Cornwall and the Scilly Isles.

Sailing

Sailing has always been popular in the UK, which has a history of producing famous sailors, from Sir Francis Drake to Sir Francis Chichester. There are sailing clubs (around 1,500) and schools in all areas of the UK and boats of all shapes and sizes can be hired, from ocean-going racing yachts to dinghies (if you don't like water, there are land yachts). In recent years, there has been a marina boom in the south-east and, if you're a sailing enthusiast, it's possible to purchase a home where you can moor your boat outside your front door. Many inland lakes have a maximum speed limit of 16kph (10mph) for power boats. There has been a huge increase in stolen boats and equipment in the last few years (outboard motors, navigational and other electronic equipment are the most popular targets). Ensure you have good security and adequate insurance for your boat. Websites such as ⌨ www.uksail.com can provide detailed information of brokers.

The Royal Yachting Association (RYA) runs excellent courses for sailors wishing to become safe and proficient skippers. The Coastal Skippers and Yachtmaster courses lead to qualifications for commercial and racing skippers, but there are also courses for power-boaters and coastal 'potterers'. For details visit the RYA website (: www.rya.org.uk).

Information

Visit Britain publishes a leaflet about residential water sports holidays in the UK, which includes canoeing, power boating, rafting, sailing, surfing, waterskiing and windsurfing. Many magazines (over 20) are dedicated to boating and yachting, plus some ten more to various other water sports.

No experience, test, safety training or equipment is required to take to the waters in and around the UK, and many people needlessly risk their lives and carry no safety equipment. e.g. flares, life jackets or radios. Don't get caught unprepared and be sure to observe all warning signs on waterways.

MISCELLANEOUS SPORTS

The following is a selection of other popular sports, which are served by private clubs with their own facilities or use those provided at public leisure centres. For the addresses and telephone numbers of national sports associations contact Sport England (⌨ www.sportengland.org) or the Central Council of Physical Recreation (⌨ www.ccpr.org.uk).

- **Archery** – Archery is still a popular sport, many years after the British army was issued with more modern weapons. The UK is still searching for a modern Robin Hood who can win an elusive Olympic gold medal. Crossbow shooting is also practised in some clubs.

- **Athletics** – Most towns and villages have local athletics clubs and organise competitions and sports days. Competitive running has a strong following and jogging is also popular. Races, from fun runs of a few miles to half and full marathons are organised throughout the year, and all finishers in important races are awarded commemorative medals. The UK has a distinguished international record in athletics, particularly in middle-distance running, and top athletes now earn hundreds of thousands of pounds a year.

- **Basketball** – A sport specially created for giants (black American giants in particular), basketball is becoming increasingly popular in the UK (there are over 1,000 clubs). Basketball doesn't have a strong following as a professional sport, although the top teams participate in the European Clubs Championship.

- **Bowls** – Bowls has its origins in the 13th century and numbers Sir Francis Drake among its past enthusiasts. Once regarded mainly as a pastime for the elderly and retired, bowls is becoming increasingly popular with people of all ages, particularly the young (who are ruining the game's image). In addition to outdoor greens, often provided in local council parks, there are also many private and indoor bowling clubs, including facilities in some leisure centres. Bowls isn't to be confused with ten-pin bowling (see below). For a list of bowls clubs visit 🖳 www bowls-clubs.co.uk.

- **Boxing** – Legalised punch-ups for violent types, boxing is popular throughout the country, particularly as a spectator 'sport' (many people enjoy watching a good fight, as long as they're out of harm's way). Most towns have a boxing club and gymnasia for budding professionals are common in the main cities. The UK has produced a stream of world champions over the years.

- **Croquet** – The UK's answer to American football, except that all bodily contact is strictly forbidden (even tripping opponents with your mallet is frowned upon). An extremely genteel sport which is mandatory at English garden parties and unlikely ever to catch on among football hooligans.

- **Darts** – Not actually a sport, darts is an excuse to get drunk (have you ever seen anyone playing darts in a milk bar?). Around 5 million people play darts regularly in the UK (which dominates the world championship), usually in pubs, most of which have teams playing in local leagues.

- **Fencing** – Although fencing is a sport which has lost a lot of its popularity since the invention of the gun, a hard core of enthusiast swordsmen are holding out in a small number of clubs.

- **Frisbee** – Believe it or not, throwing plastic discs around has actually developed into a competitive 'sport', with national and local league and cup competitions.

- **Gymnastics** – Gymnastics is another popular sport, with most schools and sports centres having 'gym' clubs. Participation in sports centres costs from £1 to £5 a session.

- **Hockey** – Hockey is a very old sport in the UK and has gained wider appeal since Great Britain won the Olympic gold medal in Seoul in 1988, although it still faces an uphill battle to woo youngsters away from soccer, rugby and cricket. It's equally popular among both sexes.

- **Horse Racing** – Watching horse racing is popular – not because the British are a nation of equestrians or horse lovers, but rather of inveterate gamblers. Horse racing is known as 'the sport of kings' and you certainly need a king's ransom to buy and keep a horse in training. An extensive programme of events is organised throughout the year consisting of national hunt racing (steeplechasing and hurdles races), where horses must jump fences, from August to April and flat racing, in which there are no fences, from March to October.

- **Horse Riding** – Equestrianism is popular and needn't be expensive unless you wish to own your own horse. There are around 2,300 riding schools in the UK, although many have closed in recent years owing to falling interest and increasing costs. It's important to wear a helmet (and a back protector when riding cross-country courses), as people are killed and paralysed in riding accidents every year. The UK has a proud tradition of breeding and horsemanship and is one of the world's leading show jumping nations.

- **Lacrosse** – Lacrosse is similar to hockey and although thought of as strictly a women's game (whose training ground is the playing fields of the UK's most exclusive private girls schools), lacrosse is played by men and women.

- **Martial Arts** – Unarmed combat 'arts' such as Aikido, Judo, Karate, Kung Fu, Kushido, Taekwon-Do and T'ai Chi Ch'uan are taught and practised in many leisure centres and clubs. Judo is the most popular martial art and a sport in which the UK has had considerable international success.

- **Polo** – Polo is a minority sport for princes and millionaires. Similar to croquet on horseback, it involves players attempting to hit a ball into a goal while riding at speeds of up to 40mph. It's played indoors and outdoors. A modern variation for commoners is bicycle polo – the sport of princes from the seat of a pushbike.

- **Rollerskating & Skateboarding** – Rinks and specially designed circuits are provided in many towns for skateboarding. Children can start at around seven, but participants of all ages should be protected against falls with crash helmets and elbow and knee pads. It's difficult to hire equipment, as it's too easily stolen, although BMX bikes can usually be hired. The cost of using purpose-built facilities is around £2 to £5 (including the hire of a bike) or nearer £1 if you provide your own bike.

  Rollerskating rinks are widely available and are sometimes located in leisure centres. Skates can be hired, coaches are to hand, and roller-discos for teenagers are often organised. Inline skating – using skates on which the wheels are set in a line – was a craze for a while. It's now less popular and its practice has been curbed on public paths due to the risks to cyclists and pedestrians (some of whom have been killed in collisions). Keen rollerskaters and inline skaters often play roller hockey.

- **Shooting** – Shooting clubs, whose members confine their sport almost exclusively to private ranges, are popular in the UK. The country does well in international competition. Clubs enforce strict rules regarding the handling and storage of firearms, which the general public aren't usually permitted to store at home without a licence. Clay pigeon shooting is also popular among the well-heeled and costs around £200 to £250 a day.

- **Tenpin Bowling** – There are tenpin bowling centres in all major cities (around 100 with up to 48 lanes) and, after a decline in the '70s, the sport made a comeback at the end of the 20th century. A game costs around £2 for adults (but may be dearer in the evening), £1.50 for under-16s and £1 for shoe hire. Most centres are open from around 10am to midnight or later. There are tenpin bowling leagues and clubs everywhere and many companies have teams. Many centres have a restaurant, licensed bar, snack bar, nursery facilities, amusement machines and pool tables.

- **Trampolining** – Trampolining is a popular sport among high fliers and gymnasts with a large number of clubs (junior and senior) thriving around the UK. Courses are organised for all ages.

- **Volleyball** – Volleyball is a really fun game for all the family, deserving much wider popularity. It's often played on beaches (beach volleyball).

- **Weightlifting** – There are weightlifting clubs in most large towns in the UK, many using the facilities of a local leisure centre or fitness club.

- **Wrestling** – This refers to the real sport of wrestling (as practised in the Olympics) rather than the cabaret stuff shown on TV. However, when it comes to mass popularity, showbiz wrestling is streets ahead.

Other Sports

Many foreign sports and pastimes have a group of expatriate fanatics in the UK, including American football, baseball, boccia, boules (and pétanque), Gaelic sports (hurling, Gaelic football), handball and softball. For information, enquire at council offices, libraries, Tourist Information Centres, expatriate social clubs, embassies and consulates.

17.

SHOPPING

The choice, quality and variety of goods on sale in British shops are all excellent, particularly in London, which is one of the great shopping cities of the world. Not only is the UK, in the words of Napoleon, 'a nation of shopkeepers', but it's also a country of compulsive shoppers; shopping being the number one 'leisure' activity (after watching television). In the UK, you often hear references made to the 'High Street' (e.g. high street shops and high street banks), which isn't usually a reference to the name of a street (although many towns do have a High Street), but a collective term for any businesses commonly found in most town centres (although no longer necessarily on the High Street itself). Shops in main centres vary from huge department stores, selling just about everything (e.g. Harrods and Selfridges in London), to small high-class specialist retailers in Georgian or Victorian-style arcades. The traditional high street – now slipping into history in many areas – encompasses a number of small shops, including a butcher, baker, greengrocer, grocer, newsagent, chemist (pharmacy), bank, post office and the inevitable pub (or two).

In larger towns (again less often than formerly), shops may include a fishmonger (fresh fish shop), ironmonger (hardware, household wares), launderette (laundromat), off-licence (alcoholic beverages), turf accountant (betting shop), fish and chip shop, dry cleaners, hairdresser, book shop, health food shop, ladies' and men's clothes shops, shoe shop, take-away restaurants, banks and building societies. Larger centres also have one or more supermarkets and department stores and most country towns have a market on at least one day a week. Outside main shopping centres, there are 'corner shops', which are general stores or mini-supermarkets selling a wide range of food and household products. Prices in small shops are necessarily higher than in supermarkets, with the exception of those belonging to Happy Shopper, Spar or VG buying groups, where they're quite reasonable.

There's generally no bargaining or bartering in the UK although, if you intend to spend a lot of money or buy something expensive (e.g. a hi-fi, television, computer or furniture), you should shop around and shouldn't be shy about asking for a discount (except in most department stores, chain stores and supermarkets, where prices are usually fixed). It's advantageous to pay cash when you do so. Many shops also meet any genuine advertised price.

Value Added Tax (VAT– see page 381) at 17.5 per cent is included in the price of most goods with the exception of food, books and children's clothes, and the advertised price is usually the price you pay (there are no hidden extras). Some items such as personal computers (PC) and electronic goods may be advertised exclusive of VAT, as these items are often purchased by businesses that can reclaim VAT. Always shop around before buying and, when comparing prices, remember to add VAT if it isn't included. The chain store Dixons has a stranglehold on the home electronics trade (they also own Currys and PC World) and charge high prices. They've been criticised by competitors such as John Lewis and Comet for this in the past, but the entire computer retailing market was officially investigated a few years ago by the Office of Fair Trading and nothing untoward was found. However, it's definitely much cheaper to buy a computer from a direct marketing company, such as Compaq, Dell or Gateway. PCs cost up to a third more than in the US and even many Europeans can buy them for less than in the UK. When comparing prices, make sure that you're comparing similar goods or services, as it's easy to 'save' money by purchasing inferior products.

Most shops accept major credit cards, although in some stores they may accept only cash, debit cards and their own account or credit cards. To ensure that customers continue digging into their pockets, many major retailers offer instant credit (e.g. over 12 or 24 months, which may be interest-free) of up to £2,000 on a range of goods, such as home appliances, electrical and electronic equipment, and furniture. Always shop around for the best deal and compare the annual percentage rate (APR) charged (see **Loans** on page 374) if you don't receive interest-free credit – but beware, as some interest-free deals are anything but, and designed to con you into paying interest. When buying electronic and electrical products, you may be offered an expensive extended warranty deal, which is a rip-off and a waste of money. The Office of Fair Trading has published a damning report on this subject. A large proportion of some companies' profits are made by selling these warranties, so don't be surprised if you're pressurised by sales staff trying to meet quotas.

Most city shops hold sales at various times of the year, the largest of which are held in January and July, when bargains abound (many newspapers publish sales guides). Sales are also held in spring and autumn (most shops will hold one at the drop of a hat). Some shops seem to have a permanent sale, although retailers aren't permitted to describe goods as reduced when they've never been sold at the fanciful initial price. Goods may, however, have been advertised at a higher price for a short time simply to get around the law. Beware of bogus bargains. A number of websites provide UK price comparisons, including 🖳 www.kelkoo.co.uk. In addition to sales, you can also shop at hundreds of factory shops around the UK, where prices are much lower than at retailers, particularly if products are flawed in some way (called 'seconds'). Ask your friends and neighbours if there are any factory shops in your area and look out for them on your travels. Factory malls (another American import) have sprung up in recent years, many specialising in fashion 'seconds' and end-of-line goods from top names such as Aquascutum, Jaeger and Ralph Lauren. Prices are typically at least 30 per cent below normal retail prices. A number of internet sites provide comprehensive details of factory shops, including 🖳 www.shoppingvillages. com and 🖳 www.retailrebel.com.

Most retailers offer club or loyalty cards giving a discount (from 1 to 10 per cent) to cardholders. Others participate in Air Miles schemes. Coupons in national and local newspapers and leaflets delivered to your home also enable you to gain discounts. Everywhere, shops run by charitable organisations, such as Oxfam, Helping Hand, and Imperial Cancer Research, sell new and second-hand items and are great places to find bargains.

Shopping guides can be obtained from Tourist Information Centres in many areas. Very comprehensive guides for those who live in or around London include the *Time Out Shopping Guide* (Time Out) and *Shopping in London* (Insight Guides). Websites focussing on shopping in London are many and include 🖳 www.123london. com and 🖳 www.21stcenturyvillage.com. Some shops, particularly department and chain stores, provide free catalogues at Christmas and other times of the year. If you're looking for a particular item or anything unusual, you will find it in yellow pages, a directory which saves you lots of time, trouble and shoe leather.

If you have any questions about your rights as a consumer, contact your local trading standards department (🖳 www.tradingstandards.gov.uk), consumer advice centre or Citizens Advice Bureau (🖳 www.citizensadvice.org.uk). Most department and chain stores exchange goods or give a refund without question (although the British rarely complain or return goods), but smaller retailers aren't so enthusiastic.

The Sale & Supply of Goods to the Consumer Regulations 2002 came into force in 2003 and give you increased rights regarding remedies for faulty goods and guarantees. The seller bears increased responsibility for advertising claims which may be made by the manufacturers: for example, he bears the risk in the goods while they're being delivered to the buyer and guarantees must be couched in plain language and not 'legalese'. The UK officially converted to metrication on 1st October 1995 and all retailers must now price goods in kilograms, litres and metres. (Some who have failed to do so have been prosecuted and one market trader in Sunderland has passed into history as 'the metric martyr'). These are the only official measurements despite the fact that a large minority of Britons still haven't got a clue whether a pound (454g) weighs more or less than a kilogram (1,000g). However, British measures, such as pounds, pints and feet, may be used alongside metric ones and shops often display conversion tables. For those who aren't used to buying goods with British measures and sizes, a list of comparative weights and measures are included in **Appendix D**.

COMPETITION

There have been numerous price-fixing allegations and revelations over the past decade encompassing a wide range of products, such as computer games and equipment, electrical goods, branded foods, watches, cameras, designer clothing, sports shoes, furniture, compact discs (CD's), cars (and parts and servicing), perfumes and sports equipment. Britons also get ripped off when buying services such as pensions, banking, insurance and savings products. High profile media campaigns focussing on 'rip-off' Britain have been commonplace, and the government's competition policy has been derided. A combination of corporate greed, invisible price cartels and the apathy of consumers (plus less competition as a result of takeovers and mergers) helps to ensure that British consumers receive one of the worst deals in Europe. However, where there's genuine competition, such as in telephone services and air fares, costs in the UK are among Europe's lowest.

Suspicions about illegal price-fixing are widespread because the price of many branded goods are identical, or vary by only a tiny fraction (typically from 1p to £1, depending on the item's price), between retailers the length and breadth of the country. Anyone who attempts to discount goods risks being blacklisted and unable to obtain further supplies. Price-fixing by manufacturers, who insist that retailers stick to recommended prices, is difficult to prevent and the manufacturers know it. Discount shops have difficulty buying goods from manufacturers, who usually refuse to supply them on some pretext or other (a problem faced by foreign, low-cost supermarkets in recent years). The final end of overt price-fixing occurred in May 2001, when the price of some over-the-counter drugs fell by as much as 50 per cent as a result.

If you want to save money, you can shop on the continent or in the US (see **Shopping Abroad** on page 477), either in perosn, by mail-order or via the internet (see **Internet Shopping** on page 476). However, bear in mind when shopping outside the EU you (or the person sending goods by mail) must make a customs declaration and duty and taxes may make a big hole oe even wipe out any savings.

SHOPPING HOURS

Shopping hours are usually from around 9 or 9.30am to 5.30 or 6pm, Mondays to Saturdays. In England and Wales, large shops are allowed to open for six hours on Sundays, while smaller ones can suit themselves. Sunday shopping has become popular in recent years and most shops in large towns are open and busy. Large supermarkets also open on public holidays until around 4pm. In larger towns these may remain open 24 hours a day except for Sundays. Many supermarkets and superstores otherwise open from 8am until 10pm from Mondays to Saturdays and 10am to 4pm (or 11am to 5pm) on Sundays. In smaller towns, shops and businesses may close for lunch (usually noon to 1pm) and, in common with counterparts in cities, remain open until around 8pm one evening a week, usually on Wednesdays, Thursdays or Fridays. Shops also extend opening times in the weeks before Christmas. Peak shopping days are Saturdays and Sundays, which are, therefore, best avoided if possible.

Small, privately-owned grocery shops and supermarkets in cities, towns and sometimes even villages, are often open until 10pm and also at weekends, which is usually the only way they can make a living and compete with supermarkets. There are even small 24-hour convenience shops in some towns. Over the Christmas and New Year period, all shops are closed on Christmas Day (25th December), although 'experimental' opening has taken place even then, and some are closed on New Year's Day (1st January). However, an increasing number of shops open on Boxing Day (26th December), which is when many start their 'new year' sales.

SHOPPING CENTRES & MARKETS

In the last decade or so, numerous vast out-of-town, indoor shopping centres (malls) have sprung up throughout the UK. There, it's possible to do all your weekly shopping under one roof (nirvana or shopping hell, depending on your viewpoint). Centres usually contain a huge selection of shops, including all the famous high street names. Among the most popular shopping centres are Merry Hill in the Midlands (🖳 www.westfield.com/merryhill), Lakeside in the south-east (🖳 www.lakeside.uk.com), Meadowhall in Yorkshire (🖳 www.meadowhall.co.uk), The Mall Galleries in Bristol (🖳 www.themall.co.uk) and the MetroCentre in the north-east (🖳 www.metro-centre.co.uk), which draw shoppers from up to 80km (50mi) around and excursion trippers from as far as 330km (circa 200mi) away. More recent developments include the Trafford Centre in Manchester (🖳 www.trafford centre.co.uk), with its 1.4 million ft^2 of shopping and leisure space and 280 shops;

and Bluewater (🖥 www.bluewater.co.uk) in north Kent, which opened in 1999 and contains three 'malls' covering over 1.5 million ft^2, and has 13,000 parking spaces, as well as a 'kid's village' and crèche. The description 'Europe's largest shopping complex' is one which is used frequently in relation to many such developments, in the UK and abroad, accurate or not. Well over 25 per cent of retail sales are now made in such out-of-town malls. There has also been a proliferation of out-of-town supermarket superstores (they exceed 1,000), similar in size to continental hypermarkets, and often selling everything from food and clothes, to home furnishings and electrical goods (see **Food & Supermarkets** below).

The main attractions of shopping centres are one-stop shopping, protection from the British climate and free parking, which usually means you can simply wheel your trolley full of purchases to your car. The largest shopping centres incorporate a wide range of leisure attractions, including multiplex cinemas, ten-pin bowling alleys, games arcades, children's play areas, and lots of restaurants and bars. Like American malls, most aren't designed for those without cars, although many are served by bus services from nearby towns. Most urban centres also have covered shopping precincts, but parking is expensive and difficult to find, particularly on Saturdays, and may be located quite some distance from shops – so much so that park-and-ride facilities are often laid on for shoppers.

An unequal battle has raged between high streets and out-of-town centres for many years, which towns have been losing hands down, although some are belatedly fighting back. Malls have turned many places into ghost towns. This is an increasing problem throughout western Europe and has led some countries to restrict any further such developments. In the UK, too, political opinion has turned sharply against them in recent years and, as a result, it's becoming difficult to obtain planning permission to build more shopping centres and malls.

Markets

Most small towns have markets on one or two days a week (Wednesdays and Saturdays are most popular) and in larger centres, there may be one on a permanent basis. Markets are cheap, colourful and interesting, and often a good place for shrewd shopping, although you must sometimes be careful what you buy (beware of fakes). Items for sale include fruit and vegetables (especially cheap at the end of the day), foods from specialist retailers, clothes, handicrafts, household goods and second-hand books, records, antiques and bric-a-brac. Huge and famous outdoor Sunday markets include Petticoat Lane in London. Farmers' markets, where producers sell directly to the public, are becoming very popular and even take place in London suburbs such as Uxbridge. Check with your local library, council or Tourist Information Centre for information.

FOOD & SUPERMARKETS

The quality and variety of food in British supermarkets (which sell well over 75 per cent of the country's provisions) have increased in leaps and bounds in recent decades, and are now among the world's best. Supermarkets excel in efficiency of supply, maintaining hygiene and safety standards, offering fresh produce even though it comes from every corner of the globe, and in the convenience and ambience of the shopping environment they create, which is designed to maximise the temptation to buy. Major supermarkets have also branched out into fields such as banking and financial services.

British supermarkets are also among the world's most expensive; among developed countries, only Scandinavia, Switzerland and Japan have long-term higher food prices. All the neighbouring countries are cheaper. It's claimed that the European Union (EU) Common Agricultural Policy (CAP) exacerbates this situation, but it doesn't have such an effect on the continent. British supermarkets have huge mark-ups on many foods (around 45 per cent on meat and up to 60 per cent on some other products) and accusations of profiteering aren't unusual, prompting the Office of Fair Trading to investigate in the past. Savings (e.g. by bulk buying or when commodity prices fall) are rarely, if ever, passed onto the consumer. For example, meat prices bear no relation to the price paid to producers; supermarkets can charge more for a single lamb chop than they pay farmers for a whole lamb! Not surprisingly, British supermarkets are also the world's most profitable. In a survey by the Food Standards Agency in 2006, 52 per cent of people said low price was their primary consideration when food shopping, while less than a third of this number mentioned quality.

The German discount supermarket Aldi, which works on super-thin profit margins, is an exception to much of this. As elsewhere in Europe, its no-frills layouts, focus on its own brands and high turnover enable it to offer rock bottom prices. It is, however, still only a minor player in the British market.

The major supermarket chains (not all are national) include Tesco, Sainsbury's, Asda/Wallmart, Co-op, Iceland, Morrisons, Somerfield, and Waitrose. Some department and chain stores are also famous for their food halls, including Harrods, Selfridges and Fortnum and Mason in London, and Marks and Spencer (M&S) nationwide. The latter offers a smaller grocery range than supermarkets, but one renowned for its quality, particularly that of their convenience (prepared) meals range. Supermarkets were quick to copy this M&S innovation.

Superstores

The largest supermarket chains such as Sainsbury's, Tesco, Asda and Morrisons have built over 1,000 huge out-of-town superstores in the last decade or so, which offer, in addition to the traditional supermarket selections, a range of shops-within-a-shop, often including a newsagent, florist, delicatessen, cheese counter, bakery, fishmonger, chemist, butcher and market-style stalls. In 2005/2006 supermarket giant Tesco's annual profits broke through the £2bn bracket and continue to rise causing a certain un-ease with local traders. Superstores are also providing competition for department stores, not least because their lower overheads and higher purchasing power allow them to cut prices when they want to. Their size also allows them to stock a wider range of goods. Most superstores provide store plans, so that you don't need to spend a week looking for butter or tea, and (very necessary) also help find lost children. If possible, you should avoid shopping after 6pm, particularly on Friday evenings, at any time on Saturdays, and on Monday mornings, when stocks run down following the weekend stampede.

Quality & Choice

Whatever you may have heard about the British junk food diet, it can hardly be laid at the door of the supermarkets. Their fresh food range is as good as, or better than that available in most European counterparts (although more continentals shop in street markets). They also offer a wide range of wholesome fare produced using traditional methods. Many foreign foods can be found in supermarkets and you don't have to look very hard. Most have a separate delicatessen where these predominate. High turnover of stock ensures that produce is fresh (although it may have been stored for up to a year in special bunkers to prevent spoilage), and many supermarkets bake their own bread on the premises (although it isn't 'real' bread!). Most have fresh fish, meat and dairy counters, and offer an array of frozen products. However, many towns also have a freezer shop (e.g. Iceland), which generally offers a wider choice and lower prices if you buy in bulk. In most areas, a 'milkman' delivers milk to your door, and often other groceries, although these must be ordered in advance. Ask your neighbours for information or contact local dairies.

Prices

The highest savings can be made on own-brand goods, wine and spirits. Manufacturers have been shrinking the size of popular brands to hide price increases (the packaging may remain the same while the contents are reduced by up to 10 per cent). Always note the price actually charged for special offers and check it against the offer price, as mistakes are common. Among the cheapest supermarkets are Asda/Wallmart and Aldi. Savings made by taking part in retailer loyalty card schemes (used to reward frequent customers), amount to around 1 per cent and you're far better off shopping around for the lowest prices. These cards have become more popular than credit cards, with a majority of shoppers having one or more. Most supermarkets accept personal cheques (with a cheque card), debit cards and credit cards. If you have a few items only (usually around ten) or one small basket and are paying by cash, you can use an express check-out (of which there are usually too few).

Labelling

The latest supermarket battle is being fought over who provides the 'greenest' products, i.e. organically-produced food, environmentally-friendly products, and food that doesn't contain potentially harmful ingredients, e.g. preservatives. You usually pay a premium for anything labelled 'low fat', 'free-range' or 'low calorie', and many such descriptions are bogus (see 🖥 www.foodstandards.gov.uk for further information). Many manufacturers make unsubstantiated claims for 'health' foods and supposedly environmentally-friendly 'green' products, which are deliberately misleading. More stringent rules on food labelling are being imposed, but some manufacturers will always try to bend them. Many processed foods, in particular, contain high salt and sugar levels (even so-called 'low-fat' products). The fierce debate about genetically-modified (GM) food (or 'Frankenstein food' as it's known in some sections of the press) has been roundly lost by its proponents. As a result of public fears, many supermarkets have refused to stock GM products as far as possible. Irradiated food (irradiation is used to kill germs and extend the shelf-life of foods) initially caused concern, but this has now faded.

Alcohol

Almost all large supermarkets have a wide selection of wine (including own label) and other alcoholic drinks, although you should shop around, as prices and choice vary considerably. The very cheap German supermarket chain Aldi (🖥 http://uk.aldi.com) has low prices on food and wine, which compare favourably with continental prices. Don't always go for wines with fancy names or reputations, but experiment with some of the cheaper plonk priced from £2.50 to £4 a bottle, which is often good value.

Many wine merchants make free home deliveries. However, the best place to buy wine and spirits isn't in the UK, but on a day trip to France (see **Shopping Abroad** on page 477). You can also buy wine via the internet (e.g. 🖥 www.chateau online.co.uk) and save up to 30 per cent on UK prices. All wine buffs should have a copy of *Superplonk* by Malcolm Gluck (Collins), a supermarket wine guide listing 1,000 best buys.

Miscellaneous

Many supermarkets provide free plastic carrier bags and boxes, and some have staff to help you pack your purchases – although you may need to ask. If you want a heavy-duty carrier bag, there's usually a small fee. All supermarkets provide trolleys, which shouldn't be removed from supermarkets or their environs, e.g. car parks. Most don't require a deposit. Supermarkets generally take orders by telephone, fax or via the internet (see **Internet Shopping** on page 476), which can then be collected from a shop or delivered to your home. This may be free if you spend a minimum amount, ranging from £25 to £99. Many supermarkets provide recycling collection sites at shops, where you can take your old bottles, paper and cans. If you're having a party, large supermarkets provide a party service and a variety of prepared cold food trays plus drinks, snacks, party-ware, gifts and prizes, sandwiches and sweets. Some also provide glasses on free loan (or for a nominal fee), if you buy a large quantity of alcohol from them. Most supermarkets have a notice board where details of items for sale or services on offer can be posted free of charge.

DEPARTMENT & CHAIN STORES

The UK has many excellent department and chain stores. A department store is a large shop, usually on several floors, which sells almost everything, and sometimes includes a food hall. Each floor may be dedicated to a particular type of goods, such as ladies' or men's fashions or furniture. Department stores usually have restaurants or cafeterias, telephones and toilets (although you may need to pay to use a toilet in some shops). The major department store groups include the Army & Navy, Debenhams, House of Fraser, Bhs and John Lewis. John Lewis (owned wholly by its staff) is the father of all department stores and has a reputation for fair trading and value for money. Among London's many department stores are the renowned Harrods and Selfridges, two of the largest in the world. (Harrods, by the way, has a dress code and spending a penny there actually costs a pound). The floor at street level is designated the ground floor, not the 1st floor, and the floor above the ground floor is the 1st floor; the floor below the ground floor being usually called the basement.

A chain store is one with a number of branches, usually in different towns, e.g. Woolworths (⌨ www.woolworths.co.uk). There are dozens of them in the UK, selling everything from electrical goods to books and clothes. One of the most acclaimed is Marks and Spencer, noted for its clothes (the reputation of which sank in public esteem for a few years because of outdated designs, but has now begun to recover somewhat well with new ranges for the younger generation), home furnishings and excellent food halls. They have a reputation for good quality and exchanging anything without question, a practice which other shops have emulated.

Over the last couple of decades or so, catalogue shops (e.g. Argos and Index), where customers select their purchases from catalogues rather than a display, have become popular, because of the wide range offered, which is similar to a department store; the competitive pricing; and a policy that allows you to return anything unconditionally within a limited period for any reason (so you can test something in the comfort of your home and take it back if you don't like it!).

Most department and chain stores provide customer accounts (e.g. Debenhams, House of Fraser, John Lewis, Marks and Spencer) and allow balances to be repaid over a lengthy period, although this isn't wise, as the APR (see **Loans** on page 374) is usually very high. However, some shops offer up to 55 days free credit, e.g. Marks and Spencer (which otherwise has a high APR), and this can be worth using. Marks and Spencer made news recently for planning to transform its store cards into credit cards without asking customers' permission, but intervention by the Office of Fair Trading helped prevent this. Account customers can often take advantage of special offers and discounts and some shops arrange special shopping evenings. Many department and chain stores sell gift vouchers that can be redeemed for goods at any branch.

Department stores (and many smaller shops) provide a gift-wrapping service, particularly at Christmas, and deliver goods locally or post them, domestically and worldwide. Some shops also have a Mister Minit workshop where shoe repairs, key cutting and engraving is done while you wait.

CLOTHES

The clothing industry is extremely competitive, and London is one of the world's leading fashion centres, particularly for the young. What London lacks in *haute couture* houses, it more than makes up for by the sheer variety, energy, innovation and vitality of its fashion scene. It's renowned for schools, such as St Martin's and the Royal College of Art, which produce a continuous stream of excellent young designers. Clothes shops offer a wide range of attire, from traditional made-to-measure clothing to the latest ready-to-wear fashions, with prices ranging from a few to a few thousand pounds. Top quality and exclusive (i.e. expensive) ladies' and men's fashion shops (many chains sell ladies' and men's clothes) include Aquascutum, Burberry's, Gucci, Jaeger, Liberty and Yves St Laurent.

More middle-of-the-road ladies' fashions (with regard to price and quality) can be found at Army & Navy, Benetton, Country Casuals, Dorothy Perkins, Etam, DH Evans, Gap, Hennes (H&M), House of Fraser, Laura Ashley, Monsoon, Next, Miss Selfridge, Principles, Richards and Wallis. Miss Selfridge and River Island cater primarily for teenagers and those in their 20s and 30s. Clothes for the less affluent shopper can be found at Bhs and Debenhams. Marks and Spencer (M&S) clothes are generally more expensive than those sold by other large 'own brand' chain stores, and have hitherto enjoyed a reputation for quality and durability. However, whereas M&S formerly bought most of its stock from long-established British manufacturers, it currently sources from developing countries and the existence of any special distinguishing features in its clothes is now highly arguable. Although M&S have become more adventurous in recent years, they still cater essentially for the more conservative, older buyer, looking for stylish classics, rather than young trend-setters.

Top quality men's clothing shops include Cecil Gee, Austin Reed, Harrods and Selfridges (in London), Horne Brothers and Moss Bros. For the young man about town, there's a wide range of fashion shops, including Burtons, Ciro Cittero, Gap, Next for Men, Principles for Men, River Island and Top Man. All main centres also boast a profusion of independent shops covering the fashion spectrum and every price bracket. Markets are often a good place to shop for cheap clothes, and mail-order offers (e.g. in Saturday and Sunday newspaper magazines) also usually provide good value too. Some clothes shops don't have changing rooms, but allow you to return anything which doesn't fit (see **Appendix D** for a comparison of British, continental and US sizes).

Clothes are generally of good quality, particularly those from famous English manufacturers (e.g. Aquascutum, Burberry, Jaeger and Liberty), who produce classic styles and traditional clothes that are made to last (and outlast ever-changing fashions). Cheaper clothes are largely made abroad (e.g. in the Far East), as it's simply too expensive to produce them in the UK. Although the quality of such clothes may occasionally be suspect, you usually get what you pay for. Most shops provide an alteration service (for a small fee) and many also provide a made-to-measure tailoring service.

The most renowned men's tailors are to be found in London's Savile Row, while Jermyn Street is famous for handmade shirts and Bond Street is one of Europe's premier locales for ladies fashion. Unless you're wealthy, beware of shops that don't price their window displays (as when buying a Rolls-Royce, if you must ask the price, you cannot afford it!).

When clothes have been fitted with a security tag, check that it hasn't left a small hole, which could lead to a much larger hole later on, in which case you would be entitled to exchange them or claim a refund.

There are also ladies' and men's clothes hire shops in many towns, where you can rent everything from a ball gown to top hat and tails.

Although you can buy shoes in some clothes shops, specialist retailers are varied and abundant. These range from the top quality (and top price) Russell & Bromley, Ravel, Bally and Charles Jourdan chains, to the more affordable Dolcis, Barrats, K Shoes, Milwards and Saxone. Like good quality English clothes, English shoes (famous makers include Crockett & Jones and Church's) are made to last, although few manufacturers remain. Two other famous English brand names are Clarks and Startrite, both of which make excellent children's shoes in a wide range of fittings, as well as good quality, reasonably-priced footwear for adults.

Sportswear shops exist in most towns, specialising in trainers, which are particularly fashionable among the young. Shoe repair shops can be found in most towns and many department stores and high streets have a Mister Minit shop, where repairs are carried out while you wait. The quality of repairs from an established family cobbler may be superior to that of an instant repair shop.

NEWSPAPERS, MAGAZINES & BOOKS

The British are a nation of inveterate newspaper readers. When city and regional newspapers are included, there are around 130 daily and Sunday newspapers, over 2,000 weekly free or paid-for newspapers and over 7,000 other periodicals published in the UK. According to the Office of National Statistics Social Trends, 55 per cent of people aged over 15 read a national newspaper each weekday (59 per cent of men and 50 per cent of women) while 80 per cent read a regional or local paper each week. The British buy rather less than 15 million national newspapers and over five million regional morning and evening newspapers each day, more than in nearly any other country in the world. However, the readership of the national papers has been declining inexorably since the early '80s. There's no tax on newspapers, magazines or books.

Most major newspapers traditionally support the Conservative party, although this has changed somewhat in recent years with the election of a Labour government, and loyalties are slightly less clear-cut. Allegiances did, in fact, become surprisingly fluid for a period, but are now tending to gradually revert to type. Daily and Sunday newspapers range from the 'quality' press for serious readers to the popular tabloids for those who just like to look at pictures (including those of half-naked ladies). The daily newspapers include (roughly in order of average sales, highest first), the *Daily Telegraph*, *The Times*, *The Guardian*, *The Independent* and the *Financial Times*. The equivalents in Scotland are the *Glasgow Herald* and the *Scotsman*. Until recently the description 'broadsheet' was used for them, as they were all difficult to read in confined spaces, but now *The Independent* has gone over to a 'compact' format and

The Times appears in two sizes. (The term 'tabloid' has been avoided like the plague). The popular tabloid daily press (also sometimes referred to by less flattering names for their cheap sensationalist exposés) includes the *Sun*, the *Daily Mirror*, the *Daily Mail*, the *Daily Express*, the *Star*, and the *Daily Record* (which replaces its stable-mate the *Daily Mirror* in Scotland).

On Sundays, the quality newspapers are *The Sunday Times*, *Sunday Telegraph*, *The Observer*, *Independent on Sunday* (and, in Scotland, the *Sunday Herald* and *Scotland on Sunday*), which are good sources of advertisements for quality cars, executive appointments, property (in the UK and abroad), entertainment, travel and holidays. The popular Sunday tabloids are the *News of the World*, *Sunday Mirror*, *People*, *Mail on Sunday*, *Sunday Express* and *Sunday Sport* (which is a 'fictional' newspaper). Most Sunday and many daily newspapers include a colour magazine (usually with the Saturday edition in the case of the latter), some of which have earned a reputation for quality journalism in their own right, e.g. *The Sunday Times Colour Magazine*. There are regional daily and evening newspapers in most areas. Free weekly newspapers are delivered to homes throughout the UK and numerous magazines are on sale, including many popular European and North American titles.

If you prefer to have publications delivered to your doorstep, most newsagents do this for a small fee (e.g. £1 to £2 a week). You can also take out subscriptions to your favourite magazines, which is cheaper than buying them from newsagents. However, new magazines come and go with amazing frequency and have a tendency to go bust just after you've sent them a cheque! In cities, newspapers are sold from kiosks or simply from the pavement, particularly Sunday papers which are available from late on Saturday nights. A selection of the foreign press, such as the *International Herald Tribune*, *Wall Street Journal Europe*, *USA Today*, the *Frankfurter Allgemeine Zeitung* and *Le Monde,* is to be found on newsstands in urban centres, often on the day of publication, and European editions of *Newsweek* and *Time* are sold by most newsagents. If you're willing to wait a few days for delivery, many such foreign publications can be bought on subscription at a large saving over newsagent prices.

Books

There are excellent book shops in most towns (hopefully all selling this book) and, in addition to WH Smith (who alone account for roughly around 15 per cent of all UK book sales), larger towns and cities usually have one or more branches of the major chains, such as Dillons, Blackwell, Waterstones, Ottakers or Hammicks. Department stores may also offer a limited range, while John Menzies and Martin, both large newsagent chains, sell paperback novels. In cities, some book shops are usually open until around 8pm or even later each evening.

As you would expect, London has a multitude of book shops, including the world-famous Foyles (utter chaos, but good for browsing), where you will find volumes on just about anything. Others specialise in art and design, feminist and ethnic interests, science fiction, sport, law, medicine, travel, politics, economics and foreign literature. The availability of foreign language books is otherwise limited to larger centres. Cut-price book shops, where 'remaindered' books that have been sold off by publishers can be bought at discount prices, are commonplace, while second-hand book shops, such as the one featured in the film *84 Charing Cross Road*, usually full of collectors and bargain hunters, are becoming rarer.

Although books may not be particularly cheap in the UK, they're often cheaper than elsewhere (particularly textbooks). Students can also save money by buying the latter from other students or second-hand book shops. Prices, formerly fixed, are now widely discounted (at least as far as best sellers are concerned, although less than in the US) and books even appear on supermarket shelves. Mail-order book clubs proliferate (see **Home Shopping** on page 475), most of which provide introductory offers and books at discounted prices. Some are general interest, while others stick to a particular subject, e.g. photography, computers or mediaeval history. (Many clubs advertise in the press, particularly in Sunday newspaper magazines). The market is dominated by Book Club Associates (BCA), owned by Bertelsman, which operates 31 separate clubs with over 2 million members, and which offers discounts of from 25 to 50 per cent.

Book tokens are a popular present for people of all ages and are sold and accepted by most book shops. Many organisations operate their own specialist libraries, which focus on matters technical. While larger public libraries have impressive book selections (see **Libraries** on page 427), smaller ones tend to be more populist than formerly in their choices.

FURNITURE

Furniture is usually good value in the UK and top quality furniture is often cheaper than in many other European countries. There's a huge choice of modern and traditional designs in every price range although, as with most things, you generally get what you pay for. Exclusive *avant garde* designs from Italy, Denmark and many other countries are available (usually with equally exclusive prices), but imports also include reasonably-priced quality leather suites and a wide range of cane furniture from the Far East. Among the largest furniture chain stores in the UK are Harveys, Heal's and Trends, all of which offer a wide range of top quality British furniture from manufacturers such as Ercol, G-Plan and Parker Knoll.

Oak is the most common wood used for traditional British quality furniture and pine, which can be bought stained or unstained, is also popular. When ordering furniture, you may need to wait weeks or months for delivery, so you should try to find a shop which has what you want in stock or which will give you a guaranteed delivery date (after which you can cancel and receive a full refund). Many manufacturers sell directly to the public, although you shouldn't assume that this will result in huge savings, and should compare prices and quality before buying. Shops specialising in beds, and leather, reproduction or antique furniture also exist, along with many companies manufacturing and installing fitted bedrooms, bathrooms and kitchens. Fitted kitchens, especially, are an extremely competitive business and you should be wary of cowboy companies who are specialists in shoddy workmanship.

If you want reasonably-priced, good quality, modern furniture, there are a number of companies selling items for home assembly (which helps keep down prices), e.g. MFI, Habitat and Ikea, the last being the world's only global furniture chain. Assembly instructions are generally easy to follow (although some people think Rubik's cube is easier) and some companies print instructions in a number of languages.

All large furniture retailers publish catalogues, which are generally distributed free of charge. Some shops offer £50 or £100 for your old suite, when you buy a new one from them. However, this may not be much of a bargain (particularly if your suite is worth more than the amount offered) and shopping around for the best deal is preferable. Furniture and home furnishings are very competitive businesses and you can often reduce the price by some judicious haggling, particularly if you're spending a large amount. Another way to save money is to wait for the sales to come round. If you cannot wait and don't want (or cannot afford) to pay cash, look for an interest-free credit deal. Check the advertisements in local newspapers and national home and design magazines such as *House & Garden*, *Country Homes & Interiors* and *Ideal Home*.

HOUSEHOLD APPLIANCES

Large household appliances, such as cookers and refrigerators, are usually provided in rented accommodation and may also be fitted in new homes. Many homeowners include fitted kitchen appliances such as a cooker, refrigerator, dishwasher and washing machine when selling their house or apartment, although you may need to pay for them separately. If you wish to bring large appliances with you, such as a refrigerator, washing machine or dishwasher, remember that the standard British unit width (60cm) isn't always the same as in other countries. Check the size and the latest British safety regulations before shipping these items to the UK or buying them abroad, as they may need expensive modifications. A wide range of household appliances is available, from British and foreign manufacturers, with larger shops also selling American-style refrigerators, in which you can store a year's supply of dairy products for a family of 14 (and a few pets). Most large appliances such as refrigerators and dishwashers have an energy efficiency rating; choose one with an A rating for the lowest running costs.

If you already own small household appliances, it's worthwhile bringing them to the UK, as usually all that's required is a change of plug, but check first. If you're coming from a country with a 110/115V electricity supply (e.g. the US), you will need a lot of expensive transformers (see **Electricity** on page 126). Don't bring a television to the UK from the continent or the US, as it won't work (see **Standards** on page 183). Smaller appliances, such as vacuum cleaners, grills, toasters and electric irons, aren't expensive and are usually of excellent quality. If you want to buy a ceramic or halogen hob, bear in mind that it may be necessary to replace all your saucepans. Before buying household appliances, whether large or small, check the test reports and surveys in *Which?* magazine (see **Consumers' Association** on page 479) at your local library.

Shops such as Comet, Power Warehouse and warehouse clubs such as Costco and Cargo offer among the best prices for household goods. You should also try Empire Direct (🖳 www.empiredirect.co.uk). A one-year guarantee is normally provided, which can usually be extended by a further two or four years. However, although extended warranties may provide additional peace of mind, they're usually a waste of money and should definitely be avoided. If you need kitchen measuring equipment and cannot cope with decimal measures, you will have to bring your own measuring scales, jugs, cups (US and British recipe cups aren't the same size) and thermometers (see also **Appendix D**). British pillows and duvets aren't the same size or shape as in many other countries.

SECOND-HAND BARGAINS

There's a lively second-hand market for almost everything, from antiques to motor cars, and computers to photographic equipment (the British spend well over £5 billion a year on second-hand goods). You name it and somebody will be selling it second-hand. The internet auction site eBay (💻 www.ebay.co.uk) is particularly popular and is a source for anything anyone could ever think of and some they cannot. With such a large second-hand market, there are often bargains to be found, particularly if you're quick off the mark. Many towns have a junk shop and an Oxfam, Imperial Cancer Research or Sue Ryder shop, which sells new and second-hand articles for charity (with most of your money going to help those in need). There's a number of national and regional weekly newspapers devoted to bargain hunters, including *Exchange & Mart*, *Dalton's Weekly* (both are national and include advertisements for just about everything) and *Loot* (a daily newspaper published in various editions for different areas – advertisements are free to non-traders).

There are also many magazines dedicated to second-hand cars. If you're looking for a particular item, such as a camera, boat or motorcycle, you may be better off looking through the small advertisements in specialist, rather than more general, publications. The classified advertisements in local newspapers are also a good source of bargains, particularly for furniture and household appliances, as are expatriate club newsletters, where such items are often sold cheaply by those returning home. Shopping centre, newsagents and company notice boards can also prove fruitful. Another place to pick up a bargain is at an auction, although it helps to be knowledgeable about what you're buying (you will probably be competing with experts). Auctions are held throughout the year for everything from antiques and paintings to motorcars and property. The UK has some of the world's most famous auction houses, including Sotheby's, Christie's and Philips, all of which hold local antique valuation days throughout the country. On a slightly less grand social level, computer equipment auctions are profuse and, given that so much good quality, but not quite up-to-the-minute kit is constantly being phased out in the UK annually, great bargains can be found. Auctions of all sorts are widely advertised in local newspapers and through leaflets.

Antique shops are encountered in many towns, and antique street markets (e.g. Portobello Road and Camden Passage in London) and fairs are held regularly. For information about local events, inquire at your Tourist Information Centre or library. Car boot (trunk) sales, where people sell practically anything from the boots of their cars, are popular throughout the UK and the best place to acquire real bargains and loads of junk without any consumer protection. Ensure you arrive early. Sales are customarily held on Sundays and may be advertised in local newspapers and signposted on roads.

HOME SHOPPING

Shopping by mail-order and telephone has always been popular and shopping via the internet is expanding, although the revolution in buying habits predicted a few years ago is only now beginning to shows signs of materialising. Sales doubled in the last 12 months. Catalogue and television (TV) shopping by mail, telephone and the internet is big business and is worth over £11 billion a year. Direct retailing by companies (cutting out the middleman) has become more widespread than agency catalogue sales, particularly for computers, office equipment, and services such as insurance. Along with the increasing importance of electronic shopping, TV shopping is becoming more popular (products sold through infomercials are a huge success).

Mail-order Catalogues

There are many companies in the UK selling exclusively by mail-order. Customers are provided with a (usually free) colour catalogue, and can often also act as agents, collecting orders from other customers and receiving a commission. The major mail-order catalogues contain almost everything you would expect to find in a department store, although your choice is more limited and prices may be higher. The main attraction is that goods are bought on approval and can usually be paid for over a period of 6 or 12 months at no extra cost. The cost of postage is usually paid by the mail-order company.

Among the major mail-order companies are Empire Stores, Freemans, JD Williams and Littlewoods. (Littlewoods also publishes other catalogues, such as Index Extra and Peter Craig. The latter contains the same goods as Index Extra, but they cost more!). Newcomers include direct-selling clothes manufacturers, such as Cotton Traders, Damart, Hawkshead, Lands' End and Next Directory. Most mail-order companies also accept orders from overseas customers, although there's usually a charge for a catalogue (e.g. £5). The quality of own brand goods, particularly clothes, is sometimes found wanting, and some companies are difficult to contact and slow to send goods or refunds.

Some major shops also publish mail-order catalogues and send goods anywhere in the world, e.g. Fortnum & Masons, Habitat, Harrods and Selfridges. Most major food retailers accept orders by telephone, fax or via the internet, including Iceland, Asda, Safeway, Sainsbury's, Somerfield and Tesco. Most shops provide account facilities and accept payment by international credit and charge cards. Many charities, institutions and organisations, e.g. Amnesty International, the British Heart Foundation, the National Trust, the Natural History Museum, Oxfam, Save the Children, the Science Museum and the World Wildlife Fund, also publish mail-order catalogues. The added bonus for buyers is that, in addition to buying beautiful, exclusive and often unusual handmade items from around the world, you can also contribute to a good cause.

Mail-order Clubs

A number of companies operate mail-order clubs for books, CDs, computer software and video cassettes, with new members being offered a number of items at a nominal introductory price (e.g. £1 each) or the chance to pay for one of five or seven items, in return for an agreement to purchase a further number of items (usually three to six) at full price during the following one or two years. There's no catch, although there may be a restricted choice and, if you want to resign before you've fulfilled your side of the bargain, you're usually required to repay the savings made on the introductory offer.

Before committing yourself to buying anything by post, make sure you know what you're signing and don't send cash through the post or pay for anything in advance, unless absolutely necessary. It's foolish to do this in response to an advertisement unless you're sure that the company is reputable and offers a cast-iron money-back guarantee. Customers who buy goods or services in response to advertisements in reputable publications are usually covered by the Safe Home Ordering Protection Scheme (SHOPS), 18a King Street, Maidenhead, SL6 1EF (☎ 01628-641 930, 🖳 www.shops-uk.org.uk), which provides a money-back guarantee. Check in advance that a periodical is covered. This may be indicated by a SHOPS logo. If purchases aren't covered by a guarantee, you may find it extremely difficult to obtain any redress. When you buy goods by post, you're usually protected by the Sale of Goods Act and by the codes of practice operating in the mail-order business.

Internet Shopping

Shopping via the internet has suddenly begun to take off in reality following the premature predictions of an explosion in this area before the collapse of the dot-com bubble a few years ago. The UK has become Europe's biggest online shopping market, overtaking Germany, UK shoppers spent 9.79bn euros (£6.7bn; $12.2bn) online in 2006.

Competition between internet providers has lowered the cost of fast broadband services, making it easier for consumers to shop online with total internet sales in Europe rising by 51% to 40.2bn euros in 2006.

There are numerous sites, including 🖳 www.shopguide.co.uk and 🖳 www.virgin.net, which provide a good directory of British shopping sites. One of the best bargain websites is 🖳 www.buy.com, which offers over 10,000 electronic items at discount prices and has forced UK high street retailers to cut theirs. Another site which provides links to all the UK's major retailers is 🖳 www.shopping.net, while another useful site is 🖳 www.onlineclothesshops.co.uk. Price comparison sites are numerous and include 🖳 www.computerprices.co.uk, 🖳 www.pricechecker.co.uk, 🖳 www.bookbrain.co.uk (for books), 🖳 www.cameratag.co.uk (for cameras) and 🖳 www.price-tracker.co.uk (for video-games).

With internet shopping, the world is your oyster and savings can be made on a wide range of goods and services, including holidays and travel. Small, high-price, high-tech items (e.g. cameras, watches and portable computers) can usually be bought more cheaply in the US of the Far East, with delivery within a few days.

However, while shopping on the internet is sometimes claimed to be **very** secure, research has shown that your credit card details are more likely to be discovered by thieves when shopping via the internet than when doing so by telephone or mail-order. The limitations of assurances given by over-confident experts were underlined in February 2003, when a computer hacker gained access to over 5m Visa and MasterCard credit accounts in the US.

Buying Overseas

When buying goods overseas, ensure that you're dealing with a bona fide company and that the goods will work in the UK. If possible, **always** pay by credit card when buying by mail-order or over the internet because, for bills between £100 and £30,000, the credit card issuer is generally jointly liable with the supplier under the Consumer Credit Act 1974. However, many card companies claim that the law doesn't cover overseas purchases, although some consider claims up to the value of the goods purchased (and they **could** also be liable in law for consequential loss). When you buy expensive goods abroad, always have them insured for their full value.

VAT & Duty

When buying overseas, take into account shipping costs, duty and VAT. There's no duty or tax on goods purchased within the European Union or on goods from most other countries worth £18 or less (or £36, if a gift). Don't buy alcohol or cigarettes outside the EU, as the duty is usually too high to make it pay. When VAT or duty is payable on a parcel, the payment is usually collected by the post office or courier company on delivery.

SHOPPING ABROAD

Shopping abroad for most British people consists of a day trip to Calais or Boulogne, and a visit to a French hypermarket (similar to a British superstore). Considerable savings can be made on a wide variety of goods, including food (e.g. cheese, ground coffee, chocolate, cooked meats and patés), alcohol (beer, wine and spirits), toys, housewares (e.g. hardware, glassware and kitchenware) and clothing (if you take your car, you can also save on servicing). Don't forget your passports or identity cards, car papers, foreign currency and credit cards. Many French shops accept sterling, but usually give you a worse exchange rate than a bank. It's usually best to use a credit card when shopping abroad and on board ferries, as you receive a better exchange rate (and can delay payment). In towns much frequented by British shoppers and tourists, the price of some goods may be higher than in inland towns.

From 1st January 1993, there have been no cross-border shopping restrictions within the European Union for goods purchased duty and tax paid, provided all goods are for personal consumption or use and not for resale. Although there are no restrictions, there are 'indicative levels' for certain items, above which goods may be classified as commercial quantities. For example, people aged 17 or over entering the UK may import the following amounts of alcohol and tobacco without question:

● 10 litres of spirits (over 22° proof);

● 20 litres of fortified wine such as port or sherry (under 22° proof);

● 90 litres of wine (or 120 x 0.75 litre bottles/10 cases) of which a maximum of 60 litres may be sparkling wine;

● 110 litres of beer;

● 3,200 cigarettes, 400 cigarillos, 200 cigars and 3kg of smoking tobacco.

There's no limit on perfume or toilet water. If you exceed the above amounts, you may need to convince the customs authorities that you aren't planning to sell the goods. There are huge fines for anyone who re-sells alcohol and tobacco, imported under this concession, which is classed as smuggling. The vast cross-Channel shopping business is made possible by ridiculously cheap off-season ferry trips costing as little as £10 return for a car and £1 for foot passengers. Most special offers are available during off-peak periods only and are often offered via coupons provided in daily newspapers. Cross-Channel shopping has led a number of British companies to open outlets in Calais, including Sainsbury's, Tesco, Victoria Wine and The Wine Society. If you don't fancy a trip to France, you can buy wine direct from vineyards and breweries in Austria, France, Germany, Italy and Spain (and beer direct from Belgium) via local intermediaries, making large savings on British high street prices.

Alcohol and tobacco are favourite tax targets of the Chancellor of the Exchequer although, if too many people hit the Calais trail, he may be forced to rethink some of his taxation policies. The revenue loss to the British government through tobacco brought illicitly into the country is estimated at well over £3.7 billion, while approaching 1 billion pounds is lost as a result of legal importation. Cross-Channel shopping has also had a huge impact on pubs and off-licences in the south-east of England (over 180 million litres of wine are personally imported into the UK each year). However, only some four per cent of alcohol, as against circa 20 per cent of cigarettes and tobacco, is imported illegally. The radical increases in cigarette prices in France will impact heavily on this situation.

DUTY-FREE ALLOWANCES

Duty-free shopping within the EU ended in 1999, but is still available when travelling further afield or to the Canary Islands, the Channel Islands and Gibraltar. For each such journey, travellers aged 17 or over are entitled to import the following goods purchased duty-free:

- Two litres of still table wine;

- One litre of alcohol over 22° volume or 38.8 per cent proof (e.g. spirits and strong liquors) **or** two litres not over 22° volume (e.g. low strength liquors or fortified or sparkling wines);

- 200 cigarettes **or** 100 cigarillos **or** 50 cigars **or** 250 grammes of tobacco;

- 60cc/ml (50gr or 2fl oz) of perfume;

- 250cc/ml (8fl oz) of toilet water;

- Other goods (including gifts, souvenirs, beer and cider) to the value of £145.

Duty-free allowances apply on outward and return journeys, even if both are made on the same day, and the combined total (i.e. double the above limits) can be imported into your home country. Since 1993, duty-free sales have been vendor-controlled, meaning that vendors are responsible for ensuring that the amount of duty-free goods sold to individuals doesn't exceed their entitlement. Duty-free goods purchased on board ferries are noted on boarding cards, which must be presented with each purchase.

CONSUMERS' ASSOCIATION

The Consumers' Association (which trendily styles itself without the definite article) is the most acclaimed and respected independent consumer organisation in the UK, with over a million members. It publishes an excellent monthly magazine (available on subscription only) entitled *Which?*, containing invaluable information about a wide range of goods and services (just about everything is tested at some time or other). All tests are organised independently by the Consumers' Association and cover financial services (e.g. insurance, banking, pensions and investment); cars; leisure products; food and health; household and domestic appliances; and items of public interest. Dangerous products are highlighted, best buys are recommended and, most importantly, you're told how to obtain your legal rights when things go wrong.

It's indispensable to anyone who's interested in obtaining value for money and their rights as consumers. Fortunately for the many companies which provide poor value for money, shoddy goods and indifferent or terrible service (in particular after-sales service), the vast majority of British people prefer to throw their money away. A subscription to *Which?* costs £75 a year which, although it may appear expensive, is excellent value considering the savings to be made in time and money (not to mention peace of mind). Advertisements and leaflets appear regularly in magazines (especially Sunday newspaper supplements), offering a free three-month trial period, and can also be accessed on their website (www.which.net). *Which?* magazines and books can also be found in the reference sections of public libraries.

The Consumers' Association also publishes similar magazines, including *Gardening Which?*, *Holiday Which?* and *Health Which?*, for which introductory offers are also available, along with a wide range of books on subjects ranging from *Starting Your Own Business* to *Making the Most of Retirement* (☎ 0845-307 4000, 🖳 www. which.co.uk).

18.

ODDS & ENDS

This chapter contains miscellaneous information. Although all topics aren't of vital importance, most are of general interest to anyone living or working in the UK, including everything you ever wanted to know (but were afraid to ask) about tipping and toilets.

BRITISH CITIZENSHIP

Apart from those born to a foreign diplomat, anyone born in the UK before 1983 automatically qualifies for British citizenship. A person born abroad before 1983 whose father was born or adopted in the UK (or had become a British citizen in the UK) and who was married to their mother, is automatically a British citizen through descent from his father. A person born in the UK after 1982 becomes a British citizen automatically only if either parent was a British citizen or a permanent resident (settled) at the time of their birth. Anyone born after 1982 with a parent who was born or adopted in the UK (or who had become a British citizen in the UK) is automatically a British citizen by descent from either parent. If the parents were not married at the time of birth, the mother's status is relevant.

In February 2002, people who continued to hold British Dependent Territories' citizenship, despite changes such as the sovereignty of Hong Kong passing to China, became British Overseas Territories' citizens. In May 2002, they then became British citizens automatically under the British Overseas Territories Act 2002, unless their status was connected with sovereign bases in Cyprus.

Any foreign national over 18, including a Commonwealth or Irish citizen, can apply to become a British citizen (called 'naturalisation'). To qualify you must have been permitted to live as a permanent resident in the UK for a minimum of one year; have lived in the UK legally for a total of at least five years, without being absent from the country for more than 450 days and with no more than 90 days' absence in the year before the application; plan to continue living in the UK (i.e. you cannot apply for British citizenship in order to qualify to live elsewhere in the European Union (EU)); have sufficient knowledge of the English, Welsh or Scottish (Gaelic) language; be of good character (e.g. no criminal record); and pay a fee. Parents of non-British children who qualify under the above rules can apply on their behalf (called 'registration') for which there's a reduced fee.

Anyone over 18 and married to a British citizen can apply for naturalisation provided he's permitted to live in the UK as a permanent resident and has lived in the UK legally for a total of at least three years, without being absent from the country for more than 270 days, and not more than 90 days' absence in the year before the application. He must also plan to continue living in the UK, be of good character and pay a fee. It currently takes an average of 6 to 12 months to become a naturalised British citizen.

For further details contact the Home Office Immigration and Nationality Directorate, Reliance House, 20 Water Street, Liverpool L3 8XU (☎ 0151-237 0405, 🖳 www.ind.homeoffice.gov.uk).

There are often delays in issuing passports and you should apply in person if you need a passport quickly. Current processing times are given in recorded messages, the telephone numbers of which are provided on application forms. These are available from main post offices and should be sent by post to your local passport office (listed on the form). Enclose with the completed form the fee, any relevant documents (such as your birth certificate), two passport-size photographs and your old passport (if applicable). An application form for a British passport must be signed by a person of professional standing in the community who knows you well, e.g. a doctor, Member of Parliament or a justice of the peace. Your family doctor may charge you around £5 to complete a passport form.

CLIMATE

The UK has a generally mild and temperate climate, although it's extremely changeable and usually damp at any time of year. Because of the prevailing south-westerly winds, the weather is variable and is affected mainly by depressions moving eastwards across the Atlantic Ocean (which make British weather reports depressing). This maritime influence means that the west of the country tends to have wetter, but also milder, weather than the east. The amount of rainfall also increases with altitude and the 'mountainous' areas of the north and west have more rain (around 2,000mm in the Lake District and the western Highlands of Scotland with almost as much in the Pennines) than the lowlands of the south and east, where the average is 700mm. Rain is fairly evenly distributed throughout the year in all areas. It may feel as though it rains most of the time, but in fact, according to the Meteorological Office, it does so only on one day in every three. The driest months are usually March to June and the wettest September to January. For many, spring is the most pleasant time of year, although early spring is often very wet, particularly in Scotland.

In winter, temperatures are higher in the south and west than in the east, and winters are often harsh in Scotland and on high ground in Wales and northern England, where snow is usual. December and February are traditionally the severest months, when it's often cold, wet and windy. When it snows, the whole country comes to a grinding halt (except for the kids, who love it) and people complain that the authorities were unprepared. Although temperatures drop below freezing in winter, particularly at night, it's rarely below freezing during the day, although the average temperature hovers around a cold 4°C (39°F). Regional variations are noticeable: it's 2°C (35.6°F) in Edinburgh, 3°C (37.4°F) in Manchester and, at over 5°C (41°F), distinctly warmer in London.

The most unpleasant features of British winters are freezing fog and black ice, both of which make driving hazardous. The 'pea-soup' fog which was usually the result of smog and pollution, and which many foreigners still associate with the UK, is generally a thing of the past. The warmest areas in summer are the south and inland areas, where temperatures are often around 26°C (75°F) and occasionally rise above 30°C (86°F), although the average temperature is 15°C to 18°C (60°F to 65°F). Fine autumn weather is often preceded by early morning fog, which may last until midday. Early autumn is often mild, particularly in Scotland. Average daily temperatures in London are: winter just over 5°C (41°F), spring 11°C (51.8°F), summer just below 18°C (64.4°F) and autumn just over 12°C (53.6°F).

The most depressing thing about British weather (at almost any time of year) is the frequent drizzle (light rain) and the almost permanent grey skies. Roughly translated into layman's terms, British weather is terrible (if it was fine day after boring day, whatever would the British people find to talk about?). British winter weather has given rise to a condition known as seasonal affective disorder (SAD), which is brought on by the dark, depressing days of winter and causes lethargy, fatigue and low spirits. However, there's **some** good news. British winters are becoming milder and in recent years winters have been nothing like as severe as in earlier decades – although whether this is a permanent change is unclear.

In fact, British weather is becoming warmer all round, with recent years experiencing some of the driest summers since records began in 1659. To add a little spice to the usual diet of cold and rain, in the last two decades, the UK has been afflicted with gales and torrential rain (including the infamous storms of 1987 and 1990), which caused severe damage and flooding in many areas. Tornadoes do occur in the UK, but are extremely rare. There's much debate among weather experts and scientists as to whether the climatic changes (not just in the UK, but worldwide) are a result of global warming or just a temporary change. If present trends continue, some scientists predict that temperatures will increase considerably in the next century and the south-west region could become frost-free).

Weather forecasts appear designed to be deliberately evasive, as if the meteorologists are continually hedging their bets; therefore most forecasts include scattered showers and sunny periods, at the very least. In fact, meteorologists are the only people who are paid for being wrong most of the time. They usually find it particularly difficult to forecast abrupt changes or extremes of weather (which are common). A style of weather report which made an appearance in the last decade introduced percentage forecasting, such as a 70 per cent chance of rain, a 50 per cent likelihood of frost overnight and a 10 per cent probability of sunny periods (and a 100 per cent chance that it will all be wrong!). The Meteorological Office (Met Office) sells its long-term weather predictions to industry, agriculture and tourism (if they have any sense, they will insist on a guarantee: the Met Office has been accused of fiddling its success-rate figures).

Detailed forecasts for just about any country or region are available on the internet, but the best sites for the UK are 🖥 www.met-office.gov.uk, 🖥 www.weather.org.uk, 🖥 www.bbc.co.uk/weather and 🖥 www.weatherweb.net. Detailed weather forecasts can also be obtained by telephone from Weatherweb on ☎ 01902-895 252 or the Automobile Association, ☎ 09003-401 100 (calls cost up to 60p a minute), which provides five-day regional forecasts. The weather forecast is also available via the television (TV) teletext services, in daily newspapers, on the internet, and on TV and radio broadcasts (usually after the news). Warnings of dangerous weather conditions affecting motoring, e.g. fog and ice, are broadcast regularly on all BBC national and local radio stations.

The most detailed weather forecasts are broadcast on BBC Radio 2 and BBC Radio 4 (which also broadcasts weather forecasts for shipping). Many newspapers also include temperatures and the weather outlook in European and world capitals,

European holiday centres, and in winter, the weather and snow conditions in major ski resorts. During early summer, when pollens are released in large quantities, the pollen count is given on radio and TV weather forecasts and in daily newspapers. In summer, the maximum exposure time for the fair-skinned is included in TV weather forecasts.

CRIME

According to official statistics, the overall number of crimes being committed is reducing, although crimes of violence, burglary, drug-related crimes, gun crimes, anti-social behaviour and domestic violence have risen sharply in recent years. The actual police figures and those issued by the British Crime Survey (BCS) are contradictory. There were officially some 5.6m cruimes commited in 2005-06, of which around 75 per cent were crimes against property such as burglery or theft. The BCS estimates that there were 10.9m crimes, although this a fall of 8.4m from the peak in 1995. This is largely because people are simply not reporting crime, considering it a waste of time; the clear-up rate or number of crimes solved is around 25 per cent nationally and far lower in some areas. The main exception is car theft, because reporting it to the police is necessary for insurance purposes. **Crime has been exacerbated in recent years by the large number of criminals who have invaded Britain's cities from Eastern Europe since the expansion of the EU.**

In the last decade, there has been an upsurge in car joy-riding (where cars are stolen by kids for 'fun'), muggings, pickpocketing, car crime, burglary, robbery, fraud, rape and school crime. Murders have increased and are approaching 750 a year. Violent crime has reached shocking proportions in some cities and it's becoming more common among children. It's true that you're more likely to choke to death on your food than you are to meet a violent end in the UK, and the public are told that crime rates are still relatively low compared with many other countries, but there are so many variables involved that this isn't always reassuring.

Many crimes are drug-related and are due to the huge increase in drugs flooding into the UK in recent years. The use of hard drugs (particularly cocaine and crack) is a major problem in most cities, where gangs increasingly use guns to settle their differences. The police warn people (particularly young women) against tempting fate by walking alone in dark and deserted areas late at night, and the increasing rate of assaults on female students has prompted many universities to issue them with rape (screech) alarms.

For many people, crime is their number one concern and in some areas, people are afraid to leave the relative safety of their homes at any time of day or night. The increase in crime in many areas is attributed by psychologists to poverty, the breakdown of traditional family life, the loss of community and social values in society, and a growing lack of parental responsibility and skills. The failure to deal with juvenile crime is a major threat facing the UK and many children are out of control by the age of ten or even younger. Riots occasionally occur and are often sparked by a breakdown in relations between police and youths.

Crimes against property are escalating, particularly car thefts and thefts from vehicles. The number of cars stolen and burglary is the highest (per capita) in Western Europe. If you work or live in a major city and park your car there, you have a one in four chance of having it stolen or broken into. In London (where around 20 per cent of all crime takes place), professional thieves even steal antique paving stones, railings and antique doors and door casings. Fraud or so-called 'white-collar' crime (which includes credit card fraud, income tax evasion and VAT fraud), costs billions of pounds a year and accounts for larger sums than the total of all other robberies, burglaries and thefts.

The authorities' response to the crime wave sweeping the UK has been to 'get tough' with offenders and sentence an increasing number of people to prison terms, particularly women. Unfortunately, British courts still imprison people for petty crimes, e.g. non-payment of TV licences and council tax. Justice is weighed heavily against women, who are often treated much more harshly than men for the same crimes. The rate of increase of women in prison has been strikingly sharp over the past decade. Their routine imprisonment for petty offences seems to be a fixed feature of the legal system. Another anomaly causing concern is the disproportionate number of black prisoners, which has led to accusations of racial bias in the courts. The UK sends more people to prison for more offences and sentences more people to life imprisonment than any other country in Western Europe.

Although the foregoing catalogue of crime may paint a depressing picture of the UK, it's generally a safe place to live. Crimes of violence are still relatively rare in much of the country, and you can walk safely in great swathes of it, day or night. In comparison with many other countries, the UK's crime rate doesn't stand out and the overall incidence of violent crime is low. If you take care of your property and take precautions against crime (including avoiding potential high crime areas), your chances of becoming a victim are small. The rate of crime varies vastly from area to area and anyone coming to live in the UK should avoid high crime areas if humanly possible.

Information

Police forces, central government, local authorities and security companies all publish information and provide advice on crime prevention. All police forces have a local crime prevention officer whose job is to provide free advice to individuals, homeowners and businesses. Most police forces publish comprehensive police *Crime Prevention Manuals*. The Central Office of Information and the Home Office also publish numerous brochures and booklets about crime prevention, including *Your Practical Guide to Crime Prevention*, available from police stations, libraries and council offices.

GEOGRAPHY

The title of this book may cause some confusion, particularly as there are occasional references to the United Kingdom, England, Scotland, Wales, Ireland

and Northern Ireland. The term Britain, as used in this book, comprises Great Britain (the island which includes England, Wales and Scotland) and Northern Ireland, the full name of which is the 'United Kingdom of Great Britain and Northern Ireland', usually shortened to just UK. The British Isles is the geographical term for the group of islands, which includes Great Britain, Ireland and many smaller islands surrounding Britain.

The UK covers an area of 242,432km^2 (93,600mi^2) and is around the same size as New Zealand or Uganda and half the size of France. It's some 1,000km (600mi) from the south coast to the northernmost point of Scotland and under 500km (around 300mi) across in the widest part. Nowhere in the UK is more than 120km (75mi) from the sea and the coastline, which is strikingly varied and one of the most beautiful in the world. The UK has a varied landscape: most of England is fairly flat and low-lying (particularly East Anglia), with the exception of the north and south-west, while much of Scotland and Wales is mountainous. If the most dire predictions of global warming become a reality, many regions of the UK will be flooded as the sea level rises. The highest mountains are Ben Nevis in Scotland at 1,343m (4,406ft) and Snowdon in Wales at 1,085m (3,560ft). The country can roughly be divided into a highland region in the north and west, and a lowland region in the south and east, approximately delimited by the mouths of the River Exe (Exeter) in the south-west and the River Tees (Teeside) in the north-east. The UK has around 1,931km^2 (1,200mi^2) of inland waters, the most famous and largest area being the Lake District in the north-west of England.

GOVERNMENT

The UK is a constitutional monarchy, under which the country is governed by ministers of the crown in the name of the sovereign (Queen Elizabeth II), who's head of the state and the government. Nowadays, the monarchy has no real power and its duties are restricted to ceremonial and advisory ones only, although there are certain acts of government that require the participation of the sovereign, such as the opening and dissolving of parliament and giving royal assent to bills. Parliament is the ultimate law-making authority in the UK (although the Channel Islands and the Isle of Man make their own laws on island affairs) and consists of two houses or chambers, the House of Commons and the House of Lords, which together make up the Houses of Parliament.

Parliament sits in the Palace of Westminster in London, which was built in the 19th century after the previous building was destroyed by fire, and whose clock, Big Ben (actually the name of the large bell), is London's most famous landmark. The roots of the UK's democratic traditions date from 1265 (when King Henry III was forced to acknowledge the first Parliament). Westminster, which is often referred to as the mother of parliaments, is the model for many democracies around the world.

The House of Commons is the assembly chamber for the 651 Members of Parliament (MPs) who are commoners (i.e. not Lords or titled people), elected by the people of the UK in a general election, that must be held every five years if parliament isn't dissolved earlier. Each MP represents an area called a constituency, of which there are 523 in England, 73 in Scotland, 38 in Wales and 17 in Northern Ireland. If an MP resigns, retires or dies during the term of a government, a by-election is held to choose a new MP. Any British subject or citizen of the Irish Republic over the age of 21 can stand for election as an MP, with the exception of disqualified people, i.e. undischarged bankrupts, those sentenced to more than one year's imprisonment, most clergy, members of the armed forces and holders of certain public offices. (Contrary to popular belief, insanity isn't a requirement for office and lunatics are disbarred from standing for Parliament). To deter 'jokers' or no-hopers from standing for election, each candidate must make a deposit of £500 with the returning officer, which is forfeited if he receives less than 5 per cent of the vote. There's a limit on the amount a candidate can spend on a general election campaign, depending on the number of registered voters in a constituency (in stark contrast to the US, where it's virtually unlimited).

All British and Commonwealth citizens and citizens of the Republic of Ireland over the age of 18 and resident in the UK can vote in parliamentary elections, provided they're registered voters. To be eligible to vote, your name must appear in a register of electors maintained and updated annually in autumn by councils. If you fail to register, you're liable to a maximum fine of £1000. Voting isn't compulsory and there's no penalty for not voting (but don't complain about the government if you don't vote). Between 70 and 80 per cent of people usually vote in general elections. British citizens who have been living abroad for less than 10 years also have the right to vote in parliamentary elections. While they're still eligible to vote in the UK, they can also vote there in local and European elections, or they can opt to do so in their country of residence, if it's in the EU.

Anyone who's a registered voter and who's away from his constituency during parliamentary, European or local government elections, can vote by post or appoint a proxy to vote on his behalf.

The government of the day is formed by the political party that wins the largest number of seats at a general election. If no party has a clear majority, i.e. 326 seats, then a coalition government may be formed between a number of parties. This is extremely rare as, unlike other countries in Western Europe, the UK doesn't have a system of proportional representation. The candidate in each constituency who polls the most votes is declared the winner ('first past the post'). All votes cast for other candidates are disregarded, which means that a party such as the Liberal Democrats (the third force in British politics) often receives millions of votes and ends up with just a few seats. Many people believe this system is outdated and undemocratic (particularly the Liberal Democrats), although it's difficult to see the major parties changing the system voluntarily (Labour went through the motions of investigating electoral reform on entering government, but then quietly forgot all about it). MPs hold weekly or fortnightly 'surgeries' (like doctors!) in their constituencies, when constituents can visit them and discuss their problems. Constituents can also write to their MP and telephone or visit him at the House of Commons.

The head of the government is the Prime Minister (PM), who's the leader of the party with the majority of seats (or the leader of the principal party in a coalition) and who chooses an inner cabinet of around 20 ministers. In addition to the cabinet, the government also appoints around 80 junior ministers, of which there may be two to five in each ministry. (The number is tending to increase as satisfying colleagues' ambitions is a useful political tool.) Every few years (or months if cabinet members resign suddenly), a game of musical ministries takes place, in which the Prime Minister's more loyal supporters get promoted and those who are lukewarm about his policies are consigned to the backbenches. The Leader of the Opposition, who's the head of the largest defeated party (and not part of a government coalition), appoints a shadow cabinet of shadow ministers, whose job is to respond to government ministers in Parliament and to act as the party's spokespeople. MPs who are members of the cabinet or shadow cabinet sit on the front benches (on opposite sides) in the House of Commons. All other MPs are known as backbenchers.

The House of Commons is presided over by the Speaker, who's the spokesman and president of the chamber and who controls proceedings (or attempts to). The Speaker is an MP of either party who's elected by the House at the start of each parliament or when the previous speaker retires or dies. He neither speaks in debates nor votes on a bill except when voting is equal (when he has the deciding vote). The Speaker has an apartment in the Palace of Westminster.

The highlight of the week in the House of Commons is question time, during which MPs can question Ministers (and which often becomes heated when the PM and the leader of the opposition trade insults). The proceedings of both houses are public (except for rare occasions involving national security) and both houses have a public gallery. Television was introduced into Parliament in 1989, although strict rules apply which are designed to hide the fact that the chambers are often sparsely attended. There are three main national parties in the UK: the Conservatives or Tories, Labour (or New Labour as it prefers to be called) and the Liberal Democrats. There are a few other smaller parties, most of which contest seats in particular regions or constituencies only. These include the Scottish Nationalist Party (SNP); the Ulster Unionist Party, the Democratic Unionist Party, the Social and Democratic Labour Party (SDLP) and Sinn Fein, all of Northern Ireland; Plaid Cymru (Welsh nationalists); the Green Party and the Communist Party of Great Britain (as distinct from just the Communist Party which is now defunct).

The UK was long plagued by its predominantly two-party system, with its extremes of left (Labour) and right (Conservatives) and very little in between. Now, however, the difference often seems more a battle for personal power than ideology. The Conservatives remain – more or less – the party of big business, from which they receive the vast majority of their finances (although this connection has been muted during the current predominance of New Labour, with which business has sought to maintain reasonable relations, and which anyway often seems quite right-wing). The Conservatives are loth to do anything to interfere with the profitable operation of business (which leads to accusations that they allow their paymasters to flout the law with regard to pollution, monopolies, price maintenance and tax loopholes). The Labour party was traditionally the party of the workers and still receives most of its funds from the trade unions, although this connection has been thrown in doubt, and it now appears more to represent the interests of public sector professionals, of which there are many. It seems an age since it believed in the public ownership of industry (nationalisation).

The House of Lords is referred to as the 'Other Place' in the House of Commons and is the geriatric ward of the constitution, where retired MPs and a declining number of blue-blooded landowners spend their days in retirement. The Lords consists of the Lords Spiritual (archbishops and bishops) and Temporal, which includes a fixed number of 90 hereditary peers and peeresses, all life peers and peeresses, and the Law Lords, with the precise total depending on the number of life peers the prime minister chooses to create. Until the beginning of the 20th century, the House of Lords had extensive powers and could veto any bill submitted to it by the House of Commons. It still retains powers to block government legislation temporarily, which sometimes can have the same result in practice. It remains the highest court of appeal in the UK, with the exception of criminal cases in Scotland, but proposals to replace it with a Supreme Court are under consideration. Members of the House of Lords are unpaid, although they receive travelling and other expenses when on parliamentary business within the UK.

The House of Lords is presided over by the Lord Chancellor, who's the ex-officio Speaker of the House, although there have been discussions about abolishing this ancient office. The House of Lords has long been considered an anachronism and has been partially reformed – until a few years ago all hereditary peers belonged to it – but currently nobody knows what to do about it. It could be replaced by an elected second house (similar to the US Senate), or a completely appointed house, but the likelihood is that it will continue in some form similar to its present one for the time being. New Labour plans to get rid of the remaining hereditary peers, but it's easy to imagine circumstances in which this doesn't happen.

Devolution

In 1999, the 129-member Scottish Parliament came into existence, and the Scottish Executive, which is formed by the majority party or a coalition based on a parliamentary majority, exercises power. The Scottish Parliament is responsible for local matters such as education, housing, health, and tourism and has taken decisions which differentiate Scotland from England in a number of areas. For example, student fees have been abolished and doctors in Scotland can pescribe drugs on the NHS that are unavailable to patients in England and Wales. Its mode of election is a complicated blend of the 'first past the post' and proportional representation systems. The Labour party, the Liberal Democrats and the Scottish Nationalist Party (SNP) are the main parties, with the Conservatives thin on the ground.

The Welsh Assembly has far more restricted powers than the Scottish Parliament. It has very limited tax-raising powers, for example, while the former is largely a talking shop. It decides on how the funds formerly at the disposal of the Welsh Office in London and allocated to it by central government should be spent. This is significant, but as its creation was supported by only a quarter of Welsh people – another quarter were opposed and half didn't vote – it has yet to convince them that it's worth taking seriously.

The Northern Ireland Assembly appears and disappears with alarming frequency, but in one form or another, its future is secure because it's a consequence of the Good Friday peace agreement, the fruits of which are appreciated by nearly everyone in the province (although some wouldn't admit it). Putting devolved government in question longer term would recreate instability. Its electoral and procedural arrangements are highly idiosyncratic, reflecting the unusual situation of Northern Ireland.

Local Government

The administration of local affairs in the UK is performed by local government or local authorities. In most areas of England and Wales, services are divided between two authorities, a district council and a county council. In large cities, services are usually provided by a single authority, e.g. a borough council in London and a metropolitan district or city council elsewhere. London is divided into 32 boroughs and the Corporation of the City of London. In Scotland, services are usually divided between district, regional or island councils, and in Northern Ireland between district councils, area boards and central government. England and Wales is divided into 53 counties which are subdivided into 369 districts. All districts and 47 of the (non-metropolitan) counties have locally-elected councils with separate functions. In Scotland, there are nine regions that are divided into 52 districts, each with its own area council.

County & Borough Councils

County and borough councils in England, Wales and Northern Ireland and regional councils in Scotland provide the main local government services that require planning and administration over wide areas, or that require substantial resources. These include the police, fire service, libraries and museums, traffic regulation, magistrates courts, the probation service, waste disposal, highways and road safety, trading standards and personal social services. Other essential services include area health authorities funded by central government.

Local Councils

District councils are responsible for local services which usually include local planning, industrial development, public housing, council tax collection, street cleaning and refuse collection, enforcing environmental health regulations and administering car parks and leisure facilities. There are also parish councils which, although they have no specific duties, may have certain responsibilities such as cemeteries and crematoria, recreation, local planning consultations, public conveniences, allotments, footpaths, village halls and any other function delegated by county or district councils.

County councils, London borough councils and around two-thirds of non-metropolitan district councils hold elections every four years. The remaining districts, including metropolitan districts, are elected in each of the three years in between county council elections. All local government councils are organised along party political lines, although some councillors are independent. All councils elect a chairman, who, in boroughs or cities, has the ceremonial title of mayor (or Lord Mayor in the City of London and other large cities). The turnout in local government elections is usually much lower than for parliamentary elections (around 30 per cent). Voting qualifications are broadly the same as for parliamentary elections, but additionally EU citizens can participate. Councillors are unpaid, although they can claim an allowance for attending council meetings and travel and subsistence allowances. Local authority finances come from a variety of sources that include around 25 per cent from council tax (see page 380), a further 25 per cent from the uniform business rate and the remainder from central government. Over 2 million people are employed by local authorities in the UK.

LEGAL SYSTEM

England and Wales, Scotland and Northern Ireland all have their own separate legal systems and law courts and, although there are a lot of similarities, there are also considerable differences. In Northern Ireland, procedure closely follows that of England and Wales, but Scottish law differs in many respects and is based on a different legal tradition from English law. Differences include the buying and selling of property, consumer rights, inheritance and the rights of young people. Even so, much modern legislation applies throughout the UK and there's a common distinction between criminal law (acts harmful to others or the community) and civil law (disputes between individuals) in all regions. Under the British legal system, you're innocent until proven guilty, although you may sometimes get the impression that not everybody is aware of this.

In the UK, less serious cases are dealt with by a magistrates court (a 'people's court', although there are professional stipendiary magistrates), which handles civil and criminal cases. A magistrates court normally consists of three lay magistrates, known as justices of the peace (JPs), who are advised on points of law and procedure by a legally-qualified clerk or assistant. Cases involving children under 17 are heard in juvenile courts. Minor civil claims such as small debts, are heard in a county court, of which there are around 300 in England and Wales. A person convicted by a magistrates court has the right of appeal to a crown court (criminal cases) against the sentence imposed (if he pleaded guilty) or the conviction if he pleaded not guilty, or to a high court in a civil case. Civil cases may be dealt with by a Queen's Bench, Family division or Chancery division court, depending on the subject matter.

Magistrates are usually unpaid local volunteers, chosen for their character and judgment, and they aren't usually legal professionals. Sentences in magistrates courts often vary considerably for the same offences and magistrates have considerable discretion in the fines they impose for certain offences, such as motoring offences. Moves are afoot to make sentencing more consistent and to match fines to a defendant's ability to pay (one London prostitute complained "How can I pay my fines, when every time I go to the West End to earn some money I get arrested?"). There's a chronic shortage of magistrates in some areas, particularly in blue-collar districts. A defendant in a magistrates court can sometimes opt for a crown court trial by jury.

More serious criminal offences, such as murder, manslaughter, rape and robbery with violence, are tried by a crown court before a judge and a jury of 12 people (15 in Scotland), or in a civil case, a high court. Every local or parliamentary elector between the age of 18 and 65 who has been resident in the UK for at least five years since the age of 13, can be called on to serve on a jury unless ineligible or disqualified (for a variety of reasons). If you're found guilty in a crown court or a high court, you have the right of further appeal against conviction or sentence to a court of appeal, criminal or civil division, depending on the case. All courts have a huge backlog of cases waiting to be heard.

In criminal and civil cases involving a point of general public importance, you may be given leave to appeal to the House of Lords (see page 489), the highest and final court of appeal in the UK. In cases involving or conflicting with EU regulations or the European Convention on Human Rights, you can appeal to the European court (Luxembourg) or the European court of human rights (Strasbourg), although they cannot enforce fines or impose their rulings on member states, and are often seen as something of a white elephant. Only one in four appeals in any court are successful, so that often the only winners are the lawyers.

Legal Representation

It isn't always necessary to have legal representation in court, particularly in a small claims court (see below), although in a serious case only a foolish person (or someone who's legally competent) would attempt to defend himself. A solicitor is a qualified lawyer who usually gives legal advice and defends cases in lower courts, such as magistrates and county courts although, with the introduction of the Court and Legal Services Bill in 1990, solicitor advocates can now practise in higher courts. A barrister (or advocate) is a solicitor who has been 'called to the bar', which, before 1990, was necessary in order to practise in higher courts. A Queen's Counsel (QC) is a barrister who has been appointed by the Lord Chancellor. He's the most experienced and expensive of all legal advisors and generally acts only for the very rich and the crown. Barristers (and QCs in particular) can earn around £1 million a year and professionally are above the law – it's impossible to sue a barrister who makes a mess of your case, as he's immune from negligence claims.

Cost

The high cost of legal representation often ensures that, unless you qualify for legal aid, you're unable to pursue justice, which leads to the accusation that 'real' justice is available only to the very rich and the very poor. Solicitors' fees have soared in recent years and leading solicitors charge clients hundred of pounds an hour, with top barristers charging £650+ an hour to prepare a case and £3,000 a day in court. Cases of overcharging and fraud are commonplace. The civil justice system is geared to enriching lawyers rather than serving justice and many observers believe that legal costs are a cancer eating at its heart. When forced to go to court, an increasing number of people (do-it-yourself litigants) handle their own cases, usually concerning bankruptcy, divorce and disputes involving custody of children. However, many have no idea how to present their cases adequately and are courting disaster.

As a general rule, you should never go to court unless you're forced to, as a dispute over a small sum can cost you many, many times more than anything you're likely to gain. Even a relatively straightforward case such as a divorce can cost an arm and a leg. If you decide to obtain advice from a solicitor, check in advance what it costs, as seeing a solicitor is often akin to signing a blank cheque. There are plans to deliver cheap and fast justice through a fast-track courts system in order to remedy the huge problems of cost, delay, complexity and inequality in the civil justice system. However, such plans have a tendency to remain hot air, because the present system serves the interests of lawyers nicely and many politicians are also lawyers.

Free Legal Advice

There are many organisations that provide free legal advice and general information on a vast range of subjects. Before taking the, often expensive, step of obtaining legal advice from a solicitor, you should contact one of the organisations listed below, all of which provide free or low-cost advice to everyone, irrespective of nationality or how long you've been in the UK. British people aren't usually in the habit of suing each other at the drop of a hat and whenever possible it's better to seek other avenues of redress rather than pursue someone through the courts. Many companies have internal complaints procedures and most professions and trades have independent arbitration schemes and ombudsmen (independent arbitrators). Only when these fail, should you consider taking legal action, provided, of course, that you have a good case and the necessary financial resources. Often the threat of legal action or issuing a summons is sufficient to force someone to concede.

Wherever you obtain legal advice, whether from a Citizens' Advice Bureau (CAB), a law centre or a solicitor, if it's a civil matter involving a lot of money or a criminal matter where your liberty is at stake, you should obtain a second opinion. If you're given, and follow, bad advice (particularly free advice) there may be no redress later. If you're in doubt about your rights or obligations, check with a solicitor or lawyer before signing anything. Contracts are usually drawn up by solicitors and some may deliberately contain a number of traps in the small print designed specifically to rob you (legally of course) of your rights. The National Consumer Council would like to outlaw 'gobbledegook' in contracts. If in doubt, ask a CAB or law centre for help in interpreting contracts and legal documents.

Legal advice is also available by telephone from the CompactLawline (☎ 01707-640 944), which is approved and endorsed by the Law Society. It provides information on a wide range of legal, domestic and consumer matters. Although no substitute for personal advice from a solicitor, it's a lot cheaper. The current fixed fee for a first enquiry is £45, including VAT. After a short message pointing out that you may qualify for public funding, you're connected to a practising solicitor. The ensuing conversation is, of course, confidential. The same company also operates a website (🖳 www.compactlaw.co.uk) dispensing free information on a wide range of legal topics. There are also many useful books, including *420 Legal Problems Solved* (Which? Books).

Citizens Advice Bureau

The Citizens Advice Bureau (CAB) was founded in 1939 to provide an emergency service during the second world war. It's an independent organisation which provides free confidential information and advice on almost any kind of problem or subject. These include Social Security; consumer and debt problems; housing; family and personal difficulties; employment; justice; local information; health; immigration and nationality; and taxes. There are over 1,200 CAB offices in England, Wales and Northern Ireland. If you would like to know more about the CAB, contact the National Association of Citizens Advice Bureaux, Myddelton House, 115-123 Pentonville Road, London N1 9LZ (☎ 020-7833 7154, 🖳 www.nacab.org.uk). In Scotland, there's a separate Citizens Advice Scotland service with 70 offices, which can be contacted at Spectrum House, 2 Powderhall Road, Edinburgh EH7 4GB (☎ 0131-550 1000, 🖳 www.cas.org.uk).

Small Claims Court

If you have a claim of up to £5,000 (with a few exceptions), you can use the simplified small claims procedure. Under this system, you take out the summons yourself and do your own prosecuting. No costs are awarded to either side, as no lawyers are required, similar to private arbitration. If you do use a lawyer in a small claims court, it can cost you thousands of pounds in legal fees. The fee for taking out a county court summons varies depending on the size of your claim from £30 to £120, but if you win, your fees are paid by the other party. A free booklet (form EX50) is available from your local county court explaining how to sue and defend actions without a solicitor.

Ombudsmen

These are industry watchdogs appointed by the government, and are completely independent arbitrators who mediate in disputes between companies (or government departments) and individuals. Usually complaints can be referred to an ombudsman only after all other complaints procedures have been exhausted. For further information ask at your local CAB or law centre.

MARRIAGE & DIVORCE

In 1995, the law regarding where a marriage can take place was changed and consequently, in addition to a church or registry office (civil ceremony), you can get married anywhere that's approved by the local authorities, including boats, stately homes, castles, hotels, restaurants, zoos and sports venues. The bride and groom must be at least 18 years old or 16 if they have parental consent (which also applies to foreigners who get married in the UK).

Foreigners living in the UK who are married, divorced or widowed should have a valid marriage licence, divorce papers or death certificate, which is usually necessary to confirm their marital status with the authorities, e.g. to receive certain legal or social benefits. A blood test isn't required to get married. Marriage according to the rites of the Church of England can be by banns, by licence (common or special) or under a superintendent registrar's certificate. If you get married in a church or place of worship, you must give notice to the local registry office, but you aren't required to undergo a civil wedding service.

The average church wedding costs around £10,000. The alternative is to be married in a registry office or another venue licensed to stage civil weddings under a superintendent registrar's certificate, which is much simpler and cheaper than a church wedding (though without the religious significance). To be married in a registry office, the bride or groom must live within its official area. You can be married under a certificate (without licence) or a licence.

A certificate is for those who don't want to have a church ceremony, but perhaps wish to invite a lot of guests and have a wedding reception. Each partner must show his or her birth certificate and pay the fee to the local registry office (if you've been married before, you must produce a decree absolute or a death certificate) at least 21 days, but not more than three months before the date on which you wish to be married (book early if you want to be married on a Saturday).

A licence is for those who wish to be married quickly and who want the minimum amount of fuss and ceremony. To be married under a licence, you and your partner must take your documents (and the fee) to the registry office at least one day before the day on which you wish to be married. Both partners must have been living in the registry office area for at least 15 days. On the wedding day, you must have two witnesses (anyone will do). A ring isn't required for a registry wedding, although most couples use one. The ceremony lasts around ten minutes after which you both sign the register (when it's too late to change your mind). 'Marriages of convenience', where a foreigner marries a British subject in order to remain in the UK, are illegal and subject to intense scrutiny by the Home Office.

To be divorced, a couple must have been married for at least one year. Under British law, it's unnecessary to prove that one marriage partner has committed an act which gives grounds for divorce (thus depriving private detectives of much lucrative work), but a marriage must have broken down beyond repair. To prove a marriage has 'irretrievably broken down' (in legal terminology) and obtain a divorce, a couple must fulfil certain legal requirements such as living apart for two years when both partners want a divorce (or five years when only one partner wants a divorce). There are many other grounds for divorce such as desertion, the behaviour of one partner in such a way that the couple cannot live together, or adultery.

If possible, it's best to deal with a divorce yourself, as involving solicitors is very expensive and messy. However, if you **must** involve a lawyer, be sure to engage a good divorce lawyer, particularly if the divorce will be contested and there's a lot of property and the legal custody of children at stake. Shared or joint custody of children isn't common in the UK, although visiting rights are normally arranged.

A couple can also obtain an 'undefended divorce' (a free booklet is available from county courts) and dispense with lawyers, for example when there are no children and neither partner is claiming maintenance.

When a divorce is granted, the court issues a decree nisi and an application for a decree absolute (which makes the divorce final) can be made six weeks later and is usually a formality. Both partners receive a divorce certificate from the county court or divorce registry that proves the divorce and which is necessary if you wish to remarry. The UK is top of the European divorce league and almost half of all marriages end in divorce. The Child Support Agency forces absent and frequently unwilling parents to pay child maintenance, often by making deductions directly from salary or Social Security payments. There are many organisations that provide marriage counselling (e.g. Relate) and advice for couples contemplating divorce. Many books are published about divorce, including *The Which? Guide to Divorce* by Helen Garlick (Which? Books).

MILITARY SERVICE

There's no conscription (draft) in the UK, where all members of the armed forces are volunteers. Engagements for non-commissioned ranks are from 3 to 22 years and, subject to a minimum period of from three to nine years, servicemen may quit the service at any time provided they give 12 or 18 months' notice. Discharge is also permitted for compassionate reasons, grounds of conscience (conscientious objection) or purchase. Reservists are entitled to register as conscientious objectors if called up for military service. Short, medium and long-term commissions (as officers) are based on educational and personal qualifications, and all services have a range of educational sponsorship schemes.

Conscription was abolished during the '60s and there's little likelihood of it being reintroduced short of a major war. The UK is unusual in Europe in having no national service, the belief being that professional armed services are better equipped to cope in times of crisis. In addition to its full-time military services, the UK has a regular reserve force totalling over 200,000 and volunteer reserve and auxiliary forces of around 100,000 (which train at weekends and for a few weeks each year). The UK is one of the main contributors to NATO and spends almost £30 billion on defence and a higher proportion of its GDP than all NATO countries except the US. The UK has reduced its armed forces in the last few years as part of the so-called 'peace dividend' resulting from the thaw in east-west relations. However, following the Iraq war and peacekeeping duties elsewhere in the world, along with continued commitment in Northern Ireland, they're currently being overstretched.

THE MONARCHY

The British royal family is the longest reigning monarchy in the world and certainly the most famous. Its continuity, apart from the period from 1649 to 1660, remains unbroken for a thousand years. The head of the royal family is the monarch or sovereign, Her Majesty (HM) Queen Elizabeth II, who's married to His Royal Highness (HRH) the Duke of Edinburgh, Prince Philip (who's the son of Princess Andrew of Greece). The monarch is head of state and head of the British Commonwealth, although these are ceremonial titles involving no real power. The UK is governed by HM Government in the name of the Queen.

The Queen and Prince Philip have four children. Prince Charles (the Prince of Wales), who's the heir to the throne (and who married Camilla, now the Duchess of Cornwall, after having been divorced from the late Diana, Princess of Wales); Princess Anne (the Princess Royal); Prince Andrew (the Duke of York, divorced from Sarah Ferguson, the Duchess of York); and Prince Edward (who married Sophie Rhys-Jones in 1999). The most popular member of the Royal Family by far was the late Queen Elizabeth the Queen Mother, who died aged 101 in 2002. The Queen's sister, Princess Margaret (who was married to the Earl of Snowdon – formerly Anthony Armstrong-Jones), died in the same year. The Royal Family includes other major and minor royals, many of whom are descended from King George V's other children, Henry (the 1st Duke of Gloucester), George (the 1st Duke of Kent) and Mary.

Many members of the royal family work tirelessly for charities, in particular the Princess Royal, who travels the world in her work as patron of the Save the Children Fund. The Prince of Wales has earned a reputation as the defender of the UK's architectural heritage and a champion of traditional building design, with a TV programme and a book to his credit (although what many architects think about his pronouncements are unprintable). He has also initiated a number of projects to help the UK's youth (e.g. the Prince's Youth Business Trust) and regenerate the rundown inner cities.

The most important functions of the Queen are ceremonial and include the state opening of Parliament; giving Royal Assent to bills; the reception of diplomats; entertaining foreign dignitaries; conferring peerages, knighthoods and other honours; the appointment of important office-holders; chairing meetings of the Privy Council; and sorting out family squabbles. She also attends numerous artistic, industrial, scientific and charitable events of national and local interest. The Queen and other members of the royal family are patrons or honorary heads of many leading charities and organisations and the royal faimly undertake over 3,000 official duties each year. The sovereign's official birthday is celebrated in June with the Trooping of the Colour ceremony on Horse Guards Parade. Each year the Queen and other members of the royal family visit many areas of the UK and undertake state visits and royal tours of foreign and Commonwealth countries.

Around 85 per cent of the cost of the royal family's official duties is met by public departments, including the upkeep of royal palaces, the Queen's flight and the royal train. The Queen's public expenditure on staff and the expenses incurred in carrying out her official duties is financed from the Civil List, which is approved by Parliament. Annual allowances are made in the Civil List to other members of the royal family, with the exception of the Prince of Wales, who as the Duke of Cornwall receives the net revenue of the estate of the Duchy of Cornwall. The Queen is estimated to be the richest person in the UK, although a lot of the property attributed to her actually belongs to the state.

The antics of the British royal family are the longest-running soap opera in the world and hundreds of column inches of newsprint are devoted to their affairs, in the UK by the tabloids (or popular press, who delight in printing sensational stories about royalty and anyone famous) and abroad (e.g. France, Germany and Italy). Nonetheless, as the overwhelming public enthusiasm for the Queen's Golden Jubilee celebrations showed recently, despite the vicissitudes of life which she has endured, she's still a focus for abiding affection and real respect.

PETS

The UK is generally regarded abroad as a country of animal lovers and has over 14 million pet owners (including some 7 million dog owners). This is attested to by the number of bequests received by the Royal Society for the Prevention of Cruelty to Animals (RSPCA), which far exceeds the amount left to the National Society for the Prevention of Cruelty to Children (NSPCC). The British are almost uniquely sentimental about animals, even those reared for food. Protests about various forms of commercial cruelty to animals make headline news at regular intervals. Britons are also prominent in international animal protection organisations that attempt to ban cruel sports and practices in which animals are mistreated (such as bullfighting).

Quarantine

The UK has the toughest quarantine regulations in the world in order to guard against the importation of rabies and other animal diseases, and has been virtually free of rabies for over 60 years. Apart from those participating in the Pet Travel Scheme (PETS, see below), all mammals, other than specific breeds of horses and livestock, must normally spend a period of six months in quarantine in an approved kennel to ensure they're free of rabies and Newcastle disease. Rabies is a serious hazard throughout the world, including many parts of Europe. You can catch this disease if you're bitten, scratched or even licked by an infected dog, cat, fox, monkey, bat or other animal. Quarantine regulations also apply to guide dogs for the blind and hearing dogs.

If you're coming to the UK for a short period only, it may not be worth the trouble and expense of bringing your pet and you may prefer to leave it with friends or relatives during your stay. Before deciding to import an animal, check the website of the Department for Environment, Food and Rural Affairs (see below) or contact the them at Nobel House, 17 Smith Square, London SW1P 3JR (☎ 020-7238 6951 or ☎ 08459-335 577, 💻 www.defra.gov.uk) for the latest regulations, application forms, and a list of approved quarantine kennels and catteries. (The ministry also publishes a number of free brochures about rabies).

Applications for the importation of dogs, cats and other mammals, should be made at least eight weeks before the proposed date of importation. To obtain a licence to import your pet, you must have a confirmed booking at an approved kennel, have enlisted the services of an authorised carrying agent (who transport your pet from the port to the quarantine kennels), and your pet must arrive at an approved port or airport. Animals must be transported in approved containers, available from air transport companies and pet shops, and must be shipped within six months of the date specified by the licence.

The cost of quarantine is from £250 to £320 a month for a dog, depending on its size (and what it eats) and around £200 a month for a cat. Prices of kennels and catteries outside the London area can be cheaper. You must also pay for any vaccinations and veterinary costs incurred during your pet's quarantine period. You're permitted, in fact encouraged, to visit your pet in quarantine, but won't be able to take it out for exercise. There are different regulations for some creatures. Birds, for example, serve a shorter quarantine period than other animals, until it's established that there's no danger of psittacosis. Pet rabbits must be inoculated against rabies and cannot be imported from the US. There's no quarantine for cold-blooded animals such as fish and reptiles. Around 5,000 dogs and 3,000 cats are quarantined each year.

The Pet Travel Scheme

This was introduced recently and enables you to bring your dog or cat into the UK, or re-enter the country with it, and avoid quarantining, **but only under stringently controlled conditions.** Animals must be microchipped; have a 'passport' listing their vaccinations and other necessary veterinary treatments; an officially approved blood test no less than six months previously; have an official PETS certificate from a government-authorised vet; come from certain countries only and only on certain routes from those countries, and on certain specified flights, ferries or railways. Their owner must also sign a declaration that the pet has not been outside of any of the countries participating in the scheme (most of which are listed here) during the past six months.

The specified countries include Australia, Austria, Bahrain, Belgium, Canada, Cyprus, Czech Republic, Denmark, Estonia, Finland, France, Germany, Greece, Holland, Hungary, Iceland, Ireland, Italy, Jamaica, Japan, Latvia, Luxembourg, Malta, New Zealand, Norway, Poland, Portugal, Singapore, Slovakia, Slovenia, Spain,

Sweden, Switzerland, the mainland US, the Vatican and a variety of dependent territories of European powers.

The list is growing and it's **essential** in any event to check the DEFRA website (💻 www.defra.gov.uk/animals/quarantine/index.htm) to ensure that your country is still covered by the scheme, and to elicit all the other fine detail connected with it. There are additional demands made on people travelling from certain countries, which vary according to the country in question. Other regulations of a general nature pertaining to animal welfare while travelling also apply and are given in detail on the website.

For some domestic animals, e.g. horses, of which only certain breeds are kept in quarantine, an import licence and a veterinary examination is required. Dangerous animals (e.g. poisonous snakes, big cats and crocodiles) require a special import licence. You require a licence from your local council to keep a poisonous snake or other dangerous wild animal, which must be properly caged with an adequate exercise area, and must pose no risk to public health and safety. **It's a criminal offence to attempt to smuggle an animal into the UK and it's almost always discovered.** Illegally imported animals are exported immediately or destroyed and the owners are always prosecuted.

Owners face (and invariably receive) a heavy fine of up to £1,000 or an unlimited fine and up to a year's imprisonment for deliberate offences. There's no VAT or duty on animals brought into the UK as part of your 'personal belongings' although, if you import an animal after your arrival, VAT and duty may need to be paid on its value.

If you don't have a friend or relative who will look after your dog or cat while you're on holiday, you must board it in a kennel or cattery. If you leave a pet with a friend, always provide full instructions regarding diet, exercise and vets. Ask your friends, neighbours or colleagues if they can recommend somewhere (if they cannot help you, ask your vet). It's important not to take pot luck, as standards vary from excellent to poor. If a kennel or cattery isn't highly recommended, check it personally before boarding your pet and ask what services are charged as extras, such as grooming, medicine and special diets. Any veterinary fees incurred while boarding are charged to the owner. If you plan to leave your pet at a kennel or cattery, book well in advance, particularly for school holiday periods. Dogs left at kennels may need to be vaccinated against certain diseases, although the requirements vary depending on the kennel.

You can take your dog or cat to a veterinary surgeon (vet) for a course of vaccinations, boosters, spaying, and neutering for kittens, the cost of which varies greatly depending on the region and the particular vet. It isn't mandatory to have your dog (or any pet) vaccinated against any disease in the UK, although most dog owners have dogs vaccinated against a number of them, including distemper, hepatitis, and leptospirosis. After the initial primary vaccinations (fee around £20 to £30), annual boosters are necessary. You receive a 'record of primary and booster vaccination' from your vet.

Shop around, compare fees and always agree one in advance. These vary greatly in different parts of the country, London being the most expensive. A list of local vets can be obtained from the Royal College of Veterinary Surgeons, Belgravia

House, 62-64 Horeseferry Road, London SW1P 2AF (☎ 020-7222 2001) or the British Veterinary Association (BVA), 7 Mansfield Street, London W1G 9NQ (☎ 020-7636 6541), which publishes a series of booklets on pet care. If you cannot afford a vet's fees, the People's Dispensary for Sick Animals, Whitechapel Way, Priorslee, Telford, Shropshire TF2 9PQ (☎ 01952-290 999) may provide free treatment. They have a network of centres throughout the country and you can also call their information line free on ☎ 0800-917 2509.

The RSPCA, Wilberforce Way, Southwater, Horsham, West Sussex RH12 9RS (☎ 0870-333 5999) is the main organisation for animal protection and welfare and operates a number of animal clinics and welfare centres. Many Britons are also concerned about the survival of wild animals and there's even a British Hedgehog Preservation Society (BHPS), although they have yet to teach the creatures how to cross roads safely. The work of the RSPCA is complemented by the National Canine Defence League (NCDL), a national charity devoted to the welfare of dogs, which takes in lost, abandoned and abused dogs, and turns them into healthy, well-adjusted pets. No healthy dog is ever destroyed by the NCDL (Dogs Trust, 17 Wakely Street, London EC1V 7RQ, ☎ 020-7837 0006). There are over 40 animal shelters in the UK, including those run by the Cats Protection League, The Dogs Home (Battersea), the NCDL, the RSPCA and the Wood Green Animal Shelters.

After a series of vicious attacks on children, the British government introduced a controversial ban on the ownership of certain breeds of dog bred for fighting. These include pit bull terriers, Japanese tosas, dogo argentinos and fila brazilieros, all of which can no longer be imported or bred in the UK (males must be neutered), and must be registered and muzzled in public. If the law is broken, a dog can be destroyed and if it attacks anyone you're liable to a fine (and your dog may also be destroyed). You can be fined up to £400 (in addition to compensation) if your dog kills or injures livestock and a farmer can legally shoot a dog that molests farm animals.

There isn't a dog registration or licence scheme in England, Wales or Scotland. In Northern Ireland, a dog licence must be obtained from your local district council office for a dog over six months old.

POLICE

The UK doesn't have a national police force, but 52 regional police forces (43 in England and Wales, 8 in Scotland and 1 in Northern Ireland), each responsible for a county (or a region in Scotland) or a metropolitan area such as London. There are no special uniformed traffic or tourist police, all routine duties being performed by standard policemen and policewomen.

Police forces in England, Scotland and Wales are among the few in the world that don't carry firearms (their only weapon is a truncheon), although in recent years an increasing number of policemen have been armed for special services such as the prevention of terrorism and when dealing with armed suspects. This is a controversial issue, as a number of innocent people have been shot dead by police marksmen over the past decade. Some police forces have also been issued with telescopic truncheons that can cause severe injuries and pepper sprays that in extreme cases can cause blindness. After the deaths of a number of police officers on duty in recent years, there has been an intense debate among the police concerning the carrying of arms. However, the great majority of police officers are against routinely carrying them and many would leave the force rather than do so. In Northern Ireland, the police (Royal Ulster Constabulary) have always been armed and the emergency situation in combating the Irish Republican Army (IRA) in the last few decades has scuttled any plans to alter this.

The uniform worn by police forces is generally the same throughout the UK and male bobbies (police officers) on the beat in England and Wales wear the famous British police helmet. Other police officers wear a flat cap with a chequered black and white band. Although Scotland has a different legal system, your rights regarding the police are roughly the same as in the rest of the UK. In addition to full-time police officers, each force has a part-time attachment of unpaid volunteer special constables. Traffic wardens are responsible for traffic and parking and come under the control of the local police force. There's also an auxiliary force of security wardens in some urban areas with fewer powers than police officers.

British policemen used to be the most respected in the world, not least by the British people. However, in recent years they've had a bad press in England and Wales and their reputation has been badly tarnished. According to a number of surveys, many people have lost faith in the integrity and efficiency of their police force. Many are unhappy about police responses when they ring 999 or their local police station, and over half the victims of crime are dissatisfied with the police response. There has been an increase in complaints against the police, many concerning prejudice, harassment, and even brutal and violent treatment. Even more worrying, a public inquiry into the handling of the murder investigation of a black teenager (Stephen Lawrence) found that racism was rife in the Metropolitan Police force. Too few members of Britains' black and Asian communities are joining the police force, which isn't suprising considering they they're often subject to racial abuse and prejudice from their white colleagues (and are also more likely to be arrested than whites which tends to alienate ethnic communities).

The police in England and Wales have consistently refused to allow independent investigations of complaints, which means that successful complaints against the police are extremely rare. Most people don't even bother to complain, as they consider it a waste of time. The Police Complaints' Authority (PCA) claims to be independent, yet investigations into complaints against police are carried out by police officers. If you're seeking compensation against the police in England or Wales, you must usually seek redress in a county court, as the Independent Police Complaints Commission (IPCC) cannot ensure that you receive compensation. The level of compensation paid by the police to the victims of illegal arrest and police brutality is increasing, often as a result of civil actions for damages. To make a complaint against a police officer, you can write to the Chief Constable of the force involved, go to any police station or write directly to the IPCC, 90 High Holborn, London WC1V 6BH (☎ 0845-300 2002). In Scotland, complaints against the police involving criminal conduct are investigated by independent public prosecutors, and in Northern Ireland complaints involving death or serious injury are supervised by the Independent Commission for Police Complaints.

A spate of well-publicised cases in the last decade or so have included framed defendants, planting or withholding of evidence, confessions extracted under duress, corruption, incompetence, police assaults, racism and discrimination, all of which have reduced public confidence. As a result the police are finding it harder to secure convictions against guilty criminals when the prosecution case relies mainly on uncorroborated police evidence or confessions, and many cases are thrown out by juries. In England and Wales, it's possible to convict someone solely on the strength of their own confession (but not in Scotland), such as happened in a number of cases involving 'IRA terrorists'. A number of infamous cases in which alleged IRA terrorists were jailed for planting bombs were overturned on appeal (after many appeals) when their convictions were judged to be unsafe.

If the foregoing catalogue of complaints has given the impression of an incompetent, prejudiced and dishonest police force, it would be quite wrong. The UK still has one of the best police forces in the world and the vast majority of people rate the police performance as good or very good. What is evident is that the actions of a small minority of officers are increasingly bringing the whole force into disrepute. Unlike some countries, the British public expects its police to be above reproach and, although it may seem old-fashioned in the 21st century, are unwilling to accept anything less than absolute honesty, impartiality and efficiency from their police officers.

POPULATION

The population of the UK was 60,209,500 according to the 2006 census, and it's estimated that it will reach 61,619,000 by 2010, (compared with 38.2 million in 1901); the 21st largest in the world, inhabiting an area of 242,432km². England is the most populous part of the UK, with over 49 million inhabitants and a density of 380 people per km², while Scotland with a total of just over 5 million people, has a density of 65 people per km². Greater London has a density of 4,560 people per km². Northern Ireland has a population approaching 1.7 million souls with a density of 124 people per km² and Wales 2.9 million with a population density of 140 per km². Overall the population density of the UK is 240 people per km², which is roughly the same as Germany and 2.5 times that of France.

The central belt, which stretches across England from London to North Yorkshire, contains around half of the UK's population. Outside this area there are a few high-density areas which include Bristol, the south coast, and Tyne and Tees in England; south-east Wales; and Clydeside in Scotland. Some 90 per cent of the UK's population live in urban areas, half of them inhabiting cities of over 500,000. In the last decade, there has been a movement of people away from London and the south-east (which contains around 17.7 million people or around 30 per cent of the UK's population), to East Anglia, Wales, the north of England and Scotland, but immigration has balanced this out.

RELIGION

The UK has a tradition of religious tolerance and every resident has total freedom of religion without hindrance by the state or community. The British, with a few notable exceptions, aren't particularly pious (church attendance has been declining for years), which perhaps explains their traditional tolerance towards the faiths of others. However, discrimination does raise its ugly head occasionally and Muslims and more rarely Jews have been the targets of bigots in recent years. (England was notably anti-semitic in the 12th century, but helped to atone for events then by giving refuge to numerous Jews escaping persecution in the late 19th and 20th centuries). The UK has few of the fire-eating bible-thumping Evangelists to be found in North America and religious programmes on television are mainly confined to a few televised church services on Sunday, none of which make pleas for pots of money to pay for your salvation (or the preacher's high life).

The vast majority of the world's religious and philosophical movements have religious centres or meeting places in London and other major cities. Over 50 per cent of the British population theoretically belongs to the Church of England (or its counterparts), of which the Queen is the head and the religious leader is the Archbishop of Canterbury, who's the 'Primate of all England' (the Archbishop of York is the 'Primate of England'). The Church in England was founded by St Augustine in AD 597 and, following the 16th century Reformation, emerged as the established Church of England. Around 10 per cent, or some 5 million, of the population of the UK is Roman Catholic.

Other Christian groups or 'free churches' include various Presbyterian denominations, Congregational churches, Evangelicals, Methodists, Baptists, Pentecostals, United Reformed Church adherents and the Salvation Army, all of which admit men and women to the ministry. The Church of Scotland is Presbyterian and more puritanical than the Church of England. Scotland also has a substantial number of Roman Catholics. The Methodists have a strong following in Wales. In Northern Ireland, where Protestants have long outnumbered Roman Catholics, the latter are fast catching up. Census figures show that in 1951 there were twice as many Protestants as Catholics, but in 2001, the Protestant community was little over 11 per cent more numerous. The UK also has around 1.5 million Muslims, 300,000 Sikhs and 470,000 Hindus, most originating from the Indian subcontinent, and around 252,000 Jews, the second largest number of any European country. Other religions represented in the UK include the Baha'i Faith, Buddhism, Christian Science, Jehovah's Witnesses, Mormonism, the Quakers, Seventh-day Adventists, Sufis, Theosophists and Unitarians, to name but a few.

British churches include some of the oldest and most magnificent buildings in the world, particularly the great cathedrals, many dating from the 11th or 12th centuries. You don't need to be religious to enjoy the splendid architecture and grandeur of these buildings, although many are in a state of disrepair. The church receives no public funds and relies on public contributions for the upkeep and restoration of its buildings (so please give generously when visiting them). Most cathedrals have gift shops and many also have a tea room or restaurant, where profits go towards the cathedral's upkeep. Some cathedrals have introduced an entrance fee in recent years.

Cathedrals provide free organ and choral recitals throughout the year, and many take part in a series of concerts performed by the London Festival Orchestra. Contact your local library or tourist information centre for church information and service times or telephone for information (look under *Places of Worship* in the yellow pages). British state schools teach 'religious education' as part of the curriculum, when classes comprising more than simple bible study are segregated by denomination. Parents can, however, request permission for their children not to attend religious education classes.

SOCIAL CUSTOMS

All countries have their own particular social customs and the UK is no exception. As with most things in the UK, social customs, behaviour and rules are based on class, but unless you move in very distinguished circles you won't have to worry too much about them. However, good manners, politeness and consideration for others are considered important. The British are generally informal in their relationships and won't be too put out if you break the social rules, provided your behaviour isn't too outrageous. As a foreigner you may be forgiven if you accidentally insult your host, but you may not be invited again. The following are a few British social customs:

● When introduced to someone, you generally follow the cue of the person performing the introduction, i.e. if someone is introduced as Tom you can usually call him Tom, however, if someone is introduced as Lord Montague Downton-Cuddlethorpe, it might not be wise to address him as 'Cuddles' (unless he asks you to). Most people usually say 'Please call me Tom' or whatever, after a short time. After you've been introduced to someone, you usually say something like, 'How do you do?', 'Pleased to meet you' or 'My pleasure' and shake hands. When saying goodbye, it isn't customary to shake hands again, although some people do. In formal circles, gentlemen may be expected to bow and kiss the back of a lady's hand, while in informal gatherings strangers are more inclined simply to shake hands. Among friends, it's becoming more common for men to kiss ladies on the cheek (or once on either cheek). Men don't usually kiss or embrace each other in Britain (unless they're gay).

● If you're invited to dinner, it's customary to take a small present of flowers, a plant, chocolates or a bottle of wine. Flowers can be tricky as, to some people, carnations mean bad luck, chrysanthemums are for cemeteries and roses signify love. Maybe you should stick to plastic, silk or dried flowers, or a nice bunch of weeds. Wine can also be a problem, particularly if you're a miser and bring a bottle of cheap Italian plonk and your hosts are wine connoisseurs (they almost certainly won't invite you again). It's customary to serve wine brought by guests at the meal, although don't expect your hosts to serve your cheap Italian red stuff (particularly if they're serving fish). If you stay with someone as a guest for a few days, it's customary to give your host or hostess a small gift when you leave.

- When planning a party, it's polite to notify your neighbours (and perhaps invite them if they're particularly attractive).

- When going anywhere that may be remotely formal (or particularly informal), it's wise to ask in advance what you're expected to wear. Usually when dress is formal, such as evening dress or dinner jacket, it's stated in the invitation and you're unlikely to be admitted if you turn up in the wrong attire. If you're invited to a wedding, enquire about the dress, unless you want to stick out like a sore thumb. Black or dark dress is almost always worn at funerals.

- Guests are normally expected to be punctual with the exception of certain society parties when late arrival is *de rigueur* (unless you arrive after the celebrity guest) and at weddings (when the bride is often late). Dinner invitations are often phrased as 8pm for 8.30pm, which means arrive at 8pm for drinks and dinner will be served (usually promptly) at 8.30pm. Anyone who arrives very late for dinner (unless his house has burnt down) or, horror of horrors, doesn't turn up at all (when death is a good excuse), should expect to be excluded from future guest lists. If you're confused by a multitude of knives, forks and spoons, don't panic, but just copy what your neighbour is doing. If he's another ignorant foreigner, you will at least have some company in the social wilderness, to which you will both be consigned (the rule is to start at the outside and work in).

- It isn't necessary to supply someone who's working at your home with endless cups of tea and biscuits, although a cup of tea or coffee is appreciated and it may help speed their efforts and discourage them from leaving a mess (but whatever you do, **don't** serve them alcohol).

- If you move in formal circles, such as the diplomatic corps, British government or the higher echelons of the City of London, you had better bone up on etiquette before arriving in the UK. Obtain a copy of *Debrett's New Guide to Etiquette and Modern Manners* edited by John Morgan (Headline), in order to learn the customary way of doing things, and *Debrett's Correct Form*, which explains the correct forms of address, in speech and writing. If you address the Queen as 'Liz', pass the port or snuff to your right, or start a letter to the Archbishop of Canterbury as 'Dear Archie', you could create a nasty diplomatic incident or at the very least be banned from the croquet club.

TIME DIFFERENCE

The UK is on British Summer Time (BST) in summer and Greenwich Mean Time (GMT) in winter. The clocks go back at 1am on the last Sunday of October. The change to BST is made in the spring (usually at the end of March),when people put their clocks forward one hour. Time changes are announced in local newspapers and on radio and TV. The time is given on the telephone 'speaking clock' service number and on televisions with teletext services (most remote controls have a 'time' button). When making international telephone calls or travelling long distance by air, check the local time difference, which is shown in the International Dialling section of telephone directories. The time difference between the UK (when it's noon GMT, the time on which the BBC World Service operates) and some major international cities is shown below:

LONDON	CAPE TOWN	BOMBAY	TOKYO	LOS ANGELES	NEW YORK
Noon	2pm	5.30pm	9pm	4am	7am

In recent years, there has been talk about bringing British time into line with continental Europe, of which the majority of people (some 95 per cent) in England, Wales and Northern Ireland approve (in Scotland around 85 per cent take the opposite view, as they would have even darker mornings).

Naturally there are two sides to every argument, and although the continentals gain an hour of light at the end of the day, they also have an extra hour of darkness in the morning (the further north you live, the later the sun rises). However, research has shown that twice as many road accidents occur when people travel home in the dark, as when they set out in the dark in the morning. The Royal Society for the Prevention of Accidents estimates that, if we had BST permanently, road casualties would be dramatically reduced. It's hardly surprising that the UK isn't on Central European Time, as the UK is out of step with Europe on most other things.

TIPPING

Whether you tip or not is a personal choice and may depend on whether you think you've received exceptional service or good value for money. The situation with regard to tipping is anything but clear and can often be embarrassing. Tipping is customary in restaurants (when service isn't included) and when using taxis, when a tip of around 10 to 15 per cent is normal (the fare is usually rounded up to the nearest pound). The tipping of hotel staff (e.g. hotel chambermaids) and porters is more discretionary, although most people tip hotel and other porters 50p to £1 per suitcase, or around the same to a doorman who gets you a taxi (Visit Britain recommends a tip of 10 to 15 per cent for hotel staff when service isn't included in the price). Tipping in hotels depends whether you're staying at Claridges or some back street hovel. Tipping hairdressers (£1 or £2 or 10 per cent of the bill, depending on the service), cloakroom attendants and garage staff (who clean your car's windscreen, or check its oil or tyre pressures) is fairly common.

Most Britons are anti-tipping (but usually too timid not to leave a tip) and would like to see it abolished and replaced with a universal service charge. Many restaurant owners exploit the situation and intentionally pay low wages on the expectation that employees will supplement their wages with tips. If you don't tip a waiter he may not starve (unless the restaurant's food is particularly bad), but he may struggle to survive on his meagre salary. Many bills have 'service not included' printed on them, which is an open invitation for you to leave a tip. Even when service is included in the bill, this doesn't mean that the percentage added for service goes to the staff, although 'service included' deters most people from leaving a tip.

Don't be shy about asking whether service is included (which should be shown on the menu). Restaurant tips can be included in cheque or credit card payments or given as cash. The total on credit card counterfoils is often left blank, even when service was included in the price, to encourage you to leave a tip; don't forget to fill in the total before signing it. (If you don't leave a tip and the waiter tips the soup in your lap on your return, you will know why). It isn't customary to tip a barman in a pub, although you can offer to buy him a drink if you've been propping up the bar for a few hours. It is, however, customary to tip in bars and hotels when drinks are served at a table.

TOILETS

Although public toilets are usually free and are better than many found on the continent, the general standard is pretty awful. The most sanitary (even luxurious) toilets are found in hotels, restaurants and department stores, and are for customers only. Toilets in public offices, museums and galleries are also usually clean; railway stations, bus stations, airports, multi-storey car parks and petrol stations generally have reasonably clean toilets; while pub toilets vary from bad to excellent. Toilets provided by local councils are located in towns, parks, car parks and on beaches, and are generally among the worst anywhere (the financial squeeze on local authorities in recent years has also meant the closure of many public toilets).

There's a charge of 20p to use toilets at London's mainline rail stations and in some department stores. Entrance is through a turnstile or via a coin machine on the door. A change machine isn't usually provided and naturally the attendant will be absent when you're desperate and lack a 20p coin. Some public toilets require payment of 10p or more.

People in the UK don't usually use the American euphemisms powder room, wash room or bathroom when referring to a toilet, which is also known colloquially as the loo (as well as by numerous other less polite names). WCs are fitted with a variety of flushing methods, including chains to pull, buttons to push (located on the WC or on the wall), knobs to pull and foot buttons to tread on. Some even flush automatically. Men's urinals may also have a knob to be pushed, pulled or trodden on (which many people neglect to do), although most are automatic.

Toilets are fitted with a variety of hand-washing facilities (or none at all) which include wash basins with knobs you hold down to obtain water, which may be cold. There may be a bar of soap, although soap is usually provided in liquid or powder form from a dispenser. Hand-drying facilities include disposable paper towels, roll linen towels and hot air dryers, which may operate manually via a button or automatically (and which always stop just before your hands are dry). Often public toilets provide no soap or hand-drying facilities and may even have no running water or toilet paper. An increasing number of department stores, large supermarkets, large chemists, Mothercare, chemists (such as Boots), restaurants, pubs and public toilets for motorists provide nappy-changing facilities or facilities for nursing mothers (breastfeeding isn't usually performed in public). Many shopping centres have special toilets for the disabled, as do airports and major railway stations. However, most public toilets for motorists aren't accessible to disabled drivers.

19.

THE BRITISH

Who are the British? What are they like? Let's take a candid and totally prejudiced look at the British people, **tongue firmly in cheek**, and hope they forgive my flippancy or that they don't read this bit (which is why it's hidden away at the back of the book).

The typical Briton is introspective, patriotic, insular, xenophobic, brave, small-minded, polite, insecure, arrogant, a compulsive gambler, humorous, reserved, conservative, reticent, hypocritical, a racist, boring, a royalist, condescending, depressed, a keen gardener, semi-literate, hard-working, unambitious, ironic, passionless, cosmopolitan, a whinger, hard-headed, liberal, a traditionalist, a couch potato, obsequious, a masochist, complacent, homely, pragmatic, cynical, decent, melancholic, unhealthy, a poor cook, pompous, eccentric, inebriated, proud, self-deprecating, tolerant, inhibited, a shopaholic, conceited, courageous, idiosyncratic, mean (a bad tipper), courteous, jingoistic, stuffy, overweight, well-mannered, pessimistic, disciplined, a habitual queuer, stoic, modest, gloomy, shy, serious, apathetic, honest, wimpish, fair, snobbish, friendly, quaint, decadent, civilised, dogmatic, scruffy, prejudiced, class conscious and a soccer hooligan.

If the above list contains a few contradictions, it's because there's no such thing as a typical Briton and very few people conform to the standard British stereotype (whatever that is). Apart from the multifarious differences in character between the people from different parts of England (particularly between those from the north and south), the population of the UK encompasses a disparate mixture of Scots, Welsh, Irish and assorted ethnic groups originating from throughout the British Commonwealth, other EU countries (including hundreds of thousands from new member countries in recent years), plus miscellaneous foreigners from all corners of the globe who have chosen to make the UK their home (London is the most ethnically diverse city in the world).

One of the things which initially confuses foreigners living in the UK is its class system, which is a curious British affectation. Entry to the upper class echelons is rooted in birthright and ill-bred upstarts with pots of 'new' money (particularly foreigners with unpronounceable names), find they're unable to buy entry to the most exclusive clubs and homes of England (even when they're **seriously** rich). Many Britons are obsessed with class and for some, maintaining or improving their position on the social ladder is a full-time occupation (the ultimate aim being to acquire a knighthood or peerage). The rest of us pretend we're a 'better' class than we actually are, with the exception of a few politicians who are busy trying to live down their privileged past in order to court popularity with the underprivileged masses.

At the top of the heap there's the upper class (the 'blue-bloods' or aristocracy), crowned by the British royal family, followed at a respectable distance by the middle class (which is subdivided into upper middle class, middle middle class, and lower middle class), the working class or lower class, and two relatively new categories that are the inevitable legacy of the unbridled market economy of the last two decades: the underclass and the beggar class. In the UK, people were traditionally officially classified according to their occupations under classes A to E. However, owing to the burgeoning of the middle class in the last few decades (we are all middle class now), the government has introduced no fewer than 17 new classes (including a meritocratic super class of top professionals and managers earning zillions a year).

Class is, of course, wholly unimportant in the UK, provided you attended public school, speak with the right accent and have pots of inherited money.

The UK has been uncharitably described (with a hint of truth) as a society based on privilege, inherited wealth and contacts. Class is also what divides the bosses from the workers in the UK and the class struggle is at the root of many industrial disputes. It has certainly re-ignited over the past couple of years. A blue-collar (manual) worker must never accept a position that elevates him to the ranks of the lower middle class (a white-collar job), otherwise his workmates will no longer speak to him and he will be banned from the local working men's club. (As a consolation he may be accepted as a member at the Conservative club). Similarly, middle-class management must never concede an inch to the workers and, most importantly, must never have direct discussions with them about anything, particularly pay rises or a reduction in working hours.

One thing that would probably cause a strike in any country is British food, particularly in most company canteens and restaurants, where everything is served with chips or ice-cream. Of course, British food isn't **always** as bad as it's painted by foreigners. (What can people who eat anything that crawls, jumps, swims or flies, possibly know about **real** food?). While it's true that British food is often bland, may look terrible and can make you sick, for most people it's just a matter of getting used to it. (What's wrong with a diet of brown sauce, chips, biscuits and tea, anyway?). After all, it's usually necessary to become acclimatised to the food in most foreign countries.

However, it's difficult not to have some sympathy with foreigners who think that many British 'restaurants' should post health warnings and be equipped with an emergency medical centre. (There's nothing wrong with British food that a good stomach pump cannot cure). It may come as a surprise to many foreigners to learn that British bookshops are bursting with cookery books and they **aren't** all written by foreigners. The UK also has many popular television cookery programmes that usually feature eccentric (and excellent) chefs and scrumptious looking food. The British can console themselves with the knowledge that they (or some of them) at least know how to behave **at** the table, even if they don't have much idea what to serve **on** it.

To compensate for their deficiencies in the kitchen, the British are famous for their love of wine (or anything alcoholic) and are among the world's foremost (self-appointed) experts on the character and qualities of good wine, although they're often better talkers than drinkers. In the UK, a wine may be described as having intense aromas and flavours of berries, bramble-jelly, morello cherries, peppery spices, mint, toffee and a hint of honey. The secret of dining in the UK is to drink a lot as, when you're drunk, most food tastes okay. The British even make their own wine; not only home-brewed stuff made from elderberries and other strange fruit, but also real commercially-produced wine made from grapes! Although it isn't exactly causing panic among continental wine producers, some of it's quite palatable.

Contrary to popular belief, the British aren't **all** drunks and are languishing in a fairly lowly 12th position in the alcohol consumption league among the world's top 30 developed countries. The British do at least know how to make a good cuppa (tea) and don't believe in polluting it with lemon or herbs (just milk and/or sugar). The British recipe for any national disaster, whether it's a cricket thrashing at the hands of the Aussies or a power cut during *Coronation Street*, is to make a 'nice cup of tea'. Tea is drunk at almost any time (approaching 200 million cups a day), not just in the morning or 'afternoon tea'. Many Britons drink tea in the same quantities as other Europeans drink mineral water or wine.

Unfortunately, coffee is a different matter altogether and although the British have been drinking it since the 16th century (long before tea), they have yet to master the art of brewing a half-decent pot, which just goes to show that practice **doesn't** always make perfect. The British don't do anything by halves and their coffee, almost always instant, is easily the worst in the world (it would help if they actually used **real coffee beans**).

You may sometimes get the impression that the British are an unfriendly lot, as your neighbours won't always say hello and probably won't drop by or invite you to their home for a cup of tea. (If they offer coffee, invent an urgent appointment!). As an outsider, it may be left to you to make the first move, although if you drop by uninvited, your neighbours may think that you're being pushy and just trying to sneak a look at their home. Northerners are generally friendly and warm-hearted, particularly when compared with the detached and aloof southerners who won't usually give you the time of day. If your southern neighbour does condescend to speak to you, he's likely to greet you with the ritual "How are you?" This doesn't, of course, mean "How are you feeling mentally, physically or spiritually?", but simply "Hello". The questioner usually couldn't care less whether you're fighting fit or on your death bed. The ritual answer is (even if you've just had a heart and lung transplant) "Fine, thank you – how are you?"

If you wish to start a conversation with your neighbour (or anyone), a remark such as "nice weather" usually elicits a response (particularly if it's raining cats and dogs). The weather is a hallowed topic and it's the duty of every upstanding citizen to make daily weather predictions because of the awful hash made of it by the meteorologists. The UK has rather a lot of weather and there's often rain, gales, fog, snow and a heat wave in the same day (although the weather is always described as 'nice' or 'not very nice'). When it snows, everyone and everything is paralysed and people start predicting the end of civilisation as we know it.

The British stick steadfastly to their Fahrenheit temperature measures and many people haven't a clue whether 20°C is boiling hot, lukewarm or freezing. The seasons are a mite erratic, but, as a rough guide, winter lasts for around 11 months, with a break of a couple of weeks for spring and autumn, and (in a good year) a couple of days for summer. There is, however, no truth in the rumour that **all** the world's bad weather originates in the British Isles (some of it **must** come from somewhere else!). The British will do anything to escape for a few weeks to sunnier climes (whatever do they find to talk about on holiday when the sky is boringly blue each day?), even going so far as to spend days in an airport lounge for the dubious pleasure of a few weeks in a half-built hotel, bathing in polluted seas and getting sick on foreign food. The fact that no people anywhere have shown such a consistent desire to emigrate as the British may have more than a little to do with the climate.

It's a common misconception among many foreigners that the British all speak English. There are numerous accents and dialects, half of which are so thick that you could be forgiven for thinking that people are conversing in an ancient secret language. A Briton's accent and choice of words is usually a dead giveaway as to his upbringing. For example, you can safely bet that someone who says, "One feels that one has a certain obligation to one's social peers to attend Royal Ascot, even though one doesn't really care for horse racing oneself", isn't from London's East End. One-third of the British use such long words that most of us cannot even pronounce them (let alone understand them) and some 25 per cent are immigrants who speak only Hindi, Bengali, Chinese, French, Gujarati, Arabic, Xhosa, Russian, Punjabi, Swahili, Urdu, Italian, Turkish, Spanish, Esperanto, Yiddish or Polish.

The rest are tourists, who usually speak the best English of all, but unfortunately don't remain in one place long enough to hold a conversation with anyone. Some foreigners actually pay real money to come to England to learn English, which is part of a grand plot to get them to teach us how to talk proper at their expense. If you're a foreigner and speak good English, you can always practise with other foreigners who you will understand perfectly. If you have a few problems writing English and tend to get all the words mixed up (to say nothing of the damned spelling), fear not; you will be in excellent company as many British are barely literate (the average Briton's vocabulary is around 1,000 words or 500 for tabloid newspaper readers). The best compliment a foreigner can receive from a native is that his English is rather unusual or unorthodox, as he will then blend in with the rest of us and won't be taken for an alien. (If you speak perfect English you will be instantly exposed as a foreigner).

Many Britons are prejudiced against all foreigners and the English are also prejudiced against English from other regions, Irish, Scots, Welsh, Yanks, Europeans, most other foreigners and anyone who speaks with a different (i.e. lower class) accent. However, don't be concerned, as British xenophobia always refers to 'the others' and present company is usually excepted. The British, in common with most other races, don't have a lot of time for foreigners, particularly rich tourists and foreigners who buy up all the best property, and who should all stay at home. Most Britons' image of foreigners is gleaned from the stereotypes portrayed on television. For example, every Briton knows that **all** Americans are millionaires with flash cars, murderers or policemen (or all three), drive like maniacs and make love with their clothes on in full make-up. However, it's the Germans and Japanese who, despite providing us with reliable cars and other things that work, remain the baddest of baddies and are still portrayed as 'the enemy' in weekly television (TV) reruns of World War II.

The British are masters of the understatement and rarely rave about anything. If they're excited about something they sometimes enthuse "that's nice" and, on the rare occasion when they're deliriously happy, they've been known to exclaim "I say, that's rather good". On the other hand, if something disastrous happens (such as their house burns down) it might be termed "a spot of bother". The end of the world will probably be pronounced "unfortunate" or, if there was something particularly good on TV that evening, it may even be greeted as "a jolly bad show" (the ultimate tragedy). The true character of the British is, however, revealed when they're at play, particularly when they're engaged in sport.

The British are sports mad, although most people confine their interest to watching or gambling rather than taking part. The British, or at least the English, are famous for their sense of fair play and playing by the rules – cheating is considered very bad form. Football (soccer) is the UK's national sport and if we hadn't taught all the other nations to play we might even be world champions. However, the real character and true sporting traditions of the English (other Brits have better things to do) are embodied in the game of cricket, a study of which provides a valuable insight into these strange islanders (and their attitude towards tea parties, religion, sex and foreigners). Foreigners may, at first, have a bit of difficulty understanding what cricket is all about (although it's far easier to understand than British politics), but after a few decades, most get the hang of it (unlike British politics which remain a complete mystery). The first thing you must understand is that cricket is a game for gentlemen, embodying the great British traditions of fair play, honour and sportsmanship (except when played by Australians, who haven't the remotest concept of these things).

It's tempting (although fairly pointless) to make comparisons between cricket and a minority sport played in the US, called baseball. (The nearest equivalent in the UK is rounders, a sissy game played by girls). Imagine if you can, a baseball match that lasts five days with interminable breaks for breakfast, drinks, rain, streakers (naked runners), lunch, injuries, stray dogs, more rain, rest days, more drinks, tea, bad light, dinner, supper, and even more rain, and always ends in a draw (if not abandoned due to rain) – and you will have a rough idea what it's all about. Despite the length of a cricket match, which varies from one to five days, it's an enthralling and thrilling sport. On the rare occasions when things get just a teensy bit boring, there's always something exciting to liven things up such as a newspaper blowing across the pitch, a stray dog or pigeon on the field or, on a good day, a streaker. The commentators do a sterling job and keep the audience spellbound with the most amazing and fascinating statistics and anecdotes about cricket's legendary heroes.

The rules of cricket are a little complicated (Einstein's theory of relativity is much easier to understand), so I won't bore you by trying to explain them in detail (fascinating though they are). A cricket team consists of 11 players and a 12th man who has the most important job of all – carrying the drinks tray. He's also sometimes called on to play when one of his team-mates collapses from frostbite or is overcome by excitement. Like baseball, one team bats and the other team attempts to get them out (or committed to hospital) by hurling a ball at the batsman's head. The team in the field (not batting) stands around in set positions with peculiar names such as gulley, slips, short leg, square leg, long leg, peg leg, cover point, third man (they made a film about him), mid-off, mid-on and oddest of all – silly mid-off and silly mid-on. Only someone who's a few pence short of a pound stands directly in front of a batsman as he's about to hit a very hard ball in your direction at around 100mph (160kph).

When the bowler strikes the wicket or the batsman with the ball everyone shouts in unison "Howzat" (very loudly, on the assumption that the umpire is asleep, hard of hearing, short-sighted or all three). Cricketers play in a white uniform and the only colourful things about the game are the ball (red) and the language used by the batsman (blue) when he's hit by the ball or when the umpire gives him out leg before wicket (lbw) to a ball that didn't touch him, and in any case was a million miles away from the wicket. One of the unwritten rules of cricket is that the players (gentlemen) never argue with the umpire, no matter how shortsighted, biased and totally ignorant of the rules the idiot is.

The Aussies (Australians), whom everyone knows have no respect for tradition (and couldn't give a XXXX for anything that doesn't emanate from a tinny or a barrel), have attempted to brighten up the game's image by dressing like clowns for one-day matches (yet another sacrilege to the old school). One of the worst mistakes the English ever made was to teach foreigners how to play cricket (or any other sport), as the ungrateful blighters get a sadistic delight from rubbing their mentors' noses in the dirt. One of the problems with foreigners is that they have no concept of how gentlemen should behave and fail to realise that the real purpose of sport is taking part and **nothing at all to do with winning**. Gallant losers are feted as heroes in the UK and heroic defeats against overwhelming odds are infinitely preferable to easy (hollow) victories.

The British have a passion for queuing (lining up) and appear to outsiders to have endless patience – as you would expect from a nation that can endure a five-day cricket match. The British queue everywhere for everything, including football tickets, sales (when people queue for days or weeks), buses, trains, aircraft, fast food (or slow food if there's a long queue), post offices, government offices, hospital beds, concerts, cafeterias, doctors' and dentists' waiting rooms, groceries, supermarkets, theatre tickets, banks and payphones. The other form of queue popular in the UK is the traffic jam. Many motorists spend their weekdays bumper to bumper driving round and round the M25 motorway, which is circular to make it easier to get back to where you started. At weekends, motorists often get withdrawal symptoms and go for a drive with the family, friends, relatives and the dog, in search of a traffic jam, usually to be found anywhere near coastal areas from spring to autumn, particularly on public holiday weekends.

Queuing isn't always a necessity, but simply a herd instinct that compels people to huddle together (in winter it helps to keep warm), except of course when travelling by public transport, when the rules are somewhat different. On public transport you must never sit next to anyone when an empty seat is available and you must spread yourself and your belongings over two or three seats and never move for anyone. (The best way is to feign sleep with a belligerent expression on your face - most people wouldn't dare disturb you). You must avoid looking at your fellow passengers at all costs (in case a stranger smiles at you), usually achieved by staring fixedly at the back of a newspaper or out of the window. Whatever you do, don't open a window and let in any nasty fresh air, which will cause a riot.

There's not a word of truth in the rumour that British men are lousy lovers (or all gay), which is a cheap lie put about by sex-mad Latinos so that they can keep all the women for themselves. Slanderous foreign propagandists have calculated that the British make love an average of twice a month. To add insult to injury they also estimate this is more often than we bathe (which is a damn insult, as the average Briton washes at least once a week). If you find a foreigner under your bed or in your bath don't be alarmed, he'll only be conducting a sex survey for *Paris Match* or *Der Spiegel*.

Although perhaps not the most romantic of lovers (but **much** better than those unctuous Italians, who are all talk and no trousers and have the lowest birth-rate in Europe), the British know what it's for and don't need a ruler to measure their manhood (neither do we **all** get our kicks flashing, mooning or being whipped by women in leather underwear). Judging by the illegitimate birth rate (around 40 per cent of all births), many Britons don't wait until they're married to find out what sex is all about either. 'No Sex Please, We're British' is simply a challenge to women who have had their fill of Latinos with short fat hairy legs (how does a woman make love to someone who only comes up to her knees anyway?). Sex is definitely not simply a person's gender and most Britons take more than a hot-water bottle to bed with them.

British women are among the most emancipated in the world – not that the weaker sex (men) gave in graciously – and are allowed to vote and drive cars. Nevertheless, it's difficult, if not impossible, for women to claw their way to the top of most professions or into boardrooms, which remain bastions of male chauvinism. Of course, no self-respecting man would allow himself to be dominated by a mere woman, unless of course he's a wimp and she's a handbag-wielding, belligerent battler. If British (male) politicians learnt nothing else during the Thatcher years, it was the utter havoc a woman can wreak in the boardroom.

The main problem with the British economy (apart from the ineptitude of British politicians) is that many Britons lack ambition. They certainly want 'loadsamoney', but would rather do almost anything than work for it (contrary to the popularly held misconception that 'hard work never did anyone any harm', the British know only too well that it can prove fatal). The British are reluctant entrepreneurs and many succeed in their own business only when forced into it.

Most people prefer to try their luck at gambling (rather than work) and will bet on almost anything, including the national lottery, football pools, horse and greyhound racing, bingo, casinos, names of royal babies or ships, public appointments, election results and who the Prime Minister will sack next (or who will resign) – you name it and someone will make a book on it. (One of the reasons that gambling is so popular in Britain is that gambling debts are unenforceable in law). However, the attitude to gambling is changing. Nowadays, someone who wins a fortune on the lottery is unlikely to declare that it won't change his life and that he'll be keeping his job as a £50 a week farm labourer (instead he'll buy a villa in Spain, a yacht and a Ferrari). If the British injected as much energy into work and business as they do into gambling, they might even be able to compete with the Germans and Japanese.

The UK's electoral system is of course unique (nobody would be daft enough to copy it) and elections are decided by the first horse (or ass) past the post. This means that the party in power rarely has more than around 40 per cent of the total vote and minority parties can poll 25 per cent of the vote and end up with only a handful of seats. Of course, nobody in the UK actually votes **for** a political party, particularly the one that wins the election (or at least nobody admits to it). Most are registering a protest vote or voting for the party they hope will do the least damage. Despite their singular lack of success, the minority parties battle manfully on and include such defenders of democracy as the Monster Raving Loony Party (the only British political party with an honest name).

Surprisingly few women are MPs, which proves conclusively that they're more intelligent than men and have better things to do with their lives than hurl insults at each other (politicians are the only children who immature with age). The calibre of British politicians may have something to do with the fact that politicking is the only job that doesn't require any qualifications, training or brains. Nonetheless, as with most charlatans and confidence tricksters, there's honour among politicians who rarely stab each other in the back (when someone is looking). Although British politicians seldom tell the truth and government statistics are all but meaningless due to the myriad ways of calculating and distorting them, politicians never in fact tell lies. A politician may accuse another honourable member only of being economical with the truth, but never of lying.

One of the favourite pastimes of British politicians (when not playing golf or holidaying in exotic places at taxpayers' expense) is sitting on committees, which after weeks of intense discussions and meetings (standing, select, joint, sitting, party, etc.), produce volumes of recommendations. So as not to waste any more time and taxpayers' money, these are promptly filed in the dustbin and forgotten about. British politics are totally incomprehensible and deadly boring to all foreigners – and almost everyone else.

Some people (usually foreigners) think that the British are out of step with their 'partners' in the European Union (EU). Of course, as any Briton will tell you, the only reason we don't always see eye to eye with the damn foreigners (who make up the insignificant part of the EU) is that they refuse to listen to us and do as we tell them. (Whatever happened to the good old days when Johnny Foreigner knew his place?). It must be obvious to everyone that we know best; just look at our manufacturing industry, modern infrastructure, culinary traditions, public services, roads, cricket team; of course, having a transport system and things that work isn't everything.

The notion that the UK doesn't always know best is ridiculous and if there's to be a united Europe, those foreign bounders had better mend their ways. (We didn't fight two world wars so that Jerry and the Frogs – who we bailed out twice – could tell us what to do!). They can start by adopting British time, driving on the left, making English their national language, anglicising their ridiculous names and moving the EU headquarters and parliament to London - which every civilised person knows is the centre of the universe. **Perhaps then we would all get on much better!** If they don't agree, we can always fill in our end of the Channel Tunnel and refuse to answer the telephone. Many Britons firmly believe that the UK is still a world power, when in reality it doesn't have a lot of influence in the modern world. This 'little England' attitude means that, to most Britons, Europe is a place full of foreigners where the sun shines when they go on holiday. Most are unaware of, or choose to ignore, the fact that the UK is actually part of it (at least geographically).

The secret of life in the UK is to maintain a sense of humour (and carry a big umbrella). Most Brits have a lively sense of humour and a keen sense of the ridiculous, which helps make life in the UK bearable. (The worst insult is to accuse someone of having no sense of humour). One of the things that endears the British most to foreigners is their ability to poke fun at themselves (the British don't take themselves too seriously) and everyone else, as typified in TV programmes such as *Monty Python* and *Dead Ringers*. Nothing escapes the barbs of the satirists: from the Pope to the Prime Minister, the President of the US to the Royal Family, everyone is lampooned with equal affection.

It's often difficult for foreigners to understand British humour or to recognise when someone is being serious or joking, although the subject at hand usually offers a clue. Generally, the more earnest or solemn the topic, the more likely they are to be joking. Amazingly, some foreigners think that the British have no sense of humour, usually Americans who don't understand our subtle way with words and cannot understand **real** English anyway. Many foreigners believe the British are at least a little eccentric and, at their worst, stark staring bonkers.

Enough of this flippancy – now for the serious bit! The UK has its fair share of problems and is still failing in many vital areas, including transport, health and manufacturing (apart from those industries we've sold to foreigners). However, we are still world leaders in pageantry, binge drinking and football hooliganism. Major concerns include rising crime (particularly juvenile and violent crime), the uneven quality of state education, a flourishing drugs culture, the failing health service, inequality (the growing gulf between rich and poor), a looming pensions crisis, pollution, awful public transport, homelessness, overcrowded roads, urban blight, a spiralling cost of living and a burgeoning underclass. Apart from that everything is perfect.

The worst crisis is among the UK's young working class males, among whom a lack of a sense of purpose and unemployment commonplace in widespread. This is reflected in their suicide rate, which has risen sharply in the last decade. Perhaps the most serious decline in British life is shown in the combined effects of loss of social cohesion and sense of community, and the breakdown of the family unit. Almost half of marriages end in divorce and some 40 per cent of all births are to unmarried mothers, which has resulted in a high proportion of one-parent families.

However, not everything is depressing in Britain and the quality of life is considered by many foreigners to be excellent and among the best in the world. In the last two decades, the UK has become a more entrepreneurial society, in which people are increasingly ready to take risks and are less dependent on the state. It has also become a more European nation, less afraid of European bogeymen and domination by foreigners (although the euro is still a hard sell).

Most Britons are better off today than they've ever been and optimism about the future has characterised the last decade. This has largely coincided with the election of a dynamic and up-beat Labour government to replace the discredited Conservatives in 1997, although ten years down the road the two are almost indistinguishable. Labout have tried hard to improve things – although not as hard as they have worked to line their own pockets – but it seems that everything they touch turns to ashes. An obsession with political spin-doctoring and public relations has tended to obscure any positive improvements, which in any case have been over-shadowed by the disastrous Iraq war. The conscious branding of the country as 'cool Britannia' now looks a little dated, but nonetheless the underlying reality remains the same. Good restaurants flourish and fashion, music, nightlife and style are all fields in which the UK can now hold its own with the world's best.

The British enjoy superb entertainment, leisure, sports and cultural facilities, which for their sheer variety and accessibility are among the best in the world (but increasingly expensive). The quality and huge choice of goods in the shops is excellent and explains why many people travel from far and wide simply to shop in Britain. British television has no equal, national and local radio is excellent, and the country has an unrivalled choice of quality newspapers, magazines and literature. The UK is a caring society, highlighted by the abundance of charitable and voluntary organisations, unparalleled in any other country, all of which do invaluable work (nationally and internationally). The UK remains a centre of scientific excellence underlined by its number of Nobel prize-winners. It's also one of the least corrupt and most civilised countries in the world.

The British have more freedom from government interference than the people of most countries to do, say and act any way they like, something most of them take for granted. The UK is still a great enlightened power (if a little frayed at the edges) and a positive influence in the world and London remains the centre of the English-speaking world. Whatever else it may be, life in the UK is spiritually, mentally and intellectually stimulating and rarely dull. Although foreigners may occasionally complain about Britain and the British weather, most feel they're privileged to live there and wouldn't dream of leaving.

Last, but certainly not least, there are the British people, who, although they can be infuriating at times, will charm and delight you with their sense of humour and idiosyncrasies. When your patience with the UK and the British is stretched to breaking point, simply take yourself off to the nearest pub and order a pint of ale or a large gin and tonic: the UK looks an even nicer place through the bottom of a (rose-tinted) glass, and, with a bit of luck, you won't even notice that it's still raining.

Long Live Britain! God Save the Queen!

20.

MOVING HOUSE OR LEAVING BRITAIN

When moving house or leaving the UK, there are many things to be considered and a 'million' people to be informed. The checklists contained in this chapter are designed to make the task easier and help prevent an ulcer or a nervous breakdown (provided, of course, you don't leave everything to the last minute). Only divorce or bereavement can cause more stress than moving house! (See also **Relocation Consultants** on page 117.)

MOVING HOUSE

When moving house within the UK, the following items should be considered:

- If you live in rented accommodation you must give your landlord notice (the period depends on your contract). You may need to remain until a minimum period has elapsed, e.g. six months for an assured shorthold tenancy. If you don't give your landlord sufficient notice, you're required to pay rent until the end of your contract or for the full notice period. This also applies if you have a separate contract for a garage or other rented property (e.g. a holiday home).

- Inform the following:

  - Your employer.

  - If moving to a new district or borough council area, you must inform your present council when you move and re-register in your new council area after arrival. When moving to a new county or borough you may be entitled to a refund of a portion of your council tax.

  - If you're registered with the police (see page 109), you must inform them of your new address or re-register at the nearest police station in your new area.

  - The electricity, gas and water companies.

  - Inform your telephone company, if you have a telephone.

  - Your insurance companies (for example health, car, home contents and private pension); banks, building societies, post office (e.g. savings or Giro account), stockbroker and other financial institutions; credit card, charge card and hire purchase companies; solicitor and accountant; and local businesses where you have accounts.

  - Your family doctor, dentist and other health practitioners. Health records should be transferred to your new doctor and dentist, if applicable.

  - Your children's (and your) schools. If applicable, arrange for schooling in your new area. Try to give a term's notice and obtain a copy of any relevant school reports or records from your children's current schools.

  - All regular correspondents, subscriptions, social and sports clubs, professional and trade journals, and friends and relatives. Give or send them your new address and telephone number. Arrange to have your mail redirected by the post office (see **Change of Address** on page 149).

– If you have a British driving licence or a British-registered car, inform the Vehicle License Registration Office as soon as possible after moving.

– Your local consulate or embassy if you're registered with them (see page 110).

● Return any library books or anything borrowed.

● Arrange removal of your furniture and belongings by booking a removal company well in advance. If you have only a few items of furniture, you may prefer to move them yourself, in which case you may need to hire a van.

● Arrange for a cleaning company and/or decorating company for rented accommodation, if necessary.

● If renting, contact your landlord or the letting agency to have your deposit returned (with interest, if applicable).

● Cancel milk and newspaper deliveries.

● Ask yourself (again): 'Is it really worth all this trouble?'

LEAVING BRITAIN

Before leaving the UK permanently or for an indefinite period, the following items should be considered **in addition** to those listed above under **Moving House**:

● Give notice to your employer, if applicable.

● Check that your own and your family's passports are valid.

● Check whether any special requirements (e.g. visas, permits or inoculations) are necessary for entry into your country of destination, by contacting the local embassy or consulate in the UK. An exit permit or visa isn't required to leave the UK.

● Book a removal company well in advance. International removal companies usually provide a wealth of information and may also be able to advise on various matters concerning your relocation. Find out the exact procedure for shipping your belongings to your country of destination from the local embassy or consulate in the UK of the country to which you're moving (don't rely entirely on your shipping company). Special forms may need to be completed before arrival.

● You may qualify for a rebate on your tax and national insurance contributions (check with your local tax office). If you're leaving the UK permanently and have been a member of a company pension scheme (or have a personal pension plan), your contributions remain in the fund and you receive a reduced pension on retirement (see page 340). Contact your company personnel office, local tax office, or pension company for information.

- Arrange to sell anything you aren't taking with you (e.g. house, car and furniture) and to ship your belongings. If you've been living in the UK for less than a year, you're required to export all personal effects, including furniture and vehicles, that were imported tax and duty-free.

- If you have a British registered car which you're permanently exporting, you should complete a 'permanent export certificate' (available from the DVLA, Swansea SA99 1DA) and register the vehicle in your new country of residence on arrival (as necessary).

- Depending on your destination, your pets may require special inoculations or may be required to go into quarantine for a period (see page 501).

- Contact your telephone company well in advance, particularly if you need to get a deposit reimbursed (see **Chapter 7**).

- Arrange health, travel and other insurance, as necessary (see **Chapter 13**).

- Depending on your destination, arrange health and dental check-ups for your family before leaving the UK. Obtain a copy of all health and dental records and a statement from your health insurance company stating your present level of cover.

- Terminate any British loan, lease or hire purchase contracts and pay all outstanding bills (allow plenty of time, as some companies may be slow to respond).

- Check whether you're entitled to a rebate on your road tax, car and other insurance. Obtain a letter from your British motor insurance company stating your number of years of no-claims discount.

- Sell your house, apartment or other property, or arrange to let it through a friend or a letting agency (see **Chapter 5**). If you own more than one property in the UK, you must pay capital gains on any profits from the sale of a second home above a certain amount (see page 394).

- Check whether you need an international driving licence or a translation of your British or foreign driving licence for your country of destination or any countries you pass through.

- Give friends and business associates in the UK a temporary address and telephone number where you can be contacted abroad.

- If you are travelling or living abroad for an extended period, you may wish to give someone 'power of attorney' over your financial affairs in the UK, so that they can act for you in your absence. This can be for a fixed period or open-ended and can be for a specific purpose only. **You should take legal advice before doing this.**

- If you're travelling by air, allow plenty of time to get to the airport, check-in your luggage and to clear security and immigration.

- Buy a copy of **_Living and Working in_** ******** before leaving the UK. If we haven't written it yet, drop us a line and we'll start on it right away!

Have a safe journey.

APPENDICES

APPENDIX A: **FURTHER INFORMATION**

Embassies & Consulates

A selection of foreign embassies and high commissions (Commonwealth countries) in London are listed below. Many countries also have consulates in other cities e.g. Belfast, Birmingham, Cardiff, Edinburgh, Glasgow and Manchester), which are listed in telephone books. All London embassies are listed in *The London Diplomatic List* (The Stationery Office).

Antigua: 2nd Floor, 45, Crawford Place, London W1H 4LP (☎ 20-7258 0070).

Argentina: 65, Brook St, Westminster, London W1U 3JT (☎ 020-7318 1300).

Australia: Australia House, Strand, London WC2B 4LA (☎ 020-7379 4334).

Austria: 18 Belgrave Mews West, London SW1X 8HU (☎ 020-7235 3731).

Bahamas: 10 Chesterfield Street, London W1J 5JL (☎ 020-7408 4488).

Bangladesh: 28 Queen's Gate, London SW7 5JA (☎ 020-7584 0081).

Barbados: 1 Great Russell Street, WC1B 3ND (☎ 020-7631 4975).

Belgium: 17, Grosvenor Crescent, London SW1 7EE (☎ 020-7470 3700).

Belize: 45, Crawford Place, London SW1H 4LP (☎ 020-7723 3603).

Bolivia: 106 Eaton Square, London SW1W 9AD (☎ 020-7235 4248/2257).

Bosnia & Herzegovina: 5-7, Lexham Gardens, London W8 5JJ (☎ 020-7373 0867).

Brazil: 32 Green Street, Mayfair, London W1Y 7AT (☎ 020-7499 0877).

Brunei: 19/20 Belgrave Square, London SW1X 8PG (☎ 020-7581 0521).

Bulgaria: 186–88 Queen's Gate, London SW7 5HL (☎ 020-7584 9400).

Cameroon: 84 Holland Park, London W11 3SB (☎ 020-7727 0771).

Canada: MacDonald House, 1 Grosvenor Square, London W1K 4AB (☎ 020-7258 6600).

Chile: 12 Devonshire Street, London W1G 7DS (☎ 020-7580 1023).

China: 49–1 Portland Place, London W1N 4JL (☎ 020-7299 4049).

Colombia: Flat 3a, 3 Hans Crescent, London SW1X 0LN (☎ 020-7589 9177).

Croatia: 21 Conway Street, London W1T 6BN (☎ 020-7387 2022).

Cuba: 167 High Holborn, London WC1 6PA (☎ 020-7240 2488).

Cyprus: 93 Park Street, London W1K 7ET (☎ 020-7499 8272).

Czech Republic: 26, Kensington Palace Gardens, London W8 4QY (☎ 020-7243-1115).

Denmark: 55 Sloane Street, London SW1X 9SR (☎ 020-7333 0200).

Dominica: 1 Collingham Gardens, South Kensington, London SW5 0HW (☎ 020-7370 5194).

Ecuador: Flat 3b, 3 Hans Crescent, Knightsbridge, London SW1X 0LS (☎ 020-7584 2648).

Egypt: 26, South St, Westminster, London SW1X (☎ 020-7499 2401).

El Salvador: 8, Dorset Sq. London NW1 6PU (☎ 020-7224 9800).

Fiji: 34 Hyde Park Gate, London SW7 5DN (☎ 020-7584 3661).

Finland: 38 Chesham Place, London SW1X 8HW (☎ 020-7838 6200).

France: 58 Knightsbridge, London SW1X 7JT (☎ 020-7073 1000).

The Gambia: 57 Kensington Court, Kensington, London W8 5DG (☎ 020-7937 6316).

Germany: 23 Belgrave Square, 1 Chesham Place, London SW1X 8PZ (☎ 020-7824 1300).

Ghana: 13 Belgrave Square, London SW1X 8PN (☎ 020-7201 5900).

Greece: 1A Holland Park, London W11 3TP (☎ 020-7229 3850).

Grenada: The Chapel, Archel Road, West Kensington, London W14 (☎ 020-7385 4277).

Guatemala: 13 Fawcett Street, London SW10 9HN (☎ 020-7351 3042).

Guyana: 3 Palace Court, Bayswater Road, London W2 4LP (☎ 020-7229 7684).

Holy See: Apostolic Nunciature, 54 Parkside, London SW19 5NF (☎ 020-8944 7189).

Honduras: 115 Gloucester Place, London W1U 6JT (☎ 020-7486 4880).

Hungary: 35 Eaton Place, London SW1X 8BY (☎ 020-7201 3440).

Iceland: 2a Hans Street, London SW1X (☎ 020-7259 3999).

India: India House, Aldwych, London WC2B 4NA (☎ 020-7836 8484).

Indonesia: 38 Grosvenor Square, London W1K 2HW (☎ 020-7499 7661).

Iran: 16 Prince's Gate, London SW7 1PT (☎ 020-7225 3000).

Ireland: 17 Grosvenor Place, London SW1X 7HR (☎ 020-7235 2171).

Israel: 2 Palace Green, Kensington, London W8 4QB (☎ 020-7957 9500).

Italy: 14 Three Kings Yard, Davies Street, London W1K 4EH (☎ 020-7312 2200).

Jamaica: 1–2 Prince Consort Road, London SW7 2BZ (☎ 020-7823 9911).

Japan: 101–104 Piccadilly, London W1J 7JT (☎ 020-7465 6500).

Jordan: 6 Upper Phillimore Gardens, Kensington, London W8 7HB (☎ 020-7937 3685).

Kenya: 45 Portland Place, London W1B 1AS (☎ 020-7636 2371).

Korea (South): 60 Buckingham Gate, London SW1E 6AJ (☎ 020-7227 5500).

Kuwait: 2 Albert Gate, London SW1X 7JU (☎ 020-7590 3400).

Lebanon: 15–21 Palace Gardens Mews, London W8 8QM (☎ 020-7229 7265).

Lesotho: 7 Chesham Place, Belgravia, London SW1X 8HN (☎ 020-7235 5686).

Luxembourg: 27 Wilton Crescent, London SW1X 8SD (☎ 020-7235 6961).

Malawi: 33 Grosvenor Street, London W1K 4QT (☎ 020-7491 4172).

Malaysia: 45 Belgrave Square, London SW1X 8QT (☎ 020-7235 8033).

Malta: Malta House, 36–38 Piccadilly, London W1J 0LE (☎ 020-7292 4800).

Mauritius: 32/33 Elvaston Place, London SW7 5NW (☎ 020-7581 0294).

Mexico: 42 Hertford Street, Mayfair, London W1Y 7JR (☎ 020-7499 8586).

Morocco: 49 Queen's Gate Gardens, London SW7 5NE (☎ 020-7581 5001).

Mozambique: 21 Fitzroy Square, London W1T 6EL (☎ 020-7383 3800).

Namibia: 6 Chandos Street, London W1G 9LU (☎ 020-7636 6244).

Nepal: 12a Kensington Palace Gardens, London W8 4QU (☎ 020-7229 6231).

Netherlands: 38 Hyde Park Gate, London SW7 5DP (☎ 020-7590 3200).

New Zealand: New Zealand House, Haymarket, London SW1Y 4TQ (☎ 020-7930 8422).

Nigeria: Nigeria House, 9 Northumberland Avenue, London WC2N 5BX (☎ 020-7839 1244).

Norway: 25 Belgrave Square, London SW1X 8QD (☎ 020-7591 5500).

Oman: 167 Queen's Gate, London SW7 5HE (☎ 020-7225 0001).

Pakistan: 35/36 Lowndes Square, London SW1X 9JN (☎ 020-7664 9200).

Panama: Panama House, 40 Herford Street, London W1J 7SH (☎ 020-7409 2255).

Papua New Guinea: Ground Floor, 14 Waterloo Place, London SW1Y 4AR (☎ 020-7930 0922).

Paraguay: 344, High St., Kensington, London W14 8NS (☎ 020-7610 4180).

Peru: 52 Sloane Street, London SW1X 9SP (☎ 020-7235 1917).

Philippines: 9a Palace Green, London W8 4QE (☎ 020-7937 1600).

Poland: 47 Portland Place, London W1B 1JH (☎ 020-7580 4324).

Portugal: 11 Belgrave Square, London SW1X 8PP (☎ 020-7235 5331).

Qatar: 1 South Audley Street, London W1K 1NB (☎ 020-7493 2200).

Romania: Arundel House, 4 Palace Green, London W8 4QD (☎ 020-7937 9666).

Russia: 6-7 Kensington Palace Gardens, London W8 4QP (☎ 020-7229 2666).

Saudi Arabia: 30 Charles Street, Mayfair, London W1X 7PM (☎ 020-7917 3000).

Serbian Republic: 28, Belgrave Square, London, SW1 X (☎ 020-7235 9049).

Sierra Leone: 41, Eagle St., Holborn, London WC14TL (☎ 020-7404 0140).

Singapore: 9 Wilton Crescent, London SW1X 8RW (☎ 020-7235 8315).

Slovak Republic: 25 Kensington Palace Gardens, London W8 4QY (☎ 020-7243 0803).

Slovenia: 10 Little College Street, London SW1P (☎ 020-7222 5400).

South Africa: South Africa House, Trafalgar Square, London WC2N 5DP (☎ 020-7451 7299).

Spain: 39 Chesham Place, London SW1X 8SB (☎ 020-7235 5555).

Sri Lanka: 13 Hyde Park Gardens, London W2 2LU (☎ 020-7262 1841).

Swaziland: 20 Buckingham Gate, London SW1E 6LB (☎ 020-7630 6611).

Sweden: 11 Montagu Place, London W1H 2AL (☎ 020-7917 6400).

Switzerland: 16–18 Montagu Place, London W1H 2BQ (☎ 020-7616 6000).

Syria: 8 Belgrave Square, London SW1X 8PH (☎ 020-7245 9012).

Tanzania: 43 Hertford Street, London W1Y 8DB (☎ 020-7499 8951).

Thailand: 29/30 Queen's Gate, London SW7 5JB (☎ 020-7589 2944).

Tonga: 36 Molyneux Street, London W1H 6AB (☎ 020-7724 5828).

Trinidad & Tobago: 42 Belgrave Square, London SW1X 8NT (☎ 020-7245 9351).

Turkey: 43 Belgrave Square, London SW1X 8PA (☎ 020-7393 0202).

Uganda: Uganda House, 58/59 Trafalgar Square, London WC2N 5DX (☎ 020-7839 5783).

Ukraine: 60 Holland Park, London W11 3SJ (☎ 020-7727 6312).

United Arab Emirates: 30 Prince's Gate, London SW7 1PT (☎ 020-7581 1281).

United States Of America: 24 Grosvenor Square, London W1A 1AE (☎ 020-7499 9000).

Uruguay: 2nd Floor, 140 Brompton Road, London SW3 1HY (☎ 020-7589 8735).

Venezuela: 1 Cromwell Road, London SW7 2HW (☎ 020-7584 4206).

Zaire: 26 Chesham Place, London SW1X 8HH (☎ 020-7235 6137).

Zambia: 2 Palace Gate, Kensington, London W8 5NG (☎ 020-7589 6655).

Zimbabwe: Zimbabwe House, 429 Strand, London WC2R 0SA (☎ 020-7836 7755).

Government Departments

Department for Culture, Media & Sport, 2–4 Cockspur Street, London SW1Y 5DH (☎ 020-7211 6200).

Department for Education & Skills, Sanctuary Buildings, Great Smith Street, London SW1P 3BT (☎ 0870-000 2288).

Department for the Environment, Food and Rural Affairs, Nobel House, 17 Smith Square, London SW1P 3JR (☎ 0845-933 5577).

Department of Health, Richmond House, 79 Whitehall, London SW1A 2NL (☎ 020-7210 4850).

Department for International Development, 1 Palace Street, London SW1E 5HE (☎ 0845-300 4100).

Department of Trade and Industry, 1 Victoria Street, London SW1H 0ET (☎ 020-7215 5000).

Department for Transport, Great Minster House, 76 Marsham Street, London SW1P 4DR (☎ 020-7944 8300).

Department for Work & Pensions, The Adelphi, 1–11 John Adam Street, London WC2N 6HT (☎ 020-7712 2171).

Foreign & Commonwealth Office, King Charles Street, London SW1A 2AH (☎ 020-7008 1500).

Home Office, 50 Queen Anne's Gate, London SW1H 9AT (☎ 0870-000 1585).

Ministry of Defence, Main Building, Whitehall, London SW1A 2HB (☎ 020-7218 9000).

Northern Ireland Office, Stormont Castle, Belfast BT4 3ST (☎ 028-9052 0700).

Scotland Office, Dover House, Whitehall, London SW1A 2AU (☎ 020-7270 6754).

Wales Office, Cathays Park, Cardiff CF1 3NQ (☎ 029-2082 5111).

Tourist Information

Visit Britain, Thames Tower, Black's Road, London W6 9EL (☎ 020-8846 9000).

Irish Tourist Board, 150 New Bond Street, London W1S 2AQ (☎ 020-7493 3201).

Scottish Tourist Board, 19 Cockspur Street, London SW1Y 5BL (☎ 020-7930 8661).

Welsh Tourist Board, 1 Regent Street, London, SW1Y 4NR (☎ 020-7808 3838).

Travel

Association of British Travel Agents, 55–57 Newman Street, London W1T 3AH (☎ 020-7637 2444).

British Airports Authority, Corporate Office, 130 Wilton Road, London SW1V 1LQ (☎ 020-7834 9449).

British Airways, Customer Relations, PO Box 5619, Sudbury, Suffolk O10 2PG (☎ 0870-850 9850).

British Midland, Head Office, Donington Hall, Castle Donington, Derby DE74 2SB (☎ 01332-854 000).

London Transport, 55 Broadway, London SW1H 0BD (☎ 020-7222 5600).

National Express, Head Office, 75 Davies Street, London W1K 5HT (☎ 0870-580 8080).

P&O, 77–91 New Oxford Street, London WC1A 1PP (☎ 020-7800 2222).

Miscellaneous

Automobile Association (AA), Fanum House, PO Box 50, Basingstoke, Hampshire RG21 4EA (☎ 020-7637 2444).

British Council, 10 Spring Gardens, London SW1A 2BN (☎ 020-7930 8466).

British Broadcasting Corporation (BBC), Broadcasting House, Portland Place, London W1A 1AA (☎ 020-7580 4468).

BBC Television Centre, Wood Lane, London W12 7RJ (☎ 020-8743 8000).

British Telecom, 81 Newgate Street, London EC1A 7AJ (☎ 020-7356 6666).

Central Office of Information, Hercules Road, London SE1 7DU (☎ 020-7928 2345).

Confederation of British Industry (CBI), Centre Point, 103 New Oxford Street, London WC1A 1DU (☎ 020-7379 7400).

Consumers' Association, Which?, Castlemead, Gascoyne Way, Hertford SG14 1LH (☎ 020-7379 7400).

Driver and Vehicle Licensing Agency (DVLA), Sandringham Park, Swansea SA7 0EE (☎ 0870-240 0009).

Good Housekeeping Institute, National Magazine House, 72 Broadwick Street, London W1F 9EP (☎ 020-7439 5000).

HM Customs and Excise, New King's Beam House, 22 Upper Ground, London SE1 9PJ (☎ 020-7620 1313).

Inland Revenue, Somerset House, Strand, London WC2R 1LB (☎ 020-7438 6622).

National Archives, Ruskin Avenue, Kew, Richmond, Surrey TW9 4DU (☎ 020-8876 3444).

National Association of Citizens Advice Bureaux, Myddelton House, 115–123 Pentonville Road, London N1 9LZ (☎ 020-7833 2181).

National Consumer Council, 20 Grosvenor Gardens, London SW1W 0DH (☎ 020-7730 3469).

National Federation of Women's Institutes, 104 New Kings Road, London SW6 4LY (☎ 020-7371 9300).

Office of Fair Trading, Fleetbank House, 2–6 Salisbury Square, London EC4Y 8JX (☎ 020-7211 8000).

Office for National Statistics, 1 Drummond Gate, London SW1V 2QQ (☎ 0845-601 3034).

RAC Motoring Services, Head Office, 1 Forest Road, Feltham, Middlesex TW13 7RR (☎ 020-8917 2500).

The Stationery Office Ltd, National Publishing, 51 Nine Elms Lane, Vauxhall, London SW8 5DR (☎ 020-7873 8787, ⌨ www.tso.co.uk).

APPENDIX B: FURTHER READING

There are many useful reference books for anyone seeking general information about the UK and the British including *Whitaker's Almanack* (The Stationery Office). Published annually since 1868, *Whitaker's Almanack* contains a wealth of information about the British government, finances, population, commerce and general statistics of the nations of the world. Newcomers to the UK may also be interested in *Britain* (The Stationery Office), an annual reference book describing many features of life in the UK, including the workings of the government and other major institutions.

In the list below, the publication title is followed by the author's name and the publisher (in brackets). All books prefixed with an asterisk (*) are recommended by the author.

Tourist Guides

*AA Explorer Britain (AA Publishing)

*Baedeker's AA Great Britain (Baedeker/AA)

Birnbaum's Great Britain (Houghton Mifflin)

*Blue Guide: England Ian Ousby (A & C Black)

*Blue Guide: Ireland Ian Robertson (A & C Black)

*Britain Travel Survival Kit (Lonely Planet)

Britain at its Best Robert S. Kane (Passport Books)

*The Complete Guide to London (Nicholson)

Days Out in Britain & Ireland (AA Publishing)

Eyewitness Travel Guide London (Dorling Kindersley)

*Fodor's Great Britain E. Fodor (Hodder & Stoughton)

Frommer's Great Britain Darwin Porter (Frommer's)

*The Good Walks Guide (Which? Books)

*The Good Weekend Guide (Vermillion)

Great Britain (Insight Guides)

Great Britain and Ireland (Phaidon Press)

Hachette Guide to Great Britain (Hachette)

*Let's Go: Britain & Ireland (Pan)

*Let's Go: London (Pan)

*Michelin Green Guide to Great Britain (Michelin)

*Reader's Digest Touring Guide to Britain (Reader's Digest)

*Rough Guide to England (The Rough Guides)

*Weekend Breaks in Britain (Which? Books)

*Welcome to Britain (Collins)

General

*A-Z London Guide (Geographers' A-Z Map Co. Ltd)

Best Behaviour Mary Killen (Century)

*Britain in Figures (The Economist)

*A Class Act: The Myth of Britain's Classless Society Andrew Adonis and Stephen Pollard (Hamilton)

*Daily Mail Year Book (Chapmans)

Debrett's New Guide to Etiquette and Modern Manners edited by John Morgan (Headline)

Discover Britain Christine Lindop and Dominic Fisher (Cambridge University Press)

*The English Jeremy Paxman (Michael Joseph)

The Guinness UK Data Book (Guinness Publishing)

*How to be a Brit George Mikes (Andre Deutsch)

The New British State (The Times)

*Notes From a Small Island Bill Bryson (Doubleday)

Statlas UK (Ordnance Survey)

*Time Out London Guide (Time Out Magazine Ltd)

*Top Towns (Guinness Publishing)

*We British: Britain Under the Moriscope Erik Jacobs & Robert Worcester (Weidenfeld & Nicholson)

*Whitaker's Almanack (The Stationery Office)

APPENDIX C: USEFUL WEBSITES

The following lists of internet sites are by no means definitive, but include many sites that will be of help and interest to those planning to live or work in the UK.

Professional Associations

Building Societies' Association (🖥 www.bsa.org.uk). Central representative body for building societies.

Council for Licensed Conveyancers (🖥 www.theclc.gov.uk). Alternative conveyancers to solicitors.

Council of Mortgage Lenders (🖥 www.cml.org.uk). Trade association for mortgage lenders.

Federation of Master Builders (🖥 www.fmb.org.uk). Includes a directory of members.

Land Registry (🖥 www.landreg.gov.uk). Practical information about registering land and land registry archives.

Land Registers of Northern Ireland (🖥 www.lrni.gov.uk). The Land Registry in Northern Ireland.

The Law Society (🖥 www.lawsoc.org.uk). Professional body for solicitors in England and Wales.

The Law Society, Scotland (🖥 www.lawscot.org.uk). Professional body for solicitors in Scotland.

National Association of Estate Agents/NAEA (🖥 www. naea.co.uk). The main organisation for estate agents.

Ombudsman for Estate Agents (🖥 www.oea.co.uk). Independent arbitration for property buyers with complaints about registered estate agents.

Registers of Scotland (🖥 www.ros.gov.uk). The Land Registry in Scotland.

Mortgages

Charcol Online (🖥 www.charcolonline.co.uk). Online mortgage brokers.

Council of Mortgage Lenders (🖳 www.cml.org.uk). The trade association for mortgage lenders.

Finance for Professionals (🖳 www.f4p.com). Finance for members of certain professions, e.g. architects, engineers and teachers.

Home Buyer & Mortgage Advisor magazine (🖳 www.homebuyermag.co.uk). The UK's most popular mortgage magazine. Good general information about buying and selling property.

Market Place (🖳 www.marketplace.co.uk). Search for the best mortgage deals.

Money Extra (🖳 www.moneyextra.co.uk). Financial services, including best mortgage deals.

Money Net (🖳 www.moneynet.co.uk). Financial services, including best mortgage deals.

Money Quest (🖳 www.moneyquest.co.uk). Mortgage brokers.

Money Supermarket (🖳 www.moneysupermarket.com). General finance including mortgages.

Mortgage Next (🖳 www.mortgage-next.com). Financial advisers.

This is Money (🖳 www.thisismoney.co.uk). Data and statistics on money matters as well as useful money guides.

Virgin Money (🖳 http://uk.virginmoney.com). The Virgin Group's financial services online.

What Mortgage Magazine (🖳 www.whatmortgageonline.co.uk). Mortgage information and comprehensive advice on buying a property.

Your Mortgage Magazine (🖳 www.yourmortgage.co.uk). Provides a wealth of information about mortgages and all aspects of buying and selling property.

Neighbourhood Information

Environment Agency (🖳 www.environment-agency.gov.uk). Check the occurrence of flooding in an area.

Enviro Search (🖳 www.home-envirosearch.info). Check whether a property is adversely affected by environmental factors.

Get-a-map (⌨ www.getamap.co.uk). Free downloadable Ordnance Survey neighbourhood maps.

Home Check (⌨ www.homecheck.co.uk). Local information about the risks of flooding, landslip, pollution, radon gas, landfill, waste sites, etc. Also provides general information about neighbourhoods.

Hometrack (⌨ www.hometrack.co.uk). Online property reports.

Knowhere (⌨ www.knowhere.co.uk). An alternative look at over 2,000 UK towns.

My Village (⌨ www.myvillage.com). Community sites for London and 20 other cities.

Neighbourhood Statistics (⌨ http://neighbourhood.statistics.gov.uk). Contains a wide range of statistics for neighbourhoods in England and Wales.

Proviser (⌨ www.proviser.com). Local property prices and street maps for England and Wales.

UK Online (⌨ www.ukonline.gov.uk). Comprehensive information about local services and neighbourhoods, including local schools, health, housing and crime statistics.

Up My Street (⌨ www.upmystreet.co.uk). Information about neighbourhoods, including property prices, local services, schools, local government, etc.

Estate Agents

Asserta Home (⌨ www.assertahome.com). Large database of properties for sale around the country.

Find a Property (⌨ www.findaproperty.com). Property for sale in London and surrounding counties.

Fish4homes (⌨ www.fish4homes.co.uk). Selection of properties and directory of estate agents around the UK.

Foxtons (⌨ www.foxtons.co.uk). London's largest chain of estate and letting agents.

Home Sale (⌨ www.home-sale.co.uk). National network of over 700 estate agents.

Hot Property (💻 www.hotproperty.co.uk). The Hot Property magazine website featuring property in London and the south-east.

House Web (💻 www.houseweb.co.uk). Independent property website that contains comprehensive advice and tips for the homebuyer.

London Property Guide (💻 www.londonpropertyguide.co.uk). Buy, sell or rent in London.

My Property (💻 www.mypropertyforsale.co.uk). Internet estate agent.

New-Homes (💻 www.new-homes.co.uk). Comprehensive database of new home developments throughout the UK.

Number One 4 Property (💻 www.numberone4property.co.uk). Property.

Property Finder (💻 www.propertyfinder.co.uk). Internet estate agent.

Property Live (💻 www.propertylive.co.uk). The National Association of Estate Agents' property website.

Prime Location (💻 www.primelocation.com). Consortium of estate agents advertising properties.

Right Move (💻 www.rightmove.co.uk). Buying, selling and letting.

Smart Estates (💻 www.smartestates.com). Independent property website selling new and resale property.

Smart New Homes (💻 www.smartnewhomes.co.uk). Search for new homes.

Vebra (💻 www.vebra.com). One of the UK's most visited property sites run by a consortium of estate agents.

Ugly Properties (💻 www.uglyproperties.com). Specialists in selling vandalised and empty properties, 'brownfield' development land and just plain ugly-looking homes.

Winkworth (💻 www.winkworth.co.uk). Property database for London and Yorkshire.

Private Sales

The following websites are online property agents who advertise property for sale, usually for a modest one-time fee (many also contain comprehensive general information):

4 Sale By Owner (💻 www.4salebyowner.co.uk).

DIY House (💻 www.diyhousesales.com). Property in Northern Ireland.

Estate Agent (💻 www.estateagent.co.uk). Advertise free of charge.

Home Pages (💻 www.homepages.co.uk).

Home Sale Network (💻 www.home-sale.co.uk).

House Web (💻 www.houseweb.co.uk).

Internet Homes (💻 www.internethomes.co.uk).

My Property for Sale (💻 www.mypropertyforsale.co.uk).

Private House for Sale (💻 www.privatehousesforsale.co.uk).

Property Broker (💻 www.propertybroker.co.uk).

Property Finder (💻 www.propertyfinder.co.uk).

Smart Estates (💻 www.smartestates.com).

Use the Mouse (💻 www.use-the-mouse.com).

Moving Resources

British Association of Removers (💻 www.bar.co.uk). Association of removal companies offering a professional service with a conciliation and arbitration service.

I Am Moving (💻 www.iammoving.com). Will inform companies on your behalf that you are moving.

Really Moving (💻 www.reallymoving.com). Excellent information about property including home-moving services and a property finder.

The Move Channel (💻 www.themovechannel.com). General property website containing everything you need to know about moving house.

General

Au Pair Forum (💻 www.aupair-forum.com). Experiences of au pairs and tips for those thinking of becoming one.

Australia Shop (⌨ www.australia.shop.com). Expatriate shopping for homesick Australians.

BBC Homes (⌨ www.bbc.co.uk/homes). Lifestyle homes from the BBC.

British Expatriates (⌨ www.britishexpat.com and ⌨ www.ukworld wide.com). Two sites designed to keep British expatriates in touch with events in and information about the UK.

Direct Moving (⌨ www.directmoving.com). General expatriate information, tips and advice, and numerous links.

Escape Artist (⌨ www.escapeartist.com). One of the most comprehensive expatriate sites, including resources, links and directories covering most expatriate destinations. You can also subscribe to the free monthly online expatriate magazine, Escape from America.

ExpatBoards (⌨ www.expatboards.com). A comprehensive site for expatriates, with popular discussion boards and special areas for Britons and Americans.

Expat Exchange (⌨ www.expatexchange.com). Reportedly the largest online 'community' for English-speaking expatriates, including articles on relocation and a question and answer facility.

Expat Expert (⌨ www.expatexpert.com). Run by expatriate expert Robin Pascoe, providing advice and support.

ExpatNetwork (⌨ www.expatnetwork.com). The UK's leading expatriate website, which is essentially an employment network for expatriates, although it also includes numerous support services and a monthly online magazine, Nexus.

Expat World (⌨ www.expatworld.net). Information for American and British expatriates, including a subscription newsletter.

Global People (⌨ www.peoplegoingglobal.com). Includes country-specific information with a particular emphasis on social and political issues.

Home Pages (⌨ www.homepages.co.uk). Comprehensive property database and information about buying and selling.

Homes Online (⌨ www.homes-on-line.com). Useful information about buying, selling, home improvements and financing a property.

Living Abroad (⌨ www.livingabroad.com). Includes an extensive list of country profiles, which are available only on payment.

The Move Channel (⌨ www.themovechannel.com). Comprehensive information on all aspects of buying and selling property.

Outpost Information Centre (⌨ www.outpostexpat.nl). Contains extensive country-specific information and links operated by the Shell Petroleum Company for its expatriate workers, but available to everyone.

Plot Finder (⌨ www.plotfinder.net). Land and renovations for sale.

Property Investor (⌨ www.propertyinvestor.co.uk). Buying, selling and letting property for profit plus information about Property Investor shows.

PropertySpy Group (⌨ www.propertymarket.co.uk). Specialises in land for sale in England.

Property Telegraph (⌨ www.property.telegraph.co.uk). Comprehensive property information including advice, prices and latest news and developments.

Real Post Reports (⌨ www.realpostreports.com). Includes relocation services, recommended reading lists and 'real-life' stories written by expatriates in cities throughout the world.

Save Britain's Heritage (⌨ www.savebritainsheritage.org). Conservation of historic buildings.

SaveWealth Travel (⌨ www.savewealth.com/travel/warnings). Travel information and warnings.

Scoot (⌨ www.scoot.co.uk). Find essential services for homeowners.

Shelternet (⌨ www.shelternet.co.uk). The website of Shelter, a charity for the homeless and the leading provider of independent housing advice in the UK.

Trade Partners (⌨ www.tradepartners.gov.uk). A UK government-sponsored site providing trade and investment (and general) information about most countries, including the US.

The Travel Doctor (⌨ www.tmvc.com.au/info10.html). Includes a country by country vaccination guide.

Travelfinders (⌨ www.travelfinders.com). Travel information with warnings about danger areas.

World Health Organization (⌨ www.who.int). Health information.

The World Press (⌨ www.theworldpress.com). Links to media sites in practically every country in the world's media.

World Travel Guide (🖥 www.wtgonline.com). A general website for world travellers and expatriates.

Yankee Doodle (🖥 www.yankeedoodle.co.uk). Import American products.

Your New Home Magazine (🖥 www.yournewhome.co.uk). The magazine for new homebuyers.

Websites for Women

Third Culture Kids (🖥 www.tckworld.com). Designed for expatriate children.

Worldwise Directory (🖥 www.suzylamplugh.org/worldwise). Run by the Suzy Lamplugh charity for personal safety, the site provides practical information about a number of countries with special emphasis on safety, particularly for women.

APPENDIX D: WEIGHTS & MEASURES

Britain officially converted to the international metric system of measurement on 1st October 1995, although many goods have been sold in metric sizes for many years. The use of imperial measures was officially due to finish at the end of 1999, but has been given a reprieve until end of 2009. Therefore you can expect to find goods sold in imperial (and other British) measures or metric units or marked in both! Many foreigners will find the tables on the following pages useful. Some comparisons shown are approximate only, but are close enough for most everyday uses.

Women's Clothes

Continental	34	36	38	40	42	44	46	48	50	52
UK	8	10	12	14	16	18	20	22	24	26
US	6	8	10	12	14	16	18	20	22	24

Pullovers

	Women's						Men's					
Continental	40	42	44	46	48	50	44	46	48	50	52	54
UK	34	36	38	40	42	44	34	36	38	40	42	44
US	34	36	38	40	42	44	sm	med	lar	xl		

Men's Shirts

Continental	36	37	38	39	40	41	42	43	44	46
UK/US	14	14	15	15	16	16	17	17	18	-

Men's Underwear

Continental	5	6	7	8	9	10
UK	34	36	38	40	42	44
US	sm	med		lar	xl	

Note: sm = small, med = medium, lar = large, xl = extra large

Children's Clothes

Continental	92	104	116	128	140	152
UK	16/18	20/22	24/26	28/30	32/34	36/38
US	2	4	6	8	10	12

Children's Shoes

Continental	18	19	20	21	22	23	24	25	26	27	28	29	30	31	32
UK/US	2	3	4	4	5	6	7	7	8	9	10	11	11	12	13

Continental	33	34	35	36	37	38
UK/US	1	2	2	3	4	5

Shoes (Women's and Men's)

Continental	35	36	37	37	38	39	40	41	42	42	43	44
UK	2	3	3	4	4	5	6	7	7	8	9	9
US	4	5	5	6	6	7	8	9	9	10	10	11

Weight

Imperial	Metric	Metric	Imperial
1oz	28.35g	1g	0.035oz
1lb*	454g	100g	3.5oz
1cwt	50.8kg	250g	9oz
1 ton	1,016kg	500g	18oz
2,205lb	1 tonne	1kg	2.2lb

Length

Imperial	Metric	Metric	Imperial
1in	2.54cm	1cm	0.39in
1ft	30.48cm	1m	3ft 3.25in
1yd	91.44cm	1km	0.62mi
1mi	1.6km	8km	5mi

Capacity

Imperial	Metric	Metric	Imperial
1 UK pint	0.57 litre	1 litre	1.75 UK pints
1 US pint	0.47 litre	1 litre	2.13 US pints
1 UK gallon	4.54 litres	1 litre	0.22 UK gallon
1 US gallon	3.78 litres	1 litre	0.26 US gallon

Note: An American 'cup' = around 250ml or 0.25 litre.

Area

Imperial	Metric	Metric	Imperial
1 sq. in	0.45 sq. cm	1 sq. cm	0.15 sq. in
1 sq. ft	0.09 sq. m	1 sq. m	10.76 sq. ft
1 sq. yd	0.84 sq. m	1 sq. m	1.2 sq. yds
1 acre	0.4 hectares	1 hectare	2.47 acres
1 sq. mile	2.56 sq. km	1 sq. km	0.39 sq. mile

Temperature

Celsius	Fahrenheit	
0	32	(freezing point of water)
5	41	
10	50	
15	59	
20	68	
25	77	
30	86	
35	95	
40	104	
50	122	

Notes: The boiling point of water is 100C / 212F.

Normal body temperature (if you're alive and well) is 37C / 98.4F.

Temperature Conversion

Celsius to Fahrenheit: multiply by 9, divide by 5 and add 32. (For a quick and approximate conversion, double the Celsius temperature and add 30.)

Fahrenheit to Celsius: subtract 32, multiply by 5 and divide by 9. (For a quick and approximate conversion, subtract 30 from the Fahrenheit temperature and divide by 2.)

Oven Temperatures

Gas	Electric	
	F	C
-	225–250	110–120
1	275	140
2	300	150
3	325	160
4	350	180
5	375	190
6	400	200
7	425	220
8	450	230
9	475	240

Air Pressure

PSI	Bar
10	0.5
20	1.4
30	2
40	2.8

APPENDIX E: MAP OF BRITAIN

The map of Britain opposite shows the counties of England, Wales, Scotland and Northern Ireland (listed below). The list shows the abbreviations (in brackets) in common use for many English counties.

England

Avon
Bedfordshire (Beds)
Berkshire (Berks)
Buckinghamshire (Bucks)
Cambridgeshire (Cambs)
Cheshire
Cleveland
Cornwall
Cumbria
Derbyshire (Derby)
Devon
Dorset
Durham
East Sussex (E. Sussex)
Essex
Gloucestershire (Glos)
Greater Manchester
Hampshire (Hants)
Hereford & Worcestershire (Worcs)
Hertfordshire (Herts)
Isle of Wight
Kent
Lancashire (Lancs)
Leicestershire (Leics)
Lincolnshire (Lincs)
London
Merseyside
Norfolk
North Yorkshire (N. Yorks)
Northamptonshire (Northants)
Northumberland
Nottinghamshire (Notts)
Oxfordshire (Oxon)
Shropshire (Salop)
Somerset
South Yorkshire (S. Yorks)
Staffordshire (Staffs)
Suffolk

Surrey
Warwickshire (Warks)
West Midlands
West Sussex (W. Sussex)
West Yorkshire (W. Yorks)
Wiltshire (Wilts)

Wales

Clwyd
Dyfed
Glamorgan
Gwent
Gwynedd
Powys

Scotland

Borders
Central
Dumfries & Galloway
Fife
Grampian
Highland
Lothian
Orkney Islands
Shetland Islands
Strathclyde
Tayside
Western Isles

Northern Ireland

Antrim
Armagh
Down
Fermanagh
Londonderry
Tyrone

INDEX

A

B

C

F

G

H

Y

LIVING AND WORKING SERIES

Our 'Living and Working' books are essential reading for anyone planning to spend time abroad, including holiday-home owners, retirees, long-term visitors, business people, transferees, students and even extra-terrestrials! They're packed with important and useful information designed to help you **avoid costly mistakes and save both time and money.** Topics covered include how to:

- Find a job with a good salary & conditions
- Avoid and overcome problems
- Find your dream home
- Get the best education for your family
- Make the best use of public transport
- Endure local motoring habits
- Obtain the best health treatment
- Stretch your money further
- Make the most of your leisure time
- Enjoy the local sporting life
- Find the best shopping bargains
- Insure yourself against most eventualities
- Do numerous other things not listed above

Our 'Living and Working' books are the most comprehensive and up-to-date source of practical information available about everyday life abroad. They aren't, however, boring text books, but interesting and entertaining guides written in a highly readable style.

Read these books and discover what it's really like to live and work abroad!

Order your copies today by phone, fax, post or email from: Survival Books, PO Box 3780, YEOVIL, BA21 5WX, United Kingdom (☎/▤ +44 (0)1935-700060, ✉ sales@survivalbooks.net, 🖥 www.survivalbooks.net).